KV-645-194

SEARCHING FOR AGRARIAN REFORM IN LATIN AMERICA

Thematic Studies in Latin America

SERIES EDITOR
Gilbert W. Merkx,
Director
Latin American Institute, University of New Mexico

The Political Economy of Revolutionary Nicaragua
By Rose J. Spalding

Women on the U.S.–Mexico Border: Responses to Change
Edited by Vicki L. Ruiz and Susan Tiano

The Jewish Presence in Latin America
Edited by Judith Laikin Elkin and Gilbert W. Merkx

Policymaking in Mexico: From Boom to Crisis
By Judith A. Teichman

Land, Power, and Poverty: Agrarian Transformation and Political Conflict in Central America
By Charles D. Brockett

Pinochet: The Politics of Power
By Genaro Arriagada with translation by Nancy Morris

The Chilean Political Process
By Manuel Antonio Garreton with translation by Sharon Kellum

Searching for Agrarian Reform in Latin America
Edited by William C. Thiesenhusen

Additional titles in preparation

Searching for Agrarian Reform in Latin America

EDITED BY

William C. Thiesenhusen

Boston
UNWIN HYMAN
London Sydney Wellington

Unwin Hyman, Inc.
8 Winchester Place, Winchester, MA 01890, USA

Published by the Academic Division of
Unwin Hyman, Ltd,
15/17 Broadwick Street, London W1V 1FP, UK

Allen & Unwin Australia Pty Ltd.,
8 Napier Street, North Sydney, NSW 2060, Australia

Allen & Unwin (New Zealand) Ltd., in association with the Port Nicholson Press Ltd., 60 Cambridge Terrace, Wellington, New Zealand

First published in 1989

Library of Congress Cataloging-in Publication Data

Searching for agrarian reform in Latin America / edited by William C. Thiesenhusen.
p. cm. — (Thematic studies in Latin America)
Includes index.
ISBN 0-04-497017-X.
1. Land reform—Latin America—Case studies. I. Thiesenhusen, William C. II. Series.
HD 13333.L29S43 1988 88-9602
333.3'1'8—dc19 CIP

British Library Cataloging-in Publication Data

Searching for agrarian reform in Latin America.
—(Thematic studies in Latin America).
1. America. Agricultural industries
I. Thiesenhusen, William C., *1936 –*
338.1'098

ISBN 0-04-497017-X

Typeset in 10/12 point Palatino
Printed in Great Britain at
The University Press, Cambridge

Many of the ideas in this book were inspired by Ray Penn;
this volume is dedicated to his memory.

CONTENTS

ACKNOWLEDGMENTS

All the authors whose work appears in this book have asked me to express appreciation to colleagues who have read and commented upon their chapters, to staff members of their respective institutions who have helped them with typing and syntax, and to their families for their forbearance.

I must express particular appreciation to the staff of the Land Tenure Center at the University of Wisconsin-Madison, including John Bruce, its director, and Jane B. Knowles, assistant director, for their assistance in the completion of the overall manuscript. Elizabeth Dunn and Monica Sella, Research assistants and graduate students in the Department of Agricultural Economics, commented on the manuscripts, helped with final references and footnote checking, and provided feedback to me and to the other authors.

Ms. Jane Dennis-Collins not only was in charge of the manuscript typing, but provided her extremely valued reaction on all of the pieces in this book. Her superlative work was beyond the call of the duties of her job. I also thank the other staff members of the Land Tenure Center for their help and assistance—and their patience with my impatience: Eugenia Loyster, Don Esser, Patty Grubb, and Linda Smith. The help of Beverly Phillips, Land Tenure Center librarian, and her cheerful staff, who were always willing to answer bibliographic questions, is gratefully acknowledged. I also thank my colleagues in the Departments of Agricultural Economics and Agricultural Journalism and graduate students in these departments and in the Doctoral Program in Development Studies.

Special funding from the Agency for International Development and the University of Wisconsin Graduate School was essential. Appreciated encouragement was provided by Peter Dorner, Bryant Kearl, David Atwood, Joan Atherton, Gil Merkx, Lisa Freeman, and John Michel.

Of course, I personally and formally thank the case-study authors for putting up with my interminable tinkering with their prose. Most treated these annoyances quietly and with solemnity, while the levity introduced by those who did not was also appreciated.

Chapter 1

Introduction: Searching for Agrarian Reform in Latin America

William C. Thiesenhusen

Though land reform has been a topic of heated discussion in nearly all countries of Latin America for the past several decades, only occasionally does the concept intrude upon the consciousness of North Americans. One purpose of this book is to increase the visibility of land reform policies and to highlight their dimensions for purposes of debate and discussion. As economic recovery returns to Latin America, issues that involve distribution (like land reform) are bound to reappear in public policy debate. To Latin American countries, which lack social safety nets and effective affirmative action legislation, land reform has the potential of being as vital as social security, unemployment insurance, and school busing all rolled up into one.[1]

In the absence of the income-transfer programs that are so common in industrial countries, one Third World alternative is to rely on coupling the rural poor with other, underutilized resources to allow for employment, acceptable standards of living, and insurance for infirmity and old age. Where affirmative action in industrial countries is a conscious, government-sanctioned policy to redistribute opportunities more equitably, in predominantly agrarian countries agrarian reform is a policy to distribute land, which is a major source of employment.

Judgments on issues such as land reform tend to be value laden and polarized. In accounts of current events, land reform is often associated with discussions of democratization in the Third World, the enclosures of nineteenth century England (which paved the way for a spurt of industrial growth unlike any seen before), and the liberating elixir of the French Revolution. The United States fostered massive land redistribution in Japan after World War II, and increased productivity ensued. Land reforms also occurred in South Korea and Taiwan, where economic success today is the stuff of legend. As such, one may be led to the value judgment that land reform is a "good thing," a policy to be universally sought.

On the other hand, since the issue is as intertwined with the histories of the Warsaw Pact nations as it is with those of Western Europe, if it comes up in the context of a discussion of the East-West conflict, the brutality attendant upon Soviet collectivization is often recalled (Conquest 1986). Similarly, since Fidel Castro organized a sweeping land reform in Cuba, the idea may be regarded as radical and even subversive. Or it may be thought of in connection with right-wing activities in a more recent and clouded period of our own history, the "pacification" in Vietnam.

Distilling lessons from historical analogy is a strained exercise. It is probably impossible to draw much more than gross generalities from the experience of already developed countries, since the setting for contemporary less developed countries (LDCs) is so different. And comparison between land reform in Latin America and land reform in Asia, where peasant manager-operatorship on rental land is the common prereform land-tenure category, is similarly fraught with difficulty.[2] More fruitful exposition of the issue is probably based on more contemporary experiences and in countries with similar extant institutions.

This volume is an effort to draw together in a series of cases, written by field researchers in countries where reforms have taken place, contemporary experiences with land reform in Latin America. From the perspectives of scholars from different social science disciplines, an attempt is made to define agrarian reform through various country experiences and to outline its goals, assess its accomplishments, and distill (or at least speculate upon) what its lessons may be. Each chapter does not deal in equal depth with each of these issues; the authors did not write to a preset outline. The coverage, rather, presents an analysis of the issues as the authors see them—an agenda of their own choosing.

This chapter sets the stage by (1) indicating conditions which have given rise to demands for land reform in Latin America, (2) defining some of the terms and issues attendant upon land reform in Latin America, (3) describing some of the contributions of small-farm agriculture in the region, (4) developing a brief history of the *latifundio–minifundio* complex, (5) noting some of the recent macroeconomic conditions that will eventually put land reform back on the policy agenda, and (6) referring to some recent writing on land reform in Latin America.

WHAT GIVES RISE TO LAND REFORM DEMANDS?

Given the rapid rate of population growth in Latin America, the work force in much of the region is due to grow rapidly for at least fifteen more years. Even if this growth rate were to slow substantially tomorrow, members of the work force for the next decade and a half have already been born. Currently, the Latin American labor force is increasing by 2.7 percent per year because of the exceedingly high population growth rate of the 1960s and early 1970s. Even prior to the recession slide in 1981, the Economic Commission for Latin America calculated (by reducing underemployment to unemployment equivalents and adding these to overt unemployment) the underutilization of the labor force at 30 million, or one-quarter of the 1980 labor force (Terra 1983,85). This represents an enormous waste of resources and is a potential source for political disruption. It also means that these countries cannot be indifferent to the development of the manufacturing, construction, and service sectors. While agrarian reform may provide the institutional context to absorb another generation of people in productive employment in farming, this gain will be short lived. New jobs must also be created in other sectors, which is where the future of the region lies (Terra 1983, 83–87).

The problem of rapid population growth is compounded by the fact that often, but not always, land taken for reform is inefficiently—even wastefully—utilized by its original owners despite frequent food shortfalls in Latin America. Some economists blame this on an unfavorable, farm-level cost-price ratio given the needs of urban areas (whose officials and entrepreneurs wish to avoid civic protest and upward pressures of the wage bill) for inexpensive foodstuffs; others say the problem is inherent in the institutional structure of agriculture itself, which fosters landlord sloth and indolence as well as capital flight, conspicuous consumption (instead of savings and investment), and lack of interest in the local community and its institutions (the landlords live in cities where, for example, their children receive an education and health care). Whatever the case, the best land in most Latin American countries is presently concentrated in a few hands while agricultural underemployment is rampant, as Alan Riding described for Guatemala:

> Each generation, therefore, must endlessly subdivide family farms among sons. In addition, their farmlands are exhausted and yields have fallen sharply. At best, the small holdings now produce enough corn and beans to last the average family six months of the year. So, to survive, the Indians must migrate to the plantations on the Southern Coast.
>
> Not only is 70 percent of land owned by 2 percent of the population, but the best land is given over to coffee, cotton and sugar, all labor-extensive

crops destined for export. And with producers paying low wages at home and obtaining good prices abroad, a few Guatemalan families have made vast fortunes. (Riding 1980, 20)

In a land reform, the hope is that those rural people who have been denied a decent livelihood for a long period of the country's history (the poor farmers or peasants, usually called campesinos in Latin America) will use the land more intensively and productively than the current owners and that the campesinos' incomes will increase.

Unfortunately, most governments of Latin America—even the relatively progressive ones—have not been anxious to reform their land tenure structures; landholding groups and their allies are still politically potent in the region. In the last several decades, however, there have been increasing demands for land reform, often from poorer classes at the grass-roots level buoyed up by alliances with dissident groups from within the middle classes. The land reform process is often wrenching, as is illustrated by an account from Brazil in mid-1986:

During a [funeral] ceremony charged with emotion, the bloodstained garments of the young priest, shot by an unknown gunman three days earlier, were held up at the altar. "He is a martyr to land reform," said one of the bishops. Josimo Moraes was one of the 20 Brazilians who die each month in a modern-day tropical version of the range wars between the cattlemen and the small farmers of the North American prairies during the last century.... Land reform was a key political promise in the campaign that led to the arrival of President Jose Sarney after 20 years of military rule. But a year into his administration, the civilian President finds his...coalition caught between conflicting interests of landed and landless. Many recall that a similar reform was a catalyst in the 1964 coup. (House 1986, 28)

The difficulty of the issue has been further highlighted recently by an account from Paraguay:

Clashes between landless peasants and the armed forces have increased here in recent weeks, claiming the lives of two squatters. In mid-August, some 100 landless peasants...took over a large section of farmland that had been abandoned, threw up makeshift huts and began to plant yucca, corn, beans and vegetables....Ramón Rolón, a peasant who participated in the land takeover, explained why the group decided to invade the land: "We're farmers, and farming is the only work we know. Since we don't have our land to work, some families and neighbors got together and came here to this big empty place to sow some seed and provide food for our families....As Paraguayans we know there's lots of idle land available for those who want to work it. We don't have money to buy land, so the only thing we can do is to come here and start farming so we can survive." (Silvero 1986, 1)

Clearly, then, increasing demands for land reform that have sprung from the grass-roots level have come up against some rather fierce opposition. The backlash that has occurred against affirmative action and welfare programs in industrial countries and against land reform in less developed nations is in some ways similar. Those who are well entrenched in the system resist policies that transfer some of their income and prestige to others. Some may lower their resistance when they finally realize that the pressure for change is so persistent that, unless they give up something, they will lose everything. This perception, as contemporary South Africa illustrates so vividly, is often late in coming. Measures to thwart reform run the gamut from administrative delay and interminable paperwork (in Spanish, *trámites*) to coups and counterreform.

One form of intransigent politics that may block reform is illustrated in present-day Guatemala:

> [Newly inaugurated President Marco Vinício] Cerezo refuses to investigate military officers accused of past human rights abuses. He has rejected the idea of a land reform.... These actions sit oddly on the shoulders of a reformist leader. But the shadows of Guatemala's violent history dim hopes for quick change.... [There are political factors] behind Cerezo's reluctance to embark on any serious land reform, even in a country where a small minority controls 70 percent of the cultivable land, while a poverty-stricken peasantry clamors for a few acres. Cerezo justifies his stand by pointing to neighboring El Salvador, where fellow Christian Democratic President José Napoleón Duarte's efforts at land reform "have set the private enterprise entirely against him, while on the other hand the guerrillas are still there." (Ford 1986, 1, 12)

But land reform came up several months later in 1986 and Cerezo found it a difficult issue to dodge:

> When Guatemala's new civilian president, Marco Vinício Cerezo Arévalo, announced in September that he would begin distributing unused land to migrant farm workers, many Guatemalans were thunderstruck. Mr. Cerezo, in office less than a year, was defying an age-old taboo. The last Guatemalan President who dared tamper with his country's feudal land-tenure system—Jacobo Guzmán Arbenz, 32 years ago—was overthrown for his trouble. In the years since, a succession of military cliques has ruled Guatemala with an iron hand, murdering thousands and suppressing talk of reform with a savagery that made the country an international pariah....What was he doing now, demanded outraged plantation owners. What he was doing, Mr. Cerezo replied, with the slightest hint of a smile, was not land reform at all, but, rather, "rural development." (Kinzer 1986, 32)

In some Latin American countries, land for the reforms of the 1960s and 1970s came largely from the public domain. In other countries, Chile and Peru, for example, the private sector was significantly affected. The procedure of expropriating present owners to utilize their land in agrarian reform is similar to condemning land for public use in industrial countries. In the United States, land can be legally taken by the government for uses deemed to be in the common good: power lines, military establishments, and roads, for example. But in Latin American agrarian reforms, "public good" is defined somewhat more broadly to include the basic sustenance of large groups in rural society that were formerly relegated to low-productivity employment—and unemployment. Indemnification is paid to owners of condemned property in industrial countries; in Latin America this is usually also the case, but sometimes expropriated property is merely confiscated (as in Bolivia in 1953, for example; in Mexico, reform guidelines included landlord compensation, but it was never paid). Sometimes, in a move redolent with poetic justice, the amount of payment for land is set as the amount the owner had declared for tax purposes. Payment may be made in industrial-sector bonds to stimulate creation of urban investments and city jobs. Often agrarian reform laws provide larger payments in cash (if the expropriated land was farmed reasonably well) and larger payments in bonds (if there was much arable land that stood idle).

In arguments opposing land reform, detractors may plead the sanctity of private property, suggest that production will fall precipitously during reform, advertise that there is plenty of idle land at the frontier to colonize, or imply that there already is too much government intervention in agriculture and that agrarian reform would provide the straw of inefficiency that breaks the camel's back. Others argue against reform because "uneducated peasants are unable to make rational management decisions." This, in fact, is the most common argument against reform by the landowners in Latin America. One frequently hears it expressed by the dominant elite in Ecuador:

> [L]andowners such as former President Galo Plazo Lasso [1948–1952] expressed their disapproval of land redistribution. "If a *latifundio* is being inefficiently farmed it should be subject to redistribution. All too often, however, the most productive estates are turned over to peasants who don't know how to farm them." (Handelman 1981, 6)

These assertions usually disregard the nonformal and life-experience learning in which the campesinos have abundantly participated.

In a real sense, the property redistributed during land reform may be considered redress, just as job preference in affirmative action is explicitly given to minorities and women as recompense for years of maltreatment. Agricultural production in Latin America has thrived lately due to many factors, among them the hard work—even in the face of menial rewards—of the peasants in the region. The system could continue in this manner and production might continue to grow more or less in step with population growth and income increases. (Though countries of the region exhibited varying performance in the twenty years ending with 1984, food production per capita in Latin America grew by an average of 0.9 percent annually.) But there would doubtless be just as much economic growth if more justice were done and those who did the work also obtained the fruits of their labor. So, in addition to equity and justice, there is the thought that the new landholders, as well as those favored by affirmative action in industrial countries, are as able—perhaps more so—to be as productive in their new jobs as the former occupants of these positions. Thus, there are inseparable elements of equity and "production" in both affirmative action and land reform.

AGRARIAN REFORM AND LAND-TENURE CONCEPTS

For the uninitiated student of agrarian reform in Latin America, a brief introduction to the subject is in order. The term "agrarian reform" will be used frequently; unlike its use in de Janvry (1981), here it will be synonymous with land reform. In Spanish there are no separate terms for land and agrarian reform. The entire matter is covered by *reforma agraria*. Technically, utilization of the two terms is a recognition that reform of the land-tenure pattern is only half of the battle. The implication of "agrarian" is that other institutions must be redirected and reshaped at the same time that land is redistributed to insure that services, inputs, research, irrigation water and facilities, credit, and marketing assistance go to the beneficiaries of land reform. If this is not the case (as in some of the cases described in this volume), land-reform efforts flounder. As reforms progress, farmers throughout the world have done their best when they have been assisted by a certain amount of public services; these subsidies are justified in that the resultant food supply is then abundant and low priced for all.

At the same time, it is difficult for the agencies that administer reforms to calculate how many services will be needed for a reform to succeed. Provision of too many services may extend the life of state paternalism; if too much is spent on current beneficiaries, lack of funds will stop the spread of reform to new beneficiaries. Indeed, a call for "consolidation" of the reform—providing more services to a constant number of beneficiaries—is one way in which Latin American conservatives have halted reforms. Enlightened reformers must try to calculate the intensity of the investment-technology push needed to propel the beneficiaries into self-sufficiency. A major agrarian reform problem has been the lavish expenditures on a few, which pushes beneficiaries far in debt. Sometimes, governments forgive this debt only to see the cycle begin anew. New landholders must, as soon as possible, convert to receiving only those state services that are available to all producers in the sector. No Latin American nation can afford to have land reform beneficiaries as permanent wards of the state. It may be necessary to extend credit and enable beneficiaries to buy productive inputs but little else; houses and community infrastructure should then be provided with savings generated from the incomes of the farmers themselves (though this does depend on weather conditions, housing left over from the previous landownership pattern, etc.). The sooner beneficiaries are weaned of necessary start-up subsidies (a difficult but necessary tapering-off process should begin very soon after granting land, and these "rules of the game" should be clear to all who are settled when they receive their land), the more the pool of beneficiaries can be expanded, if the political will to do so exists. The institution of a land tax or, alternatively, amortization schedules can help repay the beneficiaries' public debts. This does not make light of the need for attaining a proper balance: it makes no sense to set up farmers on land of their own if they do not have enough credit and inputs to cultivate their property.

In fact, then, "agrarian reform" involves much more than simply distributing land. Indeed, a land-tenure system can be likened to a prism through which government policy must pass on its way to delivering a product or a service to the recipient farmer. In traditional Latin American land-tenure systems, government policy is refracted so that most of its benefits go to an elite group of farm people, the large landowners. Subsidized credit, extension help, market breaks, less expensive inputs, and agricultural research tend to benefit the dominant elites, the major resource holders. What land reform does is change the shape of the prism so that the rays fall on a wider group of farm people, including, at least, some of the poor. (See Table 1.)

The prism, however, does not broaden its focus easily. As Kanel teaches (1971), Third World land-tenure systems often reflect the social structure and, hence, cannot be changed capriciously. It is not correct to think of alterations of land tenure in the way one thinks of manipulating other economic variables in the course of agricultural development; changing these institutions is different from the addition of more fertilizer or the modification of an irrigation system. (And changing land-tenure institutions in the Third World is far different than such alterations in developed countries, where land-tenure patterns have been stripped of their social implications and are primarily responsive to technological imperatives.) What Kanel implies is that unless the social system in the Third World country in question is fundamentally changed, the land-tenure system is likely to remain de facto, if not de jure: similar to what it always was, perhaps with power concentrated in a slightly different manner. Experience has shown that land reform is the culmination of a long and subtle process of social transformation. What baffles the outside observer is the presumed suddenness of the event. Indeed, land reform is a matter that frequently comes upon the scene abruptly and (to all but the most alert of observers) unpredictably. The catalyst can be the death of a dictator, the eclipse of an especially repressive military regime, the advent of a reformist military, the politicization of religious groups, the invasion of land by organized peasants, international pressures or pacts, the split of a coalition or class, the demonstration effect offered by other countries, guerrilla movements, martyrdom, or even an election—or more than one of these occurring in some fortuitous combination.

One irony is that reform tends to require a very large concentration of power and/or a fairly wide consensus among several classes of people to bring it about; afterward, however, a wide sharing of access and power is assumed to be necessary. This transition is a tricky one; if it isn't achieved, reform will be criticized as being too autocratic, too centralized, and not "participatory" enough.

Another difficulty can occur if land reform is accompanied by long periods of disruptive social change in those countries with a democratic form of government. City dwellers will not put up for long with chaos in the rural areas. If the reform process is perceived as anarchic, especially if it seems to result in fewer and more expensive wage goods entering the market or in a higher-than-normal rate of rural-to-urban migration (which strains city resources), urban pressures will stop the reform process abruptly. As in Chile in 1973, the intent will be to reverse reform as much as possible and to reinstitute the *status quo ante,* "when times were better"—for city dwellers, at least (Rosenberg 1986, 24, 29).

Land reform is no panacea. Its main purpose is to make certain that the benefits of growth are directed to a wider group than the present elite. When reform succeeds, there should be fewer rural tensions (to the extent that the resource and income-distribution patterns are improved and rural people have the opportunity to become a more productive work force). In the best of worlds, production will increase and greater incomes among the poor will lead to a wider market for domestic goods. This will not necessarily follow (1) if the private sector and/or the government takes a basically antagonistic or indifferent stance vis-à-vis the beneficiary sector and is unresponsive after reform or (2) if forces of reaction are strong. After agrarian reform, the social

TABLE 1
Selected countries of Latin America and the Caribbean:
Areas affected by the agrarian reform and number of peasant families benefited[a]

Country	Forest and agricultural surface[b] (thousands of hectares)			Number of farming families		
	Total	Affected	Percentage	Total	Benefited	Percentage
Bolivia	3,275.0[c]	2,730.0[d]	83.4	516,200[e]	384,560[d]	74.5
Chile	28,759.0[f]	2,940.0[g]	10.2	412,000[e]	38,000[g]	9.2
Costa Rica	3,122.4[h]	221.6[h]	7.1	155,200[e]	8,349[h]	5.4
Dominican Republic	2,676.7[i]	374.6[i]	14.0	697,800[e]	59,411[i]	8.5
Ecuador	7,949.0[j]	718.1[k]	9.0	749,000[e]	78,088[k]	10.4
Mexico	139,868.0[j]	60,724.0[l]	43.4	4,629,400[e]	1,986,000[l]	42.9
Panama	2,253.9[m]	493.2[n]	21.9	132,800[e]	17,703[n]	13.3
Peru	23,545.0[j]	9,255.6[o]	39.3	1,419,400[e]	431,982[o]	30.4
Venezuela	26,470.0[j]	5,118.7[p]	19.3	561,800[e]	171,861[p]	30.6

[a] Source: Prepared by the ECLAC/FAO Joint Agricultural Division, in Inter-American Development Bank, *Economic and Social Progress in Latin America, 1986 Report* (Washington, IADB, 1986), p. 130.
[b] Corresponds to the total surface of the exploitations.
[c] 1950 figures.
[d] Up to 1977, according to E. Ortega, *La agricultura y las relaciones intersectorales: El caso de Bolivia*, E/CEPAL/R.205 (Santiago, Chile, 1979).
[e] According to FAO data.
[f] According to INE, *V Censo nacional agropecuario* (Santiago, Chile, 1981).
[g] Up to 1982, according to A. Rojas, "Campesinado y mercado de alimentos en un modelo de economía abierta, *Estudios e Informes de la CEPAL* (Santiago, Chile), no. 35, 1984.
[h] Corresponds to the peasant settlements created by the Instituto de Tierras y Colonización up to 1980, according to SEPSA, *Información básica del sector agropecuario y de recursos naturales renovables de Costa Rica, número 2* (Guadalupe, 1982).

[i] 1983 data, according to S. Moquete, *La agricultura campesina y el mercado de alimentos: el caso de República Dominicana, Estudios e Informes de la CEPAL* (Santiago, Chile), no. 39, 1984.

[j] According to FAO, *Censo agropecuario mundial de 1970: análisis y comparación internacional de los resultados del censo agropecuario mundial de 1970* (Rome, 1981).

[k] Up to 1983, according to O. Barsky, *La reforma agraria ecuatoriana, Biblioteca de Ciencias Sociales*, vol. 3, (Quito, FLACSO, 1984).

[l] 1970 figures, according to Eckstein et al. (1978, 11).

[m] According to R. Pérez, *Estudio sobre la ganadería bovina de carne de Panamá*, mimeograph, n.d.

[n] 1977 data, according to PREALC, *La evolución de la pobreza rural en Panamá* (Santiago, Chile, 1983).

[o] Up to 1982, according to the Ministry of Agriculture, *Informe sobre la marcha de las actividades en el sector de la reforma agraria y el desarrollo rural en el Perú* (for the FAO Conference of 1983, Lima).

[p] Up to 1979, according to S. Marta, *La pobreza agrícola y rural en Venezuela* (Caracas, 1983).

scientist's models and tools are not only useful, they are indispensable. Land-reform beneficiaries will then probably live in a fairly neoclassical economic world: they will be discouraged by prices that are too low, operating costs that are too high, inflation that is too acute, an export market that is too sluggish, credit that is inappropriate, and so on.

Land reform, then, is a fundamental reordering of a land-tenure pattern that, in view of the aforementioned problems, occurs sometimes by revolution, sometimes by alliances between the peasants and the middle class which pressure the government, sometimes by less straightforward coalitions involving the Church and the military, and sometimes even through technological change. The general idea of a land reform is not only that society should change, but also that the rural poor should benefit in the process. The extent to which agrarian reforms have fulfilled such revolutionary aspirations is a matter for speculation. While most would agree, for example, that the Cuban agrarian reform was revolutionary, some would add Mexico and Bolivia to the Latin American list, together with Nicaragua and Chile under Allende. Some would add Peru after the 1969 military coup, up until about 1973, and El Salvador; others would omit all of these except, of course, Cuba. Those who believe that Cuba had the only true revolution tend to disparage the remaining reforms of Latin America: they argue that these were of the right wing and, hence, served merely to co-opt the activist peasantry. In response, the right wing often accuses reformers of all stripes of being lackeys of the Soviet bloc.

In this volume, we use the term *land tenure* to refer to the manner in which land is owned and operated and the behavior which flows from that institutional pattern. Land and agrarian reform is a basic restructuring of the land-tenure system. While in North America the predominant form of land tenure from colonial times has been the family farm under owner-operatorship, in Latin America it has been the hacienda system or, more properly, the *latifundio–minifundio* system. This pattern is dominated by very large and, increasingly, middle-sized estates, sometimes efficiently farmed and commercially oriented, sometimes not. This pattern, grosso modo, has prevailed in the Latin American agricultural scene from colonial times; in some parts of the region (as in central Mexico), the argument can be made that the die was cast in the days of the Aztecs, before the Spanish arrived.

Production on large contemporary estates is no longer predominantly based on a resident or service-tenure labor force—those who are given a plot and a small cash wage for working on the main fields (demesne) of the hacienda. Because landlords are mechanizing their operations in parts of the continent and engaging more in enterprises in which a full-time, year-round labor force is not needed, resident labor on the hacienda is disappearing. With this modernization, edged on by the green revolution technology of the last several decades, the social rationale for existing land-tenure patterns in Latin America (Kanel 1971) is being gradually replaced by a technological imperative. Now, most of the labor needed by haciendas comes from a work force that lives off the farm. Hacienda territory is usually interspersed with communities of scattered *minifundios*, tiny owner-operator or renter-operator farms. These plots are too small to provide sustenance to a family, so the *minifundistas* either have to search out wage work on the haciendas to supplement their incomes or have to migrate to the cities. So many have migrated to the cities that, in the last several decades, the region has gone from a predominantly rural to a predominantly urban area (see Table 2). Semiproletarianization of these *minifundista* families is a growing trend (de Janvry 1981). Some, that is, spend a portion—sometimes most—of their time on wage work elsewhere (often on haciendas) and spend the remaining time on farming their own land. At times the children work for neighboring haciendas while their parents labor on the subsistence home farm. The *latifundios* tap this nearby, compliant labor force. Unlike an earlier era, when the hacienda supported a year-round labor force, mechanization has made it possible for some of this subsistence expense to be thrown back on the *minifundios*. This is the essence of de Janvry's functional dualism (de Janvry 1981).

This *latifundio–minifundio* land-tenure system is the basis of a patron-client relationship within Latin American agriculture, a reciprocal social contract which favors the landlord (the patron), who grants small favors, condescension, and some employment, while the client (the peasant) gives his labor power and obeisance. The landlord makes the best credit risk for bankers, is the best customer for inputs, and has better access to government assistance. Credit, extension help, and agricultural research, important assets in these days of the green revolution, are available to small-scale producers with much more difficulty. Occasionally, landlords may broker these for the peasants.

The *latifundio–minifundio* land-tenure system has been condemned over the years because it has led to a bimodal agrarian structure[3] and highly inegalitarian resource- and income-distribution patterns (see Table 3). A few control the best land and, often, the most remunerative agricultural exports (that is, export crops that are quite lucrative during the time of price upswings in the international market). The suggestion is that there is "sectoral disarticulation." The export market drives the economy forward; development of a national market is, to elites, unnecessary in economic terms and this leaves those who pull the levers of economic progress indifferent to the plight of the poor (de

Table 2
Total and rural population and rural percentage by country, 1960 and 1980[a]

Country	Total (thousands)		Rural (thousands)		Rural percentage	
	1960	1980	1960	1980	1960	1980
Argentina	20,611	27,947	5,439	5,338	26.4	19.1
Bahamas	119	224	40	100	33.6	44.6
Barbados	230	263	164	176	71.3	66.9
Bolivia	3,294	5,600	2,407	3,051	73.1	54.5
Brazil	72,325	118,998	39,257	38,371	54.3	32.2
Chile	7,596	11,104	2,578	2,090	33.9	18.8
Colombia	15,557	24,933	8,090	8,006	52.0	32.1
Costa Rica	1,320	2,217	910	1,202	68.9	54.2
Dominican Republic	3,441	5,546	2,303	2,939	66.9	53.0
Ecuador	4,429	8,051	2,914	4,237	65.8	52.6
El Salvador	2,661	4,513	1,726	2,869	64.9	63.6
Guatemala	3,921	6,913	2,574	4,665	65.6	67.5
Guyana	604	787	444	576	73.5	73.2
Haiti	3,575	5,016	3,187	3,751	89.1	74.8
Honduras	1,988	3,707	1,550	2,372	78.0	64.0
Jamaica	1,682	2,188	1,301	1,234	77.3	56.4
Mexico	37,073	68,544	18,258	23,912	49.2	34.9
Nicaragua	1,503	2,767	881	1,216	58.6	43.9
Panama	1,220	1,955	779	917	63.9	46.9
Paraguay	1,778	3,168	1,173	1,786	66.0	56.4
Peru	10,385	17,325	5,755	6,239	55.4	36.0
Suriname	290	388	153	211	52.8	54.4
Trinidad and Tobago	842	1,094	539	539	64.0	49.3
Uruguay	2,538	2,859	591	487	23.3	17.0
Venezuela	7,963	15,024	2,859	3,866	35.9	25.7
Latin America	206,945	341,131	105,872	120,150	51.2	35.2

[a] Source: Inter-American Development Bank, from official country statistics.

Janvry 1981). Export-crop production in the 1964–1984 period grew at twice the rate of subsistence crops, as illustrated in Table 4.

The majority of farmers operates very small, soil-poor, often sadly undercapitalized hillside plots. This group tends to grow staples and often raises some chickens or other small animals that provide the family with protein sources and act as scavengers so no potential food scraps are wasted. *Minifundistas* will grow some crops for sale and some for direct consumption. For needs over and above that, they seek wage labor as semiproletarians. Usually, such labor is demanded only during planting and harvesting for the dominant export crops of the country and often involves seasonal within-country migration. These rural poor are often adversely affected by prices of domestic staples, which tend to be kept uniformly low by the government in order to subsidize the urban consumer and city industrialist. In addition, because of the large numbers and extant underemployment in the peasant sector, labor can be sold very cheaply; the poverty that ensues cannot be easily alleviated given that social welfare programs are rarely available.[4] Furthermore, those who manage these economies need the campesino's labor participation—and regard their lack of purchasing power with indifference.

In response to such unequal resource-distribution patterns, income distribution is also inegalitarian. As one remedy, agrarian reform has been advocated throughout the region. Yet, one of the reasons why agrarian reform is so difficult in contemporary times, and so often seems to fall short of expectations, is that it must satisfy so many diverse goals: those of justice, equity, and growth. A land reform that is merely a kind of affirmative action or just a welfare program brought about by resource and, hence, income transfers would be inadequate for Latin America. In countries where domestic food supplies have been characteristically short and agriculture supplies substantial export earnings, ignoring agricultural production in a search for equity would be a fatal omission and would defeat the program before it started. If redistribution brings stagnation, reform will fail. A frequent problem, however, is that as one goal is attained, others escape the policymaker's grasp. For example, to assure that marketable production remains high, transitional or "richer" peasants are often favored as land reform beneficiaries; while this helps to keep production levels acceptable, if

Table 3
***Minifundios* and *latifundios* in the Agrarian Structure of Selected Latin American Countries, 1970[a]**

	Minifundios		*Latifundios*	
Country	Percentage of farms	Percentage of occupied land	Percentage of farms	Percentage of occupied land
Argentina	43.2	3.4	0.8	36.9
Brazil	22.5	0.5	4.7	59.5
Colombia	64.0	4.9	1.3	49.5
Chile	36.9	0.2	6.9	81.3
Ecuador	89.9	16.6	0.4	45.1
Guatemala	88.4	14.3	0.1	40.8
Peru	88.0	7.4	1.1	82.4

[a] Source: Michael Todaro, *Economic Development in the Third World*, 2nd ed. (London, New York: Longmans, 1985), p. 295.

Table 4
Latin America: Selected indicators of agricultural sector production, 1960–1985[a]

Value added (growth rates)[b]	1960–1970	1970–1980	1980–1985	1960–1985
Latin American total GDP[c]	5.5[b]	6.0	0.8	4.7
Agriculture	3.5	3.7	2.4	3.3
Agriculture per capita[d]	0.9	1.2	0.0	0.8
Production (growth rates)[b]	**1964–1970**	**1970–1980**	**1980–1984**	**1964–1984**
Crops	3.0	3.5	2.5	3.1
Livestock	4.4	4.8	–0.3	3.3
Food	4.0	3.8	1.7	3.4
Food per capita[d]	1.4	1.3	–0.7	0.9
Subsistence crops	3.8	1.4	0.8	2.0
Export crops	2.4	5.5	3.1	4.1
Agricultural trade (millions of dollars)	**1970**	**1980**	**1984**	**Growth rates 1970–1984**
Balance	4,912	14,326	16,900	—
Exports	6,743	26,864	26,820	10.4
Imports	1,831	12,538	9,920	12.8

[a] Sources: Value added, Inter-American Development Bank, based on national statistics; production, U.S. Department of Agriculture; trade, U.N. Food and Agriculture Organization. Inter-American Development Bank, *Economic and Social Progress in Latin America, 1986 Report* (Washington, IADB, 1986), p. 74.
[b] All growth rates are given as percentages.
[c] GDP, Gross domestic product.
[d] Population growth rates: 1960–1970, 2.6 percent; 1970–1980, 2.5 percent; 1980–1985, 2.4 percent.

lower income peasants do not benefit, the goals of equity and justice are shortchanged.

THE ECONOMICS AND POLITICS OF LAND REFORM

Leaving aside arguments of social justice, which hold that it is immoral for governments to omit poverty-stricken, rural-group majorities from participation in a growing national income, those concerned with development in LDCs often find themselves at odds when discussing the value of land reform.

Many who argue for agrarian reform as a desirable policy in these contemporary times tilt their advocacy arguments (if not actual programs) more toward equity than productivity. After all, some countries have exhibited rather impressive and consistent economic growth rates with a traditional land-tenure system—Brazil, for example. Indeed, many Latin American countries have come across with fairly impressive marketable surpluses to stoke the manufacturing process at one time or another during the last several decades, either on the upswing of the trade cycle or in response to some combination of lower farm-level input prices and rewarding producer prices.

For their part, traditional neoclassical economists are often critical of land reform and the policies needed to attain it. They feel that as institutions are consciously reshaped by governmental policies or pressures, the system becomes increasingly insecure. Interruptions in savings and investment and the decline of production are then likely to occur. Economists of this belief feel that, although reforms are important, technology and market forces will mold institutions in due time and the poor eventually will obtain jobs as industry progresses and workers are attracted by the wages that are offered. The driving forces for this model are technology (as it is in Marxian economics), factor endowments, and product demand; the model accepts the extant institutions as sufficiently flexible and supple to accommodate changing technology. The poor obtain jobs to the extent that agriculture expands.[5] These economists (for example, Schultz 1964; Bauer 1986) would also argue that economists should confine themselves to the use of their disciplinary tools and leave institutional tinkering and speculation to political scientists and policymakers. Hence, macroeconomists frequently omit issues dealing with agrarian reform from any discussion of economic growth or recovery. For them, the issue is irrelevant.[6]

Antireformists often also include some ideas on distribution, couching their arguments in terms of the larger numbers of urban workers who would lose out if food production were lower after a reform than the number of rural dwellers who would benefit from that reform. If production failed, this would lead to higher food prices in town unless the country used foreign exchange to bring in food, which is also a costly alternative in terms of foregone industrial development. Higher food prices would lead to a stifling of investment because of greater wage bills and leaner profits. Moreover, if agroexports fell, this would represent a sacrifice of the foreign exchange needed for overall economic growth.

But whether production will fall or not after agrarian reform in Latin America is a matter for some speculation. Politicians, for example, can be expected to pronounce differently upon results, as they do on social and economic policies almost everywhere. In his campaign while running for the presidency of Ecuador, León Febres Cordero noted, "Agrarian reform should better the quality of life of Ecuadorean campesinos and improve production and productivity.... We have had more than twenty years of agrarian reform and it has done nothing positive."[7] Authors of several case studies in this volume disagree with Febres and offer data to support their views.

The crux of the antireform argument is that land reform involves too radical an alteration of the production structure for output to be maintained. Antireformists claim that given the existing Latin American institutions, land reform in that region cannot be expected to reproduce the results of the productivity-enhancing reforms in Taiwan, South Korea, and, even earlier, Japan. Postreform farm-management problems in Latin America are indeed radically different from those in East Asia, where managerial tenants were making the bulk of economic decisions before reform and agrarian transformation meant cutting the ownership ties to the landlord and transferring the land they already farmed to the occupant beneficiaries. The campesino in Latin America is in a much different situation. In the *latifundio–minifundio* land-tenure system, key decisions are usually made by a managerial staff of administrators and foremen, sometimes in consultation with the landowner. The campesinos, for their part, are more uneducated (in formal terms) now than at least their Japanese counterparts were before their agrarian reform. They tend to follow orders formulated and meted out in a hierarchical administrative structure, similar to that of the armed services, and to work under the constant vigilance of the landlord's foremen. When the prereform structure is based on the large farm, how overhead capital is treated is also an important consideration. If land reform was conceived as giving each qualifying campesino family an individual plot, initial division costs of infrastructure (fences, roads, irrigation adjustments, electrical installations) would be extremely high. Also, some claim a superiority of large-farm agriculture because of the economies of scale inherent in some crops, that is, in their husbandry (for example, planting, aerial spraying, harvesting), in their processing (coffee, cotton, sugar), and in their international marketing.

Those who felt agrarian reform was necessary, but accepted these latter arguments as compelling, tended to favor the production cooperative as a postreform institution for Latin American agrarian reform. Others argued that economies of scale are not really decisive in some farming enterprises and that, if they existed, peasants working together could overcome them, just as threshing crews did in the Midwest of the United States before the days of the combine. Infrastructural adjustments could be accomplished gradually.

In fact, campesinos on their own small properties—even on *minifundios*—have been shown in some sense to be more efficient in their operations than large haciendas: they tend to maximize production yielded by their scarce resources, land and capital. More than 25 years ago, the economic argument for the inverse relationship between farm size and productivity was clearly articulated (Arulpragasam 1961); Dorner and Kanel (1971) later formulated the argument for Latin America. It was again emphasized by Robert McNamara as president of the World Bank:

> It has often been suggested that the productivity of small-scale holdings is inherently low. But that is simply not true. Not only do we have the overwhelming evidence of Japan to disprove that proposition, but a number of recent studies on developing countries also demonstrate that, given the proper conditions, small farms can be as productive as large farms. For example, output per hectare in Guatemala, the Republic of China, India, and Brazil was substantially greater on smaller farms than on larger ones. And it is, of course, output per hectare which is the relevant measure of agricultural productivity in land-scarce, labor-surplus economies, not output per worker. (McNamara 1973, 15)

The argument is that small farms in these labor-surplus, capital-scarce LDCs use more labor per hectare than do large farms—up to the point where an additional laborer will add very little to output, the point of near-zero marginal productivity. These small farmers, in order to add to output, have no choice but to use unpaid family labor in this way. They tend to press all arable land into production. They may even graze animals on nonarable land and feed them with by-products that would normally be wasted in a large-farm enterprise. They use farm-produced inputs (substituting manure for commercial fertilizer) to lower their production costs. They tend to reduce or shorten the fallow period. Weather permitting, they extract as many crops per year as they can. They may grow higher value crops and certainly cultivate those most needed for their subsistence. If they have secure access to their land, they also have every incentive to take measures to conserve it. This is all possible and necessary because *minifundios* are a kind of family farm that usually does not hire labor; *minifundistas* raise and utilize their own labor force, and it is often kept in farming for lack of alternatives. Large farms that hire labor, on the other hand, must maximize profits. They do not press production beyond the point where the wage equals the marginal product of the last laborer hired.

The green revolution has given the inverse-relationship argument another twist and made it more complex: green revolution crops require more fertilizer, hybrid cultivars, water, and skill in some crucial combination. These inputs are usually considered highly divisible, so they should be as readily available on small farms as on large ones. To the extent that this is true, the argument is reinforced: there should be a stronger inverse relationship between size of farm and productivity after the green revolution than before. But this expected result may be mitigated if (1) credit is available only in relatively large quantities to wealthy producers; (2) irrigation, a category of capital which is not divisible, requires a costly infrastructure and water use can be controlled by a few, say, by upstream users; (3) machines are needed for precision seedbed preparation or to speed up turnaround time between one seeding and another if double cropping is to be achieved (this is the exceptional case; labor with simple tools can usually do the job satisfactorily even where weather conditions are demanding); and (4) a high-value (usually export) crop is raised and only a few have access to the seeds, the technology of growing them, and the required milling and processing facilities (as in cash crops such as tea, coffee, and sugarcane).

Some who criticize this line of thought on the superior efficiency of family farming believe (see chapter 10 in this volume) that capitalism punishes the farm family unfairly—in labor-surplus, alternative-sparse economies, especially—by exploiting its labor power. Others may accept the "inverse-relationship" hypothesis but still not believe that these minuscule operations can fulfill the developmental role of transferring sufficient food to the urban sector at a low enough cost to keep up the pace of industrialization, since smaller farm peasants tend to consume more of their output than owners of larger farms.

The latter was not true to any debilitating sense in the Republic of Korea, where few farms exceed 3 hectares (the average size of holding was only 0.9 hectares after the land reform). This experience shows that when farm people receive inputs on an equitable basis and have marketing facilities available at reasonable prices, small farmers can both consume more and transfer surpluses to industry, thereby spurring the overall development process (Lee 1979).[8]

A study by Giovanni Andrea Cornia involving three Latin American countries, Mexico, Barbados, and Peru, sheds more light on the farm size-productivity issue. While he could not confirm the relationship with Peru, a strong negative relationship between production per hectare and size of farm was evident in Mexico and Barbados (Cornia 1985). His production-function analysis shows constant returns to scale except for Mexico, where he reports *decreasing* returns to scale. Berry and Cline (1979) confirmed the "inverse" relationship for Mexico and Brazil. Parthasarathy (1979, chap. 2) also finds an inverse relationship in the Brazilian data.

CONTRIBUTIONS OF PEASANT AGRICULTURE

Emiliano Ortega looks at peasant production of market-bound crops and argues that it is not correct to assume that the contribution of peasants is small. In 1972 it was shown, for example, that 30 percent of marketed agricultural products in the region were attributable to small farms. Ortega classifies less than one-fifth of the agricultural area in Latin America as "peasant agriculture." He also shows that increases in income tend to call forth greater amounts of marketed crops. Before the revolution, 10 percent of all maize grown in Bolivia was sold; that increased to 75 percent after the agrarian reform in 1953.

In 1970, peasant agriculture in Mexico contributed nearly 70 percent of maize production, two-thirds of the production of beans, one-third of the production of wheat, and nearly half of the fruit production (Ortega 1982, 75–111, esp. 82–94; Ortega 1985). Table 5 shows how small-farm agriculture contributes to the food needs of the area.

Peasant farms also make contributions to the export market. It has been estimated that in Costa Rica, nearly 30 percent of agricultural exports is contributed by campesino producers; in Honduras, this figure is 25.5 percent. In Brazil and Colombia, 40 and 30 percent,

Table 5
Latin America: Provisional estimates of dimensions of entrepreneurial and small-producer agriculture at the beginning of the 1980s[a], [b]

Indicators	Entrepreneurial agriculture	Small producer[c]
Number of economic units	22	78
Total area covered by the units	82	18
Cultivable area covered by the units	63	37
Area utilized by the units[d]	56	44
Domestic consumption	59	41
Export	68	32
Permanent crops	59	41
Short-cycle crops	47	53
Maize	49	51
Beans	23	77
Potatoes	39	61
Rice	68	32
Coffee	59	41
Sugarcane	79	21
Cattle	76	24
Pigs	22	78

[a] Source: Luis López Cordovez, "Trends and Recent Changes in the Latin American Food and Agriculture Situation," *CEPAL Review*, no. 16, April 1982, p. 26, prepared with national agricultural census data.
[b] All estimates are given as percentages.
[c] The "small producer" column covers family-type units. To differentiate between them and the entrepreneurial units, criteria of size were used.
[d] Includes area used for crops and does not in
clude pastureland.

respectively, of production is from peasant farms. In Mexico, Venezuela, and Bolivia, it is 54, 63, and 75 percent, respectively (Ortega 1982, 1985). If small farms already add so much to a nation's production, creating more of them through land reform should not, one would think, be detrimental to production.

A catalog of *potential* economic benefits of land reform can be made, with the recognition that there is ample scope for any one of them to go awry. All agrarian reform programs are not likely to show progress in each. In a well-designed land reform program (1) production per acre should rise, (2) ownership should imply more stewardship of resources than do other land-tenure forms, (3) year-round in situ employment should be provided so that labor transference costs and city infrastructural costs may be kept lower than otherwise, (4) income distribution should improve as resource distribution is improved, (5) peasants should come to demand more products of industry, thus stimulating other sectors of the economy as their incomes rise (of course, if other sectors are not responsive, inflation will doubtless result), (6) on-farm savings and investment should increase, and (7) communities should develop as their members, with increased incomes, are more willing and able to support local public institutions and businesses.

As the following cases show, the agrarian reform models utilized by Latin American countries in the 1960s and 1970s have not worked as smoothly as this implies. They may have been too partial, too paternalistic, too lacking in farmer incentives, and too short of credit, inputs, research, and extension; prices may have been too unfavorable to the beneficiaries, payments expected from new landholders may have been too high, and the government, private industry and international community may have been too unkind or even overtly negative to the process. And sometimes these problems are found in combination. The net result has often been that policymakers and researchers have pronounced agrarian reform to be a failure or, at least, passé.

The epitaph may be premature. Some of these reforms may have snuffed out the revolutionary spark of the peasantry and co-opted them. On the other hand, it is possible that reforms in the 1960s and 1970s have simply shown campesinos what promises the future holds and added frustration to their rising expectations. Viewed in this manner, agrarian reforms since the 1960s may have paved the way for more complete reforms in decades to come.

Notwithstanding the economic shortcomings of the agrarian reform models utilized by Latin American countries in the 1960s and 1970s, there is a class of political benefits that reform can bring about: land reform can garner peasant support for whatever government gives them land. Almost all land reform seems to have this "patronage" characteristic. In Chile, in the homes of peasants benefited by the Eduardo Frei reforms of the 1960s, one would often see a picture on the wall of either Frei or John F. Kennedy (who established the land reform "conditionality" of the Alliance for Progress, that is, the idea that countries attempting agrarian reforms could receive U.S. assistance). As Salvador Allende's reform proceeded, those who got land under his administration would support him fervently.

Even in more revolutionary situations, the politics of land reform need to be understood. In Nicaragua, for example,

> Nicaragua's Sandinista government is wooing peasants with land and rifles in an effort to gain support in case of a possible U.S.-backed *contra* incursion. In the belief that peasants—a majority of the population—could help turn back the rebels by simply defending what they own, the government plans to create 20,000 new landowners this year. (*World Press Review* 1986, 6)

Huntington (1968) believes that the political advantage of land reform is often what induces policymakers to implement such a program.[9] He argues that a suffering peasantry is profoundly revolutionary; when peasantries own land of their own, in contrast, they are a generally conservative force in politics:

> The peasantry...may be the bulwark of the status quo or the shock troops of revolution. Which role the peasant plays is determined by the extent to which the existing system meets his immediate economic and material needs as he sees them. These needs normally focus on land tenure and tenancy, taxes and prices. Where the conditions of landownership are equitable and provide a viable living for the peasant, revolution is unlikely. Where they are inequitable and where the peasant lives in poverty and suffering, revolution is likely, if not inevitable, unless the government takes prompt measures to remedy these conditions. No social group is more conservative than a landowning peasantry, and none is more revolutionary than a peasantry which owns too little land or pays too high a rental. The stability of government in modernizing countries is thus, in some measure, dependent upon its ability to promote reform in the countryside.... Land reform carried out by revolution or by other means thus turns the peasantry from a potential source of revolution into a fundamentally conservative social force....(Huntington 1968, 375)

After land is distributed and the distribution is publicized, the pressure on government from the grass roots, or from whatever advocacy group is promoting agrarian reform, is relieved. Rather than encouraging continued pressures and complaints, land distribution is often the coup de grace to campesino organizations, which tend to be disbanded or at least considerably weakened after land is given out and

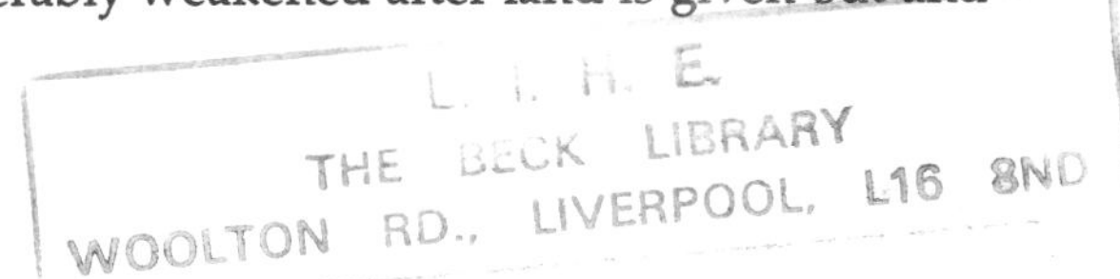

their *raison d'être* disappears. Only in a few cases (in contemporary Nicaragua, in Honduras, and in Chile most notably under Frei and Allende) has this pressure been sustained. Once a goal is fulfilled, continuation can occur only when the organization can quickly pick up the cudgels for another cause (such as beneficiary welfare). Governments—even progressive ones—often discourage grass-roots organization after reform, as before, so that they can focus on other sectors of the economy, those which more often contain the economic growth points.

THE DEMAND FOR BETTER CONDITIONS

As literacy increases, as communications networks penetrate more effectively into rural areas, and as population continues to rise, demands for better countryside living conditions will likely mount in Latin America. When 1980 is compared with 1960, social indicators demonstrate that more people now live into old age and that infant mortality has dropped. Furthermore, many more migrate not only to urban areas but also to other rural areas (often to obtain harvest-time jobs) and out of the country (frequently to return), more are literate, more are becoming organized into unions and political parties, and more are becoming aware of the generally improved living standards in the twentieth century through the mass media. For example, simple averages of data from the twenty-five Latin American countries surveyed by the World Bank show that the rate of infant mortality dropped about 40 percent between 1960 and 1980, primary school attendance ratios rose 51 percent, secondary school attendance ratios rose 150 percent, the adult literacy rate rose 20 percent, and the rate of radio-receiver ownership rose 250 percent. Since upper and middle classes within countries had fairly high levels of all of these by 1960, we can only assume that this represented a higher percentage gain in the lower income classes than in the upper classes (social indicator figures are not available by income class). Another indication of this is that if one separates the upper middle-income countries from the lower middle-income countries, more progress is registered in the lower income countries for most of these indicators (calculated from World Bank 1983). All of these changes tend to raise expectations of peasant groups.

Despite such changes, however, in most Latin American countries income distribution seems to have become more concentrated in the 20 years in question, thus implying that upper classes reaped more income from growing economies and that lower classes more often just held their own (Thiesenhusen 1983, 242–250).

To counteract pressures for change, repression in many parts of Latin America is much stronger in the 1980s than it needed to be in the 1960s. In some countries the pressure itself has been somewhat relieved by a "return to democracy," which has the effect of placing the material hopes and desires of the poor some place in the foreseeable future. In the 1970s, particularly, a number of Central American countries were governed by spurts of repression and small structural reforms (which tended not to challenge the status quo). In the 1980s this was followed by more overt repression and what has come to be known as low-intensity conflict (LIC) in Central America (Klare 1986; Trager and Scully 1981). How long the new and varied strategies, which range from putting down dissent with force to implementing democratic forms which promise the poor benefits sometime in the future, can overwhelm the desires of the poor for progress can only be surmised.

HISTORICAL ANTECEDENTS

What the conquerors had to perform upon their arrival in the New World was a social engineering feat of the first order. Theirs was the challenge of removing metals to Iberia while governing an immense, relatively sparsely settled territory.

When feasible, Iberia aimed at controlling the New World and its indigenous populations through existing institutions. Indeed, the secret of colonization was to use indigenous institutions as much as possible but to replace the chiefs with Iberian leaders. The purpose was to stabilize the indigenous population as a captive labor force. In cases where local institutions were lacking, the conquerors were forced to mold their own institutions of social control to what they found. Institutions of colonial control (Martín 1974, 14) were to be the *encomienda* (a trust over labor); *repartimiento* or, in the Andes, *mita; mercedes* (land grants); and debt peonage (peasants took out consumption loans which they were continually renewing and, through labor, attempting to pay off). These were not used at the same time, of course. Debt peonage, for example, came to make sense only after land grants were given out, the *estancia* or hacienda flowered, and labor was scarce. In lowland areas and/or where populations were nomadic, *encomiendas, resguardos* (reservations), *missiones, rescate* (ransom), and outright slavery were utilized to tie labor to the land. Slavery and quasi-slavery were not anathema to those among the conquering group who thought that they saw in the New World an illustration of the Aristotelian doctrine of natural slavery—the idea that part of society was destined to serve a class born into a life of virtue and relative ease.

It is probable that contemporary *minifundio* communities were of several origins: (1) some foot soldiers were given small properties (*peonías*) as a reward of conquest, (2) peripheral resident hacienda labor was probably released from haciendas from time to time during a slack period in the business cycle or for other reasons (like social pressure), and (3) at times haciendas disintegrated and were recombined with others, doubtlessly freeing some labor in the process.

According to Service (1955, 411) and Pearse (1975, 4–37), the conquerors encountered four basic situations upon their arrival in the New World; they modified their strategies of governance and suppression of the local population accordingly.

First, in highland America they encountered settled, fairly sophisticated, hierarchically organized societies. To bring the populations to submission, they took over "the apex positions in the society." Indeed, the Aztec and Incan social structures were so pyramidal that their civilizations were immobilized once the Spanish had destroyed their rulers. So it was easy for the Spanish to substitute their own for the traditional symbols of social control and allow lower levels of social organization to persist; the Spaniards collected their tributes in goods and in labor.

In the highland areas of Mexico, this blending of Iberian and local social structures took place easily. Chevalier, the foremost historian of the period, claims that "late conquests of the Aztecs made the Spaniards' task easier; the latter found willing accomplices in states defeated or threatened by the Aztecs, so that subsequently to get hold of the tribute or certain lands they merely had to step into the shoes of the former masters. The substitution was all the easier since authority was strongly centralized..." (Chevalier 1963, 16).

In Peru in 1533, the Incan emperor was allowed only figurehead status acting under the supervision and command of Pizarro. Moreover, most of those who accompanied Pizarro were not members of the aristocracy in Spain but were anxious to use the land to form a local agriculture-based elite. In Spain they had seen land used as the basis for power and status; while social climbing was difficult if not impossible at home (Pizarro was an illiterate worker on a large feudal estate in Extremadura until he joined the party of Balboa in its journey that ended with the discovery of the Pacific Ocean), they were determined to be included in the social register of the New World. According to Preston James, "Such adventurers passionately desired the opportunity to acquire land and so to gain a portion of prestige. Grants of land by the Spanish crown, therefore, soon led to the creation of vast private estates and to the formation of a new aristocracy" (James 1959, 167).

As the historian Luís Martín notes,

> To help support them in their new role as city fathers, Pizarro began distributing generous land grants and homesteads among them. In an effort to accelerate the transformation of soldiers and adventurers into settlers, Pizarro also introduced in Peru the institution of the *encomienda*, a legal system of trusteeship by which a Spanish overlord or *encomendero* was entrusted with the care and protection of a group of Indians. The encomendero was morally bound to work for the welfare of his Indians, to protect them from the greed of other Spaniards, and to teach them Christianity. To compensate him for these services, the encomendero was legally entitled to collect from the Indians and keep for himself the royal tribute imposed on them as new subjects of the crown. Pizarro was indeed generous with his companions, making many of them not only powerful landlords but also lords over thousands of Indians. The land grants, the homesteads, and the encomienda, unjust as they certainly were from the point of view of the conquered Indians, helped root the Spaniards in the land and fostered the early development of an orderly society of settlers. (Martín 1974, 32–33)

Land grants (*mercedes*) were made in the name of the crown; *encomiendas* were to provide the labor force. Land usually continued to be farmed as before with the rent or tribute now paid to the new owner. It was the indigenous populations working the land who gave it value to the Spanish. Both the Spanish and the Portuguese were attracted less by the prospect of earning a living by their own toil than by the opportunities for profit (Pendle 1963, 29); while they engaged in speculative mining ventures, however, they had to be fed. Over time, the concepts of land grant and labor grant merged (the mechanics of this merger are debated by historians as part of the capitalism versus feudalism discussion); if properties changed hands, both land and Indians were sold together. Indeed, even into the mid-twentieth century in some Latin American countries, workers were sold with the land. A Santiago, Chile, resident in the early 1960s, for example, could read an advertisement in the daily, *El Mercurio*, telling of a farm of, say, 2,000 hectares with 100 resident laborers that was being offered for sale.

Conquest and control were made easier because the Iberian plunderers found an economic and political system similar to their own already set in place. Among the Aztecs and the Incas there existed a division of labor; they both had landholding villages (the *calpulli* and the *ayllu*, respectively), though the *calpulli* were more complex, as Chevalier points out (1963, 16–23). There were religious leaders, farming families labored to produce a surplus and transfer it to another group that was socially superior, some families were much "better off" than others, in some areas what appeared to be private property was beginning to evolve, artisan crafts were practiced, there were warriors to protect the community, and, furthermore, there were government functionaries. In other words, these were in no way egalitarian societies; as such, they cannot be held up as egalitarian models (as some have done) for what an agrarian reform might produce. Speaking of New Spain, James notes, "The ruling Aztecs exploited the labor of people they had conquered, and the Spanish merely carried on where the Aztecs left off. In many instances the same units were taken over, a Spanish officer taking the place of an Aztec lord without further dislocation of the system" (James 1959:591).

This first pattern, superimposition of a colonist master upon a preexisting social system, is easiest to understand, but there were three other scenarios that, in terms of the territory they covered, were more important. A second pattern thrived in such areas as the islands and coastal areas of the Caribbean, in much of Brazil, in coastal Peru, southern and western Bolivia, central Chile, and Paraguay, where the Iberians encountered peoples at lower levels of technology with much less social organization. Often, these people were engaged in swidden or slash-and-burn agriculture; in addition, some hunted and fished and were organized into small, fairly egalitarian kinship or tribal groups. This pattern had little in common with any set of institutions with which the conqueror was familiar, so indirect rule was impossible.

The frustrating characteristic for the Iberians was that there was little scope within these decentralized fragments of society for producing the agricultural surplus that the conquerors needed. The local labor force that might have been cajoled for a time into providing labor would soon escape into the forests where it could replicate its simple life style, leaving settlers without labor. Establishing domestic slavery was one method the conquerors attempted in an effort to rectify this problem; sometimes this was done through the missions as a sort of penalty for the refusal of the Indians to accept Christianity. Slavery did not work well, however, because a great deal of supervision was required. Furthermore, the Church's representatives in the New World sometimes became indignant at the miserable conditions of forced labor that this required and reported as much to the crown, the Indians could easily escape, and the labor force was decimated as it contracted European diseases. In some of these areas, Pearse (1975, 5–8) points out that "the more sparsely populated and remote the area of settlement, the less feasible it was to maintain even domestic slavery." A once-and-for-all technique (and, for this reason, different from slavery)—ransom (*rescate*)—was also attempted. It took many forms; one was that Indian villagers were incarcerated and left without food, being promised release by the conquerors if they paid a head tax in gold for every family member. In some sparsely populated backwaters, as in the highland areas, an institution called the *encomienda* (defined as a trust over Indians who lived in a particular area) was attempted, but it worked better if male settlers married Indians and simply reproduced their own work force.

When there was a strong demand for export crops, a third scenario was possible. This option required a good port for product shipment and fairly fertile and even irrigable soil near the port to grow the crop, as in northeastern Brazil, some of the Caribbean islands, northern coastal Peru, and Colombia. Sugar is a good example of this kind of enterprise. While the natural conditions were favorable, however, there were seldom enough Indians located nearby in these unforgiving climates; labor scarcity was a problem. In an attempt to meet the labor demand, African slaves were shipped from other parts of the New World to these coastal regions, and when that supply was exhausted they were brought from the African continent itself. Utilizing African slaves instead of Indians proved more efficient, in that those foreigners were less able to escape since they knew neither the terrain nor the languages of the New World. Also they were paid little heed by the Church, which considered them so foreign that they were out of its evangelical ken. Illness and death from tropical diseases among the laborers was a hallmark of this type of colonization.

A fourth situation was that in which the conquerors encountered the very simplest of hunter-gatherer societies, often egalitarian and usually nomadic to some extent. The control which the Iberian colonial institution could exert was least in this fourth group. Sometimes, these indigenous groups were rounded up into reservations in order that their labor might be exploited; when enslaved, however, these local people often became ill. Largely they disappeared, gradually at times, sometimes after absorption into the families of their conquerors. In places like Argentina, northern Mexico, southern Chile, Uruguay, and parts of Colombia and even Venezuela, assimilation and extermination left vast areas open to new waves of European settlement, especially from Germany and Italy.

Ultimately, the Europeans, in the 75 years after the first Spanish conquest, discovered more land than in the previous thousand. The Spanish alone conquered a region larger than forty Spains. How these four scenarios ultimately led to the creation of a rather predominating hacienda (or in Brazil, *fazenda*) system throughout Latin America is the subject of much historic debate; all we can see in colonial history is the rough outline, the cameo appearance. The resilience of this predominating hacienda system from independence up to the twentieth century, however, is clearly evident. Despite changing governing coalitions, the formation of new political parties, and the evolution of democracies and dictatorships, the essence of the system's hierarchical structure and its patron-client relationship remained intact.

Indeed, this extraordinarily durable set of institutions left in its wake a bimodal society in which the strong, primarily European, could always prevail over the weak, primarily indigenous or imported slave. Not until economic growth occurred in the twentieth century was a recognizable middle class established. Intermarriage with the indigenous populations to produce a large group of mestizos or ladinos (or with blacks imported from Africa to work in agriculture when native peoples died upon being exposed to European diseases) occurred more frequently in Latin American than in North American settlements.

Today, although the hacienda is progressively being eroded by wave upon wave of capitalistic endeavor, such constant change continues to occur within the broad outlines of a resilient and still paternalistic *latifundio* system. In the early postcolonial period, markets for nearly all outputs were established. As technology produced off-farm inputs for farming and the green revolution came to Latin America, market control of agriculture increased. Land and labor were the last factors to be subjected to market control. Labor now is bought and sold separately from land. Nonetheless, land is still not entirely subject to the organized market, for remnants of the landed elites still survive and are strong in some countries and regions.[10]

The period from 1850 to 1930 reinforced the bimodal character of the agrarian structure in Latin America. Most countries came to rely on the export of one or several primary commodities to the industrial centers of the time and to depend on these centers, in turn, for imports of other primary commodities or simple manufactures. Demand generated by increased population encouraged landowners to put more land into cultivation; sometimes, this meant obtaining it from indigenous communities or other *minifundistas.* More land meant that the production pressures in what was still a very labor-intensive process were placed on service and share tenants and other wage laborers.[11]

Export-based agriculture augmented the power of the landlord, the prime producer of these goods. The state, anxious for foreign exchange, advanced the interests of these property holders, encouraging infrastructural development, establishing subsidies for inputs and services, and granting credit to meet production costs. The exporting, landowning elite, thus allied with the state and commercial agents, foreign investors, and often importers, tightened its grip on land as its hold on capital and labor became more secure. Production for the domestic market continued more slowly; exporting—first to Iberia, then to England, then to North America—was the driving force in agriculture.

Industrialization followed upon the collapse of mining and agriculture in the 1930s. As urbanization increased, especially in the largest and most advanced Latin American countries, the power of landlords weakened somewhat; they no longer could maintain hegemonic dominance in much of Latin America. To maintain their status, landholding groups frequently invested in commerce and manufacturing. Thus, by moving aggressively into some of their country's new growth points, the agricultural elite often managed to maintain enough power to inhibit the reform of rural social relations. The way in which agricultural modernization occurred, together with the manner in which commercial and service institutions were already geared to the elites, meant that little fundamental change occurred to the structure of agriculture in Latin America, though it did have to accommodate some new forces: increased rural organization, left-wing political movements, and intellectual critiques of the 1960s and 1970s.

It is partly this historic legacy, the tied-labor patterns and the nonnegotiability of land throughout much of this century, that makes land reform so difficult to understand and even more difficult to enact. Land reform affects agrarian institutions that reach far back into the histories of the most highly settled cultures of the Americas. As such, these agrarian institutions are one of the best outward manifestations of social class: they reflect status within society, they reflect privilege, they reflect power.

RECENT IDEAS: AGRARIAN REFORM AND RURAL DEVELOPMENT POLICY

Much research on land reform has been done in the last several decades; the most valuable type of inquiry has investigated the reform process over time in one country or has compared land reform in several countries of the region.[12] Before that, field work on land reform and agrarian structure was the ken of anthropologists and sociologists who tended to write on single-country experiences. Classic works, rich in detail and emphasizing benefits that land reform could bring or was then in the process of delivering, were written on Chile (McBride 1936), Peru (Ford 1955), and Mexico (McBride 1923; Whetten 1948). The Inter-American Committee on Agricultural Development (*Comité Interamericano de Desarrollo Agrícola*, CIDA) reports of the 1960s[13] and Peter Dorner's edited volume on Land Tenure Center research during a comparable period[14] broke this pattern in favor of more multicountry treatment.

Several careful and comprehensive volumes have appeared quite recently with views on the importance of land reform over the period that tend to be less sanguine than those of the CIDA and Dorner, who both feel that a fairly thorough land reform would help the region distribute its resources more equitably and that production could be affected positively. These works were undertaken in the 1970s when the mood was decidedly more pessimistic; the analysis was also more dynamic, as it was then realized that the peasant sector of the economy was characterized by a great deal of change while the basic, anachronistic features of the *latifundio-minifundio* structure still prevailed. Thus, the change that was occurring tended not to bring much benefit to a wide group of campesinos.

Pearse (1975) documents the changing, modernizing world which the peasantry faces and concludes that positive policy has a role to play, but that the present reforms do not augur well for the future given "the incorporative forces" of an expanding urban-industrial complex. The Bolivian agrarian reform of 1953, for example, tended to replace one set of despots with another; there was little to make Pearse think that other Latin American land reforms would have better results. Here, he draws conclusions similar to those of Heath (1970, 1973), an anthropologist, who said that the new kingpins of Bolivia should be considered *hacendados* with bad table manners. Pearse examines land reform in the partial manner in which it occurred in Latin America; he depicts the way in which such reform made it possible for new social differentiation to appear and for new elites to emerge, elites no more anxious for change than the group they replaced.[15]

De Janvry (1981) believes that land reform in Latin America has been one more tool that the state has consciously used to pave the way from feudalism to capitalism. He asserts that most production increases that happen as a result of land reform occur on the nonexpropriated farms or on those parts of expropriated farms still in the hands of the old landlords. Landholders can and do evade land reform legally by showing authorities that their land is utilized efficiently. (The fact that efficient land is exempted from reform may be taken as "proof" that the reform has been set in motion by capitalists to help capitalists and not to assist peasants out of their poverty; the fact that all of this can be done in the name of alleviating poverty keeps this fact well hidden from the "glare of publicity" and prevents the effort from being scorned.) De Janvry notes that since land reforms are not integral efforts, that is, since they are not accompanied by the services and capital that beneficiaries need to make progress, the old landlords are not displaced in the reform. In fact, de Janvry notes, after the reforms of the 1960s and 1970s, Latin American social fabric remained pretty much what it was before the reform. The land reform served some important political goals, however. Land was given to a small group of peasantry that became the conservative agrarian petite bourgeoisie (those who have control over the physical means of production, investment, and resource allocation, but who have no control over the labor power of contributors other than the family). This group, being protective of its land resource, could act as a conservative buffer against countryside change; it was, and is, relied upon as a force for countryside stability.

For all of this, capitalism is the healthier: not much has to be paid for the reform, farming is more efficient as a result, beneficiaries protect the system, and, since beneficiaries cannot produce much more efficiently than *minifundistas*, they soon seek off-farm labor and are snapped up by landlords who want to hire wage workers. As old landlords mechanize, they need labor only for part of the year, and those who are semiproletarianized do not need to be supported year-round on the hacienda. Land reform beneficiaries and *minifundistas* thus find themselves tied with landlords into a system of functional dualism.[16]

Grindle (1986) likewise takes a jaundiced view of land reform in Latin America, but she does not agree with the elite-as-state-manipulator model of de Janvry. She feels that the state does not simply reflect and reproduce class relations within society: Grindle places state elites, "those who are formal incumbents in decision- and policy-making positions," more centrally. For Grindle, state elites have more a life of their own, more autonomy, than for de Janvry; they have not been captured to as great an extent by the dominant class. Rather, state elites on their own seem to make up a class in Grindle's view.

However, Grindle does agree with de Janvry on the extant agricultural structural situation that has resulted in the region. She recognizes, for instance, the importance and the relative privilege (especially in terms of state expenditures for technology, and so on) granted to capitalist agriculture and its primarily agroexport nature. She also decries the neglect of the domestic subsistence sector, concluding that this has led to the bifurcation of agriculture. Her conception is that state-elite influence has been growing in the region; it now laps over into many social and political areas as well as economic areas. Indeed, the state, in the four decades she analyzes, has increasingly taken charge of the region's agriculture, having reached some sort of a zenith in the late 1970s. Moreover, the state elite has a role as mediator in social conflict between the dominant class and the poor; it frequently uses repression and sometimes co-opts groups, thus promoting the social stability that both the dominant class and the state elite require.

Grindle argues that because of the need for the region to import so many staples in the 1960s, peasants were "rediscovered" in many countries of the region. In that decade there emerged the agrarian reform initiatives concerned with modifying the structural nature of the agrarian economy. Yet, by the 1970s and with the green revolution, some countries altered their emphasis from structural to technological issues; they no longer talked of land reform. This shifted the focus back to the large-farm entrepreneurial sector. Through this period, it became obvious to the state elite that the dominant private-sector elite was consistently subverting economic growth and social stability. However, the state elite had to take account of the still-powerful landlord class, and this meant looking upon reform—especially in times of financial stringency—as risky, expensive, politically volatile, and difficult to implement. Some partial reforms, nonetheless, were implemented and served to increase state-elite power by encouraging new social divisions in the countryside; this inhibited the rise of class-based protest.

Integrated rural development (IRD), one of the catchphrase programs of the 1970s, attempted development without land reform in a single geographic area and in relative isolation from commercial agriculture; it claimed that the trickle-down theory in agriculture was obsolete. But, without land, IRD could not address the issue of rural underemployment. IRD, as the state-sponsored agrarian reforms that occurred earlier, increased state control and management over rural areas and the people who lived there.

Rather a variant on de Janvry than a new direction, Grindle believes that IRD and agrarian reform are the culmination of an effort by the state (technocrats and public managers) to gain control over the economy. She regards what agrarian reform the region has seen (in the four Latin American countries she studied) as a palliative. Expansion of state power does not mean that the poor will be helped—far from it. The state benefits from agrarian reform as its bureaucracy swells to accommodate it: the rural poor will get something for themselves only in a sort of political version of "trickle down."[17]

RATIONALE FOR THIS VOLUME

In this spirit, what we attempt in this volume is to shed light on cases of agrarian reform in Latin America over the past 25 years. This entails covering one facet of the growth-distribution debate that is claimed by many social science disciplines but often not systematically studied by any of them. Agrarian reform in Latin America is frequently found where two or more of the social science disciplines—often economics and political science—overlap and become inseparable. For that reason, the subject matter of this book is necessarily interdisciplinary.

The rationale for presenting the essays in this volume is to inform opinion and provide several guideposts for future public policy on agrarian reform in Latin America. In the expository cases to be presented, specific land reforms do not appear as either completely pure or wholly tarnished efforts. As in most issues of public policy, positive and well-intentioned work is usually alloyed with baser substances.

Usually, land reforms do not accomplish all they set out to do. Often, accomplishment on one score is mixed with less satisfactory results on another; sometimes, to the chagrin and embarrassment of all, results are nearly the opposite of what was intended. As these cases are examined, we find that political expedience is more frequent than altruism. Furthermore, mixed motives—and sometimes even accidents—occur more often than perceptive foresight; pragmatism is more common than ideological purity.

NOTES

1. Poor countries do not have the luxury of the social welfare-antidiscrimination programs. The numbers of those in poverty are so large in less developed countries (LDCs) that governments cannot make the necessary expenditures, even if they had the political will to do so, without generating runaway inflation, to say nothing of enormous bureaucracies.

2. Comparing one of the few sharecropping areas of Latin America, such as the Guayas Basin in Ecuador where Redclift (1978) shows that the agrarian reform of 1971 had favorable effects on rice production, with some tenanted rice areas of Southeast Asia might yield interesting results. Comparisons have been made also in Ghose (1983).

3. This term was coined by Theodore Schultz (1964) to characterize the contrast between the Soviet Union's large-scale, mechanized collective farms and the very small, highly labor-intensive private plots cultivated as a sideline activity by members of a collective farm. Bruce Johnston began using this term to characterize contrasting patterns of agricultural development policies, using "bimodal" in the case of Mexico and "unimodal" to refer to Japan's development strategy (see Johnston 1966, 251–312; Johnston and Cownie 1969). For more recent treatment, see Johnston and Clark (1982, 70–72).

4. At the same time, large farms, on which the best farmland is typically located, may be utilized for extensive agricultural pursuits, for agroindustry, or for export crops. Theoretically, there is nothing wrong with this land-use pattern for large properties in countries where unemployment and underemployment are infrequent, other sectors are dynamic, and public resources are amply available to redress the lack of opportunities. But in Latin America, the industrial sector is usually not growing rapidly enough to absorb excess population, agricultural growth on large haciendas or *fazendas* implies that fewer rather than more workers will be needed with the passage of time, technology adoption in the economy means that progressively less labor per unit of output is the rule, and the frontier has been settled. In this situation, agrarian reform will come up as a policy option sooner or later.

5. "Institutions are the rules of a society or of organizations that facilitate coordination among people by helping them form expectations which each person can reasonably hold in dealing with others. They reflect the conditions that have evolved in different societies regarding the behavior of individuals and groups relative to their own behavior and the behavior of others. In the area of

economic relations they have a crucial role in establishing expectations about the rights to use resources in economic activities and about the partitioning of the income streams resulting from economic activity. Carlisle Ford Runge has noted that 'institutions provide assurance respecting the actions of others, and give order and stability to expectations in the complex and uncertain world of economic relations' [Runge 1981, xvi]. Our perspective on the sources of demand for institutional change is similar to the traditional Marxian view [Marx 1913, 11–12]. Marx considered technological change as the primary source of institutional change. Our view is somewhat more complex in that we consider that changes in factor endowments and product demand are equally important sources of institutional change. Nor is our definition of institutional change limited to the dramatic or revolutionary changes of the type anticipated by Marx.... [W]e share...the view that basic institutions such as property rights and markets are more typically altered through the cumulation of 'secondary' or incremental institutional changes such as modifications in contractual relations or shifts in the boundaries between market and nonmarket activities." (Hayami and Ruttan 1985, 94–96)

6. For a recent example, see Balassa et al. (1986).

7. See *El Comercio*, Quito, 23 March 1984.

8. A less sanguine view of an East Asian reform (Taiwan) is available (see Apthorpe 1979).

9. Because land reform can serve to buy favor, a word on matters of ethics and land reform is needed. Indeed, land reform may be an immoral policy expedient where (1) land reform buys support of the peasantry for a corrupt regime, (2) the postreform structure is not in keeping with standards of environmental conservation, (3) reform gives land to some poor as it deprives other poor of land or, worse, allows the rich to benefit at the expense of the poor, (4) reform freezes the peasantry on worn-out land for which insufficient yield-increasing inputs are made available, (5) short-term gains for the peasantry (which roughly correspond to the period during which the government needs support until it can develop repressive capacity) are offset by massive, probable, long-term losses, (6) the land-taking confiscatory process is brutal and even inhumane, and (7) reform involves public deceit so that a few obtain land and the remainder of the land hungry receive highly publicized promises.

10. See López Cordóvez (1982) and Ortega (1982).

11. This and the following three paragraphs are based on Grindle (1986, 34–44).

12. See FAO (1976), LTC (1974).

13. The director of the first set of these studies was Solon Barraclough; another set was directed by Thomas Carroll. Much research documentation came from this careful field work (see, for example, Barraclough and Domike 1966, Barraclough 1973, Feder 1971, and Eckstein et al. 1978).

14. See Dorner (1971, 1972); see also Griffin (1976), King (1977), and FAO (1979).

15. Pearse sees much disruption for the peasant in the urbanization of Latin America that is occurring and the concomitant pressures it generates. As the principal sociologist on the team of groundbreaking CIDA social

scientists who examined agrarian structure of Latin America, his view of agrarian reform, a measure recommended by CIDA as one which might ameliorate the peasant's plight, is circumspect and even skeptical. Based primarily on events in various colonization schemes on which he did field work as well as on Bolivia's land reform, Pearse sees little merit in any solution to ameliorate the peasant's plight that governments might propose; negative forces to enduring reform are too powerful. Pearse's treatment of the Latin American peasant shows how traditional institutions have undergone change and disintegration as they have come into contact with modern society. It is pessimistic. In Pearse, one has the feeling that reverting to an earlier age and to the comfortable days when the peasant family grew just what was needed for subsistence would be the best remedy for peasants' current problems. The critic of Pearse's important work might challenge it on the basis that there is little or no evidence that these past days were so comfortable and much evidence to suggest that they were miserable; in the second place, as Pearse himself would doubtless agree, it is unrealistic to think one can ever recover a halcyon and more idyllic period.

16. Like Pearse, but placing the campesino within a neo-Marxist theoretical framework, de Janvry distinguishes between the "center" or socially and sectorally articulated economies—those in the developed world—and the "periphery" or disarticulated economies of the Third World. For Pearse the market bodes little good for peasant welfare; de Janvry specifies why the market exploits. For Pearse, the impersonality of the market is a problem as is the fact that, in obtaining the inputs necessary for agriculture, needed credit is available only through exploitative middlemen; in de Janvry, the market is rigged against the campesino; it virtually conspires against the peasant as it serves the causes of the capitalist farmer-landlord.

17. Like de Janvry, Grindle is concerned with the place of the state in the process of development. In her study, which involves examining governmental policies in several Latin American countries in the four decades ending in 1980, she concludes that the state role is so extensive that it cannot be explained merely on the basis of capital accumulation and crisis management. The pursuit of national development by state elites serves to ensure the continued existence of the regime they serve. She concludes that it is the technocrats and public managers—the state elites—who "allocate resources in a way that expands their own power and wealth." For de Janvry, one gets the impression that the state does not have a life of its own: it is dependent upon the needs of the ruling elites. For Grindle, the expansion of the state is evidence that the state not only breathes for itself but also aggrandizes in and of itself. As such, it has carved out for itself an increasingly larger role in the agricultural sector. Agrarian reform and IRD are seen by Grindle as the culmination of an effort begun at the end of the Great Depression to put power from agriculture into the hands of the state, which could then utilize the legal, bureaucratic, and coercive apparatus to gain control over the economy. Since both programs require state participation, they could also become methods of control by the state. State expansionism paralleled the growth of state capitalism in Latin America. And, with expansion of state power, the problems of the rural poor were not satisfactorily addressed. Grindle feels that because of resource

constraints, lack of administrative capacity, and political opposition, land reform will never be massively implemented and will, therefore, serve the sector only as a palliative. The state will benefit first, and only then will the rural masses be touched, in a sort of political "trickle down."

REFERENCES

Apthorpe, Raymond. 1979. The burden of land reform in Taiwan: An Asian model land reform re-analyzed. *World Development* 7:519-530.

Arulpragasam, L.C. 1966. A consideration of the problems arising from the size and subdivision of paddy holdings in Ceylon. *Ceylon Journal of Historical and Social Studies* 4(1):59–70.

Balassa, Bela, Geraldo Bueno, Pedro-Pablo Kucynski, and Mario Henrique Simonsen. 1986. *Toward renewed growth in Latin America.* Washington: Institute for International Economics.

Barraclough, Solon L., ed. 1973. *Agrarian structure in Latin America* (in collaboration with Juan Carlos Collarte). Lexington, Mass.: Heath.

Barraclough, Solon L., and Arthur L. Domike. 1966. Agrarian structure in seven Latin American countries. *Land Economics* 42(4):391-424.

Bauer, Peter. 1986. Anything goes. *New York Review of Books*, 20 November.

Berry, R. Albert, and William S. Cline. 1979. *Agrarian structure and productivity in developing countries.* Baltimore: Johns Hopkins Univ. Press.

Chevalier, François. 1963. *Land and society in colonial Mexico: The great hacienda,* edited by Lesley Byrd Simpson, translated by Alvin Eustis. Berkeley: Univ. of California Press.

Conquest, Robert. 1986. *The harvest of sorrow: Soviet collectivization and the terror-famine.* New York: Oxford Univ. Press.

Cornia, Giovanni Andrea. 1985. Farm size, land yields and the agricultural production function: An analysis of fifteen developing countries. *World Development 13*(4):513–534.

de Janvry, Alain. 1981. *The agrarian question and reformism in Latin America.* Baltimore: Johns Hopkins Univ. Press.

Dorner, Peter, ed. 1971. *Land reform in Latin America: Issues and cases. Land Economics* Monograph Series, no. 3. Madison: Published by *Land Economics* for the Land Tenure Center at the University of Wisconsin.

——.1972. *Land reform and economic development.* Baltimore: Penguin Books.

Dorner, Peter, and Don Kanel. 1971. The economic case for land reform. In *Land reform in Latin America: Issues and cases,* edited by Peter Dorner, pp. 41–56. *Land Economics* Monograph Series, no. 3. Madison: Published by *Land Economics* for the Land Tenure Center at the University of Wisconsin.

Eckstein, Shlomo, Gordon Donald, Douglas Horton, and Thomas Carroll. 1978. *Land reform in Latin America: Bolivia, Chile, Mexico, Peru, and Venezuela.* World Bank, Staff Working Paper, no. 275. Washington: World Bank, April.

El Comercio (Quito), 23 March 1984.

FAO (Food and Agriculture Organization). 1976. *Progress in land reform: Sixth report. New York: FAO.*

——.1979. World conference on agrarian reform and rural development (WCARRD). *Review and analysis of agrarian reform and rural development in the developing countries since the mid-1960s.* WCARRD/INF.3. Rome: FAO.

Feder, Ernest. 1971. *The rape of the peasantry: Latin America's landholding system.* Garden City, N.J.: Doubleday.

Ford, Peter. 1986. Guatemala inches forward. *Christian Science Monitor,* 23 June.

Ford, Thomas R. 1955. *Man and land in Peru.* Gainesville: Univ. of Florida Press.

Ghose, Ajit, ed. 1983. *Agrarian reform in contemporary developing countries.* London: Croom Helm.

Griffin, Keith. 1976. *Land concentration and rural poverty.* New York: Macmillan.

Grindle, Merilee S. 1986. *State and countryside: Development policy and agrarian politics in Latin America.* Baltimore: Johns Hopkins Univ. Press.

Handelman, Howard. 1981. Ecuadorian reform: The politics of limited change. In *The politics of agrarian change in Asia and Latin America,* edited by Howard Handelman, pp. 63–81. Bloomington: Indiana Univ. Press.

Hayami, Yujiro, and Vernon W. Ruttan. 1985. *Agricultural development: An international perspective.* 2nd ed. Baltimore: Johns Hopkins Univ. Press.

Heath, Dwight. 1970. Hacendados with bad table manners: Campesino syndicates as surrogate landlords. *Inter-American Economic Affairs* 24(1):3–13.

——.1973. New patrons for old: Changing patron-client relationships in the Bolivian yungas. *Ethnology* 12(1):75–98.

House, Richard. 1986. Casualties of a bloody land war. *South* (July), pp. 28–30.

Huntington, Samuel P. 1968. *Political order in changing societies.* New Haven, Conn.: Yale Univ. Press.

James, Preston E. 1959. *Latin America.* 3rd ed. New York: Odyssey Press.

Johnston, Bruce F. 1966. Agriculture and economic development: The relevance of the Japanese experience. *Food Research Institute Studies,* no. 3. Stanford, Calif.: Food Research Institute.

Johnston, Bruce F., and and William C. Clark. 1982. *Redesigning rural development: A strategic perspective.* Baltimore: Johns Hopkins Univ. Press.

Johnston, Bruce F., and J. Cownie. 1969. The seed-fertilizer revolution and labor force absorption. *American Economic Review* 59(4):569-582.

Kanel, Don. 1971. Land tenure reform as a policy issue in the modernization of traditional societies. In *Land reform in Latin America: Issues and cases,* edited by Peter Dorner, pp. 23–35. *Land Economics* Monograph Series, no. 3. Madison: Published by *Land Economics* for the Land Tenure Center at the University of Wisconsin.

King, Russell. 1977. *Land reform: A world survey.* Leicester (U.K.): Univ. of Leicester.

Kinzer, Stephen. 1986. Walking the tightrope in Guatemala. *New York Times Magazine,* 9 Nov.

Klare, Michael T. 1985–1986. Low-intensity conflict: The new U.S. strategic doctrine. *Nation,* 28 Dec. 1985/4 Jan. 1986, pp. 710–716.

Lee, E. 1979. Egalitarian peasant farming and rural development: The case of South Korea. *World Development* 7:493–517.

López Cordovez, Luis. 1982. Trends and recent changes in the Latin American food and agriculture situation. *CEPAL Review*, no. 16, April, pp. 7–41.

LTC (Land Tenure Center). 1974. *Agrarian reform in Latin America: An annotated bibliography. Land Economics* Monograph Series, no. 5. Madison: Univ. of Wisconsin Press.

McBride, George McCutchen. 1923. *Land systems of Mexico*. American Geographical Society Research Series, no. 12. (Reprint, New York: Octagon Books, 1971.)

——.1936. *Chile: Land and society*. American Geographical Society Research Series, no. 19. (Reprint, Port Washington, N.Y.: Kennikat Press, 1971.)

McNamara, Robert S. 1973. Address to the board of governors, Nairobi, Kenya, 24 September 1973. Washington: International Bank for Reconstruction and Development.

Martín, Luis. 1974. *The kingdom of the sun: A short history of Peru*. New York: Scribners.

Marx, Karl. 1913. *A contribution to the critique of political economy*. Chicago: Charles H. Kerr and Co.

Ortega, Emiliano. 1982. Peasant agriculture in Latin America: Citation lost. *CEPAL Review*, no. 16, April, pp. 75–111.

——.1985. Campesinado y producción agrícola: La agricultura campesino en América Latina. Typescript. Distribución restringida, Santiago. (Update of 1982 *CEPAL Review* article.)

Parthasarathy, Gorgula. 1979. Understanding agriculture: Growth and current concerns. Mimeograph. Rome.

Pearse, Andrew. 1975. *The Latin American peasant*. London: Frank Cass.

Pendle, George. 1963. *A history of Latin America*. Baltimore: Penguin Books.

Redclift, Michael R. 1978. *Agrarian reform and peasant organization on the Ecuadorian coast*. London: Athlone Press, Univ. of London.

Riding, Alan. 1980. Guatemala: State of siege. *New York Times Magazine*, 24 August.

Rosenberg, Tina. 1986. The moral limits of self-interest. *Atlantic Monthly*, December.

Runge, Carlisle Ford. 1981. Institutions and common property externalities: The assurance problem in economic development. Ph.D. dissertation, Univ. of Wisconsin-Madison.

Schultz, Theodore W. 1964. *Transforming traditional agriculture*. Chicago: Univ. of Chicago Press.

Service, Elman R. 1955. Indian-European relations in colonial Latin America. *American Anthropologist* 57:411–425.

Silvero, Ignacio. 1986. Paraguay: Violence erupts in peasant land takeovers. *Latin America Press*, 23 October.

Terra, Juan Pablo. 1983. The role of education in relation to employment problems. *CEPAL Review*, no. 21, December, pp. 83–87.

Thiesenhusen, William C. 1983. Economic effects of technology in agriculture in less developed countries. In *Technology and social change in rural areas,* edited by Gene F. Summers, pp. 235–252. A Festschrift for Eugene A. Wilkening. Boulder, Colo.: Westview Press.

Trager, Frank N., and William L. Scully. 1981. Low-intensity conflict: The U.S. response. In *U.S. policy and low-intensity conflict,* edited by Sam C. Sarkesian and William L. Scully, pp. 175–198. New York: National Strategy Information Center.

Whetten, Nathan. 1948. *Rural Mexico*. Chicago: Univ. of Chicago Press.

World Bank. 1983. *World tables, vol. 2, social data,* 3rd ed. Baltimore: Johns Hopkins Univ. Press.

World Press Review. 1986. Early warning. December.

Chapter 2

Agrarian Reform and Structural Change: Ecuador Since 1964

José Vicente Zevallos L.

This chapter examines the implementation of agrarian reform policies in Ecuador since 1964 and assesses subsequent impacts on the land-tenure system, rural social relations, and technological change.[1] Agrarian reform is analyzed in the context of other policies and processes that have shaped the evolution of the agrarian structure. Particular attention is paid to colonization and to trends set in motion by the oil boom during the 1970s.

THE LEGAL BASIS FOR THE TRANSFORMATION OF SOCIAL RELATIONS IN AGRICULTURE, 1964–1970

The traditional hacienda was the typical production unit in Ecuadorian agriculture until the 1940s on the Coast (where mainly export crops were produced) and until the 1960s in the Highlands (where primarily crops for domestic consumption were grown). Hacienda laborers generally received land in usufruct, and in exchange they worked for the landlord without pay or for nominal wages. Landlords controlled the laborers not only economically but also politically. The landlords were able to manipulate legislators, state officials, and local authorities to their own advantage, so that when peasant movements arose, the police would quickly intervene (Hurtado 1977, 73, 165).

Wage relations spread rapidly in the coastal region during the 1950s as a result of the expansion of banana and sugar plantations and cattle ranching. As early as 1954, landless wage laborers accounted for over half of the agrarian work force in the coastal lowlands. The development of capitalist agriculture in the Highlands, meanwhile, lagged considerably behind. In 1954, landless wage laborers represented only 2 percent of the agrarian work force of this region (CIDA 1965, 16-17).

Two state interventions contributed significantly to the elimination of precapitalist relations in agriculture: (1) a reform implemented in the Andean highlands by authority of the Agrarian Reform Law of 1964, and (2) a reform implemented in the coastal lowlands based on a special 1970 decree, *Decreto* 1001. The Agrarian Reform Law of 1964 followed the general objectives of the "Alliance for Progress," promoted at the time by the U.S. State Department. The law proscribed the *huasipungo* and *arrimado* systems and other precapitalist arrangements, referred to under the generic name of *precarismo. Huasipungueros* were peasants who exchanged labor on haciendas for usufruct on a plot of land and, theoretically, a small wage. In practice, this system was often a form of debt peonage, as landlords gave their laborers credit against future wages, put hacienda livestock in their charge and made them financially responsible for animals that got lost or died, or held them otherwise liable for hacienda property that was damaged. *Arrimados* also exchanged labor for usufruct on hacienda land, but, in contrast, they received no wages. An additional difference between the two systems is that the former entailed the right to use the land through generations, while the peasant in the latter system had no security either to keep the land or to transmit use rights to heirs (Hurtado 1971, 32).

The 1964 law established that the *precaristas* were to receive formal title to land. Although officially the regulation was to be applied throughout the country, the law actually was implemented only in the Highlands, where around 17,000 plots were awarded between 1964 and 1971 (Velasco 1979, 99). These plots, which averaged about 3.5 hectares, were usually of lower quality than those that *huasipungueros* and *arrimados* had worked prior to the reform. In subsequent years, the plots were divided further through inheritance and used primarily for subsistence farming.

The law also specified a maximum landholding size, but, de facto, no farms were expropriated solely for this reason.[2] Land redistribution was restricted to haciendas belonging to the government's *Asistencia Social* (Social Assistance) and to haciendas owned by the Catholic Church, which were handed over to the state voluntarily.[3] The most important impact of the reform, then, was its contribution to the spread of impersonal wage relations in highland agriculture. Even so, the role of reform in this process should not be overemphasized. Wage relations had been growing in importance prior to 1964; the reform merely accelerated an existing trend.[4]

Decreto 1001 was the second piece of legislation that affected social relations in agriculture. This 1970 decree proscribed rice *precarismo*, a precapitalist arrangement that was prevalent in the Guayas Basin and had been unaffected by the 1964 reform.[5] Rice *precarismo* had developed after the "cacao crisis" of the 1920s as a result of the reduction of foreign demand for cacao and the opening of new production zones in Brazil and Africa. Until then, most haciendas in the Guayas Basin had grown cacao; but, after the collapse in the world market price, many hacienda owners had simply failed to plant. When this happened, former hacienda laborers began to cultivate rice on the abandoned floodplain.

From the 1930s to the 1960s, rice *precarismo* evolved in ways that were clearly advantageous to the landowners. First, *precaristas* became obliged to share their harvest of rice in exchange for the use of land. Usually, the *precarista* was assigned 7 hectares, while the owner charged from 3 to 6 hundredweight of milled rice or its equivalent value in local currency (sucres) for every hectare. In order to meet production costs and subsistence expenses, especially in the preharvest months, the *precarista* had to borrow from the landowner or from a moneylender, known as a *fomentador*. These loans carried usurious interest rates and were payable in full at the time of harvest. Second, the landowners became mill owners, enabling them to buy rice from their tenants at depressed prices and to sell the crop for a handsome profit (Redclift and Preston 1980, 56–17).

Pressure for reform in the rice zones began to grow in the late 1960s as a result of two main factors. The first was because agitation by tenants, who demanded land of their own, had understandably mounted; the second was because domestic rice shortages, which were attributed to the inefficient production, processing, and marketing of rice, had occurred (Redclift and Preston 1980, 57). With *Decreto* 1001, all riceland cultivated under "precarious tenure" was declared to be of public utility and subject to expropriation and immediate occupation by *precaristas*. Titles to land were not to be given to individuals (as in the 1964 reform) but to agrarian cooperatives; in practice, the cooperatives rarely functioned as such.[6]

Decreto 1001 immediately broke the old ties between landowners and peasants, but the process of granting titles to cooperatives was very slow. Most of this task was carried out by the Guillermo Rodríguez regime between 1973 and 1975. As in the case of the 1964 reform, *Decreto* 1001 did not bring about a significant redistribution of land. Tenants simply acquired legal, collective titles to the land that they were already working. *Decreto* 1001, like the 1964 reform, contributed mainly to the generalization of wage relations in agriculture.[7]

Data from the last two agricultural censuses (1954 and 1974) confirm the limited redistributive impact of both reforms. As Table 1 shows, the most important change in the land-distribution pattern during the intercensal period was a decline in the relative importance of properties over 500 hectares in size, resulting mainly from subdivision and private sales.

TABLE 1
Number and area of farms classified by size, 1954 and 1974[a]

Size of holding (in hectares)	Percentage of total number of holdings		Percentage of total national farm area	
	1954	1974	1954	1974
<5	73.1	69.7	7.2	7.8
5–20	16.7	18.5	9.4	13.0
20–100	8.0	9.9	19.0	28.6
100–500	1.7	11.6	19.3	20.6
>500	0.4	0.3	45.2	30.0

[a] Source: LTC (Land Tenure Center) Library, *Land Concentration in the Third World: Statistics on Number and Area of Farms Classified by Size of Farms*, Training and Methods Series, No. 28 (Madison: Land Tenure Center, University of Wisconsin, April 1979), pp. 144–146.

REFORMING THE NONREFORM SECTOR: AGRARIAN REFORM LAW OF 1973

Another agrarian reform law was issued in October 1973.[8] Its stated objective was to achieve social justice and sustained agricultural growth simultaneously: "Agrarian reform implies a process through which a redistribution of land and income occurs, permitting the elimination of the *latifundio*, integration of *minifundio*...and an increase in agricultural production" [MAG 1974, 5 (author's translation)]. While social justice and agricultural growth appear to be given equal importance in this preamble, the provisions of the law suggest that the latter was its primary objective. In fact, no limit was set on the size of farm as long as the enterprise was operated efficiently.[9] The real target of the reform was what de Janvry (1981) has called the "nonreform sector," that is, all farmland that was neither expropriated for redistributive purposes nor awarded to peasants through colonization programs.

The law contained several provisions to encourage increased productivity and efficient land use in the nonreform sector, the most important of which were Articles 25 and 30. Article 25 established that a farm was to be considered inefficient—and thus subject to expropriation—if it failed to meet any of the following three requirements: (1) by January, 1976, at least 80 percent of the land appropriate for agriculture was to be efficiently utilized according to the geographic and ecological conditions of the zone in which it was located; (2) the productivity of the farm was to reach at least the government-established average for its zone; and (3) the farm was to be equipped with the physical infrastructure necessary for its economic utilization.[10] Article 30 discouraged absentee landownership by declaring that all farms not administered directly were also subject to expropriation. And direct administration was defined as that which was carried out by the owner, by the owner's relatives, or by administrators if the owner were a company or legal entity. Besides absenteeism and inefficiency, the law provided for expropriation in three other instances: (1) farms that were located in areas affected by "great demographic pressure" (areas in which the neighboring population was unable to subsist on agricultural activities),[11] (2) farms that did not conserve natural resources adequately, and (3) farms that violated labor laws.

Of all these rules, the large landowners perceived Article 25 to be the greatest threat to their interests, particularly in its requirement that all farmers must utilize at least 80 percent of their land efficiently in order to avoid expropriation. But this article was never applied, mainly because of successful opposition campaigns launched by the *Cámaras de Agricultura*, organizations representing the interests of the large landowners, and because of difficulties inherent in determining the meaning of "efficiently utilized" (see Zevallos 1985, chaps. 3 and 4).[12] Expropriations of land on the basis of other provisions were few and generally occurred after peasants had invaded land that had been abandoned by the owner, thus forcing the Agrarian Reform Institute (*Instituto Ecuatoriano de Reforma Agraria y Colonización*, IERAC) to intervene so that the law could be applied.

THE USE OF OIL REVENUE IN THE CONTEXT OF UNEQUAL DISTRIBUTED LAND

Soon after the promulgation of the Agrarian Reform Law of 1973, the military government, headed by President Rodríguez, began implementing an agricultural promotion policy (*política de fomento agropecuario*) aimed at promoting production through the provision of subsidized credit, technical assistance, infrastructure, and tax advantages.[13] The government hoped that these benefits would increase the profit margin of agricultural producers and that the profits would be reinvested in better agricultural technology. If productivity improved, the government could also expect a slower rate of inflation.

The rise in oil prices and export earnings, beginning in 1973,[14] increased the financial capacity of the state and made possible an expansion of its role in the economy. Government agricultural programs, conceived as part of the *política de fomento,* grew in size and scope. As a result, state expenditures in agriculture rose rapidly from 74 million sucres in 1970 (1.4 percent of total expenditures) to 2,033 million sucres in 1979 (7.5 percent of total expenditures). In real terms this represented a ninefold increase (CONADE 1982, Table 120; Vega 1980, Table 2–2).[15] The expanded financial resources were spread among the Ministry of Agriculture (MAG), two marketing enterprises, four decentralized agencies, and four regional agencies.[16] Unfortunately, much of the MAG budget was used for bureaucratic growth of little or no consequence to those in the rural sector.[17] Technical assistance provided by MAG focused on commodities produced predominantly on medium and large farms and was generally ill adapted to most small-farmer needs (Zevallos 1985, 180–181; World Bank 1979, 398).

The two marketing enterprises—the National Agency for Storage and Marketing of Agricultural Products (*Empresa Nacional de Almacenamiento y Comercialización de Productos Agrícolas,* ENAC) and the National Agency for Basic Foods (*Empresa Nacional de Productos Vitales,* ENPROVIT), a government-owned supermarket chain—were among the most heavily subsidized state ventures during the oil boom (de la Torre 1984, 16). Subsidies were primarily consumer oriented and often wasteful.[18] Expenditures allocated to irrigation projects by the decentralized and regional agencies were used mainly to build primary and secondary systems.[19] Tertiary or on-farm water-distribution systems were rarely developed. This focus limited the access of poorer farmers (who did not have the means to build their own distribution systems) to the major irrigation works (JUNAPLA 1979, 136-139; World Bank 1979, 152–155, 403). Technologies developed by the Ecuadorian Research Institute (*Instituto Ecuatoriano de Investigaciones Agropecuarias,* INIAP), were likewise too sophisticated for most small farmers (World Bank 1979, 404).

The sheer growth of agricultural credit was impressive: the value of loans totaled 9.2 billion sucres in 1979, up 429 percent (or 229 percent in constant 1970 prices) from the 1972 figure of 1.7 billion sucres (BCE 1984, 39).[20] This growth primarily reflected the expansion of public credit, which was distributed by the National Development Bank (*Banco Nacional de Fomento,* BNF) and the Central Bank (*Banco Central*). About one-third of the total amount loaned by the BNF went to lower income campesinos (World Bank 1979, 165). Credit from the Central Bank went almost exclusively to medium and large producers, for most of it was channeled through private banks. These banks only rarely gave credit to campesinos, who were considered a high-risk group. In 1978 the Central Bank began a conscious effort to reach small producers through the Fund for the Development of the Marginal Rural

Sector (*Fondo para el Desarrollo Rural Marginal*, FODERUMA), which channeled about 476 million sucres to small agricultural producers between 1978 and 1980, an amount that represented less than 5 percent of the total credit granted by the Central Bank during that period.[21]

Taking BNF and Central Bank credit together, the peasant sector received only about 15 percent of total agricultural credit during the period from 1972 to 1980 (Cosse 1984, Table 11). Case study evidence shows that within the peasant sector, credit benefited mostly the so-called *campesinos capitalizados* (capitalized peasants) such as rice producers on the Coast and potato producers in the Highlands.[22] The poorest sectors of the peasantry were excluded from formal sources of credit—except for the modest FODERUMA program—and continued to rely primarily on informal credit sources. These lenders charged interest rates as high as 40 percent per year (CSA 1979, 35).

In sum, the growth of state expenditures during the oil boom benefited mainly medium and large landowners. Petrol-generated state services and subsidies in the agricultural sector did little for the rural poor and probably accentuated rural inequality. This outcome reflected not only the intentional actions of the government but also the fact that increased state spending occurred in the context of an already highly unequal distribution of land. Those farmers with the largest properties received disproportionately more state services and subsidies. State efforts to bring about technological change rarely addressed small-farmer needs. In the absence of a significant land reform, the landless and near-landless were usually outside the reach of state programs.

In terms of growth, the increased allocation of state revenue to agriculture had disappointing results. From 1972 to 1979, the sector grew at an average annual rate of only 2.7 percent (Zevallos 1985, Table 5). This rate is lower than that for Latin America as a whole during the 1970s (3.6 percent) and lower than that of Ecuador during the preceding ten years (4.3 percent) (IADB 1984, 195). Crop production was uneven, but on the whole it stagnated. Increases in industrial-crop production were offset by the poor performance of most food crops (Zevallos 1985, chap. 6). Livestock production increased, but productivity per hectare (a better measure of the impact of state services) did not improve significantly.[23]

An important reason the expansion of state spending did not yield results is that credit, one of the major spending items, may have partly gone to nonagricultural activities. State officials interviewed by this author believed that credit must have been diverted, although they could not prove it. Anecdotically, I was told that some farmers borrowed cattle to show to BNF inspectors and thereby gain access to credit earmarked for livestock production; they then used the credit to contribute to the urban real-estate boom.[24] These stories are credible considering (1) the lower interest rates for agricultural credit vis-à-vis public credit for other activities, (2) the greater risks of agricultural investments compared to most urban businesses, (3) the poor investment returns in some agricultural subsectors relative to those attainable in the booming sectors of the urban economy at the time (real estate, construction, and import-substituting industries), and (4) the lack of effective controls on the part of the lending agencies to prevent the diversion of credit.[25]

COLONIZATION AS AN ALTERNATIVE TO REFORM

Until the 1970s, most colonization in Ecuador had been spontaneous. In the most common pattern, self-selected agricultural producers settled along state-opened roads on their own initiative. Later, the state moved in to organize and legalize the occupation and to provide certain services to the newly colonized areas. Finally, settlers moved to outlying areas, filling in the "empty spaces" between roads.

Colonization became a key policy issue during the 1972–1979 period of military rule. The military favored colonization in all areas of the country that had potential for extending the agrarian frontier, but they believed that the colonization of the Amazon region should be the government's priority. This region was considered to be the one with greatest potential for colonization projects. The military was convinced, moreover, that colonization of the Amazon was the best way to defend this territory against a possible Peruvian invasion.[26]

The military also hoped that colonization would relieve population pressure in the Highlands. As General Oliverio Vásconez put it in a 1983 interview, "Colonization in the Oriente is the logical way to solve the problem of land scarcity in the Highlands. The Oriente is almost half of our territory, while its population is less than 3 percent of the national total. And since this region contains land that is appropriate for agriculture, we had to colonize it."[27]

In this manner, colonization became an alternative to agrarian reform. Instead of further fragmenting land in the Highlands, the landless peasants and *minifundistas* were expected to relocate in the virgin Amazonian lowlands.

This strategy had been favored by the *Cámaras de Agricultura* for many years. The solution to the problem of population pressure in the Highlands, the landowners had argued, was not seizure and division of their properties but colonization of the Amazon. The government never publicly agreed with this proposal; officially, colonization was defined as a complement to land reform, not as a substitute. However, the emphasis placed on colonization in the 1970s and the concurrent lack of political will to expropriate land demonstrated the military's practical agreement with the landowners' thesis.

To attain the dual objective of reducing population pressure in the Highlands and securing border territories, the military implemented five ambitious projects of "directed colonization"—planned, sponsored, and aided by the state.[28] In order to institutionalize directed colonization, the Law of Colonization of the Amazon Region was issued in 1977.[29] This law also created the Institute of Colonization of the Amazon Region (*Instituto Nacional de Colonización de la Región Amazónica*, INCRAE) to direct, plan, and finance Amazonian colonization projects. Execution of these projects fell to the various national ministries.[30]

The Law of Colonization of the Amazon Region established that land titles in colonization areas could be granted only to agricultural cooperatives.[31] In practice, however, the cooperatives did not farm their lands collectively. Their members tended to divide the properties and work them individually, rarely engaging in joint activities. Cooperative ventures consisted mostly of marketing agricultural products, building basic infrastructure for common use, and pressuring the state to provide services. From the governmental point of view, cooperatives facilitated the allocation of state resources and services in colonization areas (Barsky et al. 1982, 70–71).

Most members of the cooperatives were highland peasants. As Chiriboga (1984, 102) has pointed out, however, some land was also awarded to cooperatives whose members were of urban middle-class origin, especially military officers.

POLICY IMPACT: THE SIZE AND STRUCTURE OF THE REFORM SECTOR

From 1964 to 1985, about 8 percent of all agricultural land in the country (744,395 hectares) was adjudicated through land reform to 99,673 families (IERAC 1985, 1986). The average size of the plots awarded was 7.5 hectares. For about 30 percent of the total area involved, however, peasants acquired legal rights to land that they had previously worked under precapitalist arrangements.[32] By subtracting these entitlements, a more exact estimate of the amount of land actually redistributed would be about 520,000 hectares or 5.4 percent of total agricultural land.

Land reform was relatively more important in the Highlands than on the Coast. In the Highlands, land awarded through reform between

1964 and 1985 accounted for 5.1 percent of the total agricultural area. On the Coast, meanwhile, land reform during the same period affected only 2.6 percent of the total agricultural area (IERAC 1985, 1986). The greater importance of land reform in the Highlands reflects the fact that the development of capitalist agriculture was slower in the Highlands and peasant pressure for land was greater. Within each region, however, the impact of land reform was not homogeneous. In the Highlands, land was awarded mainly in the southern provinces of Chimborazo and Loja, where the development of capitalist agriculture had been slowest and peasant movements had been strongest (IERAC 1985).[33] On the Coast, land redistribution occurred primarily in the rice zone, where peasant mobilization was greatest.[34]

During the same period, 1964 to 1985, over 2.5 million hectares in colonization areas were granted to about 60,000 families (IERAC 1985). The average size of these units (42 hectares) was considerably greater than that of farms awarded through land reform (7.5 hectares). The main site of colonization was the Amazon, where about one-half of the colonized land was located (IERAC 1985, 1986); colonization resulted from both "directed" efforts of the government and spontaneous migratory movements that followed the opening of roads for oil exploration and extraction.

Other important sites of colonization were on the Coast, particularly in the provinces of Esmeraldas and Manabí and in some "intermediate zones" between the Highlands and the Coast.[35] The importance of colonization in the Highlands relative to other regions dropped from 45 percent during the 1960s, to 15 percent during the 1970s, to 12 percent in the 1980s (Haney and Haney 1984, 17; IERAC 1985, 1986). Colonization was spontaneous both in the Highlands and on the Coast. State action was restricted to granting titles and providing services after settlement had occurred.

By 1985 the size of the reform sector (the farms created by awarding land reform and colonization lands) was about 3.3 million hectares.[36] This area represented nearly 30 percent of total national farmland (see Table 2).

Over three-fourths of the reform sector was comprised of colonization lands while the rest consisted of properties awarded through various land reform programs. The predominance of colonization became even greater during the last five years of the 1964–1985 period (see Table 3).

The size and the structure of the reform sector are indications of the direct impact that agrarian reform and colonization activities had on land distribution. As I will show, however, land reform legislation and other aspects of agrarian policies affected agrarian and productive structures in a more indirect way.

Table 2
Size of reform sector, 1964–1985[a]

Period	Hectares[b]	Percentage of total 1985 agricultural land[c]
1964–1971	692.1	7.1
1972–1979	1,362.7	14.0
1980–1985	1,269.7	13.1
1964–1985	3,324.5	34.2

[a] Source: Instituto Ecuatoriano de Reforma Agraria y Colonización, *La nueva reforma agraria,* 1985 (Quito: IERAC, 1985); Instituto Ecuatoriano de Reforma Agraria y Colonización, "Adjudicaciones legalizadas de tierras en colonización y en reforma agraria por provincias: 1985," mimeograph (Quito: Departamento Técnico, IERAC, 1986).
[b] × 1000.
[c] Total farmland in 1985 (9,702,189 hectares) was calculated by adding the 7,955,249 hectares identified in the 1974 census as total farmland to the 1,746,940 hectares awarded through colonization from 1975 to 1985.

Table 3
Land awarded through land reform and colonization, 1964–1985[a]

	Land reform		Colonization		Total	
Period	Area[b]	Percentage	Area[b]	Percentage	Area[b]	Percentage
1964–1971	174.0	25.1	518.1	74.9	692.1	100
1972–1979	349.8	25.7	1,012.9	74.3	1,362.7	100
1980–1985	220.6	17.4	1,049.1	82.6	1,269.7	100
1964–1985	744.4	22.4	2,580.1	77.6	3,324.5	100

[a] Source: Instituto Ecuatoriano de Reforma Agraria y Colonización, *La nueva reforma agraria,* 1985 (Quito: IERAC, 1985); Instituto Ecuatoriano de Reforma Agraria y Colonización, "Adjudicaciones legalizadas de tierras en colonización y en reforma agraria por provincias: 1985," mimeograph (Quito: Departamento Técnico, IERAC, 1986).
[b] Hectares (× 1000).

AGRARIAN POLICY AND THE "JUNKER ROAD" OF CAPITALIST DEVELOPMENT

De Janvry (1981, 208) describes the Ecuadorian agrarian reform during the 1960s as one that induced a transition from the precapitalist *latifundia* to capitalist ("Junker") enterprises that hired wage laborers.[37]

This was accomplished, according to de Janvry, by proscribing labor services in exchange for usufruct on land and by giving peasants who performed such services titles to small plots. While this description is correct in general terms, it requires some clarification. First, the elimination of the *huasipungo* began prior to the 1964 reform as an initiative of owners of more modernized haciendas. The 1964 reform merely forced more traditional landowners to follow suit.[38] Second, the hiring of wage labor was already a generalized practice in coastal agriculture when the 1964 law was enacted; in the few areas where precapitalist relations had survived, the 1964 reform had little effect. It was only in 1971, when *Decreto* 1001 was issued, that agrarian reform legislation began to have a significant effect on the Coast. Third, capitalization and technological change were slow on both highland and coastal haciendas in the 1960s.

During the 1970s, however, modernization of large estates became a rapid and general trend. This occurred under the influence of three main factors: the Agrarian Reform Law of 1973, the agricultural promotion policy, and the oil boom. The 1973 law threatened inefficient properties with expropriation. Although this provision of the law was only occasionally applied,[39] the mere threat of expropriation was often enough to induce landowners to intensify production and to farm more efficiently. This trend was most evident on the modernized coastal plantations and the agroindustrial haciendas in the Highlands, as will be discussed shortly. The agricultural promotion policy induced modernization by providing landowners with cheap loans, tax advantages, infrastructural improvements, subsidies, and duty-free imported inputs. The oil boom increased the demand for industrial crops, food crops, meat, and dairy products, thereby creating opportunities for growth and incentives for modernization among agricultural enterprises producing for the domestic market.

The development of capitalist farming occurred at a different pace in various areas of the country. For analytical purposes, four categories of haciendas that underwent "Junker" development during the 1970s can be distinguished: the "agroindustrial haciendas" of the Highlands, the "modernized plantations" of the Coast, the "adapted haciendas" of both regions, and the "traditional haciendas" of the Coast.[40] The agroindustrial haciendas of the Highlands modernized rapidly, while their size was either maintained or reduced through sales of marginal lands. In the most common pattern, land on hillsides was divided into small plots which were then sold to peasants, while better, lower lands were retained by the owner.[41] Agroindustrial activities developed as a response to a rising urban demand for dairy products and other processed foodstuffs during the oil boom. Crop cultivation by traditional methods was largely abandoned, thereby reducing labor needs.[42]

The second category of "Junker" development is the modernized plantation of the Coast. This type of unit underwent rapid technological change, while its size was either maintained or expanded. The banana, African palm, sugar, and abaca plantations located in Guayas, El Oro, eastern Los Rís, and the Santo Domingo-Quinindé area fall into this category. The trend toward expansion was clearest in the Santo Domingo-Quinindé area, where modern plantations bought land from impoverished peasants (MAG 1979b,26).

The third category is the adapted hacienda of the Highlands and the Coast. This kind of hacienda modernized more slowly, either maintaining its size or selling off its marginal lands. An owner's decision to sell marginal lands, however, was usually made in response to threatened or actual peasant invasions.[43]

The fourth category is the traditional hacienda of the Coast. Technological change was slowest on these properties, and farm size was unaffected. This situation was characteristic of eastern Guayas (Naranjal area) and various parts of Manabí and Esmeraldas.[44]

In general, technological change was more often implemented to reduce labor needs than to improve land use. While fertilizer consumption roughly doubled from 1972–1973 to 1978–1979, the dollar value of imported capital goods for agriculture increased sevenfold during the same period.[45] Mechanization was a logical response to low fuel prices, exemption from import duties, rising wages, the flight of labor to the cities, and the threat of expropriation for farmers who did not comply with labor regulations.

While the threat of expropriation and the new economic conditions created by the oil boom provided the incentives for some landowners to modernize, they inspired others to subdivide and sell all or part of their farms.[46] The division of haciendas into medium and small units, which were then sold to local merchants or rich peasants, was a common phenomenon both in the Highlands and on the Coast.[47] The highland haciendas that were fractionated in this manner usually had one or more of the following three characteristics. First, they were located in areas where population pressure was high and the peasant movement was strong. Second, they employed traditional, extensive agricultural practices. Third, they were located far from the urban markets. These haciendas could neither take advantage of the investment incentives granted by the state nor profit easily from the growth of urban demand for food. They chose not to modernize and did not adapt to the new conditions created by the oil boom. In turn, their unwillingness or inability to adjust their operations made large areas, left abandoned and uncultivated, vulnerable to campesino invasion and expropriation.

Thus, many highland landowners divided and sold their farms, transferring their capital to urban ventures, which they saw as less risky and more profitable. It is important to note that urban investments in the rapidly growing construction, import-substitution, and real-estate businesses were very attractive throughout the 1970s. Although the agricultural capital that was transferred to urban activities is not quantifiable, it is safe to assume that many of the new industrialists and real-estate owners of the 1970s were the "backward" landowners of the 1960s.

Subdivisions and sales on the Coast were also a reaction both to the threat of agrarian reform and to the emergence of new urban investment opportunities, particularly in Guayaquil. In comparison with the Highlands, however, the subdivision of land on the Coast was less severe, primarily because peasant pressure for land was not as intense.

Taking account of hacienda subdivision into medium and small farms throughout the 1970s, de Janvry's "Junker road" apparently was not the dominant path of capitalist development in Ecuadorian agriculture. Such a characterization might have been appropriate until the early 1970s, but small and medium farms have grown in number since then. As a result, the "farmer" and "peasant" roads of development have acquired equal or, perhaps, even greater importance. Although this change cannot be quantified in the absence of new census data, a likely guess is that, by now, farms above 500 hectares control about 20 percent of the agricultural land, reduced from 30 percent in 1974 (LTC 1979, 144).[48]

CHANGING PRODUCTIVE STRUCTURE

The transformation of the traditional hacienda system was accompanied by changes in the productive structure of both highland and coastal agriculture. In the Highlands, farmers tended to shift from grain cultivation to dairy farming; on the Coast, traditional export crops declined in importance relative to raising cattle and producing industrial crops.

The decline of grain production in the Highlands began in the 1960s when wheat producers were forced to compete with lower priced wheat imported under U.S. Public Law 480.[49] Because of this competition, the price of domestic wheat fell in real terms, production costs rose, and profit margins declined (CENDES 1982, 70, 352–353). When the international price of wheat began to climb in 1973, the government established a subsidy on imported wheat. This subsidy, which was maintained throughout the decade, further diminished the profitability of local wheat production; as a result, cultivation of wheat decreased nearly 60 percent from 1970 to 1980 and was largely relegated to the peasant sector.[50] By making bread and other wheat products relatively cheap, the subsidy led to a sharp increase in their consumption (Zevallos 1985, Table 8) at the expense of products made with the traditional subsistence crops, barley and maize. Demand for these other grains fell, profitability declined, and their cultivation was abandoned.[51] Between 1970 and 1980, the area planted to barley and maize declined 80 percent and 72 percent, respectively (Jara 1984, 65). As in the case of wheat, most of the remaining production of maize and barley occurred on peasant farms. Grainfields on medium and large farms were generally converted to pastures as their owners moved into livestock.

The tendency to move away from traditional export crops (bananas, coffee, and cacao) on the Coast was a response to unfavorable international prices in the late 1960s. Prices improved in the 1970s, but derived benefits were offset by internal monetary policy. From 1972 to 1977, the government fixed the exchange rate at 24.85 sucres per dollar, resulting in a 27 percent overvaluation of the sucre in real terms with respect to the dollar (CEPAL 1979, Table 74). This made Ecuadorian exports less competitive abroad and less profitable at home.[52] Banana production suffered most: between 1970 and 1980, it declined 22 percent in value despite productivity gains and a 226 percent increase in international prices (Zevallos 1985, Tables 13, 15; World Bank 1979, 150–151; MAG 1978, 89–91). Large banana areas, particularly those located far from export centers, were replanted with more profitable industrial crops, such as African palm and soybean, or converted into pastures for livestock.

The shift toward livestock production, both in the Highlands and on the Coast, was promoted by the state through favorable tax and credit policies.[53] In addition, income expansion among the urban middle class during the oil boom had raised the demand for animal protein and made meat production and dairy farming more profitable.[54] This shift from crop cultivation to livestock farming can also be interpreted as an unintended effect of the Agrarian Reform Law of 1973. As stated earlier, the law threatened farmers with expropriation if they did not comply with labor regulations, the most important of which was a minimum wage. The minimum-wage requirement had not previously been enforced, particularly in the Highlands. But hacienda workers responded to the establishment of expropriation as a penalty by organizing, often to claim hacienda lands. Landowners reacted by reducing their labor needs via mechanization (taking advantage of duty-free machinery imports and low-interest credit for agricultural imports) and by transforming labor-intensive crop areas into pastures.

Farmers who felt threatened by the regulation that at least 80 percent of their land had to be used efficiently to avoid expropriation often converted uncultivated land into pastures. In the process, landowners created more pastures than their cattle required. As a result, the area used for pastures during the 1970s grew faster than the number of cattle, and thus the number of head per hectare declined (Zevallos 1985, Table 11).

TRENDS IN THE PEASANT SECTOR

The transformation of the traditional hacienda was accompanied by changes within peasant agriculture. Peasant farms can be defined as those that function on the basis of labor obtained primarily outside of the formal labor market, from family members and through networks of informal contacts.[55] By 1972, peasant farms in Ecuador were, with few exceptions, external to the large estates. Subsistence plots within the traditional haciendas (mainly huasipungos in the Highlands and sharecropping plots on the Coast) had been practically eliminated with the application of the Agrarian Reform Law of 1964 in the Highlands and *Decreto* 1001 of 1970 on the Coast.

Peasant farms can be divided into two types according to size: (1) *family farms*, that is, farms large enough to meet the needs for maintenance and reproduction of the peasant family, and (2) *subfamily farms*, that is, farms too small to permit the survival of the peasant household on the basis of agricultural production alone. In the latter case, the peasant family must rely on other sources of income such as wage labor and artisan work, which gives them semiproletarian status.[56] De Janvry (1981) maintains that family farms are largely absent from the Latin American agrarian structure. When family farmers (a rural petty bourgeoisie) appear, they are not likely to remain in that status for long; most become semiproletarians:

> Blocked by unfavorable prices, unable to translate cheap food into cheap semiproletarian labor because it is at most only a small employer, and excluded from control of the state, this fraction of a class [the rural petty bourgeoisie] is incapable of insuring the going rate of profit to its capital or a normal rent to its land. To face up to competition from the landed elite and the bourgeoisie, the household on the family farm is forced to overexploit its own labor to a great degree. This group is highly unstable and quickly differentiates into farmers and semiproletarian peasants, with the largest mass being drawn to the latter. (de Janvry 1981, 112)

According to de Janvry, semiproletarians have two main origins in Latin America. Parts of this class originate when peasants who are expelled from estates undergoing a "Junker" type of transformation resettle on subsistence plots. Other parts are formed after the subdivision of family farms, which are "increasingly pulverized under the pressure of demographic growth and insufficient employment opportunities, which reduce off-farm migration" (de Janvry 1981, 113).

De Janvry's characterization of family and subfamily farms fits well with the evolution of the reform sector in the Highlands. The peasant plots awarded to *huasipungueros* and *arrimados* were usually located on poor quality, marginal lands. These plots, which were initially very small, were then subdivided through inheritance. Insufficient land and soil erosion led to semiproletarianization of all or some of the members of the peasant family. A similar evolution can be observed on existing *minifundios*, especially on poor quality land.[57]

De Janvry's model, however, does not apply well to dominant trends in the evolution of the reform sector on the Coast. Here, peasants were not relocated as in the Highlands. Rice tenants were given property rights over plots they had been cultivating prior to reform. The plots awarded through land reform were larger than those in the Highlands, and the land was of good quality. In addition, the reform beneficiaries gained immediate access to credit and received technical assistance from the state. These factors, combined with a favorable price policy, enabled many peasant producers to increase output and productivity levels. In fact, rice production (most of which was in the hands of land-reform beneficiaries) increased threefold during the 1970s.[58] This growth in production as well as other evidence[59] suggests that most rice-producing peasants increased their marketable surplus and became capitalized after the 1970 reform.

Peasant farms also did well in some of the colonization areas and where the dissolution of the traditional hacienda had given peasants access to good quality, well-located land. These instances—which were not isolated cases—again contradict de Janvry's pessimistic view of the evolution of the peasant sector since peasant farms tended to capitalize and even to expand in size. This process has been documented in the area of Quinindé (Barsky et al. 1982), in the Huachi Grande *parroquia* in Tungurahua (Pachano 1977), and in the San Gabriel *parroquia* in El Carchi (Lehmann 1986; Barsky 1984b).

This progress by a substantial sector of peasant farms during the 1970s was related to the oil boom in three principal ways. First, prices for wage goods, produced primarily in the peasant sector, improved in the 1970s as a result of the growth in urban demand during the oil boom. Second, the rapid growth of the industrial and commercial sectors during the 1970s created new employment opportunities outside agriculture, increasing off-farm migration and reducing labor supply in the agricultural sector. In turn, farm wages rose,[60] and the peasant sector became more competitive with large landowners in the production of labor-intensive crops. This partially explains why the large landowners moved away from crop production and tended to specialize in dairy farming and cattle raising during the 1970s.[61] Third, oil revenues enabled the state to provide more credit and technical assistance to some small producers, as Redclift (1978) and Barsky (1984b, 76–78) have documented for the cases of rice and potato producers, respectively. Technological innovations, marketing improvements, increased incomes, and more on-farm investment followed.

In sum, the de Janvry model does not give us a clear guide to understanding the changing structure of Ecuadorian agriculture during the 1970s. Some producers were able to take advantage of low-interest credit, technical assistance, and growing demand for their products, while others underwent increasing semiproletarianization and even pauperization. Producers of potatoes in El Carchi, of rice in the Guayas Basin, and of fruits in Tungurahua generally exemplify the former case; the former *precaristas* of the Highlands (ex-*huasipungueros* and ex-*arrimados*) generally follow the latter pattern. Two factors appear to be particularly important in explaining these different regional outcomes. First, the size and quality of the farms influenced the extent to which peasants were able to take advantage of expanded state services such as low-interest credit and technical assistance. A clear illustration of this phenomenon may be found in the different evolutionary trajectories of the reform sectors in the Highlands (where plots were quite small and of low quality) and on the Coast (where plots were larger and of better quality). The second factor, the location of the peasant farm with respect to the main markets, determined the extent to which peasant producers were able to take advantage of the growing urban demand for food during the oil boom.

CONCLUSIONS

Agrarian reform during the 1960s and early 1970s led mainly to a generalization of wage relations in agriculture. Land distribution was largely unaffected. But, after the 1973 Agrarian Reform Law was passed and revenues from the oil boom increased the state's capacity to intervene in the agricultural sector, significant changes occurred in both peasant and capitalist agriculture. Increased state expenditure primarily benefited medium and large landowners. State efforts rarely addressed the needs of small farmers. The impact of state intervention on agricultural growth was generally disappointing, with the food-production subsector of agriculture performing the most poorly. Colonization policies were the state's response to peasant demands for land in the absence of significant redistribution. Modernization of the larger estates accelerated in the 1970s under the influence of threats of expropriation contained in the 1973 Agrarian Reform Law, pressure from peasants, the agricultural promotion policy, and the oil boom. While these factors gave some landowners the incentives they needed to modernize, other owners divided up and sold all or part of their land, frequently transferring capital to urban pursuits. This trend increased the relative importance of medium and small farms. The development of the peasant sector was uneven, depending on the size, quality, and location of the peasant farm.

NOTES

1. The author is a recent graduate of the Development Studies Program at the University of Wisconsin-Madison. This chapter is based in part on his Ph.D. thesis, "Oil, Power, and Rural Change in Ecuador: 1972–1979," written under the supervision of Professor William C. Thiesenhusen. Research was jointly funded by the Inter-American Foundation and the Social Science Research Council. All statements and conclusions, however, are personal and do not necessarily represent the views of these organizations. The author extends special thanks to Beverly Phillips, Director, Land Tenure Center Library, University of Wisconsin-Madison, for substantive and editorial comments that aided the revision of this paper.

2. Limits were 2,500 hectares on the Coast and 800 hectares in the Highlands, to which another 1,000 hectares of natural pastures or *páramos* could be added.

3. *Asistencia Social* was the Ecuadorian social security agency that preceded the current *Instituto Ecuatoriano de Seguridad Social*. The haciendas owned by *Asistencia Social* were expropriated by the government from the Catholic Church in the early part of the twentieth century (Handelman 1980, 8).

4. See Barsky (1978).

5. The 1964 statute outlawed not only "precarious tenure" arrangements that were typical of the Highlands (*huasipungo* and *arrimazgo*) but also others common in coastal agriculture such as *redención* and *finquería*. In the former system, peasants planted crops such as coffee and cacao and the landowners "redeemed" the plants for a previously agreed upon amount in cash. Under *finquería* the peasants cultivated permanent crops (cacao, coffee, or bananas) and paid the landowners a rent in cash, crops, or labor. However, the law did not prohibit sharecropping (*aparcería*), which had become common in the coastal region, particularly in the rice zone. Instead, it regulated the ways in which this arrangement could be practiced. The law's provisions relating to coastal agriculture were never applied, however, partly because of the political influence of coastal landowners and agroexporters. This influence derived from the state's dependence on revenues from taxes on agricultural exports and from its need to encourage these exports, which were Ecuador's primary source of foreign exchange prior to the oil boom.

6. For an analysis of the evolution of the cooperative system, see Redclift (1978).

7. *Decreto* 1001 was preceded in September 1970 by *Decreto* 373, *Ley de Abolición del Trabajo Precario en la Agricultura*. This decree abolished all forms of "precarious tenure," including some, such as sharecropping, that had been excluded from the 1964 Agrarian Reform Law. The decree stated that peasants who had worked for at least three years under any precarious tenure arrangement had the right to demand that the Agrarian Reform Institute expropriate the land they were cultivating and sell it to them at cadastral value. In response to *Decreto* 373, many landowners in the Guayas Basin tried to evict tenants from their estates and refused to grow rice. Faced with the prospects of a rice-production crisis and a widespread confrontation between landlords and tenants, the government issued Decreto 1001, a more radical and effective measure (Redclift 1978, 86–87).

8. *Decreto* 1172, *Ley de Reforma Agraria*, was issued by the military regime headed by Guillermo Rodríguez.

9. The law established that *acaparamiento* (hoarding) of land was a reason for expropriation. However, the *reglamento* of the law, issued 11 months later, established that *acaparamiento* existed only if the land being hoarded did not have an adequate productivity level. Article 18 reads: "There will be *acaparamiento* if landholdings with more than 200 hectares of usable land do not have a productivity level 15 percent above the average established by the Ministry of Agriculture for the zone in which they are located. This productivity level must be 20 percent above the average in the case of properties with more than 500 hectares and 25 percent above the average in the case of properties with more than 1,000 hectares...." Therefore, as Barsky (1984a, 219) has pointed out, a landowner was allowed to own an unlimited amount of land as long as the productivity of the land was adequate.

10. *The Reglamento General para la Aplicación de la Ley de Reforma Agraria*, issued in September, 1974, specified the meaning of the first requirement by saying that 80 percent of the land must be "effectively utilized." Thus, land left fallow was included in the remaining 20 percent. With respect to the second requirement, the *reglamento* established a provisional measure that would be effective until the Ministry of Agriculture had determined average levels of productivity for the various ecological areas. Provisionally, all farms not achieving a production level equivalent to at least 80 percent of the "real average production" of the area were considered to be inefficient and, thus, subject to expropriation (*Reglamento*, Art. 7). This rule is still in effect, since the Ministry of Agriculture never established average levels of productivity.

11. Article 30, Sec. 9 of the first version of the 1973 law, and Art. 46, Sec. 9 of the 1979 version.

12. In addition to landowner opposition, the transfer of power to the military triumvirate in January 1976—when Art. 25 was to go into effect—worked against the application of the law. The triumvirate was politically more conservative than the preceding military regime headed by Rodríguez. But even under the best of political conditions, the application of Art. 25 regarding efficient cultivation would not have been a simple task. Further regulations were needed to deal with the technical problems posed by application of the

article, especially in the Highlands where the topography is very irregular and the quality of land varies greatly. But the military triumvirate did not address these problems because it lacked the political will either to redistribute land to the campesinos or to conflict with the landowners.

13. Some specific measures were taken: the elimination of taxes on commercial transactions involving agricultural goods, the elimination of taxes on imported inputs for the agricultural sector, the creation of a subsidy for the importation of fertilizers, and the creation of "centers of agricultural mechanization," experimental farms, and laboratories.

14. The price of oil jumped from $2.50 (U.S. dollars) a barrel in August 1972 to $13.90 a barrel in January 1973. As a result, the value of oil exports rose from $59 million in 1972 to $609 million in 1974.

15. The 1979 figure of 2,033 million current sucres is equivalent to 708.2 million constant 1970 sucres, which is 9.6 times greater than the 1970 figure. Constant sucres were calculated on the basis of CONADE's consumer price index (CONADE 1982, 101).

16. For a more detailed description of state expenditures, see Zevallos (1985, 177).

17. From 1973 to 1976, for example, the personnel of MAG expanded by 18 percent. However, most of the increase was in support staff; professional and technical staff grew by only 2.7 percent. Professional/technical personnel thereby declined as a proportion of total staff from 66 percent in 1973 to 55 percent in 1976. Because of this pattern, MAG's output grew more slowly than the costs of total staff and more slowly than its budget increases would suggest. For example, the number of hectares receiving technical assistance from MAG grew by only 9 percent from 1973 to 1976, while the ministry's current expenditures increased by 75 percent in constant 1970 prices (World Bank 1979, 410–411).

18. ENAC's biggest subsidy was for the importation of wheat, a support mechanism designed to keep consumer prices low. As the international price of wheat increased, significant amounts of subsidized wheat flour were sold in Colombia and Peru by smugglers, particularly after 1975. The beneficiaries of ENPROVIT's expenditures were mainly urban consumers (Luzuriaga and Zuvekas 1983, 184).

19. The agencies that provided irrigation systems were the Ecuadorian Institute of Water Resources (*Instituto Ecuatoriano de Recursos Hidráulicos*, INERHI), the Center for the Rehabilitation of Manabí (*Centro para la Rehabilitación de Manabí*, CRM), and the Research Commission for the Development of the Guayas Basin (*Comisión de Estudios para el Desarrollo de la Cuenca del Río Guayas*, CEDEGE).

20. Constant 1970 prices were calculated on the basis of CONADE's consumer price index (CONADE 1982, 101).

21. One-third of BNF's portfolio was devoted to *crédito de capacitación*, which goes to lower income campesinos; the remainder was granted as *crédito bancario*, which is given to medium and large farms (JUNAPLA 1979, Table 28; Cosse 1984, Table 10). This proportion represents a sharp increase over the years preceding the oil boom when the fraction of total loan volume going to lower income campesinos was just one-tenth. The main reason for the greater

participation of small campesinos in BNF credit was the democratization of BNF after 1972. At that time, peasants without title to their land (*posesionarios*) gained access to BNF credit. This was an important gain for most agrarian reform beneficiaries, who lacked title to their land because titling was (and still is) a complicated process that takes several years to complete.

22. See Barsky (1984b) and Redclift (1978).

23. See World Bank (1979, 144) and CENDES (1982, 213). Both show that dairy farming and cattle ranching have a long way to go before reaching satisfactory productivity levels. CENDES (1982, 214) estimates that, by 1982, daily milk production per cow averaged 4 liters (as compared to an average of over 20 liters in countries where dairy farming is technologically advanced).

24. Interviews, Felipe Orellana, 21 Oct. 1982; Marcos Rojas, 6 May 1983; Pedro Aguayo, 14 July 1983 (see Zevallos 1985, 231).

25. Although there were regulations for obtaining and utilizing state-subsidized agricultural credit, landowners found ways to circumvent the rules (interview, Marcos Rojas, 6 May 1983).

26. General Oliverio Vásconez, Minister of Agriculture, 1976-1979, noted in a 1983 interview (Zevallos 1985, 275–279): "Nearly half of Ecuador is made up of the Amazonian lowlands. It is from the oil in those lowlands that the government gets half of its budget. A significant part of that territory was lost to Peru in the 1941 invasion. Since it was unsettled, it was easy for Peru to take it. Thus, the best defense of our territory is colonization; only through colonization projects will there be people to defend those lands."

27. Interview, General Vásconez, 2 August 1983.

28. The first of these projects was initiated in 1972. This project, Shushufindi, comprised an area of 3,500 hectares and was planned for 80 settler families. A second effort, the Payamino Project, began in late 1975 and was jointly supported by IERAC and a Swiss-based private aid organization. This 16,000-hectare project was planned to accommodate 400 families (World Bank 1979, 207–208). The third project, San Miguel, was initiated by IERAC in 1976 and continued by the Institute of Colonization of the Amazon Region after 1978. This project was made up of 18,000 hectares and was planned for 360 families. Also in 1976, the Center for the Economic Reconversion of Azuay, Cañar, and Morona (a regional institution, in Santiago, attached to the Ministry of Agriculture) initiated the Morona Project, comprising 300,000 hectares and expected to provide farms for over 4,000 families. Finally, in 1977, the Program for the Development of the Southern Region of Ecuador, another regional agency attached to MAG, initiated a project for the valleys of Zamora and Nangaritza. The Zamora Valley already had a spontaneous settler population of about 4,000 families; the Nangaritza Valley had only a few settlers but offered considerable settlement potential. The project was to support both existing and prospective settlers (see World Bank 1979, 207–213).

29. The Law of Colonization of the Amazon Region stated that it was the policy of the state "to favor the diversion of persons from the most populated zones in the Highlands and on the Coast to the Amazonian Region." Article 6 noted that colonization projects "will give priority to aspects related to the security and the defense of the territorial integrity of the country."

30. After the creation of INCRAE, only colonization outside of the Amazon remained in IERAC's domain.

31. Article 31, *Ley de colonización de la región amazónica ecuatoriana* (IERAC 1980).

32. This figure is a rough approximation based on data of CONADE (1982, Table 118) for the 1964–1979 period.

33. The greater importance of land reform programs in the least developed agricultural areas of the Highlands has been noted by Chiriboga (1984, 111–113).

34. See Redclift (1978).

35. The Santo Domingo-Quinindé area has been the most important of these intermediate zones.

36. For an elaboration of the concept "reform sector," see de Janvry (1981, 203–204).

37. For an elaboration of the concepts "Junker road" and "farmer road" and their relevance for the analysis of Latin American agriculture, see de Janvry (1981, 106-109).

38. See Barsky (1978).

39. The law specifies two categories that permit expropriation (*afectación*) for inefficiency: *expropiación* and *reversión*. Within *expropiación*, there are ten reasons for initiating legal action against a landowner; of these, only two relate to inefficient production practices. Within *reversión*, land reverts to the state if the landowner has not been involved in production for two or more years. This category can include cases of abandonment of property or cases where the property is worked by persons independent of the owner. Available statistics do not specify which reasons invoked expropriation in specific cases. Since regulations concerning expropriation in the case of inefficiency were difficult to apply (see Zevallos 1985, 88–91), we can conclude that most expropriations due to inefficiency fell into the *reversión* category. According to the latest available data, published in a 1979 evaluation of the agrarian reform (MAG 1979c,203–204), a total of 920 cases of *reversión* were resolved between 1973 and 1975, affecting a total of 36,000 hectares.

40. This typology is based on MAG (1979a, 1979b, 1980). MAG's nomenclature, however, is slightly different from mine. MAG refers to the agroindustrial hacienda of the Highlands as the "*hacienda empresarial de la sierra*," to the modernized plantation of the Coast as the "*hacienda empresarial de la Costa*," and to the adapted hacienda as the "*hacienda tradicional adaptada*."

41. The sale of marginal lands was a trend that began during the 1950s and 1960s; in the 1970s, this trend accelerated as a result of the faster pace of modernization on most haciendas.

42. This pattern of change was characteristic of the dairy farms located in the valleys of Machachi and Latacunga (provinces of Pichincha and Cotopaxi) and in the Cumbe area (Province of Azuay). Similar transformations occurred in the sugar-producing areas of the Catamaño Valley (Province of Loja). For a detailed description of the development trends in the areas of the Highlands dominated by modern agroindustrial units (*haciendas empresariales*), see MAG (1979a).

43. This path of transformation was characteristic of highland haciendas in the Andean part of El Carchi, in the Canton of Otavalo, in the area

of Angochagua-Olmedo and Cayambe, on the edges of the Machachi and Latacunga valleys, in the area of Santa Rosa-Yaruquí, in several parts of Chimborazo, and in the Andean region of Loja (see MAG 1979a, chap. 4). A similar evolution occurred among haciendas in the coastal rice zone.

44. See MAG (1979b).

45. Fertilizer consumption in 1972/73 was 42,000 metric tons. It rose to 86,000 in 1977/78 and declined to 70,000 in 1978/79 (FAO 1979, 119). The importation of capital goods for agriculture grew from $4.4 million in 1970 to $31.2 million in 1979 (CONADE 1982, 89).

46. Although there are no data to quantify private sales of land during the 1970s (the last agricultural census was in 1974), the importance of this phenomenon has been documented in several studies done at the local level. Evidence of sales of hacienda lands to peasants has been found in Chimborazo (Haney and Haney 1984; MAG 1979a, 91), Cotopaxi (Martínez 1980), Loja (MAG 1979a, 105,194), Tungurahua (MAG 1979a, 73), Pichincha (Archetti and Stolen 1980), El Carchi (Barsky 1984b), and Bolívar (FEPP 1978). These studies, my own observations in the field, and evidence that I gathered during interviews suggest that private sales of land during the 1970s were more important in terms of reducing land concentration than land reform.

47. For details on areas where the traditional hacienda has disintegrated, see Zevallos (1985, 120,134,n. 20) and MAG (1979a, 1979b).

48. A safe assumption is that, as a result of subdivisions and sales, the number of medium and small farms (ranging from 20 to 500 hectares) has been increasing since 1972 at the expense of units of over 500 hectares (see Zevallos 1985, 133–134,n. 19).

49. *El Comercio*, 30 April 1972, pp. 1 and 14. The price of domestic wheat was higher than that of imported wheat throughout the period from 1963 to 1972 (CENDES 1982, 352). This imbalance of price reflected both the higher productivity of U.S. wheat farming and the fact that U.S. wheat was subsidized by the government (Marchán 1983:26).

50. See Jara (1984:65). Units of 10 hectares or fewer accounted for 88 percent of the cultivated area of wheat in 1982, up from 51 percent in 1975 (JUNAPLA 1979, Table 11a; CENDES 1982, 70).

51. During the 1970s, while demand for soft maize and barley dropped, prices for the products increased slowly and production costs rose. CEPAL (1979, 100) estimates that production costs for barley and soft maize increased 154 and 105 percent, respectively, between 1973 and 1975. Meanwhile, their prices increased only 39 and 30 percent, respectively.

52. It is true that the overvalued sucre decreased the cost of imported inputs. However, since traditional export crops are not highly input dependent, the impact of this price reduction on profitability was not significant, a conclusion supported by production trends documented by Zevallos (1985, chap. 6).

53. Cattle imports were exempted from taxes and facilitated through the *Programa de Repoblación Ganadera* (Livestock Restocking Program), initiated by the Ministry of Agriculture in 1973. Credit from the *Banco de Fomento* was earmarked for the importation of cattle and the construction of silos.

54. See Moncada (1978, 97) and World Bank (1979, 144). Livestock production did not suffer from the competition of imports as grain production

did. Although Ecuador imported powdered milk during the oil boom, this importation did not depress the price of milk to the degree that wheat imports depressed the price of domestic grains. Besides, dairy farmers were able to divert fluid milk into more profitable dairy products such as butter, cheese, and yogurt, which were not subject to strict price controls or to competition from imports.

55. Networks of informal contacts and ties of primary loyalty or kinship are particularly important labor sources in areas such as that studied by Lehmann in El Carchi (Lehmann 1986), where sharecropping is generalized among small producers.

56. See de Janvry (1981, 112–113). Lehmann's argument that peasant farms often function by combining family labor with labor obtained through informal and kinship ties does not invalidate this distinction. Whether the labor used is family labor or labor obtained informally is irrelevant for establishing whether a given farm's resources are sufficient to enable its owners to reproduce on the basis of agricultural income alone. Use of nonfamily labor obtained through reciprocal arrangements may increase the efficiency of labor inputs, but the potential of the farm to satisfy the reproductive needs of its owners does not change, given varying labor needs during the year. In the end, if the resources of a farm do not permit the reproduction of the resident family (with or without help obtained through reciprocal arrangements), additional sources of income will be required. Thus, even farmers who obtain outside labor through informal channels may be operating subfamily units.

57. Such is the case, for example, of the areas Sigsig-Nabón and Gualaceo (Azuay), parts of Pelileo canton (Tungurahua), Azoguez sector (Cañar), and some *minifundio* areas in Manabí.

58. See Zevallos (1985, Table 7).

59. Zuvekas (1976), Redclift (1978), and my own observations in Vinces and Baba cantons, Los Ríos province.

60. According to the World Bank (1979, 138), the average daily wage for farm labor rose from 15 to 20 sucres in 1972/73 to around 70 sucres in 1976.

61. See Zevallos (1985, chap. 6).

REFERENCES

Archetti, Eduardo B., and Kristi Stolen. 1980. Burguesía rural y campesinado en la sierra ecuatoriana. *Cahiers du Monde Hispanique et Luso-Brésilien* (Université de Toulouse), 34, pp. 57–82.

Barsky, Osvaldo. 1978. Iniciativa terrateniente en las transformaciones de la sierra ecuatoriana: 1959–1964. Master's thesis, Rural Sociology, CLACSO-Catholic University of Ecuador.

———.1984a. *La reforma agraria ecuatoriana.* Quito: Corporación Editora Nacional.

———.1984b. *Acumulación campesina en el Ecuador.* Quito: FLACSO.

Barsky, Osvaldo, Eugenio Díaz Bonilla, Carlos Furche, and Roberto Mizrahi. 1982. *Políticas agrarias, colonización y desarrollo rural en Ecuador.* Quito: Ediciones CEPLAES.

BCE (Banco Central del Ecuador). 1984. *Boletín anuario,* no. 7. Quito: BCE.

CENDES (Centro de Desarrollo Industrial del Ecuador) and ILIS (Instituto Latinoamericano de Investigaciones Sociales). 1982. *Diagnóstico de la agro-industria ecuatoriana*. Quito: CENDES.

CEPAL (Comisión Económica para América Latina). 1979. *Ecuador: Desafíos y logros de la política económica en la fase de expansión petrolera.* Santiago, Chile: CEPAL.

Chiriboga, Manuel. 1984. El estado y las políticas hacia el sector rural (1979–1982). In *Ecuador agrario: Ensayos de interpretación,* edited by M. Chiriboga et al., pp. 94–141. Quito: Editorial El Conejo.

CIDA (Comité Interamericano de Desarrollo Agrícola). 1965. *Ecuador: Tenencia de la tierra y desarrollo socio-económico del sector agrícola.* Washington: Unión Panamericana.

CONADE (Consejo Nacional de Desarrollo). 1982. *Indicadores socio-económicos*. Quito: CONADE.

Cosse, Gustavo. 1984. *Estado y agro en el Ecuador*. Quito: Corporación Editora Nacional.

CSA (Comisión para el Sector Agropecuario). 1979. *El sector agropecuario del Ecuador: Resumen del diagnóstico preliminar*. Quito: CSA.

De Janvry, Alain. 1981. *The agrarian question and reformism in Latin America*. Baltimore: Johns Hopkins Univ. Press.

De la Torre, Augusto. 1984. Stabilization and resource allocation aspects of a petroleum boom: Ecuador 1972–76. Paper presented at Development Workshop, held at University of Notre Dame, Notre Dame, Indiana, February.

El Comercio. 1972. Quito, 30 April.

FAO (Food and Agriculture Organization). 1979. *Fertilizer yearbook*. Rome: FAO.

FEPP (Fondo Ecuatoriano Populorum Progressio). 1978. *Proyecto "Fondo Bolívar."* Quito: FEPP.

Handelman, Howard. 1980. *Ecuadorian agrarian reform: The politics of limited change*. South America reports, no. 20. Hanover, N.H.: American Universities Field Staff.

Haney, Emil, and Wava Haney. 1984. Cambios recientes y tendencias actuales en la estructura agraria del Ecuador: Algunas líneas generales de actuación y sus consecuencias: Parte 1. Typescript. Madison: Land Tenure Center, University of Wisconsin, April.

Hurtado, Osvaldo. 1971. *Dos mundo superpuestos*. Quito: Instituto Ecuatoriano de Desarrollo.

———.1977. *El poder político en el Ecuador*. Quito: Ediciones de la Universidad Católica.

IADB (Inter-American Development Bank). 1984. *Economic and social progress in Latin America*. Washington: IADB.

IERAC (Instituto Ecuatoriano de Reforma Agraria y Colonización). 1980. *Recopilación de leyes agrarias*. Quito: IERAC.

———.1985. *La nueva reforma agraria,* 1985. Quito: IERAC.

———.1986. Adjudicaciones legalizadas de tierras en colonización y en agraria por provincias: 1985. Mimeograph. Quito: Departamento Técnico, IERAC.

Jara, Carlos. 1984. El modelo de modernización y la crisis del agro. In *Ecuador agrario: Ensayos de interpretación,* edited by Manuel Chiriboga et al., pp. 26–71. Quito: Editorial El Conejo.

JUNAPLA (Junta Nacional de Planificación y Coordinación Económica). 1979. *Estrategia de desarrollo (dimensión rural).* Quito: JUNAPLA.

Lehmann, David. 1986. Sharecropping and the capitalist transition in agriculture: Some evidence from the Highlands of Ecuador. *Journal of Development Economics* 23(2):333–354.

LTC (Land Tenure Center) Library. 1979. *Land concentration in the third world: Statistics on number and area of farms classified by size of farms.* Training and Methods Series, no. 28. Madison: Land Tenure Center, University of Wisconsin, April.

Luzuriaga, Carlos, and Clarence Zuvekas. 1983. *Income distribution and poverty in rural Ecuador, 1950–1979.* Tempe: Arizona State Univ. Press.

MAG (Ministerio de Agricultura y Ganadería). 1974. *Reforma agraria, ley y reglamento.* Quito: MAG.

———.1978. *Política agropecuaria.* Quito: MAG.

———.1979a. *Las zonas socio-económicas actualmente homogéneas de la sierra.* Diagnóstico socio-económico del medio rural ecuatoriano, vol. B. Quito: MAG.

———.1979b. *Las zonas socio-económicas actualmente homogéneas de la costa.* Diagnóstico socio-económico del medio rural ecuatoriano, vol. C. Quito: MAG.

———.1979c. *Informe general de la evaluación de la reforma agraria ecuatoriana.* Quito: MAG.

———.1980. *Las zonas socio-económicas actualmente homogéneas de la región amazónica ecuatoriana.* Diagnóstico socio-económico del medio rural ecuatoriano, vol. D. Quito: MAG.

Marchán, Carlos. 1983. La producción agrícola para el mercado interno. Mimeograph. Quito: Banco Central del Ecuador.

Martínez, Luciano. 1980. *Descomposición del campesinado en la sierra ecuatoriana: Un estudio de caso.* Quito: Editorial El Conejo.

———.1984. Pobreza rural y migración. In *Ecuador agrario: Ensayos de interpretación,* edited by M. Chiriboga et al., pp. 72–93. Quito: Editorial El Conejo.

Moncada, José. 1978. Las perspectivas de evolución del Ecuador hacia fines del presente siglo. In *Ecuador, hoy,* edited by Gerald Drekonja, pp. 91–133. Bogotá: Siglo Vigésimo Primero.

Pachano, Simón. 1977. Diferenciación campesina: Un caso de capitalización. Master's thesis, PUCE-FLACSO, Quito.

Redclift, Michael. 1978. *Agrarian reform and peasant organization on the Ecuadorian Coast.* London: Athlone Press.

Redclift, Michael, and David Preston. 1980. Agrarian reform and rural change in Ecuador. In *Environment, society and rural change in Latin America,* edited by D. Preston, pp. 53–63. New York: John Wiley and Sons.

Vega, Néstor. 1980. *La economía ecuatoriana en la década de los alos 70 y perspectivas futuras.* Quito: Editorial La Unión.

Velasco, Fernando. 1979. *Reforma agraria y movimiento campesino indígena en la sierra*. Quito: Editorial El Conejo.

World Bank. 1979. *Ecuador: Development problems and prospects*. Washington: World Bank.

Zevallos, José Vicente. 1985. Oil, power and rural change in Ecuador: 1972–1979. Ph.D. dissertation, University of Wisconsin-Madison.

Zuvekas, Clarence, Jr. 1976. Agrarian reform in Ecuador's Guayas River Basin. *Land Economics* 52:314–319.

Chapter 3

The Agrarian Transition in Highland Ecuador: From Precapitalism to Agrarian Capitalism in Chimborazo

Emil B. Haney Jr. and Wava G. Haney*

This chapter summarizes recent changes in agrarian structure in one province in the Central Highlands (Sierra) of Ecuador. Prior to the initiation of Ecuador's agrarian reform program in 1964, the Province of Chimborazo was said to have one of the most anachronistic agrarian structures in the country, if not in the entire hemisphere. Drawing from secondary data and from survey data collected in 1983, we argue that the agrarian reform measures implemented in that province were facilitated and enhanced by changes already under way as a result of market forces and other national policies. We examine some of the trends in the province's agrarian structure and their implications for rural development policy.

THE HACIENDA SYSTEM IN HIGHLAND ECUADOR

In the Ecuadorian Sierra, the classical hacienda system based on debt peonage became the dominant land-tenure form during the Spanish colonial period. Although modified somewhat during the "liberal revolution" of the first two decades of the twentieth century, this system tied a large portion of the rural, highland, indigenous, and mestizo populations into precapitalist labor arrangements until the 1960s. When *concertaje* (bonded labor) was abolished, it was

* Currently, the authors are Professor of Business and Economics and Associate Professor of Sociology, respectively, with the University of Wisconsin Centers at Baraboo and Richland. At the time of study, they were both Visiting Associate Professors with the Land Tenure Center, University of Wisconsin-Madison.

replaced by *huasipunguaje* (service tenancy) and related, precapitalist, land-tenure forms. In exchange for work obligations to the hacienda and the *hacendado's* family, the *huasipunguero* (service tenant) and his family received usufruct rights to a *huasipungo* (subsistence plot, usually no larger than 2–5 hectares) and, typically, some restricted access to forests, pastureland, and water elsewhere on the hacienda. Ostensibly, the *huasipungueros* also received very modest wages for services performed; *arrimados* (tied laborers) did not.

The *huasipungueros* typically spent five or six days per week working for the *hacendado*, while older sons labored as peons (day laborers) or as assistants to their fathers (Farga Hernández 1981). Because the men were occupied with hacienda work obligations, women often took major responsibility for tending the *huasipungo* and any animals. During planting and harvesting seasons, the women usually joined the hacienda workforce (Likes and Salamea n.d.). Guerrero (1975) argues that the servile work required of the *huasipunguero* and his family were too demanding to permit ample subsistence to nuclear families; this obligated various families to pool their labor and become involved in secondary tenancy relationships. The extended *huasipunguero* family assured reproduction and provided the *hacendado* with a supplemental labor force.

As the rural population of the Sierra increased and some tenants acquired permanent property rights, an "independent" campesino (peasant) sector emerged beside the hacienda-*huasipungo* system. Since the land resources of these "smallholders" were usually too meager to provide the basic necessities or absorb available family labor, many of the campesinos became dependent upon the hacienda for supplementary employment and additional land as well as for firewood, water, and pasture rights (Farga Hernández 1981). This collateral peasantry played a vital role in the maintenance and renewal of the *latifundio-minifundio* complex.

THE REFORM PERIOD

Despite serious disagreement on how far the nation should go in responding to growing pressures to reorganize its agrarian structure, a general consensus emerged on the need for state action to modify traditional labor forms and redistribute some public lands (Handelman 1980, 7). The initial response to these pressures came in 1959 in the form of a National Emergency Decree, which followed the attempts by many other Latin American countries to promote spontaneous and directed colonization on unsettled public lands. With the help of foreign financing and technical assistance, Ecuador encouraged settlement in its piedmont regions and on *Asistencia Público* (public welfare) haciendas acquired from the Catholic Church in the Sierra. After four years of further acrimonious national debate, the ruling military junta finally passed the country's first Agrarian Reform Law in July 1964.

The 1964 law was ostensibly intended to promote improved living standards and increased productivity through the transfer of inefficiently used hacienda lands to campesinos and the integration of smallholders into the national economy via production cooperatives. In practice, the law concentrated on de facto titling of the remaining *huasipungos* and *arrimados* in the Sierra, creating production cooperatives on public welfare lands and land titling in areas of spontaneous colonization (Cosse 1980, 61). By the end of the decade, the Agrarian Reform Institute (*Instituto Ecuatoriano de Reforma Agraria y Colonización,* IERAC) had expropriated only fourteen haciendas (nine without compensation) and sold land to campesinos on another thirty-six haciendas (Blankstein and Zuvekas 1973, 15).[1]

During the first eight years of the agrarian reform, over 90 percent of the beneficiaries and nearly 80 percent of the land were in the Sierra (see Table 1). The average amount of land received by sierra family beneficiaries during this period was fewer than 5 hectares. During this period, IERAC adjudicated nearly 3 hectares of colonization land for every 1 hectare of agrarian reform land. Because of the relatively large number of *huasipungueros* and *arrimados* who received titles to small plots during the initial years of the program, the ratio of agrarian reform to colonization beneficiaries during this time span was about two to one.

The 1973 Agrarian Reform Law, which superseded all previous agrarian reform legislation, was not a departure from that of 1964. While it opened the door for increased public and private participation in rural infrastructural development and agricultural modernization, it did not address the problem of land maldistribution (Handelman 1980, 10). The new law called for the abolition of precapitalist labor forms, but its major thrust was to bring more land under cultivation and to increase production on existing agricultural land through the application of modern technology.[2]

The 1979 Agricultural Development Law further emphasized improved agricultural output and productivity through more efficient use of human and natural resources, research, technology, credit, and development of infrastructure. It also imposed significant constraints on the agrarian reform process by relaxing the criterion of "efficient use" as a basis for expropriation and by excluding participants in land invasions from receiving benefits from IERAC (Barsky et al. 1982, 57–59). The law delighted the large landowners while leaving most

Table 1
Amount of land adjudicated (in hectares) and number of families benefited through official agrarian reform actions in Ecuador, 1964–82, by period and region[a]

	Sierra		Coast		Total	
	Hectares	Families	Hectares	Families	Hectares	Families
1964–1966 (military government)	68,448	17,018	17,155	1,142	85,603	18,160
1967–1971 (civilian government)	72,191	12,102	21,105	1,198	93,296	13,300
1972–1979 (military government)	253,239	22,377	122,670	12,683	376,407[b]	35,069[b]
1980–1982 (civilian government)	83,482	6,115	46,834	3,598	130,557[c]	9,717[c]
Total (1964–1982)	477,360	57,612	207,764	18,621	685,863[d]	76,246[d]

[a] Sources: Instituto Ecuatoriano de Reforma Agraria y Colonización, *Estadísticas de las adjudicaciones legalizadas en reforma agraria y colonización* (Quito: Departamento de Evaluación y Estadística del IERAC, 1979), pp. 1–2; unpublished data compiled by Departamento de Evaluación y Estadística del IERAC (Quito, 1983).
[b] This includes 498 hectares adjudicated to nine beneficiaries in the Oriente.
[c] This includes 186 hectares adjudicated to three beneficiaries in the Oriente and 55 hectares adjudicated to one beneficiary in the Galápagos Archipelago.
[d] This includes 684 hectares adjudicated to twelve beneficiaries in the Oriente and 55 hectares adjudicated to one beneficiary in the Galápagos Archipelago.

peasant leaders disenchanted (Handelman 1980, 10). Symbolically, the law may have formally marked the end of what de Janvry (1981, 224) labels "agrarian reformism via land reform" and marked the beginning of "agrarian reformism via rural development projects."

By the end of 1982, IERAC reported that approximately 2.5 million hectares had been adjudicated to about 120,000 beneficiaries. About three-fourths of this total area and one-third of the beneficiaries were in colonization projects, most of which involved the simple titling of de facto squatter-settled lands in the public domain (Barsky et al. 1982, 68). Discounting extensive areas of almost totally unproductive land and the differing results of beneficiary enumeration by IERAC, we estimate that agrarian reform and colonization activities may have affected as much as 18 percent of the country's total agricultural land and 15 percent of the country's farm families. While these percentages compare favorably with those in other Latin America countries such as Colombia and Venezuela, they are relatively low when compared with Mexico, Bolivia, and Peru where the emphasis was more clearly upon distributive reforms. This observation is reinforced by the fact that nearly 25 percent of the total area adjudicated by IERAC was already in the hands of the state when the 1964 law was enacted. Much of what was called "agrarian reform," then, was simply the ratification of an existing situation.

AGRARIAN STRUCTURE IN CHIMBORAZO: EVOLUTION AND CURRENT TRENDS

While it would be impossible to identify a single province to represent the agrarian structure of the Ecuadorian Sierra, Chimborazo has many characteristics and problems which are common to the country's highland region and to other parts of the Andes. It also has some features that are unique, but which are rich with implications for rural development in Ecuador and elsewhere.

Chimborazo was the first area in present-day Ecuador to be colonized by the Spanish. In the early 1960s, it was thought to have the most traditional agrarian structure and the most backward rural areas in Ecuador (CIDA 1965, 275). However, Chimborazo was most affected by the country's agrarian reform program in terms of land area and beneficiary numbers. In part this high level of public intervention was a response to intense political pressures from the province's large indigenous population, which was organized by leaders of the *Federación Ecuatoriana de Indios* and Bishop Leonidas E. Proaño ("el Obispo de los Indios") from Riobamba.

The province's rugged topography is accentuated by two major cordilleras with four snowcapped peaks. Except for some alluvial terraces along the two major rivers, most of the land is rolling to very steep. Despite the fact that many of the soils are of relatively recent volcanic origin with good permeability and natural fertility, topography poses a severe constraint on agricultural activity. Increasing demographic pressure and intensive land use have taken a heavy toll on the province's natural resource base. In many areas, accelerated erosion has caused irreversible damage.

As in most parts of the Sierra, the natural forests of Chimborazo have been all but obliterated. In 1981 about one-third of the province's land was cultivated or lying fallow, a little over one-third was pasture, and the remaining one-third was *paramo* and wasteland. Although most of the pasture is unimproved and overgrazing is pervasive throughout the province, some pastureland could be used more intensively. Such areas of inverted land use are vestiges of the hacienda system, which allocated the best lands to the owners' crops and cattle; marginal lands were assigned to sheep production and to tenants for subsistence and sharecropping.

Despite heavy out-migration from most rural areas and small towns toward Riobamba, Chimborazo remains very rural, with nearly seven out of every ten inhabitants living in the countryside. While considerable improvements have been made in Chimborazo's infrastructure during the past decade or so, the province still lags behind other regions of the country in public infrastructure and services. In recent decades, much of the province's out-migration has flowed toward the country's two largest cities, Guayaquil and Quito. The 1982 population census showed that the number of Chimborazo-born persons living outside the province nearly equaled the number of urban inhabitants living in the province.

Farm Size and Ownership

The 1954 agricultural census showed a very skewed land-distribution pattern for Chimborazo. Over 85 percent of the farms was under 5 hectares and controlled only one-sixth of the total farmland in the province (see Table 2), and 94 percent was under 10 hectares, or "subfamily" units (CIDA 1965, 14) before agrarian reform. Chimborazo was a province of *minifundios*.

At the other extreme, only forty-six farms (0.15 percent of the total) controlled about two-fifths of the total farmland, and the eighty-four farms (0.3 percent of the total) with 500 hectares or more controlled

Table 2
Distribution of agricultural production units and farmland, by farm size, Chimborazo, 1954[a]

Size category (hectares)	Number of production units[b]		Total farmland (hectares)[b]		Mean size (hectares)
< than 5 hectares	28,625	(86.1)	52,300	(17.0)	1.8
5–19.9 hectares	3,486	(10.5)	29,800	(9.0)	8.5
20–99.9 hectares	790	(2.4)	32,900	(10.0)	41.6
100–499.9 hectares	236	(0.7)	50,700	(16.0)	214.8
> than 500 hectares	84	(0.3)	149,900	(48.0)	1,784.5
Total	33,221	(100.0)	315,600	(100.0)	9.5

[a] Source: Instituto Nacional de Estadística y Censos, *I censo agropecuario nacional de 1954* (Quito: INEC, n.d.).
[b] The numbers in parentheses represent percentages.

nearly one-half of the province's farmland. So, before the agrarian reform, Chimborazo was also a province of *latifundios*.

While the middle categories were numerically lean, farms in the 100–500 hectare range were six times more prevalent than those in the 500–1,000 hectare group and controlled twice as much land. And even though the medium-sized farms in the 20–100 hectare range accounted for slightly over 2 percent of the total, they controlled 10 percent of the total farmland. This suggests that inheritance patterns and land markets had begun to create a significant number of family-sized units before the agrarian reform (see Table 2).

Abolition of service tenancy meant immediate changes in the agrarian structure of Chimborazo as the 1964 Agrarian Reform Law was implemented, but the effects of land redistribution and colonization dragged into the 1970s and 1980s. While the 1974 agricultural census reported nearly a 25 percent increase in the number of production units and nearly a 20 percent increase in farmland over the 1954 census, these changes cannot be attributed solely to the reform. Beginning in the early 1970s, the country's "petroleum boom" fostered nearly a decade of rapid economic growth. Although the growth focused on urban areas, it generated some positive "trickle-down" effects for peripheral regions like Chimborazo through increased off-farm employment opportunities and increased demand for farm products (Haney and Haney 1987; Commander and Peek 1986).

Even though the proportion of farms under 5 hectares decreased slightly from 1954, the 1974 census indicated a 20 percent numerical increase (see Table 3). Production units smaller than 1 hectare increased by one-half. Farms of 5–20 hectares increased dramatically in number (63 percent) and in area (82 percent); within the subcategory of 10–20 hectares, the number of farms quadrupled. Medium-sized farms, however, decreased slightly in number, in area, and in average size. While the number and area of large farms was stable (the reform established several large-scale properties as *comunas* or cooperatives) and some of the larger size categories gave up land area during the 20-year period, overall the average size of large farms increased by 400 hectares.

The census data suggest that Chimborazo continued to be, even after the agrarian reform, a province of very large and very small farms. Compared with the nation and the Sierra, Chimborazo in 1974 had a larger proportion of small units, which in turn held a larger proportion of farmland. The province also had a lower proportion of medium-sized units, which controlled a much lower proportion of farmland.[3] Holdings with 500 hectares or more controlled nearly one-half of the land in the province compared with a little over one-fourth nationally and about one-third for the Sierra.

Table 3

Distribution of agricultural production units and farmland by farm size, Chimborazo, 1974, and changes from 1954 to 1974[a]

Size category[b]	1974 Number of production units[c]		1954–1974 Change (number of units)[c]		1974 Total farmland (hectares)[c]		1954–1974 Change (total farmland, in hectares)[c]		1974 Mean size (in hectares)
< 5	34,234	(83.3)	5,609	(20.0)	59,950	(16.0)	7,650	(15.0)	1.75
5–19.9	5,692	(13.8)	2,206	(63.0)	54,276	(14.0)	24,476	(82.0)	9.5
20–99.9	845	(2.1)	55	(7.0)	28,569	(8.0)	−4,331	(−13.0)	33.8
100–499.9	234	(0.6)	−2	(−1.0)	47,969	(13.0)	−2,731	(−5.0)	205.0
> 500	83	(0.2)	−1	(−1.0)	180,297	(49.0)	30,397	(20.0)	2,172.3
Total	41,088	(100.0)	7,867	(24.0)	371,061	(100.0)	55,461	(18.0)	9.0

[a] Sources: Instituto Nacional de Estadística y Censos, *I censo agropecuario nacional de 1954* (Quito: INEC, n.d.), and *II censo agropecuario nacional de 1974* (Quito: INEC, 1979).

[b] In hectares.

[c] The numbers in parentheses are percentages.

Table 4

Distribution of agricultural production units and farmland by farm size, Chimborazo, 1980, and change from 1974–1980[a]

Size category[b]	1980 Number of production units[c]	1974–1980 Change (Number of units)[c]	1980 Total farmland (hectares)[c]	1974–1980 Change (total farmland, in hectares)[c]	1980 Mean size (hectares)
<5	37,013 (76.0)	2,779 (8.0)	64,319 (17.0)	4,369 (7.0)	1.74
5–19.9	9,449 (19.4)	3,757 (66.0)	90,085 (24.0)	35,809 (66.0)	9.53
20–99.9	1,864 (4.0)	1,019 (121.0)	69,832 (18.0)	41,263 (144.0)	37.5
100–499.9	240 (0.5)	6 (3.0)	50,279 (13.0)	2,310 (5.0)	209.5
>500	47 (0.1)	−36 (−43.0)	105,813 (28.0)	−74,484 (−41.0)	2,251.3
Total	48,613 (100.0)	7,525 (18.0)	380,328 (100.0)	9,267 (3.0)	7.8

[a] Sources: Instituto Nacional de Estadística y Censos, *II censo agropecuario de 1974* (Quito: INEC, 1979); 1980 estimates done by Banco Central del Ecuador, Subgerencia de Estudios Especiales, based on data from Instituto Ecuatoriano de Reforma Agraria y Colonización, Departamento de Programación y Evaluación Estadística de Jefatura Regional Centro-Oriente, reported in Centro de Desarrollo Industrial de Ecuador, *Comercialización de productos agrícolas para la provincia de Chimborazo* (Quito: CENDES/Banco Central/Centro Agrícola de Riobamba, 1983), p. 39.

[b] In hectares.

[c] The numbers in parentheses are percentages.

Some 1980 data on the agrarian structure of Chimborazo were generated by the Ecuadorian Central Bank as part of a provincial marketing study (CENDES 1983). These data show a significant increase in the number and prominence of medium-sized farms when compared with 1974. Between 1974 and 1980, the number of farms with 20–100 hectares doubled, as did the amount of farmland they controlled (see Table 4). Yet, in 1980, Chimborazo still had a lower proportion of medium-sized farms than did either the country or the Sierra in 1974. Much of the growth in medium-sized farms is related to sharp losses in the size of the largest holdings, especially those with 1,000 hectares or more; a 20 percent drop in the amount of farmland they controlled is recorded. At the other end of the scale, small-sized farms increased in absolute numbers but decreased in proportion of the total. Thus, in 1980, the proportions of small units in Chimborazo was still higher than that of the nation but about the same as in other sierra provinces. The amount of farmland small farmers controlled was stable, and the average size of holdings remained the same.

Labor Use

Staple foods, accounting for about 60 percent of total hectares in cropland in 1974, increased 20 percent in area and more than doubled in production between 1954 and 1974. During the same period, the area devoted to edible legume seeds and vegetables increased 33 percent in Chimborazo, while production expanded nearly sevenfold. Tubers, forage crops, and pome fruits (for example, apples, pears, plums) also doubled in production over the last two decades.

As might be expected from the previous discussion, the 1974 census showed the agricultural labor force of Chimborazo to be composed predominantly of independent agricultural producers who, in addition to their own labor, relied heavily on unpaid family labor and occasionally employed wage labor. Most of the members of the agricultural wage-labor force were part-time workers. The average number of part-time agricultural laborers was more than twice that of full-time workers. A 1975–1978 survey of labor utilization (MAG et al. 1982) found that in Chimborazo most of the full-time wage labor was employed in large units. While both small and large producers hire seasonal wage labor, especially for crop production, the medium and large units depend on occasional wage workers for two-fifths to two-thirds of their labor requirement.

The division of labor by gender reported in the 1974 population census suggested that women's involvement in agricultural production was quite small. Only 15 percent of the rural women were considered "economically active," and only 5 percent of the agricultural labor force was female. However, the 1975–1978 survey revealed a different picture in terms of both the types of activities performed and the form of employment (MAG et al. 1982, 199–256).[4] It showed that rural women in the Sierra accounted for about two-fifths of total family labor in agricultural production and 4 and 12 percent, respectively, of the occasional and full-time wage labor.[5] Among the sierra provinces, rural women from Chimborazo made the heaviest relative contribution to the family labor pool. Overall they contributed nearly 50 percent of total family labor spent on the family plot. Women's labor accounted for about one-third of the family labor devoted to crops and two-thirds devoted to livestock production. Their labor input to family crop and livestock production was highest on units under 10 hectares, but their wage-labor input to crops was highest as occasional laborers on medium units and to livestock as full-time workers on large units (Haney 1985).

POSTREFORM AGRARIAN STRUCTURE: FIELD STUDY ANALYSIS

The objective of this section is to analyze the economic organization of agricultural production and employment in rural Chimborazo with data gathered nearly twenty years after the country's first agrarian reform law was promulgated. We will compare the employment and income strategies of 522 sample households from three regions of the province that were affected in different ways by the agrarian reform program.[6] In the northern region of the province, most of the present-day farms were derived from old haciendas through land sales and inheritance, with relatively little direct intervention of the agrarian reform program. In contrast, much of the central region was subdivided by the agrarian reform. At the time of the 1964 law, the extensive public welfare holdings were being rented to individuals who operated them as large haciendas with *huasipungueros* and other forms of service tenancy. Distribution of land to these *huasipungueros* was an important part of the first few years of the agrarian reform. Finally, in the southern region the agrarian reform program's actions were more modest. Although quite rugged and isolated, this region has undergone considerable subdivision in recent years through land sales and inheritance along with some agrarian reform colonization projects.

Farm Size and Tenure

The most prevalent type of producer was the owner-operator. While the current generation of proprietors is more numerous, it has far less power and wealth than the preceding generation of landowners. Only 6 percent of the households did not own any land and only about 15 percent reported that they worked on land owned by others.[7] In the north, about 85 percent of the owner-operators owned fewer than 5 hectares, 66 percent owned fewer than 5 hectares in the central region, and about 55 percent owned fewer than 5 hectares in the south. The mean amount of land owned was 2.2 hectares in the north, 2.7 hectares in the central region, and 3.5 hectares in the south.

Many production units have become seriously fragmented, especially in the north. Two-fifths of the farms in the north are composed of three or more parcels, twice the proportion for each of the other regions. About two-thirds of the parcels owned in 1983 were acquired by purchase; the remaining one-third were either inherited or acquired through agrarian reform. Overall, the land quality of two-thirds of the farms was classified by the respondents as average or poor. Only one-third of the producers had any irrigation.

Labor Patterns

As might be expected from the prevalence of *minifundios* and the poor soil quality in Chimborazo, most families relied heavily on off-farm employment for sustenance. In over two-thirds of the sample families, the husband, the wife, or both worked off the farm. In the northern and central regions, this figure rose to 80 percent overall and was about 85 percent among families who operated fewer than 5 hectares. The proportion of families with off-farm employment dropped precipitously as farm size increased. In these regions, husbands were most likely to work off the farm (about one-half of the families), while both husband and wife held off-farm jobs in one-fifth of the households. The men tended to combine the operation of the farms with agricultural wage labor, small-scale commercial or artisan activities, or construction work. While household work was the primary responsibility of women, about two-thirds of them combined this with agricultural production on the farm and, in a few cases, with agricultural wage labor.

A more detailed analysis of labor by gender in sample households reveals five major configurations of occupations for the sample couples: (1) both husband and wife engage in agricultural activities, including agricultural wage labor off the farm (about one-half), (2) husband works off the farm while wife is sole or principal agricultural producer (about 10 percent), (3) wife has nonagricultural occupation while husband is primarily responsible for the farm (about 10 percent), (4) primary occupations of both husband and wife are nonagricultural while husband manages the farm (about 10 percent), and (5) husband is responsible for the farm and wife is not involved in agricultural production (about 10 percent). The pattern is similar across all regions with the exception that wives are more likely to be the sole or principal agricultural producer in the central region (about 25 percent compared with 15 percent in the north and only 4 percent in the south) and much less likely to be involved in agricultural production in the south (25 percent compared with 10 percent in each of the other regions).

Family Income

Farm income was positively correlated with farm size, but both gross and net farm income fell for the top size categories in all three regions of the province. The average gross farm income for the two smallest size groups was quite similar for all three regions. The 1–2 hectare category earned about twice as much gross farm income as the group with less than 1 hectare in the north and central regions and about three times as much as the same group in the south. With more than 2 hectares, the average gross farm income increased faster by farm size in the north than in the other two regions. This is attributable to the importance of intensive vegetable production on the 2–10 hectare units in the north.

Overall, crops were about three to four times as important as livestock in generating gross farm income in the north and south, respectively. In the central region, livestock was somewhat more important than crops in generating gross farm income. Partly because of its relative isolation and generally poor soils, the original haciendas of the central region were heavily oriented toward livestock production, especially cattle and sheep. Apparently, agrarian reform made enough land available to campesinos to allow them to continue with livestock activities.

Income analysis confirms that nonfarm employment is a relatively more important survival strategy among households in the north than in the other two regions. On average, net farm income contributed only 40 percent of gross family income in this region. Wages and salaries contributed one-third while commerce and artisan activities provided about one-fourth. In the north, farming has become a secondary occupation for most rural families.

Extensive land subdivision in the north of Chimborazo goes back several decades, and since the agrarian reform program was relatively inactive in this part of the province, extensive nonfarm employment may have both contributed to and resulted from the characteristic *minifundio* problem. Most rural families in this region appear to perceive that they are better off clinging to their small parcel of land in the countryside and putting up with the uncertainties of the volatile artisan and labor markets than moving their families to face even more uncertainties in town.

Commerce and artisan activities as survival strategies were relatively insignificant for families in the central region, but wage labor, usually either temporary agricultural labor or construction work, was quite important. Except for a few cases, farming activities provided the most important source of gross family income in the central region. This is significant because the averages for both gross and net family incomes compare quite favorably with the corresponding size categories in the north and south. Since the central region of Chimborazo has long been considered among the poorest in the nation and since the agrarian reform was especially intense in this region, it appears that agrarian reform has had a positive impact on incomes.

With the exception of the poorest farms in the south, which forced owners to derive nearly all of their income from wages, farming activities constituted the major source of gross family income for respondents—78 percent for the region as a whole. It should be pointed out, however, that farm income for this region was adversely affected by a prolonged and severe rainy season at the time of the study. While this probably exacerbated the tendency of the small farms to obtain a low net family income, it did not appear to change their ordinal ranking relative to small farms in other regions.

These income data suggest several general conclusions. With two exceptions, the gross family income averaged above the official annual minimum wage for an urban worker in 1983 (28,500 sucres, or about $315 in U.S. dollars). While this level of income is hardly adequate to provide the necessities for a family of five or six members, it is probably more than many rural families could expect to receive immediately upon moving to a city in Ecuador.

It appears from the data that families in Chimborazo must hold about 5 hectares of land before they can generate (from all sources) the equivalent of two minimum wages for an urban worker. With 10 or more hectares, rural families in Chimborazo can compete quite favorably with the income-earning capacity of unskilled urban workers.

Using net family income as a rough approximation of the savings potential for families, most of Chimborazo's rural families are living at or near the "break-even point" or "zero level" of savings. In some years, they may come out ahead; in other years, they probably operate at a loss. Again, 5 hectares of land seems to represent a threshold level below which any savings potential disappears.

In the north, 21 percent of the families registered a negative net income; the figures for the central and south were 15 and 39 percent, respectively. The number of families earning 10,000 sucres (about $110) or less of net income in the north, central, and south was 52, 44, and 54 percent, respectively. These negative and low-positive net family income figures confirm the precarious situation of most rural families.

On the other hand, 11, 8, and 21 percent of the sample families in the north, central, and south, respectively, earned at least 50,000 sucres (about $550) of net income. This shows that some rural families—those with access to reasonable amounts of productive resources—fare quite well in a very difficult environment.

Reform versus Nonreform Sectors

Data from the central and southern regions of Chimborazo suggest that families in the reform sector compare favorably with those in the nonreform sector in terms of income (see Table 5). In the central region, average gross farm income for agrarian reform beneficiaries was more than twice that of the sample families in the nonreform sector. The difference was particularly apparent in livestock production, from which average gross receipts of beneficiaries were more than five times those of nonbeneficiaries. While the difference in average gross farm income between the reform and the nonreform sectors in the south was not as great as in the central region, the agrarian reform beneficiaries of the south still showed an advantage over nonbeneficiaries.

Likewise, average net farm income was considerably higher for the reform properties in both the central and the southern regions. In the central region, agrarian reform beneficiaries had, on the average, more than twice as much net farm income and only one-half as much salary income as nonbeneficiaries. On the other hand, the beneficiaries earned significantly more income than nonbeneficiaries from other sources, including distributions from cooperatives.

Contrary to popular opinion advanced by antireform interests in Ecuador, the agrarian reform apparently had increased income and employment opportunities over prereform levels in some rural areas. The permanent and temporary exodus of rural people into the cities, at least in the first generation of beneficiaries, is taking place mainly among those who still lack reasonable access to land and other productive resources.[8] If net family income is a reasonable proxy for the family's ability to save, then the evidence once again points favorably toward land redistribution as a means to promote capital formation.

Whether successive generations of agrarian reform beneficiaries will continue to have an edge over their nonbeneficiary counterparts in the rural areas, however, remains to be seen. Reform in the south is recent. However, some evidence from the central region suggests a polarized effect among the offspring of agrarian reform beneficiaries, which is not unlike that found in the rural population generally. Those beneficiaries who received more and better quality land tend to educate their children to help them become better established in nonfarm occupations. The children of families who did not receive reform benefits are more likely to be totally or partially engaged in unskilled work in both rural and urban areas.

Table 5
Farm and family income analysis of reform and nonreform properties in current sucres, by region, Chimborazo, 1983[a]

	Central[b]		South[b]	
Farm and family income	Reform (N = 38)	Nonreform (N = 100)	Reform (N = 50)	Nonreform (N = 138)
Value of gross farm production				
Crops	20,055	17,794	99,040	72,427
Livestock	42,180	8,321	15,662	19,778
Total	62,235	26,115	114,702	92,205
Production costs				
Crops	5,771	3,253	13,504	14,051
Livestock	7,128	902	749	5,552
Other	11,466	4,428	9,500	13,691
Total	24,365	8,583	23,753	33,294
Net farm income	37,870	17,532	90,949	58,911
Family income sources				
Net farm income	37,870	17,532	90,949	58,911
Wages and salaries	8,153	17,166	5,914	16,167
Artisan/commercial activities	2,608	3,325	3,188	1,028
Other	12,021	1,108	1,618	4,091
Total	60,652	39,131	101,669	80,197
Family consumption	29,687	24,482	49,850	41,269
Net family income	30,965	14,649	51,819	38,928

[a] Source: Survey EEAE. Survey of the "Estudio sobre la estructura agraria del Ecuador," conducted by the Instituto Ecuatoriano de Reforma Agraria y Colonización, in collaboration with the Land Tenure Center, University of Wisconsin-Madison, 1983–1984.
[b] Missing data: Central, nine cases (all reform properties); south, nineteen cases.

SUMMARY

The evolution of Chimborazo's agrarian structure during the past two decades and its apparent direction of change today closely parallel alterations elsewhere in Ecuador and in other parts of the world. Despite a sluggish beginning, the agrarian reform program was an important factor in the transformation of Chimborazo's agrarian structure. However, many of the changes were already in progress when agrarian reform began. Indeed, these trends helped to justify the reforms.

It should not be surprising that the traditional hacienda and its associated forms of service tenancy have all but disappeared in Chimborazo. Land, labor, and capital markets in the rural areas have become increasingly vigorous and complex, as the heirs of the traditional landed gentry modernize or abandon the countryside in favor of urban-based professions and part of the burgeoning peasantry strives to obtain a more secure hedge in the rural areas against the vagaries of urban subsistence. Meanwhile, growing urban markets for agricultural products—along with the widespread availability of new agricultural technology and the penetration of the countryside by urban-based bureaucracies—have virtually eliminated rural self-sufficiency. As a consequence of these pressures, land subdivision has continued at unprecedented rates, and the land is cultivated ever more intensively.

Perhaps the most salient features of the agrarian transition in Chimborazo over the past two decades are the increasing minifundization and semiproletarianization of the countryside. *Minifundistas* with off-farm employment have become the norm in the province. For the province as a whole, 60 percent of the gross family income came from agricultural production while 25 percent came from wages. In the smaller but more densely settled northern region, where 88 percent of the farms was under 5 hectares in size, only 40 percent of the gross family income came from farming. However, two-thirds of the families—all with farms under 5 hectares—received an average annual income from all sources at or below the official annual minimum wage.

Traditionally, artisan activities (such as weaving, knitting, rug making) provided an important source of supplementary earning, but these products are being replaced by manufactured goods produced by urban-based, capital-intensive industries. Mechanization of the coastal agroexport industries and the emergence of surplus-labor supplies in that region have likewise virtually eliminated another traditional source of supplementary income for the Chimborazo peasantry.

This means that the rural families of Chimborazo are increasingly dependent on precarious service activities in Quito and Guayaquil. As artisan activities decline, women are also forced into agricultural wage labor in Chimborazo and into domestic service in the cities. As husbands and sons devote ever more time outside the household to wage earning, women have also assumed a growing responsibility for farming operations.

If the agrarian transition has either lowered or held most rural families to the margin of poverty, it has been quite benign to others. In contrast to the near landless, the small group of landed peasantry—the one-fifth of the sample with 5 to 20 hectares—earn markedly higher incomes from fewer sources. Those with at least 10 hectares earn about 90 percent of their income from farming. This group of rich campesinos, along with the small and medium farmers who managed to acquire and hold good land, is now benefiting from public rural development projects, abundant cheap labor, and a growing demand for food. While evidence of sustained individual accumulation for those owning between 5 and 10 hectares is weaker, these peasant and farm families nevertheless are investing in the education of their children and in urban assets. Those with larger farms—whether heirs who have modernized remnants of defunct haciendas or successful climbers—are clearly the major beneficiaries of the new agrarian structure which still favors those who control the most productive resources.

Our study suggests that relatively little of the private accumulation generated by successful adapters is being captured and returned to the land and to rural communities. Rural services such as health and education have improved immensely, largely through external infusions of public revenues. The new farmers are investing in homes, means of transport, clothing, diets, and the education of their children, but they are not sanguine about the future of the countryside. Rural villages reflect this prevailing attitude. They show a declining vitality as their citizens reach ever farther for their sustenance and as the terms of trade between countryside and city continue to deteriorate. Short of massive public transfers to create jobs and to forestall environmental degradation in the rural areas of Chimborazo, the prospects for increased production and income look bleak.

POSSIBLE POLICY RESPONSES

Agrarian reform was a long time coming to Chimborazo. When it arrived in the mid-1960s, the structural conditions were seriously polarized. Temporary and permanent migration, voluntary land subdivision, and yield-increasing technology simply were not keeping pace with a burgeoning rural population on a deteriorating resource base. Agrarian reform provided an additional escape valve.

In the northern part of Chimborazo, where most of the traditional haciendas were already in various stages of dissolution and where a market for intensive fruit and vegetable production was established, agrarian reform amounted to little more than a legitimation of de facto subdivision. After twenty years of agrarian reform, the north, with its preponderance of *minifundios*, still has a number of holdings with 100 hectares or more of productive land in unimproved pastures devoted to extensive grazing. Many of these holdings have absentee owners who run dairy operations with administrators and hired labor. With proper soil and water management, agrarian reform could lead to significant production increases on these holdings. An expansion of agricultural processing facilities and other employment opportunities could fortify the region's economy, which is already heavily oriented toward intensive part-time farming.

While our study and others, such as the agricultural marketing study of the Central Bank (CENDES 1983), verify the importance of the area's farms in generating additional employment and income, they also point to many bottlenecks in this sector. In addition to the structural impediments to increased output, technological and financial inputs are notably deficient. For example, about 20 percent of the households in our sample used institutional credit. To address these needs and to create additional nonfarm employment opportunities, the Ecuadorian government has given heavy emphasis to integrated rural development projects in the northern and central regions of the province. To date, however, the projects have been very costly and have directly benefited only a small portion of the target group. Although IERAC has been involved in the projects, agrarian reform has been limited primarily to a "cleaning up" of land titles.

In the central and southern regions, reform activities have been and continue to be a much more dominant force in changing the agrarian structure. The central region experienced more agrarian reform intervention than any other area of the country. Our study confirms that most of these activities produced a positive impact on income, employment, and the general welfare of the people in the region. But the creation of a campesino economy has also seriously taxed the region's natural environment and, so far, has failed to establish a sustainable growth pattern for the region.

The land in these regions is quite fragile. While most of the recent land-redistribution efforts have been based on sound land-use planning principles, closer attention to better land use and improved agricultural production techniques, including good soil and water conservation measures, is essential if the region is to support a productive system of small- and medium-scale agriculture oriented to the urban markets.

As in the north, a large number of families in the central and southern regions still do not have clear title to their land and, therefore, do not qualify for institutional credit and other essential inputs. At the same time, many of the collective properties and campesino organizations created by the reform process have collapsed in the face of strong pressures for individually owned properties. While it would be naive and perhaps counterproductive to resist this individualization trend, to let it continue without constraints invites rampant minifundization and exacerbated threats to the fragile environment. These problems beg IERAC and other public agencies to rethink and reorganize collective properties to preserve any economies of scale and to foster social benefits associated with collective action.

In general our analysis supports findings from other postreform studies in Latin America. In those areas where reform activities were significant, the beneficiaries and the communities show decided improvement. On the other hand, the reform certainly did not eliminate the gross inequities in the agrarian structure of Chimborazo. If the precapitalist estates and their tied labor force no longer exist, thousands of rural families still live on the brink of poverty, lacking sufficient resources to eke out a decent living. To ensure a higher level of employment and income to these families will take more public support and less resistance to agrarian reform and rural development.

NOTES

1. The new Agrarian Reform Law issued in September 1970 called for the elimination of all rental arrangements and other insecure tenure forms that had been excluded from the 1964 law. Two other decrees were issued that year in response to the increasingly tense situation in the rice-growing areas of the Coast. However, data for the early 1970s show few changes in the tempo of reform activity. For further detail on this period, see José Zevallos, chap. 2 in this volume.

2. For further analysis of the 1973 law, see chap. 2 in this volume.

3. The 1974 census data for the province of Chimborazo compared with the national data are as follows. In Chimborazo, 83 percent of the production units was under 5 hectares compared with 67 percent for the nation and 78 percent for the Sierra; units under 5 hectares in Chimborazo held 16 percent of the farmland compared with 7 and 12 percent for the nation and the Sierra, respectively. In Chimborazo, 2 percent of the units was from 20 to 100 hectares in size compared with 12.5 and 6 percent for the nation and the Sierra, respectively; these medium-size units in Chimborazo controlled only 8 percent of the farmland compared with 33 percent for the nation and 26 percent for the Sierra.

4. The study reported the number of days spent by men and women on the following agricultural activities: planting, weeding, and harvesting crops; clearing land; tending livestock; generally maintaining the farm; gathering firewood; processing farm products; marketing farm products; exchanging reciprocal labor; laboring on agricultural production cooperatives; working for the landlord; and contributing on collective infrastructure projects such as roads and schools (*minga*). The type of labor performed was divided into four types: family labor (on the family plot whether owned or not), temporary wage (occasional agricultural day labor), permanent wage (full-time agricultural labor), and nonmonetary reciprocal labor exchange including assistance given by family members, typically by children to parents.

5. Sierra women contributed a greater proportion of total family labor as well as occasional and full-time wage labor than did rural Ecuadorian women

as a whole. Nationally, rural Ecuadorian women accounted for one-third of the family labor and 2 percent of both the occasional and full-time wage labor.

6. Lacking an a priori listing of the production units in Chimborazo, we established an area sample frame based largely on the work of Dubly et al. (1982). Representative area samples were established independently for each of the three general agropolitical regions of the province. Within each of the three regions, the dominant land-use areas were identified by using land-use maps from the Ministry of Agriculture. The study areas or interview blocks, consisting of 25 hectares each, were drawn randomly from each area and transposed to recent air photos to facilitate field identification. We attempted to interview all of the households owning and/or operating land that fell within each interview block. A sufficient number of blocks were identified and interviewed sequentially to account for approximately 5–10 percent of the total estimated households in each land-use area. Sparsely settled forested areas, wasteland, and *paramos* were excluded from the study, as were blocks falling on more densely populated villages. The northern region is dominated by a mixture of small and medium farms producing commercial vegetable and tuber crops and some milk, along with a proliferation of *minifundios* producing barley and corn on marginal land. The central region is composed of marginal land, much of it very badly eroded. The dominant agricultural enterprises are tuber crops, small grains, cattle, swine, and sheep. In the southern region, the smaller holdings are devoted primarily to tuber crops and small grains, while the medium and large holdings are heavily oriented toward cattle. The subtropical area is dominated by small and medium holdings producing fruit and livestock. (For a more detailed treatment of the findings of this research study, see Haney and Haney 1987.)

7. Because of the negative connotation of tenancy in the postreform period, we suspect that the instance of tenancy revealed in the interviews is substantially understated. Legally, cash rent is the only form of tenancy permitted other than individual or collective ownership and various share arrangements within families. All cash-rent contracts are supposed to be authorized by the Agrarian Reform Institute. Another semantic discrepancy arises in the interpretation of *escritura* (deed). In Chimborazo, at least, families often consider provisional titles, and even collective titles (for communal properties) granted by the Agrarian Reform Institute, the same as an *escritura*. In fact, many of them have apparently acquired *escrituras* to such land with the assistance of private lawyers, who see that the properties are recorded with the local *registros de propiedad*. It is unlikely that many private parties or government officials would contest this procedure.

8. Of the male and female migrants, 80 percent came from sample families that owned fewer than 10 hectares. Of those 14 years of age and older, 35 percent of the sons and 30 percent of the daughters from families with less than 10 hectares had migrated, primarily to Quito and Guayaquil. Among the nonmigrant sons, about one-third were secondary school students while an additional one-fourth were employed principally as agricultural wage laborers within the province.

REFERENCES

Barsky, Osvaldo, Eugenio Díaz Bonilla, Carlos Furche, and Roberto Mizrahi. 1982. *Políticas agrarias, colonización y desarrollo rural en Ecuador.* Quito: OEA/CEPLAES.

Blankstein, Charles S., and Clarence Zuvekas, Jr. 1973. Agrarian reform in Ecuador. *Economic Development and Cultural Change* 22:73–94.

CENDES (Centro de Desarrollo Industrial de Ecuador). 1983. *Comercialización de productos agrícolas para la provincia de Chimborazo.* Quito: CENDES/Banco Central/Centro Agrícola de Riobamba.

CIDA (Comité Interamericano de Desarrollo Agrícola). 1965. *Tenencia de la tierra y desarrollo socio-económico del sector agrícola: Ecuador.* Washington: Organization of American States.

Commander, Simon, and Peter Peek. 1986. Oil exports, agrarian change and the rural labor process: The Ecuadorian Sierra in the 1970s. *World Development* 14(1):79–96.

Cosse, Gustavo. 1980. Reflexiones acerca del estado, el proceso político y la política agraria en el caso ecuatoriano, 1964–1977. *Estudios Rurales Latinoamericanos* 3(1):51–83.

de Janvry, Alain. 1981. *The agrarian question and reformism in Latin America.* Baltimore: Johns Hopkins Univ. Press.

Dubly, Alain et al. 1982. La situación campesino en el Ecuador. Mimeograph. Quito: CESA.

Farga Hernández, M. Cristina. 1981. *Semiproletarización y estrategias de reproducción campesina: El caso de una comunidad de ex-huasipungueros de la provincia de Imbabura.* Otavalo: Instituto Otavaleño de Antropología.

Buerro, Andrés. 1975. La hacienda precapitalista y la clase terrateniente en América Latina y su inserción en el modo de producción capitalista: El caso ecuatoriano. Quito: Universidad Central.

Handelman, Howard. 1980. *Ecuadorian agrarian reform: The politics of limited change.* AUFS paper, no. 49. Hanover, N.H.: American Universities Field Staff.

Haney, Wava G. 1985. Women in highland Ecuador: Work and family. Paper presented at annual meeting of Midwest Sociological Society, St. Louis, Mo., April.

Haney, Emil B., and Wava G. Haney. 1987. *Transformation of the agrarian structure in Ecuador with specific reference to the province of Chimborazo.* LTC Research Paper, no. 86. Madison: Land Tenure Center, University of Wisconsin, January.

Likes, Mary Frances, and Lucía Salamea. n.d. The changing role of rural women in Ecuador. Mimeograph. Quito.

MAG (Ministerio de Agricultura), PRONAREG (Programa Nacional de Regionalización Agrícola), ORSTOM (Office de Recherche Scientifique et Technique Outre-Mer), and ILDIS (Instituto Latinoamericano de Investigaciones Sociales). 1982. *Diagnóstico socio-económico del medio rural ecuatoriano: Descomposición de la mano de obra agropecuaria.* Quito: MAG.

Chapter 4

Minifundistas in Tungurahua, Ecuador: Survival on the Agricultural Ladder[1]

Nancy R. Forster*

Persistent inequality of landownership and fragmentation of "smallholdings" by population pressure are central problems for development in Latin America. At the same time, development specialists frequently argue that *minifundio* holdings of fewer than 5 hectares are commercially unviable and contend that the position of smallholders has deteriorated rapidly in recent decades. In the words of Erich Jacoby, the "agricultural ladder" has been replaced by a descending escalator (Jacoby 1980, 301).[2] This chapter examines the *minifundio* community of Santa Lucía Arriba in highland Ecuador over the course of two generations to determine the effects of population pressure and commercialization on landholding patterns. At the time of study, 80 percent of the households in the community owned less than 1 hectare of land or were landless. Yet, 61 percent had purchased land over and above what they had inherited. Therefore, evidence from Santa Lucía does not suggest a uniform pattern of deterioration in the status of the peasantry under the pressure of increased population and commercialization. In fact, commercialization enables some peasants to buy land and move up the structural ladder in rural society.

Development policy to promote commercialization has usually been directed at larger units while *minifundios* have been regarded as residual employment sources, their operations being treated as poor credit risks and their owners often assumed to be bound for unskilled jobs in the urban economy. Marxist theory predicts the disappearance of peasant smallholders. Commercialization of peasant economies, according to Marx and Lenin, will increase socioeconomic

* Ph.D. candidate in the Development Studies Program, University of Wisconsin-Madison.

differentiation and eventually lead to a division of the peasantry into an agrarian bourgeoisie (a small group of viable farmers who use hired labor and consolidate larger holdings because of their commercial success) and a mass of landless peasants (a large group of proletarians who provide wage labor for both rural and urban enterprises). Updating the model to current conditions, some contend that because of the incomplete, dependent nature of Latin American capitalism, marginalized peasants cannot be fully absorbed into the work force (de Janvry 1981). Therefore, these peasants will cling to their minuscule holdings and work as part-time wage laborers in a semiproletarianized condition, with neither outside employment nor the land alone being able to support them.

Undoubtedly, smallholders with fewer than 5 hectares are economically vulnerable, and many must secure external employment to survive. Yet, a small but growing body of empirical research indicates instances of upward mobility for this group. Some of the most lively debates over commercialization's impact on peasant economies have focused on rural India. David Attwood's longitudinal study of peasant and landlord families over a 50-year period in a commercialized area of western India argues that, contrary to Marxist theory, landownership had not become more concentrated. The Gini coefficient comparing landholding in 1920 and 1970 remained virtually unchanged (Attwood 1979, 502). At the same time, there was a great deal of upward and downward mobility during this period, with landlords, on average, losing a greater percentage of land through partition and sales than smallholders. Attwood found that 44 percent of families with land in 1920 was landless by 1970, while 25 percent of the landed peasant families in 1970 had been landless 50 years earlier.[3] Other studies of India indicate similar patterns of upward mobility by some peasants (Rao 1972; Vyas 1980). Until now, cases of capital accumulation by landless or smallholders in Latin America have generally been treated as "exceptions." Yet, a growing number of these exceptions are appearing in the literature. Research in Carchi, Ecuador, shows significant land purchases by the rural lower classes during a period of hacienda decline and smallholder commercial-potato expansion (Barsky 1984; Lehmann 1986).

Rural Ecuador has traditionally been highly stratified. Inequality in the agrarian structure of the Highlands diminished only slightly between 1954 and 1974 despite land reform efforts in 1964, 1970, and 1973. In 1954, 82 percent of the units had fewer than 5 hectares and 11 percent of the land, while slightly more than 1 percent of the units was larger than 100 hectares and controlled 64 percent of the land.[4] By 1974, the relative status of *minifundistas* had improved slightly, since that group had dropped to 77 percent of all farm units and had nearly 13 percent of the area. Furthermore, the monopoly of the largest *hacendados* had been somewhat weakened. *Latifundia,* accounting for slightly over 1 percent of the units, controlled 43 percent of the land. The greatest relative gains in landholding were made by the middle strata with holdings between 10 and 500 hectares (Barsky 1978, 77). Comparing static pictures of the agrarian structure over time does not monitor the social mobility of individual households or the fortunes of particular family lines. Nor does it indicate whether there has been a rotation of rural actors, whereby older elites are replaced by the nouveau riche and bourgeoisie. This study emphasizes the importance of regional patterns of development in highland Ecuador and focuses on the upward and downward mobility of particular peasant households in a *minifundio* zone during a period of increasing commercialization of the nation's agricultural economy.

ECONOMIC CHANGE AND THE LEGACY OF *LATIFUNDISM* IN ECUADOR

Although Ecuador was incorporated into world markets from colonial times, by the second half of the twentieth century the volume and value of exports had increased dramatically and the pace of economic change quickened. Growing export revenues, first from bananas in the 1950s and then from petroleum after 1973, stimulated economic growth and social change. During the 1950s and 1960s, an increasing part of that export revenue was directed toward public employment. The consolidation of the state bureaucracy under the Galo Plaza government (1948–1952) and some incipient import-substitution industrialization contributed to greater middle-class purchasing power (Barsky 1978, 101–102). Cueva (1975, 59) estimates the size of the middle class to have been 23 percent of Ecuador's population in 1956, earning one-third of the national income. Between 1961 and 1966, as population grew by 3.4 percent annually, employment increased and net private consumption grew at a yearly rate of 5.3 percent, giving Ecuador one of Latin America's highest growth rates (Robalino Gonzago 1969, 159). This expansion heightened demand for agricultural products which, along with modest agrarian reform policies and state credit, contributed to the eventual technological transformation and increased commercialization of highland agriculture.

Researchers for the seminal Interamerican Committee on Agricultural Development (*Comité Interamericano de Desarrollo Agrícola,* CIDA) study of land tenure in Latin America characterized agriculture in the Ecuadorian Sierra at the beginning of this period as stagnant and blamed the extremely skewed agrarian structure, which was a reflection of a fairly rigid class structure (CIDA 1965). Furthermore, the CIDA investigators maintained that the complex interdependence between *latifundia* and *minifundios* discouraged development. The large haciendas were weighed down by precapitalist labor relations (generally defined as *precarismo*) such as *huasipungo* (peasants are allotted plots of land within the hacienda in exchange for a set amount of labor), allowing the *huasipungueros'* extended family (the *arrimados* or *apegados*) to live on the hacienda in exchange for labor, as well as *yanapa* or *ayuda* (by which peasants outside the hacienda are allowed access to estate resources such as pasture, water, and firewood in exchange for labor). By the early 1960s, these arrangements permitted peasant economies based within the hacienda to compete, in a sense, with the economic activity carried out in the demesne, thus plaguing the haciendas with absenteeism and low productivity. At the same time, CIDA researchers reported, by definition, that peasants confined to *minifundios* outside the haciendas had too little land to support a household and were dependent on the large holdings for pasture, fuel, and water. At the time of study, the only sign of budding capitalism was displayed by a few *terratenientes* (landlords) who were modernizing dairy production. Other, more traditional haciendas were in decay, under siege from within by *huasipungueros* and from without by *minifundistas* (Baraona 1965, 692–695).

CIDA researchers doubted that peasants could make significant commercial advances due to structural and market constraints (Barraclough 1973, 214–215; Baraona 1965, 688, 695). Furthermore, Baraona (1965, 688, 695–696) feared that continued landlord modernization would displace peasants who were highly dependent on estate resources. As *hacendados* dissolved precapitalist labor relations by ceding plots to *huasipungueros* (absolving themselves of debt and further social obligation), peasants lost access to pastureland, thereby eliminating sheep raising, the most prevalent strategy for peasant capital formation at the time. Thus, it seemed unlikely that peasant economies could prosper in areas where *hacendados* were modernizing. Campesino success, they argued, depended on the passivity or incompetence of landlords. Furthermore, the CIDA authors warned that peasant farm economies in densely populated *minifundio* zones were deteriorating because of high rates of migration and off-farm employment (Baraona 1965, 691).

HACIENDA CAPITALISM: THE JUNKER MODEL OF AGRARIAN TRANSITION

Some scholars contend that Ecuador's transition to capitalism has followed Lenin's Prussian or "Junker" path because a small group of northern and central sierra landlords in the 1950s and 1960s initiated social and technological changes in agriculture and, subsequently, played an important role in braking the agrarian reform (Murmis 1980; de Janvry 1981, 208).[5] The dramatic technological conversion of a fraction of traditional haciendas to dairy suggested to many researchers that this sector was the leading edge of the capitalist transformation in the Ecuadorian Highlands (Barsky 1978; Barsky et al. 1980).[6] This contention was supported by the following data. Between 1954 and 1973, the area of improved pasture increased by more than 800 percent, constituting 40 percent of all highland pasture by the end of the period (Barril 1980,325). The sierra dairy-cattle population increased at an annual rate of 5 percent during that period, and milk output per cow more than doubled (from 3.8 to 8.3 liters) between 1966 and 1974 (Barril 1980,325).

At the same time, labor relations in the dairy areas were being transformed. Fears of a Cuban-style revolution, pressures from the Alliance for Progress, and evidence that neofeudal relationships were no longer profitable convinced some modernizing landlords to terminate labor arrangements such as *huasipungaje* on their holdings. In the 5 years preceding the passage of Ecuador's 1964 Agrarian Reform Law (which banned *precarismo*), 15 percent of all *huasipungo* relationships were dissolved voluntarily by landlords who ceded land to their peasants. An additional small number of labor arrangements were terminated without granting land (Barsky 1978, 116). These transfers were particularly prevalent in the Sierra's three northernmost provinces—Pichincha, Imbabura, and Carchi—where the transformation to dairy production was most pronounced. While these provinces had less than half the nation's *huasipunguero* population in 1959, they were the site of nearly 90 percent of the land settlements prior to the agrarian reform.[7]

The initiative of the modernizing dairy landlords enabled them, along with some coastal estate owners, to circumvent the agrarian reform process and set the terms of the agrarian reform debate. On average, lots ceded before the agrarian reform were smaller than those later adjudicated by the law (Barsky 1978, 115). More importantly, northern *hacendados* were able to keep the most productive portions of their estates, consolidating capital-intensive production on valuable bottom lands while ceding plots of marginal quality to the peasants. In the southern and south-central Sierra, however, absentee landlords and those dependent on neofeudal labor relations lost far more—sometimes their entire haciendas—through the agrarian reform (Barsky 1980).

By the 1970s, as petroleum revenues pumped new resources into the economy, many landlords took advantage of state credit policies to incorporate new technology and further expand dairy production. The *Banco Nacional de Fomento* opened a special line of credit for mechanization, while the government offered tax incentives for planting improved pasture. Landlord response was immediate and dramatic. From 1973 to 1974, the number of tractors used in agriculture rose from 3,348 to 4,553, with tractor imports for that single year amounting to over half the number imported from 1962 to 1972 (Barril 1980, 223–234). Between 1966 and 1976, 181 milking machines were imported, with 95 percent of them coming into the country after 1972 (Barril 1980, 234). *Banco de Fomento* loans for pasture development increased 350 percent, from 273 million sucres in 1972 to 967.7 million sucres in 1974 (Arcos and Marchán 1978, 15). This massive conversion of cropland to pasture adversely affected national cereal production. Ministry of Agriculture estimates indicated that from 1970 to 1978, areas devoted to wheat and barley each dropped 46 percent in acreage (Barril 1980, 236).

The dramatic expansion of hacienda dairy production and *hacendado* monopoly of state credit prompted criticism of Ecuador's high-cost agricultural development model, one based on massive capital investment. The state, these critics suggested, had become the financial motor of misshapen development (Martínez 1983), stimulating production of "luxury" (dairy) items that were beyond the reach of most consumers and of benefit to only a small number of producers who, in any case, were more affluent initially. This, in combination with the modernizing elite's domination of the political process, convinced many scholars that a Junker-style agrarian transition was taking place, which would cause long-term political and economic development to suffer.

Elite domination was blamed for the agrarian reform's failure to reach many peasants in need of land and, according to some critics, for actually worsening conditions for many of the "beneficiaries." Not only did peasants who reached settlements with landlords prior to 1964 receive smaller plots than those subsequently adjudicated by the Agrarian Reform Institute (*Instituto Ecuatoriano de Reforma Agraria y Colonización*, IERAC), but the distributed land also tended to be of poorer quality than that which *huasipungueros* had cultivated in usufruct under the earlier neofeudal arrangements (Costales and Costales 1971, 129; Barsky 1978, 115; Salamea 1980, 265; Sáenz 1980, 316). Furthermore, analysts contended that reform benefited but a fraction of the peasantry and a minority of those dependent on the haciendas. Others in "precarious" tenure relations, such as *arrimados* (part of the extended *huasipunguero* family dependent on the usufruct plot) and *yanaperos* (free peasants who exchanged labor for access to hacienda resources), both lost their traditional rights through the reform process and received little or no compensatory land transfer. The net result of the reform, critics insisted, was a significant increase in migration to cities and the coast and more dependence on off-farm income for the campesinos who remained in farming (Salamea 1980, 266; Sáenz 1980, 320–321).

Without doubt, modernization of the dairy sector from the late 1950s displaced a great deal of labor. A close look at the scope of this transformation helps determine its overall impact on the highland peasantry. The 1954 Agrarian Census showed that *huasipunguero* families made up less than 8 percent of the Sierra's rural population, while 77 percent was smallholders or had mixed tenancy (they supplemented income earned on private holdings with that from sharecropping and/or cash renting) (CIDA 1965, 17). Furthermore, most highland peasants do not live near the modernizing haciendas. The technically advanced dairy areas are located in a few ecologically favored valleys: Cayambe, Machachi, and Los Chillos (near Quito) and the central valley in Cotopaxi Province. Therefore, the agrarian transition in these areas is quite different from that of other sierra regions. In looking beyond the dairy zones, therefore, one obtains a broader view of the peasantry's role in the commercialization of highland agriculture.

PEASANT CAPITAL ACCUMULATION: TRAVELING THE CHAQUIÑAN (FOOTPATH) IN THE AGRARIAN TRANSITION

Upward social and economic mobility of the peasantry is a minor theme in Latin American studies; the usual assumption is that, for campesinos, the direction of movement is downward. Looking at cases of peasant land purchases, however, may lead to more optimistic conclusions. As early as the turn of the century in the Otavalo region of northern Ecuador, one observer noted peasants buying hacienda lands:

> By forming societies they have bought *fundos* of the value of twenty-three thousand sucres, of twenty thousand, et cetera....Day by day, the Indian is taking over the lands of the Canton, albeit by fair purchase; having taken possession of them on a larger scale, by cultivating them with care he will achieve a well-being that will make him scorn the laborer's wage [Salomon 1973, 488].

While this chronicler cited by Salomon did not indicate the source of capital for these early purchases, later studies indicate that the Otavaleño strategy judiciously combined subsistence crop production with commercialized artisan weaving to earn cash (Buitrón 1947; Salomon 1973; Meier 1982). The 1974 Agricultural Census showed that 83 percent of smallholder units in Otavalo Canton produced primarily or exclusively for home consumption (Meier 1982, 132). Their success in purchasing land was determined largely by the amount of time that could be devoted to weaving in order to generate capital.[8]

Other evidence indicating peasant land acquisitions early in the twentieth century comes from Mejía Canton in Pichincha Province (Archetti and Stolen 1981) and Guaytacama Parish in Cotopaxi (Arcos and Marchán 1978). In 1918, as a result of the abolition of *concertaje* (debt peonage), ex-*conciertos* were free to take advantage of higher coastal wages.[9] The subsequent labor shortages forced landlords to offer highland peasants more inducements in order to guarantee a stable and reliable work force.

Contemporary research reveals that peasant land acquisition has probably become more frequent in recent decades, especially during the 1960s and 1970s, and cash purchases have replaced labor as the means of securing land. Furthermore, land sales and transfers from *hacendados* to *campesinos* in this period have frequently been associated with the intense social and political pressure surrounding the agrarian reform. It is not clear, however, how the benefits have been spread. Some researchers contend that the recent sales and transfers have favored only a minority and have hastened the process of differentiation within peasant communities. None of the studies reviewed here quantifies the portion of winners and losers in the scramble for land. They do make it abundantly clear, however, that the peasantry has been actively involved in the breakup of the haciendas and that an important portion of estate land has passed to smallholders.

A study of the northern highland communities of San Pablo del Lago (Ibarra Province), located in one of the most important centers of *hacendado*-initiated dairy modernization, demonstrates the effects of peasant pressure. Seeking to purchase tranquility in the countryside, landlords in this area had turned over many *huasipungo* plots to their resident laborers prior to agrarian reform. Neighboring *comunas* were not satisfied, however, because that settlement denied them access to the hacienda-controlled *páramo* (high pasture) lands, a part of which they claimed on the basis of a 1751 allotment (*repartimiento*) by the Spanish crown (Rosero Garcés 1982, 68). Unsuccessful litigation to reclaim the *páramo* dated from the early part of the century.

In the late 1960s the community of Gualaví, with the aid of two advocacy groups [the Ecuadorian Federation of Indians (*Federación Ecuatoriana de Indios*) and the Andean Mission (*Misión Andina*)], invaded the area's most vulnerable estate, the absentee-owned Hacienda Cusín. Its American proprietor sold the *comuna* 144 hectares at only 5 sucres per hectare, hoping to "end all further land claims" (Rosero Garcés 1982, 100). Quite the contrary, the settlement seemed to whet land-hungry peasants' appetites. In 1970, members of two

Gualaví cooperatives bought an additional 160 hectares of the Cusín. *Comuneros* outside the cooperatives were promptly denied access to fuel and hay, initiating a new phase in the land struggle, pitting peasant against peasant under rules of the free market. Peasants who failed to benefit from the land sales continued to defend communitarian values, arguing that such sales were illegal since, according to the colonial title, the *páramo* belonged to the entire community (Rosero Garcés 1982, 102–103).

Rosero Garcés (1982, 91) emphasizes that unequal success in urban employment, which had promoted differentiation within the community prior to the land sales, resulted in unequal access to the cooperatives and, in turn, to hacienda lands. The poorest *comuneros* could not even afford the cooperative's entrance fee, much less buy land. Thus, the pace of differentiation quickened (Rosero Garcés 1982, 107).

In a high-altitude zone in the central Sierra (Cotopaxi Province), a study of three communities bordering a hacienda formerly owned by the Church shows how the threat of agrarian reform enabled some peasants to acquire land. Martínez (1983, 112–178) emphasizes, however, that benefits were inequitably spread. To avoid IERAC's intervention, the Church initially divided the large hacienda between two dioceses, which later divested themselves of the rural properties. In 1971, the Diocese of Ambato handed over its legacy, the 1,100-hectare Hacienda Cotopilaló, to the Ecuadorian Center for Agricultural Services (*Central Ecuatoriana de Servicios Agrícolas*, CESA), a church-based, community-organizing group, which formed a livestock cooperative incorporating many ex-*huasipungueros* and *arrimados*. After a few years, members of the cooperative gradually arranged to buy the hacienda with their earnings. As peasants gained decision-making power, livestock activities contracted and household-based agriculture, especially market-oriented potato production, expanded (Martínez 1983, 141–142). In addition, by 1980 one-fourth of the cooperative's members had also independently purchased 193 hectares outside of Cotopilaló (Martínez 1983, 140, n.).

Developments in the Diocese of Latacunga's legacy, the 1,665 hectare Hacienda Rasuyacu, were less favorable for the peasantry. In 1969, the diocese sold the estate to its former *mayordomo* (a man of peasant origins who had also sharecropped and rented hacienda land). The new owner reestablished precapitalist ties with the ex-*huasipungueros*, exchanging access to *páramo* pasture for one day's labor per week. Martínez argues that the *hacendado's* monopsonistic control of labor and his virtual monopoly over land in the area (he subsequently bought three additional haciendas) were detrimental to peasant welfare, diminishing the possibility of a "*vía campesina.*" Yet, even under these circumstances, some ex-*huasipungueros* had purchased from Rasuyacu's owner a total of 239 hectares of land, albeit mostly *páramo* (Martínez 1983, 122–123).

Peasants who benefited least from the breakup of Church estate were smallholders in the community of Pilacumbi, who had been linked to the hacienda only through *yanapa*. Even though some peasants had accumulated capital through migration earnings, hacienda property was not available to them for purchase. Consequently, 42 percent of the household heads worked 5 days per week off farm. Other families had migrated into a nearby tropical colonization zone (Martínez 1983, 132).

In another high-altitude area above the Machachi Valley dairy lands in Pichincha, Archetti and Stolen (1981) found a strong trend toward repeasantization of landless workers. Their survey of 70 landowning peasants indicated that only 5 percent had inherited their holdings; the remainder had purchased their plots. Prior to buying land, 76 percent of the peasants sampled had been salaried rural workers, as was 60 percent of their fathers for the entirety of their lives (Archetti and Stolen 1981, 314). In this transformation, agrarian reform played an important role. Seventy percent of the land had been purchased between 1966 and 1976, mostly by peasant cooperatives organized for the purpose of securing IERAC support in pressuring landlords to sell their property. Cooperative members subsequently secured individual titles to the land and dissolved the collective organizations (Archetti and Stolen 1981, 315).

Recent studies in Carchi, the country's northernmost province, indicate that the historic decline of that region's great estates fostered peasant land acquisition (Barsky 1984; Lehmann 1986). The breakup of *latifundia* in Carchi began as early as the 1930s, but was greatly accelerated in the 1960s and 1970s by the threat of agrarian reform (Lehmann 1986, 337). Barsky's San Gabriel Parish survey of fifty smallholders who had purchased land showed that 66 percent of the sample's parents was landed, yet only 10 percent of the 422 hectares owned had been inherited. Most land (71 percent) had been purchased on the open market, while an additional 14 percent came from buying lots previously held in insecure tenancy, mostly in *huasipungaje*. Peasants began to acquire land on the open market in the 1930s, but 87 percent was purchased after 1955, with the largest percentage (27 percent) obtained between 1975 and 1979 (Barsky 1984, 71–77).

The Carchi studies found that, far from the pernicious relationship common in South Asia, sharecropping in northern Ecuador was a common means of capital accumulation. In Barsky's sample, 82 percent had entered at some time into such an arrangement (Barsky 1984, 86). Lehmann maintains that, in Carchi, sharecropping relationships tended to be relatively egalitarian and served to minimize risk for both parties as they participated in the volatile commercial potato market

(Lehmann 1986, 338–339). Sharecropping enabled producers to invest scarce capital in directly productive activities rather than tying it up in land (Barsky 1984, 83). Only after accumulating a certain amount of savings did peasants seek the greater security of landownership.

The expansion of potato production, despite its requirements for high investment in chemical inputs (fertilizers and pesticides), offered many Carchi peasants a vehicle for economic progress. Barsky found that in the 1960s, small units (less than 20 hectares) produced 45 percent of San Gabriel's potatoes. By 1974, their contribution had risen to 76 percent (Barsky 1984, 66). This increase came partly from an expansion of the area planted in potatoes, but was primarily due to intensification of capital (agrochemical) and labor inputs. Most of the additional production was marketed.

This brief summary of peasant land purchases indicates that there has been a transformation of peasant agriculture paralleling the more obvious capitalization of the Sierra's large holdings. This transformation has been aided both directly and indirectly by agrarian reform, and, in some areas, it was supported by the organizing efforts of advocate groups. Whatever the reason, there has been an independent response by the peasantry to the expanding national economy manifested in the last decades by smallholders' market participation and their drive for land. During a period when national potato production was increasing fivefold, from an annual average of 100,000 metric tons in the 1950s to 500,000 metric tons in the 1970s, the peasant share of that production was also growing (Barsky 1984, 59). Nationally, the portion produced on units of less than 20 hectares rose from less than 40 percent in 1954 to 60 percent in 1974. At the same time, the share of potatoes produced on units of over 50 hectares dropped from 52 to 31 percent (Barsky 1984, 60). Furthermore, the increase in smallholder production during this period was accomplished mainly through intensification (primarily through greater use of agrochemicals); the smallholding area planted in potatoes (58 percent in 1954 and 62 percent in 1974) remained almost constant (Barsky 1984, 59).

Almost all of the studies reviewed here emphasize that economic change in recent decades has increased differentiation within peasant communities. While they concede that some peasants purchased land, most argue that the majority did not, just as the majority failed to benefit from the economic boom of the 1970s. They contend, furthermore, that peasant economies are in a state of disintegration. Much of the research pointing to the state of crisis among rural smallholders uses rates of migration and off-farm employment as indicators. Yet, it cannot be assumed that these phenomena always reflect peasant impoverishment. Commander and Peek (1986) argue that for *minifundistas* in Ecuador, diversified employment during the period of high economic growth in the 1970s, especially migration to construction work, contributed to the survival and consolidation of the small-farm sector. For the period of economic expansion, they find a decline in the rate of increase in the number and proportion of landless households and an expansion in the number of small farms (Commander and Peek 1986, 79, 93).

ECONOMIC STRATEGIES IN THE COMUNA SANTA LUCÍA ARRIBA

The data presented here trace economic strategies and measure changes in landownership for two generations of highland *comuneros* in Santa Lucía Arriba, located at an altitude of 3,000–3,500 meters in Tisaleo Parish, Tungurahua Province. Tungurahua was chosen because it has a history of commercial agriculture and a predominantly *minifundista* population. Since commercialization of agriculture and *minifundism* are often seen as undermining smallholder economies, the region seemed particularly apt for this study.

The 1974 Agrarian Census showed that minuscule parcels, often classified as "subfamily holdings," predominated in Tungurahua. Over three-fourths of the holdings were less than 2 hectares and occupied only 12 percent of the land. Pressure on the land was even greater in Tisaleo. In 1974, nearly two-thirds of the farm units in the parish were less than 1 hectare and 81 percent were less than 2 hectares. The census showed that farm units of less than 5 hectares (96 percent of the total) subsisted on only 11 percent of Tisaleo's land area. Yet, this extreme pressure on the land in Tisaleo was not the result of *latifundista's* monopoly over resources. In 1974, private units with more than 5 hectares comprised 4 percent of all holdings and controlled only 8 percent of the area. The overwhelming majority (81 percent) of the land in the parish is *páramo*, which until recently was preserved as communal grazing land for all contiguous *comunas* in Tisaleo. The preponderance of communal land in Tisaleo distinguishes it from Ambato Canton and from the province as a whole, where only 30 and 16 percent, respectively, of the total land was under community control and haciendas 200 hectares and larger had approximately one-third of the land. Despite the absence of large private holdings in Tisaleo, *comuneros* in Santa Lucía had to deal with haciendas in neighboring Mocha Parish.

One cannot dismiss either the area or Santa Lucía as atypically affluent. Using 1974 data to measure rural standards of living in Ecuador, Luzuriaga and Zuvekas (1983) ranked Ambato Canton as eightieth of the nation's ninety-four sierra and coastal cantons in standard of living and fifty-third in per capita income. Within Ambato

Canton, Santa Lucía ranks somewhere in the middle, since it is not nearly as prosperous as many fruit-cultivating communities at lower altitudes (Pachano 1980) nor as poor as some villages on the slopes of the western cordillera (CESA 1982).

The household units in Santa Lucía are almost entirely *minifundios* (fewer than 5 hectares). In addition, a number of holdings larger than 5 hectares and a small number of "haciendas" of 20–30 hectares are dispersed throughout the area. Since owners of the larger holdings do not live in the commune, their economic activities are not included in the quantitative analysis.

I conducted the community study over a period of eleven months in 1983–1984, with a 20-percent household sample of the *comuna* drawn randomly from a list stratified by key informants according to land available (which included land owned, rented, and/or sharecropped in or out, along with that available in usufruct). Of the present-generation sample, 19 percent was totally landless, while 61 percent owned less than 1 hectare. Between 1 and 2 hectares were owned by 9 percent, and 11 percent had between 2 and 5.6 hectares. With the addition of *páramo* plots for private usufruct between 1979 and 1984, the available land in the community more than doubled, and distribution, though still skewed, became somewhat more equitable. For analysis in this chapter, present-generation households are divided into four groups according to land availability: the highest (N = 10) had between 2.8 and 6.5 hectares, medium high (N = 13) between 1.7 to 2.4 hectares, medium low (N = 18) between 0.8 to 1.6 hectares, low (N = 12) between 0.04 to 0.6 hectare.

While it was relatively easy to gather quantitative data from informants for two generations of *comuneros*, obtaining the economic history of third-generation forebearers was more difficult. Families with more successful parents and grandparents had preserved much more information than the poor, who often had difficulty remembering details of their parents' lives. The oral histories I gathered indicate that, in the late nineteenth and early twentieth centuries, the area had a low population density and new families had immigrated to the area. Informants' accounts suggest that, in those times, there was less equitable land distribution than today. Furthermore, grandparents of mestizo members of the sample tended to own larger amounts of land than their indigenous counterparts. At the turn of the century, mestizos were not *comuneros* and were usually prevented from using communal resources. Also in contrast to the present period, the Quichua language was widely used, and there was a greater sense of cultural separateness. In the late nineteenth and early twentieth centuries, grandparents of many in the sample worked as hacienda peons or day laborers, supplementing their meager incomes from small plots. At the same time, a small but dynamic group of independent smallholders and hacienda sharecroppers in the community, both indigenous and mestizo, were accumulating capital from agricultural production and trading.

Early Peasant Capital Accumulation

In the late nineteenth and early twentieth centuries in the Santa Lucía area as well as in other parts of the province, two occupations offered peasants economic opportunity: that of muleteer (*viajero*), trading products between the Sierra and the Coast, and that of sharecropper, which was especially profitable for those who could get access to the long-fallow lands of absentee landlords. Both mestizo and indigenous entrepreneurs used strategies that were wedded to the peasant agrolivestock complex, which even in that period (and possibly earlier) was partially commercialized and, for some, generated a surplus for land purchases.

Specifically, the first strategy combined agricultural production and commerce and is illustrated by the case of Miguel, born the son of a landed, local *cacique* (indigenous leader) in the late 1860s.[10] With his wife, Miguel was among those who went to court in 1883 to defend the communal *páramo* against agricultural expansion by *hacendados*. The battle was a persistent and continuing one, and, in 1927, members of the extended family again actively opposed hacienda encroachments.[11] Miguel, several of his brothers, and later his nephews spent much of their lives as *viajeros*, transporting products to and from the hot and humid area of Bodegas (now Babahoyo), in Los Ríos Province, where the Andean foothills meet the Guayas Basin. Trade was most intense during the coastal summer, since mountain trails were nearly impassable during the winter rainy season. Selling part of his own production as well as that of others, Miguel kept ten burros, using half each week with the help of two peons, to transport potatoes, *mellocos* (an Andean tuber), *habas* (broad beans), and pork from the temperate, cool Sierra, returning with oranges, sugar, rice, and *panela* (crude brown sugar) from the Coast. Meanwhile, Miguel's wife, with the aid of peons, worked the land, in an informant's words, "as hard as any man." This pattern of farming and trading apparently paid off for Miguel and his wife, for they invested in real estate. An examination of selected years from the cantonal property registry in Ambato reveals that, between 1892 and 1934, Miguel bought land twenty times and sold land out of the family four times.[12] In their will, he and his wife left 32 *cuadras* (22.6 hectares), granting 21 hectares to their daughter (the one child of six who survived them) and the remainder to a son-in-law.

A second strategy, illustrated by Antonio, was based fully on agrolivestock production, aided by a precarious tenancy relationship. Born in 1887, the son of landed peasants and the grandson of an indigenous immigrant from Cuenca, Antonio spent a few years as a *viajero* before marrying. Shortly thereafter, he and his wife were asked to become sharecroppers by an absentee owner who inherited land in Santa Lucía. The apparently intense search for sharecroppers at the time and the cultivation of lands previously in fallow suggest that increased demand, stimulated by capitalist development on the Coast, was making agriculture in Tungurahua a more profitable venture. The difficulty of finding labor at the time was partly due to low population density and to higher coastal wages, which were attracting highland workers.[13]

Antonio's production on the long-fallowed "hacienda" land was fairly high by the standards of that era. By age 25, a few years after hiring on as a sharecropper, he had purchased 5 cuadras (3.5 hectares) from his employers.[14] By the late 1920s, Antonio had become one of the larger commercial producers in Santa Lucía. Using 200 sheep and 22 larger animals to fertilize his fields (and later to sell when fattened), he marketed a yearly average of 100 quintals of potatoes, 15–30 quintals of wheat, 20 quintals of barley, 12 quintals of lentils, and 4–6 quintals of dried peas, representing nearly one-half of his total production.[15] A portion of these products was sold in Ambato, the provincial capital, and, to a lesser extent, in Cevallos or Pelileo (nearby secondary market towns). At that time, many consumers also came directly to the farm to buy products. Some paid as early as six months in advance for barley, indicating a high demand. Like Miguel, Antonio purchased property with his profits. The survey of selected years of the property registry showed that, between 1916 and 1946, he bought land sixteen times and sold outside of the family only once. He and his wife left 20 cuadras (14 hectares) to their nine children.

Both Miguel and Antonio (and their extended families) bought relatively small quantities of land each time and usually purchased from indigenous sellers. One of Antonio's sons recalled how *naturales* (indigenous people) came to his father in 1928, during a severe drought, and begged to exchange land for a sheep or a cow. The indigenous entrepreneurs also bought from the local bourgeoisie and from absentee heirs of the colonial elite.[16] At least part of the time, they also joined in mainstream capitalist practices of the day, officially registering land in Ambato as collateral for credit they either extended or received. Foreclosure on land when a loan was in default was not unknown.[17]

The Peasant Advance in the First Half of the Twentieth Century

The landholding history of ancestors of the present-generation sample suggests that the cases of Miguel and Antonio were not unique. Throughout the first half of the century, there was a trickle of land into the market, as *hacendados* moved to the city or as absentee heirs sold property to support their Ambato lifestyles or to rid themselves of fractionalized inheritances. Those sharecroppers with the closest personal ties to owners who had decided to sell had a "foot in the door" and were in a good position to buy if they had some savings. Thus, peasant land purchases were fairly common during the first half of the century. Most of the present-generation sample was born during this era, and this was the period in which their parents reached their most productive years.[18] Only 15 percent of the parent group was landless; 85 percent owned land, with a mean of 1.6 hectares, 69 percent of which was purchased.

Informants contended that it was easy to buy land in those days, and there is some evidence suggesting that landowners preferred selling to the peasantry. A local *hacendado* recounted how, as a bachelor in the 1940s, he had to sell 15.5 hectares to settle a gambling debt. He had an offer of 11,000 sucres from a leading landowner in the area but, on the advice of a friend, made greater profit by selling to local peasants in parcels of 0.5–3 cuadras (0.35–2 hectares).[19]

By mid-century, even more land was available in the market as the provincial bourgeoisie responded to the increasingly dynamic national economy and moved to Ambato (to set up workshops or commercial establishments), Quito (to enter professions or commerce), or to other locations. Tisaleo suffered a 19 percent decline in population between 1950 and 1962, partly reflecting peasant out-migration, but with a significant portion due to the flight of the rural bourgeoisie (Hoffmeyer n.d., 8–9).

Many parents of the current generation of *comuneros* responded to opportunities brought about by the rural exodus; 64 percent of them bought land. At the same time, an important segment of the parents failed to gain land, and 5 percent of the total group fell from landed to landless status. On average, however, a greater portion of the parents moved from landless to landed status than vice versa. Twenty-four of the parent group (26 percent) received no inheritance. Of those, only nine remained landless throughout their lives, while nine made small purchases ranging between 0.03 to 0.71 hectare (with a mean of 0.26 hectare) and six achieved dramatic upward mobility, purchasing between 2.5 and 8.5 hectares (with a mean of 6.3 hectares). In all, 71 percent of those parents who inherited no land (or 17 percent of all parents) gained landed status in their lifetimes.

Economic opportunity in the first half of the century thus brought forth a new peasant "elite" in the community. The five wealthiest males of the present generation each had parents who began their productive careers with landless or near-landless status (one had inherited only 0.09 hectare). Through a combination of strategies, including sharecropping, animal sales, commerce (buying and selling crops), and even day labor, four of those parents bought between 5.2 and 8.5 hectares each.

Of that group of land purchasers, Celidonio was the only parent also to inherit. His own father had been a muleteer at a time when profits were low due to increased competition from train and motor transport. In the 1930s, Celidonio became a *partidario* (sharecropper) for an absentee heiress of a nineteenth century elite family (part of which left Ambato to form the *Banco de Préstamos* in Quito). Until 1948, she had twelve sharecroppers, with slightly over 4 hectares each, on her 75-hectare inheritance. Celidonio planted his allotment mostly in peas and wheat, using peons and *randín* (labor exchange) with the other sharecroppers. Before 1948, he began buying land with his earnings; but when the hacienda was rented and the *partidarios* were evicted, he began to buy in earnest, purchasing a total of 5.2 hectares on eight occasions.

While one of his four children, José María, the wealthiest member of my sample, said he owed his success to God's good will, the entrepreneurial training his father had given him clearly also helped, as did the land he inherited from Celidonio. Though José María worked on the Coast during most of his adolescence solely for room and board, he eventually secured more lucrative coastal work and later engaged in commerce, transporting produce between ecological zones. In 1983/84 the family owned 5.6 hectares (and farmed an additional hectare in usufruct) and netted an estimated 338,000 sucres (over $3,000, including the value of home consumption), with some 93 percent derived from agrolivestock production and the remainder from rental of their tractor.

Landholding Patterns of Present-Generation *Comuneros* Compared to Their Parents

There is an obvious methodological problem in comparing a sample of households, which may be at any point in their life cycles, with the household heads' parents, who have ended or nearly ended their productive years. I have controlled for this—albeit imperfectly—by separating the present-generation sample into groups above and below age 35, since at that point some *comuneros* had begun to buy land, and limited the intergenerational analysis to respondents above age 35 and their parents. With the adjustment, there is little difference in the mean age of the four current-generation strata defined by land available.[20]

The data to follow point out a number of important tendencies. (1) On average, members of the present generation own less land than their parents. The difference is due to the lower average amount of land purchased by current-generation households rather than to less inheritance. (2) The downturn in peasant landholding does not seem to indicate imminent crisis and increasing proletarianization. The rate of landlessness did not increase in the second generation, and the percentage of households that bought land is nearly the same for the two generations. (3) There is no marked tendency for wealthy *minifundio* families in Santa Lucía to become wealthier. (4) Only a small percentage of households at the bottom of the economic ladder have been stuck in poverty over both generations studied.

The most striking difference between the two generations is the dramatic drop in the average amount of land owned. The average present-generation household with a family head over age 35 owned 44 percent less land than the average parent household (see Table 1). The two poorest strata experienced the greatest decline in landownership compared to their parents. On average, they owned 68–70 percent less land, while the upper middle group owned 54 percent less land. The average amount of land owned by the highest stratum was only slightly smaller than the parents', slipping 13 percent.

Table 1 shows that, on average, the present generation inherited nearly the same amount as their parents had inherited: 0.52 and 0.54 hectare, respectively, due to the parents' success in buying land. Thus, the deterioration in the amount of land owned by the contemporary generation is due to its poorer record (up to the point of the survey) in the land market. As of 1984, current-generation *comuneros* had purchased 62 percent less land than their parents. The poorest stratum acquired only 1 percent of its land in the market, contrasted with 87 percent for the parent group. Members of the lower middle group also bought significantly less land than their parents, obtaining, on average, only 28 percent of their land in the market, compared to 57 percent for the former generation. The two upper groups purchased 54 percent, compared to 69 percent for the previous generation.

The fact that the present generation bought less land may be partially explained by its incomplete life cycle, but the difference is also due to more land entering the market during the parents' productive years as the rural elite and bourgeoisie turned away from agricultural interests. The parents, therefore, were able to take advantage of economic opportunities that are less available to their children. Since land was cheaper, campesinos could afford more than they can presently. At the same time, the addition of the usufruct plots in the *páramo* to the present generation's land pool has meant that this group is under less pressure to buy land than their parents.

While the average amount of land owned has markedly dropped over the two generations, other factors caution against concluding that the community is in a mounting state of crisis. The rate of landlessness (owning no land) remained nearly constant during the period under study. Of present-generation households (including those

Table 1
Landownership patterns of present generation compared to their parents[a]

Land available	N	Present generation[b] Inherited (mean hectares)		Purchased (mean hectares)		Owned (mean hectares)		N	Parents[b] Inherited (mean hectares)		Purchased (mean hectares)		Owned (mean hectares)		Percentage change in land owned (parents to children)
High	10	1.18	(46)	1.37	(54)	2.55	(100)	19	0.90	(31)	2.02	(69)	2.92	(100)	−13
Medium high	11	0.31	(46)	0.36	(54)	0.67	(100)	20	0.44	(31)	1.00	(69)	1.44	(100)	−54
Medium low	9	0.34	(72)	0.13	(28)	0.47	(100)	15	0.63	(43)	0.85	(57)	1.48	(100)	−68
Low	11	0.272	(99)	0.004	(1)	0.276	(100)	15	0.117	(13)	0.791	(87)	0.908	(100)	−70
Total > age 35	41	0.52	(53)	0.46	(47)	0.98	(100)	69[c]	0.54	(31)	1.20	(69)	1.74	(100)	−44
Present generation < age 35	12	0.05	(77)	0.015	(23)	0.065	(100)	22	0.54	(43)	0.71	(57)	1.25	(100)	−95
Total	53							91							

[a] The present generation has been divided at age 35. Those above age 35 are stratified according to land available and compared to their parents (who are not separately stratified).
[b] Numbers in parentheses are percentages.
[c] No data = 6.

with family heads below age 35), 19 percent is landless, compared to 15 percent of the parent group. In addition, the percentage of families that purchased or sold land is identical for the current generation over age 35 and their parents. Of each group, 61 percent purchased land, 19 percent inherited land but made no further purchases or sales, and 10 percent sold all or part of their inheritance (7 percent of the parents sold the entirety). In both groups, 10 percent consistently remained landless.

This pattern suggests that commercialization of this *minifundio* economy did not result in its steady deterioration. Instead, commercialization apparently facilitated land purchases and the community's survival. At the same time, forces were at work to brake the process of land accumulation by *minifundistas*, for less land has been acquired by the present generation than by their parents.

Table 2 constitutes a more stringent test of mobility; it examines whether the present generation surpassed its parents in landownership. The data indicate no strong trend for the contemporary group over age 35 either to move beyond or to fall behind their parents' status; 45 percent owned more land than their parents and 44 percent owned less. The lower middle stratum showed the least ability to exceed parents' status. For the other strata, the contemporary households tended to surpass rather than fall behind parents in landholding.

Table 2
Economic mobility of present generation vis-à-vis parents[a]

Land available	*N*	More land than parents (%)	Less land than parents (%)	Landed, no change (%)	Landless no change (%)
High	20	55	35	10	0
Medium high	20	50	45	5	0
Medium low	16	31	63	0	6
Low	17	41	35	12	12
Total > age 35	73[b]	45	44	7	4
Present generation <age 35	22[c]	5	85	5	5

[a] Percentage of present-generation households above and below age 35 owning more or less land than parents. Present-generation married couples were compared separately to each set of parents.
[b] No data = 2.
[c] Total *N* = 95.

These data reveal a great deal of vitality in the present generation. Despite the contracting land market, 61 percent expanded their holdings beyond inheritance, 45 percent surpassed their parents in landholding, and three times more of the second-generation families gained landed status than lost it. At the same time, there was no strong trend for wealthier heirs in the contemporary group to accumulate more land than *comuneros* with less inheritance. On the contrary, evidence suggests that downward mobility was very common among children of wealthier parents. The top 20 percent of the parents of respondents over age 35 ($N = 15$) owned between 3.5 and 8.5 hectares (with a mean of 5.8 hectares). Of their offspring, 87 percent owned less than they did, with totals ranging between 0.6 and 5.6 hectares (with a mean of 1.8 hectares). This pattern appears contrary to the Leninist premise that richer peasants profit during the process of commercialization. Yet, it is not totally surprising, given the Andean tradition of equal partition of inheritance and the intense effort expended by smallholder households to achieve upward mobility. *Minifundio* families that are successful in buying land are often large, making children's inheritances relatively small.

Regression analysis further discredits the notion that wealthier heirs are more likely to purchase land. For both the present generation and the parent group, the variables, inheritance and land purchases, together explain nearly all of the difference in the amount of land owned within each group. Yet, there is no significant relationship between these two independent variables. The amount of land inherited and the amount of land purchased in the market did not significantly correlate for either the current generation or parent households.[21] Thus, in each generation, wealthier heirs were not more apt to expand their holdings than were those with little or no inheritance.

The preceding analysis suggests that there was a great deal of socioeconomic mobility and differentiation during the parents' generation. There is no evidence to suggest that this stratification, however, is rigid and prevents social and economic mobility of the younger generation. On the contrary, second-generation differentiation appears to be less severe.[22] While larger landholdings are fractionalized through inheritance, marriage alliances and land purchases improve the status of some poorer heirs.

A certain amount of differentiation apparently has even played a vital role in the maintenance and long-term survival of this *minifundio* community. In each generation, households that accumulated capital acquired property from the declining rural bourgeoisie or fallen elite, thereby bringing new land (which was rarely sold again to outsiders) into the community. In this way, larger holdings were progressively broken into smaller pieces, parts of which became available to *comunero* households with lower purchasing power. Within Santa Lucía, more permanent differentiation did not develop, since the internal dynamic of Andean *minifundism* shattered holdings through inheritance, preventing the emergence of a viable "farmer" class. Thus, the *minifundio* community of Santa Lucía appears to subsist in a state of dynamic equilibrium.

At the lower end of the economic scale, a small portion of *comuneros* did not participate in the generational cycle of upward and downward mobility but stagnated in poverty. Of the household heads in the current generation, 6 percent was second-generation landless, and an equal portion subsisted with minuscule holdings and had made no purchases (some had even sold land) during the period under study.

The Role of Migration in the *Minifundio* Community

While the majority of present generation *comuneros* had been able to purchase land, does the strong downward trend in the average amount of land owned over two generations imply an inpending crisis? That tendency, and the fact that 55 percent of the heads of households had migrated to seek work outside the community and 83 percent had worked as wage laborers at some time in their lives, might seem to reinforce the view that proletarianization will soon develop from semiproletarianism.

While high rates of migration sometimes indicate a process of community disintegration, qualitative information about migration patterns cautions against hasty conclusions. Interviews show that migration is motivated by a variety of goals, which include capital accumulation as well as survival. The most frequent migrants are the young; extrazonal jobs, especially those on the Coast, offer higher wages than local day labor. Also, many young people use temporary migration as a rite of passage, a way of learning about the world and a means of breaking away from the desultory chore of contributing labor to their parents' land unit. Teenagers frequently steal away from home and, when young and single, rarely save. In Santa Lucía, those who managed to accumulate capital generally did so after marriage and after securing better paying jobs on the Coast—working in the sugar mills, laying rail tracks in the cane fields, or loading cane. Those who cut cane, harvested rice, or worked on smaller *fincas* in the Milagro-Quevedo colonization zone frequently returned to their homes with little or no savings.

Those who had been temporary migrants were more likely to be part of the highest rather than the lowest economic group; 28 percent was in the top economic stratum and only 14 percent was in the bottom group at the time of study. Of those who never migrated, 8 percent was in the highest stratum and 33 percent in the lowest. The very poorest were the least likely to have ever migrated and, at the same time, were the most proletarianized. Family histories of the very poor indicated that they tended to opt for security by establishing patron-client ties within the zone. This strategy permitted them to work for only a few people; it negatively affected their earnings and, therefore, savings available for purchasing land. These *comuneros* often depended primarily on wage labor most of their lives.

Table 3 shows that 28 percent of the present generation derived more than half of their income from day labor. Such dependence was particularly acute in the poorest group, in which 83 percent subsisted as *jornaleros* (day laborers). Of the lower middle group, 22 percent, and virtually none of the top two groups, relied heavily on daily wages.

At the time of study, *comuneros* of Santa Lucía, with few exceptions, had ceased seeking employment outside of the region. As of 1975, they obtained land by collectively farming the communal *páramo* where, after 1979, they were also ceded individual usufruct lots. Members of the association that worked the common lands were required to reside in the village and spend one day per week on collective labor in the *páramo*. These developments put an upward pressure on day wages in the area. Even so, richer farmers complained that no one wanted to work for day wages after the private *páramo* lots were granted. Expansion of agriculture into the *páramo* represents the latest in a series of opportunities which seem to have saved the peasantry of Santa Lucía from proletarianization.

Table 3
Percent of present generation dependent on day wages[a]

Land available	*N*	Dependent on day wages (%)	Occasional or no wage labor (%)
High	10	0	100
Medium high	13	8	92
Medium low	18	22	78
Low	12	83	17
Total	53	28	72

[a] Defined as households with 50 percent or more of total family income derived from day wages.

Opening the *Páramo*—The Newest Source of Land

Located roughly above 3,200 meters and often shrouded in clouds, the undulating *páramo* is thickly covered with grasses and a variety of low-growing plants. Soils are acidic but rich in organic matter. From the colonial period and into this century, indigenous communities and Spaniards used the area primarily for grazing sheep. Large tracts were ceded by the Spanish crown in *repartimientos* to the communities. By the late nineteenth century, *hacendados* in Santa Lucía were interested in the *páramo's* potential for cultivation, since the natural fertility of the soil allows two to three years of very high yields if the crops escape frost. Haciendas began encroaching on communal lands for potato production, and, on at least two occasions (1883 and 1927), the indigenous communities of Tisaleo reversed this expansion.

While the *comuneros* defended their traditional rights to maintain animals in the commons, they were also aware of the *páramo's* rich potential for agriculture. Informants contended that there was interest in cropping as early as the 1920s. By the early 1970s, the Rodríguez Lara military government was actively encouraging such a move. Ministry of Agriculture representatives visited Santa Lucía yearly to press for "more productive land use." However, powerful *comuneros*, who were accumulating capital from grazing livestock, opposed the change. Some villagers had herds of up to 200 sheep in the *páramo* as late as the 1960s. Cultivating a part of the area would mean that livestock owners would be liable for their animals' damage to crops.

In 1973, under protection of police sent by the governor, a small number from the "farmer" interest group broke the *páramo* sod to plant trees. Two years later, the most powerful members of the opposition grazing group united with farmers in order to crop communally. Although the entrance fee for the production cooperative was just 10 sucres in the first year, only a small group of relatively better off *comuneros* joined in the backbreaking work of opening the thick turf with hoes. Poorer peasants who were dependent on their wage, which purchased subsistence on a daily basis, could not wait for semiannual returns from potato production, nor could they afford the cash assessments for inputs. Other *comuneros* remained outside the association, arguing that because the *páramo* technically belonged to the state, crops grown there might be appropriated.

In 1979, subdivision of lots for private usufruct by association members sparked opposition of nonmember *comuneros*, including residents of other villages that shared the common lands of Tisaleo. To avoid opening membership to peasants outside of Santa Lucía Arriba, a part of the opposition group was permitted into the association and community boundaries were officially drawn up by IERAC. This exercise resulted in the exclusion of communities with lands not contiguous to the *páramo*. A civil suit by the lower altitude *comunas* was initiated.

By December 1983, a potential total of four *páramo* lots for private use had been ceded for a nominal fee to each of those who had joined the association. With the addition of just three (of four) *páramo* plots, the present generation was compensated for its lack of land purchases.[23] The average amount of land available to the present generation totaled 1.71 hectares. Thus, with their usufruct lots, inheritance, and land purchases, the current generation surpassed the average parent's private holding of 1.62 hectares.[24]

Benefits from the *páramo* allotments, however, were not distributed equally in the community. Because the sample has been stratified according to land available, "poverty" for the present generation reflects both a failure to buy land and, more importantly, a failure to join the work association. While 75 percent of the community as a whole were members of the work association, only one household in twelve (8 percent) from the poorest group joined. If *páramo* lots for usufruct are excluded, the lower middle and low strata had nearly equal amounts of land available, 0.29 and 0.26 hectare, respectively. However, since members of the lower middle group joined the association in higher numbers, they increased their average available land fourfold, giving them the greatest relative gain among the four groups. Despite the lower middle stratum's dramatic increase in land, however, those peasants cultivated only 57 percent of their available *páramo*. The member households from the poorest group used an even smaller amount, cropping only 33 percent. The low utilization of *páramo* land by poorer work-association members can be partially explained by that group's higher percentage of young households, which typically lacked labor and working capital. Furthermore, because they joined the association more recently than older members, they had had less time to open lots for cultivation. Finally, the high dependence of some of the young on daily wages exacerbated the problem, leaving them little time for their family plots.

In contrast, it appears that the two upper strata realized considerable advantage from farming their private lots in the commons, even though their relative gains were less than the lower middle group. The top group in the sample increased its available land 64 percent with the addition of the usufruct lots, while the upper middle group expanded its area by 155 percent. *Comuneros* in the top group had the largest average *páramo* allotment (1.7 hectares) due to their greater success in enrolling unmarried children in the association, while the upper middle group averaged 1.2 hectares. The two top strata also farmed some 80 percent of their *páramo* land, a portion significantly higher than poorer association members.

Since poverty for the present generation is all but synonymous with remaining outside the work association, it is important to determine what has kept them from joining. The poorest *comuneros'* high dependence on day wages left little time for other responsibilities. Also, by 1984, there were barriers to joining the production cooperative; a 30,000-sucre entrance fee effectively excluded most day laborers. Age was also a factor. The lowest stratum had a mean age of 60 years, the oldest of the four groups and, therefore, the least likely to generate capital through migratory or artisan work. Equally important, however, is the fact that the poorest *comuneros* were missing the family-support system so important for peasant survival and accumulation. Table 4 shows a high percentage of single-head and female-head households in the poorest group, and 50 percent of single, divorced, or widowed households and 42 percent of those headed by women fell within the lowest stratum. Only 9 percent of households headed by married couples was in the poorest group.

While an important segment of this *minifundio* community was passed over in the government-sponsored effort to augment land, some success was apparent in the program. Among landless or near-landless households, *comuneros* who had managed to join the production cooperative insisted that they were eating better, that their children were sick less often, and that they had more to sell in the marketplace. Moreover, the addition of the *páramo* land had provided some redress for agrarian structure inequalities. Table 5, comparing inequality of land owned with land available, shows that with the addition of the *páramo*, the portion of the land available to the very poorest declined from 7 to 4 percent, but the shares available to other groups became more equal. While 19 percent of the landholders owned 62 percent of the area, their share dropped to 46 percent when *páramo* lots were included. The middle groups, constituting 58 percent of the sample, owned 31 percent of the land but increased their share to 50 percent when the *páramo* land was added.

Although the addition of *páramo* lots more than doubled the land available for Santa Lucía, the new lands were not necessarily equal in quality to lower altitude private holdings. The *páramo* is distant, necessitating more travel time, and slopes are steep. By 1984, erosion was robbing topsoil from hilltops. Most importantly, risk was great in the high-altitude commons, since frost seriously damaged an average of one harvest in four. Potatoes were the most common crop in the early years and remained popular because they could be used both for market and for subsistence. But potato production was being cut back as pests invaded the virgin land and agrochemical prices rose (especially after the devaluation of the sucre, beginning in the early 1980s). In 1983/84, greater profits were realized in *páramo* plots with *mellocos* and *habas*,

Table 4
Status of present-generation household heads

Land available	Married head of household (%)[a]	Single head of household (%)[b]	Female head of household (%)[c]
High	23	11	8
Medium high	34	6	8
Medium low	34	33	42
Low	9	50	42
Total	100	100	100

[a] $N = 35$.
[b] Widowed, divorced, or single. $N = 18$.
[c] $N = 12$.

Table 5
Agrarian structure, Santa Lucía Arriba, 1983/84: Comparison of inequality with and without *páramo*

Land available	Owners[a] (%)	Area Owned[b] (%)	Total area available[c, d] (%)
High	19	62	46
Medium high	24	19	26
Medium low	34	12	24
Low	23	7	4
Total	100	100	100

[a] $N = 53$.
[b] Total area owned by sample = 41.0 hectares.
[c] Total area available to sample = 90.8 hectares.
[d] Includes *páramo* in usufruct and total land owned; excludes land rented and sharecropped in and out.

both of which required little fertilizer and pesticide and brought good returns in the market.

One of the most successful farming strategies for land-short households was to relegate *páramo* land to subsistence, or to crops with low input costs, and to cultivate more valuable products, such as blackberries or onions, on the lower altitude private lands. The greatest earnings could be realized with purple *paiteña* onions, which did exceptionally well at high altitudes. Some *comuneros* had even grown *paiteña* onions in the *páramo*, but, because of their potentially great value, most were planted close to the house. Risk was incurred in the onion market because seed and product prices tended to fluctuate wildly (Hanssen-Bauer 1982, 279–287). Individuals lucky enough to sell when the market was high made astonishing earnings. One middle-income peasant made a gross sale of 320,000 sucres (nearly $3,500) from a 0.17-hectare lot—and promptly bought a Chevrolet pickup truck. Others went into debt when the market worked against them, and one family even had to sell a cuadra of land to cover its losses. Because of high input costs and great risk, poorer peasants participated only minimally in the onion "lottery."

For the present generation, the *páramo* has provided a needed population safety valve, has helped to avoid proletarianization, has maintained the community, and has increased the prosperity of the village. Although production cooperative members complain about losing a day each week to communal labor, they have realized some benefits. Community labor and profits from collective production have been invested in building village infrastructure, including roads, a school, a community meeting house, a clinic, and a chapel. Individual usufruct lots have increased household food production, drawn members into greater market participation, and promoted more equality in the agrarian structure. Since lower middle peasants made the greatest gains in their holdings by securing use of the *páramo*, some younger households will probably be able to accumulate capital as a result.

These developments coincide with a rapid rise in property values in Santa Lucía, making it increasingly difficult to buy land. Prices in 1984 rose as high as 400,000 sucres per cuadra (more than $5,600 per hectare). This increase was due to greater demand for property (especially from successful onion producers) and the absentee bourgeoisie's decreased willingness to part with their inheritance in hopes of larger, future gains from real estate. Though the *páramo* offers opportunity, many peasants do not feel secure with the additional risk and the fact that they are now dealing with market forces which are uncontrollable and increasingly subject to violent fluctuations.

CONCLUSIONS

This research emphasizes the importance of longitudinal studies of peasants and landlords to determine development trends. The study has examined forces for change at work in a smallholder community over a two-generation period. The challenges of *minifundism* (due to population pressure) and commercialization in Santa Lucía have not uniformly produced peasant impoverishment. Instead, the *minifundio* community has been perpetuated. Commercialization of production and labor allowed a majority of the two generations under study to mitigate the effects of population growth through land purchases. Their success was possible because small, affordable pieces of property were available in the land market, principally due to the exodus of the landed bourgeoisie who sought higher returns in other rural and/or urban investments. On average, parents purchased larger amounts of land than their children, accounting for the downturn in the average amount of land owned by the present generation.

Differentiation is inherent within the process of commercialization. A small percentage of the community advances economically more than the rest. Yet, in this *minifundio* community, differentiation did not increase in step with greater commercialization; differences in landownership were more pronounced within the parent group than among the children. This was partly because land was more available to the first generation and partly because a pattern of constant land acquisition is difficult to sustain in a *minifundio* economy. The offspring of the most successful first-generation families did not surpass their parents in landholding. The larger quantities of land acquired by the parents were broken up at their death, and heirs did not regain comparably sized holdings. Economic success was not confined to those with larger inheritances; even some landless peasants were able to purchase land. There was no correlation between the amount of land inherited and the quantity of land purchased by households.

A small percentage of the sample remained in chronic poverty for both generations studied. The lowest economic group had the highest percentage of *comuneros* who had never migrated to coastal jobs, was (on average) older, and had the highest percentage of household heads who were female, single, divorced, or widowed. Population pressure led to proletarianization of family labor in many of those households.

A government-sponsored program of supporting cultivation of the communal *páramo* provided a crucial safety valve for land-short Santa Lucía and made up for the deficit of land purchases by the present generation. In theory, state-supported change has great potential to help poorer peasants; in this instance, it fell short. Because of the labor investments and financial requirements necessary for joining the production cooperative, some 25 percent of the community, most of them older and without adequate incomes or family support, did not benefit. Indeed, their position deteriorated vis-à-vis the remaining *comuneros*, whose ability to commercialize production increased.

This study has demonstrated that cases of peasant upward mobility occurred in a region that is favored economically by its location and its dynamic peasant markets. Yet, the study area was not atypically affluent. Virtually all of the sample examined here owned fewer than 5 hectares; 80 percent owned less than 1 hectare or were landless. Clearly, they were *minifundistas.* Mere survival in a *minifundio* economy requires some success in the market, whether selling labor, crafts, or agrolivestock production. Without some land purchases, fractured inheritances cannot provide even a minimal income, especially when families are large. More significant advances require that *minifundistas* exhibit creativity vis-à-vis markets. Strategies must change as new opportunities appear. The findings in Santa Lucía show that when opportunities open, peasants are able to grasp them and to move up the "structural ladder." They also show that Andean inheritance patterns inhibit the development of a "farmer" class. Finally, this study demonstrates that serious constraints prevent some of the very poorest from significantly improving their lot.

NOTES

1. Revised version of a paper presented at the annual meetings of the Latin American Studies Association, held in Albuquerque, New Mexico, 17–20 Apr. 1985. Funding for this research was provided by the Fulbright-Hays Training Program, the Inter-American Foundation, the Social Science Research Council, and the American Council of Learned Societies.

2. The concept of the "agricultural ladder" was proposed early in this century in the United States by W. J. Spillman (1919), who noted that farmers tended to pass through different roles with increasing age, progressing from unpaid family worker to wage laborer (or sharecropper or tenant) to owner-operator to, eventually, landlord. This idea was similar to Chayanov's observation in Russia that peasants passed through life cycles and, as children provided more labor, the household amassed more land (Chayanov 1925). Both theories relating age to mobility emerged in regions with relatively low population densities and an available supply of common land or frontier. Subsequent research in more densely populated, stratified societies has made it clear that additional determinants affect upward and downward mobility in most areas of the world today.

3. Of the total sample, 18 percent had acquired landed status, 46 percent remained landed throughout their lives (including families whose holdings had increased or decreased), and 36 percent had been forced off the land. Attwood found that economic rank order in the 1920s was not a strong predictor of rank fifty years later. With a Spearman coefficient of .256, a family's rank in 1920 explained only 7 percent of the variance in ranking for 1970.

4. Discussions of Ecuador's agrarian structure generally do not distinguish between large holdings controlled corporately by indigenous communities and those under private ownership. Data from the *1974 Agricultural Census* (INEC 1979) show that 10 percent of the Sierra's land was communal, ranging from 3 percent in Pichincha Province to 16 percent in Tungurahua, Chimborazo, and Cañar (INEC 1979, Table 3). Since almost all of the communal holdings were larger than 200 hectares, the extent of land concentration in the hands

of *latifundistas* has been somewhat overstated, especially in some highland provinces.

5. This model is based on developments in sixteenth century East Prussia, where feudal "Junkers" released their serfs from labor obligations and converted their estates to efficient grain-growing enterprises. Since the economic and political power of the landlords was never broken by pressure from below, Lenin designated this as a conservative path. For further discussion of the various "roads" in the development of capitalism in agriculture, see de Janvry (1981, 106-109).

6. Historical investigations have revealed that initial experiments in dairy modernization (genetic improvement of the herds, pasture rotations, use of mineral and organic fertilizers, and limited mechanization) had begun as early as the first decades of the twentieth century in Pichincha and Cotopaxi provinces and other selected areas (Buitrón and Salisbury 1947; Arcos and Marchán 1978). Most scholars agree, however, that the most far-reaching changes date from the 1950s (Barsky 1978; Archetti and Stolen 1981, 309).

7. Of the 19,665 *huasipungueros* in Ecuador in 1959, Pichincha had 32.7 percent, Imbabura had 9.6 percent, and Carchi had 5.6 percent. The central province of Cotopaxi had 12.1 percent, and south-central Chimborazo had 20.2 percent (Costales and Costales 1971, 123). Of the 3,019 *huasipungueros* who received land prior to the agrarian reform, however, 58.3 percent was in Pichincha, 15 percent in Imbabura, and 16.5 percent in Carchi, while Chimborazo had only 4.4 percent and Cotopaxi had 5.2 percent (Costales and Costales 1971, 117).

8. Both Buitrón (1947) and Salomon (1973) noted a high degree of differentiation in landownership. Buitrón maintained that peasants with valley holdings, where cultivation was relatively easy, were more successful than those with plots scattered through different microclimates on mountain slopes, where more labor was required and greater ecological risk was incurred (Buitrón 1947, 45–67).

9. Established in 1601, *concertaje* originally functioned as a way to contract both short- and long-term Indian labor in exchange for loans of cash or products or a subsistence plot. The exchange of labor for land eventually evolved into *huasipungo*, which was not abolished until 1964. *Concertaje*, defined in its narrowest sense, described the system of indebting Indians in order to extract their labor under threat of prison (Hurtado 1980, 48–49).

10. These cases were chosen because they had a high number of descendants who provided detailed information which could be cross-checked. In addition, the life stories of these entrepreneurs reveal patterns and activities which are frequently not treated in the histories of Andean indigenous peoples.

11. I have used pseudonyms for members of the community and their forefathers and actual names for nonmembers. The community suit in 1883 was against Mariano and Jacinto Lalama, heirs to a fragment of the family's holdings secured during the late colonial period [*Archivo del Banco Central Ambato* (ABCA), *Juicios Civiles* no. 7672]. The action in 1927 involved violence and resulted in the deaths of ten to twelve *comuneros*. The 1927 suit was against Joaquín E. Arias (descendant of colonial elite), Inocencio Gonzales (provincial bourgeoisie), and Alcides Peralvo (*parroquia teniente político* and descendant

of an upwardly mobile mestizo family, originally from near Ambato) (ABCA, *Juicios Civiles* no. 7120).

12. The sample from the *Registro de Propiedades*, Ambato, included the years 1891–1899, 1906-1912, 1916-1917, 1921, 1926, 1928, 1934–1938, 1946-1949, 1964-1983. A minor percentage of the sales in the registry are really inheritance transactions, transferring land for a nominal price to heirs.

13. Informants spoke of labor shortages in Santa Lucía well into the 1920s and 1930s. "Hacienda" lands (that is, holdings of 20 or more hectares) were often in fallow. *Hacendados* who cultivated their land often had to bring in labor from more densely populated areas (principally the western cordillera) and eventually established sharecropping relationships with local families to get access to their labor. Yet, even then, one informant said, women did most of the sharecropping work since men stayed for long periods on the Coast and only came back to help during critical times.

14. *Registro de Propiedades*, Ambato, 1912, no. 182; Index entry no. 176.

15. Informants recounted that less than a quarter of the barley was sold in the market. Most was reserved for peons and family members, who ate máchica (toasted barley flour) and *arroz de cebada* nearly every day.

16. The extended families purchased land from Tomás López Naranjo (heir of colonial elite) in 1891 and from Joaquín E. Arias in the late 1920s and early 1930s. The latter, following loss of the law suit, gave up 43.7 disputed hectares to the *comuna* of Tisaleo (Registro de Propiedades, Ambato, 1979, no. 1541). Shortly thereafter, he sold the remainder of his lands in Santa Lucía in twenty-three small and medium sales (between 50 and 1,200 sucres) and in one final sale of the hacienda core, in 1939, for 9,000 sucres to Juan Paredes, member of the provincial bourgeoisie. In the 1950s and 1960s, Paredes sold more parcels to the local peasantry.

17. *Registro de Hipotecas*, Ambato, 1911, no. 6; Index no. 505.

18. Forty-one of fifty-three household heads' birth dates were between 1898 and 1949, with a mean birth date of 1930. The remaining twelve respondents were under age 35 and were separated from the analysis for part of the following section. Parents of the latter group, on average, reached their most productive years during the 1950s and 1960s.

19. Interview, Antonio Martínez, September 1984.

20. The total sample over 35 years had an average age of 53, while the mean ages for the four economic groups were the following: high, 53; medium high, 47; medium low, 50; low, 63. *Comuneros* below 35 years of age had an average age of 29.

21. The present generation inherited an average of 0.41 hectare of land (median = 0.13, range = 3.0, standard deviation = 0.61). That group purchased an average of 0.37 hectare (median = 0.07, range = 4.6, standard deviation = 0.81). The independent variables, inheritance and land purchases, together explain 98 percent of the difference in the amount of land owned within the present generation (significant at a $< .01$ level of probability), with about equal portions explained by each variable. However, for the current generation, the ordinary least-squares regression of inheritance on land purchases yields the equation $y = .28 + .21x$ [standard error of beta (s.e.b.) = .18] with a 95 percent confidence interval of $-.15$ to .58, which is not significant. Further analysis,

adjusting for cases without land purchases, did not result in significance. The parent group inherited an average of 0.54 hectare (median = 0.18, range = 3.5, standard deviation = 0.81) and purchased an average of 1.1 hectares (median = 0.17, range = 9.2, standard deviation = 1.9). The two independent variables, inheritance and land purchases, explain all the difference (16 and 84 percent, respectively) within the parent group in the amount of land owned (significant at a $< .01$ level). Yet, like the relationship found for the present generation, the parent group's least squares regression of inheritance on land purchases, $y = 1.02 + .12x$ (s.e.b. = .25) with a 95 percent confidence interval of $-.37$ to .63, is not significant.

22. The rate of differentiation appears to have slowed in the second generation. The most successful entrepreneurs among the parents achieved relatively great leaps in landholding status compared to their children, causing greater variance in landownership among parents than among their offspring. The standard deviation for land owned by parents is 2.1, compared to 1.0 for their children.

23. The fourth lot was ceded in December 1983 and is not included in this analysis since it was not cleared for cropping.

24. This comparison does not include land that parents had available through sharecropping. That area was often substantial but varied at different periods in families' life cycles and was difficult to quantify. If the present generation's sharecropped land is included, their average amount of land available rises to 1.78 hectares. Informants may have underreported sharecropped land since the arrangement was illegal and government extension agents kept a watchful eye for violators.

REFERENCES

Archetti, Eduardo P., and Kristi Anne Stolen. 1981. Burguesía rural y campesinado en la sierra ecuatoriana. In *Campesinado y estructuras agrarias en América Latina*, edited by Eduardo P. Archetti, pp. 297–325. Quito: CEPLAES.

Arcos, Carlos, and Carlos Marchán. 1978. Apuntos para una discusión sobre los cambios en la estructura agraria serrana. *Revista Ciencias Sociales* 2:13–51.

Attwood, D.W. 1979. Why some of the poor get richer: Economic change and mobility in rural western India. *Current Anthropology* 20:495–516.

Baraona, Rafael. 1965. Una tipología de haciendas en la sierra ecuatoriana. In *Reformas agrarias en América Latina*, edited by Oscar Delgado, pp. 688–696. Mexico City: Fondo de Cultura Económica.

Barraclough, Solon, ed. 1973. *Agrarian structure in Latin America*. Lexington, Mass.: D.C. Heath and Co.

Barril, Alex. 1980. Desarrollo tecnológico, producción agropecuaria y relaciones de producción en la sierra ecuatoriana. In *Ecuador: Cambios en el agro serrano*, edited by Osvaldo Barsky et al., pp. 207–247. Quito: FLACSO-CEPLAES.

Barsky, Osvaldo. 1978. Iniciativa terrateniente en la reestructuración de las relaciones de producción en la sierra ecuatoriana: 1959-1964. *Revista Ciencias Sociales* 2(5):74–126.

———.1980. Los terratenientes serranos y el debate político previo al dictado de la Ley de Reforma Agraria de 1964 en el Ecuador. In *Ecuador: Cambios en el agro serrano,* edited by Osvaldo Barsky et al., pp. 133–205. Quito: FLACSO-CEPLAES.

———.1984. *Acumulación campesina en el Ecuador*. Quito: FLACSO.

Barsky, Osvaldo et al., ed. 1980. *Ecuador: Cambios en el agro serrano*. Quito: FLACSO-CEPLAES.

Buitrón, Aníbal. 1947. Situación económica y social del indio otavaleño. *América Indígena* 7:45–67.

Buitrón, Aníbal, and Barbara Salisbury. 1947. *El campesino de la provincia de Pichincha*. Quito: Caja del Seguro.

Chayanov, A.V. 1925. *Peasant farm organization*. Moscow: Co-operative Publishing House. Reprinted in *The theory of peasant economy,* edited by D. Thorner, B. Kerblay, and R.E.F. Smith, pp. 29–277. Homewood, Ill.: Richard D. Irwin, 1966.

CESA (Central Ecuatoriana de Servicios Agrícolas). 1982. Políticas y economías campesinas en ecosistemas de altura: Caso Pilahuín, zona interandina, Ecuador. Paper prepared for regional seminar, Peasant Survival in High Altitude Eco-Systems, organized by Economic Commission for Latin America (CEPAL), the United Nations, and the Ministry of Agriculture, Ecuador.

CIDA (Comité Interamericano de Desarrollo Agrícola). 1965. *Ecuador: Tenencia de la tierra y desarrollo socio económico del sector agrícola*. Washington: Organization of American States.

Commander, Simon, and Peter Peek. 1986. Oil exports, agrarian change and the rural labor process: The Ecuadorian Sierra in the 1970s. *World Development* 14(1):79–96.

Costales, Piedad, and Alfredo Costales. 1971. *Historia social del Ecuador: Reforma agraria*. Quito: Casa de la Cultura Ecuatoriana.

Cueva, Agustín. 1975. *El proceso de dominación política en el Ecuador*. Quito: Solitierra.

de Janvry, Alain. 1981. *The agrarian question and reformism in Latin America*. Baltimore: Johns Hopkins Univ. Press.

Hanssen-Bauer, Jon. 1982. *Plaza Pachano: Market integration, intermediaries and rural differentiation in Tungurahua, Ecuador*. Occasional papers in social anthropology, no. 5. Oslo: Department of Social Anthropology, Univ. of Oslo.

Hoffmeyer, Hans. n.d. Pérfil de la subarea Tisaleo, proyecto DRI Tungurahua. Report prepared for Integrated Rural Development Project, Tungurahua.

Hurtado, Osvaldo. 1980. *Political power in Ecuador*. Albuquerque: Univ. of New Mexico Press.

INEC (Instituto Nacional de Estadística y Censos). 1979. *II censo agropecuario de 1974*. Quito: INEC.

Jacoby, Erich H. 1980. Has land reform become obsolete? In *Peasants in history: Essays in honour of Daniel Thorner,* edited by E.J. Hobsbawn, W. Kula, A. Mitra, K.N. Raj, I. Sachs, pp. 296–305. Bombay: Oxford Univ. Press.

Lehmann, David. 1986. Sharecropping and the capitalist transition in agriculture: Some evidence from the Highlands of Ecuador. *Journal of Development Economics* 23(2):333–354. (See also Working papers, no. 40. Cambridge: Centre of Latin American Studies, Univ. of Cambridge.)

Luzuriaga, Carlos, and Clarence Zuvekas, Jr. 1983. *Income distribution and poverty in rural Ecuador, 1950–1979*. Tempe: Center for Latin American Studies, Arizona State University.

Martínez, Luciano. 1983. *De campesinos a proletarios*. Quito: Editorial El Conejo.

Meier, Peter C. 1982. Artesanía campesina e integración al mercado: Algunos ejemplos de Otavalo. In *Estructuras agrarias y reproducción campesina: Lecturas sobre transformaciones capitalistas en el agro ecuatoriano*, edited by Cristián Sepúlveda, pp. 121–147. Quito: IIE and PUCE.

Murmis, Miguel. 1980. El agro serrano y la vía prusiana de desarrollo capitalista. In *Ecuador: Cambios en el agro serrano*, edited by Osvaldo Barsky et al., pp. 7–50. Quito: FLACSO-CEPLAES.

Pachano, Simón. 1980. Capitalización de campesinos: Organización y estrategias. In *Ecuador: Cambios en el agro serrano*, edited by Osvaldo Barsky et al., pp. 461–499. Quito: FLACSO-CEPLAES.

Rao, V.M. 1972. Land transfers in rural communities: Some findings in a Ryotwari region. *Economic and Political Weekly*, 30 September, pp. A133-A144.

Robalino Gonzago, César Raúl. 1969. *El desarrollo económico del Ecuador*. Quito: JUNAPLA.

Rosero Garcés, Fernando. 1982. El proceso de transformación-conservación de la comunidad andina: El caso de las comunas de San Pablo del Lago. In *Estructuras agrarias y reproducción campesina: Lecturas sobre transformaciones capitalistas en el agro ecuatoriano*, edited by Cristián Sepúlveda, pp. 65–119. Quito: IIE and PUCE.

Sáenz, Alvaro. 1980. Expulsión de fuerza de trabajo agrícola y migración diferencial. In *Ecuador: Cambios en el agro serrano*, edited by Osvaldo Barsky et al., pp. 301–340. Quito: FLACSO-CEPLAES.

Salamea, Lucía. 1980. La transformación de la hacienda y los cambios en la condición campesina. In *Ecuador: Cambios en el agro serrano*, edited by Osvaldo Barsky et al., pp. 249–300. Quito: FLACSO-CEPLAES.

Salomon, Frank. 1973. Weavers of Otavalo. In *Peoples and cultures of native South America*, edited by Daniel R. Gross, pp. 463–492. Garden City, N.Y.: Doubleday and Natural History Press.

Spillman, W.J. 1919. The agricultural ladder. *American Economic Review* 9, (supplement, no. 1):29–38.

Vyas, V.S. 1980. Changes in land ownership pattern: Structural changes in Indian agriculture. In *Peasants in history: Essays in honour of Daniel Thorner*, edited by E.J. Hobsbawn, W. Kula, A. Mitra, K.N. Raj, I. Sachs, pp. 181–193. Bombay: Oxford Univ. Press.

Chapter 5

Agrarian Reforms of the 1960s and 1970s in Peru

Susana Lastarria-Cornhiel*

Land reform has been a political issue in Peru since the 1920s when the American Popular Revolutionary Alliance (*Alianza Popular Revolucionaria Americana,* APRA) party advocated a widespread structural change as a part of its platform. While the reform was also supported by other, smaller populist parties, the ruling classes found both APRA and land reform anathema. An agrarian reform law was not passed until 1964, during the presidency of Fernando Belaúnde Terry.

As with most legislation of this type in Latin America, the 1964 Peruvian law had so many exclusions and exceptions, and offered such high compensation to landowners, that its implementation was difficult and its impact was ambiguous. In fact, the law accomplished little. When the military government of Juan Velasco Alvarado took over in late 1968, one of its priorities was an effective agrarian reform, and, in June 1969 it decreed and immediately began to implement one of Latin America's most extensive land reforms. In spite of the military government's determination, results are mixed, with some successes and some failures. Today, that land reform is undergoing fundamental changes, particularly on the Coast (see chap. 6 in this volume).

In this chapter, I will (1) describe the class structure and agricultural production in Peru leading up to the 1964 Land Reform Law, (2) review Belaúnde's agrarian reform and its accomplishments, and (3) describe Velasco's 1969 agrarian reform and evaluate the results of the military government's policies.

* Susana Lastarria-Cornhiel is a Research Associate with the Land Tenure Center, University of Wisconsin-Madison.

AGRICULTURAL PRODUCTION AND STRUCTURE PRIOR TO THE 1960s

Peru's agriculture—indeed, its entire economy—has been described as dualistic: modern and traditional, capitalist and precapitalist (Fitz-Gerald 1979; Thorp and Bertram 1978, 9–19). While there is an argument that this characterization hides many interrelationships (de Janvry 1981), two very different interrelated systems of production have undeniably existed in Peru since at least the beginning of the century.

In part, this distinction is tied to Peru's geography: the coastal areas, particularly around Lima, are modern and capitalized; the farther one gets from the Coast, the more traditional and precapitalist production becomes. Peru has three distinct geographic regions: Coast, Sierra, and Jungle (Selva). The jungle area will not be dealt with here because, although the largest of the three, it contains a small proportion of the country's population and only a small proportion of its land is in production. It should be mentioned that Peru's agricultural resources in relation to its land area are minimal. Arable land per capita in Peru is only 0.18 hectare as compared with 0.50 for all of South America, 0.20 for Asia, and 2.03 for North America (Alberts 1983, 9). Of the coastal and sierra regions, which represent 37 percent of total land surface, only 6.4 percent is arable land (Kay 1982, 142). While the Coast is very fertile, it is also a desert; without irrigation, it produces nothing. Since water must be brought from the mountains, irrigation projects are expensive. The Sierra, on the other hand, has a different set of problems. Its topography is mountainous, the land is poor (except for valley bottoms), and the rainfall is often inadequate. These geographical characteristics mean that agricultural production in Peru faces a number of formidable natural obstacles.

Coastal agriculture is capitalist and export oriented. Until recently, large- and medium-sized farms using wage labor, advanced technology, and formal credit predominated. There are also a number of market-oriented peasant farmers. Until the mid-1970s, production was primarily for export (sugar and cotton) and agroindustry (industrial corn and rice), with some intensive livestock raising, mainly of dairy cattle. High yields per worker and per hectare are obtained. By 1969, coastal agriculture represented 43 percent of the country's arable land (in standardized units), produced 43 percent of its gross agricultural output, and employed 16 percent of its agricultural labor force (Caballero 1981b, 27).

In contrast, sierra agriculture has had mainly a *latifundio-minifundio* structure and, until the 1969 agrarian reform, used precapitalist arrangements to mobilize labor from peasant communities. The agriculture consists of a combination of subsistence and cash-crop production, with some production for export (wool) but most of it for regional markets. Livestock raising (cattle, sheep, llama, and alpaca) predominates and, unlike the Coast, is extensive, with the livestock grazing mainly on natural pasture. Crop cultivation (potatoes, corn, wheat, and barley), representing a small proportion of production, is located primarily in the inter-Andean valleys. While there are some isolated, capitalist crop and livestock farms, sierra agriculture has been usually characterized by low technology levels and little formal credit. Low productivity per worker and per hectare is the rule. By 1969, sierra agriculture represented 47 percent of the arable land (in standardized units), produced 42 percent of the gross agricultural output, and employed 73 percent of the agricultural labor force (Caballero 1981b, 27).

The one characteristic that both regions shared was concentration of land in the hands of a small number of owners. Data from the 1961 agricultural census showed that while 83 percent of all farms (those under 5 hectares) occupied 5.7 percent of the total farmland, 1 percent of the farms (those over 100 hectares) controlled 84 percent of the farmland. By 1970, 78 percent of the farms (under 5 hectares) occupied 6.5 percent of the land, and 1 percent of the farms (over 100 hectares) controlled 76 percent of the land (de Janvry 1981, 138–139). The shifts that occurred during the decade were due primarily to the growth of medium-sized farms (5–20 hectares) at the expense of larger ones. Most of the land of the large sierra haciendas was of marginal quality; when this was converted to standardized hectares, the degree of concentration was reduced. However, control of land, even marginal land, was important for the sierra *hacendados* as a means of capturing labor from peasant families: due to hacienda monopolization of the basic agricultural resource, peasants were forced to enter into service-tenancy arrangements with the landlords.

One effect of land concentration and duality was a very skewed distribution of income between classes, between regions, and between rural and urban sectors. Using Webb's 1961 income-distribution figures, 80 percent of the labor force in the lowest quartile ($0 to $120 per year in U.S. dollars) consisted of sierra rural workers. In the highest quartile (over $540), 59 percent was wage earners (mostly coastal blue-collar workers, both rural and urban) and white-collar workers. Of the labor force in the lowest quartile, 87 percent was rural, while 72 percent in the highest quartile was urban. If we compare the poorest area of the country (La Mancha India) with the richest (Lima), 51 percent of the population in Apurimac, Ayacucho, Cuzco, Huancavelica, and Puno, but only 4 percent of that in Lima, fell into the lowest quartile, while

54 percent of Lima's labor force was in the highest quartile (Webb 1977, 10–11). In summary, the agricultural structure in Peru until very recently was characterized by duality, land concentration, and gross income inequality.

Rural Labor

Although the Coast and Sierra have thus far been characterized as capitalist and traditional, respectively, one cannot conclude that social relations of production on the Coast were completely proletarianized while those in the Sierra remained purely precapitalist. The peasantry was greatly differentiated in both areas.

The coastal haciendas have historically suffered from a shortage of labor. Before the 1900s, the labor problem was solved initially by importing black slaves and then, after slavery was abolished, by importing indentured Chinese laborers. By the twentieth century, *yanaconaje*, *enganche*, seasonal labor, and wage labor were the principal forms of coastal labor relations.

Yanaconaje was a way of attracting peasants to the coastal haciendas. A small amount of land was rented to a campesino family, often in an uncleared area of the hacienda. In return for usufruct rights to the land, the *yanacona* family was obliged to pay in labor, in kind, and/or in cash. In general, the family worked for the landowner without pay, selling its surplus crops to the owner, improving the lands that it rented, purchasing its subsistence commodities from the owner (often at inflated prices), and returning the land to the owner upon request (Roel 1961, 199–200). In the early 1900s, the *yanaconas* began to unionize, and in 1947 they formed a national federation. Through the unions, the *yanaconas* fought for better conditions (for example, more days of free labor) and against increasing demands by the landowner or his threats of expulsion. Nonetheless, expelling *yanaconas* became a prevalent practice as sugar haciendas became more and more mechanized. Under these conditions, the sugarcane *hacendados* preferred salaried labor and direct control of the land. A typical pattern was for the landowner to expel the *yanaconas* to work the land directly. Then they hired the ex-*yanaconas* back as wage laborers (Matos Mar 1976).

The *enganche*, also a way of securing a stable labor force, was frequently used in the more industrial, agricultural firms that processed cane into refined sugar. The hacienda employed a labor contractor (*enganchador*), who would travel through the highland communities offering loans that could be repaid only by working for the hacienda. Once the peasant was tied through debt peonage to the hacienda, the labor contractor deducted 10–15 percent of his salary as interest, thus making the loan more difficult to repay. As migration from the Sierra to the Coast increased, wage labor (both permanent and temporary) became easier to obtain and the *yanaconaje* and *enganche* systems declined.

Eventuales, seasonal workers, were a third component of the coastal labor force. They were landless peasants or, sometimes, *minifundistas* who worked part-time mainly on the cotton estates and the fruit-producing haciendas. Many *eventuales* were *minifundistas* from the Highlands looking for part-time work on the Coast because their plots could no longer support them.

The Highlands also produced a differentiated labor force which was located principally around livestock (cattle, sheep, and alpaca) haciendas. Traditionally, labor on these haciendas was supplied by *huacchillero* shepherds, who were paid a token salary and were allowed to graze their own livestock on hacienda pasture. Because pasturelands were very scarce and concentrated in the Sierra, grazing rights were important to the *huacchilleros*. But the rise in the world market price for wool encouraged the *hacendados* to improve their breeding practices and to increase their own herds. This meant elimination of the *huacchillero*, whose animals were lowering the quality of the landlord's herd by breeding with hacienda livestock. Attempts to replace the *huacchilleros* with salaried labor met strong resistance from organized *huacchilleros* (Martínez Alier 1973; Campaña and Rivera 1979).

Most sierra haciendas used part of their land to produce foodstuffs for regional markets. A *colono* labor system was used for this crop production. *Colonos*, service tenants who lived on the hacienda, were given usufruct rights to a parcel of land on which they could construct living quarters and grow food. In return, the *colono* and his family would work on the hacienda demesne and in the *hacendado's* house. Additional duties might include transporting the hacienda's harvest to market or providing the *hacendado's* family with poultry and eggs (Vásquez 1961). As urban areas expanded and their populations grew, foodstuffs became increasingly important, and the *hacendados* used various means to increase the hacienda's production. These measures included pushing *colonos* onto marginal lands and claiming better lands that belonged to indigenous communities. In a few cases, traditional haciendas were converted to modern farms by selling off marginal lands and keeping the best lands in production; replacing *colonos* with wage labor; investing in improved seeds, animal breeds, and machinery; and specializing in a single product, such as milk for urban areas (Deere 1978). In spite of conflicts between the *hacendados*, the *colonos*, and neighboring communities and the fact that landowners paid token salaries (since Peruvian law prohibited the use of unpaid labor), this form of labor peonage did not change substantially for years.

Also producing foodstuffs in the Sierra was a large sector of small, independent peasants who produced for subsistence needs as well as for local and regional markets. In some areas, the Sierra of Arequipa, for example, the small-farm sector was predominant and produced foodstuffs primarily for the national market. Labor in this sector was supplied mostly by family and part-time laborers. Also common among these small peasants was *ayni* labor; that is, labor given in exchange for work for a specified period and returned at a later date.

Alongside and interspersed with these forms of production, the indigenous communities persisted, often forced into marginal areas and robbed of their lands at the whim of local hacienda owners who dominated the local power structures and the market channels. Indigenous communities on arable land frequently evolved into communities of independent peasant families. The development of markets both in the Sierra and on the Coast resulted in differentiation within the peasant community; some concentration of land and resources allowed a few peasants to become relatively richer, while most became poorer (Long and Roberts 1978). Some capitalist producers emerged from these peasant families. These entrepreneurial peasants, by accumulating land and resources and by taking advantage of communal land and labor practices, produced for both national and regional markets (Campaña and Rivera 1978; Mallon 1983).

Export and Internal Markets

Peru's agricultural exports (sugar, cotton, coffee, wool) do not stimulate sustained, relatively autonomous, diversified growth outside of the export sector; only economic groups immediately involved tend to benefit (Thorp and Bertram 1978, 70–71). By 1930, sugar production had become concentrated on the northern Coast and was monopolized by a small number of firms. During the 1930s and 1940s, cotton changed from *yanaconaje* production to direct ownership (using wage labor) and cash-rental arrangements. Although there were some large-scale cotton haciendas, cotton production, in contrast to sugarcane, was grown largely on smaller scale units and was dependent on seasonal labor at peak periods (Eguren López 1981, 43–54). Although some spin-off industries developed from both of these crops (for example, textiles, paper), the price of and demand for Peru's export crops (as well as other exports such as minerals) were determined by supply and demand in the international market (Thorp and Bertram 1978, 170–187).

During the 1940s, landowning classes began to lose economic and political power while other, more urban classes were gaining strength and trying to achieve control of the state apparatus. While a series of policies beneficial to agroexporters and foreign investment (such as unrestricted foreign exchange and trade, reduction of taxes in sectors dominated by foreign investment, and repression of APRA and other left-wing parties and their unions) were implemented, other policies (including control of food prices and food imports to keep prices low and concentration of credit in coastal agriculture) were in opposition to the interests of sierra landowners (Cotler 1978, 273–287). By 1950, the landowning class in the Sierra, often called the traditional landowning oligarchy (*gamonales*), had lost political power and was able to survive only through support from and alliance with more progressive coastal landowners.

Policies that were beneficial to one group of landowners while being detrimental to another were indicative of the changes occurring in Peru's social and economic structure from the late 1940s through the early 1960s. The tendencies in the industrialized sector that had begun in the 1930s were now obvious. An import-substitution process was taking place. Foreign capital concentration was changing as investments were becoming more diversified. Certain sectors of the middle class as well as other groups (for example, the Roman Catholic Church and the Peruvian Army) were developing a developmentalist (*desarrollista*) and nationalist ideology and, concomitantly, were organizing political parties. Meanwhile the old, dominant landowning and commercial classes were losing economic and political power. The political legitimacy of the landowning classes was threatened by numerous peasant uprisings throughout the 1950s and 1960s (Pease García 1977, 32–34).

Meanwhile, agriculture's significance was shrinking while other productive sectors were becoming more important. Agriculture's share of gross domestic production (GDP) dropped from 22.5 percent in 1960 to 16.1 percent in 1970 (Horton 1974, 11). Although the index of dollar earnings from agricultural exports increased from 89 in 1945 to 569 in 1965, agriculture's share of exports declined from 56.2 to 34.3 percent (Thorp and Bertram 1978, 208). Both the rural population and the agricultural labor force were declining in relative terms, the former dropping from 65 percent in 1940 to 53 percent in 1961 and to 40 percent in 1972. The agricultural labor force dropped to less than half (49.1 percent) of the total labor force by 1961 and to 43.8 percent by 1971.

Meanwhile, agriculture was less and less able to feed the nation's population, and more food imports were needed each year. Although total agricultural production had increased by an average of 2.5 percent between 1950 and 1970, the index of per capita food production declined from 100 for the 1952–1956 period to 95 in 1972 (Horton 1974, 11). With the exception of rice, there was no government initiative to expand food production. Indeed, public policy had turned instead to price controls and food imports in order to keep prices low for urban consumers. There is evidence that the incomes for vast sectors of the population grew very slowly or not at all, thus keeping consumption and demand for food at a low level. A study of agricultural production from 1944 to 1969 reveals an agricultural sector in decline, but a closer and more detailed analysis shows more complexity (Hopkins 1981). While the export crops (sugar, cotton, and coffee) increased in volume from 1944 to a peak in 1963, they steadily declined from 1963 to 1969 (Hopkins 1981, 67). The behavior of each crop was dependent on world prices and demand as well as on an inelastic supply of irrigated land (Thorp and Bertram 1978, 254).

Even more interesting are trends in agricultural production for the domestic market. Production for the urban market more than doubled in volume in the 1944–1969 period. In contrast, production for the rural market increased rapidly until the mid-1950s yet fell drastically in 1956 because of a severe drought. While production for the rural market increased in the early 1960s, by 1969 it had not regained its 1954 level. Another aspect of production for the internal market was the production of agroindustrial products, such as hard corn for animal feed, milk for canned milk, barley for beer, cotton for internal textile factories, and sugar and coffee for internal consumption. The value of these crops increased from 5.9 percent of gross agricultural production in the 1948–1952 period to 13.3 percent in the 1967–1971 period, while the value of other foods for the urban market increased from 22.8 to 41.3 percent. Production value for the rural market decreased by 36.5 percent between 1948–1952 and 1967–1971 (Hopkins 1981, 67–69).

Changing Economic and Political Power

As agriculture declined, other sectors of the economy experienced rapid growth during the 1950s and 1960s. Production in both mining and fishing increased rapidly, and, because both are export oriented, they replaced agriculture as the main source of foreign exchange. Combined, these two industries increased their share of exports from 17.9 percent in 1945 to nearly 70 percent in 1970. However, only a minuscule portion of the country's labor force was employed by these two industries: 2.9 percent in 1961 and 2.5 percent in 1971 (IBRD 1973, 114). Manufacturing (oriented toward the internal market) also experienced growth during the 1950s and 1960s, although its growth was not as dramatic as that of mining and fishing. Between 1950 and 1970, the manufacturing industry grew at an average annual rate of 7.4 percent (Brundenius 1976, 2) and increased its share of GDP from 16.6 percent in 1960 to 20.9 percent in 1970 (Quijano 1971, 122). Meanwhile, manufacturing increased its share of total employment from 13 percent in 1950 to only 14.5 percent in 1970.

Industrialization was becoming both increasingly diversified and more controlled by foreign capital, especially after the 1959 Industrial

Promotion Law created certain tax exemptions for industry. In 1968, 33.5 percent of nondurable consumer goods, 57.6 percent of intermediate goods, and 44.1 percent of metal goods (*metal-mecánica*) were produced by large- and medium-sized foreign and mixed companies (Thorp and Bertram 1978, 268). An import-substitution process was taking place in enclaves, transforming ore into metals, sugarcane into alcohol and paper, and cotton into textiles. Import substitution was also producing durable consumer goods, mostly in Lima. As in other countries, the import-substitution industry eventually came to be dependent on the importation of machinery, inputs, and technology from the industrialized countries (FitzGerald 1979, 96–99). By 1968, three-quarters of mining, one-half of fishing, and two-thirds of sugar industries, as well as one-half of the cotton and wool processing plants, were owned by foreign enterprises (FitzGerald 1976, 20). The industrialization process slowed in the mid-1960s because of a lack of markets—the lack of dynamism in effective domestic demand (due to concentration of personal income and the end of the fishing boom) and the failure of manufactures for export to compete successfully (FitzGerald 1976, 18). In other words, the limits of import-substitution industrialization were reached quickly due to Peru's very small internal market.

The political scene was also changing: new and progressive sectors of the middle class were becoming politically important. Economic changes, together with the growing militancy and political activism of the lower and middle classes, caused the legitimacy of the traditionally dominant classes to be questioned by the industrial class and progressive sectors of the middle class. Professionals, white-collar workers, Church groups, and the Army saw the agroexport and mining enclaves, the growing involvement of foreign capital in the economy, the backward Sierra society, and the state of agricultural production as obstacles to Peru's development of varying importance (Cotler 1978,303–329). Whereas the Sierra had previously provided cheap foodstuffs for the labor force, now mass migrations from the Sierra and industry's inability to absorb this labor power created unemployment and underemployment in the urban areas. Foreign capital also came under attack, and demands for the nationalization of Peru's extractive sectors were made. New progressive parties were organized; they called for an agrarian reform to end precapitalist production relations, an expansion of the internal market through invigorated industrialization, and a strong state that could control and direct the development of the economy.

In August 1956, the Presidential Commission for Agrarian Reform and Housing (*Comisión para la Reforma Agraria y Vivienda,* CRAV) was named to design an agrarian reform law. The members of CRAV were, for the most part, *hacendados* or agricultural sector supporters; a few members represented politically liberal groups. After four years, the commission proposed an agrarian reform law that focused on colonization and the use of modern inputs as solutions to Peru's agricultural difficulties while recommending a very limited land redistribution. Progressive groups sharply criticized the proposed law and offered alternatives. Although some colonization and irrigation projects were undertaken, the law was never passed (Matos Mar and Mejía 1980, 83–90).

The largest and most important peasant movement was that of *La Convención y Lares*, in southern Peru (Blanco 1972; Fioravanti 1974; Handelman 1975). When this movement began in the late 1950s, the police were sent to exercise control. They were incapable, however, of putting down the movement, which spread rapidly and became better organized. In time, the peasants of *La Convención* gained control of the area, expelled the landowners, and implemented their own land reform. Eventually, the Army was called to "restore order." This was the first time in recent Peruvian history that the military became involved in repressing a grass-roots movement in the interior of the country; while there was brutality, some of the officers were deeply moved by what they had seen. They could now confirm the pitiful conditions under which peasants worked, and they reported that demands made by the campesinos were quite justified—some of the labor relations still practiced by landlords were blatantly illegal. This experience convinced the more progressive elements of the military that an agrarian reform was necessary to end the backwardness of Peru's socioeconomic structure and to avoid future popular uprisings (Villanueva 1973, 266).

BELAÚNDE'S AGRARIAN REFORM

The presidential election of 1963 was a turning point. Although APRA for years had called for agrarian and other progressive reforms, it had sullied its reputation on these matters by becoming allied with the oligarchic, dominant classes in previous governments. A three-way contest for the presidency resulted in the election of Fernando Belaúnde Terry. His party lacked a majority in Congress, however, and a coalition formed between agroexporters and APRA to frustrate Belaúnde's efforts. Because of opposing pressures from both internal and external conservative groups, Belaúnde was not able to implement reforms that he had promised.

The interests of the dominant classes had begun to diverge in the 1940s, and the contradictions among them became especially evident during Belaúnde's presidency. The agroexport landowners were finally forced to concede that an agrarian reform was needed—but only for the traditional hacienda and not, of course, for the "efficient" commercial enterprises engaged in exporting. The split was between the coastal *hacendados* and the backward, landowning class of the Sierra, the former supporting Belaúnde's call for agrarian reform and the latter resisting any change in the land-tenure structure. A third dominant group, the urban industrialists, was dependent upon foreign capital and technology and, hence, on the agroexport sector for foreign exchange. It vacillated between aligning itself with the progressive middle class in supporting a strong state program of industrial development independent of foreign control, on the one hand, and helping the exporters, on the other. Being economically and politically weak and ideologically liberal vis-à-vis other dominant groups, the industrialists usually opted for whatever short-range advantage they could obtain.

Although Belaúnde pushed an agrarian reform law through Congress, the groups opposing him were able to modify it so that whatever "reform" remained was both difficult and expensive to implement and allowed many exceptions, both explicitly and through various loopholes. The agrarian reform bill recognized the need to modernize the agricultural sector in order to promote industrial development and clearly intended to modify significantly the land-tenure structure. The bill limited the extent of landownership to 150 hectares of permanently irrigated land or its equivalent (300 hectares of seasonally irrigated land, 450 hectares of rain-fed land, and 1,500 hectares of natural pasture) and allowed for payments to the landowners in the form of agrarian reform bonds. However, Belaúnde's reform bill also exonerated those haciendas that were highly efficient and capital intensive. And, while it also prohibited personal services in exchange for access to land, it did allow cash rentals of land. With regard to how the land was to be distributed and adjudicated, the bill intended for the land to be distributed to individual persons, peasant communities, and, in some cases, cooperatives (Matos Mar and Mejía 1980, 94–102). Individual private ownership, rather than collective ownership and working of the land, was the envisioned modality of land tenure.

The opposing political parties in Congress, such as the *Unión Nacional Odriísta* (UNO) and the APRA party representing the modern coastal landowners and other exporting groups, were able to insert enough provisions to make the law practically ineffectual. The most important difficulties were (1) compensation for landlords was to be quite generous, (2) each expropriation necessitated a great deal of paperwork, including a presidential decree, (3) exceptions were made for efficient and commercial haciendas (and the evidence for placing farms in these categories was equivocal or at least debatable), and

(4) private parcellation was allowed. Through this last measure, a landowner could divide his property among relatives and friends and, in practice, maintain as much control over the entire enterprise as before.

From 1964 when Belaúnde's agrarian reform law was passed to October 1968 when Velasco's military government took over, little was accomplished. Exceptions to this were some expropriations where popular unrest was rampant, several isolated areas on the Coast where sharecropping was prevalent, and some haciendas owned by the Church and other institutions. Acreage and beneficiary numbers were small, however. As of 1968, 384,254 hectares were distributed to 14,345 peasants. This represented 4 percent of the land that could have been transferred with the legal instruments available and less than 2 percent of the peasants in need of land (Matos Mar and Mejía 1980, 94–105). The National Planning Institute (*Instituto Nacional de Planificación*, INP) estimated that, at that rate, it would have taken a hundred years to carry out the agrarian reform (Matos Mar and Mejía 1980, 103).

Another major problem during Belaúnde's presidency was the 1966/67 fiscal crisis which resulted from a large government deficit, caused by parliamentary pressure for increased public expenditure together with refusal to vote tax increases, and a balance-of-payments deficit, caused by imports that rose in value terms faster than exports (FitzGerald 1976, 5–6; Thorp and Bertram 1978, 286–294). The conservative coalition in Congress passed deflationary measures and devalued the national currency. The effects of the crisis became most evident at the end of the Belaúnde period, in late 1967 and early 1968.

Belaúnde failed at carrying out an effective land reform to curb the political and economic power of the landowning classes, at administering an economic policy favorable to industrial development and an integrated national economy, and at negotiating an acceptable agreement with the International Petroleum Company (IPC). Through these problems, Belaúnde undermined the coalition of the middle-class groups that had put him in power; some simply became more radical and withdrew their support (Cotler 1978, 360–361; Pease García 1977, 62–68). The weaknesses of the Belaúnde government, a growing lack of support for the president, and a strong and unacceptable possibility that APRA would win in the upcoming elections convinced the more progressive elements of the Peruvian army that they would have to take control of the state.

VELASCO'S AGRARIAN REFORM

From the day General Juan Velasco Alvarado and a group of army officers took over the government in 1968, there has been debate as to the nature of Peru's military government and its reforms, particularly the agrarian reform. Critics range from those who branded the government revolutionary (Delgado 1972), to bourgeois (Petras and Havens 1979), to reactionary (Dore and Weeks 1976). As to the effectiveness of the reforms, some analysts maintain that great transformations were achieved (Cotler 1975, 44; FitzGerald 1976, 2), while others aver that Velasco's regime simply continued previous policies and that no profound change occurred (Schydlowsky and Wicht 1979, 33; Webb 1977, 77–90). During the first few years, the military tried to live up to its self-denomination as a revolutionary regime: it expropriated a number of foreign firms (for example, within a week the IPC was nationalized) and rapidly put a number of reforms into effect, including an agrarian reform.

The 1969 Agrarian Reform Law was the first of several reforms that the government decreed and implemented. While the military government did not have a well thought-out, integrated national development strategy on which to base the reforms, the more progressive groups within the government believed that recent economic crises could be overcome only by a series of structural reforms that would facilitate industrial development (Zimmerman Zavala n.d., 105–123). The military felt that this could be done by eliminating the dominant classes with interests tied to the export agriculture and extractive sectors: the oligarchy's free-trade ideology and restrictive monetary policies limited industrial development (Delgado 1972, 152–177). Those whose economic interests hampered industrialization included not only backward landowners in the Sierra who produced mainly for the internal market, but also capitalist agriculturists on the Coast who produced for export (Cotler 1975, 44–46).

Reform Enterprises

The Agrarian Reform Law of 1969 was radical in the sense that (1) all landholdings above a certain size (150 hectares on the Coast and 15–55 hectares in the Sierra) were, without exception, subject to expropriation (land reforms in other countries such as Chile—and, it will be recalled, the 1964 Peruvian Land Reform Law—allowed exceptions for hard-to-document factors such as efficiency, while the Mexican reform had excepted certain industrial crops), (2) landowners were required to live and work on the land, (3) industrial plants directly connected with the expropriated landholdings (such as sugar mills) were expropriated, (4) postreform large estates were to be owned and worked as cooperative enterprises, (5) idle lands or those not providing conditions to workers as specified in labor legislation were made subject to expropriation, (6) compensation was based on the value declared by the landowner for tax purposes, (7) reimbursement to landlords for land was paid primarily in government bonds, and (8) an Agrarian Tribunal with autonomy from the traditional judiciary system and with complete authority to decide on land reform cases was created. While the effectiveness and results of this agrarian reform have been the subject of much debate, the one result on which there is no quarrel is that the Peruvian elites who had based their power on landholding were eliminated.

As of September 1979, most of the expropriated land (63.9 percent) was redistributed as production cooperatives, mainly *Cooperativas Agrícolas de Producción* (CAPs) and *Sociedades Agrícolas de Interés Social* (SAIS).[1] Also, 4.3 percent of the land had been assigned to individual families and 31.5 percent to peasant groups and communities. These latter groups tended to farm and own livestock individually, while their pastureland was held collectively. If hectares are standardized to compensate for differences in land quality (such as irrigated land versus pastureland), the proportions of land in each category change somewhat. Cooperatives received 65.2 percent, individuals obtained 12.6 percent, and the peasant groups and communities got 22.2 percent of the land distributed (Caballero and Alvarez 1980, 26).

CAPs were organized from crop-producing haciendas and, in nonadjusted hectares, received 26.1 percent of the land redistributed. Since this land had good potential (much of it was irrigated, rich coastal land), in standardized hectares it represented 51.8 percent. The permanent workers of these haciendas became cooperative members and they worked the land together as a single production unit. In the Sierra, while group farming was predominant, CAP members were often allowed to keep their usufruct plots for farming individually.

The SAIS were organized from large livestock haciendas in the Sierra and received 34.7 percent of the redistributed land. Since most of this land was pasture, in standardized hectares it consisted of only 11.9 percent of redistributed land. The SAIS were to include ex-hacienda workers and members of the surrounding peasant communities. Over the years, many of these livestock haciendas had long and bitter struggles with neighboring communities because of their "encroachment" on community lands. The SAIS were to be farmed and administered by the former workers, and the communities were to receive a share of the profits not deemed necessary for reinvestment.

A breakdown of the reform's beneficiaries shows that 27 percent was former permanent workers on haciendas, mostly on the Coast; on average they received the equivalent of 3.8 standardized hectares. *Colonos, huacchilleros,* and others in service tenancy before the reform, mostly in the Sierra, represent 25.3 percent of the beneficiaries; they received, on average, 2.1 standardized hectares apiece. Members of peasant communities make up 38.3 percent of the beneficiaries but received an average of 0.4 standardized hectares (mostly pastureland).

Beneficiaries who received land individually represent 9.4 percent of the total; they received, on average, 2.6 standardized hectares (Caballero and Alvarez 1980, 45).

A useful typology of these cooperative enterprises, based on the characteristics and organization of the haciendas that they replaced, is that of José María Caballero (1981b, 38–40). The first type consists of the thirteen largest sugarcane haciendas. These operations were highly centralized, their labor relations were fully capitalist, their technology was advanced, and their productivity was high (Scott 1979, 59–68). All were agroindustrial enterprises producing sugar and some by-products (for example, alcohol, paper). All became CAPs.

A second type of cooperative enterprise is the CAPs organized from the remaining haciendas on the Coast and from some of the crop-producing haciendas in the Sierra. Before the reform, these enterprises, although not highly centralized, were large, modern, commercial farms producing cotton, corn, rice, vegetables, and fruits. They combined wage labor and service tenancy arrangements, used modern technology and inputs, and had moderately high yields. The CAPs organized from these haciendas incorporated their former permanent work force in addition to some temporary labor and sharecroppers who could verify that they had previously worked on the farm. As with the sugarcane CAPs, production was centralized but some members were allowed private plots.

A third type of cooperative enterprise is the SAIS (and a few CAPs) organized from the modern livestock haciendas of the Sierra. While wage labor predominated, some service tenancy was also used. These farms were, and continue to be, very large enterprises, with a mean of about 90,000 hectares of pastureland, 100,000 head of livestock, and 200 full-time workers. The livestock (mostly sheep but some cattle) was generally of high quality; modern technology and breeding practices were employed. The workers were allowed to graze their own livestock on SAIS land, but their cattle were kept separate from the SAIS herd because of inferior quality.

The last types are of collective enterprise are the CAPs and SAIS which were formed from traditional haciendas and which represented the majority of the Sierra haciendas. The crop-producing haciendas consisted of a relatively small area of centralized production in which *colonos* did the work under the supervision of a *hacendado* or his/her representative; a rather large amount of land was occupied by the *colonos*, sharecroppers, or cash renters for their individual cultivation. The crops grown and the technology utilized on both were more-or-less traditional. Previously, the livestock haciendas had consisted of large extensions of land where both hacienda and *huacchillero* livestock grazed and interbred, with little quality control over the herd or attention to improved pasture. Organizing CAPs and SAIS on these traditional haciendas did little to change the form of production itself (Caballero 1981a). CAP members kept the plots they had possessed before, and SAIS members continued to graze their livestock on SAIS land. There was pressure from the beneficiary families from the beginning for more individual production and less collective land.

While the reform's emphasis was on the organization of large units to be worked cooperatively and not subdivided, accomplishing this goal was more difficult than initially anticipated. Consequently, a fairly large percentage of the reform land was not managed centrally. In standardized hectares, 82 percent of the redistributed land on the Coast was in centralized production at the time the land was turned over. In the Sierra, however, only 41 percent of production was centralized at the time (Caballero and Alvarez 1980:32). The increasing decentralization of collective enterprises on the Coast due to parcellation began in the early 1980s (see chap. 6 in this volume).

How did these CAPs and SAIS fare economically? Evidence indicates an uneven performance (Caballero 1981b; Thorp and Bertram 1978; Alvarez 1983b). The reform enterprises that produced for the export market did well when international prices were favorable. The sugar-producing CAPs, for instance, maintained high productivity and reasonable profits until sugar prices fell in the mid-1970s; then a drought hit the Coast from 1976 to 1980. The SAIS did satisfactorily when wool prices started to increase in the late 1970s, but profits for distribution were low. Commercial CAPs producing for both export (cotton) and internal (rice, corn, fruits, vegetables) markets have done poorly and, almost from their inception, received subsidized credit from the Agrarian Bank. The traditional CAPs and SAIS did not do well, though they are difficult to evaluate since most of the land is not under centralized production, technology levels are minimal, and capital investment is low.

Reform Objectives

Have the objectives of the 1969 agrarian reform been achieved? Alvarez (1983a, 112–113) lists three agrarian reform objectives stated in the text of the law: (1) to bring social justice to the rural areas, (2) to support an enlargement of the internal market, and (3) to contribute to the capital formation necessary for rapid industrialization. While these are commendable objectives, it may be unrealistic to expect an agrarian reform to accomplish all three; furthermore, one can envision situations in which the last objective is in conflict with the first two.

Measuring the reform's achievements by these objectives yields a demonstration of limited success. Reform did eliminate the large landowning class, and it did redistribute more land and benefit more rural families than any agrarian reform in South America to date. Even so, the coverage of the reform was smaller than had been expected, and the manner in which land was redistributed conserved some basic inequities of the countryside. At the time the law was decreed, it was estimated that 59 percent of agricultural land and pastures (17 million hectares) would be affected (Matos Mar and Mejía 1980, 115). But a very small percentage of the land in the Sierra—and even on the Coast—was suitable for crop production; most of the land in the Sierra was natural pasture. With this limitation, and recognizing that a high proportion of Peru's population was rural, there was really not much land to distribute. As of September, 1979, when the expropriation and distribution process had been practically completed, 38.3 percent of the agricultural land included in the 1972 census had been distributed to 20.9 percent of the agricultural families (or 31.5 percent of families in need of land) (Caballero and Alvarez 1980, 13–53). Alvarez feels that the reason for the shortfall was a lack of basic information about the agricultural sector at the time of reform (Alvarez 1983a, 112). The amount of land appropriate for agriculture was greatly overestimated, especially in the Sierra. A great proportion of the hacienda land in this region was marginal: these lands were expropriated but not redistributed. Another overestimation concerned the degree of land concentration, especially in the Sierra. A misinterpretation of census data and an assumption that the political and social importance of sierra *gamonales* was necessarily based on land concentration led many authors, social scientists, and politicians to overestimate land concentration (Caballero 1981a, 92–95).

The problem of how and to whom the land was to be distributed was a second factor that limited the effect of land reform. Hacienda land was redistributed to former permanent workers: salaried workers, *colonos*, *huacchilleros*, and sharecroppers; seasonal workers and *minifundistas* were excluded. The SAIS model was an attempt to include families that lived near the collective enterprise but was not very successful in this respect. Also, land was redistributed within both the modern and the traditional sectors (Webb and Figueroa 1975, 134). This benefited the workers of the coastal haciendas much more than the sierra peasant families, whose haciendas were much poorer. Within the coastal CAPs, members of the capital-rich, sugarcane cooperatives received the most benefits; the peasant families of the poor southern Sierra received little. Besides affecting a small percentage of the rural labor force, the reform failed to divert capital and other resources from modern to traditional agriculture.

A positive evaluation of the reform's ostensible second objective, internal market expansion, would show productive employment and incomes increasing in the rural sector. There is conflicting evidence on this matter (Caballero 1978; Scott 1979). The state pressured for as many workers as possible to be included as collective enterprise members (*socios*). For their part, however, *socios*, in an attempt to keep benefits for themselves, resisted the addition of more members, preferring to hire seasonal labor at much lower wages than to divide profits among more full-timers. Other cooperatives preferred mechanization to either enlarging the cooperative membership or hiring seasonal or part-time labor. Some writers argue that even hiring temporary labor redistributed some of the cooperative's income (Scott 1981, 303–304). In fact, however, these workers received wages that were much lower than the salaries and dividends accruing to cooperative members. What is more, both Adolfo Figueroa and Richard Webb, after an extensive study of income data, conclude that a minimal amount of income was redistributed as a result of the agrarian reform (Figueroa 1983; Webb 1977; Webb and Figueroa 1975). Webb (1977, 77–90) maintains that redistributive efforts toward the very poor under Velasco were similar to those under Belaúnde and that, under both regimes, very little was accomplished. First of all, as with the agrarian reform, redistributive policies and reforms caused incomes to be redistributed within sectors (urban, rural, modern, traditional), not across sectors, and, while in most cases the distributional direction was downward (toward those with lower incomes), considering the gross income inequalities that already existed, the amounts transferred were very small. Second, as in the distribution of land and resources, those groups that benefited most from income transfers were those that already had relatively high incomes, such as urban workers in capital-intensive firms and rural workers in the sugarcane haciendas. Thus, in general, the rural sector gained much less than the urban sector, and the rural workers in modern enterprises within the rural sector gained more than peasants in traditional enterprises. Figueroa also observes that income redistribution occurred within sectors. He concludes that the agrarian reform transferred between 1 and 2 percent of national income to 15 percent of the labor force. And the greater part of this was transferred to the richest quartile of the working population (Webb and Figueroa 1975, 128–134).

The third objective of reform was to add to capital formation in manufacturing. Funds were made directly available for industrial development through government compensation to landlords and payment of the agrarian debt by beneficiaries. The bonds that *hacendados* received in partial payment for their lands could be redeemed at any time prior to their maturity by investing the funds in industrial projects. Few expropriated landlords, however, chose this option. Despite the military government's emphasis on industrialization, capitalists in Peru were wary of the "revolutionary" government and its reformism. Peru's industrialists seemed too dependent on foreign capital and technology. They were unwilling to risk their own capital in the type of independent development that the military government advocated (FitzGerald 1979, 60). Because the declared tax value—on which basis landlords were compensated—was low and because inflation wiped out the value of the nonadjusted bonds, the use of bonds for investment purposes failed (Alvarez 1983a, 135–136). The other source of investment capital in industrialization was the beneficiaries' agrarian debt payments. This likewise turned out to be insignificant; as inflation accelerated, the remittances became minimal. In 1979, the agrarian debt was forgiven. Alvarez maintains that the reform's contributions to industrialization were indirect; the government's policies channeled funds from rural to urban sectors through price controls, taxes, subsidies, monetary adjustments, and marketing mechanisms (Alvarez 1983b).

Overall, therefore, Peru's agrarian reform failed to achieve its stated objectives. In a sense, this failure affirms that classes and class structure cannot be abolished by decree, that revolutionary transformations are attained through reform only with great difficulty, and that Peru's economy cannot be restructured without substantial investment. Furthermore, the capital-starved agricultural sector must be reinvigorated before being squeezed for purposes of capital formation.

Food and Export Production

One measure of a reform's success must be whether or not production increased concomitantly with agrarian reform. A number of structural and political factors have influenced reform-enterprise production of foodstuffs and industrial inputs. CAPs and SAIS that inherited modern haciendas with substantial capitalization performed better as centralized enterprises than those that were organized from traditional haciendas, which typically had low levels of technology and minimal capital investment. A second factor was the government's failure to transfer resources between sectors and its continued support of export agriculture; these policies kept the production of different crops and livestock at output levels similar to those of the prereform period (Alvarez 1983a, 128–130). The third factor, the military government's priorities of industrial development and low food prices (Caballero 1984b), influenced the agricultural sector in different ways, as Alvarez shows in her work on governmental policies and how they affected agricultural production during the 1970s (Alvarez 1980, 1983a, 1983b).

In fact, the military government's commitment to industrialization and its expectation that the rural sector could contribute to that development did not waiver much during the 1970s. In its efforts to assure cheap foodstuffs so that urban workers would not exert upward wage pressures, the government penalized agriculture through policies such as price controls and competitive food imports; it did not invest to stimulate food production and increase productivity. These official policies were, of course, not new; previous governments had faced the problem of declining per capita food production by importing cheap grains and imposing price controls (Hopkins 1981). The military government simply continued and expanded these policies, at least until 1977 when Peru experienced a serious fiscal crisis and was close to bankruptcy.

The military government increasingly resorted to price controls, especially on processed foods, in an attempt to control the urban foodstuffs market. These controls were successful until 1973: food prices increased more slowly than the general consumer price index. After 1973, however, food prices increased more rapidly, at which time the government started paying subsidies on a number of foods and food inputs. Most of the subsidies were for imported inputs such as wheat and powdered milk. While the subsidies meant lower food prices for the urban population (mostly in metropolitan Lima), agroindustrial firms derived the primary benefit. When the subsidies were eliminated in the late 1970s, prices for processed foods increased at a rate higher than both the general consumer price index and the food price index (Alvarez 1983b, 116-164).

Tax policy before and after agrarian reform did not differ significantly. The agricultural sector's contribution to tax revenue came mostly from export crops, and this revenue had declined during the 1960s (Scott 1979, 74–75). The creation of CAPs and SAIS by the agrarian reform facilitated the collection of taxes (private *hacendados* often kept no accurate records; CAPs and SAIS, as public entities, had registry systems), but taxes were not extended to all reform enterprises until the mid-1970s. With the exception of some private commercial farms, the rest of the agricultural sector did not pay direct taxes. With regard to state investment in agriculture, it consisted mainly of irrigation projects on the Coast; investments in the sierra and jungle regions were minimal (Eguren López 1977, 249; Alvarez 1983b, 173–188).

When considering credit policy, it should be remembered that only a small proportion of rural producers in Peru utilize credit to purchase inputs, most of which are imported. Only 12.5 percent of agricultural land received credit during the 1970s (Alvarez 1983b, 198). In other words, the majority of Peru's farmers produces within a logic of production (noncommercial, subsistence) that precludes the use of official credit as capital. Therefore, government scope for affecting agricultural production in general through credit was minimal. Essentially, military-government credit policies during the 1970s were the same as the credit policies of the 1960s (Eguren López

1977, 247; Alvarez 1983b, 192–213). During the 1960s, the agricultural production value financed through credit fluctuated between 16 and 18 percent. Most of this credit was concentrated on the Coast and was for a limited number of crops. During the 1960s, total credit in real terms increased; within this, the ratio of state credit to total credit increased (from 48 percent in 1960 to 76 percent in 1970) while that of private banks decreased (from 52 to 24 percent). Also, the percentage of credit invested in urban food production increased (to 50 percent by the 1965–1969 period), credit for export crops decreased (to 38 percent by 1965–1969), and the proportion of credit for sierra crops remained small (12 percent in 1965–1969) (Alvarez 1983b, 193, 199).

During the 1970s, these credit trends more or less continued: the coastal CAPs received the most credit. The amount of credit, in real terms, for agriculture continued to rise; the percentage of agricultural credit financed by the state increased to 96 percent by 1979; credit for export crops continued to decline (from 38 percent to 20 percent), increased for urban food production (from 50 percent to 68 percent), and remained the same (at 12 percent) for rural food crops (Alvarez 1983b, 193–199). While state credit during the early 1970s was utilized to support the newly organized reform enterprises at low interest rates regardless of their commercial viability, the economic crisis of the mid-1970s reoriented credit policy and conditions for its receipt. The interest rate subsidy was halved, credit was extended to those enterprises perceived as able to repay, and penalties were imposed against default (Alvarez 1983b, 208, 213–215).

How did these policies affect production for the internal food market and for the export crop market? Agricultural production apparently followed the same trends that had become evident during the 1960s. Although agricultural production in general increased during the 1969–1979 period, it grew at a slower annual rate than GDP (1.7 percent versus 3.2 percent) or population increase (2.9 percent) (Alvarez 1983b, 36). Alvarez shows, as had Hopkins (1981) for the prereform period, that crops destined for various markets performed differently. Production for direct urban consumption (for example, rice, poultry, beef, milk) increased by 3.5 percent annually between 1969 and 1979. Most of this growth was due to the spectacular increases in rice and chicken production that resulted from favorable government policies (Alvarez 1983b, 37–43). The production of agroindustrial inputs (for urban food production) also increased dramatically, mostly because of growth in the chicken industry. In contrast, production of food for the rural market decreased during the period at an average rate of 0.8 annually, probably because of a paucity of resources channeled toward highland agriculture and overall policies that favored production for the urban market (Alvarez 1983b, 44). The growth in production of export crops followed the downward trend that had begun in the mid-1960s: sugar, cotton, and coffee production increased at an average annual rate of only 1.8 percent (Alvarez 1983b, 46). During this period, internal consumption of the traditional export crops—sugar and cotton—continued to increase, and the importance of these crops for foreign exchange diminished.

A comparison of these four groups by marketing type (direct urban, agroindustrial input, rural, and export crop) with regard to their share of agricultural production and land use demonstrates their varying importance during the 1969–1979 period. Production for direct urban consumption increased as a share of agricultural production value from 41.3 percent in 1967–1971 to 47.2 percent in 1976; agroindustrial inputs increased from 13.1 to 17.9 percent during this period. In contrast, production for the rural market decreased in its share of agricultural production value from 30.8 percent in 1967–1971 to 27 percent in 1976, and export crops decreased from 14.8 to 7.9 percent (Alvarez 1983b, 47–48). These trends were evident already in the prereform period. The amount of land utilized to produce these different types of crops reflects production changes. Thus, in 1971, 16.7 percent of the land was used to produce food for direct urban consumption, and 19.9 percent was used to produce agroindustrial inputs. In 1979, these shares had increased to 18.7 and 25.4 percent, respectively. Meanwhile, land in rural food production decreased from 53 percent in 1971 to 45.9 percent in 1979 (Alvarez 1983b, 49–50). While land in export-crop production decreased very little (from 10.4 percent in 1971 to 10 percent in 1979), more and more of this output was being internally consumed.

The positive experience the government had in promoting rice production (Caballero 1984b, 18) would seem to indicate what can be accomplished if the government implements policies that promote the production of crops. Starting in the 1960s, state revenues were used to stimulate rice production for internal consumption: irrigation projects were undertaken, credit programs were set up, and a guaranteed price was offered to rice producers. The state also took over the milling and marketing of rice in order to guarantee the provision of this staple for urban markets. The result was that the production of rice between 1969 and 1976 increased at an average annual rate of 4.5 percent, surpassed only by poultry production in the list of urban foodstuffs (Alvarez 1983b, 39–42).

Class Conflict

The military government had several other objectives when it drafted the 1969 Agrarian Reform Law. First of all, it clearly expected to eliminate rural classes and defuse class conflict; it also expected to stimulate production for the internal urban market and earn foreign exchange, especially for industrial development. The military's view that obliterating the economic bases of the rural elite would eliminate class conflict proved simplistic. Changing ownership relations transforms but one aspect of the production system. Agricultural production under reform remained part and parcel of Peru's capitalist economy.

Indeed, the reform process itself was influenced by class conflict, which, in turn, effected changes and modifications in the law (Havens et al. 1983). Some changes resulted from a clash of interests between former hacienda peasantry or agricultural workers and landowners; these tended to make the law more radical. Other modifications resulted from pressure by independent, medium-sized farmers; these made the law more conservative. A change of the former type was the repeal of the provision that allowed haciendas to be subdivided and sold by the owner as small farms. Some holdings had been distributed among the owners' relatives and friends, thus permitting the landowners de jure subdivision and de facto single ownership. Peasant strikes protesting this turn of events were instrumental in obtaining an end to this provision in November, 1969, five months after the law had been decreed. In February, 1971, after more than a year of conflict between the peasantry and the landowners, with each group trying to pressure a different faction of the military government, parcellations that had been authorized between June and November, 1969, were annulled.

Conservative opposition to the agrarian reform came mainly from a more commercialized group of peasants, located mostly on the Coast. The large landowners were not able to oppose the land reform effectively because the most powerful owners, the coastal sugarcane *hacendados*, were expelled from their lands within the first few months of reform. Without their leadership, the other large landowning groups were unable to stop land takeovers. In 1973, a law was passed which allowed small- (up to 50 hectares) and medium-sized (from 50 to 150 hectares) landowners to certify themselves as small or medium landowners and thus guarantee that their holdings would not be subject to expropriation in the future.

Another important legal change that the small peasantry brought about was to lower the ceiling for the landholding size judged immune from expropriation. When the law was decreed in 1969, the upper limit for landownership was 150 hectares on the Coast and 15–55 hectares (depending on whether the land was irrigated or not) in the Sierra and the Ceja de Selva (high jungle). When both the peasantry and the government realized that there was not enough land to distribute, the peasantry pressured for lower ceilings. In 1969, the military government apparently had believed that, by subjecting just the very largest estates to reform, 10 million (out of a total of 24 million) hectares could be expropriated and 300,0000 families could benefit (FitzGerald 1976, 31). By the end of 1974, however, only 4.8 million hectares had been affected, 200,000 families had benefited, and the reform process had already reached into the middle-sized landholdings. In 1975, the limits were lowered to 50 irrigated hectares on the Coast and 30 irrigated hectares in the Sierra.

Contradictory objectives within the reform enterprise sector presented another problem that illustrates the persistence of class conflict. CAPs and SAIS alike suffered the tension of being basically capitalist enterprises, functioning efficiently and turning a profit, yet at the same time accomplishing social goals such as providing employment, generating egalitarian income patterns, and supplying other welfare benefits to both present and potential members (Caballero 1981b, 41–45). The other main contradiction of the SAIS and CAPs is embodied within the peasantry itself. Except for the sugarcane enterprises, a significant number—if not the majority—of the work force on the haciendas had peasant (as distinguished from wage worker) backgrounds. This resulted in pressures from members to expand production on family plots. Demands arose for more land to be assigned to individuals and less to be assigned in common.

Thus, although the reform did eliminate the large landowning class which had existed up to 1969, the attempt to blur the rural class structure failed. The rural proletarian and peasant classes remained; the state was substituted for the landed elite. The fact that the reform enterprises are state created and state controlled, and that they function within a capitalist market system, means that they cannot escape the class structure of a state capitalist system. Still, today, the struggles between the classes continue in the Peruvian countryside.

Perhaps as important as what was happening within the reformed sector of agriculture is what was happening outside this sector. An important trend which began in the 1960s and continued into the 1970s—in spite of or perhaps because of the agrarian reform—was the growing importance of medium-sized landowners as agricultural producers, particularly of urban foodstuffs. The medium-sized landowners produced 50.4 percent of agricultural production value in 1977 and 62.7 percent of the food produced for direct urban consumption (Alvarez 1983b, 54). The conclusion to be drawn affirms de Janvry's assertion (1981, 214–218): the most dynamic sector of agriculture was the private (as opposed to the reform) sector and, within this sector, the medium-sized landowners, in this case those who produced rice and poultry on the Coast and coffee in the jungle foothills, performed the best. These medium-sized landowners were mostly ex-*hacendados* who intensified their pattern of production on the land left them by the agrarian reform and medium-sized peasantry who had not been affected by the reform but who had enough land and resources to invest in commercial agriculture.[2]

CONCLUSIONS

Much of this chapter can be placed within the framework of de Janvry's model. Of the three types of agrarian reform outlined by de Janvry (redistribution within precapitalism, transition to capitalism, and reform within capitalism), Peru's first two reforms (1964 and 1969), described in this chapter, were of the second type. The third type of reform (the subject of the following chapter) is presently taking place (de Janvry 1981, 202–211).

Agriculture in Peru through the early twentieth century was largely precapitalist: large estates with noncapitalist labor relations and small subsistence farms. Capitalist development in agriculture up to the advent of agrarian reform was minimal and consisted of both Junker development and farmer agriculture. In Junker agriculture, landlords transformed their precapitalist estates into capitalist enterprises using a wage-labor workforce. This type of capitalist development occurred mainly on the Coast (on the sugarcane haciendas) and in some isolated sierra areas (such as the dairy farms in Cajamarca). Commercial farms also developed in some areas, such as the central Sierra and Arequipa valleys. This evolution of capitalist development was limited, however. Precapitalist estates and subsistence peasant farms continued to dominate Peru's agriculture.

Implementation of Belaúnde's 1964 reform promoted further development of Junker-type agriculture. Even before agrarian reform, the threat of the law's eventual passage was enough to cause some landlords to begin selling off marginal parts of their estates and to start adopting capitalist innovations. Wage labor was hired and replaced precapitalist relations, infrastructural investments were made, and specialized production for urban or export markets displaced diversified production for rural markets. The outlawing of precapitalist labor relations and the expropriation of inefficient estates by Belaúnde's agrarian reform accelerated the transition to large-scale capitalist estates. What this reform attempted to accomplish was not the elimination of landlords but their transformation from a precapitalist to a capitalist class.

The weakness of Belaúnde's reform and the difficulties in its implementation convinced the progressive sectors of the military that the landlord class had to be eliminated in order to clear the way for capitalist development in agriculture. De Janvry calls this type of reform a transition from Junker to farmer capitalism. Landlords' holdings were drastically reduced in the process, and individual landowners were personally obliged to supervise the management of their holdings. In de Janvry's terminology, the landlords were transformed from Junker to farmer capitalists.

But how do the reform enterprises themselves, which represent a significant portion of Peru's agriculture, fit within this scheme? For the large number of CAPs and SAIS (particularly those in the Sierra) which had been formed from traditional haciendas, the low level of centralized production, infrastructure, and capital investment, together with their virtual neglect by the government, meant that they never really became production cooperatives. Production in these reform enterprises remained virtually the same as before the reform: peasant household production. With regard to those CAPs and SAIS formed from the more modern haciendas that were able to function as centralized production units, the majority failed to become viable. This failure was due in part to contradictory state policies that, on average, favored investments in urban industrial development and assured cheap foodstuffs for the urban population. These reform enterprises were also doomed to fail partly because the *socios* were actually fully proletarianized agricultural workers who required too high a price for their labor: their members had to receive wages that covered their year-round subsistence and reproduction. The collective enterprises became even more expensive when they tried to provide their members with basic services, such as education and health, that the state failed to deliver.

Many small peasant holdings have been neglected by the agrarian reform process and the state. The families who farm these holdings must try to produce within a capitalist system but with little capital and few resources. They are forced, therefore, to look for other sources of income to supplement their limited earnings from the land. The semiproletarianized labor of this small peasantry is cheaper than that of permanent workers in two ways: the production of food for the internal market on small peasant plots is cheaper than that on capitalist enterprises utilizing wage labor (Vergopolous 1978; Caballero 1984a, 349–350), and the temporary or seasonal labor of the small peasantry on capitalist enterprises such as the CAPs and SAIS is cheaper than that of permanent wage labor (de Janvry 1981, 83–84, 103–104). Thus, it is not surprising that the CAPs and SAIS have been judged "inefficient" and are pressuring—and being pressured—for parcellation into small peasant farms.

NOTES

1. The CAPs were crop-producing enterprises, owned and worked collectively by the cooperative members, the former permanent workers of the haciendas. Ownership of land and capital goods was in the hands of the cooperative, not individuals. Management of the enterprise was implemented through a General Assembly of all the cooperative members and an Administrative Council, whose members were elected by the General Assembly. The SAIS were livestock enterprises, owned and worked collectively by the former permanent workers of the haciendas. However, in this case, the cooperative members consisted not only of the workers but also of the surrounding communities. This was done because many of the livestock haciendas had, over the decades, encroached on peasant community lands, and the ensuing disputes and conflicts in most cases had never been resolved. It was thought that by making these surrounding community families part of the SAIS, the conflicts would cease. The other collective enterprise created by the agrarian reform was the Social Property Enterprise (*Empresa de Propiedad Social*, EPS). While the ownership of the EPS was collective, the management and profit-distribution structure were more similar to the urban social property enterprises created in the mid-1970s. The EPS represented only 3.1 percent of the land affected by the agrarian reform (Caballero and Alvarez 1980, 26).

2. The potential expansion and development of the medium-sized landholdings on the Coast, as a result of the parcellation of the CAPs, is briefly treated in chapter 6 of this volume.

REFERENCES

Alberts, Tom. 1983. *Agrarian reform and rural poverty*. Boulder, Colo.: Westview Press.

Alvarez, Elena. 1980. *Política agraria y estancamiento de la agricultura, 1969–1977*. Lima: Instituto de Estudios Peruanos.

———.1983a. Government policies and the persistence of rural poverty, 1960–1980. Ph.D. dissertation, New School for Social Research, New York.

———.1983b. *Política económica y agricultura en el Perú, 1969–1979*. Lima: Instituto de Estudios Peruanos.

Blanco, Hugo. 1972. *Tierra o muerte: Las luchas campesinas en el Perú*. Mexico City: Siglo Veintiuno Editores.

Brundenius, Claes. 1976. *Patrón de crecimiento de la economía peruana*. Lima: Instituto Nacional de Planificación.

Caballero, José María. 1978. *Los eventuales en las cooperativas costeñas peruanos: Un modelo analítico*. Lima: Departamento de Economía, Pontificia Universidad Católica del Perú.

———.1981a. *Economía agraria de la sierra peruana*. Lima: Instituto de Estudios Peruanos.

———.1981b. *From Belaunde to Belaunde: Peru's military experiment in third-roadism*. Working papers, no. 36. Cambridge, U.K.: Centre of Latin

American Studies, Univ. of Cambridge.

———.1984a. Unequal pricing and unequal exchange between the peasant and capitalist economies. *Cambridge Journal of Economics* 3:347–359.

———.1984b. Agriculture and the peasantry under industrialization pressures: Lessons from the Peruvian experience. *Latin American Research Review Review* 19 (2): 3–41.

Caballero, José María, and Elena Alvarez. 1980. *Aspectos cuantitativos de la reforma agraria (1969–1979)*. Lima: Instituto de Estudios Peruanos.

Campaña, Pilar, and Rigoberto Rivera. 1979. Los huacchilleros y la Cerro de Pasco Co. *Estudios Rurales Latinoamericanos* 2(1):111–121.

———.1978. El proceso de descampesinización en la Sierra Central del Perú. *Estudios Rurales Latinoamericanos* 1(2):71–100.

Cotler, Julio. 1978. *Clases, estado y nación en el Perú*. Lima: Instituto de Estudios Peruanos.

———.1975. The new mode of political domination in Peru. In *The Peruvian experiment*, edited by Abraham F. Lowenthal, pp. 44–78. Princeton, N.J.: Princeton Univ. Press.

Deere, Carmen Diana. 1978. The development of capitalism in agriculture and the division of labor by sex: A study of the northern Peruvian Sierra. Ph.D. dissertation, Univ. of California-Berkeley.

de Janvry, Alain. 1981. *The agrarian question and reformism in Latin America*. Baltimore: Johns Hopkins Univ. Press.

Delgado, Carlos. 1972. *El proceso revolucionario peruano: Testimonio de lucha*. Mexico City: Siglo Veintiuno Editores.

Dore, Elizabeth, and John Weeks. 1976. The intensification of the assault against the working class in "revolutionary" Peru. *Latin American Perspectives* 3(1):55–83.

Eguren López, Fernando. 1977. Política agraria y estructura agraria. In *Estado y política agraria*, pp. 217–255. Lima: DESCO.

———.1981. Evolución de la producción algodonera. In *Producción algodonera e industria en el Perú*, pp. 11–125. Lima: DESCO.

Figueroa, Adolfo. 1983. *La economía campesina de la sierra del Perú*. Lima: Pontificia Universidad Católica de Perú.

Fioravanti, Eduardo. 1974. *Latifundio y sindicalismo agrario en el Perú*. Lima: Instituto de Estudios Peruanos.

FitzGerald, E.V.K. 1976. *The state and economic development*. Occasional paper, no. 49. Cambridge, U.K.: Cambridge Univ. Press.

———.1979. *The political economy of Peru, 1956–78*. Cambridge, U.K.: Cambridge Univ. Press.

Handelman, Howard. 1975. *Struggle in the Andes*. Austin: Univ. of Texas Press.

Havens, A. Eugene, Susana Lastarria-Cornhiel, and Gerardo Otero. 1983. Class struggle and the agrarian reform process. In *Military reformism and social classes*, edited by David Booth and Bernardo Sorj, pp. 14–39. London: Macmillan.

Hopkins, Raúl. 1981. *Desarrollo desigual y crisis en la agricultura peruana, 1944–1969*. Lima: Instituto de Estudios Peruanos.

Horton, Douglas. 1974. Land reform and reform enterprises in Peru. LTC/IBRD report. Madison: Land Tenure Center, University of Wisconsin.

IBRD (International Bank for Reconstruction and Development). 1973. *The current economic position and prospects of Peru*. Washington: IBRD.

Kay, Cristóbal. 1982. Achievements and contradictions of the Peruvian agrarian reform. *Journal of Development Studies 18*(2):141–170.

Long, Norman, and Byran R. Roberts. 1978. Peasant cooperation and underdevelopment in central Peru. In *Peasant cooperation and capitalist expansion in central Peru,* edited by N. Long and B.R. Roberts, pp. 297–328. Austin: Univ. of Texas Press.

Mallon, Florence E. 1983. *In defense of community in Peru's central Highlands: Peasant struggle and capitalist transition, 1860–1940*. Princeton, N.J.: Princeton Univ. Press.

Martínez Alier, Juan. 1973. *Los huacchilleros del Perú*. Lima: Instituto de Estudios Peruanos.

Matos Mar, José. 1976. *Yanaconaje y reforma agraria en el Perú*. Lima: Instituto de Estudios Peruanos.

Matos Mar, José, and José Manuel Mejía. 1980. *La reforma agraria en el Perú*. Lima: Instituto de Estudios Peruanos.

Pease García, Henry. 1977. La reforma agraria peruana en la crisis del estado oligárquico. In *Estado y política agraria,* pp. 13–136. Lima: DESCO.

Petras, James, and A. Eugene Havens. 1979. Peru: Economic crisis and class confrontation. *Monthly Review 30*(9), February, pp. 25–41.

Quijano, Anibal. 1971. Nationalism and capitalism in Peru. *Monthly Review* 23(3), July-August, pp. 1–122.

Roel, Virgilio. 1961. *La economía agraria peruana*. Lima: Instituto de Promoción Humana.

Schydlowsky, Daniel, and Juan J. Wicht. 1979. *Anatomía de un fracaso económico,* Perú 1968–1978. Lima: Universidad del Pacífico, Centro de Investigación.

Scott, Chris. 1979. The labour process, class conflict and politics in the Peruvian sugar industry. *Development and Change 10*(1):57–89.

———.1981. Agrarian reform and seasonal employment in coastal Peruvian agriculture. *Journal of Development Studies 17*(4):282–306.

Thorp, Rosemary, and Geoffrey Bertram. 1978. *Peru, 1890–1977: Growth and policy in an open economy*. New York: Columbia Univ. Press.

Vásquez, Mario. 1961. *Hacienda, peonaje y servidumbre en los Andes peruanos*. Lima: Editorial Estudios Andinos.

Vergopolous, Kostas. 1978. Capitalism and peasant productivity. *Journal of Peasant Studies* 5(4):446–465.

Villanueva, Victor. 1973. *Ejército peruano*. Lima: Editorial Juan Mejía Baca.

Webb, Richard Charles. 1977. *Government policy and the distribution of income in Peru, 1963–1973*. Cambridge, Mass.: Harvard Univ. Press.

Webb, Richard Charles, and Adolfo Figueroa. 1975. *Distribución del ingreso en el Perú*. Lima: Instituto de Estudios Peruanos.

Zimmermann Zavala, Augusto. n.d. *El plan Inca-Obejetio: revolución peruana*. Lima: Empresa Editora del Diario Oficial "El Peruano."

Chapter 6

Changing Paths: The Decollectivization of Agrarian Reform Agriculture in Coastal Peru

Michael R. Carter and Elena Alvarez*

The structure of Peruvian coastal agriculture in 1980 reflected the ambitious changes wrought by the agrarian reform initiated by Juan Velasco Alvarado's military government in 1969. Nearly every private coastal holding larger than 50 hectares had been reassigned as the collective property of its permanent workers (see chap. 5 in this volume). The newly organized *Cooperativas Agrarias de Producción* (CAPs) functioned as large-scale, integrated production cooperatives. While subject to government regulation, CAPs were labor-managed firms.

Despite the wrenching change of the Velasco reforms, beginning in 1981 coastal agriculture underwent yet another transformation as the CAPs began to be subdivided into individual holdings. Each CAP member typically received a 4–6 hectare parcel. The process of subdivision, or parcellation, had extended to about three-fourths of coastal CAPs by 1986. While this reform of the agrarian reform occurred quickly and relatively quietly, with no explicit program, it profoundly altered the scale of agriculture in an area where large-scale organization had dominated for centuries.

The shift to small-scale agriculture raises questions about the productivity, stability, and economic viability of the new coastal agrarian structure.[1] Proponents view parcellation as a consolidation of the agrarian reform which will result in a dynamic and productive yet still fundamentally egalitarian agricultural sector. Opponents doubt

* Carter is Associate Professor of Agricultural Economics, University of Wisconsin-Madison. Alvarez, an economist, has just completed a fellowship at the Helen Kellogg Institute, University of Notre Dame. Carter's research was supported by a grant from the Graduate School, University of Wisconsin-Madison.

the economic feasibility of modernized, small-scale agriculture and see parcellation as leading to either inegalitarian land reconcentration or a plethora of low-productivity *minifundios*. These positions reflect the extremes of the general debate in Peru about the organization of agriculture for economic development. The goal of this chapter is to explore these changing strategies of agrarian reform in Peru and to identify the likely impact of parcellation on agricultural productivity and income distribution.

DECOLLECTIVIZATION OF COASTAL AGRICULTURE

Agricultural decollectivization has quickly changed the appearance of Peru's coast. Valleys which only a few years ago were uninterrupted expanses of a single commercial crop are now patchworks of fields, footpaths, and residences. To illustrate the impact of parcellation on coastal agrarian structure, Table 1 shows the change in farm-size distribution since 1980 in two valleys, Cañete and Chincha (which are discussed later). Parcellation has almost completely obliterated large-farm agriculture, most recently composed of CAPs, which previously controlled nearly 50 percent of agricultural land. CAP size averaged 710 hectares in these two valleys. Holdings between 3 and 10 hectares now dominate the agrarian structure: this size stratum contains 60 percent of the cultivated area.

The Sociopolitical and Legal Setting

The issue of what to do with the reform sector had been on the agenda of different Peruvian administrations, but it became more pressing by the second presidency of Fernando Belaúnde Terry. At Belaúnde's inauguration in mid-1980, many reform enterprises were in virtual bankruptcy (Munaíz and González 1979; Matos Mar and Mejía 1980; González 1985). The president's stance on the issue was complicated by the fact that he had never supported the collectivist reforms of the Velasco government. During his first presidential term in the mid-1960s, Belaúnde had espoused an individual, family-farm model of reform. During his second term, not surprisingly, he did little to stop (and much to facilitate) the subdivision of production cooperatives.

Parcellation of agrarian reform enterprises after 1980 had been preceded by attempts to restructure collective enterprises in both coastal (Piura, Chiclayo, Trujillo) and highland (Cusco, Ayacucho, Cajamarca, Cerro de Pasco) regions. These attempts were often triggered by financial instability of enterprises and member dissatisfaction with enterprise performance (Castillo 1980, 86–94). The restructuring process was explicitly considered by the Francisco Morales Bermúdez administration in its *1976 Plan Tupac Amaru*. Restructuring, according to the plan, would entail changes in size and type of enterprise as well as the implementation of new advisory and monitoring systems to oversee production (Castillo 1980, 86). The first official regulations for restructuring reform enterprises were issued in early 1978 and affected approximately 200 enterprises (Castillo 1980, 86; Vidal 1985, 178).

Table 1
Change in agrarian structure with parcellations, 1980–1986[a]

Farm size (hectares)	1980[b]				1986[b]			
	Number of farm units		Area[c]		Number of farm units		Area[c]	
Valley of Cañete								
< 3	5,007	(84.2)	3,049	(13.2)	5,007	(63.2)	3,049	(13.2)
3–10	694	(11.7)	4,439	(19.2)	2,679	(33.9)	14,752	(63.8)
10–50	201	(3.4)	3,550	(15.4)	201	(2.5)	3,550	(15.4)
> 50	25	(0.4)	1,760	(7.6)	25	(0.3)	1,760	(7.6)
CAPs	16	(0.3)	10,313	(44.6)	0	(0.0)	0	(0.0)
Total	5,943	(100.0)	23,111	(100.0)	7,912	(100.0)	23,111	(100.0)
Valley of Chincha								
< 3	8,500	(86.5)	3,665	(14.0)	8,500	(74.5)	3,655	(14.0)
3-10	1,136	(11.6)	4,573	(17.5)	2,739	(24.0)	13,596	(52.0)
10–50	140	(1.4)	2,755	(10.5)	140	(1.2)	2,755	(10.5)
> 50	33	(0.3)	2,737	(10.5)	33	(0.3)	2,737	(10.5)
CAPs	16	(0.2)	12,435	(47.5)	4	(0.04)	3,412	(13.0)
Total	9,825	(100.0)	26,155	(100.0)	11,416	(100.0)	26,155	(100.0)

[a] Sources: Figures for 1980 elaborated on the basis of information in Centro de Estudios de Desarrollo y Participación, "Diagnóstico técnico-económico de la actividad agrícola de los principales valles de la costa peruana" (Lima: CEDEP, 1985), and "Diagnóstico técnico-económico de la actividad agropecuario del Valle de China" (Lima: CEDEP, 1985), assuming that the structure of nonreform land was the same in 1980 as in 1985 and that all CAP land was farmed as a single collective unit. Information on parcellation was taken from CEDEP, "Diagnóstico técnico-económico de la actividad agropecuario del Valle de China" (Lima: CEDEP, 1985); Ministero de Agricultura, "Informes de la revisión de los procedimientos administrativas sobre el cambio de modelo empresarial asociativas agrarias" (Lima, 1986); M. Eresue et al., El proceso de parcelación de las cooperativas agrarias del valles de Cañete (Lima: Ministerio de Agricultura, 1985). In calculating postparcellation farm size, we assumed that all CAP land was parceled and that only legal reform beneficiaries received plots.

[b] The numbers in parentheses are percentages.

[c] In hectares.

The legal basis for governmental enterprise restructuring lay in the Velasco Agrarian Reform Law [*Decreto Ley* (D.L.) 17716] and its supplementary bill [*Decreto Supremo* (D.S.) 240–69-AP]. According to these laws, the government and enterprise members were co-owners of the property until the mortgage on the land was paid (Pasara 1978, 53; Vidal 1985, 178). After the 1979 Constitution forgave the agrarian debt, internal autonomy and undivided ownership rights were ceded to reform enterprises. Enterprise members were to obtain property titles from the government (D.L. 22748). While these changes ended formal governmental efforts to restructure agrarian reform enterprises, subsequent legislation opened the door to a thorough overhaul of the enterprises and their subdivision into individual properties.

In November 1980, the Belaúnde administration passed the laws needed for parcellation of reform enterprises. Most significantly, the new Law for the Promotion and Development of Agriculture, D.L. 2, permitted CAP members, by majority vote, to change the organization of their enterprise (Article 80). In addition, the law reinvigorated the land market by allowing the enterprise and its assets to be used as collateral for loans and agrarian reform land to be sold in payment for debts (Articles 49 and 53). Neither action had been permitted by previous agrarian reform legislation. In addition, Article 46 removed the CAP's preferential access to subsidized government credit. Until that time, the government had been the sole source of production credit for CAPs (Alvarez 1983a, 214–227).

Revesz (1985) argues that the overall strategy of the Belaúnde administration was to eliminate the CAPs and consolidate agriculture around an agrarian bourgeoisie of medium-sized producers. But the legal changes initiated by D.L. 2 did not comprise a particularly aggressive approach to reforming the agrarian reform for such an apparently bold design. The government essentially followed a "hands-off" policy and only established the legal preconditions for such a structural overhaul. Eresue et al. (1985, 2:7) argue that the Belaúnde administration was genuinely taken aback by the rapidity of the structural change which occurred under its laissez-faire rereform policy.

The wildfire spread of parcellation led to legal modifications designed to regulate and mitigate the side effects of the rapid structural change. Additional bills were issued to supplement D.L. 2, adding confusion to an increasingly complex body of agricultural legislation.[2] Laws issued in December 1984, changed the legal framework regulating parcellation. Vidal (1985, 180) enumerates a number of the new provisions: (1) a service cooperative must be created which, among other things, helps to maintain indivisible production assets such as dairy stables, (2) members opposed to parcellation are entitled to a multifamily agricultural unit for collective management, (3) only those enterprises which own their assets are entitled to convert, (4) criteria for changing an enterprise structure must protect the rights of both member and nonmember workers, (5) the Agricultural Bank (*Banco Agrario*) must provide an enterprise with the funding necessary to carry out the studies required before subdivision, (6) government approval of the parcellation plan and the subsequent property titling is required as collateral for members to obtain government loans, and (7) *parceleros* must be registered in the record of irrigation users (*padrón de regantes*). In practice, while many coastal CAPs are already subdivided, few have respected all these strictures (Vidal 1985, 177).

The Decollectivization of Coastal Agriculture, 1980–1986

Because of the unplanned nature of the process of change, no single, centralized source documents agricultural decollectivization in Peru. The rate of parcellation within any area seems to depend on local circumstances. Both Eresue et al. (1985) on Cañete and Torre (1985) on Lambayeque identify one specific CAP within their respective regions that functioned as the parcellation "demonstration plot." CAP Casimiro Chuman in the Chancay Valley initiated the first systematic reform of the cooperative model in Lambayeque when it subdivided in 1978 into a number of smaller groups. By 1980, Casimiro Chuman had moved toward one-plot-one-family parcellation.[3]

Neighboring CAPs slowly began to follow the lead of Casimiro Chuman. Some initial timidity (created in part by legal uncertainties) quickly gave way. By 1984, twenty-three of the thirty-nine nonagro-industrial CAPs in Lambayeque had been parceled.

In Cañete, CAP Tupac Amaru was subdivided in mid-1981 after intensive public debate. By late 1982, other Cañete CAPs followed. Within a year, fourteen of the sixteen CAPs in Cañete had decided to subdivide; by 1986 the remaining two had followed suit. A government study of the parcellation process in the Department of Ica (located just south of Cañete) notes that parcellation spread southward like a "contagion" (*Ministerio de Agricultura* 1986). Both Eresue et al. (1985) and Torre (1985) note that leaders from CAPs Casimiro Chuman and Tupac Amaru had participated in the assemblies during which neighboring CAPs chose to parcel. In the southern valleys, further testimony in favor of subdivision was given by *parceleros* of Lurinchincha (in the Chincha Valley), a fairly successful parceled farm dating from the 1960s and modeled on the Israeli *moshav*.

Parcellation spread throughout the Peruvian coast much as it had in Lambayeque and Cañete. Eresue et al. (1985, 8) estimate that by the end of 1984, 60 percent of the coastal CAPs had been parceled. Based on the *Centro de Estudios de Desarrollo y Participación* (CEDEP) studies of sixteen coastal valleys (CEDEP 1985a), Martínez (1986b) states that 75 percent were parceled as of mid-1985. A survey of the 214 delegates to the inaugural meeting of the Peruvian *Parcelero*

Association in December, 1985, yielded an average parcellation level of 72 percent for the eighteen valleys represented at the conference (ONA 1986). Government reports are entirely consistent with these figures (see MAG 1986).

In response to concerns about the possibility of pernicious effects of parcellation (for example, abandonment of dairies and other hard-to-subdivide assets), the government of Alan García Pérez announced a temporary halt to subdivision shortly after assuming power in mid-1985. By that time, an articulate opposition to the pattern of unbridled parcellation had coalesced.[4] García ordered the Ministry of Agriculture to undertake a review of parcellation and its effects. Although García subsequently rescinded his parcellation freeze (following opposition from would-be *parceleros*), the subdivision debate continues.

AN ECONOMIC ANALYSIS OF THE PARCELLATION DEBATE: THEORETICAL PERSPECTIVES ON THE PRODUCTIVITY CONSEQUENCES OF PARCELLATION

Because parcellation divides a large production cooperative into many individual units, it potentially affects resource allocation and use. The debate about subdivision and owner-operatorship concerns, inter alia, whether having many small decision-making units, as opposed to a single large one, intrinsically inhibits or promotes agricultural productivity. Drawing on the theoretical literature about agrarian markets and organization in an effort to clarify the issues involved, this section analyzes the microeconomics of parcellation and identifies hypotheses about the economic effects of subdivision.

Parcellation assigns to individuals the basic property rights to agrarian reform land that had been held collectively. Use and management rights pass unencumbered to individuals, along with rights to the receipt of income produced on assigned land. Correspondingly, individuals lose management and income rights on land assigned to others.

The shift in property rights with parcellation implies four changes that are of potential economic significance:

1. Work incentives are clear and irrefutable under parcellation.
2. The insurance devices, which were implicit in the joint ownership and income sharing of the CAPs, are eliminated.
3. The scale of the new primary decision-making unit is smaller than the optimal operational scale for some indivisible inputs.
4. Production is under the control of a household which has a different access to markets and which faces different effective prices than did the CAP.[5]

Uncertainty about the combined effects of these changes on the efficiency of resource allocation and use underlies the parcellation controversy.

A shift from large-scale cooperative to small-group production and then to individual-farm production represents a progression from ambiguous and indirect recompense to direct material reward in return for provision of labor and other inputs. Under owner-operatorship, the producer receives full value of increments to production created by his or her effort. Incentives to produce are undiluted by the realization that, in a production cooperative, product is shared among the other cooperative members more or less equally, regardless of quantity and quality of individual labor contribution.[6] Sharpening or concentrating otherwise dilute CAP incentives is one of the major changes wrought by parcellation. This change would, one might anticipate, elicit increased effort.

Clear incentives for individual parcel holders comprise a benefit against which must be balanced the disappearance of the implicit insurance received by a beneficiary when his or her income is averaged with those of all other members in a CAP. In the CAP, an individual's income is based on the average yield of a diversified portfolio of perhaps two hundred 4–5 hectare "plots." Still further diversification is possible in that each plot may be planted to several crops. This insurance scheme serves as a safety net of sorts for the mediocre or the luckless. Their misfortune is shared in the final income accounting, and their income is stabilized and increased by the superior performance of the fortunate or the skilled. Under parcellation, in contrast, income is tied to the yields of a single plot. The increase in risk of low income (and capital loss) that this change implies depends upon the degree of yield variation among plots. If all yields and incomes are fairly near the mean, then risk is not substantially accentuated by the move to individual farms.

To date, there has been no systematic study of the degree of cross-plot variation and the increase in risk due to parcellation. But two available case studies have shown that considerable differences in farming practice, skill, luck, and climate become manifest in marked interplot variation. Vergarra's (1986, 51) sample of 60 *parceleros* in the Chincha Valley, for example, shows that 7 percent had cotton yields below 30 quintals per hectare, 25 percent had yields between 30 and 40 quintals, 43 percent had yields between 40 and 50 quintals, and 25 percent had yields greater than 50 quintals. Carter's (1987) data from parceled, irrigated rice enterprises in the Dominican Republic show a coefficient of variation for yields of 16 percent, with a coefficient of variation of over 60 percent for net income. Figures of this magnitude are consistent with the hypothesis that some individual *parceleros* receive low or negative net incomes, even while other individuals, also former members of the same production cooperative, receive incomes that are highly positive.

Risk borne by an individual campesino would be of no allocational significance if a crop-insurance program from the government or an independent insurance provider were available. A well-functioning credit market, where *parceleros* could borrow to assure subsistence in bad times, could also serve to insure *parceleros* against risk. However, crop-insurance schemes are all but nonexistent in Peru, and access to the credit market for *parceleros* is tenuous. Carter (1987) shows that the complete sacrifice of CAP insurance in exchange for the undiluted incentives of parcellation is inferior, from the *parcelero's* point of view, to a mixed scheme that maintains some insurance at the cost of weaker incentives.

Insurance loss as a result of CAP breakup could also have negative social effects. If individual *parceleros* react fearfully to risk, they may "self-insure" by pursuing safer, and perhaps less remunerative and socially suboptimal cropping strategies. Under such circumstances, individual producers may shift to a cropping pattern that guarantees subsistence or minimizes cash exposure. Imagine, for example, a cash crop which requires large doses of purchased inputs. The danger of low revenues, caused by declines in either yield or price, could induce the risk-averting producer to reallocate land to low-value food crops which at least guarantee family needs if all else fails. Such a reallocation would be socially undesirable if average returns are higher on the risky cash crop. It might even jeopardize production of a marketable surplus needed to feed cities or generate export earnings.

A third economic feature of parcellation is that land is allocated in units smaller than the scale needed for optimal use or management of certain inputs. Such scale-sensitive, indivisible inputs include machinery, irrigation infrastructure, and agronomic knowledge (which few skilled individuals possess). CAPs were usually large enough to own or otherwise directly take advantage of these inputs, but small parcel size does not by itself indicate that scale economies will impair parcel productivity. Smallholders can potentially access some scale-sensitive inputs through rental arrangements (for example, custom plowing). However, market relations for other scale-sensitive inputs can be subject to productivity-reducing enforcement problems which occur when the small-scale buyer is unable to ascertain input quality (and compel its use) in advance. Technical assistance is one input likely to be so burdened. Market relations for other scale-sensitive inputs which require coordination between contiguous plots (for example, aerial application of pesticides) are prone to be rendered ineffective by negotiation problems. The overall efficiency of market relations in delivering scale-sensitive inputs to small farms affects both the productivity and distributional consequences of parcellation.

In a theoretical model, Eswaran and Kotwal (1985) show how enforcement problems (like those with technical assistance) can lead to the emergence of share contracts in spite of inherent incentive, productivity, and distributional problems with this contractual form. Despite these shortcomings, share contracts provide at least some incentives for both parties to the contract to provide hard-to-measure inputs (such as labor by a landowner and technical expertise by an agronomist). Also, where the market must be depended upon to supply necessary inputs, landownership rights by themselves may not result in substantially enhanced living standards,[7] as Kritsman noted in his 1920s analysis of land reform in the Soviet Union (see Cox 1984). In Kritsman's view, egalitarian distribution of land rights did not markedly improve peasants' economic position because the peasants remained vulnerable to having their rents extracted by monopolistic owners of traction power.

The fourth economic implication of parcellation concerns the small scale of farm units, since access to various markets (credit, input, or product) may be stratified by farm size. Small producers may, for example, find some markets completely closed to them. In other markets, terms of trade may be relatively unfavorable for small transactions. In a theoretical model, Carter (1988) shows how the costliness of collecting information from a large number of small producers may lead a competitive, profit-maximizing banking system that supplies credit at highly discriminatory terms or simply refuses loans to small farmers. Binswanger and Sillers (1983) argue that credit will be offered to small farmers only at terms that discourage its use. Furthermore, fixed transaction costs may raise the effective per-dollar cost of credit to small borrowers to prohibitive levels (see Adams and Nehman 1979).

The effect of differential market access on small-farm resource allocation and productivity has been analyzed by Feder (1985), Eswaran and Kotwal (1986), and Carter and Kalfayan (1987).[8] As opposed to their credit market problems, small farms are likely to enjoy relatively favorable access to the family labor "market." Because more child and self-supervising family labor may be utilized than on CAPs, small-scale landowners effectively have access to cheaper labor. The disadvantages of a hard-to-access credit market need to be balanced against the advantages of cheap labor. Feder (1985) shows that these two factors may offset each other and that small-farm and large-farm productivity per land unit may be similar. When crops differ in working-capital intensity and when credit markets must substitute for nonexistent crop-insurance programs, however, cheap labor does not completely cancel out the fact that credit is expensive or unavailable. Because of stratified access to labor and capital markets, shifts toward a safer, labor-using, capital-saving, product mix may be anticipated on parceled farms. Land productivity could fall on smaller units if capital constraints are severe enough (see Carter and Kalfayan 1987).

Access to other input and product markets is also likely to be stratified by farm size. Unfavorable terms of access to these markets for small farms has long been seen as a rationale for organizing service cooperatives. In Peru, the legacy of distrust of cooperatives brought on by the collapse of the CAP model makes this type of market-access problem likely.

In summary, microeconomic decision making is being restructured by reform of the Peruvian agrarian reform sector. Subdivision of CAPs results in changes in incentives, risk bearing, scale, and market access. From a theoretical point of view, the net effect of these changes on reform sector productivity is ambiguous. Parcellation provides a potent incentive structure, but the ability of *parceleros* to exploit scale and risk-sharing advantages (either indirectly through market relations or directly through cooperative organization) is open to question. Even when contractual relations are devised to substitute for the large scale of the CAPs, rents previously captured by CAPs may be redistributed away from reform beneficiaries and toward input suppliers and other middlemen. The immediate impact of parcellation on agricultural productivity and income distribution is thus uncertain.

Evolution of Agrarian Structure and Dynamic Aspects of the Parcellation Debate

Parcellation also has longer run implications for the stability and evolution of the reform sector. Correspondingly, the parcellation debate offers competing theories of structural evolution. Proponents of parcellation foresee a stable, small-farm system of land tenure rooted in an unambiguous incentive structure and with high production per land unit. Opponents argue that parceled agriculture will face endogenous economic pressure for further structural change, perhaps toward land reconcentration, on the one hand, and "minifundization," on the other. According to this latter view, irrigated coastal agriculture necessarily tends toward large-scale farming (Méndez 1986).

The shift to a smaller scale of agriculture in the transverse valleys on Peru's coast is startling by historical standards. Archaeological evidence traces the origins of agriculture based on large-scale irrigation back 2,000 years (Keith 1976). Indeed, the area irrigated by the precolonial system probably exceeded the contemporary cultivated area. Keith presents coastal Peru as one of Karl Wittfogel's classic "waterworks despotism" cases, where the fundamental necessity of large-scale irrigation dictates a pattern of centralized organization and control.

The relationship between large-scale waterworks and actual farm production organization in the precolonial period is not known. Better documented is the evolution of agrarian structure in the period since the Spanish conquest. Historical accounts discuss the appearance and consolidation of hacienda agriculture in the colonial period. Keith (1976) notes that middle-sized farms were rapidly swallowed up by emerging haciendas in the late sixteenth and early seventeenth centuries. Additional waves of land concentration occurred in the postcolonial nineteenth and twentieth centuries, with cycles of commercial boom and bust in sugar, cotton, and rice (see Arroyo 1981; Burga 1976; Klaren 1983). Klaren describes the decline of the small farmer and the destruction of small-town society in nineteenth century Chicama. Similarly, Burga documents the elimination of small-scale agriculture in the Lambayeque Valley. As more and more land fell under hacienda control, hacienda sharecroppers were simultaneously and systematically expelled and proletarianized.

This pattern of land concentration is consistent with de Janvry's (1981) vision of "functional dualism" in Latin America's agrarian structure; de Janvry hypothesizes that modern capitalist growth occurs in a large-scale "Junker" sector. The subordinate small-farm sector is deemed incapable of sustained growth, given the constraints and strategy options faced by its occupants. But, to what extent is this growth pattern the result of the intrinsic, technical weakness of small-scale agriculture? Or is this debility better explained by the social and political power of large-scale agriculture, which results in economic policy favorable to that sector's growth?

In Peru, evidence on these questions is mixed. Ramírez-Horton (1977) explains the historic pattern of land concentration in terms of the elites' political power which allowed them favored access to labor, irrigation water, and land. Klaren (1983) focuses on the power of elites to monopolize irrigation water, particularly in drought years. Because smallholders lacked access to capital markets, a bad year triggered by drought brought bankruptcy and resulted in land sales and further concentration. Like Klaren, Burga (1976) interprets unequal access to capital as the constraint that explains which farms survived and even expanded during cyclical downturns. Unequal market access has clearly been a compelling factor in the emergence and persistence of large-scale agriculture in Peru.

Yet there is little in this interpretation that forecloses the possible economic vitality of the small-scale agriculture that is appearing today. Burga (1976) explains that even the expansion of sugar plantations in nineteenth century Jequetepeque left some opportunity for smallholders who were able to obtain contracts for sugar production. *Minifundio* agriculture prospered from 1932 to 1962 as formal credit expanded and domestic food demand increased. Davies (1984) presents a history of colonial agriculture in Arequipa, a region where haciendas did not dominate, and shows that smaller scale agriculture can at least coexist with the organizational imperatives of large-scale waterworks. Fonseca's (1983) discussion of traditional, collective water-control institutions in Cañete leads to the same conclusion.

What the historical record of land concentration implies for the economic viability of parcellation is thus unclear. Privileged access to water and credit was clearly an important precursor of land concentration. But when access to water and credit was even partially democratized, and terms of trade were favorable, smaller scale agriculture became reasonably productive and able to survive.

THE DECISION TO PARCEL: MACRO- AND MICROECONOMIC FACTORS

Financial difficulties were experienced by the agrarian reform enterprises from the late 1970s through 1982, when parcellation began on a large scale. The financial crisis of the early 1980s is indisputable. Gross profits per CAP member (expressed in 1983 U.S. dollars) peaked in 1979 and then declined sharply. CAPs exhibited large losses in 1981 and 1982. Even the gross profits of the group of Cañete CAPs identified by Eresue et al. (1985, 2:129–132) as being the strongest socially and economically experienced a severe economic shock. CAPs in ten additional coastal valleys covered in the CEDEP (1985b) study reveal a similar pattern. In all ten valleys, average gross profits were negative in 1981 and 1982. Positive average gross profits were recorded in five of the ten valleys for 1978, in eight valleys for 1979, but in only three valleys for 1980.

To what extent is this financial distress and subsequent parcellation explained by the failure of the CAP organizational form? Following Putterman (1985), problems with cooperative production that lead to parcellation will be divided into (1) those that resulted from factors intrinsic to the cooperative model itself and (2) those that were extrinsic to the organization, that is, those created by more-or-less spurious external circumstances and policy. A similar classification of reasons for parcellation characterizes other writings on the Peruvian experience (for example, Gols 1985; González and Torre 1985; Martínez 1986b; Méndez 1986).

The Extrinsic Factors: The Macroeconomic and Policy Environment

The 1969 reform was part of an urban-industrial, import-substitution development strategy. Within this model, agrarian reform was expected to fulfill several objectives, among them (1) to enlarge the internal market (through increasing the effective demand of peasants by redistribution), (2) to contribute to capital formation for the rapid industrialization of the country, and, above all, (3) to bring peace and social equity (through a fairer distribution of wealth and income).

As part of its industrialist development model, the military government implemented a number of measures that affected, particularly in the reform sector, agricultural prices, marketing, taxes, and credit. The overall effect of these measures was to assure cheap foodstuffs for urban areas and to transfer surpluses from the most affluent of agricultural producers (that is, coastal cooperatives) to the urban industrial sector. In this context the reform enterprises were only a small subsystem, subordinate to the macroeconomic policies of the larger development model. Among these macroeconomic policies were measures designed to have a direct impact on agriculture, including price and credit policies. Other measures devised for the macroeconomic management of the entire economy, such as exchange rate, fiscal, monetary, and trade policies, indirectly affected agriculture. These latter measures were particularly important to the coastal reform sector because of its large share of agricultural exports.[9] This section briefly discusses the impact of the macroeconomic policies which had a direct impact on the financial status of the CAPs.

Government intervention in pricing and marketing has been widespread in Peru throughout this century. The government has imposed prices and has even marketed fertilizers, urban foodstuffs, key agricultural exports, and agroindustrial products. The 1968–1980 period saw a dramatic increase in government intervention. A decrease occurred with Belaúnde after 1980.

Regulations initiated in 1968 differed from those of previous administrations in at least three ways: (1) the military government established a new administrative structure, representing more government intervention in price regulation of urban, consumed items, (2) most agroindustrial inputs were regulated through the Public Agency for Agricultural Services (*Empresa Pública de Servicios Agrícolas*, EPSA), and (3) the government monopolized marketing for major agricultural exports produced by the CAPs (sugar, cotton, and coffee) and fixed domestic currency prices for these same goods.[10]

Through its market control over sugar, cotton, and coffee production, the government negatively affected incomes of agricultural producers. For sugar and cotton produced by CAPs, the government fixed both price and amounts to be sold internally; only residual production could be exported. Therefore, producers were unable to benefit from higher international prices (Valdes and Alvarez 1984). A number of deductions were made from the price of exported goods to cover marketing costs. Sugar cooperatives were required to sell to the domestic market at a fixed price during the 1971–1975 period, while their export earnings were heavily taxed. If the sugar CAPs had been allowed to sell sugar at the prevailing external market price, their estimated average gross profits would have been 130 percent higher than what they actually were (Alvarez 1983b, 257). Instead, sugar CAPs registered negative profits for the 1976-1980 period (Amat y León and Martínez 1986, chap. 3). In cotton, estimates showed that producers barely covered production costs during the 1975–1979 period (Alvarez 1983b, 246–249; Amat y León and Martínez 1986, chap. 3). The result was an income transfer from the cooperatives to both the state and consumers. Another indication of the negative price policy that was applied to CAPs is the evolution of terms of trade, defined as the ratio of farm-gate price to agricultural cost of production for export crops and agroindustrial crops. Terms-of-trade calculations indicate a steadily deteriorating trend during the 1970s (Alvarez 1983a, 259–260; Billone et al. 1982, 68).

The Belaúnde administration liberalized the macroeconomic climate within which the CAPs operated. The exchange rate was devalued, potentially improving domestic currency receipts for exports. Price controls were relaxed for some crops grown by the CAPs. However, this liberalization policy did not generally succeed in reversing the severe decline in agriculture's terms of trade. Indeed, coincident with liberalization in 1981, the decline *accelerated* for many crops (see Eresue et al. 1985; Amat y León and Martínez 1986). [Rice was an exception to this pattern—see Franklin et al. (1985).] In 1972, 499 kilos of cotton were sufficient to pay for a fixed, 1-hectare input package; in 1979, 623 kilos were needed to buy the same package; in 1982, 1,246 kilos were necessary (Eresue et al. 1985, 2:33).

Tax laws written after the 1969 Agrarian Reform Law was enacted reveal the state's intention to increase agriculture's contribution to public revenue. This applied with particular force to the coastal reformed agroexport sector, which paid the bulk of agriculture's indirect taxes (Alvarez 1983b, 175–189). The reform sector could not evade taxes, since the state had access to CAP accounting records. Internal data from the Sugar Cooperatives Financial Management Office show that total taxes paid by CAPs in the 5-year period after 1971 fluctuated between 24.2 percent (1972) and 72.6 percent (1975) of gross profits. Data collected by the *Instituto de Estudios Peruanos* from 183 CAPs in 1978 indicate that coastal CAPs paid taxes at a rate seven times higher than the reform enterprises in the Highlands and the Ceja de la Selva (upper jungle) (Alvarez 1983b, 187). From 1980 to 1985, the Belaúnde administration reduced financial pressure on coastal CAPs by decreasing the percentage and/or eliminating many of the export and other taxes charged to the CAPs (Priale 1982, 27; Martínez 1986a, 487).

The credit policy was probably the one positive measure, aside from the land distribution itself, which the military governments applied to CAPs throughout the 1970s. CAPs were given government preference in obtaining loans, often at negative real interest rates. In 1970 about 27 percent of the credit granted through the Agrarian Bank went to the CAPs; by 1975 this figure had risen to 66 percent, and in 1978 it was still high at 61 percent (Alvarez 1983c, 12).[11] In this matter, CAPs did more poorly under Belaúnde. Their share in Agrarian Bank credit fell to 47 percent in 1981/82; by the mid-1980s, it was 34 percent. As total real credit was also contracting at this time, CAPs faced severe cutbacks in formal credit. In addition, beginning in 1981, real interest rates became positive. Eresue et al. (1985) and Amat y León and Martínez (1986) show that financial costs rose to extraordinary proportions of total production costs during this time, in excess of 35 percent in some instances.

In summary, reform enterprises were, from their creation, subordinate to extractive policies designed to foment industrial capital accumulation. Economic liberalization in the early 1980s failed to reverse agriculture's unfavorable macroeconomic environment. To compound the problem, drought conditions prevailed during 1982/83 in the northern Coast, where sugar and a large share of cotton and rice are produced. This history of extrinsic factors undoubtedly explains much of the CAP financial crisis.

Intrinsic Factors: Microequilibrium in the CAP

The nature of agricultural production makes assurance of labor inputs a difficult task under any institutional regime, but agricultural production cooperatives have intrinsic problems with achieving a disciplined labor supply. Like the haciendas before them, CAPs must assure effective labor inputs in order to utilize resources efficiently. Piece rates and direct supervision both are devices to encourage more effort, and they can be used by either CAPs or haciendas. The specific problem of CAPs lies in the difficulty which CAPs have in generating the *authority* (or, alternatively, esprit de corps) to enforce (or entice) ample work for the tasks at hand.

In contrast to the CAPs, the *hacendado* had relatively unambiguous authority, which was enforceable through his ability to withhold payment in the face of a generally pliable and unorganized labor force. While elimination of the *hacendado's* power was a reform goal, the authority gap created must be filled with some other institutional mechanism. One alternative is democratic authority empowered to enforce work and payment rules. However, enforcement of any kind of supervisory authority among peers is difficult, even by elected officers. The effectiveness of direct supervision was further undercut by essentially egalitarian payment rules which were adopted on many CAPs. Even the piece-rate scheme attempted on some CAPs failed to elicit the necessary work effort, because work-quality norms were not enforced (McClintock 1981).

A second alternative to *hacendado* authority is bonds of mutual social obligation and commitment, which elicit work effort without the need for intense supervision or precise reward-penalty payment rules. Family labor is typically portrayed to operate on such a principle. However, the large-scale CAPs lacked the apparently natural and given social ties of the family unit that make such a labor-control system work.

While endemic to agricultural production cooperatives, the authority problem is not insolvable. Carter (1985b) describes CAPs where efficient resource utilization was achieved through either effective rule-enforcing authority or bonds of mutual social obligation. But these mechanisms are far from automatic, and many CAPs apparently had problems maintaining any pattern of coordination or control of labor (Carter 1984). The misincentives which can lead CAP productivity to deteriorate when authority mechanisms are absent can be briefly explained.

If a CAP member assumes that others will work diligently, he may slacken off and "free ride" on the efforts of others. With everyone working hard, the individual will experience little loss of income from his own indifferent work habits while appropriating all the benefits of increased on-the-job leisure. If, on the other hand, the other workers provide only minimal labor, the individual will still profit by negligent rather than diligent behavior. For if he worked hard, he could be described as being exploited by the others. If all individuals follow this strategy and slack off regardless of other's behavior, overall production and member income levels would suffer.

In a formal model of cooperative production, Carter (1987) demonstrates that the internal equilibrium of the CAP will, without authority devices, tend toward this low-effort, low-income position over time. While the individual CAP member would find this position unambiguously inferior to a high-effort, high-income equilibrium, the preferred equilibrium position is unstable and cannot be maintained because, in the absence of effective institutional devices to control opportunistic behavior, individuals constantly face incentives to free ride. Within the context of this model, parcellation appears as an individually rational response to the inferiority of the CAP equilibrium.[12]

In 1986, interviews with members of parceled CAPs in the Huaral Valley north of Lima uncovered personal commentaries that reflected the model's implications. One *parcelero* described the enthusiasm born of the agrarian reform, which initially had motivated individuals to work hard—even on Sundays. By 1977, however, cooperative hard work and solidarity had given way to minimal effort.[13] Informal interviews in 1981 revealed that on central coastal CAPs, members may have worked no more than a 4- to 6-hour day. CAPs responded to this low labor effort by hiring nonmember wage workers—a reaction that helped maintain farm yields while reducing the net farm incomes of individual members (operating costs were higher with the new wage bill).[14] In the Cañete Valley, Gols (1985) reports that use of hired labor became so extensive that, by 1981, over two-thirds of all CAPs averaged fewer than 3 hectares per full-time labor unit, even though the reform had assigned more than 4 hectares per CAP member in Cañete.

This low-effort, low-income equilibrium would not lead to parcellation if CAP members preferred this position to higher effort alternatives. But "revealed preferences" of CAP members after parcellation document its perceived inferiority. Interviewed *parceleros* report large increases in both hours worked and personal income after parcellation. Vergarra's (1986) survey in the Chincha Valley reveals an average workday of over 9 hours on the parcel. Only 7 percent of Vergarra's respondents reported working fewer than 8 hours a day. Eresue et al. (1985, 95) calculate that their sample showed earnings at least 22 percent higher with parcellation than with CAP membership.

While CAP microequilibriums motivated parcellation from below, the social inferiority and undesirability of such an equilibrium are open to question. A side effect of labor laxity on CAPs was employment generation for individuals left out of the agrarian reform. Peru's reform, like those of many countries, has been criticized for benefiting only a privileged stratum of "upper poor" (Thiesenhusen 1979; de Janvry 1981, 220). The intrinsic labor problems of the CAP model inadvertently extended second-class reform benefits to the many individuals hired as full-time wage laborers, or "permanent-temporary" workers, as they became known. Gols's (1985, 13) figures for Cañete show that this phenomenon increased the number of reform beneficiaries by 25 percent. In this sense, parcellation is a reappropriation by original reform beneficiaries of full reform benefits.[15]

If the extension of reform benefits which resulted from labor indiscipline on CAPs is valued positively, this result must be weighed against the social cost of any economic inefficiency intrinsic to the CAPs. The hiring of nonmembers did at least partially salvage the productivity of economically scarce land resources under the CAP system. However, the available evidence does point to residual productivity problems on many CAPs.[16]

In summary, intrinsic problems with the production-cooperative model sparked CAP-member interest in parcellation. These same problems help explain the financial weaknesses of the reform enterprises. The labor-effort problem required CAPs to hire additional workers and, thus, increased their production costs. At the same time, agricultural policy, which was meant to benefit industry, left CAPs with a thin profitability margin. The sharp decline in post-1980 profitability discussed above, even in CAPs which were least burdened by intrinsic problems, points to the negative impact which macroeconomic policy played in the reform sector. While extractive macropolicy and overemployment of temporary workers provide a weaker social than individual CAP-member rationale for parcellation, no institutional pattern with a major core of individual dissatisfaction can be stable in a democratic environment.

Microeconomic Equilibrium under Parcellation

Evidence presented in the preceding section indicates that *parceleros* work more hours on their own land after parcellation. Such a reallocation of labor time is consistent with theoretical expectations based on the strong, unambiguous incentives created by parcellation. The key question remains this: "What are the economic effects of the stronger work incentives in the new system?" Earlier discussion identified constraints which potentially limit the productivity of individual small-scale agriculture. Drawing on studies and on field interviews, this section continues to sketch the microeconomics of *parcelero* production.

At least in part, increased labor inputs by *parceleros* and their families substitute for labor previously performed by hired workers. Eresue et al. (1985, 2:90) show that *parceleros* have substituted family for hired labor in all but harvesting tasks. Only 30 percent of Vergarra's 1986 sample hired any nonfamily labor. Gols's (1985, 32) data on the labor intensity of production in Cañete show that sampled *parceleros* produced corn and potatoes with almost the same number of labor days per hectare as CAPs, while parcels in cotton absorbed 20 percent more labor per hectare. If parcellation simply induces a substitution of family for hired labor, the intensity of production will not change, but there will be major distributional consequences as reform beneficiaries reappropriate their reform benefits.[17]

The 1985 survey of Eresue et al. shows that the average *parcelero* in Cañete hired 244 days of labor a year, with much variation around this mean depending on differences in family size.[18] Not only does this evidence seemingly contradict that of Gols and Vergarra, but, at this level, use of hired labor would seem to exceed that on CAPs.[19] More multiple cropping on parcels than on CAPs could explain some of this contradiction.

While data on the labor intensity of *parcelero* production are ambiguous, there is consistent evidence that machinery use declines with parcellation. Eresue et al. (1985) and Gols (1985) agree that *parceleros* use between 10 and 50 percent fewer machinery hours per hectare than did the typical CAP. This reduction may be interpreted as a planned substitution of human labor (or animal traction) for machine power. But the decline appears to result, in part, from scale and organizational problems which prevent individuals from obtaining use of machinery. Of Vergarra's sample of sixty, 30 percent named scarcity of machinery as their principal production problem (in total, second only to water scarcity) on newly parceled land.

Legal regulations, introduced in late 1984 after several years of unbridled parcellation, did require the establishment of a service cooperative (called a *Cooperativa Agraria de Usuarios*, CAU) to provide machinery and other scale-sensitive inputs and services. To meet these legal requirements, subdividing CAPs initially set aside a common area of 50-100 hectares to produce the income to finance CAU operations. Each *parcelero* was to work a day or so per week on the communal enterprise. In practice, however, the CAUs collapsed, largely because there was no mechanism obliging members to work the required number of days (see Eresue et al. 1985, 2:124; ONA 1986). In addition to faulty institutional design, the CAU demise may have been the inevitable result of the legacy of distrust in cooperation. Lacking any form of cooperation, *parceleros* thus face a stark economic environment as unorganized, small-scale farmers.[20] In this sense, parcellation in Peru has created a radical individualization of production.

One impact of this disorganized decollectivization is visible in the decapitalization of ex-CAPs. Four years after parcellation, ex-CAP San Antonio in the Chincha Valley displayed a surrealistic graveyard of broken-down machinery. Only one of the eleven tractors inherited from the CAP still functioned in 1986. The system of diesel-powered wells that had permitted farming in the dry season had deteriorated. Of twenty-two wells in operation at parcellation (1982), eleven were still working in 1984, and only two in 1986. A dairy and 75 hectares of citrus trees, which were to be maintained by the CAU, were no longer producing. The cattle had been sold, and the overgrown orchard property was subdivided. In its day, San Antonio was a well-run CAP, one that operated without marked internal strife. Its rapid demise, along with that of its CAU, is all the more startling in this context. While there are no data on the generality of the San Antonio experience, reports of scarce machinery and declining dairy production indicate that its decline is not altogether unusual (see Eresue et al. 1985, vol. 2; MAG 1986).

Radical decollectivization also means a loss of production planning. Coordinated input use between parcels is rare. Integrated pest management and aerial cotton fumigation have disappeared in Cañete and Chincha.[21] Prior CAP planning, aimed at keeping production levels in line with demand, has given way to a pattern of over- and underproduction for the Lima market, with consequent price and income instability.

Questions about the ability of each *parcelero*, individually and unaided by collective action, to obtain access to scale-sensitive inputs, technologies, and markets become more serious with a radical decollectivization. The eventual ability of the market to service the parceled sector adequately can only be conjectured at this stage. As to credit access, the *Banco Agrario* has reportedly been willing to make individual *parcelero* loans, despite huge transaction-cost increases and other disincentives. Nonetheless, the ONA *parcelero* survey (1986) reports that only 33 percent of *parceleros* is financed individually by the *Banco Agrario* (with perhaps another 15 percent financed indirectly through CAUs), despite finding that 91 percent of survey respondents desired official credit. This credit inadequacy is likely to become more grave as remaining CAUs collapse. The severity of resulting credit constraints will depend on the functioning of informal and private credit markets.

Parcelero access to technical assistance has also been problematic and will likely become more so as extreme individualization continues. In the Cañete and Chincha valleys, for example, the *Banco Agrario* provided funds for technical assistance as part of its smallholder loan package. Despite efforts to increase the supply of qualified personnel, *parceleros* indicate that the quality of the technical assistance has been unsatisfactory.

An alternative mode of *parcelero* access to credit and technical assistance was reported in the Huaral Valley, where a type of sharecropping has emerged in which the *parcelero* contributes land and labor and a second party provides capital, technical aid, and economic expertise. The logic of such arrangements is explored by Eswaran and Kotwal (1985), who argue that this sharecropping supplies some added incentive for the adequate provision of inputs such as capital and technical assistance. Adoption of a share contract corrects a weakness in small-scale agriculture, but, as with other share contracts, remains a "second-best" solution because input-provision incentives are diffuse.

A partial substitute for these sharecropping arrangements is credit provision by output buyers, which occurs more commonly. The buyers provide production credit as a cash advance against future crop purchase. Discounting the sale price for the crop pays the accumulated interest. Unfortunately, no studies have been done on the implicit interest rates of these types of contracts. An advantage of this credit form is its low transaction cost relative to formal loans (informal interviews; Eresue et al. 1985, 2:118–120).

In summary, the failure of parcellation to create a viable, co-operative service structure leaves the *parceleros* to fend for themselves in the marketplace. Wiener (1985) writes that *parceleros* have turned themselves into "little fish," waiting to be devoured, their land to be taken by the "big fish." The Eresue et al. study (1985) comes to similar but less metaphoric conclusions on the weak market position of *parceleros* relative to the agrarian elite.

To date, there have been no annual productivity comparisons between parcellation and the CAP mode with the same resource base.[22] Only scattered information on cropping patterns and yields is available. Eresue et al. (1985) describe a pattern of increased crop diversification as *parceleros* gain experience. Upon subdivision, Cañete *parceleros* produced cotton almost exclusively (as did the Chincha *parceleros* in Vergarra's 1986 study). For later seasons, Eresue et al. document a shift to a preferred cropping pattern which included subsistence and noncotton, commercial crops.[23] They describe this preferred pattern as a "safety-first" strategy, in which the *parcelero* first guarantees family subsistence against inflation and other risks and uncertainties, and only then produces cash crops. Another force for crop diversification is the need to conserve on financial and capital requirements. Short-cycle crops are planted to finance subsistence, pending the harvest of 9-month-maturity cotton. Perhaps reflecting this pattern of self-finance, Eresue et al. (1985) detect an increase in cropping intensity as *parceleros* gain experience. In their sample, the ratio of area harvested to area owned rose from 1.17 to 1.32 over the 1982/83 to 1984/85 period. Interview respondents were unanimous in reporting a greater allocation of land to subsistence food crops after parcellation. The ONA (1986) survey reports that 13 percent of *parcelero* land was devoted to family food crops. However, no such cropping shift can be discerned in unpublished Ministry of Agriculture crop statistics.

Although the statistical base is weak, several authors have concluded that crop yields have remained more or less constant under parcellation (see Gols 1985, 31; Eresue et al. 1985, 2:91). Gols surveyed ten *parceleros*, all on the same ex-CAP, for the 1983/84 crop year. Average yields obtained on the ex-CAP from 1977–1981 were about 10 percent higher than the *parcelero* averages. *Parcelero* averages were in turn about 10 percent higher than the averages for all Cañete CAPs for the 1981/82 crop year. The Eresue et al. (1985) survey gave an estimate of average *parcelero* cotton yields of 53.4 quintals per hectare over the 1982–1985 period, in contrast to a 58.3-quintal average yield on Cañete CAPs from 1977 to 1982. *Parcelero* potato yields were slightly higher than the CAP average (4.9 versus 4.7 metric tons). While all these yield averages are broadly similar, without larger samples and multivariate analysis, which controls for differences in climatic and other conditions, not much can be concluded about yields and the relative technical efficiency of *parcelero* production.

To summarize, production possibilities under parcellation are constrained by the failure of beneficiaries to maintain institutionalized cooperation and coordination. Market access to credit, machinery, and technical assistance on the part of individual parcel holders is uneven. In the CAP breakup, obvious benefits from production planning and collective marketing were inevitably lost. Despite these constraints, and despite the clear production incentives that parcellation establishes, no radical change in crop yields has been detected. Production is less capital intensive, but evidence on labor use is unclear. Cropping patterns are changing in response to credit constraints and the logic of a risk-averting subsistence strategy. Available data are insufficient to determine whether these changes represent any significant, enduring social gain or loss. Parcellation has probably created important once-and-for-all losses in productive capacity because CAUs have proved unable to maintain indivisible capital assets. Whether these organizational difficulties will create problems for future accumulation and maintenance of irrigation infrastructure remains to be seen. But the performance of individualized agriculture in Peru will depend also on the macroeconomic environment.

Macroeconomic Environment and the Viability of Parceled Agriculture

Not enough time has elapsed to assess the effect of García's agricultural policies. So far, after a short hiatus, the García administration did give a renewed "go ahead" to parcellation. But, despite popular anticipation of enormous and dramatic change, the government's initial measures have been more or less consistent with those of the military and Belaúnde administrations. The first policy effort of the García government was to assure reasonably priced, urban foodstuffs by imposition of price controls and subsidies. Marketing of these urban foodstuffs continues to be an important administrative function for government. Policy-making officials in the García administration apparently are concentrating on the short run, however, with almost no consideration of longer term goals (see Hopkins 1986). Many policies from former governments that aimed at managing the macroeconomy have simply been continued.

García's government inherited not only a very unstable political environment but also a dismal economic situation, plagued with both fiscal and external trade disequilibriums. Given this framework, it will be difficult to devise enlightened sectoral policies. García's first policies toward coastal agriculture do not seem very promising for producers: once again, the state put a brake on agricultural profitability through its price policy. Moreover, the fixed, nominal foreign exchange system that the administration imposed still taxes agricultural exporters, though it does contain inflation. This, in a sense, is giving a reprise to the policies that so devastated agricultural income and productivity in the 1960s and 1970s. If large farms had trouble then, can new and viable *parcelero* farms develop now? Any answer must be qualified. First, despite the continuing low profitability of agriculture, the new *parceleros* have little or no choice: alternative employment is not readily available—the *parceleros* must survive, whatever macroeconomic constraints the government may devise. Second, *parceleros* must be flexible enough to change their production techniques and enterprise patterns when more profitable alternatives appear. Third, coastal producers may, in the end, find economic advantage in unified pressure for more favorable policies.

TOWARD THE LONGER TERM: STRUCTURAL DYNAMICS OF PARCELLATION

The longer term evolution of Peruvian agrarian reform agriculture under parcellation is hard to divine. Resource allocation and productivity levels under the new regime are only now becoming measurable. Pending additional research,[24] we advance some preliminary ideas about the longer term consequences of the new small-farm structure.

There is no evidence of fundamental, irremediable productivity problems that threaten the economic viability of decollectivized agrarian reform farms in the short term. However, a basic, unresolved question is the ability of this sector to maintain its residual capital assets and to accumulate new ones. While the reform sector's inability to capitalize itself would have negative distributional consequences over the longer term, such a failure need not forebode a reconcentration of landownership structures if markets can be devised to deliver access to new technologies and techniques.

Assuming that postparcellation agrarian reform agriculture is fundamentally viable, differential success among *parceleros*—and not the exertion of bold political power from an outside elite—could form the basis for future structural change. Evidence on the exact degree of differentiation occurring among *parceleros* is still weak. Eresue et al.

(1985, 2:94) suggest, without supporting data, that such differentiation is substantial. Vergarra (1986) estimated income levels from his sample and found that the poorest 7 percent received gross profits of approximately $66 (U.S. dollars) per hectare, while the richest 15 percent earned gross profits of $335 per hectare.[25]

A critical issue is whether this degree of differentiation is sufficient to initiate land transfers and an unequal growth path, a process described by Lenin and others. If producers operate on a thin profit margin because of predatory macropolicies and excessively extractive input-market relations, land transfers probably will occur. As the history of hacienda land concentration in Peru shows, secure access to capital markets plays a critical role in maintaining longer term enterprise stability through periods of cyclical downturn. And credit access is not presently secure for *parceleros*.

Limited direct evidence on postparcellation structural change comes from Torre's (1985) study of the Lambayeque Valley. His figures show that 564 hectares, out of a total of 10,190 hectares that had been parceled, were subsequently sold. Torre suggests that such transactions could underlie the emergence of a new stratum of medium-sized (50–100 hectare) properties. Properties of such size could produce more stable income streams, allow better credit access (Carter 1988), and, hence, provide greater economic survivability over time than 4-hectare parcels. Whether such a process is likely to affect the postparcellation structure of Peru's agrarian reform sector, and what will happen to those who are displaced, remains to be seen.

CONCLUSION: LESSONS FROM THE PERUVIAN EXPERIENCE

The decollectivization of Peru's agrarian reform sector tests the ability of small-scale units to sustain high-productivity agriculture on socially acceptable distributional terms. To the extent that national circumstances permit land reform to appear on the political agenda, organizational questions become paramount because the rapid growth of capitalism in agriculture implies that any land to be reformed is likely already to be in high-productivity use (Lehman 1978). The need to minimize economic loss may dictate organizational choice.

In examining Peruvian decollectivization for lessons, two questions emerge: Is parcellation an improvement over the system of cooperative production established in the CAPs? Is parcellation the best possible policy alternative?

Parcellation released CAP members from a low-effort, low-income equilibrium; their own evaluation of the change has been quite positive to date. A societal evaluation of the change is ambiguous. Change in the aggregate productivity of scarce resources cannot yet be measured as either positive or negative. Parcellation strengthened the rights of the original beneficiaries of agrarian reform at the expense of the permanent-temporary workers, who had become an implicit group of reform beneficiaries on the CAPs. The longer term productivity and stability of the new sector is yet to be seen, and the net impact of parcellation on social productivity and distributional goals is still unclear.

Is there an organizational alternative superior to both fully collective or fully parceled agriculture? The seeming tragedy of restructuring Peruvian reform agriculture is that the remedy was postponed so long and was, because of beneficiary discontent, so radical. At the time of decollectivization, the CAPs, together with the "cooperative movement," lost legitimacy. Whether this loss is irreversible remains to be seen.

NOTES

1. Though parceling of reform enterprises has occurred in other regions of the country, the process elsewhere is not as extensive as in the coastal region. The current administration is also allowing the reform enterprises of the Highlands to "restructure," as in the case of reform enterprises in Puno [*Decreto Supremo* (D.S.) 006-AG, 5 Feb. 1986]. See "Informe Agrario (19)," *La República*, 4 Apr. 1986, p. 5.

2. See D.S. 147–81-AG, D.S. 001-82-AG, D.L. 85, D.L. 141; Vidal (1985, 179).

3. Decollectivization of the agrarian reform sector in the Dominican Republic also demonstrated this process of an intermediate stage of small-group production as a prelude to parcellation. See Carter and Kanel (1985) for details; see also chapter 11 in this volume.

4. Much of the debate over parcellation took shape in newspaper columns, particularly in *Observador Nacional*. Méndez (1982, 1986) and Figallo (1982) are more accessible statements of opposition to—or at least concern about—negative impacts of parcellation.

5. The fact that the new production unit is a joint production-consumption household would not affect its production logic and behavior *if* markets for all goods and services were "perfect" in the sense of neoclassical economics (see Singh et al. 1986). In practice, this stricture is unlikely to hold. While the discussion in the text does not explicitly include new household or peasant production logic, it does indicate where market imperfections are likely to cause *parcelero* production behavior to deviate from the apparent dictates of profit maximization. This indirect approach to household production is taken in order to stress that households produce "like peasants" because of constraints, not because of an innate peasant logic.

6. Few CAPs seemed effectively able to implement payment rules that link income to work effort. For more discussion of the general problem, as

well as for examples of successful alternatives, see McClintock (1981) and Carter (1985b).

7. The income distribution effects of such contractual relations in Eswaran and Kotwal's (1985) model are shaped by the agent's economic opportunities outside the contract. If the smallholder's income opportunities without contractual provision of needed inputs are weak, then he or she is liable to be squeezed down to a relatively low living standard—perhaps not all that different from that of a landless worker.

8. Eswaran and Kotwal (1986), for example, show that credit constraints may produce a class of smallholders who are unable to cultivate competitively and must exit direct production. Carter and Kalfayan (1987) have a richer model of class structure in which binding credit constraints create a class of low-productivity, semiproletarian producers.

9. For a theoretical as well as an applied analysis of the impact of these indirect policies on agriculture, see Valdes (1985, 1986). A recent study of Peruvian trade policy, agricultural prices, and food consumption with an economywide perspective during the 1960s and 1970s (Franklin et al. 1985) found, among other things, that high protection of the industrial sector affected real exchange rates and caused an effective taxation of agriculture. In particular, a deterioration in real imports was required. That is, direct and indirect measures applied to Peruvian agriculture reinforced one another to affect the economy of the CAPs negatively.

10. Coffee was produced not by CAPs but by service cooperatives (CAS) composed of individual landholders. CAS provide members with a number of services, for example, marketing of inputs and outputs, in order to foster agricultural activity.

11. Alvarez (1983b, 222–224) developed a simulation exercise to show the high dependency of reform enterprises on public-subsidized funding. The purpose was to determine the gross profitability rates necessary for CAPs to cover all financial costs and maintain fiscal equilibrium. She made diverse assumptions regarding the various financial costs encountered. The exercise showed that in the most optimistic circumstances, CAPs needed a gross profit rate of about 20 percent to obtain financial equilibrium. Under less optimistic but still realistic assumptions, the gross profit rate would have to be somewhat higher than 113 percent to guarantee enterprise survival. These high required rates are a good indicator of the permanent liquidity problems that developed in these enterprises.

12. Parcellation may be an improvement over uncoordinated collective production and income sharing, but, in formal models, Carter (1987b) and Putterman and DiGiorgio (1985) show that the individually optimal institution mixes elements of parcellation with collective production and income sharing. Carter's result is driven by the risk-sharing advantages of cooperative production, while that of Putterman and DiGiorgio reflects scale advantages available in the cooperative sector.

13. In their study of collective agriculture in the Dominican Republic, Carter and Kanel (1985) describe a similar process of demoralization and decline in effective labor supply over time. Gols (1985, 25) and Eresue et al. (1985, 2:54) report the same sequence in Cañete CAPs.

14. This equilibrium should not be interpreted to mean that CAP members consumed leisure exclusively with their spare time and energy. Sideline economic activities filled some of that time, though no documentation exists of its extent or effect on family incomes.

15. The fate of permanent-temporary workers has been a contentious issue in parcellation. Most such workers have simply been left out. In late 1984, the government required CAPs to include these workers in parcellation. In one Huaral Valley CAP, this regulation was translated into 50 hectares set aside for thirty-five permanent-temporary workers (full members received 4 hectares each). In Lambayeque, where the CAPs relied on fewer outside workers, permanent-temporary workers received 2–4 hectares versus 7–10 hectares for members. Informal interviews suggest that many CAPs have simply made no such provision, despite the law. Bruno Revesz (personal communication) noted that parcellation in one area in Piura was inhibited by kinship and community ties between CAP members and permanent-temporary workers. CAPs in that area apparently were reluctant to "fire" their compatriots through parcellation.

16. Carter's (1984) econometric analysis offers some inference on the issue of CAP productivity. He finds CAPs, on average, to be technically less efficient than private producers for the two crops studied. (His analysis does, however, implicitly impute economic value to labor.) Over the entire range of production activities, Carter finds large variation in efficiency among CAPs, which suggests that CAPs varied widely in their ability to maintain resource productivity.

17. Permanent-temporary workers were frequently relatives of CAP members. If these individuals were absorbed into the family economy of the parcel, then the distributional consequences of parcellation could be mitigated. However, one interview in Huaral suggests that such absorption is not taking place. A group of permanent-temporary workers (one-half of whom are sons of reform beneficiaries) is fighting for inclusion in the parcellation plans of a CAP in that valley.

18. It is unclear whether this figure includes any family labor. Vergarra's survey in Chincha revealed that a substantial percentage of parceleros pays wages to family laborers.

19. While there are figures on the number of permanent-temporary workers on CAPs, precise calculations of days worked by casual wage labor are not available. Thus, comparison of labor market demand between CAPs and *parceleros* is difficult. Nonetheless, the estimate of 244 hired worker-days per *parcelero* is high given that, on average, there was only one permanent-temporary worker for every four CAP members.

20. Whether the CAUs have collapsed as uniformly as most authors believe is an issue that requires more research. Torre (1985, 245) notes that some informal networks of cooperation have emerged around old social ties.

21. An exception to this observation is ex-CAP Unión Campesina in the Cañete Valley. According to Eresue et al. (1985), this farm had retained sufficient organizational vigor to coordinate production plans and technology such that collective services—aerial fumigation—could be used. In contrast, a classic "holdout" story emerged from interviews in Chincha. There, the holder of a parcel in the midst of a large cottonfield refused to pay his share

for fumigation. Under such pressure, collective efforts quickly collapsed. Also gone is an integrated, pest-management scheme in Cañete potato production (Douglas Horton, personal communication).

22. As noted in the second section, personal income is estimated to increase with parcellation. But, because parcellation also has redistributive effects, this income increase cannot be interpreted as directly indicative of a net increase in value added and social efficiency. In addition, personal income figures for CAPs exclude value of collective services (30 percent of direct income in Carter's 1984 data) and amounts stolen.

23. Eresue et al. (1985, 84) note that 70 percent of their sample monocropped cotton in the 1982/1983 season. By 1985/1986, only 38 percent monocropped, while 25 percent grew three or four different crops.

24. Several research projects have been initiated recently to study the economics of parcellation. Among these efforts is work by Figallo and Amezaga (DESCO, in Lima) and Melmed and Carter (University of Wisconsin-Madison).

25. These gross profit figures include all labor as a cost of production. Family earnings would, thus, be higher than reported figures.

REFERENCES

Adams, D., and J. Nehman. 1979. Borrowing costs and the demand for rural credit. *Journal of Development Studies* 15:165–176.

Amat y León, C., and D. Martínez. 1986. La rentabilidad de la agricultura en relación con el sistema económico. Planteamiento metodológico para simular políticas alternativas. Mimeograph. Lima: Universidad del Pacífico, Centro de Investigación.

Alvarez, E. 1983a. Government policies and the persistence of rural poverty in Peru, 1960–1980. Ph.D. dissertation, New School for Social Research, New York.

———.1983b. *Política económica y agricultura en el Perú, 1969–1979.* Lima: Instituto de Estudios Peruanos.

———.1983c. Government policies and the persistence of rural poverty in Peru, 1969–1982. Paper presented at the 11th International Congress of the Latin American Studies Association, Mexico City, Mexico, 29 Sept.-1 Oct.

Arroyo, E. 1981. *La hacienda costeña en el Perú. Lima.*

Billone, J., D. Carbonetto, and D. Martínez. 1982. *Términos de intercambio ciudad-campo, 1970-1980: Precios y excedente agrario.* Lima: CEDEP.

Binswanger, H., and D. Sillers. 1983. Risk aversion and credit constraints in farmers' decision-making: A reinterpretation. *Journal of Development Studies* 20:5–21.

Burga, M. 1976. *De la encomienda a la hacienda capitalista.* Lima: Instituto de Estudios Peruanos.

Carter, M.R. 1984. Resource allocation and use under collective rights and labour management in Peruvian coastal agriculture. *Economic Journal* 94:826–846.

———.1985a. Cooperativas, parcelación y productividad: Por una alternativa mixta. *Socialismo y Participación 29*: 45–51.

———.1985b. Revisionist lessons from the Peruvian experience with cooperative agricultural production. *Advances in the Economic Analysis of Participatory and Labor Managed Firms 1*:179–194.

———.1987. Incentives and risk sharing in the decollectivization of agriculture. *Oxford Economic Papers 39*:577–595.

———.1988. Equilibrium credit rationing of small farm agriculture. *Journal of Development Economics 28*:83–104.

Carter, M.R., and J. Kalfayan. 1987. An economic model of agrarian structure in Latin America. Department of Agricultural Economics, Staff paper, no. 279. Madison: Department of Agricultural Economics, University of Wisconsin.

Carter, M.R., and D. Kaimowitz. 1986. An economic model of agrarian class structure . Draft. Madison, Wisc.

Carter, M.R., and D. Kanel. 1985. *Collective rice production in Finca Bermúdez: Institutional performance and evolution in the Dominican agrarian reform*. LTC research paper, no. 83. Madison: Land Tenure Center, University of Wisconsin.

Castillo, H. 1980. La reestructuración de la tenencia de la tierra y de las empresas asociativas. In *Promoción agraria? para quien?*: Análisis de la Ley de Promoción y Desarrollo Agrario, edited by J.M. Mejía, pp. 84–104. Lima: Tiempo Presente.

CEDEP (Centro de Estudios de Desarrollo y Participación). 1985a. Diagnóstico técnico-económico de la actividad agrícola de los principales valles de la costa peruana. Mimeograph. Lima: CEDEP.

———.1985b. Diagnóstico técnico-económico de la actividad agropecuario del Valle de China. Mimeograph. Lima: CEDEP.

Cox, T. 1984. Class analysis of the Russian peasantry: The research of Kritsman and his school. *Journal of Peasant Studies* 11:11–60.

Davies, K. 1984. *Landowners in colonial Peru*. Austin: Univ. of Texas Press.

de Janvry, A. 1981. *The agrarian question and reformism in Latin America*. Baltimore: Johns Hopkins Univ. Press.

Eresue, M. et al. 1985. *El proceso de parcelación de las cooperativas agrarias del valles de Cañete.* 3 vols. Lima: Ministerio de Agricultura.

Eswaran, M., and A. Kotwal. 1985. A theory of contractual structure in agriculture. *American Economic Review* 75:352–367.

———.1986. Access to capital as a determinant of the organization of production and resource allocation in an agrarian economy. *Economic Journal* 96:482–498.

Feder, G. 1985. The relation between farm size and farm productivity: The role of family labor, supervision and credit constraints. *Journal of Development Economics* 18:297–313.

Figallo, F. 1982. Cuatro tesis equivocados sobre las parcelaciones. *Quehacer* 29:46–50.

Fonseca, C. 1983. El control comunal del agua en la cuenca del Río Cañete. *Allpanchis* 22:61–75.

Franklin, D., J. Leonard, and A. Valdes. 1985. *Consumption effects of agricultural policies. Peru: Trade policy, agricultural policies and food consumption: An economy-wide perspective.* Report prepared by the Sigma One Corporation for the Agency for International Development. Raleigh, N.C.: Sigma One.

Gols, J. 1985. La parcelación de las empresas asociativas de la costa peruana: El caso del Valle de Cañete. Thesis, Universidad Nacional Agraria-La Molina.

González, A. 1985. Cooperativismo agrario y parcelación en la costa del Peru. In *Las parcelaciones de las cooperativas agrarias del Perú*, edited by A. González and C. Torre, pp. 75–142. Chiclayo: Centro de Estudios Sociales Solidaridad.

González, A., and C. Torre, eds. 1985. *Las parcelaciones de las cooperativas agrarias del Perú.* Chiclayo: Centro de Estudios Sociales Solidaridad.

Hopkins, R. 1986. Atrapados en el corto plazo? *Visión* (Lima), 20 April.

Keith, R. 1976. *Conquest and agrarian change: The emergence of the hacienda system on the Peruvian coast.* Cambridge, Mass.: Harvard Univ. Press.

Klaren, P. 1983. *Modernization, dislocation and aprismo.* Austin: Univ. of Texas Press.

McClintock, C. 1981. *Peasant cooperatives and political change in Peru.* Princeton, N.J.: Princeton Univ. Press.

MAG (Ministerio de Agricultura). 1986. Informes de la revisión de los procedimientos administrativas sobre el cambio de modelo empresarial asociativas agrarias. Mimeograph. Lima: MAG.

Martínez, D. 1986a. Tributación, precios y subsidios en el agro: diagnóstico y propuesta en el corto plazo. In *Priorización y desarrollo del sector agrario en el Perú*, edited by A. Figueroa and J. Portocarrero, pp. 483–501. Lima: Fundación Friedrich Ebert.

———.1986b. Unidad productiva y desarrollo agrario. In *Priorización y desarrollo del sector agrario en el Perú*, edited by A. Figueroa and J. Portocarrero, pp. 33–49. Lima: Fundación Friedrich Ebert.

Matos, J., and J.M. Mejía. 1980. *La reforma agraria en el Perú.* Lima: Instituto de Estudios Peruanos.

Méndez, M.J. 1982. Las cooperativas agrarias de producción y las parcelaciones; Situación actual y perspectiva. In *Situación actual y perspectiva del problema agrario en el Perú*, edited by F. Eguren, pp. 95–136. Lima: DESCO.

———.1986. Cooperativas agrarias y parcelación en la costa peruana. In *Priorización y desarrollo del sector agrario en el Perú*, edited by A.

Figueroa and J. Portocarrero, pp. 253–304. Lima: Fundación Friedrich Ebert.

Munaíz, J.A., and González, A. 1979. Informe de la visita a las CAPs azucareras norteñas (15–30 enero 1979). Proyecto reforma agraria y transformaciones en el Perú. Typescript. Lima: Instituto de Estudios Peruanos.

ONA (Organización Nacional Agraria). 1986. *Resultados de encuesta a parceleros*. Informe, no. 23–85. Lima: CEAF/ONA.

Pasara, L. 1978. *Reforma agraria: Derecho y conflicto*. Lima: Instituto de Estudios Peruanos.

Priale, G. 1982. La comercialización externa de productos agrarios. In *Situación actual y perspectiva del problema agrario en el Perú*, edited by F. Eguren, pp. 259–274. Lima: DESCO.

Putterman, L. 1985. Extrinsic versus intrinsic problems of agricultural cooperation: Anti-incentivism in Tanzania and China. *Journal of Development Studies* 21:175–204.

Putterman, L., and M. DiGiorgio. 1985. Choice and efficiency in a model of democratic semi-collective agriculture. *Oxford Economic Papers* 35:33–53.

Ramírez-Horton, S. 1977. Land tenure and the economics of power in colonial Peru. Ph.D. dissertation, University of Wisconsin-Madison.

Revesz, B. 1985. La reforma de la reforma en el agro costeño. In *Las parcelaciones de las cooperativas agrarias del Perú*, edited by A. González and C. Torre, pp. 191–214. Chiclayo: Centro de Estudios Sociales Solidaridad.

Singh, I., L. Squire, and J. Strauss. 1986. *Agricultural household models*. Baltimore: Johns Hopkins Univ. Press.

Thiesenhusen, W. 1979. The eighties: Will they be the decade of the peasant? *Land Reform, Land Settlement and Cooperatives* 1:35–42.

Torre, G. 1985. La parcelación y alternativas organizativas en las cooperativas agrarias de la Costa. In *Las parcelaciones de las cooperativas agrarias del Perú*, edited by A. González and C. Torre, pp. 215–270. Chiclayo: Centro de Estudios Sociales Solidaridad.

Valdes, A. 1985. Exchange rates and trade policy: Help or hindrance to agricultural growth? Paper prepared for 19th International Conference of Agricultural Economists, Malaga, Spain, 26 Aug.-4 Sept.

———.1986. Trade and macroeconomic policies' impact on agricultural growth: The South American experience. Typescript. Washington: International Food Policy Research Institute.

Valdes, A., and E. Alvarez. 1984. Government policy and food supply management in Peru, 1950–1981. Report prepared by International Food Policy Research Institute for Inter-American Development Bank. Washington: IFPRI.

Vergarra, R. 1986. Estudio de cooperativas agrarias en el Valle de Chincha. Working paper. Lima: DESCO.

Vidal, A.M. 1985. La legalización de la parcelación en las CAPs. In *Las parcelaciones de las cooperativas agrarias del Perú*, edited by A. González and C. Torre, pp. 177–191. Chiclayo: Centro de Estudios Sociales Solidaridad.

Wiener, R. 1985. La situación de la reforma agraria y parcelación privada. In *Las parcelaciones de las cooperativas agrarias del Perú*, edited by A. González and C. Torre, pp. 143–176. Chiclayo: Centro de Estudios Sociales Solidaridad.

Chapter 7

Law, Conflict, and Change: Frei's Law and Allende's Agrarian Reform

Joseph R. Thome*

Following the inauguration of Salvador Allende as president of Chile in 1970, a process of structural change was begun which was to shake the foundations of the country's institutions. Accelerated agrarian reform was an integral part of Allende's proposed program. Allende represented the Popular Unity (*Unidad Popular*, UP) coalition in the election; his platform had espoused construction of a legal road to socialism. In short, the UP aspired to initiate a social transition by operating within the system which its administration inherited.

According to Allende, this historic opportunity was made possible by the Chilean working class, which had managed to obtain both legal recognition and enforcement of certain basic social rights. This process had produced a unique structural context which not only allowed "the people to assume the political direction of the nation" (Allende 1971a, 13) but also provided the Chilean society, or so it seemed at the time, with institutions flexible enough to adapt to new demands and conditions—indeed, to allow for their own destruction and replacement by a more socialistic system. In Allende's words: "We have made the commitment that our revolutionary program will be carried out with full respect for the 'Rule of Law.'...[T]he principles of legality and institutional power are compatible with a socialist regime" (Allende 1971b, xii).

INITIAL PERCEPTION AND POLICY FORMULATION OF THE UP's AGRARIAN REFORM

According to the 1970 platform of the Popular Unity, Chile's economy and society were stagnant because of their economic dependence

* Professor of Law, Land Tenure Center Associate, and Director, Ibero-American Studies Program, University of Wisconsin-Madison.

on the developed countries and their internal domination by landlords and other members of the bourgeoisie. This elite was tied to foreign capital and was incapable and unwilling to solve fundamental problems of the country such as those of endemic poverty; these ties derived, moreover, from class privileges and would not be given up voluntarily. The reformist policies of Allende's predecessor government, that of Eduardo Frei, had not altered the situation significantly. The alternative, according to the UP, was to end the domination by "imperialists," "monopolies," and the "landed oligarchy" and to begin a transition to socialism (UP 1971a, 151, 152, 156).

Paradoxically, the transition was to be achieved through legally sanctioned means (UP 1971a, 158). Within this context, agrarian reform was to be a simultaneous and complementary process—a key element in the transformation of Chilean society (UP 1971a, 164). The agrarian reform process was to accomplish (1) a very rapid change in the land-tenure system, eliminating *latifundia* and stimulating cooperative organizations and socialist forms of production, (2) a change in the economic relationships between agriculture and the rest of the economy, (3) a change in the productive process, (4) industrialization of the rural sector, (5) active campesino participation in the entire process of change, and (6) special assistance programs for the most neglected groups, the Mapuche Indians and the *comuneros* or communal landowners (Chonchol 1971, 217–218).

One of the principal mechanisms for accomplishing these objectives was the power of the state to expropriate rural properties and, subsequently, to redistribute this land. To this end, the agrarian reform that was "on the books" from the Frei era was to be accelerated. All farms that exceeded 80 basic irrigated hectares, including such formerly excluded holdings as fruit orchards, vineyards, and forest reserves of lumber companies, were to be taken. Furthermore, the expropriation would also include all or part of the farm's inventory, and the landowner would not be able to select the location of the reserve; in fact, the campesinos to be benefited were to decide, on a case-by-case basis, whether any reserve rights were to be granted at all. Only small- and medium-sized farms were to be excluded from expropriation (under certain conditions), and expropriations were to be carried out in priority zones rather than on a farm-by-farm basis. The beneficiaries would participate directly in the formulation and application of the expropriation policies through their campesino councils. In short, the government would operate under Law 16.640 of 1967, the Frei Agrarian Reform Law, until such time as new legislation could be moved through Parliament (UP 1971b, 165, 181-185).

Once in office, the Popular Unity government was faced with the task of translating its amorphous and somewhat idealistic agrarian reform objectives into operational policy (Barraclough 1971, 14–33). At this point, UP found itself with an institutional and political puzzle that was to affect the reform process fundamentally. First, the agrarian reform program already had an administrative agency which had been in operation for several years; most of the bureaucrats who worked there had civil service tenure. Second, legal and institutional mechanisms were available which could, through inertia, administratively limit and restrict the government's scope of action. And third, some of the provisions of the existing legislation might (and did) come into direct conflict with stated campaign objectives of the UP.

Given its commitment to legality, the government had to choose: either it could amend the existing legislation and administrative structure before initiating its own agrarian reform program and thus avoid the vices of the old program, or it could try to do as much as possible under the extant legal-institutional framework until such time as laws could be changed. Conscious of the fact that its congressional representation was in the minority and that, even in the best of cases, a new agrarian reform bill would probably suffer interminable delays, the government opted for the second alternative (Chonchol 1972, 151–152).

THE LEGAL AND INSTITUTIONAL PARAMETERS OF ACTION

Even before Allende's inauguration, Popular Unity had made commitments which curtailed its future scope of action. Although Allende had received a plurality of the popular vote (36 percent), UP still fell far short of the constitutionally required majority. Under such circumstances, the Chilean Congress had the prerogative to select the president from the top two contenders: a conservative, Jorge Alessandri (a former president), and Allende.

Because the Popular Unity coalition represented barely one-third of the total in the Congress, it had to seek an awkward and almost embarrassing alliance with Frei's Christian Democratic Party (*Partido Demócrato Cristiano*, PDC) in order to obtain confirmation of Allende as president. As it turned out, the Christian Democrats would not commit themselves until Popular Unity had once again affirmed a formal adherence to the constitution and to the existing legal structure of the country.

This commitment presaged events in Congress. Due to anomalies in Chile's electoral system, no congressional elections were scheduled until March 1973. So, from 1970 until that time, the UP government had to live with an inherited Congress in which it was a distinct minority. The difficulty of ever achieving a majority vote soon became clear.

With the exception of the popular copper nationalization, Allende did not obtain legislative enactment of any of his programs.

Fortunately for the UP government, legislation enacted in prior administrations, particularly the short-lived "socialist republic" government of Marmaduke Grove (1932), the Popular Front government of Aquirre Cerda (1938–1941), and the reformist government of Eduardo Frei (1964–1970), provided the Allende administration with sufficient legal tools to initiate the "transition toward socialism." Imaginative use of existing legal instruments permitted the UP government to proceed much further toward its goals than most had expected at the outset.[1]

This chapter examines the legal and institutional instruments available to the Allende government for carrying out its program of agrarian reform and how these mechanisms worked. First, however, a review of the Frei reform program is in order, as the legal and administrative framework from this period played an essential role in shaping Allende's agrarian reform.

THE CHRISTIAN DEMOCRATIC AGRARIAN REFORM LEGISLATION AND PROGRAMS

Law 16.640 of 1967: The Political Antecedents

In November 1965, Eduardo Frei submitted to the Chilean Congress an agrarian reform bill to supplant the previous land reform legislation, Law 15.020 of 1962. This bill, passed in 1967, had taken more than a year to draft and represented the culmination of lengthy studies and public deliberations that had involved the participation of distinguished agronomists, economists, lawyers, politicians, and sociologists (Frei and Trivelli 1967, 5).

As in the UP case, agrarian reform had been one of the primary planks of the Christian Democrats' electoral campaign. The proposed program for the Frei government had promised to initiate a process of massive redistribution of land and water property rights to benefit those who worked the land directly, together with a comprehensive program of technical assistance, credit, and education for the campesino population (Menjivar 1970, 21). Frei's goal was to redistribute land to 100,000 peasant families during his 6-year term.

There were several reasons for the prominence of agrarian reform. Perhaps the primary consideration was the prevailing socioeconomic structure in the Chilean countryside, characterized by a concentration of land and water resources in relatively few hands—3,250 large rural estates, or 2.2 percent of the total number of farm units, each over 2,000 acres, controlled 68.8 percent of the total agricultural land. At the other extreme, 185,000 rural families owned no land whatsoever, and 117,000 owned or possessed tiny or *minifundio* plots, representing 78 percent of the total number of farms but only 5 percent of the agricultural land. According to the Christian Democrats, this had resulted in inefficiency and low productivity in the agricultural sector, as reflected in an increasingly unfavorable balance of agricultural trade. Social statistics were also unfavorable. In the early 1960s, there was a 36 percent rate of illiteracy in the countryside versus 11 percent in urban areas; large peasant migrations to the cities occurred between 1940 and 1960—approximately 1 million peasants, or 10 percent of the population, had moved to urban centers (Frei and Trivelli 1967, 7–11).

But more was involved than increasing the economic share of the agricultural sector as part of the development process—more even than improving an inequitable social structure, as urged by idealists or reformers motivated by an emerging, progressive current in Roman Catholic social thought. Of growing concern was the electoral support of the peasantry, once docile and dominated by conservative parties but now becoming increasingly independent and even militant (Loveman 1976a, 200–220; McCoy 1969, 48–49).

But while Frei and his followers (the *oficialista* sector within the Christian Democratic Party) were proclaiming a goal of individual family farms, members of the "leftist" (*tercerista* or *rebelde*) wings of the PDC envisaged a land-tenure system dominated by "communitarian" farms. Many of the PDC members charged with drafting and subsequently implementing the law, such as Jacques Chonchol, belonged to the *rebelde* wings (Thome 1971, 499). The final version of the statute preserved this distinction and permitted the establishment of communitarian, cooperative, and individual tenure structures, as well as combinations of all three (Law 16.640, 1967, Articles 67, 69, 81).

Despite leftist-sounding pronouncements, the PDC hierarchy was controlled by the *oficialista*, Frei-wing of the party. The development goals that the *oficialistas* espoused involved economic growth and control of inflation, not distributive programs (Kaufman 1972, 84). Reforms were to be moderate, and close private-sector cooperation was sought. For various reasons, however, the party's *terceristas*, though far from hegemonic, played the key role in drafting the agrarian reform bill, organizing the administrative apparatus, and implementing the reform and its allied legislation (Kaufman 1972, 87).

While still before Congress, however, the agrarian reform bill and its constitutional amendment authorization became subject to an intense, protracted, almost two-year debate. The *oficialista* wing of the PDC expressed its misgivings on the bill, the amendment,[2] and the changes proposed by right-wing politicians and by leaders of the National Agricultural Society (*Sociedad Nacional de Agricultura*, SNA), the powerful landowners' association. Among the amendments eventually passed—with the combined efforts of cabinet leaders and *oficialista* congressmen—were measures that made the landlord payment system in cases of expropriation more generous, raised the amount of land to be retained by expropriated owners as "reserves," and exempted certain vineyards from expropriation altogether (Kaufman 1972, 97). Nevertheless, the law finally enacted in 1967 was basically the same bill that had been introduced in November 1965. President Frei threw the weight of his prestige and authority behind the bill and the constitutional amendment: this made even rather conservative PDC members reluctant to break rank. Radical, communist, and socialist parties also gave their support, guaranteeing an ample majority in both chambers of Congress (Kaufman 1972, 94, 106).

While the 1925 Constitution permitted some expropriation of private property for reasons of public utility, it also stipulated that full, commercial-value compensation (its amount to be determined by the courts) was to be paid before the state could enter into possession of the property. The 1967 Amendment stipulated that new expropriation procedures and norms could be established through legislation, and it made possible a quicker and more expansive expropriation process. Agrarian Reform Law 16.640 was passed by Congress and promulgated on 29 July 1967 (Thome 1971, 499–500).

Until passage of 16.640, the Frei administration's agrarian reform program was implemented under the Land Reform Law passed in 1962 during the administration of Jorge Alessandri. This law established the two institutions which later administered the agrarian reforms under both Frei and Allende: the *Corporación de Reforma Agraria* (CORA), charged with acquiring land for subsequent redistribution, and the *Instituto de Desarrollo Agropecuario* (INDAP), charged with providing credit and assistance to agrarian reform beneficiaries and other smallholders (Thome 1971, 495). In addition to requiring full cash payment (as provided by the Constitution) before CORA could take physical possession of expropriated properties (Thome 1971, 495), other procedural requirements made the expropriation process under this law slow and cumbersome.

Nonetheless, between November 1964 and July 1967, CORA was able to negotiate the acquisition of 478 large farms with a total acreage surpassing 1 million hectares. Landlords were to be paid in installments over a 10-year period. These negotiated or "voluntary" settlements were made possible by the threat of the enactment of the Frei law, under which the terms of compensation would not be nearly as favorable to the landowner (Lührs 1969a).

After July 1967, CORA began to implement Law 16.640, soon finding it to be an ambitious statute. Notwithstanding other complementary new PDC laws and programs which would improve the status of rural labor by extending rural education and providing credit and technical assistance to smallholders, the heart of the Frei agrarian reform program was that it would provide both for quickly taking property and for efficient redistribution of land among landless campesinos. It would also nationalize and reallocate water rights (in the richest agricultural area of the country, irrigation is a necessity).

Consequently, Law 16.640 was complex and lengthy; its official text—160 pages of small type—contained 357 excruciatingly detailed and legalistic articles. In addition, Law 16.640 spawned a vast number of complementary statutes, regulatory decrees, and other legal provisions (Thome 1971, 500).

The Process of Expropriation under Law 16.640

Law 16.640 empowered CORA to acquire both privately owned and public land for the purpose of subsequent redistribution to landless campesinos. Lands susceptible to agricultural production held in the public domain or owned by government corporations or entities were to be transferred gratis to CORA, with the exception of lands held by government welfare agencies. These latter were to be compensated at "market value." Certain public property, such as the land held by the Urban Development Corporation, could not be expropriated (ICIRA 1968, 10, citing Arts. 28 and 29).

The law also authorized the expropriation of privately owned rural holdings (ICIRA 1968, 11). Farms could be expropriated for reasons of their large size, deficient use, abandonment, unauthorized subdivision, corporate ownership, lack of compliance with labor laws (which also governed tenants), small size (*minifundios*), and location (such as property within reclamation or irrigation projects). In addition, CORA could buy lands offered to it.

Because of their procedural complexity (which might well lead to a court case) or high cost, most of the reasons for which expropriation could take place were seldom, if ever, invoked. The PDC government carried out expropriations under the excess-size, voluntary transfer, corporate ownership, and unauthorized subdivision provisions (see Table 1).

The excess-size provision established that rural properties larger than 80 basic irrigated hectares (BIH)[3] were subject to expropriation regardless of their productivity. Certain communal property, such as the Mapuche Indian landholdings, were exempted. Owners expropriated under the excess-size criterion had a right to retain a portion of the property (a reserve), not to exceed 80 BIH.

Properties transferred voluntarily were categorized as "expropriations" by the law in order to subject them to the law's coverage regarding compensation. CORA was prevented from purchasing properties

Table 1
Number of properties expropriated and legal grounds used in CORA expropriations, July 1967 to December 1969[a]

Expropriation dates	Excess size		Low productivity	Unauthorized subdivisions	Corporate ownership	Voluntary transfers	Carry over from previous law	Subtotal	No data available	Total number of expropriations
	A[b]	B[c]								
07/67–12/67	51	7	1	4	12	4	8	87	19	106
01/68–06/68	26	3	2	—	5	34	15	85	4	89
07/68–12/68	30	19	—	—	15	53	14	131	—	131
01/69–06/69	29	20	1	5	5	56	2	118	13	131
07/69–12/69	16	47	—	7	8	54	4	136	47	183
01/70–06/70	—	—	—	—	—	—	—	—	201[d]	201
Totals	152	96	4	16	45	201	43	557	284	841

[a] Source: German Lührs and Joseph R. Thome, unpublished data from Corporación de Reforma Agraria, Dirección de Planificación y Control; Corporación de *Reforma Agraria, Reforma agraria chilena: 1965–1970* (Santiago: M-Graphic, 1970), pp. 36 and 38.
[b] By reason of excess size alone.
[c] Excess size *plus* declaration of abandonment or inadequate exploitation.
[d] Available CORA data (1970:38) fail to distinguish between excess-size expropriations with declaration of abandonment or inadequate exploitation and expropriations solely on the gournds of inadequate exploitation. Presumably, however, the 201 expropriations in 1970 would be distributed roughly among the same categories as in previous years.

at market value, but it was given the flexibility of acquiring otherwise nonexpropriable properties offered to it. The provision encouraged landowners who feared expropriation to offer their lands to CORA voluntarily: in this manner, they would obtain more favorable compensation than if they awaited expropriation (Thome 1971, 504).

Excess size and voluntary transfer accounted for approximately 70 percent of all Frei expropriations. They were easy and exempt from judicial review. In contrast, expropriations due to low productivity or abandonment were not only subject to judicial review but also required an elaborate verification process involving technical, economic, and social criteria for establishing whether the law applied (Vodanovic 1968, 285). Though the burden of proof was on the landowner (Law 16.640, 1967, Art. 1, Sec. C), CORA lawyers had to be prepared to rebut the landowner's evidence. Less than 1 percent of all the Frei government expropriations was based exclusively on low productivity or abandonment (Table 1).

"Corporate ownership" grounds for expropriation referred to rural property owned by corporations or other legal forms of business association. Various exceptions were provided by the law, such as for campesino cooperatives (Law 16.640, 1967, Art. 6). Approximately 6 percent of all expropriations under the Frei government was carried out under this criterion (Table 1).

The "unauthorized subdivision" grounds for expropriation were designed to prevent the circumvention of the excess-size provisions of Law 16.640 through the subdivision of large landholdings among family members or straw men (ICIRA 1968, 19; Law 16.640, 1967, Art. 5 and Transitory no. 1).

The Frei government, acting under Law 15.020 until July 1967 and Law 16.640 thereafter, expropriated about 1,319 properties totaling nearly 3.5 million hectares, of which 280,000 were irrigated (CORA 1970, 36). This represented 13 percent of the land under cultivation and 14.5 percent of the productive land. Under this reform, 28,000 families, representing 5–10 percent of peasant families with no land or insufficient holdings, received land (Chonchol 1976, 606).

Farms smaller than 80 BIH were not legally expropriable unless they were abandoned or poorly exploited (Art. 15). Other types of exempted properties were experimental or educational farms (Art. 26), forests, and land approved for reforestation (Art. 27). Finally, the president could exclude certain properties or portions thereof from expropriation (Arts. 21-25).

Specifically excluded from expropriation were animals, tools and equipment, and other machinery (ICIRA 1968, 11). These provisions encouraged landowners to claim the center of their farms, with the home, barns, and outbuildings as part of their reserve, and to strip the expropriated portions of needed installations, animals, and machinery. This meant that CORA or the *asentamientos* were forced to invest scarce funds to reestablish an economic infrastructure.

Although Law 16.640 attempted to legislate for every conceivable situation, lacunae and ambiguities were still common. In the case of reserve rights, for instance, no *minimum* size was established, nor was there any provision for landowners expropriated under the excess-size grounds who failed to qualify for a reserve. The subsequent Allende government made use of loopholes to limit reserve rights to substantially less than 80 BIH.

Compensation for Expropriated Property

Regardless of the grounds for expropriation, landlord compensation was limited to the amount of the current appraisal of the land for property-tax purposes plus the market value of improvements. Both were to be determined as of the date of the expropriation decree. Once notice of appraisals were provided to affected landowners, they had a 30-day period within which to file appeals to agrarian tribunals (Law 16.640, 1967, Arts. 42 and 43).

Although the basis for compensation was identical in all cases, the forms of compensation differed according to the grounds for expropriation. Because of Chile's endemic inflation (which meant that payment in bonds, with a long-maturity, fixed-price element, was subject to great value depreciation), these differences were significant. When the acquisition was based on excess size, corporate ownership, or voluntary offers to CORA, the landowner was paid 10 percent in cash and the balance in 25-year class "A" bonds.[4] Nevertheless, if CORA could show that a property so acquired was either abandoned or inadequately exploited, then the form of compensation was 1 or 5 percent in cash, respectively, with the balance in 30-year class "C" bonds. Although an expropriation based solely on grounds of abandonment or poor exploitation gave the landowner recourse to judicial review (which could delay the process for years), this was not the case when the declaration of abandonment or poor exploitation was attached to an excess-size expropriation. As the land reform proceeded, this device became more frequent (Table 1). CORA preferred to acquire properties through amicable settlements with landowners rather than following the entire expropriation process to its lengthy and costly conclusion. The remaining types of land acquisition had a panoply of different—and prescribed—forms of compensation.

Judicial Review of Expropriation

Law 16.640 created a special agrarian court system to resolve conflicts arising from the law's application. A provincial agrarian tribunal, or trial court, was provided for each province, and nine appellate tribunals were established throughout the country. The provincial tribunals were staffed by one regular judge and two agronomists; two regular appellate judges and one agronomist sat on the appellate tribunals (Law 16.640, 1967, Arts. 136-141).

This special court system represented an attempt to keep agrarian reform conflicts out of the regular court system and to provide for a rapid, simple, and technical process of review (Frei and Trivelli 1967, 28–29). Article 145 thus provided a comprehensive list of twenty potential expropriation conflicts over which the agrarian tribunals were to have exclusive jurisdiction; it included the legal provisions regulating the grounds of expropriation, forms of payment, methods of appraisal, taking of possession, and grants of reserve rights. Appeals from the final judgments of these tribunals were to be heard exclusively by the appellate agrarian tribunals. The role of the Supreme Court was thus to be limited to disciplinary actions (ICIRA 1968, 205).

The goal of a quick and nonappealable judicial review was not fully achieved. Under the guise of reviewing petitions which complained of the agrarian courts' abuse of authority or discretion (*recursos de queja*), the Supreme Court, in effect, often decided substantive issues in terse judgments that merely declared the wrongful or correct application of a statute. The Supreme Court also accepted jurisdiction over land reform conflicts where the landowners claimed that some articles of Law 16.640 were unconstitutional, even though cases on the matter in question were concurrently being heard before agrarian tribunals. Although the Court usually found that the applications of Law 16.640 did not violate the constitution, the appeals postponed taking possession of the affected properties by CORA and established procedural precedents that became significant during the Allende government.[5]

Findings from the province of Valparaiso indicate that during the Frei government, relatively few expropriations resulted in cases put before an agrarian tribunal. Of the twenty-six expropriations in Valparaiso between July 1967 and March 1969, only six were contested in these courts (Lührs 1969a, 21). During the Allende government, however, there was a substantial increase in the number of cases contested before the agrarian tribunals.

Taking Possession of Expropriated Property

Aware that cumbersome expropriation procedures in other countries and, indeed, under Law 15.020 had represented a major obstacle to a rapid and successful agrarian reform process, the drafters of Law 16.640 attempted to provide for a procedure that would minimize the time between the expropriation decree and possession taking by CORA (Frei and Trivelli 1967, 27–28). Thus, Law 16.640 provided that

CORA would receive transfer of a property after depositing with the civil court the cash part of the compensation. This deposit had to be made within a year after publication of the expropriation decree (Law 16.640, 1967, Art. 39).

In fact, quickly taking possession was not easily achieved. Although no data are available on length of time, an approximation can be made by comparing the date of the expropriation decree with the date of *asentamiento* (land reform settlement) organization. In over 50 percent of the cases that took at least 6 months; in 10 percent of the cases, the period exceeded 1 year (Thome 1971, 510–511).

Some of these delays were CORA's fault or the fault of the exchequer for not providing funds on time for the down payment.[6] This was often a conscious tactic: because of endemic inflation, the longer a fixed cost could be delayed, the cheaper it became. In this way, CORA could stretch its limited budget and expropriate more properties. Other delays were due to problems in arriving at the appraisal figures because of the lack of trained personnel, bureaucratic inefficiencies, and difficulty in obtaining agreements with owners (Thome 1971, 510).

The landowners' legal tactics also produced transfer delays. Aided by the conservative nature of most civil court judges in Chile, landowners were quick to object to CORA's deposit on the grounds that the appraisals were incorrect. Many judges accepted these complaints, and appraisals then became subject to regular civil court procedures, notorious in Chile for their complexity and length. In many cases, appeals to higher courts occurred (Lührs 1969b).

In most cases, the effect of judicial proceedings was limited to delays; the ultimate judgments usually favored CORA (for example, Corte Suprema 1969; Corte de Apelaciones-Temuco 1969). When judgments went against CORA, it had to start over, and sometimes these judicial procedures set important precedents which were to affect CORA's future scope of action during both the Frei and the Allende administrations.

The expropriation grounds most commonly applied—excess size—were based on very objective criteria set out in great detail by the law. Article 172, the relevant section of the law, consisted of nine pages of tables in which most of the country was divided into physical and geographical categories. For each, the hectarage equivalents of 80 BIH were provided. Thus, it was quite easy to establish whether any given farm or group of farms owned by one person exceeded this maximum so as to make the overage eligible for expropriation. On the other hand, the appraisals for improvements were subjective in nature, and reasonable people could produce widely divergent figures.

The Chilean government expropriated properties which were not immediately redistributed in small plots to campesinos. There was an intermediary stage, the *asentamiento*; this was a contract arrangement under which eligible campesinos were settled on the expropriated properties for at least three years. During this time, ownership of the land was retained by CORA, and all or most of the property was operated on a "production cooperative" basis. Day-to-day management of the *asentamiento* was to be conducted by an administrative committee elected by the members (*asentados*, or settlers) from among themselves. Supervision and assistance to the committee members was to be provided by CORA technicians until the campesinos developed more experience. Most of the economic and social inputs—credits, seeds, fertilizers, machinery, education, public health, and other community services—were also to be provided by CORA, while the campesinos provided the labor. At the end of the year, operating and administrative costs were subtracted from gross farm income, and the remainder was to be distributed among the *asentados*. In reality, this last step seldom occurred, either because the bookkeeping process soon became mired in administrative inefficiency or because CORA consciously decided to subsidize inefficient *asentamientos*.

Whether an individual or a cooperative title was ultimately distributed supposedly depended on the decision of the eligible *asentados*. Thus, if they decided that all of the land was to continue to be operated as a production cooperative, then the legal title was assigned to the cooperative whose members were the prior *asentados*. Alternatively, they could decide to divide the entire property into individual farms, in which case each would receive a title. In still other instances, a mixed system was a possibility, under which the cooperative would receive title over part of the land while the rest would be divided as individual parcels, each with its title. Whatever the type of land distribution, the beneficiary had to pay for the received share of land over a 30-year period, during which time the ownership rights were subject to restraints on alienation and inheritance (ICIRA 1968, 94–104).

Once most of these policies were faced with real situations, application diverged from goals. Toward the end of the Frei period, the administration of the land distribution program bore little resemblance to a coherent plan; rather, it seemed to be guided by ad hoc, politically expedient, pragmatic responses to various pressures.

The selection of members to the *asentamiento* is a case in point. While the resident laborers (*inquilinos*) from the expropriated farm were favored, the original policy had envisaged the incorporation of many peasants who had no access to land whatsoever (Menjivar 1970, 87). In practice, the *inquilinos* took control of the selection process and, with few exceptions, would not allow outsiders to become full-fledged *asentados*. Very few non-*inquilinos* became *asentamiento* members. This practice, sanctioned by CORA's silence, resulted in fewer peasant families receiving land rights than might have been supported by the expropriated properties. It also meant that the lucky beneficiaries began, as a group, to hire temporary labor in much the same way as had the former landowners (Menjivar 1970, 156).

On this and other production decisions, the *asentados* had a great deal of autonomy. Nevertheless, CORA always retained control over such fundamental decisions as planning, investments, credits, and marketing, providing little if any opportunity for *asentado* participation in some rather key matters (Echenique 1970, 106). Furthermore, *asentados* were dependent on CORA for the cash living advances (*anticipos*) paid monthly in anticipation of the harvest. The end result was a patron-client relationship between CORA and the *asentados* in which the clients were far from powerless in matters of internal administration of their affairs but were still dependent on CORA and other state agencies for contacts outside the farm gate (Lehmann 1974, 88–89).

By 1 August 1970, 98 of 910 *asentamientos* had been divided and assigned under conditional titles to 5,688 families. The benefited family always received a provisional, individual title, at least to their house and adjoining garden plot. The data do not indicate the legal forms—cooperative or mixed—under which the remaining land was distributed, though most was doubtless assigned to cooperatives. Of the 98 assignations, 65 were made between January and August 1970, leading some to suggest that the presidential elections of September 1970 were a basic stimulus.

AGRARIAN REFORM OF THE POPULAR UNITY

The UP's Initial Operational Policy

Choosing among alternatives and establishing policies were never a smooth process for the Popular Unity government, which represented an often uneasy coalition of various parties and movements, including Social-Democrats, Christian-Marxists, Socialists, and Communists. Not only were there historic conflicts among several of these parties, but some movements themselves suffered from serious internal divisions. Every policy decision tended to be subject to a fierce ideological debate, which often made its way into the mass media. President Allende himself frequently intervened to convince or bludgeon the squabbling factions to compromise. Forging an operational policy for the agrarian reform was no exception: even after the decision had been made to operate within the existing legislation, a debate arose as to which legal instruments to use as well as how and when to use them.

One government sector favored government intervention of farms designated by CORA for land reform. Chilean legislation had long permitted the appointment of a public official as the administrator or "intervenor" of an enterprise where a serious labor or social conflict had resulted in a production standstill. Such intervention would allow a rapid taking of possession of the whole property, including its machinery or inventory, thus preventing the dismantling of capital on the farm to be expropriated. A simple government decree was all that was required to set the mechanism in operation.

But intervention also had disadvantages. It could be used only where labor conflicts existed and an intervenor was needed for each case. There weren't enough qualified personnel for a massive process of intervention. More seriously, legislation stipulated that intervention was to be temporary, lasting only until the conflict could be resolved. Title to the property remained with the intervened owner (Law 16.640, Art. 171; CORA 1972a, 27; CORA 1972b, 12). Intervention could create insecurity among both current owners and potential beneficiaries. Finally, as intervention was violently opposed by small- and medium-sized landowners, its frequent use could further increase the political opposition to agrarian reform, to the UP, and to Allende.

The Allende government, like its predecessor, ultimately decided on expropriation as the favored device for land acquisition, with intervention to be used only for special cases (Chonchol 1973a). Peasant pressure, however, eventually forced the government to intervene on farms to a greater extent than anticipated. Labor conflicts, which could be solved only through intervention, were commonly instigated (or at least given tacit approval) by some government officials who considered their use as one more weapon in the public arsenal to break landholder power.[7]

According to Jacques Chonchol, Allende's Minister of Agriculture at the time, the initial expropriation policy of the UP was more technical-economic in character than revolutionary (Chonchol 1973a). Its basic goal was to expropriate all *latifundia* (farms with an area over 80 BIH) within two-and-a-half years. Farms smaller than 80 BIH were to be expropriated only in exceptional cases. In 1970 there were still approximately 2,000 farms over 80 BIH in the country; many more had been subdivided prior to the enactment of Law 16.640 and were, thus, no longer subject to expropriation for reasons of size.[8]

The short-run goal for 1971 was to expropriate half of these, or 1,000 eligible farms, preferably before June so they would be ready for spring planting in September. The UP government was anxious to carry out a more planned and controlled agrarian reform than the PDC, so it concentrated reform in certain key regions. A controlled expropriation process would also facilitate achievement of other objectives of the reform program, such as the creation of the Agrarian Reform Centers (*Centros de Reforma Agraria*, CERA), a new and transitory form of cooperative land-tenure organization which, it was envisioned, would correct the defects of the *asentamiento*. UP leaders also felt that the new government could sacrifice some immediate agricultural production for a larger expropriation program.

This experience shows again that, no matter how rational and careful, plans formulated by technocrats and ideologues must be tested in the crucible of real life. In this instance, the impetus for change was too strong for controlled agrarian reform. Organized campesino pressure soon emerged, demanding massive expropriation, even of farms smaller than 80 BIH if they harbored social conflict. The nongovernment ultraleft supported, and probably instigated, this movement, as did some left-wing elements within the UP. They also argued, ideologically, that exempting medium-sized holdings strengthens the agrarian bourgeoisie and, hence, the capitalist system (Chonchol 1973a).

The clearest manifestations of campesino pressure were the *tomas* (the illegal invasions of farms by campesinos); these were particularly prevalent in those southern provinces with high Indian (Mapuche) populations. During 1971, approximately 1,278 farms were occupied or invaded, mostly in the harvest months of January and February; this compares to 456 in 1970 and 148 in 1969 (Kay 1973, 13).

Responding to these pressures, the Minister of Agriculture and his staff moved to the zone of conflict and, for two months, operated from headquarters in Cautín. Here, amidst summer heat and political turmoil, the government reversed its long-standing policy of sending in the police in cases of farm invasions: it ordered the expropriation or intervention of the occupied farms.

The intensity of the *tomas* caused the government to reformulate its entire expropriation policy: sociopolitical rationale was substituted for technical and economic planning. Particular attention was given to farms with symbolic or political value. Priority was given to those farms where campesino pressure was intense, as long as legal justification for expropriation could be found. From this point on, expropriation was not restricted to *latifundia*; it also included farms between 40 and 80 BIH which were poorly exploited, abandoned, offered voluntarily by their owners, or otherwise met any of the criteria for expropriation established by Law 16.640.[9] Farms smaller than 40 BIH were to be expropriated only in very unusual cases (Chonchol 1971, 219–220). At this time, chafing under real and imagined expropriation threats, landowners began to accuse the government of "manufacturing" the elements necessary for expropriation or intervention and of instigating labor conflicts.

During the remainder of 1971 and 1972, the new expropriation strategy was carried out with relative success; the number of land invasions lessened. By early 1972, the principal objective was no longer the well-publicized expropriation of a few large farms but again focused on expropriating all farms larger than 80 BIH. During 1971, expropriation actions were initiated for 1,400 farms; in 1972 an additional 2,170 farms were affected, for a total acreage during the two years of 5.5 million hectares (CORA 1973).

In terms of BIH, by July 1972, 35 percent of the agricultural land in Chile was in the reform sector.[10] Of this total, 40 percent was expropriated during the Frei government and 60 percent during the first year and a half of the Allende administration (PNUD et al. 1972, III-3 and -4).

The rate of expropriation more than doubled in comparison with the prior government; by June 1972, there were only 200 private farms larger than 80 BIH left in the country. But the situation was not perfect: some 1,500 farms larger than 80 BIH had been subdivided in 1965–1966, the period after Frei's election and before enactment of 16.040 (PNUD et al. 1972, III-1). Furthermore, the approximately 75,000 campesino families benefiting from the reform process since its inception in 1965 until December, 1972, represented only 20 percent of the total number of peasant families in Chile (Barraclough and Affonso 1973, 71).[11]

Campesino Participation in the UP Agrarian Reform

A fundamental plank in Allende's campaign platform was the active participation of the organized working class in the proposed social change. Massive popular support was always deemed by the UP as a necessary condition for achieving a qualitative change in the nature of the state. A key to success for the UP was to promote and support the development of this "popular participation" (UP 1971a, 240).

In the area of agrarian reform, the objective of popular participation was to be achieved by peasant representation at all levels of government. For instance, all state agencies dealing with rural matters were to have a campesino representative on their board of directors. These representatives were to be selected by the campesino organizations themselves and were to replace the representatives of the large landowners.

More important was the plan to establish a national network of campesino communal councils, composed of a national executive committee council, regional councils, and local councils at the county or municipal level. These representatives were to be elected by campesino organizations and were to participate actively in the formulation and implementation of agricultural development policy, including the expropriation and distribution of agricultural landholdings (UP 1971b, 132).

More than symbolic trappings, these councils represented a basic operational component within the ideological framework of the UP.

The presence of the working class within the UP government was supposed to provide popular control over political-administrative actions to prevent the formulation and implementation of policies contrary to their interests. Not the least of the councils' objectives was to raise the class consciousness of the working class and to protect against the campesinos becoming passive within a new social order (Chonchol 1971, 240).[12]

On 6 January 1971, barely two months after Allende's inauguration, Ministry of Agriculture Decree no. 481 was promulgated, establishing the campesino councils. Somewhat surprisingly, the text of the decree and its regulations expanded but then qualified somewhat the participatory role of the campesinos. Instead of stipulating that the "*Consejo Nacional Campesino* will be charged with working with the government in all agricultural matters," as most campesino organizations had suggested in line with the UP platform, the decree read, "*Consejo Nacional Campesino* will be charged with transmitting the opinion of *campesinos* to the government in regard to agricultural matters . . ." (Loveman 1976b, 268).

According to the decree, the National Peasant Council was to be composed of two representatives from each of the legally recognized rural worker unions, two representatives from the National Confederation of Peasant Cooperatives, and two representatives from a small-farmer association (Kay 1973, 6–7). Because so few campesinos were affiliated, the decree thus excluded the 85 percent of the peasants who did not belong to any legally recognized organization (Chonchol 1971, 240). Moreover, the decree practically handed control of many of the councils, in particular the National Council, to organizations which were opposed to the government, such as the PDC-controlled *asentamiento* associations (Maffei and Marchetti 1972, 130).

While this circumscription of peasant opinion and representation can be partly explained by the limitations imposed by legislation, it also was the result of pressures from within and without the UP government. The Communist Party, for example, considered that the function of the councils should be as a conduit of opinion; it preferred to maintain power within the rural unions (Cantoni 1972, 83). On the other hand, peasant organizations fought for and pressured the government for the precise language which was ultimately contained in the decree. These organizations feared, with certain reason, that a massive peasant organization dominated by independent campesinos without any affiliation would erode the power of existing campesino organizations. According to Cantoni, "These considerations were vital for the organizations controlled by or affiliated to the Christian democracy...as they were in no condition to successfully compete in a process of massive peasant organization if the basis of this new organization would be the entire peasant population" (Cantoni 1972, 83). At the same time, the leaders of the existing organizations were interested in controlling the new councils so they could be used as instruments for maintaining or increasing their power base and sphere of influence with the administrative bureaucracy.

Provincial and county councils began to organize in accordance with the provisions of Decree 481, but peasant opposition and pressure surfaced almost immediately, particularly in the Mapuche areas of Cautín. This campesino mobilization was reflected by the organization of councils constituted through the direct vote of the independent peasant, which thus ignored the norms of the decree. These councils subsequently became known as *consejos de base*.

Not surprisingly, these *consejos de base* were prone to engage in such militant actions as *tomas* and shifting of land boundaries, and other direct acts of civil disobedience designed to force the government to intervene in or expropriate rural estates not originally included in CORA's operational plans. Because of this pressure, the government was forced to increase the rate of expropriation; it did not wish, however, to resort to repression (Cantoni 1972, 84–85).

In March 1971, Chonchol achieved an agreement with the Provincial Council of Temuco by which both parties agreed to organize communal councils with both representatives from preexistent and legally recognized organizations and representatives elected directly by the peasant population or the base. These councils were designated as *consejos ampliados*, or "expanded" councils (Kay 1973, 9).

While peasant councils played a significant role during the Allende agrarian reform, they certainly were not as important as originally conceived. The statistics are impressive. By June 1972, 186 county councils had been organized throughout the country: 110 in accordance with the provisions of Decree 481, 31 directly by the peasants, and 45 under the compromise agreed upon by the Minister of Agriculture and the Temuco Provincial Council (PNUD et al. 1972, V-26).

Many of the councils provided useful services for the peasants they represented. Often, they served as mediators in the resolution of conflicts between the peasants and the government. They also served as a useful channel through which county or local problems could be brought to the attention of the appropriate state agencies. In addition, CORA often consulted campesino councils in order to establish priorities for the farms to be expropriated. In some places the councils even began to oversee the work of public civil servants or bureaucrats (PNUD et al. 1972, V-31).

But, in general, the councils did not fulfill their primary objective: the active and dynamic participation of the peasants in the decisions and execution of agrarian policy. The National Peasant Council, for example, had met six times by June 1972, only to be informed of decisions already taken by the government. The function of the provincial councils was more symbolic than real, and those councils which functioned did so basically as mediators or pressure groups (Gómez 1973a).

Within government agencies, the role of the peasant representatives in the executive council of CORA was merely one of symbolic participation. CORA's regional officials did, however, take into account the petitions of the peasants regarding the land which should be expropriated.[13]

While legal obstacles to campesino councils partially explain the situation, a more important factor was the lack of coherent operational policy on the councils. The government never clearly defined their functions. In fact, it never provided a clear-cut decision or policy on peasant participation but rather muddled through with fuzzy pronouncements or ad hoc resolutions of pressing demands. This was primarily due to the ideological differences which existed within the UP. The Communist Party advocated a limited role for the councils as a conduit of opinion. For their part, the Socialists perceived the councils' role as the genesis of a new structure of public power. Finally, the Christian Marxists (MAPU) thought that the councils should represent a consensus among the various elements of the peasant classes.

In summary, workable mechanisms and procedures necessary for guaranteeing an active and efficient participation by the peasants in the formulation and implementation of the agrarian reform policy of the Popular Unity government were never established. This lack probably contributed to increased militance among the peasants. In the process, it forced the government to adopt a case-by-case approach to conflict resolution. This not only made the implementation of a well-planned and economically rational process of agrarian reform difficult, it also provided fodder for the political opposition.

The Legal Framework and the UP Agrarian Reform

The notion of an elastic legal system became a core concept within the Allende government's "legal road to socialism." It was conceived principally by Eduardo Novoa, Allende's chief legal advisor. Once the goal of a tightly controlled and technically oriented expropriation process had to be abandoned because of strong campesino pressures, the law was subjected to a stiffer test than was originally intended. A major rationalization of the 1973 coup was, indeed, that the law had been stretched so far that it left no legal boundaries at all.

But the parties opposing the government did not simply stand by while government attorneys manipulated the legal instruments for their own advantage. Although taken aback by the government's initial aggressive strategy, the opposition was not lacking in legal talent. Far from it, the opposition was, by experience and class position, better equipped to engage in legal battles within a legal-institutional framework. Always adept themselves at bending or stretching rules for the interest of the ruling classes, opposition lawyers now proved more than worthy adversaries to government lawyers.

Thus, by the beginning of Allende's second year in government—a watershed period, marked by both Fidel Castro's visit to Chile and the clamorous middle- and upper-class women's march with pots and pans—the first successful opposition mass rally was held. Indeed, opposition forces had regrouped, closed ranks, and initiated their own counteroffensive. In agrarian reform, the legal strategy of the opposition was more of a holding action than an attempt to unravel the reform. Nevertheless, the strategy was successful in trapping thousands of expropriation cases in a bottleneck of complex litigation, preventing the establishment of new land settlements in the affected properties, and forcing CORA to expend a substantial amount of its resources and effort to defend its actions. As the social conflict and polarity intensified, the legal system became ever more subject to the manipulations of the opposing camps.

Legal and Bureaucratic Constraints to the UP Agrarian Reform

Throughout its nearly 3-year administration, the Popular Unity coalition government had to be content with a relatively weak political position. Although the UP had won the presidency and its significant executive powers, it never achieved support from any opposition party, save in the matter of copper nationalization. Moreover, the UP government never gained control of key public agencies, and it quickly found itself at loggerheads with the judiciary. Finally, the armed forces acted throughout the period as the self-proclaimed watchdog of Chilean constitutionality (and, ultimately, its destroyer).

At this point the government had no choice but to act within preexisting legal and institutional channels. This legislation imposed serious limits on the agrarian reform. The legal definition of *latifundia*, for instance, included only farms larger than 80 BIH. This somewhat arbitrary legal criterion exempted a considerable number of large farms from expropriation, even though many exceeded 1,000 hectares in actual size and clearly represented *latifundia* in economic and social terms. By mid-1972, these exempt estates, added to the reserve rights granted to expropriated landowners constituted a total of 6,000 landholdings of between 20 and 80 BIH in size, or about 40 percent of the agricultural land in Chile (Barraclough and Affonso 1973, 81). While some of this land was theoretically expropriable under other legal grounds, the process was so difficult that it rarely merited the effort.

Moreover, as already noted, expropriations had to be carried out on a farm-by-farm basis, making difficult the creation of large reform units known as CERAs (*Centros de Reforma Agraria*), a type of producer's cooperative or collective favored by the UP. Nor did expropriations include the inventory, leaving the acquired portion with an inadequate infrastructure or requiring the use of scarce funds to purchase or replace the machinery, cattle, and other essential inventory (CORA 1972c, 16-18).

Moreover, the public institutional organization for the rural sector inherited by the UP government was characterized by duplication of services and a lack of clear-cut lines of authority (Barraclough and Affonso 1973, 122). Bottlenecks in the expropriation phase of the agrarian reform exemplified this problem. Because of the accelerated rate of expropriation during the years 1971 and 1972, the minister of agriculture requested other rural-sector government agencies to allow some of its appraisers to work temporarily for CORA. The support provided fell far short of need, producing serious constraints: during 1972, CORA could not take possession of thousands of farms whose expropriations had been initiated in a timely fashion because the appraisals had not been completed. While this situation was resolved during early 1973, the resulting undefined and insecure status of these holdings adversely affected production levels (Chonchol 1973b).

Other Political Constraints to the UP Agrarian Reform

The Allende government has often been criticized for lacking a coherent and unified agrarian reform policy and program. But a neat, coherent policy was difficult to achieve in the political turmoil prevalent in Chile. Moreover, the UP was a difficult and often unstable coalition of different parties and movements which could not agree on general policies or even on the analysis of the rural sector's problems, let alone on a specific operational plan. These differences were never resolved at the national level, and this resulted in diverse orientations and lines of action in the field. Following party lines made unified action on policy almost impossible (Gómez 1973b, 8–9).

A strong political opposition to the agrarian reform process grew in size and power as the opposition parties and groups joined forces and took the initiative away from the government. Nationally, opposition was reflected, for example, by the approval in Congress of a project of constitutional reform which would have again amended Article 10 of the constitution, undermining the legal base for expropriation of land without compensation at market price.

When the president vetoed that effort, opposition parties asked for a plebiscite on the subject, which was rejected by Allende. The National Society of Agriculture (SNA), through its various divisions and lines of action, managed to organize a solid political front among a diverse group of agricultural interests (such as large-, small-, and medium-sized landowners), professional associations (such as agronomists and veterinarians), supervisory employees (such as administrators and foremen), some peasants who had been settled in lands under prior agrarian reform processes, and even some rural workers. The SNA was thus able to establish a vigorous opposition to the UP's agrarian reform (PNUD et al. 1972, V-37-V-41).

There was even some campesino opposition to the agrarian reform policy of the UP government. Most of it was carried out through the rural organizations controlled by the Christian Democrats and the right-wing National Party (PNUD et al. 1972, V-41-V43). But peasant opposition did not come solely from organized political parties in opposition to the actual government. There were cases of peasants who opposed expropriation and other elements of the reform because of the clumsy bureaucracy. At times, CORA officials never bothered to explain clearly to peasants what the agrarian reform process would mean to them.[14]

CONCLUSION

The process of agrarian reform during the Popular Unity government was conflictive. Groups on the right bitterly denounced it for creating chaos in rural areas as reflected by land invasions and government interventions in rural estates. The inefficiency of the bureaucracy rankled others (Locke and Garrido 1972, 7–14; *El Mercurio* 1972, 3). Groups on the left also were critical, some feeling that the agrarian reform process was counterrevolutionary and left the structural base of capitalist production in Chile intact (*Punto Final* 1972a, 10, 1972b, 16-19). One of the most severe leftist critiques argued that the actual process did not correspond to the original plans, objectives, and goals of the Popular Unity government as announced in Allende's platform. According to this critique, the UP's agrarian reform was virtually indistinguishable from Frei's (Rivera 1972, 2, 7).

These critiques had some basis in fact, though they were exaggerated. But even evaluations fundamentally favorable to the government have indicated various defects and problems with the process. One claimed that there were problems of inadequate agricultural production and rural unemployment, that the new types of land settlements such as the CERA were not meeting their objectives, and that agricultural planning was ineffective (Barraclough and Affonso 1973, 74–75).

Were the UP government's initial premises incorrect? The Popular Unity government had made a commitment to implement its program within the preexisting legal-institutional framework. Existing legal channels proved, in the last instance, to represent obstacles and constraints to goal attainment. The product of a liberal-capitalist value legal framework had been elaborated to reach goals only superficially similar to the goals of the Popular Unity government.[15]

The agrarian reform policy and strategy of the Popular Unity government suffered defects for which the government could blame only itself. But elements of the inherited legal framework represented factors beyond government control. They imposed their own pattern on the process of agrarian reform. Given these limitations, the Popular Unity government may have advanced as far as it could in meeting its agrarian reform objectives.

NOTES

1. After an initial period of panic and disorganization, however, the opposition forces learned how to use the legal system to their own ends, becoming perhaps even more proficient at legal maneuvering than the UP. Thus, by mid-1972, the Allende government was on the legal defensive; the existing legal-institutional framework was now being used to place limits and restrictions on its own scope of action (Novoa M. 1970–1971).

2. See, for example, PDC Senator Prado's statements to the effect that private property rights are intimately related to the values of Christian civilization but should be limited so that more people could enjoy their benefits (Chile Senate 1966, 32).

3. A basic irrigated hectare was a conversion factor whose purpose was to "equalize" all landholdings in Chile. Thus, the number of hectares equivalent to 80 basic irrigated hectares varied throughout the country. The conversion to the equivalent areas in the different zones of Chile was performed through coefficients provided in a set of tables contained in Art. 172 of the law. These tables were generally based on productivity—that is, in any one region, as many hectares would be equivalent to 80 BIH as were necessary to be as productive as 80 irrigated hectares in the Melipilla area of the province of Santiago. According to Lyon, however, "there were deviations from the productivity criterion because of political pressure and certain policy reasons. For example, the south of Chile does not have the tenancy problems in the acute form found in the central region, nor is its production as inefficient. To obtain the votes of congressmen from the south, the hectares equivalent to 80 BIH (basic irrigated hectares) in that region were greater than the criterion of productivity would justify" (Lyon 1968, 10).

4. The three classes of bonds, "A," "B," and "C," were amortized in twenty-five, five, and thirty annual payments, respectively. Each of the three classes was divided into two series. An expropriated owner received 70 percent in bonds of the first series, which were readjusted annually in accordance with the official consumer price index, and 30 percent in bonds of the second series, which were not readjusted to reflect inflation. The bonds were not negotiable but could, under certain conditions, be used to purchase stocks or to satisfy tax bills or public assessments (Law 16.640, 1967, Art. 132).

5. See, for instance, the cases of *In re* Alamos Igualt, *In re* Violeta Grebe, and *In re* Alberto Guzmán, in Corte Suprema (1968, 2, 45, and 78); also see ICIRA (1969, 102).

6. If CORA failed to make the deposit within the required year, the affected landowner could petition the court to cancel the expropriation decree. Unless CORA proved the deposit requirement had been satisfied, the court had to grant the petition and the property was made exempt from expropriation for a 3-year period (ICIRA 1968, 65–66).

7. For an analysis of interventions and other legal mechanisms available to the government, see Novoa M. (1970–1971).

8. Although Law 16.640 of 1967 provided that farms over 80 BIH which had been subdivided subsequent to 4 Nov. 1964 were subject to expropriation as if they were larger than 80 BIH, the law also provided that this ground for expropriation expired on 16 July 1970 with regard to those farms subdivided prior to 16 July 1967 (Art. 5 and Temporary Art. no. 1).

9. Nevertheless, in the period from January, 1971, to July, 1972, more than half of the expropriated estates were smaller than 80 BIH (Barraclough and Affonso 1973, 77).

10. While in almost every case the landowners were no longer in possession, and in most cases legal title to these lands had passed to CORA, a substantial number of cases were being held up in the courts through various legal maneuvers; that is, the legal determination of the respective rights and duties had not been terminated. After the 1973 coup, most of these farms where the expropriation was challenged were returned to their former owners.

11. The number of families benefited is larger than the number of peasant families residing in the expropriated farms, since during the Allende government some "outside" families were incorporated into the new land-tenure arrangements.

12. See Loveman (1976b); also, see Stanfield and Bossert (1974).

13. This judgment was based on personal field observations and various conversations with CORA officials.

14. These observations are derived from interviews with various pro-UP peasant-union officers and campesino-council members held in late 1972 and early 1973. For obvious reasons, the names are omitted.

15. For more complete analyses of the "legal road to socialism," see, among others, Viera-Gallo (1971), Novoa M. (1970–1971), and Novoa M. (1972).

REFERENCES

Allende, Salvador. 1971a. Discurso inaugural, Estadio Nacional, Santiago, 5 de noviembre de 1970. In *Nuestro camino al socialismo: La vía chilena*, pp. 9–24. Buenos Aires: Ediciones Papiro.

———.1971b. *Primer mensaje del Presidente Allende ante el congreso pleno: 21 de mayo de 1971*. Santiago: Talleres Gráficos, Servicio de Prisiones.

Barraclough, Solon. 1971. Reforma agraria: Historia y perspectivas. *Cuadernos de la Realidad Nacional* (Santiago), no. 7, March, pp. 51–83.

Barraclough, Solon, and Almino Affonso. 1973. Diagnóstico de la reforma agraria chilena. *Cuadernos de la Realidad Nacional* (Santiago), no. 16, April, pp. 71–124.

Cantoni, Wilson. 1972. Poder popular en el agro chileno. *Cuadernos de la Realidad Nacional* (Santiago), no. 11, January, pp. 80–103.

Chile Senate. 1966. Informe de la Comisión de Constitución Legislación, Justicia y Reglamento, recaido en una moción de los Honorables Senadores Señores Ampuero, Corbalán González, Chadwick y Luengo que modifica el Artículo 10, no. 10, de la constitución política del estado, relativo al derecho de propiedad. *Boletín*, no. 22,021. Santiago: Instituto Geográfico Militar.

Chonchol, Jacques. 1971. La política agrícola en una economía de transición: El caso chileno. In *El pensamiento económico del gobierno de Allende*, pp. 217–244. Santiago: Editorial Universitaria.

———.1972. La reforma agraria y la experiencia chilena. In *Transición al socialismo y experiencia chilena*, compiled by Centro de Estudios - Sociales and Cuadernos de la Realidad Nacional, pp. 149–160. Santiago: Prensa Latinoamericana.

———.1973a. Class lecture, Catholic University, Santiago, 4 July.

———.1973b. Interview, Santiago, 19 July.

———.1976. La reforma agraria en Chile. *Trimestre Económico* 43(3):599–623.

CORA (Corporación de Reforma Agraria). 1970. *Reforma agraria chilena: 1965–1970*. Santiago: M-Graphic.

———.1972a. *Boletín Jurídico*, no. 61, September.

———.1972b. *Boletín Jurídico*, no. 56, April.

———.1972c. *Boletín Jurídico*, no. 54, January.

———.1973. Comparación entre expropiaciones agrarias: Gobierno popular-gobierno D.C. Santiago: CORA, Departamento de Relaciones Públicas.

Corte de Apelaciones-Temuco. 1969. *In re* Corporación de la Reforma Agraria. In *Revista de Derecho, Jurisprudencia y Ciencias Sociales* 66(4), Sec. 2 (June):33–37.

Corte Suprema. 1968. *Revista de Derecho y Gaceta de Tribunales* 65(1), January-March, Part 2.

———.1969. *In re* Sociedad Ganadera del Aysen, S.A. In *Revista de Derecho, Jurisprudencia y Ciencias Sociales* 66(1), January-March:18–19.

Echenique, Jorge. 1970. Las expropiaciones y la organización de asentamientos en el período 1965–1970. In *Reforma agraria chilena: Seis ensayos de interpretación*, pp. 95–114. Santiago: ICIRA.

El Mercurio. 1972. Santiago, 19 August, p. 3.

Frei, Eduardo, and Hugo Trivelli. 1967. Mensaje del ejecutivo al congreso proponiendo la aprobación del proyecto de ley de reforma agraria. In *Ley de reforma agraria*, by Antonio Vodanovic, pp. 5–38. Santiago: Editorial Nascimento.

Gómez, Sergio. 1973a. Consejos campesinos: Hacia una nueva estructura de poder en el campo. Paper presented at International Conference on Law and the State in a Period of Transition, sponsored by Centro de Estudios de la Realidad Nacional, Santiago, Chile.

———.1973b. Agricultura y revolución: Diferentes puntos de vista en el seno de la izquierda. *Revista Agraria*, no. 4, April, pp. 8–9.

ICIRA (Instituto de Capacitación e Investigación en Reforma Agraria). 1968. *Exposición metódica y coordinada de la ley de reforma agraria*. Santiago: Editorial Jurídica de Chile.

———.1969. Departamento de Derecho y Legislación Agraria. *Derecho y Legislación de Reforma Agraria* (Santiago), no. 1.

Kaufman, Robert R. 1972. *The politics of land reform in Chile, 1950–1970*. Cambridge, Mass.: Harvard Univ. Press.

Kay, Cristóbal. 1973. La participación campesina en el gobierno de la Unidad Popular. Working paper. Santiago: Departamento de Estudios Socio-Económicos de la Universidad de Chile.

Lehmann, David. 1974. Agrarian reform in Chile, 1965–1972. In *Peasants, landlords and government*, edited by David Lehmann, pp. 71–119. New York: Holmes and Meier.

Locke, James, and José Garrido. 1972. La situación de la agricultura y sus perspectivas. *Portada*, no. 28, March, pp. 7–14.

Loveman, Brian. 1976a. *Struggle in the countryside: Politics and rural labor in Chile, 1919–1973*. Bloomington: Indiana Univ. Press.

———.1976b. The transformation of the Chilean countryside. In *Chile: Politics and society*, edited by Arturo Valenzuela and J. Samuel Valenzuela, pp. 238–296. New Brunswick, N.J.: Transaction Books.

Lührs, Germán. 1969a. Expropiaciones bajo las leyes 15020 y 16640. Seminar paper, University of Wisconsin-Madison Law School.

———.1969b. Proyecto de ley modificatorio de la ley 16640. Santiago: ICIRA.

Lyon, Michael. 1968. The agrarian reform law of Chile: A description of its basic elements. Mimeograph. Santiago: ICIRA.

McCoy, Terry. 1969. Agrarian reform in Chile, 1962–1968: A study of politics and the development process. Ph.D. dissertation, University of Wisconsin-Madison.

Maffei, Eugenio, and Emilio Marchetti. 1972. Estructura agraria y consejos comunales: Situación actual, análisis y estrategia. *Cuadernos de la Realidad Nacional* (Santiago), no. 14, October, pp. 126-151.

Menjivar, Rafael. 1970. *Reforma agraria chilena*. San Salvador: Editorial Universitaria.

Novoa M., Eduardo. 1970–1971. Vias legales para avanzar hacia el socialismo. *Revista de Derecho Económico* (Universidad de Chile), no. 33 and 34, Oct. 1970-March 1971, pp. 27–38.

———.1972. El difícil camino de la legalidad. *Revista de la Universidad Técnica del Estado*, no. 7, April.

PNUD (Programa de las Naciones Unidas para el Desarrollo), FAO (Food and Agriculture Organization), ICIRA (Instituto de Capacitación e Investigación en Reforma Agraria). 1972. *Diagnóstico de la reforma agraria chilena: Noviembre 1970-junio 1972*. Santiago: ICIRA.

Punto Final. 1972a. Reform agraria sin conducción. No. 152, 29 February, pp. 10–11.

———.1972b. La mitad de la tierra expropiada está improductiva. No. 167, 26 September.

Rivera, Rigoberto. 1972. El campo chileno: ¿Donde va la reforma? *Punto Final*, no. 167, supplement, 26 September, pp. 1–11.

Stanfield, J. David, and Thomas J. Bossert. 1974. The role of participation and campesino consciousness in the Chilean agrarian reform. Draft. Madison, Wisc., November. Land Tenure Center Files, University of Wisconsin.

Thome, Joseph R. 1971. Expropriation in Chile under the Frei agrarian reform. *American Journal of Comparative Law* 19(3):489–513.

UP (Unidad Popular). 1971a. Programa de la Unidad Popular. In *Nuestro camino al socialismo*, by Salvador Allende, pp. 151–174. Buenos Aires: Ediciones Papiro.

———.1971b. Los veinte puntos básicos de la reforma agraria. In *Nuestro camino al socialismo*, by Salvador Allende, pp. 181–185. Buenos Aires: Ediciones Papiro.

Viera-Gallo, José Antonio. 1971. Derecho y socialismo. *Mensaje* (Santiago), 281–289.

Vodanovic, Antonio. 1968. *Recopilación de leyes, decretos con fuerza de ley, reglamentos y decretos agrarios*. Santiago: Editorial Nascimento.

Chapter 8

Radical Reformism in Chile: 1964–1973

Marion R. Brown*

INTRODUCTION

This chapter examines the Chilean agrarian reform during its most active phase. It touches on some aspects of the Jorge Alessandri period (1958–1964), carries through the Eduardo Frei years (1964–1970), and concludes with the truncated administration of Salvador Allende (1970–1973). The analysis relies largely on primary data gathered at the farm level. Most of the data come from a longitudinal study of a sample of very large farms in Chile's central valley. In simple terms, this was a "before-after" study of the first 5 years of the Frei reform.[1] Investigation began in 1965 with a survey of a random sample (panel) of 105 large haciendas. These holdings were prime candidates for expropriation. They were drawn from a universe of the very largest and most economically and socially important rural properties in the nine provinces that comprise Chile's central valley (Table 1).

They were selected on a random basis so that expropriations, subdivisions, employment trends, and other changes observed in the panel would be representative of changes occurring throughout Chile's large-farm sector.

The baseline survey, completed before expropriations began under Frei's Agrarian Reform Law, documented existing conditions and provided a basis for monitoring the reform over time.

The "after" phase of the study began in 1970 and focused on the agricultural year 1970/71. It consisted of a resurvey of the farms studied

* Professor of Agricultural Journalism in the Land Tenure Center, and Chairman, Department of Agricultural Journalism, University of Wisconsin-Madison.

Table 1
Some characteristics of the universe sampled

	Total number of very large haciendas	Large haciendas as percent of all properties in each province	Total area in very large haciendas (in BIH)[b]	Area of large haciendas as percent of area in province (in BIH)
Aconcagua	45	1.2	12,503	34.7
Valparaíso	50	1.2	16,053	56.0
Santiago	272	3.3	84,380	54.6
O'Higgins	188	2.2	62,860	54.0
Colchagua	121	2.1	33,004	44.3
Curicó	45	1.4	10,477	29.3
Talca	130	2.6	41,199	50.1
Linares	128	1.9	53,825	49.6
Nuble[c]	88	0.5	20,771	26.3
Total	1,067	1.7	335,072	47.0

[a] Source: Comité Interamericano de Desarrollo Agrícola, *Chile: tenencia de la tierra y desarrollo socio-económico del sector agrícola* (Santiago: Talleres Gráficos Hispano Suiza, 1966), Table XI-3, p. 148.
[b] BIH = basic irrigated hectare, the standard unit of land area used in implementing the 1967 land reform law.
[c] In Nuble, data were not available for two-thirds of the province; therefore, these figures are not comparable with those for other provinces.

in 1965 and an analysis of new units of various types that emerged in the panel after 1965 as a result of expropriation and private subdivision. Data were gathered concerning the operation and management of the "central enterprises" of each of these units as well as various "satellite enterprises," such as land rented out, sharecropped, or granted to workers and reform beneficiaries as partial payment for their labor.[2] Questionnaires were also administered to a sample of the permanent resident workers on each farm unit: 259 *inquilinos* (permanent resident workers) in 1965, and 1,216 workers in 1971.

A major assumption of this analysis is that virtually all farm units in Chile had, by 1971, been affected to some degree by agrarian reform. The threat of expropriation had produced major changes on private farms: some had been subdivided, others were being more intensively managed, and a few had been virtually abandoned and were awaiting expropriation. The expropriation process itself created a new and very different kind of private farm, the *reserva* (reserve), that part of the farm left to the original owner. This analysis, therefore, deals not only with the reform sector per se, but also with the various types of private farms that evolved during the course of the reform. It focuses on (1) historical and political antecedents to the reform, (2) reform policies and procedures, and (3) resulting changes in tenure and management, intensity of resource use, production, and employment.

HISTORICAL AND POLITICAL ANTECEDENTS

Chile's agrarian structure is, in part, a legacy of Spanish colonization policies (Borde and Góngora 1956). An important result of these policies, with implications for modern landholding patterns and labor relations as well as for the land reform, was the *encomienda* system. The *encomienda* (literally, "trust") placed enormous jurisdictions of land under the control of conquistadores and other Spanish families, together with a charge to care for, protect, and Christianize the indigenous population. The *encomienderos* were allowed to "utilize" the labor of the population found in the jurisdictional area.

In addition to *encomiendas*, there were outright grants, called *mercedes*, and forced labor arrangements, known as *repartimientos*. These various forms of grants, trusts, leases, and sales differed in the security of proprietorship and degree of control which they afforded over resources and labor. Colonization was not a simple transfer of land and water rights from the Spanish crown to favored Spanish colonists. From the time of the conquest, there were complex and conflictive situations not only because of the protracted war between the Araucanians and the Spaniards but also because of the power struggle among the Spaniards themselves. These conflicts involved access to and control over labor, land, and water. During the fifteenth and sixteenth centuries, a complex structure of laws and proclamations enabled relatively privileged and politically strong families to amass ever larger tracts of land and increase their control over the lives of the indigenous population and other less fortunates. By the early 1800s, most of Chile's land had been consolidated into very large estates. For the most part, these were cattle ranches producing for the domestic market.

In the second half of the same century, new export markets opened up, especially in Peru, and *hacendados* began to shift from cattle to wheat. This required more labor, so the landowners sought to establish large resident work forces on their properties. This, according to Góngora (1960), was the beginning of *inquilinaje*, the quasi-feudal patron-client institution that was a central feature of Chile's agrarian structure for nearly a century (McBride 1936).

The *inquilinos* (literally, "renters") were attracted to haciendas by a variety of arrangements, ranging from simple rental contracts to sharecrop tenancy. While Chilean historians are divided as to the social and ethnic origins of *inquilinos*, the prevailing view is that most were of European descent: the "foot soldiers" of the conquest and members of downwardly mobile Spanish families who lost out in the early scramble for land. Families which were not able to garner a critical mass of land and other wealth could not follow the prevalent tradition of *mayorazgo* (primogeniture), in which holdings were passed from one generation to the next without any subdivision among heirs. Unable to establish multiple heirs in the professions or to subsidize them adequately from a rural wealth base, the families were forced to divide their lands, giving rise within a few generations to a large number of families with little or no land (Brown 1971a).

Many of these families, according to Góngora (1960), settled on the large estates as renters, displacing day laborers (peons and slaves), who in turn became temporary and migrant workers (*afuerinos*). Initially the *inquilinos* were tenants in the conventional sense, paying in cash or shares for their use of hacienda lands. They were not wage laborers but manager-entrepreneurs in their own right. However, as their numbers increased, and as a combination of opportunities and economic pressures stimulated the *hacendados* to take more direct control of their lands, *inquilinos* began to lose their relatively independent status. Gradually, their bargaining power eroded until they were, in fact, laborers who received part of their pay in the form of a subsistence plot and the right to pasture animals on the hacienda's lands.

Inquilinos formed the core of the resident labor force, but there were two other groups of resident workers on the traditional Chilean hacienda: (1) *empleados* (supervisory personnel) and (2) *voluntarios* (resident, occasional laborers).

Empleados were typically drawn from the *inquilino* ranks and enjoyed higher incomes, better homes, lighter work loads, and considerable prestige as representatives of the *hacendado*. *Voluntarios* formed a large group. They were usually relatives (grown children and in-laws) of the *inquilinos* and lived with them as *allegados* (boarders). *Voluntarios* filled in for *inquilinos* when they were ill or otherwise unavailable. Some enterprising *inquilinos* hired *voluntarios* to fulfill a major share of their work obligation on the haciendas in order to devote more time to their individual enterprises.

Traditionally, if the son of an *inquilino* caught the eye of the *patrón*, he was offered a house and other perquisites and promoted to *inquilino* status when he married. Women were rarely elevated to the status of *inquilina*. They worked alongside men in the fields and served as maids in the houses of the landowners, but the perquisites and prestige of *inquilinaje* almost always went to male heads-of-household. In fact, the only *inquilinas* on the farms in the panel studied here were widows or abandoned wives of *inquilinos*.

By and large, *inquilinos* were not of peon or "working class" origin. This point is critical to understanding the dynamics of the rural labor movement which preceded and greatly affected the reform process. It is also crucial to the "new class hypothesis," which depicted the reform beneficiaries as failing to form and sustain a united front with other members of the rural work force once they had received "their" land (see Roxborough 1977). From the outset, *inquilino* families constituted a growing, if downwardly mobile, rural middle class. They were geographically isolated on "their" haciendas but maintained significant social and political relationships with their counterparts on other farms through extended family networks and the union movement. *Inquilinos* saw themselves as better off than workers who migrated from farm to farm. The self-perceived social identity and the concrete economic and political interests of *inquilinos* were rarely, if ever, identical to those of *minifundistas* (subsistence farmers), *afuerinos* (temporary workers), and *Mapuches* (indigenous groups). Failure to recognize this fact was probably responsible for unrealistic expectations on the part of both social scientists and political activists in Chile. Unfounded expectations of "campesino solidarity" were especially salient during the Allende years.

By the time Chile gained its independence in the early nineteenth century, the landed aristocracy dominated politics in both rural and urban areas. This power remained virtually intact for more than a hundred years. This group was able to absorb new elements, adapt to changing conditions, and accommodate industrialization and urbanization more successfully than most rural elites in Latin America. Not until well after World War I did land reform became an issue of any real political import. And, even then, the landed aristocracy was able to maintain the status quo by making minor concessions and "deals" with the growing urban middle classes. Pressure groups, unions, and virtually every political entity in Chile entered, at one time or another, into open or tacit alliance with landed interests (Ratcliff 1973). As a result, the rural order remained essentially unchanged throughout more than half of the present century. However, the *hacendado's* ability to resist mounting pressures for change was, with each concession and each new alliance, gradually eroding. By 1964, the traditional system of rural property was under serious strain. At this point, the long struggle between the *inquilinos* and their patrons came into sharp focus. To many, the newly visible pressures for reform seemed to have emerged suddenly as a result of "agitation" by urban organizers (Brown 1971b). In fact, the agrarian crises of 1964, 1970, and 1973 were manifestations of a continuing struggle that dated back to the mid-nineteenth century (Loveman 1976).

Prior to 1964, and to a certain extent during the Frei period, the stability of the rural order depended on the ability of the landed class to avert substantial reforms. In the early 1900s and again at midcentury, governmental concessions on industrialization issues (that is, the right of urban workers to organize) garnered support (even from the communist and socialist parties) for a policy of benign neglect of the peasant sector and a systematic weakening of the rural labor movement (Brown 1971b; Loveman 1976).

The *inquilinos* were essentially unrepresented in these bargains and constantly challenged them by continuing to organize themselves into clandestine labor unions. This campesino activism was seldom recognized in the literature: most analyses of Chile's rural labor movement characterized the campesinos as complacent and acquiescent. The credibility of this docile image speaks eloquently of the effectiveness of the "low profile" suppression of the rural labor movement by landowners and by urban-based political parties, which, until the 1960s, had little to gain by allying themselves with the rural poor.

The electoral reforms of 1958 introduced the secret ballot, making it virtually impossible for landowners to continue to control the votes of the workers on their farms. The balance of voting power shifted markedly in favor of the campesinos, and they were aggressively courted by urban-based groups and parties, especially the Christian Democrats (*Partido Demócrático Cristiano*, PDC) and the Marxist coalition, then known as the *Frente de Acción Popular* (FRAP).

As the presidential election approached in 1964, Chile's agricultural sector was characterized by extreme concentration of landownership and income, underutilization of resources, lagging production, and severe underemployment (CIDA 1966). At the beginning of the Frei administration in 1965, 2 percent of the farms accounted for nearly 70 percent of the land. The legal minimum rural wage, including the value of payments in kind, was about 75 U.S. cents per day. Nearly 42 percent of the irrigable land in the central valley was in natural (unimproved) pasture. Agricultural output had increased by an average of only 1.8 percent per year since 1930, while the population had grown by nearly 2.5 percent annually during the same period. Rural underemployment was estimated at 30 percent, and some 685,000 people (29 percent of the 1950 rural population) had migrated from farm to city during the previous decade. Despite this massive rural-urban migration, the rural labor force had continued to grow in absolute terms, resulting in underemployment in the large-farm sector and accelerated subdivision of smallholdings. Statistics on rural education, literacy, nutrition, infant mortality, housing, sanitation, and health care showed that the quality of life of the majority of farm people in Chile was considerably lower than that of city dwellers.

Proposed solutions to these problems were of two basic types: (1) the neoclassical approach, which emphasized technological change and sought economic growth within the existing social and political structure, relying on market signals to guide investment and create jobs and assuming that benefits would "trickle down" to marginal groups, and (2) the reformist approach, which emphasized *social change* to ensure more equitable distribution of income and more direct political, economic, and social participation by the majority of the population in the development process (Dorner and Kanel 1971; Barraclough and Schatan 1975).

THE FREI REFORM

Frei was elected on a reformist platform that committed the Christian Democrats to a "rapid, drastic, and massive"[3] land reform which would provide 100,000 rural families with ownership rights to the land they worked. During the six ensuing years, this commitment was severely tested both by right- and left-wing opposition and by disagreements and conflicts within the Christian Democratic party. The result was a compromise populist strategy which combined reformist and neoclassical modernization policies (Kay 1977). Large, unproductive haciendas and farms experiencing intense labor conflict were expropriated at the same time that better managed and socially stable units were encouraged to modernize along conventional lines. This dual policy was reflected in Frei's land reform law and in his expropriation policies which exempted many owners outright and allowed others to subdivide their farms, to keep larger reserves, or to receive greater compensation if their farms were especially productive. It was also reflected in highly subsidized credit and machinery-importation policies designed to stimulate the modernizing commercial sector. One study reported an increase of 164 percent in machinery and equipment on a sample of private farms between 1964 and 1969 (Ringlien 1971).

The Frei agrarian reform law was preceded and followed by diverse and complex reactions on the part of landowners and campesino groups. Some landowners resigned themselves to turning their farms over to the government. Others retained their land by opting for the "carrot" that Frei held out to encourage efficient management and improved labor relation. Still others subdivided their properties into units small enough to be exempt from expropriation or carried out "private reforms," ceding significant portions of their farms to their workers and challenging the government to expropriate the resulting campesino cooperatives.

Landowner responses were matched by campesino activism. One tactic was the *toma*, the extralegal invasion and takeover of a farm by resident workers. This was rare in 1970 and 1971, but became more common during the course of the study. Only one hacienda and one reserve in the panel had been illegally occupied as of May 1971.

Frei's reform units were called *asentamientos* (settlements) and were organized and operated along production cooperative lines. The *asentamientos* typically corresponded to the expropriated farm, less any reserve left to the former owner. The *asentados* (direct beneficiaries) were, in most cases, the former *inquilinos* of the expropriated farm. Other resident workers became *socios* (associates).

The *asentamiento* was to be a temporary arrangement in which the Land Reform Agency (*Corporación de Reforma Agraria*, CORA) and a resident campesino committee (*Asemblea Campesina*) jointly managed expropriated properties during a 3- to 5-year period. According to the law, *asentados* on each *asentamiento* (typically thirty to forty families) would decide at the end of this period whether to continue with cooperative ownership and management, to divide the land into individual units, or to work out some combination of the two. The Frei government encouraged the "communitary" option. In fact, most *asentamientos* that matured during his term chose a mix of collective and family enterprises, preserving economies of scale in orchards, vineyards, and pastures while dividing up lands devoted to cereals and truck crops.

EXPROPRIATION CONCEPTS AND POLICIES

Chile's first significant agrarian reform law was passed during the regime of Jorge Alessandri in 1962. It provided for expropriation only where the government could prove very low productivity or virtual abandonment. When Frei came into office in 1965, he began to apply the Alessandri legislation and, at the same time, to press Congress for a stronger law that would greatly increase the government's expropriation powers. Surprisingly, he did nothing to forestall private subdivision until after he had published his own agrarian reform bill.

Two years passed before the Frei's agrarian reform law was approved. During this period, his reform proceeded on the basis of negotiated "purchases" of farms, not a few of which were offered for sale by their owners. With the prospect of a tougher law, some *hacendados* preferred to sell under the terms of the Alessandri legislation. As it turned out, these landowners got a better deal than those who waited, benefiting from relatively more liberal assessments, higher land prices, larger down payments, and larger reserves.

In an attempt to devise a fair system for fixing the "size" of a farm for taxation and/or expropriation purposes, the 1967 reform law created a new unit of land measurement called the basic irrigated hectare

(BIH). This determination was based on data from an aerial survey of the central zone. Soil quality was taken into consideration, but the most critical element was a distinction between arable lands below canals and lands that were neither arable nor irrigable. (Irrigation is crucial in all of the nine central valley provinces included in the study.)

The central valley was divided into zones, and "coefficients of equivalence" were established for each zone. The standard for the derived basic irrigated hectare was "one hectare of high-quality, irrigated land in the Maipo River Basin."[4] The coefficients reflected productivity and were used to adjust the "legal size" of all properties. In theory (rarely in practice), a very fertile farm of 50 hectares with plenty of water could be judged expropriable (equivalent to more than 80 BIH), while a farm of several thousand unirrigated hectares might not be considered a *latifundio*.[5]

CHANGES IN TENURE AND MANAGEMENT

By 1971, the haciendas in the original panel had evolved into four tenure types: (1) *latifundios* that had been neither expropriated nor subdivided, (2) properties that had been expropriated in their entirety, (3) farms that had been partially expropriated, and (4) haciendas that had escaped expropriation through private subdivision prior to passage of the 1967 reform law. By the end of Frei's term in 1970, the sample of 105 haciendas had changed considerably (Tables 2 and 3).

FARM SIZE

The properties that had been expropriated were clearly the larger farms in the panel. Many of these very large units had been notoriously mismanaged, and their expropriation caused little concern among other owners, many of whom supported the idea of doing away with the most glaring excesses of *latifundismo*.

The eighteen partially expropriated haciendas averaged more than 640 BIH and nearly 3,000 physical hectares. A few were truly enormous, encompassing entire river basins extending from the Argentine border in the Andes to the Pacific Ocean. One expropriated owner we interviewed acknowledged that he had no idea how much land he controlled, but that a conservative estimate would be more than 150,000 hectares.

The nineteen haciendas which Frei expropriated in their entirety were slightly smaller than those on which he left reserves, averaging just over 600 BIH (2,600 physical hectares).

Table 2
Farm Size by Type of Farm

Type of farm	*N*	Mean irrigated area in physical hectares	Mean irrigated area in BIH	Mean dry area in physical hectares	Mean dry area in BIH	Mean total area in physical hectares	Mean total area in BIH
Unexpropriated, undivided *haciendas*	41	353.1	251.1	791.0	36.6	1,144.1	287.7
Completely expropriated *haciendas*	19	869.8	538.4	1,781.3	65.9	2,651.1	604.4
Partially expropriated *haciendas*	18	539.6	589.2	2,375.7	52.9	2,915.2	642.1
Subdivided *haciendas*	27	378.1	330.5	421.9	19.4	800.0	349.9
Total	105	485.0	381.5	1,146.9	40.3	1,632.0	421.7

Table 3

Four patterns of land tenure that evolved between 1965 and 1971 in the sample[a]

Pattern of land tenure	Total area (physical hectares)		Irrigated area (physical hectares)		Area (BIH)		Number of farms in 1965		Number of farms in 1971	
Completely expropriated haciendas	50,372	(29.4)	16,527	(32.5)	11,484	(25.9)	19	(18.1)	22	(10.2)
Partially expropriated haciendas, where part of the land remained in unexpropriated parcels or in reserves	52,474	(30.6)	9,712	(19.1)	11,557	(26.1)	18	(17.1)	55	(25.6)
Subdivided haciendas, where no parcel was expropriated before May 1971	21,602	(12.6)	10,210	(20.0)	9,447	(21.3)	27	(25.7)	97	(45.1)
Haciendas with the same boundaries as in 1965/66	46,909	(27.4)	14,478	(28.4)	11,795	(26.6)	41	(39.1)	41	(19.1)
Total	171,357	(100.0)	50,927	(100.0)	44,283	(100.0)	105	(100.0)	215	(100.0)

[a] The numbers in parenthesis percentages.

The twenty-seven farms which had been subdivided were substantially smaller than those on which some expropriation had occurred—they averaged 350 BIH and 800 physical hectares before they were subdivided.

The forty-one *fundos* whose boundaries had not been affected were the smallest of the 105 studied, averaging slightly under 290 BIH.

In sum, 73 percent of the 171,357 physical hectares in the panel had undergone some tenure change through expropriation or subdivision by 1971 (Table 3). The 105 haciendas studied in 1965 had been transformed into 215 farms of widely varying types and sizes. Of the original haciendas, 41 were intact. Coincidentally, the same number of *asentamientos* had been formed. On 3 of the 19 completely expropriated haciendas, 2 *asentamientos* had been formed. Private parcels or *hijuelas* numbered 117, and 16 private reserves had been left to the owners of expropriated haciendas.

Of the 174 private units functioning in the panel in 1971, only 50 (29 percent) were under the same management with the same people owning and operating them as in 1965. Of those that changed ownership/management, in 73 (43 percent) the new owners were relatives or ex-partners of the previous owners. Representing just 10 percent of the area still in the private sector, 51 farms (29 percent) were in the hands of individuals who had no apparent family relationship with the previous owner (Table 4).

Of the 44,283 BIH in the panel of haciendas, 42 percent had been assigned to reform beneficiaries, 26 percent had been subdivided, 5 percent had been retained by original owners as reserves, and nearly 27 percent had been unaffected.

QUALITY OF LAND

The unexpropriated and undivided farms had, on average, more dry land than the subdivided farms, but the latter had more productive potential. The twenty-seven subdivided farms had the highest quality land. The partially expropriated *fundos* had land of intermediate quality, while the completely expropriated units were clearly those of poorest quality.

The better lands on partially expropriated farms stayed in the hands of the original owners. When reserves were allowed, the owner usually kept his house, the adjacent outbuildings, and a sizable parcel near the barns, house, and the main irrigation canals.

Table 4
Property and farm management transfers in the unexpropriated part of the sample[a]

Owners as of 1 May 1970	Number of farms[a]		Percentage of area not expropriated as of 1970
Same as in 1965	50	(28.7)	44.1
Family or business ties with 1965 owners			
Wife, husband, son or daughter, other relative	28	(16.1)	11.4
Limited partnerships, reorganized after 1965	16	(9.2)	18.8
Members of limited partnerships, dissolved after 1965	29	(16.7)	15.6
Subtotal	73	(42.0)	45.8
No apparent relationship with 1965 owner	51	(29.3)	10.1
Total	174	(100.0)	100.0

[a] The numbers in parenthesis are percentages.

THE PACE OF REFORM

The original sample was composed entirely of expropriable farms, and a yearly breakdown of the number and types of farms expropriated shows how the pace of expropriation varied over time under different laws and regimes (Table 5). The first 2 years (1965–1966) of the Frei period saw few expropriations. Only about 6.5 percent of the land in the panel was affected. In 1967, thirteen large farms were expropriated, accounting for 21 percent of the land in the panel.

After 1967, the rate of expropriation dropped off steadily, until in 1970 only 7.5 percent of the panel was affected.

Many observers of the Chilean reform were surprised by the slowdown during the last 3 years of Frei's regime. With the benefit of hindsight, it is clear that the right-center political alliance from which the PDC derived much of its power broke down when the reform moved on from very large, unproductive farms to modern, well-managed units. Relatively conservative elements in the party withdrew support on grounds that the program was "dangerously" insensitive to due process and overly responsive to campesino demands. The upshot was political crisis in the party and policy paralysis in the field.

Table 5

Rates of expropriation of land in the sample of large farms

Year	BIH Available for expropriation[a]	Number of farms expropriated	Average BIH per farm expropriated	Total BIH expropriated	Total BIH left in reserves	Percentage of expropriated land left in reserves[b]	Percentage of expropriable BIH actually expropriated[c]
	(1)	(2)	(3)	(4)	(5)	(6)	(7)
1965 & 1966	44,283	6	383.8	2,303	0	0	6.58
1967	41,980	13	689.5	8,963	61	0.68	21.35
1968	32,956	9	338.9	3,050	501	14.11	9.25
1969	29,405	8	406.1	3,249	656	16.80	11.05
1970	25,500	7	273.1	1,912	212	9.98	7.50
1971	23,376	31	243.6	7,553	378[d]	4.77	32.30
1972	15,445	42	190.2	7,987	252[d]	3.06	51.71
1973	7,206	n.a.[e]	n.a.	n.a.	n.a.	n.a.	n.a.
Summary	44,283	116	301.9	35,017	2,060		79.08[d]

[a] The total area in the sample is 44,283 basic irrigated hectares (BIH), all of which in 1965 was expropriable according to the law's maximum farm size of 80 BIH. The total available for expropriation each year is the total available in January of the previous year minus the area expropriated and left in reserves that year.

[b] This is by determined by dividing column (5) by the sum of columns (4) and (5).

[c] This is determined by dividing column (4) by column (1).

[d] Estimated as of January, 1973.

[e] n.a. Not available.

As the expropriation rate dropped off, so did party support for the rural labor movement, which was creating very strong pressures for more expropriation, fewer reserves, and a general acceleration of the reform process.

In 1969, the liberal wing of the PDC broke away and formed a new party, the Movement for Popular United Action (*Movimiento de Acción Popular Unido*, MAPU), which eventually allied itself with the Socialist and Communist parties to form the Popular Unity (*Unidad Popular*, UP), which elected Salvador Allende.

The pace picked up when Allende came into office and began applying Frei's legislation more forcefully. The rate of expropriation increased and the percentage of land left in reserves declined.

The terms of expropriations as related to land quality lend support to the contention that reform implementation during the Frei years was affected by the right-center alliances of the PDC. Most of Frei's expropriations (93 percent) were based on articles in the law which were relatively favorable to owners (that is, which allowed for larger cash payments and larger reserves). The Allende administration was somewhat harder on the *hacendados*. Of the land expropriations implemented during the first 2 years of his administration, 28 percent cited less favorable articles. The main difference between the two regimes, however, was in the pace of expropriation rather than in the relative "harshness" with which the law was applied.

The difference in the quality of land expropriated during the two administrations is also of interest. Frei generally took farms with land of lower quality than did Allende, which suggests that the owners of better quality farms (which also tended to be better managed) had more bargaining power with Frei than with Allende.

By September, 1970, near the end of Frei's term, the reform sector included 1,364 formerly private farms, comprising about 12 percent of Chile's irrigated land. In terms of expropriable land, Frei had affected about 46 percent of the area in the panel and more than 48 percent in the central valley. Approximately 25,000 families had been settled, representing one-fourth of Frei's original goal (Stanfield and Brown 1977, 17).

LAND USE, TECHNOLOGY, PRODUCTION, AND EMPLOYMENT

Frei's combination of classical and reformist approaches in different subsectors of a relatively homogeneous area (Chile's central valley) provides an empirical basis for testing assumptions and predictions concerning production, technology, and employment under different structural and institutional arrangements. These relationships are the foci of this part of the analysis, which examines both cross-sectional and cross-time changes in farming and employment practices. Of special interest are differences between the reformed sector (*asentamientos*) and the private sector (intact haciendas, reserves, and *hijuelas* created by private sales). To document changes over time, performance of "new" units was contrasted with that of the haciendas from which they originated.

RESOURCE USE AND PRODUCTION

The most striking land-use change was a decrease in natural pastures and an increase in cultivated crops, especially vegetables. These transformations varied significantly with tenure type. Intact haciendas hardly changed, but *asentamientos* showed a marked shift toward more intensive land-use patterns. *Hijuelas* and *reservas* showed intermediate patterns of intensification.

Under both Frei and Allende, demand for farm products increased in urban areas. Beneficiaries were in a good position to meet that demand. As *inquilinos*, they had devoted most of their *raciones* and *goces* (ceded parcels) to food crops. They were familiar with both methods of cultivation and market signals for these crops. When more land became available, they did what came naturally: they grew vegetables. Fortunately for them, vegetable markets were open and accessible. To sell other crops, *asentados* would have had to compete in a system where owners of large private farms were already well established. By producing vegetables, they could operate in local markets they understood and trusted. In sum, the *asentados* made a more radical shift than did their private-sector counterparts from extensive, lower valued crops to more intensive, higher valued crops.

Where livestock is concerned, the differences in tenure type were also significant. Livestock production (31.5 percent of total value added) was concentrated on the reserves. *Asentamientos* received only 8.8 percent of their total value added from livestock, while intact haciendas and *hijuelas* received about 19 percent from animals and animal products. Cross-time decreases in livestock production occurred in *all* tenure categories. The difference between 1965/66 and 1970/71 was almost 22 percent. On the larger units, the decline probably resulted from the fact that animals were not expropriable and were sold or slaughtered in anticipation of the reform. The relatively large decrease on *asentamientos* reflects the fact that *asentados* lacked the wherewithal to retain or rebuild livestock enterprises.

In sum, farms of different tenure types performed very differently. The *asentamientos* had the poorest land, the reserves and *hijuelas* had the best land, and the untouched haciendas had land of intermediate quality. There were no dramatic differences in productivity, but there were very significant differences in farming systems and management styles. The panel data provide compelling evidence that, as of 1971, the reform had not had a negative impact on production; indeed, output was higher than in 1966 on farms in all tenure categories (Table 6).

Four major differences between private and reformed sector units and within each sector were associated with variations in their respective performances.

First, they operated in different "service" settings. Farms in the private sector were well connected to private commercial institutions which provided credit and inputs and facilitated marketing. *Asentamientos* did not have significant access to these private institutions. Instead, they depended upon the state for credit, supply, and marketing services. Specifically, they depended upon the Agrarian Reform Corporation and the Farming and Livestock Service (*Servicios Agrícolas y Ganaderos*, SAG). And access for each *asentamiento* depended very much on its political rapport with CORA and SAG.

Personnel in state agencies were civil servants. Frei had a hard time dislodging employees contracted during or before the Alessandri regime, many of whom were antagonistic to Frei's policies but had "tenure" in their positions. By the same token, Allende could not remove Frei functionaries, who continued to show favor to "Christian Democratic" *asentamientos*. He could and did appoint new heads of these agencies who then hired new technicians to service "his" reform units. But the Allende appointees also came from different parties within the Popular Unity, each of which sought its own "*base campesina*" (rural base). And so it went. The result was a fragmented, fractious service sector. One element was private. Two were governmental. None could garner sufficient resources to adequately service "its" constituency, let alone the entire agricultural sector.

A second difference which affected performance of reformed and private farms was managerial experience. Most *asentados* had spent years working small subsistence plots they did not own. A few had gained managerial experience through sharecropping or parallel arrangements involving livestock. But very few, if any, had previously managed large units or done business with large private or state agencies and institutions. They were experienced in dealing with their traditional patrons, local moneylenders, millers, truckers, and other actors in the informal sector, but not with the bankers, extension agents, and other functionaries in the formal sector.

A third difference was management style. On private farms, decision-making responsibility and authority resided with one or a few individuals. *Asentamientos* were run by worker committees in league

Table 6
Mean value added per BIH (1970–1971) and mean change in value added per BIH (1965–1966 to 1970–1971), by tenure category[a], [b]

Tenure Category	1970–1971 total value added/BIH (1)	1970–1971 crop value added/BIH (2)	1970–1971 livestock value added/BIH (3)	Change in total value added/BIH (4)	Change in crop value added/BIH (5)	Change in livestock value added/BIH (6)
Fundo	8,641	6,930	1,580	431	1,087	−641
Asentamiento	7,031	6,611	422	1,702	2,578	−991
Reserve	8,547	6,412	2,134	4,192	3,424	769
Hijuela	7,906	6,144	1,732	2,822	2,128	679

[a] Values are in constant 1971 escudos.
[b] The F statistics were as follows: (1), 0.15; (2), 0.07; (3), 0.67; (4), 0.63; (5), 0.30; (6), 1.02. None was statistically significant.

with state functionaries of various political stripes. The managers of Frei *asentamientos* defined their problems one way, their Allendista counterparts another. Private owner-operators represented still a third style. Each saw different goals or objectives ("goods" to be attained and "ills" to be avoided), each acquired different normative information, and each dealt with different "objective realities."

A fourth variation within each general tenure type—reformed and private—reflected the continuing influence of traditional tenure patterns and patron-client relationships. As noted earlier, the reformed sector was bifurcated: some *asentamientos* were established on properties expropriated in toto, others on partially expropriated farms. On the latter, the proximity of the reserve and/or *hijuela* led to continuing personal and economic influence from the *hacendado*. The original owner kept the heart of the farm, including orchards, vineyards, and basic infrastructure. *Asentados* were "amortizing owners" of outlying lands, devoid of buildings, roads, irrigation works, and houses. Despite the stated goals of the reform, some beneficiaries found themselves locked into a continuing dependency relationship with their traditional patrons.

CHANGES IN TECHNOLOGY

In 1965/66, only 15 of the 105 haciendas in the sample reported using improved wheat or corn seed. Farms that reported using improved seed in 1965 were also more modern with respect to other factors of production. They used 125 percent more tractors and 137 percent more horsepower per BIH than did farms using more traditional cultivars. The modern group also used 18 percent fewer work animals per BIH.

These data bear out theoretical predictions of the effects of adoption of modern technology within a given tenure structure. Farm managers who adopt new varieties are also inclined to mechanize. Taking advantage of yield-increasing technology leads to increased mechanization. With mechanization, the need for labor does not necessarily drop and may even rise. However, there is a rapid change in the type of labor needed: from a large force of semiskilled workers, competent in the breeding, training, care, and use of animals (especially draft animals)—and more or less independent in terms of their own subsistence—to a smaller skilled work force (machine operators and mechanics) with large numbers of unskilled seasonal laborers.

A major advantage of the panel design is that each farm serves as its own control, showing how yield-increasing and labor-saving technologies relate to structural change. By 1970, virtually all of the units (affected and unaffected) had become "modern" in terms of the crude seed-use index used to categorize the original panel. Only four farms still used unimproved seeds in 1970/71. Mechanization had increased dramatically. Both technological modernization and structural change had occurred rapidly and simultaneously throughout the panel. Still, there were differences among tenure types.

In 1970/71, *asentamientos* had far fewer tractors per BIH than the other tenure types. Intact haciendas had somewhat more tractor power, while the *hijuelas* and reserves were, if anything, "overmechanized." As noted earlier, movable capital (especially machines) had been concentrated on vestiges of expropriated farms.

REFORM AND EMPLOYMENT

Traditional *fundo* worker categories had their counterparts within the reform sector. *Inquilinos* (and some *empleados*) became *asentados*; *voluntarios* (sons of *asentados*) became *socios* (members without land rights who received a portion of end-of-year profits). Rights to individual plots and other perquisites as well as social and status relationships between these two types were much the same as under the traditional hacienda system.

For *empleados*, expropriation had negative consequences. Where reserves were left, *empleados* sometimes continued to work for their old patrons. In a very few cases, *empleados* were incorporated into reform units. More often than not, they simply found themselves out of a job when their haciendas were expropriated.

In the decade preceding the Frei reform the number of *voluntarios* who became *inquilinos* had declined as owners replaced permanent resident workers with machines and/or temporary laborers. Increasing numbers of young people had migrated to the cities or joined the ranks of underemployed migrant farm workers. Instead of moving up to *inquilino* status, they had moved down a step and become *afuerinos*. A major goal of the reform was to reverse this trend. Some observers argue that it "failed absolutely" in this regard (Strasma 1975, 14–20). But the panel data tell a different story. Resident employment per BIH of "central enterprises" was nearly 27 percent higher in the overall panel in 1970/71 than employment on counterpart enterprises in 1965/66. The issue was not so much whether but how new families would be incorporated into the *asentamientos*. The *asentados* insisted that this was a decision only they should make. They were jealous of their gains and they aggressively resisted CORA's efforts to settle "strangers" on their cooperatives. On the other hand, they made room for their offspring and their *compadres* who had been expelled in the years of labor strife preceding the reform. They "hid" new seasonal workers, but did not hesitate to place their sons, daughters, and former neighbors on the payroll.

On completely expropriated haciendas, the number of permanent resident workers rose by 60 percent. *Asentamientos* created by partial expropriation showed a 42 percent increase. Unaffected haciendas exhibited an 18 percent increase. Only the privately subdivided units showed a decline (about 10 percent) in numbers of resident workers.

Employment also increased for *afuerinos*, but the reform was, at best, a mixed blessing for them. Typically, they did not appear on official payrolls nor were social security payments made in their behalf. This was a major disappointment to reform planners and a surprise to those who expected the campesinos to exhibit a "higher" degree of class consciousness and solidarity.

By early 1973, groups excluded by the *asentados* were becoming both more visible and more effective as a political force (Roxborough 1977). Land invasions were no longer aimed exclusively at haciendas: underpopulated *asentamientos* were increasingly targeted, often with the tacit support of factions within CORA. Radical Allendistas were challenging moderate Allendistas and Freistas to "reform the reform" (that is, to reduce the ceiling of expropriable farms from 80 to 40 or even to 20 BIH and to press existing *asentamientos* to accept new members). A second generation of reform was clearly gaining momentum in the latter part of Allende's administration—a fact that was not lost on counterreform elements that ultimately supported Pinochet's coup d'état.

In sum, the reform increased resident employment on expropriated farms and had an indirect effect on unaffected haciendas. There were both positive and negative incentives for the owners of intact haciendas to intensify their operations and to maintain harmonious labor relations. The latter influences were not felt as strongly by the owners of subdivided parcels. Splitting up the farm had the effect of breaking up labor unions, and parcel owners could then hire and fire with a freer hand. New owners were not bound by the labor contracts of their predecessors.

CONCLUSIONS

Many analysts argue that, whatever the case in 1971, farm output dropped dramatically in 1973. And they seem to attribute this drop to the Allende reform. Time and resources did not permit collection of production data on the panel farms in 1973. But our research teams were visiting these farms, refining the 1970/71 data and documenting tenure changes through August of 1973. The "chaos hypothesis" does not square with our observations. The 1972 truckers' strike certainly delayed input deliveries and very probably affected wheat yields in the south-central region. And the black market definitely diverted farm products from the conventional channels in which they could be easily counted by the statisticians who kept track of national accounts. On-farm consumption also increased. Scarcities in major cities were highly visible and very problematic, especially for people who could not pay black market prices. But the *colas* (lines of frustrated consumers) were probably more a result of shifts in purchasing power and disruptions of traditional market channels than of real declines in food production. Reports of abandoned fields, corruption, and chaos on the *asentamientos* (indeed, in the entire rural sector) were greatly exaggerated. There is little hard evidence and little reason to conclude that production per se fell significantly.

On balance, the Chilean reform is better characterized as a modest (and flawed) success than as a failure. It achieved (1) significant redistribution of wealth and income, (2) dramatic changes in rural social relations, (3) important advances in participatory development, (4) relatively stable levels of farm output, (5) significant increases in employment, and (6) visible (if soon to be reversed) momentum toward more profound changes (reduction of landlord reserves and mobilization of excluded sectors of the peasantry).

Not insignificantly, it also "invented" the *asentamiento* as a contemporary, transitional form of tenure, not unlike the collective *ejido* of Mexico (see chap. 10 in this volume). The idea has since been picked up by Panama, Peru, the Dominican Republic, and other nations of the region. Communitarian rhetoric aside, the *asentamiento* was essentially a "decapitated hacienda." It removed the *hacendado* at the same time that it preserved the campesino community, maintained the productive momentum of the farm unit, and postponed the costs of parcellation. Resident workers performed much as they had before, only in their own behalf (and to the benefit of their friends and families) rather than in behalf of their traditional patrons.

Market and sociopolitical relationships beyond the farm gate quickly became problematic for the "new owners." In their day, the *hacendados* had performed some useful functions. Their relationship with workers was greatly out of balance, but not without reciprocity (Scott and Kerkvliet 1977). With reform, CORA was, by and large, a poor substitute for the traditional patrons. Nonetheless, when the campesinos were left to their own devices, they did not fare badly. *Asentamientos* and other production cooperatives are not much in favor these days, and few would argue that they represent a viable long-term alternative. But their value as a transitional tenure form in a market-oriented economy has probably been underestimated.

The tragedy of the Chilean reform is not that it failed but rather that it was reversed. From an academic point of view, completion of the experiment would have offered insight into the land reform process that cannot now be gained. From a human point of view, sufficient progress had been demonstrated to make highly questionable the Pinochet government's efforts to turn back the process. The involvement of U.S. personnel in those efforts may prove to be one of this country's most serious policy mistakes in dealing with Chile and Latin America in the past two decades.

NOTES

1. This chapter draws on unpublished work by J. David Stanfield and Stephen M. Smith, who collaborated in the collection and the analyses of data in the panel study reported here. A complete description of the methodological design is available in Stanfield (1973). Part of the present analysis has been reported previously in Stanfield et al. (1974).

2. The central enterprise includes lands and other resources controlled directly by the owners of private farms and by the production cooperatives on reform units. "Satellite enterprises" on these units are smaller plots managed by individual workers and their families.

3. This description of the reform is attributed to Jacques Chonchol, who held appointments in the cabinets of both Frei and Allende.

4. This is an extremely fertile, irrigated valley near Santiago.

5. This word, often shortened to fundo in common usage, means "large farm." However, with the passage of the law, the term came to mean "more than 80 BIH" and, consequently, subject to expropriation.

REFERENCES

Barraclough, Solon L., and Jacobo Schatan. 1973. Technological policy and agricultural development. *Land Economics* 49(2):175–194.

Borde, Jean, and Mario Góngora. 1956. *Evolución de la propiedad rural en el Valle de Puangue,* vols. 1 and 2. Santiago: Editorial Universitaria.

Brown, Marion R. 1971a. Private efforts at reform. In *Land reform in Latin America: Issues and cases,* edited by Peter Dorner, pp. 243–257. Land Economics monograph series, no. 3. Madison: Published by *Land Economics* for the Land Tenure Center at the University of Wisconsin.

———.1971b. Peasant organizations as vehicles of reform. In *Land reform in Latin America: Issues and cases,* edited by Peter Dorner, pp. 189–206. Land Economics monograph series, no. 3. Madison: Published by *Land Economics* for the Land Tenure Center at the University of Wisconsin.

CIDA (Comité Interamericano de Desarrollo Agrícola). 1966. *Chile: Tenencia de la tierra y desarrollo socio-económico del sector agrícola.* Santiago: Talleres Gráficos Hispano Suiza.

Dorner, Peter, and Don Kanel. 1971. The economic case for land reform: Employment, income distribution, and productivity. In *Land reform in Latin*

America: Issues and cases, edited by Peter Dorner, pp. 41–56. Land Economics monograph series, no. 3. Madison: Published by *Land Economics* for the Land Tenure Center at the University of Wisconsin.

Góngora, Mario. 1960. *Origen de los inquilinos de Chile central.* Santiago: Editorial Universitaria.

Kay, Cristóbal. 1977. Two types of agrarian reform and their contradictions: The case of Chile. *Sociologia Ruralis* 17(3):203–222.

Loveman, Brian. 1976. *Struggle in the countryside: Politics and rural labor in Chile, 1919–1973.* Bloomington: Indiana Univ. Press.

McBride, George McCutchen. 1936. *Chile: Land and society.* American Geographical Society Research Series, no. 19. (Reprint, Port Washington, N.Y.: Kennikat Press, 1971.)

Ratcliff, Richard. 1973. Kinship, wealth and power: Capitalists and landowners in the Chilean upper class. Ph.D. dissertation, University of Wisconsin-Madison.

Ringlien, Wayne. 1971. Economic effects of Chilean national expropriation policy of the private commercial farm sector, 1964–1969. Ph.D. dissertation, University of Maryland, College Park.

Roxborough, Ian. 1977. The political mobilization of farm workers during the Chilean agrarian reform, 1971–73: A case study. Ph.D. dissertation, University of Wisconsin-Madison.

Scott, James C., and Benedict J. Kerkvliet. 1977. How traditional rural patrons lose legitimacy. In *Friends, followers and factions: A reader in political clientelism,* edited by Steffen W. Schmidt et al., pp. 439–458. Berkeley: Univ. of California Press.

Stanfield, J. David. 1973. Methodological notes on evaluating the impact of agrarian reform in Chile's central valley. Mimeograph. Santiago, Chile, March. Land Tenure Center files, University of Wisconsin, Madison.

Stanfield, J. David, and Marion Brown. 1977. Rural stratification and the Chilean agrarian reform. Working paper in the agrarian reform series, no. 2. Santiago and Madison: Centro para el Desarrollo Rural y Cooperativo, Terra Institute, February.

Stanfield, J. David, Marion Brown, Stephen Smith, and Thomas Bossert. 1974. The impact of agrarian reform on Chile's large farm sector. Mimeograph. Madison, Wisc. September. Land Tenure Center Files, University of Wisconsin, Madison.

Strasma, John. 1975. Agrarian reform in Chile under Frei and Allende: Some problems in evaluating resources and results. Paper presented at the Conference of the Pacific Coast Council on Latin American Studies, Fresno, Calif., October.

Chapter 9

The Unraveling of Chile's Agrarian Reform, 1973–1986

Lovell S. Jarvis*

The concentration of agricultural land in Chile, dating from the Spanish conquest until the mid-1920s, was the major factor that led to Chile's bipolar social structure. Traditional society consisted, on the one hand, of a landholding aristocracy—well-educated, highly cultured, and fully in control of national life—and, on the other, of a lower class consisting of agricultural workers, usually resident laborers on the rural estates (McBride 1936). Agrarian in origin, this distinction was later carried into the urban sector where it slowly eroded.

By the 1960s, however, Chile was predominantly an urban nation. The growth of its middle class during the 1940s and 1950s led to a society divided politically rather evenly among left, center, and right. Both the left and the center pushed increasingly for social and economic reforms, and land reform was high on the agenda. Land reform also received strong support from the Roman Catholic Church and the Alliance for Progress, as well as initial sympathy even from many industrial entrepreneurs who hoped for an expanded internal market and lower food (and, thus, wage) costs. A land reform law was passed during the Alessandri presidency in 1962. Although little used during that administration, the law set the stage for the reform effort, which began in earnest with the Frei administration (1964–1970), and intensified with the passage of a more far-reaching law in 1967.

Land reform, it was hoped, would promote both economic and social change. Reform was expected to increase agricultural production both by forcing private landowners to improve their techniques (to avoid expropriation) and by shifting underutilized land on large

* Associate Professor, Department of Agricultural Economics, University of California at Davis.

estates into the reform sector where it would be intensively used. Land reform would make the distribution of income more egalitarian by transferring agricultural land from the owners of large estates to agricultural workers at a price lower than market value. It was to reduce the political and economic strength of the large landowners at the same time that beneficiaries and other campesinos, who organized and received economic benefits (including higher wages), received greater power.

The land reform process in Chile had three distinct phases. It began with the Eduardo Frei administration, from 1964 to 1970. The reform was extended and amplified by the Salvador Allende administration, from 1970 through September 1973. It was curtailed by the military government after 1973, though its effects continue to evolve.

After the coup in late 1973, the military government stopped expropriation and began returning land that was still in government hands to the private sector. The production cooperatives, or *asentamientos,* were dismantled. Some land was returned to previous owners, other properties were parceled out to land reform beneficiaries, additional acreage was immediately auctioned off to cooperatives or to individual farmers, while some land was passed to government agencies for development purposes (often for future auction). Somewhat more than half of the land expropriated between 1964 and September 1973 was ultimately given to beneficiaries. This process was nearly complete by the end of 1976.

The effects of the land reform on land tenure did not end with the distribution of expropriated land, however; sales of parcels thus created began almost simultaneously with their distribution and increased once such sales had become legal. Other farms were also bought and sold, largely as a result of the reform and the disruptions in agricultural enterprises which it had caused. Thus land reform had both a direct and an indirect impact on the structure of landholding; the latter is still unfolding.

Military government policy toward reform beneficiaries was consistently negative. Although many beneficiaries could have succeeded as independent farmers if provided assistance during transitional years, government policy systematically denied them this help. The intent, often explicit in government pronouncements, was to cause most beneficiaries to sell their land to other (presumably) more efficient farmers.

Land reform and its aftermath had a strong impact on the structure and magnitude of agricultural employment and on agricultural wages. Only a small part of this change could be attributed directly to the expropriation and parcellation of land; the larger part resulted from ex post facto changes in labor laws which made unionization difficult and permitted the expulsion of resident farm workers on medium-sized and large farms. Currently, most agricultural laborers on such farms are employed on a "temporary" basis. They reside predominantly in villages or "urban" areas and travel to and from the farm each workday. Real agricultural wages for most workers have slipped to levels below those prevailing in 1965.

Although government policies specifically targeted at the reform sector have been harsh, the evolution of the reform sector since 1973 has also been critically affected by the macroeconomic context. Recession, unemployment, and a steadily more inegalitarian distribution of income reduced the demand for many agricultural products—especially the traditional staples most frequently produced by land reform beneficiaries. Simultaneously, fruit exports soared, creating a price boom for land on which fruit could be grown. Few beneficiaries had access to the capital or the expertise needed to invest in fruit. Squeezed economically, on the one hand, and offered high prices for land, on the other, many chose to sell out.

Finally, land reform had a great, but unexpected, political effect. Under Frei and Allende, it was expected to end the hacienda as a social and political—not only economic—institution and permit much greater public development effort in the rural sector. Instead, the turbulence, passion, and uncertainty generated by land reform were crucial elements in the events which brought the military government (and its conservative economic advisors) to power (Lehmann 1971; Cusack 1974). Similarly, after it took power, the military government implemented policies that sharply reduced the capacity of rural workers, *minifundistas*, and smallholders to influence government action, largely by impeding their ability to organize. Simultaneously, it increasingly relied on representatives of large landowners in setting its policy, thus reviving their influence. While land reform may still have some progressive impact, in the long term, effects from 1973 to date have largely reversed what the reformers had intended.

THE LAND REFORM PROCESS

The Frei and Allende governments' different policy approaches toward land reform affected implementation. The legislation passed under Frei permitted the expropriation of farms for various reasons, including inefficiency, abandonment, lack of landlord adherence to labor legislation, and excessive size. However, an attempt was made to assure landowners that efficiently operated farms smaller than 80 basic irrigated hectares (BIH) would be immune from expropriation.[1] Owners of larger farms were entitled to retain a "legal reserve" of up to 80 BIH, contingent upon their meeting other reform criteria. The purpose was to reduce opposition to land reform among the more numerous smaller farmers and to retain the marketable surplus which the skills and capital of more progressive, larger farmers could provide. Only land and fixed assets could be expropriated; machinery and livestock on expropriated farms either had to be purchased by the government at market value or could be retained by the landowner. Expropriated land was recompensed in small part in cash, with the remainder in long-term bonds. Some of the bonds were to be readjusted for inflation.

The initial impact of land reform was substantial. By September 1973, expropriation procedures had been started or completed on 5,800 farms. The area expropriated amounted to 43 percent of Chile's agricultural land, as expressed in BIH, or two-thirds of the land held in large estates prior to 1965 (Jarvis 1981c). Only about 200 farms exceeding 80 BIH escaped expropriation.[2] The remaining private sector thus consisted mainly of small and medium-sized farms (including the reserves and smaller parcels created by subdivisions from the large-farm sector) in addition to the many *minifundios*.

But rather than promoting political stability in the countryside, as had been hoped, land reform created agitation and became the focal point for a struggle of ever more polarized social forces. Expropriation hardened the resistance of landlords, who steadily incorporated the support of smaller landlords fearing the same treatment, while those workers who had not been included as beneficiaries pressed for benefits from the process. Both sides increasingly resorted to extralegal tactics. Maneuvering by political parties—each of which sought to advance its electoral position—contributed to increasing tension and uncertainty (Lehmann 1971).

Land reform also seemed to have fallen short of its agricultural production and income distribution goals. Production rose from 1965 to 1971, despite growing expropriation, but output declined sharply in 1972 and 1973 because of the increased uncertainty created by widespread social and political conflict, declining investment on the farms remaining in the private sector, a deteriorating macroeconomic situation, and the worsening economic performance of the *asentamientos*. The opponents of land reform were quick to identify the reform as the major cause of the decline.[3] Income distribution had been only marginally improved by land reform. The number of beneficiaries remained small as a proportion (15–20 percent) of the agricultural labor force, and it became increasingly clear that the permanent farm workers who benefited were the better-off rural workers, not the poorest of the rural poor. Temporary agricultural laborers and *minifundistas* were probably more harmed than helped by the changes introduced due to the reduction in both available temporary jobs and land for rent (Bloom 1973).

Land reform costs, including continuing government subsidies to reform sector beneficiaries, substantially exceeded original estimates. These costs could not be met without sacrificing other important social needs. Debate over priorities, intense during the Frei administration, remained so under Allende.

COUNTERREFORM

The military government decided quickly that the land reform should be terminated and moved to implement its decision. Its rationale was based on a desire to step up economic growth, end open social conflict, and increase the resources controlled by large-farm owners, who quickly became allies of the new government (Wright 1982; Jarvis 1985).

The government decreed a series of laws to guarantee the tenure security of private farms—first those having fewer than 40 BIH, and then those having from 40 to 80 BIH (primarily farms re-created through restitutions). Subsequently, it annulled the land reform law and abolished the land reform agency (*Corporación de Reforma Agraria*, CORA). A caretaker agency, the Office to Normalize Agriculture (*Oficina de Normalización Agrícola*, ODENA), was established to oversee the final disposition of reform-sector land.

Restrictions imposed on land transactions were gradually removed to permit the subdivision and sale of all private properties. The rental or sale of reform-sector parcels was initially prohibited, but the government covered its eyes from the illegal sales that occurred. In 1979, free transaction in such parcels was legalized.

When the military took power, the final disposition of most of the expropriated land was still undetermined. Only 96,000 BIH had been assigned to beneficiaries, in cooperative form, and many expropriations were in litigation, as landowners, who originally had sought accommodation with CORA to obtain favorable terms, had learned routinely to contest expropriations in the courts (Thome 1971). Consequently, the military government could easily restore expropriated land to 3,823 landowners. Some 1,649 expropriated farms, averaging 87 BIH, were wholly restored to their former owners. Another 2,174 farms were partially restored, with the area returned averaging 51 BIH. Including the reserves that the owners had been previously allowed to retain, these reconstituted farms also averaged about 80 BIH.

Restitution of land to previous owners was justified on three grounds. First, the government argued that many expropriations and interventions were illegal. Although the land reform law had permitted efficient farmers to retain a substantial reserve, this provision was often suppressed during the Allende administration. And some farms having less than 80 BIH had been expropriated without, it appeared, having satisfied the legal criteria. There were legal precedents for restitution of expropriated land, and the military government used them.[4]

Second, the government wished to cut the costs of subsidies to beneficiaries and interest payments on bonds issued to owners of expropriated land and to resolve the large number of law suits filed by landowners for alleged violations of the law. All landowners who accepted restorations were required to renounce all claims for damages.

Third, the government wanted to increase agricultural production as rapidly as possible. It reckoned that the best way to do this was to place a substantial amount of productive land in the hands of "experienced" farmers. It argued that the *asentados* were poorly prepared to assume independent owner-operator functions.

After its program of restitution, the military government distributed most of the land remaining in the reform sector as private parcels. Semiarid lands, suited primarily for livestock and reforestation, were sold to cooperatives or at public auction.

The government argued that most *asentados* preferred owning their own plots to being members of production cooperatives and that, judging from the serious production problems faced by the *asentamientos* during the Allende administration, individual ownership would be more efficient. The military government chose not to try to remedy the problems of poor *asentamiento* management and poor production incentives (the classic "free rider" issue) within the production cooperative context. It had an ideological aversion to cooperatives, deeming them reminiscent of socialism and, hence, the political order recently overthrown. Furthermore, some imagined that the establishment of cooperatives forestalled the exit of "inefficient" *asentados* from the sector.[5]

Of the land originally expropriated, 57 percent (in terms of productive value) remained in the reform sector under cooperative or individual management, 28 percent was returned to previous owners, 5 percent was auctioned, and 10 percent was retained in the public sector, mainly for forestation and subsequent private sale. Of 900,000 BIH expropriated between 1964 and September 1973, 500,000 BIH did go to land reform beneficiaries. Of this total, 385,000 BIH were given out as parcels to individuals; the remainder had been distributed as cooperative farms during the Frei administration. Most cooperatives were gradually converted into individual plots under the military government, whose policies strongly encouraged such privatization.

THE PROCESS OF PARCELLATION

Parcels were not distributed to all of the *asentados*. The government argued that the parcels had to have a minimum size to be economically viable. Thus, a unit of land, the *Unidad Agrícola Familiar* (UAF), was defined as the amount which could provide a family with acceptable employment and income. The UAF was set at 10 BIH, about twice as large as the parcel which would have resulted had all adult males on the *asentamientos* been given equal shares of the reform-sector land. This decision meant that roughly half of the existing *asentados* and their families—for whom no other employment arrangements were made—would be excluded.

To be eligible for a UAF, an individual had to be (1) a farm resident at the time of expropriation, (2) a head of household, and (3) someone who had not participated in any illegal land seizure carried out during the past two administrations.

The first criterion limited the potential beneficiaries largely to those who had been permanent workers (or members of their families) before expropriation. Most *asentados* fell into this category.[6] The second criterion excluded many younger *asentados* who had substantially more education than did the older generation and who might have been better farmers. For example, data show that only 25 percent of the *asentados* was functionally literate, compared to 75 percent of their adult sons. The third criterion was used as retribution by expropriated landowners both to settle old scores against their ex-workers (as well as those disputes which had arisen after the organization of the *asentamientos*) and to destroy potential unionization of farm workers by purging its leadership. Many capable *asentados* were excluded from obtaining land rights through this mechanism.

Of the approximately 61,000 *asentado* heads of household resident on *asentamientos* in September 1974, approximately 36,000 (55 percent) ultimately received land; the remaining 25,000 had to seek employment elsewhere. Nearly all of the 15,000 adult single males who were hired laborers on the *asentamientos* before the coup, primarily sons of the *asentados*, also were denied land.[7]

Choosing 36,000 adults from a pool of 76,000 suggests that the government should have been able to choose well-qualified beneficiaries. In fact, the selection process fell short. The process emphasized age, family size, work experience, and education; but the heavy preference given to workers with large numbers of dependents meant that older, more tradition-minded campesinos tended to get land. The educational level of the beneficiaries was no different from that of the pool of *asentados*. The priority given to workers with large families was justified by a concern for short-run welfare.

The series of decisions regarding eligibility and selection resulted in parcel assignment to many who were among the least able farmers in the initial pool of *asentados*—a result which made little sense if the government intended to develop a viable beneficiary sector.

Contrarily, the military government altered the legislation in 1975, permitting anyone to apply for a parcel; this was so that former farm administrators, sons of former landlords, supervisory employees, and agricultural professionals could get some land. These individuals were often well qualified, but they did not satisfy any distributional criterion.

BENEFICIARY EXPERIENCE AFTER PARCEL RECEIPT

Land was sold to the new beneficiaries at about 50 percent of its market value (DEA 1979), although there appeared to be great price variation among parcels. The purchase was financed with 30-year loans, the principal readjusted according to changes in the official cost-of-living index plus 6 percent real interest. Some felt that these terms were too soft, particularly after 1976 when interest rates elsewhere were much higher. In fact, most beneficiaries, given their lack of capital and the harsh market conditions they faced, had difficulty meeting these financial commitments.

After selection of the "new" beneficiaries, the government made almost no provision for start-up assistance—technical aid and credit—during the early, difficult, transition stage. Even today, little such assistance for the small-farm sector is available.

Beneficiaries were immediately confronted with a shortage-of-capital bottleneck. Many *asentados* began farming with no capital, a huge debt on land, and production credit loans to pay off. In addition, *asentados* were required to pay off past debts of the *asentamiento* upon its parcellation. The Land Reform Law of 1967 had provided only for the expropriation of land (Thome 1971). This meant that credit had to be made available to the *asentamientos* for the purchase of machinery and livestock, for construction, and also for working capital, including advances by government (*anticipios*) to *asentados* to tide them over from one harvest to the next. Credit was usually provided at low rates of nominal interest (inflation was so high that interest rates were frequently negative).

Most of the *asentamientos* had learned quickly that, with this interest-rate structure and given the lax repayment policies, it was "good business" to borrow, and many had accumulated substantial debts by 1973. Rather than forgiving such debts as being the result of past governmental errors, the military government required settlement. Repayment was possible only by selling existing nonfixed capital, so the *asentamientos* were inventoried and their machinery (with some livestock) was auctioned off. When proceeds fell short of debts (the usual case), the *asentados* had to assume a prorated share of the debt if they wanted land.

One ulterior motive for the equipment and livestock auctions was that such sales provided a conduit of cheap capital to reconstituted medium-sized and large farm sectors. There was some economic truth in the government's contention that the relatively small UAF would not make the most efficient use of the machinery available, but the policy to bleed the reform sector to benefit the newly reconstituted elites was simple injustice. Furthermore, it left the new beneficiary farms decapitalized. Since the medium-sized and large farmers were allowed to collude at auctions, the *asentados* received credit for only a fraction of the value of the equipment sold.

This approach was also economically inefficient. It encouraged the large-farm sector to substitute machinery for labor, despite a general abundance of the latter, due to the substantial government equipment purchases for the *asentamientos* from 1964 to 1973 (Jarvis 1985). This exercise left the *asentados* without hope of exchanging their existing machinery for smaller scaled implements or for other essentials they would need as family farmers: seeds, fertilizer, fencing, livestock, or irrigation infrastructure.

The new beneficiaries were placed in an almost impossible bind: they were expected to produce at an acceptable level yet were allowed no resources with which to do so. They began substantially in debt, dependent on more credit to produce. If they failed to repay, their credit rating was ruined; if they did pay, their families were often left without necessary subsistence.

Beginning in 1976, the economic screw was tightened. The government's new macroeconomic policies caused real interest rates to rise sharply, and, over the following 5 years, real short-term rates averaged 35 percent. Simultaneously, the prices of most agricultural products declined. Few options were open to the beneficiaries, who put into practice what survival strategies they could. Many sold whatever capital they had to pay their interest charges. Others rented part of their land for lack of funds to farm it, used the cheapest seeds available, adopted rudimentary technologies, and/or became increasingly self-sufficient (Olavarría 1978). Still others, fearful of government action if they did not succeed in an increasingly impossible situation, simply sold out, often to the previous landowner or a local merchant, while those who attempted to hold on saw their farms rented and/or sold bit by bit. This fragmentation resulted in the creation of additional *minifundios* and various other insecure tenure forms. (Pulverization of *minifundios* into ever smaller plots occurred in the indigenous communities as well, where the government, urging privatization, implemented policies which made parcellation almost mandatory.)

The number of parcel sales, which steadily increased for a time, now seems to have leveled off (there may have been a slight upturn since 1983). Of 42,500 beneficiaries (the 34,500 who received UAFs plus 8,000 who received parcels via the subdivision of cooperatives), only about half remain. Rough estimates suggest that about 15 percent had sold by June 1978 (ICIRA 1979), about 30 percent by December 1979 (Jarvis 1980), about 40 percent by August 1982 (Jarvis 1985), and about half by the end of 1986 (Gómez and Echenique 1986a).

Some reasons for parcel sale by new beneficiaries had little to do with accumulated debt. A few did not like individual farming and welcomed the opportunity to sell out and obtain capital for other activities. A few dissipated their newfound wealth in self-indulgence. Some did badly when exposed to the normal risks of farming. Still others were poor farmers. The majority who failed, however, never had a chance given the odds they faced. With a supportive government, many might have developed into capable farmers, with positive social and economic repercussions.

Much of what happened to beneficiaries is anecdotal; little data are available on their performance. The Institute for Training and Research in Agrarian Reform (*Instituto de Capacitación e Investigación en la Reforma Agraria*, ICIRA), a center founded in Frei times and officially charged with gathering and evaluating data on the reform sector, carried out sample surveys of the beneficiaries in crop years 1975/76, 1976/77, and 1977/78, with the last being the most comprehensive (ICIRA 1976, 1977, 1979). These three ICIRA reports were never released, and no later surveys were conducted. The ICIRA effort was terminated in 1979 in a government effort to avoid publicity on the beneficiaries' plight.

Available data for 1977/78 show that the net income of land-reform beneficiaries averaged $2,400 (U.S. dollars), twice the minimum wage but less than half that of *minifundistas* with similar-sized parcels. Beneficiary incomes varied widely around this mean, however; 18 percent reported negative net incomes, and 42 percent had incomes of less than $800 (Jarvis 1985). Thus, more than half had net incomes below the minimum wage.

ICIRA data also suggest that the process of land parcellation was haphazard and inequitable. Although all UAFs were supposed to be about 10 BIH, in fact, the worth of the most valuable parcels in 1977/78 was six times that of the least valuable (the best often went to the ex-landlord's son). The subsidy provided each beneficiary—as measured by the difference between the price paid and the assessed tax value—was as capriciously assigned: sometimes it was very large and, at other times, it was negative (Jarvis 1985). Similar results were found in a smaller sample conducted by Tahal (1979).

By 1978, most beneficiaries still had little nonfixed capital: 36 percent had a value of less than $1,600, and 64 percent had less than $3,200. Some (30 percent) had no machinery. Others (44 percent) harvested all of their crops by hand (ICIRA 1979).

The ICIRA surveys showed a steady decline in cropped land, suggesting a drop in production. Much of the land taken out of cultivation was simply left unused for want of credit to buy inputs. A large proportion of some of the best land in Chile (50 percent of the land distributed was classified as irrigable and another 5 percent as potentially irrigable) went into unimproved pasture. Much of the potentially irrigable land went unirrigated for lack of capital to adjust water-distribution facilities to the smaller farms created.

Beneficiaries received what credit they got primarily through the State Bank (*Banco del Estado de Chile*, BECH) from 1974 to 1976, with a guarantee from CORA. This guarantee was removed after 1976, and beneficiaries who fell behind in their payments were denied further credit. While reasonable from an accounting viewpoint, this was not logical if the government harbored any intent that the new beneficiaries become viable farmers.

After the CORA guarantee ended, bank credit was available only upon presentation of a formal mortgage, which usually cost the equivalent of about $250 (Tahal 1979). The beneficiary's equity was frequently insufficient to provide collateral. Private banks established a minimum of $50,000 for development loans, which eliminated beneficiary requests.

This government neglect of the beneficiary sector often appeared to be land-reform-sector sabotage. The Institute for Agricultural Development (*Instituto de Desarrollo Agropecuario*, INDAP) had been established under the Land Reform Law of 1967 and was responsibile for providing credit and technical assistance to small farmers and land reform beneficiaries. However, the government sharply reduced INDAP's staff and budget between 1974 and 1976 and verged on eliminating it entirely. INDAP was eventually preserved because (1) its director had access to military leaders and was able to argue his case against both the Ministry of the Treasury (with its free-market philosophy) and the Ministry of Agriculture (representing large landowners) and (2) because the U.S. Agency for International Development (USAID) provided some funding for its activities (Jarvis 1981a).

However, the government prohibited INDAP from providing land reform beneficiaries with credit between 1976 and 1978 (Jarvis 1981a), and the usefulness of the technical recommendations INDAP would offer was sharply circumscribed. Although it had nearly exclusive responsibility for official credit to small farmers, who controlled about 45 percent of Chile's land, INDAP's lending accounted for only 2 percent of total official agricultural credit in 1981, well below the absolute amount it had lent even in 1974 (Cox 1985a). And INDAP had only about 600 professionals throughout 1974 to 1981 to service approximately 300,000 *minifundios*, land reform plots, and small farms.

In 1977, the government announced a plan to provide technical services to this group through private consultants, whose fees would be partly subsidized by the state. The government argued that a private extension system (*Asistencia Técnica Empresarial*, ATE) would provide better service, at lower cost, than a public extension service, and that farmers would value its services more if they were required to pay an ever increasing share of its costs.

The ATE system was an almost complete failure because the subsidy provided was insufficient to finance the establishment of a quality service, and farmers soon became uninterested in paying for services which they deemed of little value. ATE enrolled 9,000 farmers in 1978, its first year; this shrank to 5,000 in 1982. In the meantime, no other technical assistance was provided. The government belatedly admitted that technical assistance "needed improvement." To date, a replacement system has not implemented.

Since the government justified the selection of beneficiaries largely on welfare grounds, efforts to provide them with education and training and other well-designed assistance would have been especially warranted. The military government, however, implemented no new policies to train the beneficiaries prior to land distribution and, shortly after the distribution of parcels was complete, cut back and then eliminated the existing training program run by ICIRA.

In 1979, INDAP proposed that creating small local beneficiary groups would facilitate provision of technical assistance, credit, input sales, and marketing services. This proposal was rejected by government with the argument that any such "popular" organizations were undesirable (Jarvis 1981a). Large farmers, of course, maintained numerous organizations, for example, the *Sociedad Nacional de Agricultura*, which maintained a constant dialogue with the government.

Similarly, beginning in 1978, the Institute for Agricultural Research (*Instituto de Investigación Agrícola*, INIA) undertook research to develop (small-farm) technology and established demonstration centers. However, these efforts were minuscule in relation to INIA's overall program, which was oriented to the needs of large farms. INDAP entered into agreements with INIA to encourage additional research on small-farm technology, but these and INIA's own independent work were phased out in 1982 and 1983, with full responsibility passing to INDAP, which really had no institutional capacity for such work.

INIA currently focuses on transferring technology to large farmers via organized groups, an approach specifically denied small farmers.

Neglect of small farmers is so complete that the International Corn and Wheat Improvement Center (*Centro Internacional de Mejoramiento de Maíz y Trigo*, CIMMYT), which initiated a program to increase output for small farmers in Chile, mainly in the rain-fed coastal area, cancelled this program and left Chile in 1985 because of lack of government interest.

The vast literature on land reform efforts throughout the world has long shown that beneficiaries are likely to develop successfully only if they receive support during the first decade or so after land receipt (for example, Warriner 1969). The Chilean government chose to ignore such lessons and consistently opposed helping small farmers in various ways, the most prominent of which was a rejection of all manner of subsidy. They also argued that the beneficiaries had already received more than had most members of society and that resources should instead go to other poor. Their antisubsidy attitude was inconsistent, however; for example, subsidies were maintained which paid for 100 percent or more of the costs of forestation and were destined almost exclusively to large farms and private corporations.

Initially, after the UP appointees were systematically ousted from government, agricultural policy was made by technocrats concerned with preserving and consolidating the effects of land reform and promoting rural development more generally (Cox 1985a). But this group was replaced after 1974 in response to advice from the National Society of Agriculture (*Sociedad Nacional de Agricultura*, SNA), an association which traditionally defended the positions of large farmers. The government's policies were altered markedly. After 1976, the officials of the Ministry of Agriculture were taken directly from SNA (Wright 1982). They had strongly resisted land reform and now based their policies on the assumption that it had been a mistake, and that efforts to assist the resulting small-scale farmers would compound the error. Not to have sincerely believed this would have severely compromised their cultural views that one class—their own—was destined to control the rural sector and that the other class—the workers—should do its bidding. They argued that since small farms were less efficient than large ones and since better educated farmers were more efficient than more poorly educated farmers, it was desirable to allow land to pass from small to large farms and from less educated to better educated farmers through the unfettered functioning of the free market.

Such beliefs meshed well with the neoconservative economic ideology preached most fervently by the "Chicago Boys," who assumed firm control of Chile's economic policy in 1975/76.[8] It called for strict reliance on the free market and the private sector and for minimal government intervention.

The government argued that policies which gave market forces free play were distributionally neutral. It failed to acknowledge that the existing distribution of resources, including education, training, experience, and social connections, was inherently unequal and that this inequality had been the fundamental reason for past social tensions. While pretending otherwise, the government was not an impartial mediator among factions; it took a stance which clearly favored the rich and politically conservative. The country had paid an enormous price to undertake far-reaching land reform, but the government allowed the hope and promise it had inspired to dwindle and fade.

THE EFFECTS OF LAND REFORM, LAND RESTITUTION, AND LAND SALES ON LAND STRUCTURE

Land reform caused considerable change in the structure of Chilean agriculture, as shown in Tables 1 and 2. The 1965 distribution shows the situation just as land reform began, with fewer than 5,000 producers (2 percent) controlling 55 percent of the land. Although the 1967 reform law specifically prohibited the subdivision of large farms, a number of such transfers were illicitly carried out before the reform was fully operative, in the 1965/66 period. The resultant subdivisions, often gifts from parents to children, were carried out by persuading local registrars to alter the land-title records and predate the transactions. These alterations probably shifted about 10 percent of the total area of farms exceeding 80 BIH to smaller farms.[9]

By 1972, when the expropriation process had nearly reached its peak, the ratio of large to total farms appeared much smaller than a decade earlier. Most of this reduction was due to expropriation of land and its reassignment to the reform sector. A smaller part was explained by bogus division and creation of landlord reserves.

Despite the military government's return of about 40 percent of the expropriated land to medium and large farms, parcellation of the reform sector made the size distribution of land significantly more equal in 1976 than in 1965 [the 1976 data are a projection by the Catholic University (DEA 1976)]. The area controlled by farms exceeding 80 BIH was reduced by half, while the area controlled by farms having 5–20 BIH was tripled. The change was less marked than had been intended by the reformers, but the net effect of the reform was that some 50,000 new farms had been created; this left about half of Chile's agricultural land in the hands of small farmers and *minifundistas*.

Table 1
Distribution of agricultural properties, by size categories, 1965–1986[a], [b]

Size Categories	1965	1972	1976	1979a[c]	1979b[d]	1986[d]
< 5 BIH	9.7	9.7	9.7	14.1	13.3	14.0
5–20 BIH	12.7	13.0	37.2	38.4	29.0	26.0
20–80 BIH	22.5	38.9	22.3	22.3	36.3	31.0
> 80 BIH	55.3	2.9	24.7	21.3	16.9	26.0
Other public agencies	0.0	0.0	0.0	4.0	4.0	3.0
Reform sector	0.0	35.5	9.5	0.0	0.0	0.0
Totals[f]	100.2	99.8	103.4	100.1	99.5	100.0

[a] Distributions are expressed as percentages.
[b] Sources: 1965 and 1972: Instituto de Capacitación e Investigación en Reforma Agraria, "Diagnóstico de la reforma agraria chilena, noviembre 1970-junio 1972," Documento de trabajo (Santiago: ICIRA, 1972). 1976: Departamento de Economía Agrícola, Pontificia Universidad Católica de Chile, "Chile Agricultural Sector Overview: 1964–1974," Prepared for USAID (Santiago, 1976).
[c] Sources: Lovell S. Jarvis, "La distribución de tamaño de las propiedades agrícolas chilenas en 1979," *Estudios de Economía* (Universidad de Chile), no. 17 (1981), pp. 29–61; Jarvis, *Chilean Agriculture under Military Rule: From Reform to Reaction, 1973–1980* (Berkeley: Institute of International Studies, University of California, 1985); and author's revisions. 1979a: Data taken from tax roles as published in Servicio de Impuestos Internos, "Los efectos del reavaluo de los predios agrícolas," *El Mercurio*, 13 January 1980. The category size groups differ from those for other years. They are, approximately, < 5.1, 5.1–25.5, 25.6–64, and > 64 BIH. See Jarvis, *Chilean Agriculture under Military Rule*, for explanation. The data here have been slightly revised to correct an arithmetic error in the original.
[d] Author's estimates. 1979b data were taken from tax roles as shown in 1979a and adjusted to approximate the category size groups used for other years, that is, < 5, 5–20, 20–80, > 80 BIH.
[e] Author's estimates. 1986 data are 1979b data adjusted for estimated land transactions since 1979 and for multiple holdings by individual owners. This estimate is the author's best guess of the current landownership structure but is highly subjective. See text for additional discussion.
[f] Columns may not sum to 100 due to rounding errors. However, there is a nonrounding error in 1976 which appears in the original.

Immediately after land reform ended, however, land transactions began to alter further the size distribution of agricultural properties. Emphasis is often placed on the ever-increasing number of beneficiaries who sold their parcels, but many other transactions took place involving reserves, *hijuelas*, and other farms (Gómez et al. 1979; Maffei 1978; Dorsey 1981; Gómez and Echenique 1986a). Many of those who sold had emerged from land reform without much capital and weary from the struggle; others had inherited the land and did not have the expertise, capital, or inclination to farm it efficiently. Some of those who purchased land used their access to cheap credit to speculate, but most purchasers planned on agricultural development.

Table 2
Comparison of 1965 and 1979 Distributions of Agricultural Land (with additional disaggregation for 1979)[a]

Size Categories (hectares)	1965			1979b[b]			1979a[b]		
	Number of properties	Percentage of properties	Percentage of total private land	Number of properties	Percentage of properties	Percentage of total private land	Number of properties	Percentage of properties	Percentage of total private land
< 5	189,529	81.4	9.7	250,000	72.6	13.8			
5–20	27,877	11.5	12.7	68,000	19.8	29.0			
20–80	11,633	5.1	22.5	22,000	6.4	36.3			
> 80	4,876	2.0	55.3	4,200	1.2	16.9			
Minifundios									
< 2.6							222,523	64.8	8.2
2.6–5.1							33,402	9.7	5.9
Small farms									
5.1–10.2							38,911	11.3	14.1
10.2–25.6							31,884	9.3	24.3
Medium farms									
25.6–64.0							11,376	3.3	22.3
Large farms									
> 64.0							5,426	1.6	21.2
Totals	232,955	100.0	100.0	344,200	100.0	100.0	343,522	100.0	96.0*

[a] Of privately held land in 1965, 4 percent was held by government agencies in 1979.
[b] 1979a and 1979b are defined in Table 1.

In the absence of a new agricultural cadastre, it has been impossible to measure accurately the impact of sales on the distribution of agricultural land in terms of BIH. Jarvis (1981c, 1985) used assessed property values from the agricultural tax rolls to estimate the size distribution in December 1979. The data available did not directly yield the same size categories used in previous years. Thus, two estimates are shown in Tables 1 and 2, one estimated directly from the tax-roll data (1979a) for slightly different size categories, and another converted into size categories identical with those used in previous years (1979b).

Accumulating evidence indicates that each of these distributions underestimates the concentration of land because (1) many of the land reform parcels sold between 1974 and 1979 were still registered on the tax rolls in 1979 in the original beneficiary's name because of the tax advantages this provided for the new owner, (2) a high proportion of parcels sold—perhaps half—have been bought by larger farmers, and (3) many large farms are now composed of a number of smaller, discontiguous plots registered under different names, usually of other family members.

Fear of further land reform has induced many farm operators to fragment their landholdings. Dorsey (1976) was among the first to document this. He interviewed numerous farmers in one region of the country who came to own a number of discontiguous plots with the intent of avoiding expropriation. Similar evidence is available from a random sample of farms exceeding 15 BIH undertaken in 1982 by the Department of Agricultural Economics, Catholic University of Chile (DEA 1982).

The same phenomenon can also be seen in a sample of forty-five farms studied recently by Gómez and Echenique (1986a). They selected ten outstanding farmers for study in each of five enterprises (table grapes, apples, corn, sugar beets, and rice).[10] The farms sampled ranged from 52 to 1,690 physical hectares, with most of the area irrigated. Excluding outliers, the average farm for each type was 357 hectares (table grapes), 150 hectares (apples), 110 hectares (corn), 280 hectares (sugar beets), and 128 hectares (rice). The forty-five farmers interviewed owned a total of 139 separate pieces of land, with many registered in the name of different family members. Plots belonging to the same farm operation were often geographically dispersed (up to 13 miles apart). Only sixteen farms (36 percent) were composed of a single, contiguous property. Fragmentation was most extreme among fruit growers, who owned as many as ten separate plots and averaged more than four each. Gómez and Echenique found that fear of land reform was a major factor leading to holding fragmentation.

The 1979 tax data [adjusted for the evidence from Dorsey (1976), DEA (1982), and Gómez and Echenique (1986a)], plus information regarding the ongoing sales of land reform parcels, provide a basis for my estimate of the 1986 distribution of land in Table 1, with the area controlled by large farms now 25–30 percent of the total land area.

Land reform had little impact on the number of farms exceeding 80 BIH (consistent with the intent to allow most farmers to retain a reserve), but also reduced the average size of large farms significantly less than intended—from about 235 to about 125 BIH. A considerable proportion of the land shifted out of large farms via land reform is now in medium-sized farms instead of in cooperatives or land reform parcels. The number of small farms and the area controlled by them has been significantly increased relative to 1965. The government's policy of purposeful discrimination continues to weaken and shrink that subsector.

The number of *minifundios* having fewer than 5 BIH had also increased substantially by late 1979, to about 250,000. Of these, about 225,000 contained less than 2.6 BIH (190,000 had less than 1.3 BIH) (see Table 2). The increase in *minifundios* is mainly due to (1) the distribution of house sites to some ex-*asentados* who did not receive UAF, (2) the fragmentation of beneficiary parcels, and (3) the deeding of house plots to a number of formerly permanent workers on *fundos* (Chilean haciendas) who received a house plot as part of their severance pay after changes in labor legislation made dismissal possible. Growth in the number of *minifundios*, which provide inadequate employment and income to maintain a family, reflects a strong welfare need both for small-farm technologies to increase production and for additional off-*minifundio* employment in rural areas.

GOVERNMENT POLICY TOWARD THE BENEFICIARIES

To the extent that the military government (and its civilian allies) sought to "show" that land reform had been damaging, land reform was destined to evolve in an unfavorable manner. This policy is evident in the selection of the beneficiaries, in the lack of assistance provided them, and in the treatment of excluded *asentados*.

The military government faced a substantial set of agricultural problems in 1973, but it had the power to effect solutions which would provide long-term economic and social benefits. The decisions to stop expropriations, to provide landowner restitution, and to distribute the remaining land in the reform sector as private parcels are policies which many might accept in principle. However, government action was more extreme; it consistently benefited the wealthy and the powerful at the expense of the poor and weak. Nowhere is this more clear than in its treatment of the new beneficiaries, who were given no assistance because of the cynical assumptions that most would soon fail and sell their land and that the country would be better off for it.

The degree to which properly selected and assisted beneficiaries might have become viable producers in Chile will continue to be debated for years. Nonetheless, it has been a maxim of land reform for at least two decades that land reform can be successful only if the government provides adequate support services. Even when the beneficiaries were previously tenant-operators, as in countries like Korea and Taiwan, and were accustomed to undertaking production decisions, assistance from the state to substitute for or to create those services which had been provided by the landlords was required, that is, in credit, marketing, purchase of inputs, and so on. In Chile, beneficiaries needed all of these in addition to technical assistance in making production decisions and adequate technologies for their small-scale farms. While knowing this, the government placed beneficiaries in a context where any error or misfortune by an inexperienced entrepreneur would likely spell his ruin.

The government's restitution of land to previous owners reduced the land in the hands of small farms so that the government could adopt the pretense that only large farms had productive importance. Thus, in contrast to the policies of Taiwan and South Korea, which fostered productivity for the small farms on which their economies depended, Chilean policies discriminated against them. Aggregate sector growth was sacrificed, at least in the short run, with the intent of squeezing out smaller producers.

The following would have been essential to transform *asentados* into productive small proprietors: (1) emphasize farming ability above other criteria in the beneficiary selection process, (2) provide beneficiaries with a minimum package of loaned capital (implements, livestock, and working capital) upon receipt of their property, (3) develop a unified program for government support of beneficiaries, including agricultural research, agricultural extension and training, credit, marketing assistance, and farmer organization, and (4) provide a more favorable macroeconomic context.

A growing number of nongovernmental organizations (NGOs) have attempted to extend assistance to the small-farm sector and at least partially to fill the void left by government neglect. In early 1986, about sixty NGOs were assisting small farmers (Jorge Echenique, personal communication). These have been largely church affiliated, with significant assistance from many international foreign-aid organizations. Much of this effort was initially channeled toward the maintenance or renovation of agricultural sector cooperatives, including the provision of technical assistance and credit as well as assistance with input supply and marketing. Although well intentioned, most such efforts failed badly both because the assistance provided was inappropriate and because the organizations assisted had ineffective local leadership. Current efforts, directed at developing managerial and technological packages for the individual producers, still reach only a very small proportion of farmers.

AGRICULTURAL EMPLOYMENT AND WAGES

In the 1800s, most labor on large Chilean haciendas was performed by *inquilinos*, permanent workers who provided labor services on demand in exchange for a house, land for cultivation, grazing rights, various other in-kind benefits, and small amounts of cash. The system of *inquilinaje* provided a stable farm labor force at low cash cost to the employer. Although their wages were low, their living conditions were poor, and the *inquilinos* were largely isolated from national life, their incomes were higher than those of most non-*inquilino* workers in the rural sector.

By 1965, Chile's large farms were smaller and more profit oriented than the haciendas of the previous century (Dorsey 1981). The value of land relative to labor had increased, and owners were seeking to reduce the usufruct rights provided to their *inquilinos*; landlords aimed at gradually transforming *inquilinos* into permanent, salaried workers. This change was further encouraged when the government established a minimum agricultural wage and placed limits on the percentage of the salary that could be paid in kind. Nonetheless, Valdés (1974) found that, in 1965, in-kind benefits still accounted for more than 50 percent of an *inquilino's* pay.

Legislation after 1965 sought to improve the position of rural labor significantly. The initiation of land reform was soon followed by efforts to unionize agricultural workers, which had previously been extremely difficult due to legal restrictions (Loveman 1976; Wright 1982). The minimum wage was increased, a higher proportion was required to be paid in cash, and sanctions were increased for employers who failed to make social security contributions for their workers or in other ways evaded labor legislation. Unionized workers pressed for, and usually received, wages which were even higher. Permanent workers also began to pressure CORA to expropriate the farms on which they worked, so that they could become *asentados*. During the Allende administration, when expropriation moved too slowly, workers often took over the farm, forcing CORA to act more rapidly. Such takeovers were often encouraged by political parties and even by government officials.

Under the threat of land reform, unionization, and new labor legislation, permanent workers received higher wages, improved fringe benefits, better working conditions, and almost total work security. Frequently, they became *asentados*. Temporary workers and *minifundistas* received few benefits from land reform or unionization. Through organization, the permanent workers were usually able to exclude other potential beneficiaries.

The improved situation for permanent workers was abruptly reversed when the military government assumed power in 1973. Rural labor union activity was suspended and the Law of Immobility (*Ley de Inamovilidad*), which had prohibited the firing of a laborer without substantial cause (or a severance payment equal to one month's pay for each year worked), was ignored. The government's economic team suggested that such policies—which signified a cheapening of labor—were justified by the need to improve labor allocation.

Landowners reduced their permanent labor force, first expelling workers viewed as union organizers or potential troublemakers, then discharging those who were least productive, and finally firing all but a few specialized workers to oversee the farm and supervise the temporary laborers, who now performed the bulk of the farm work.[11]

Rural unemployment rose, contributing to the fall in real wages and encouraging landowners to reduce their permanent labor force because they could be sure of finding temporary labor at an acceptable price whenever needed.[12] Urban unemployment rose in response to similar labor legislation and to a reduction in public employment. Recession in 1975 and 1976 reduced labor demand in both agricultural and nonagricultural activities.

Given the decrease in the cost of labor, substitution of labor for capital should have increased. Nonetheless, the aggregate employment data show that this did not happen, at least prior to 1984.[13] Jadresic (1986) estimates that agricultural employment fell from 621,000 in 1974 to 586,000 in 1976, then rose to 640,000 in 1981 before declining in the recession to 595,000 in 1983. The agricultural labor force grew over this period, leading to rising agricultural unemployment. Jarvis (1985) estimated open agricultural unemployment at about 15 percent in 1979 (when employment was 625,000); underemployment, which was concentrated among *minifundistas*, added a similar amount of labor underutilization.[14] Agricultural labor demand remains highly seasonal, implying that, though employment is high during the peak season, there is significant unemployment during about 5 months of the year. The unemployment situation is especially bad for landless laborers and for the many *minifundistas* who must supplement the employment and income from their small farms with off-farm employment (Monardes T. 1977, 1978).

Increased competition for employment and the use of piece-rate systems seem also to have led to more days worked and greater intensity of effort for those employed workers. While this lowered labor costs, it made finding work more difficult for the unemployed.

In 1979 a new Labor Plan (*Plan Laboral*) permitted the organization of rural labor unions, but only on farms with at least eight permanent workers (few remaining farms had a permanent labor force of this size). The law also permitted hiring of temporary workers on a regular basis for a substantial period without granting them permanent laborer status, thus effectively leaving many "permanent" laborers with diminished employment stability and fringe benefits.

These labor-market changes are reflected in agricultural workers' wages. Real wages rose sharply between 1967 and 1972 and remained high in 1973 relative to historical levels, despite some decline. Real agricultural wages then fell sharply between 1974 and 1979 to a level substantially below even those prevailing in 1965. In 1979, temporary and permanent workers were receiving wages averaging about $3.25 and $5.50 per day, or about 90 and 80 percent, respectively, of the amount received for similar work in 1965 (Jarvis 1985; Galleguillos 1981; Vargas 1982). Cox (1985b) found that, in 1982, real wages for most workers (temporary and permanent laborers, plus some specialists) remained below their comparable levels in 1965, but that a small group of permanent workers with supervisory tasks had incomes some 50 percent higher than those received by individuals performing similar tasks in 1965.[15]

Agricultural wages suffered a greater percentage decline between 1973 and 1976 than did urban wages: their recovery between 1976 and 1981 was slower and less complete (Jarvis 1985). Only from 1983 to 1986 did agricultural wages rise relative to urban wages, following a sharp increase in agricultural employment. However, in 1986, agricultural wages still remained below their comparable levels in 1965.

The employment structure also shifted substantially. The number of temporary agricultural jobs increased and the number of permanent jobs declined; the number of paid jobs declined and the number of unpaid jobs increased (as a result of the increased number of family members employed on *minifundios* and on land reform parcels). Because remuneration was lower for temporary than for permanent work (and for the implicit pay for unpaid work), these structural shifts increased the decline in the average rural wage and the worsening of the rural income distribution.

Social security coverage of workers also dropped, mainly as a result of the shifts in the employment structure. While coverage remained reasonably high through 1976, between 1976 and 1978 the proportion of rural workers covered by the social security system dropped from more than three-fourths to less than one-half (Jarvis 1985). Coverage has since remained at a low level. Many self-employed (temporary) workers seem to decide to forgo coverage because they felt unable to make the required contributions. Thus, as the dissolution of the patronal system reduced the security which was one benefit of that system, many workers have found it more difficult to obtain social assistance from the state.

The principal social and economic problem faced by Chilean agriculture today is that of landless laborers who increasingly have become a rural proletariat detached from any permanent place of work (Gómez 1986a; Ortega 1986; Cox 1985b; Rivera 1982). Many of this group would migrate to urban areas if the opportunity existed. Since it does not, landless laborers and *minifundistas,* who must supplement their incomes with outside work, eke out an existence in rural areas as best they can.

Reliance on temporary labor use continues to increase on large farms. Gómez and Echenique (1986b) found that temporary labor provided from 47 to 83 percent of the labor utilized during the 1986 harvest season; the percentage was lowest in rice and highest in table grapes. The temporary laborers are generally young, 60 percent being under 30 years of age. Of these, 40 percent live on *minifundios,* reform-sector parcels, and traditional small farms; another 40 percent live in rural hamlets and small towns; 13 percent are from large cities; and 7 percent are resident farm workers. Gómez and Echenique also document that substantial seasonal migration is occurring within the agricultural sector, with many workers traveling long distances in search of work.

Of the temporary laborers they interviewed, two-thirds had prior work experience only in agriculture; the remaining one-third had experience mainly in industry and construction. In other words, scarce agricultural jobs were attracting job seekers from urban areas despite low wage rates. Their survey also found a rising number of women in the rural labor force. Employers frequently characterized women as being better suited for some tasks, harder workers, and more docile than men. There is a greater tendency today than in the past for as many members of the family as are able to enter the work force (Ortega 1986).

In 1986, Gómez and Echenique (1986b) found that 94 percent of the temporary workers interviewed (during the peak harvest-season months, from February to April) earned between 300 and 900 pesos or, at the official exchange rate, about $1.50 to $4.50 per day. The average wage was about 550 pesos or $2.75 per day. Much of the work performed was on a piece-work basis and frequently lasted long hours.[16]

The government has not provided assistance to small producers, including *minifundistas,* because this would "waste" resources and bid up the cost of labor to medium and large farms. Similarly, little has been done to stimulate rural industrialization.

THE IMPACT OF THE MACROECONOMIC CONTEXT

Macroeconomic policy and developments in international markets affected the way in which the land reform evolved after parcels were distributed. The effects of the tight monetary policy after 1976 made it difficult for beneficiaries who began with significant debts to repay them and for those who began without capital to justify borrowing.

The domestic demand (and prices) for agricultural products most often produced by beneficiaries (basic crops and vegetables) declined because of (1) economic recession in 1975 and 1976 and again in 1982 and 1983, (2) a worsening distribution of income, (3) appreciation of the peso from 1976 through 1981, which, along with reduced tariffs, contributed to higher food imports, and (d) declining international prices of grains and milk after 1973.

Meanwhile, demand in international markets for fresh fruit products sharply increased to exacerbate the "duality" in Chilean agriculture after 1974. Trade added a new factor causing changes in landownership; it fostered land sales by some beneficiaries to those involved in fruit exports. Evidence shows that land sales have been greatest where there is the greatest difference between the income which can be earned by beneficiaries using traditional practices (basic crops and traditional technologies) and the income earned by farmers using capital-intensive modern practices. During the first 8 years of the postreform process, this occurred in areas where fruit production, especially table grapes and apples, was most profitable. While it was common to find that "new beneficiary" parcel sales had reached 80 percent in these areas, where basic crops were grown the sales were much lower, often only 20 percent.[17]

The fruit boom made it attractive and feasible for many individuals, especially those who could get exporter credits, to purchase land reform parcels and establish orchards. In contrast, most beneficiaries could not borrow. Furthermore, they had limited entrepreneurial ability and were concerned, first and foremost, with producing enough to guarantee family self-sufficiency and to make payments on the land received. Most had little familiarity with fruit or with the institutional framework essential to its development: banks, technical agents, and exporters. Many might have successfully initiated production with assistance. (Some 160 beneficiaries successfully became apple producers with INDAP assistance, but INDAP had insufficient resources to help any more.)

RETROSPECTIVE

Land reform was intended to achieve three primary goals: (1) increase agricultural output, (2) improve the distribution of income in rural areas, and (3) reduce the political power of large landowners while simultaneously increasing that of small farmers (including the reform beneficiaries) and agricultural laborers. How should the reform be evaluated using these criteria?

Other questions also are important. Is land reform simply the expropriation of land and its transfer to new owners? Does its effect include the increased efficiency which it induced on nonexpropriated private land? Was land reform responsible for bad (or good) administration of the *asentamientos*? Was it also responsible for political polarization and, ultimately, a conservative backlash? And is it, therefore, land reform that caused the new set of labor laws and economic policies which have impacted the agricultural sector during the last 13 years? The answers to these and other similar questions will largely determine the judgment formed about land reform in Chile and the lessons to be drawn from that experience.

Agricultural Production

The net effect of land reform on agricultural output seems to have been relatively small to date but may turn out to be positive in the longer run. This view is sharply at variance with that commonly expressed by many government and private sector spokespersons, and some academics, who have argued that land reform had a disastrous effect on production (for example, MAG 1979; DEA 1979). The belief that land reform damaged production was a major justification given by the military government for terminating it and distributing the land as chosen.

Land reform affected output in various ways: (1) it resulted in the direct transfer of land from expropriated large landowners to workers and changed capitalization, managerial ability, and work incentives, (2) it induced increased efficiency on private reserves as owners sought to reduce income losses due to expropriation, (3) it led to uncertainty among landlords who were not expropriated and were not clearly exempt, reducing their level of investment, (4) it required the government to provide production-increasing resources such as technical assistance, credit, technological development, and marketing to the nonreform sector, and (5) it caused intangible but important changes of inertia by the subdivision of large farms and the injection of new landowners.

The rate of growth of agricultural value added during the 25 years prior to land reform, beginning in 1940, was 2.0 percent per year (CORFO 1956, 1963; BCC 1981). Since 1965, agriculture's average annual rate of growth was above this level except for 1972 and 1973. It appears that changes in the rate of agricultural growth since 1965 have been determined primarily by changes in price policies and macroeconomic conditions and not by agrarian reform per se.

To support this assertion, it will be useful to examine five periods: (1) the Frei administration (1964–1970), (2) the Allende administration (1971 to September 1973), (3) the first year of the military government, during which time government policies were supportive of agriculture (1974), (4) the subsequent 9 years when policies were increasingly less supportive (1975–1983), and (5) the most recent years, when policies have again been more favorable (1984–1986).

During the Frei period, the annual growth rate of agricultural value added was 3.5 percent, well above the sector's prior long-term average[18] (see Table 3). Growth exceeded 9 percent annually for 1966-1968, declined (due to drought) in 1969, and recovered in 1970. Land reform was technically well implemented during the Frei administration. Of the total farmland, 18 percent was expropriated over 6 years.

Most of the output gains achieved under Frei came from the private sector; the reform prompted increased efficiency and investment on large farms by owners seeking to retain land on the basis of improved performance (Ringlien 1971). However, production also increased in the reform sector despite the need to reorganize and recapitalize farm operations (Smith 1974). Most landlords chose to withdraw their machinery and livestock when their land was expropriated; the state made large investments to replace them and also invested substantial technical and bureaucratic resources in the reform sector. Government price, credit, and technical assistance policies were all favorable to the sector, though labor legislation resulted in a substantial increase in real farm wages. The high rate of growth achieved during this period contrasts markedly with the decline in output which initially followed land reforms in other countries (Warriner 1969).

In the Allende years, official data indicate that agricultural value added declined 18 percent over three years—at an increasing rate—as the pace of land reform quickened. An additional 25 percent of Chile's farmland was expropriated, bringing the total to 43 percent. Incentives for collective work on the *asentamientos* eroded and their administration worsened (ICIRA 1972; de Janvry 1973; Valdés 1974; Gómez 1982). Nonetheless, other influences, such as price controls, input shortages, high inflation, and civil disturbances, also had negative effects on agricultural production. The rapid recovery of production in 1974 suggests either that incentive and administration problems were easily correctable or that other factors must have been more important than any land-reform-related, structural changes in explaining the output

Table 3
Evolution of agricultural production

Year	Value added[a]	Value added[b]	Gross output[c]
1964	79	85	—[d]
1965	81	84	79
1966	98	92	89
1967	101	101	92
1968	106	103	96
1969	93	92	91
1970	97	98	99
1971	95	106	100
1972	88	102	96
1973	79	83	86
1974	100	100	100
1975	105	95	96
1976	102	94	96
1977	112	105	110
1978	107	100	106
1979	113	106	110
1980	117	107	109
1981	122	113	117
1982	118	111	116
1983	116	105	—
1984	123	112	—
1985	130	117	—

[a] Sources: Banco Central de Chile, *Cuentas nacionales, 1960–1983, 1984; and Boletín Mensuales*, n.d.
[b] Source: Mario Marcel and Patricio Meller, "Empalme de las cuentas nacionales de Chile, 1960–1985: métodos alternativos y resultados," *Colección Estudios CIEPLAN* (Santiago), no. 20 (December 1986), pp. 121–146.
[c] Source: Maximiliano Cox, "Políticas y evolución del sector agro-rural en el período 1974–1982," in *Agricultura chilena, 1974–1982: políticas, evolución y campesinado*, Maximiliano Cox, ed. (Santiago: Desarrollo Campesino, 1985), pp. 1–126.
[d]— not available.

decline evident especially in 1972 and 1973. Indeed, output may have declined less than shown, being instead simply diverted into unregistered channels to evade the increasingly severe price controls which the Allende government attempted to impose (see chap. 8, this volume).

Until recently, I had accepted the view that land reform in Chile resulted in a significant decline in agricultural output, largely influenced by the decline shown in the official figures for 1972 and 1973. Brown (chap. 8, this volume) questions that view on the basis of his microeconomic data, and, after discussion with him and reexamination of the aggregate data, I believe that land reform per se seems to have caused surprisingly little reduction in output.

During the year after the coup, output recovered quickly, rising 27 percent in 1974 alone. This recovery is particularly surprising given that little new agricultural investment or change in land tenure had occurred.[19] The main changes leading to increased output seem to have been higher agricultural prices, the elimination of input shortages, the provision of credit at low real interest rates to both the private and the reform sectors, improved administration of the *asentamientos*, and the end of the uncertainty that characterized the late Allende period. Indeed, government agricultural policy in 1974 was similar to that in effect under Frei (Cox 1985a). Output was again marketed through legal channels; this could be an important factor explaining the large increase shown. The ability of the sector to recover so dramatically in one year seems to indicate that land reform by itself had not caused any dramatic decline in productive capacity. Indeed, during the 11 years of land reform prior to 1975, agricultural value added increased at an average annual rate of 2.4 percent, well above the historic trend.

The growth of agricultural value added during the next 9 years averaged 1.3 percent per year, below the level of both the prereform and the 1964–1974 periods. Land restitutions and parcel distribution were essentially complete by 1976, yet output grew less rapidly than when large, forceful land transfers had been implemented or when land had been managed under *asentamientos*, which the military government alleged were less efficient organizational units. The causes of slow growth are not hard to identify. Internal demand for agricultural products was extremely weak during the recession of 1975 and 1976, recovering gradually through 1981 only to decline again in the crisis of 1982–1983. Income distribution worsened. Price policies became progressively less favorable to agriculture after 1976, real interest rates rose and remained at high levels, and land taxes were increased. Credit and technical assistance for small farms and for land reform beneficiaries were negligible, thereby constraining production on about 45 percent of agricultural land (Gómez 1982; Jarvis 1980, 1985; Cox 1985b).

In contrast, agricultural value added grew in the 1984–1986 period by approximately 6 percent annually, a rate surpassed only during the first 4 years of land reform. The increase seems clearly linked to agricultural policies, which turned sharply favorable after 1983 as a result of devaluation and the reimposition of import protection. At the same time, outstanding farm debt was rescheduled and interest rates were lowered (Gómez 1986b). Government assistance for small farmers, including the reform beneficiaries, remained minimal, but beneficiary land-purchase debts were scaled down in 1985 as part of the process of bailing out indebted large farmers.

Whenever agricultural price policy has been favorable during the last two decades, growth has exceeded its historic trend. Further, it seems clear that agriculture's growth could have been substantially higher had either or both the Allende and the military government placed greater emphasis on achieving higher output in the reform sector. Regardless, it is remarkable that over 40 percent of Chile's agricultural land could be expropriated and placed under different management without significant output decline. Large farms in the prereform period must have had significant scope for increased efficiency and/or the *asentamientos* and land reform beneficiaries must have been able to maintain production to a higher degree than expected.[20]

Fruit production (mainly for export) has grown rapidly during the last decade. This growth might have occurred had no land reform transpired given the increase in international demand and favorable domestic price policies. However, casual empiricism suggests that reform, including the substantial land tenure changes, injected a new dynamism into the sector. While this is most clear in fruit, it is also evident in vineyards and forestry as well as in livestock production, staple crops, and a growing variety of specialty products. Workers received no benefits during the first decade of this experience, and fewer will ever receive direct benefits than was hoped. However, an increasing number should benefit if employment continues to grow.

Income Distribution

Land reform was intended to transfer land from wealthy large landowners to poorer workers and, simultaneously, pressure all agricultural employers to improve pay, fringe benefits, and working conditions for their laborers. Data presented previously indicate that 12–13 percent of the agricultural labor force became *asentados*, an additional number of their family members (about half the number of beneficiaries) received indirect benefits on the *asentamientos*, and other permanent workers (perhaps an additional 15 percent of the labor force) benefited through higher wages. Temporary workers and *minifundistas*, who amounted to roughly half the agricultural labor force, were unaffected or harmed by land reform, mainly through loss of work on expropriated land (for example, Bloom 1973).

The gains associated with reform were largely transitory. Only half the *asentados* became beneficiaries. About half the beneficiaries have now sold their land. Almost all *asentados* who did not receive land became worse off than before, as did most other agricultural workers after 1973, as labor laws became more favorable to employers. Real wages, job security, and fringe benefits were greatly reduced, and unemployment increased.

CONCLUSION

The justification given for land reform in Chile was often economic, but the process surely had its most important impact in the political realm. The reform initially pitted what was perceived as a small economic elite against the broad majority. The land reform law was passed by a coalition of urban voters, with grudging acceptance from many progressive farmers who felt that change was inevitable (Kaufman 1972). As the reform progressed and became more extreme, opposition from landowners intensified. Clamor arose from some for more radical change (Lehmann 1971), and the elite began to use the reform to rally the middle class, in both urban and rural areas, to slow social change. The dynamics of reform played a key role in bringing to power a more radical government (Allende) and then in creating a violent opposition to it, thus providing an opening for a military coup. By the time the coup occurred, large numbers of the middle class accepted its necessity and came indirectly to support policies favored by the economic and political elite.

The land reform was intended—and generally expected—to both reflect and strengthen a progressive, new political and economic structure. Instead, it contributed to a conservative backlash. In rural areas, landowners recovered much of their property and basic control over agricultural policies. Initially, landowners influenced the disposition of land in the reform sector, the development and application of labor laws, technological policy, and, more generally, the "reestablishment of order." Their ability to influence agricultural price policy increased sharply after the economic crisis of 1981–1982 discredited the Chicago Boys and their simplistic monetarist policies (Gómez 1986a; Ortega 1986; Kay 1985). *Inquilinaje* and the traditional hacienda are institutions of the past. Large Chilean farms are increasingly capital intensive and are applying new technology. However, as credit, technology, purchased inputs, and managerial skills are more important than land in determining output and income, large landowners have been able to achieve exclusionary access to these.

Perhaps the most striking change in the rural sector is the high degree of disenfranchisement of the rural poor: the lack of attention and the apparent lack of concern for them by both government and private rural leadership. Agricultural labor unions are all but impotent, and most smallholder organizations have been suppressed and/or have lapsed into inactivity. As Gómez (1982) noted, most of the cooperatives created from 1964 to 1973 were heavily dependent on government assistance; they withered when this assistance was removed. Political organizations were banned. The agricultural labor force is better educated, and it has become highly mobile in seeking seasonal employment opportunities. But, socially, politically, and even economically, the majority of agricultural workers is probably worse off than they were two decades ago before the reform process began.

NOTES

1. Land area was expressed in basic irrigated hectares, a concept elaborated in preparation for the land reform to ensure that farm size was measured in units of equivalent productive capacity. One BIH was the equivalent of 1 hectare of prime irrigated land in the central Maipo River valley. The land reform law prohibited the division, parcellation, or granting of plots to children (*hijuelación*) of any agricultural property larger than 80 BIH without the authorization of the Agrarian Reform Agency (*Corporación de Reforma Agraria*, CORA), which was empowered to oversee the expropriation process.

2. These farms were efficient, vertically integrated enterprises, such as vineyards and fruit orchards, where the fiscal cost of expropriation would have been large due to the need to pay cash for nonland assets.

3. The amount to which output fell in 1972 and 1973 and rose in 1974 remains controversial, as does the relative importance of the various possible causes. These issues are discussed in greater detail later.

4. The government initially estimated that 2,858 farms, involving a maximum of 1.5 million physical hectares, would be restored; but, once begun, the process gained momentum and restitutions were made on more than 3,800 farms and involved 3 million hectares (Cox 1985a).

5. Cooperatives were proposed for social and economic reasons to achieve economies of scale and to allow the best qualified beneficiaries to provide leadership for the least qualified. In practice, the cooperatives encountered problems in developing honest, capable leadership and maintaining individual initiative. In addition, most *asentados* wanted their own parcel.

6. Land reform legislation limited the beneficiaries to those who had been campesinos. It was expected that the beneficiaries would include the farm workers resident on each farm who wished to become *asentados*, plus other campesinos who might be included. In actual practice, the permanent farm workers were usually able to exclude other potential beneficiaries.

7. Approximately 34,500 of the 37,000 UAF distributed went to *asentados*, with the remainder distributed to others outside the reform sector including approximately 1,000 to 1,500 who were ex-farm administrators, sons of previous landowners, or agricultural professionals. Another 1,500 *asentados* organized themselves into cooperatives to purchase semiarid land.

8. This appellation was rooted in their common academic background in the University of Chicago's Department of Economics.

9. The subdivisions—*hijuelas*—were intended to escape expropriation on the basis of size (less than 80 BIH); however, even if larger, each subdivision would yield a legal right to a reserve. The process of *hijuelación* successfully increased the amount of land retained within the same family, thus evading the redistributional effect, but it did result in the creation of both

smaller landholdings and additional landowners, each of which subsequently increased land sales.

10. Farmers were selected for inclusion on the basis of interviews with knowledgeable individuals in the area, including other farmers, leaders of farm organizations, agricultural technicians, and managers of agroindustries dealing with the sector.

11. Sometimes the housing occupied by the workers was deeded to them as severance pay, which worked to retain the workers for employment when needed. Many laborers chose instead to migrate to a rural community, where they hoped for greater employment opportunities.

12. The unemployment situation was aggravated by the parcellation of reform sector land, which resulted in the expulsion of 40,000 *asentados* and their sons, representing about 7 percent of the total agricultural labor force. They found work slowly (ICIRA 1979).

13. From 1974 to 1982, the increasing demand for labor in the fruit and forestry subsectors was largely offset by declining demand in vineyards and staple crops, especially in wheat and sugar beets (Jarvis 1985). Fruit and forestry have been growing rapidly, but from a small base; each accounted for only about 6 percent of total agricultural employment in 1978. The severe recessions of 1975–1976 and 1982–1983 also reduced agricultural employment. In 1984 and 1985, agricultural employment expanded rapidly to 693,000, 11 percent above the 1974 level, partly because of continued increases in fruit and forestry production, but also because of expanded production of wheat, sugar beets, and milk that was stimulated by increased protection.

14. Dorsey (1981) found a significant increase in the number of man-days applied per BIH of land in region VI between 1965 and 1970 and, again, between 1970 and 1976. Where large farms had been transformed into land reform parcels, the increase was particularly large because cultivation was carried out by horse and by hand. However, labor use had increased even on larger farms, where mechanization had increased significantly, primarily as a result of a changing crop mix, including the shift from pasture to crops. This effect must have been specific to the region studied because national agricultural employment actually fell 6 percent between 1970 and 1976 (Jadresic 1986).

15. The education level achieved by rural workers in Chile has increased substantially during the last two decades. The failure of the rural sector to offer such individuals opportunities for economic achievement and job satisfaction is a source of growing frustration (Gómez, personal communication, 1986).

16. Real agricultural wages remained roughly constant between 1979 and 1986; the variation in U.S. dollar equivalence is due mainly to the sharp devaluation of the peso after 1983.

17. The process by which this occurred in the Putaendo Valley is detailed by Gómez (1981). Gómez (personal communication, 1986) suggests that the rate of land-reform-parcel sales increased in wheat areas throughout Chile from 1983 to 1986 after wheat prices were increased.

18. The military government's claims regarding the growth of agricultural value added have been continually overstated. Jarvis (1981b) used official data on subsector production to argue that the true growth rate could not exceed 1.7 percent, less than half the 4.8 percent published in the national accounts

for 1974–1979. The revised national accounts released subsequently (ODEPLAN 1981a, 1981b) reduced the official claims for this period to 2.3 percent, but the official figures show that production grew at only 1.1 percent and that value added is higher than this figure only because intermediate inputs were estimated to have declined (Jarvis 1985). The questionable quality of official data is raised again in note 20.

19. About 60 percent of land restitutions to previous owners took place during 1974, but the area affected was only 8 percent of total land area. About 20 percent of reform sector land was parceled out to beneficiaries (4.3 percent of total land area). In each case, most tenure changes occurred too late to affect output in 1974.

20. A recent study by Marcel and Meller (1986) suggests that the national accounts should be revised. Their own revised series for agricultural value added (included in Table 3) suggests that agricultural growth for the period 1964–1974 was 1.6 percent, below that achieved in the prereform period. The cost of land reform in terms of lost production is still very small and, assuming considerable output was "hidden" in 1972/73, probably overestimated. The annual movements in these data also suggest that slower growth from 1975 to 1983 was due mainly to macroeconomic policies.

REFERENCES

BCC (Banco Central de Chile). 1981. *Indicadores económicos, 1960–1980*. Santiago: BCC.

Bloom, Reynold Joseph, Jr. 1973. The influence of agrarian reform on small holder communities in Chile's central valley, 1965–1970. Ph.D. dissertation, University of California, Los Angeles.

CORFO (Corporación de Fomento de la Producción). 1956. *Cuentas nacionales, 1940–49*. Santiago: CORFO.

———.1963. *Cuentas nacionales, 1950–1960*. Santiago: CORFO.

Cox, Maximiliano. 1985a. Políticas y evolución del sector agro-rural en el período 1974–1982. In *Agricultura chilena, 1974–1982: Políticas, evolución y campesinado,* edited by Maximiliano Cox, part 1, pp. 1–126. Santiago: Desarrollo Campesino.

———.1985b. La pequeña agricultura chilena: Condiciones actuales y perspectivas. In *Agricultura chilena, 1974–1982: Políticas, evolución y campesinado,* edited by Maximiliano Cox, part 2, p. 183. Santiago: Desarrollo Campesino.

Cusack, David. 1974. Confrontation politics and the disintegration of Chilean democracy. *Vierteljahresberichte*, no. 58 (December), pp. 313–353.

DEA (Departamento de Economía Agrícola). 1976. Chile agricultural sector overview: 1964–1974. Prepared for USAID. Santiago: Pontificia Universidad Católica de Chile.

———.1979. 15 años de reforma agraria en Chile. *Panamorama económico de la agricultura*. Santiago: Pontificia Universidad Católica de Chile, January.

———.1982. Niveles de endeudamiento en las empresas agrícolas.

Panorama económico de la agricultura. Santiago: Pontificia Universidad Católica de Chile, November.

de Janvry, Alain. 1973. Of the importance of dialectical interactions in collective farms. Draft. Santiago.

Dorsey, Joseph F., Jr. 1976. Análisis coyuntural de la agricultura de riego de la VI región: Año agrícola 1976-1977. Santiago: CENDERCO-Terra Institute.

———.1981. Empleo de mano de obra en las haciendas del valle central de Chile: VI región, 1965, 1970, 1976. Documento de trabajo, PREALC/199. Santiago: Programa Regional del Empleo para América Latina y el Caribe, Organización Internacional del Trabajo (PREALC-OIT).

Galleguillos, Silvia. 1981. Remuneraciones agrícolas 1971–1979. Memoria de prueba. Santiago: Escuela de Economía, Universidad de Chile.

Gómez, Sergio. 1981. Transformación en un área de minifundio: Valle Putaendo, 1960–80. Documento de trabajo. Santiago: Facultad Latinoamericana de Ciencias Sociales.

———.1982. Programas de apoyo al sector campesino en Chile. Documento de trabajo. Santiago: Facultad Latinoamericana de Ciencias Sociales.

———.1986a. La organización campesina en Chile: Trayectoría y perspectivas. Programa FLACSO, Documento de trabajo, no. 300. Santiago: Facultad Latinoamericana de Ciencias Sociales, July.

———.1986b. Polémicas recientes sobre el sector agrario. Programa FLACSO, Documento de trabajo, no. 294. Santiago: Facultad Latinoamericana de Ciencias Sociales, May.

Gómez, Sergio, and Jorge Echenique. 1986a. Nuevos empresarios y empresas agrícolas en Chile. Programa FLACSO, Documento de trabajo, no. 277. Santiago: Facultad Latinoamericana de Ciencias Sociales, January.

———.1986b. Trabajadores temporeros de la agricultura moderna del Chile central. Programa FLACSO, Documento de trabajo, no. 324. Santiago: Facultad Latinoamericana de Ciencias Sociales, December.

Gómez, Sergio, José M. Arteaga, and M.E. Cruz. 1979. Reforma agraria y potenciales migrantes. Programa FLACSO, Documento de Trabajo, SCL:082. Santiago: Facultad Latinoamericana de Ciencias Sociales.

ICIRA (Instituto de Capacitación e Investigación en Reforma Agraria). 1972. Diagnóstico de la reforma agraria chilena, noviembre 1970-junio 1972. Documento de trabajo. Santiago: ICIRA.

———.1976. Análisis de la situación actual de los parceleros asignados hasta 1974. Primer diagnóstico. Documento de trabajo. Santiago: ICIRA.

———.1977. Análisis de la situación actual de los asignatarios de tierras a diciembre de 1976. Segundo diagnóstico. Documento de trabajo. Santiago: ICIRA.

———.1979. Análisis de la situación de los asignatarios de tierras a junio de 1978. Tercer diagnóstico. Documento de trabajo. Santiago: ICIRA.

Jadresic, Esteban. 1986. Evolución del empleo y desempleo en Chile, 1970–85: Series anuales y trimestrales. *Colección Estudios CIEPLAN* (Santiago), no. 20, December, pp. 145–193.

Jarvis, Lovell S. 1980. The poor in Chilean rural society today. Santiago: Programa Regional del Empleo para América Latina y el Caribe, Organización Internacional del Trabajo (PREALC-OIT).

———.1981a. Small farmers and agricultural workers in Chile, 1973–1979. Documento de trabajo. Santiago: Programa Regional del Empleo para América Latina y el Caribe, Organización Internacional del Trabajo (PREALC-OIT).

———.1981b. ¿Cual ha sido la tasa real de crecimiento en los años recientes? Una nota acerca de las cifras de producción de la agricultura chilena en el período 1973–1979. *Colección Estudios CIEPLAN* (Santiago), no. 5, December, pp. 85–116.

———.1981c. La distribución de tamaño de las propiedades agrícolas chilenas en 1979. *Estudios de Economía*, no. 17, pp. 29–61. Santiago: Departamento de Economía, Universidad de Chile.

———.1985. *Chilean agriculture under military rule: From reform to reaction, 1973–1980*. Research series, no. 59. Berkeley: Institute of International Studies, University of California.

Kaufman, Robert R. 1972. *The politics of land reform in Chile, 1950–1970*. Cambridge, Mass.: Harvard Univ. Press.

Kay, Cristóbal. 1985. The monetarist experiment in the Chilean countryside. *Third World Quarterly* 7(2):301–322.

Lehmann, David. 1971. Political incorporation versus political stability: The case of the Chilean agrarian reform, 1965–1970. *Journal of Development Studies* 7:365–395.

Loveman, Brian. 1976. *Struggle in the countryside; politics and rural labor in Chile, 1919–1973*. Bloomington: Indiana Univ. Press.

McBride, George McCutchen. 1936. *Chile: Land and society*. American Geographical Society Research Series, no. 19. (Reprint, Port Washington, N.Y.: Kennikat Press, 1971.)

Maffei, Eugenio. 1978. Cambios estructurales en el sector reformado de la agricultura, su efecto en la demanda de fuerza de trabajo campesina y en las migraciones rurales: 1964–1978. Documento de trabajo. Santiago: Facultad Latinoamericana de Ciencias Sociales (FLACSO).

MAG (Ministerio de Agricultura). 1979. Presentación del Gobierno de Chile a Conferencia Mundial sobre Reforma Agraria y Desarrollo Rural, sponsored by the Food and Agriculture Organization, Santiago, Chile.

Marcel, Mario, and Patricio Meller. 1986. Empalme de las cuentas nacionales de Chile, 1960–1985: Métodos alternativos y resultados. *Colección Estudios CIEPLAN* (Santiago), no. 20, December, pp. 121–146.

Monardes T., Alfonso. 1977. *Empleo de mano de obra, producción e ingresos en predios de pequeña agricultura del valle central de Chile*. Documento de investigación, no. 17. Santiago: Departamento de Economía, Universidad de Chile.

———.1978. *An econometric model of employment in small farm agriculture: The central valley of Chile*. Latin American Studies Program, dissertation series, no. 78. Ithaca, N.Y.: Cornell University.

ODEPLAN (Oficina de Planificación Nacional). 1981a. Metodología y serie de cuentas nacionales, 1974–1980. Santiago: ODEPLAN.

———.1981b. *Cuentas nacionales*. Revised. Santiago: ODEPLAN.

Olavarría, Carlota. 1978. *La asignación de tierras en Chile, 1973–1976, y sus efectos en empleo agrícola*. Monografías sobre empleo, no. 9. Santiago: Programa Regional del Empleo de América Latina y el Caribe, Organización

Internacional del Trabajo (PREALC-OIT).

Ortega, Emiliano. 1986. El campesinado y las transformaciones agrarias: De la participación a la desarticulación social. Draft. Santiago: CIEPLAN, August.

Ringlien, Wayne. 1971. Economic effects of Chilean national expropriation policy on the private commercial farm sector, 1964–69. Ph.D. dissertation, University of Maryland, College Park.

Rivera, Rigoberto. 1982. Poblados rurales y migración en Chile. Documento de trabajo, no. 11. Santiago: Grupo de Investigaciones Agrarias.

Smith, Stephen Michael. 1974. Changes in farming systems, intensity of operation, and factor use under an agrarian reform situation: Chile, 1965/66-1970/71. Ph.D. dissertation, University of Wisconsin-Madison.

Tahal (Tahal Consulting Engineers). 1979. Proyecto Digua y Mante Norte: Crédito. Santiago: Comisión Nacional de Riego.

Thome, Joseph R. 1971. Expropriation in Chile under the Frei agrarian reform. *American Journal of Comparative Law* 19(3):489–513.

Valdés, Alberto. 1974. The transition to socialism: Observations on the Chilean agrarian reform. In *Employment in developing nations*, edited by Edgar O. Edwards, pp. 405–418. New York: Columbia Univ. Press.

Vargas, Verónica. 1982. *Salarios agrícolas en Chile en el período 1975–1981: Estudio de casos*. Monografías sobre empleo, no. 24. Santiago: Programa Regional del Empleo para América Latina y el Caribe, Organización Internacional del Trabajo (PREALC-OIT).

Warriner, Doreen. *1969. Land reform in principle and practice*. Oxford: Oxford Univ. Press.

Wright, Thomas C. 1982. *Landowners and reform in Chile: The Sociedad Nacional de Agricultura, 1919–1940*. Urbana: Univ. of Illinois Press.

Chapter 10

Agrarian Reform in Mexico: Capitalism and the State

Gerardo Otero*

The Mexican agrarian reform is often touted by government officials as the product of a "peasant" revolution which brought justice to the rural masses. In contrast to this view, the critical history presented here argues that land redistribution in Mexico was the way chosen to develop and entrench capitalism in Mexico. The end result of Mexican agrarian reform has been a pauperization of rural people that has brought both peasant and capitalist agriculture to a crisis. Because redistribution has stopped recently, land reform has ceased to strengthen the relationship between the government and the peasantry. As a direct result, the viability of the state has become open to question.

SOCIAL ORIGINS OF THE AGRARIAN REFORM

The origins of the agrarian reform may be traced to Articles 27 and 123 of the Mexican Constitution of 1917. These two articles embody the policy essence of the revolution vis-à-vis the peasantry and the working class, respectively. They represent advanced social thought when seen in relation to postrevolutionary Mexican society. Indeed, they became the basis for future peasants' and workers' struggles, and the resulting organizations were folded into the Institutional Revolutionary Party (*Partido Revolucionario Institutional*, PRI), presently the dominant political party.

* Postdoctoral Research Fellow, Center for U.S.-Mexico Studies, University of California, San Diego.

More specifically, Article 27 was a negotiated settlement between two predominant political factions—one led by Alvaro Obregón and the other by Venustiano Carranza—in order to deprive the more radical revolutionary peasant factions—led by Emiliano Zapata and Francisco Villa—of their original demands. With the completion of this move, the radicals lost a final political battle against the reformist constitutionalists, coupled, as it was, with the military defeat of both Zapata's and Villa's armies. Thus, the Constitution of 1917 marked the rise of a new and reformist regime from a bloody revolution.

The Mexican revolution was a costly social process in which one million persons died. Those who gained from it were not the ones who sacrificed the most. The revolution primarily helped the agrarian bourgeoisie of the North, not the peasantry who had been the primary revolutionary force. On the other hand, the reformist leadership managed to form an alliance between the working class and the constitutionalist movement. Thus, some Mexican political scientists conceptualize the revolution as a political rather than a social revolution because it did away with a highly exclusionary political regime, one in which political power was based on landownership. Nonetheless, the main trajectory of the new society was capitalist development, which reformed property relations in the countryside but stopped far short of abolishing private ownership. Thus, while the revolution eliminated the barrier to capitalist development in agriculture that had been erected by the large and inefficient landholders, it did not modify property relations fundamentally (Córdova 1972).

The Reform Laws of the Porfirio Díaz Regime

The histories of the various regions that make up the Mexican republic are sufficiently distinct that the agricultural population of Mexico today is quite heterogeneous. The rural people of central Mexico had an important precolonial cultural heritage, while the North was significantly settled only in the last century.

Before the revolution, the Roman Catholic Church was the largest landowner, representing a type of feudal ownership which markedly contrasted with the liberal ideology that had emerged in other sectors. A clash resulted from the emergence of an industrial bourgeoisie which demanded the development of agriculture so that its own growth would not be stunted by increased wage demands and falling profits. Meanwhile, the Church continued to maintain large acreages of uncultivated land and represented a major fetter to development.

The liberal reforms of 1857 provided the legal instruments to expropriate the Church's landholdings. But the same law, aided by further legislation passed during the *Porfiriato* (the prerevolutionary period, 1876-1910, during which Porfirio Díaz ruled Mexico), was applied as well to Indian community land. Thus, after the liberal reform laws and during the *Porfiriato*, the Indian communities were deprived of 90 percent of their land.

Land monopolization continued at a brisk pace during the *Porfiriato*, abetted by the *baldío* laws of 1883 and 1884, which provided for the surveying and sale of "vacant" lands. For these purposes, surveying companies (*compañías deslindadoras*) were created. These companies were given the right to keep one-third of the surveyed land as payment for their work; the rest was sold by the government. The surveying companies eventually owned 49 million hectares, or one-fourth of Mexico's territory; once surveyed, the companies purchased much of the land sold by the state. They also surveyed the Indian and peasant towns and communities, arbitrarily deeming the land to be "vacant" or eligible for surveying as they went. When Indian communities lost their land, their members were converted into laborers or peons, working for the resultant haciendas or the surveying companies; many became unemployed.

The immediate outcome of the liberal reforms was thus a transfer in landownership from the Church and the Indian communities to existing and new *latifundistas*. Large holders in the private sector of Mexican agriculture saw that they could enlarge their farms at little cost. For decades that followed, they satisfied their voracious appetites for land by putting their fences around Indian communal land. They also devised ways of attaching newly landless Indian peasants to the land, for example, through various debts the workers would incur with the landowner (credits for wedding feasts, goods advanced at *tiendas de raya* or hacienda stores, and so on). These debts were inherited by the peons' children, who were not able to give up their "jobs" until they had completely paid any past-due accounts to the landlord (López Cámara 1967; Hansen 1974).

During the *Porfiriato*, the infrastructure for the development of industry was being established (for example, a large railroad network). But, paradoxically, the *Porfiriato* also maintained and reinforced feudal, and even slave, forms of labor in farming. It was only through a ruthlessly repressive dictatorship that these contradictions in economic structure were maintained for so long. In the end, the inconsistencies between capitalist development and the archaic land-tenure pattern became so antagonistic that a revolution was fought to alter the entire system.

Industry was still a nascent sector during the *Porfiriato*. As of 1910, the main capital investments were concentrated in railroads (40 percent of the total) and mining (17 percent), followed by industry (6 percent) and oil (5.9 percent). The greatest part of this investment—77 percent—was made up of foreign capital (Gilly 1974, 21).

The *Porfiriato* promoted a massive flow of North American investments into Mexico; this was a decisive step for Mexican integration into the world economy. Indeed, this occurrence, along with two others, is seen by Friederich Katz (1982) as a prime mover of the revolution. The second motivating factor was the expropriation of Indian communities; the third was the pacification of nomadic Indians on the northern frontier that transformed the area into a peaceful and permeable border with the United States. The flow of North American capital into the Mexican economy followed soon thereafter, and the downturn of the world economy in 1907 had dramatic effects in Mexico's northern states.

The revolutionary movement coalesced in different ways in the various regions of Mexico. In central Mexico, the main social rift was between the expropriated Indian communities and the *hacendados*. In the North, revolution was led by the *hacendados* who were excluded from political power during the *Porfiriato*. They formed a broad and unlikely alliance with their own peons, small farmers, ranchers, and urban middle classes. In central Mexico, specifically in Morelos, Indian peasants had been organized to oppose the *Porfiriato* since 1908, before Francisco I. Madero had even called for the revolution's first shot (Womack 1969). Unlike the broad alliance in the North which was represented by *hacendados* (like Madero), the Morelos peasantry named their leader from among their own community, Emiliano Zapata.[1] Followers of Zapata decided to ally themselves with Madero and the northern *hacendados* because an effort to air their grievances had been repulsed at the state level.

By the time of the Zapatista uprising, sharecroppers and poor farmers were ready to join with the revolutionary movement. *Peónes acasillados* (peasants resident on haciendas) preferred their current lives to the uncertainty of revolt: "Only rarely did they [the Zapatistas] recruit rebels among the *gente de casa* [resident peons], who anyway preferred their bonded security, and nowhere evidently did they excite these dependent peons to rise up and seize the plantations they worked on" (Womack 1969, 87). The most militant and combative of Zapatistas were poor peasant producers and share tenants. In 1911, once Zapatistas began to implement local land reform according to the Plan de *San Luis Potosí*, Madero's revolutionary manifesto, "armed parties of sharecroppers and poor farmers began invading fields....The defenseless plantation managers and peons resident on the land the squatters claimed had no alternative but to meet the revolutionary demands" (Womack 1969, 87).

The prerevolutionary situation in the North was distinct. La Laguna, located in the north-central region, was settled only in the last century; it did not harbor an extant, sedentary Indian population as did so much of the highlands of central Mexico. Among the difficulties faced by settlers were the repeated attacks by warrior and rootless Indian tribes of the North. These Apaches had always been outside of Aztec influence. Whereas the Laguneros had been the native settlers before 1750, their population was so decimated by the struggles against Spaniards and smallpox that, by the turn of this century, there was hardly a trace of Indian culture in La Laguna (Beals 1932).

In contrast to peons from central haciendas who tended to remain loyal to their patrons and spurn the revolution, peons and *hacendados* in the North rebelled *together* against the central government. Madero, a *hacendado* from the state of Coahuila, led the rebellion. This was partly due to the fact that, in the North, debt servitude had lost its sway since mid-nineteenth century because of the development of mining and even some industry which offered alternative employment opportunities (Katz 1982, 28–29). Even the *tiendas de raya* were different in the North. While in the center of the country they were the *hacendado*'s instrument to keep peons indebted and thus attached to the hacienda, in the North peons were not forced to purchase goods at the *tienda de raya*. Indeed, *hacendados* generally sold products there at lower prices as an additional incentive to attract labor. Also in La Laguna, agricultural wages were the highest in the country (Katz 1982, 31).

Another group in addition to those involved in the resident peon-*hacendado* relationship in La Laguna were the "colonists." They usually held greater acreages of land and more livestock than free peasants of other regions (Landsberger and Hewitt de Alcántara 1970; Craig 1986). In the state of Chihuahua, communities of colonists were established specifically to defend the frontier against Apache incursions. They had a greater internal autonomy and felt that they had not only the right but also the duty to be armed to defend themselves against Apache attacks (Nugent 1985; Wasserman 1980). Although they were not a large percentage of the rural labor force, they did get land from President Benito Juárez in 1864 after helping him fight against the French invasion. Later on, during the *Porfiriato*, the La Laguna colonists struggled with livestock *hacendados* who had deprived them of water by altering the flow of the Nazas River (Eckstein 1966, 132). Considering that the colonists had lost their land under Porfirio Díaz, it was not surprising that they became combative in the revolution and were among the first land reform beneficiaries in 1917. In Chihuahua, compared to ordinary peasant communities, colonists had become accustomed to privileges usually accorded Spaniards and Creoles. While colonists, they were land proprietors and could sell their land. But, by 1910, they had been dispossessed of their land and deprived of municipal autonomy. These aggrieved colonists were easily organized for combat (Katz 1982, 24–26).

Another important revolutionary group developed in the northwest state of Sonora. Most of the leaders of the constitutionalist movement, in fact, came from Coahuila and Sonora (Cumberland 1975). Initially headed by Venustiano Carranza, a former governor of Coahuila, the Sonora group seized control of the revolutionary state by 1920 (Matute 1980). Generals Adolfo de la Huerta, Alvaro Obregón Salido, and Plutarco Elías Calles are closely associated with the triumph of this faction of the revolution; they helped to legitimize the emerging agrarian bourgeoisie of the North. These three generals held the presidency of Mexico between 1920 and 1928, and Calles extended his reign through "puppet" administrations from 1928 to 1935 (Loyola Díaz 1980; Medin 1982). At the time of the revolution, Obregón was a small farmer while Calles came from a family of well-off merchants. Nevertheless, they soon embodied the spirit and character of what today is the northern agrarian bourgeoisie (Aguilar Camín 1977, 1982; Sanderson 1981).

Revisionist historians have pointed out enormous regional differences in types of revolutionary leadership and involvement. Barry Carr (1973, 1980), for example, has challenged the assumed "popular" character of the first decade of the revolutionary period. He emphasizes "the hegemony exercised by bourgeois groupings over most of the revolutionary coalitions" (Carr 1980, 7). In the Sonoran case, argues Carr, "an exceptionally high percentage of the state's revolutionary leadership emerged from the ranks of the *hacendado* community or from the class of prosperous capitalist farmers and ranchers that occupied such an important place in northern society" (Carr 1980, 8). In sum, the social origins of the Mexican revolution were as varied as Mexican society itself.

ARTICLE 27: A REFORMIST COMPROMISE

Article 27 of the 1917 Constitution was designed to fulfill the demands of the many peasant farmers who had been dispossessed during the *Porfiriato* while preserving the possibility of private landownership. Indeed, the land reform article to the Constitution was a reformist compromise. One of its central features was that it declared all land to be owned by the nation. The nation, in turn, had the right to transmit this land to individuals and to constitute "private property." Also, the nation had the right and the obligation to expropriate any private property when the land was deemed necessary for "public use." This article provided the postrevolutionary state with the legal instrument to carry out land redistribution. The specific ways in which an agrarian reform was to be carried out were left to be determined in a set of enabling laws which were to be designed by the national Congress (cf. Sanderson 1981, 67–69).

The *ejido* was the preferred postreform tenure for beneficiaries of land distribution after the revolution. The *ejidatario,* holder of such land title, is not a fee-simple proprietor as in English Common Law; this "owner" reaps the usufruct of the land and has the right to work the land individually. The *ejidatario,* however, is not legally enabled to transfer those rights to nonheirs (Gutelman 1974, 151). A recent modification of the Mexican Agrarian Code, however, provides for the renting of *ejidal* land by more capitalized farmers to those who lack the necessary capital (Bartra 1974, 142 fn.). Since de facto renting of *ejidal* land had become widespread anyhow, especially in the irrigation districts, the legislative modifications show how the legal apparatus follows and is adapted to real situations.

The *ejidatario* is a producer without dependency relations with large landowners. Like the *minifundista,* the *ejidatario* may transform himself into a capitalist or may become proletarianized, may accumulate or lose his means of production, and may maintain himself in the market or be eliminated. I will argue that the process of social differentiation of the peasantry in Mexico has resulted predominantly not in full proletarianization but in depeasantization. ("Depeasantization" is the process by which direct producers become separated from their means of production regardless of the land-tenure system. Thus, they are forced to rely on other economic activities, namely, wage labor, to supplement their incomes.)

STRUCTURAL REFORMS UNDER CÁRDENAS: INDIVIDUAL AND COLLECTIVE *EJIDOS*

The 1917–1935 period saw some land being slowly redistributed. During Carranza's mandate (1917–1920), much of the land that had been given out under the Zapatista laws was returned to its previous owners. Zapata himself was murdered by an officer of the Federal Army at a meeting in which the two were expected to negotiate terms for surrender of the peasant armies. Without its beloved leader, the peasant movement in Mexico gradually became impotent.

The 1920–1935 period was one of economic reconstruction and ruling group consolidation. Because the "revolutionary family" was becoming fragmented, especially after the assassination of Obregón in 1928, Calles, in 1929, sponsored the organization of all revolutionary forces into a political party called the National Revolutionary Party (*Partido Nacional Revolucionario,* PNR), a precursor of the PRI.

The outstanding features of the 1920–1935 period were a leadership based on caudillos, an ideological radicalism expressed in heavy anticlericalism, and a halt to land redistribution. Anticlericalism led to the Cristero rebellion in west-central Mexico, while the absence of significant land redistribution led to a radical agrarian movement in the state of Veracruz headed by Governor and General Adalberto Tejeda (Falcón 1977; Fowler Salamini 1979). These two threats, one from the right and the other from the left, explain the 1933 choice of Lázaro Cárdenas as its presidential candidate by the Congress of the dominant PNR (Medin 1982). Calles, the "Jefe Máximo" of the revolution, agreed to nominate Cárdenas for at least three reasons: Cárdenas's proved loyalty to him, the fact that *political* factors predominated over *ideological* or economic factors (that is, the "revolutionary family" was becoming consolidated within the PNR), and his feeling that Cárdenas's record as an agrarianist while governor of Michoacán would offset the pressures from radical Tejedismo in Veracruz.

In order to consolidate the power of his office against Calles, who attempted to retain his informal rule even after the election, Cárdenas organized the peasantry and the working class. Rather than allowing peasants and workers to organize independently, he incorporated their organizations into the official party, which became the Party of the Mexican Revolution (*Partido de la Revolución Mexicana*, PRM). This obviously required making several concessions. Cárdenas encouraged workers—within certain limits—to struggle with the other "factor of production" (that is, the capitalists) to attain an "equilibrium." His intention was not to promote rifts between classes but to encourage a "class conciliation" in which the state was the "impartial" mediator.

Before Cárdenas's administration, most land in the agrarian reform had been distributed to *ejidatarios*, with *individual* plots to each *ejido* member. But Cárdenas confronted, for the first time, the need to distribute the land of highly productive haciendas in irrigated regions where the agrarian movement was intense; he felt there were scale economies. In order to preserve the productivity of large units and to maintain an uninterrupted flow of agricultural raw materials and wage goods to industry, Cárdenas's policy was to create "collective" *ejidos*, which appeared very similar to producer cooperatives. Ultimately, about 12 percent of all *ejidos* assumed this collective form of organization (Eckstein 1966).

Although Cárdenas obliged the large-acreage ex-owners to transform themselves into capitalist agriculturists, he also respected the principle of "small private property ownership." Each time a farm was expropriated, the owner could retain the hacienda core, not to exceed 150 hectares of irrigated land; in land reform jargon, which often involves a euphemistic turn of phrase, this is a "small property" or *pequeña propiedad* (sometimes called a rancho). An important number of *latifundistas*, frightened by the climate of violence in which agrarian reform was being carried out, divided their lands themselves and sold them as "small properties." In some cases, this was done through trusted *prestanombres* ("name lenders"). The *prestanombre* might be a family member or a former employee. These cases usually implied that the original owner retained control of land that was formally "sold."

At the end of his presidential mandate, Cárdenas had granted more land to the peasants than all of his predecessors together: 17,891,577 hectares were distributed among 814,537 peasants (Gutelman 1974, 109).

THE COLLECTIVE *EJIDOS*: LA LAGUNA, EL YAQUI VALLEY, AND ATENCINGO

The Cardenista plan for La Laguna's collective *ejidos* set the example for future collectivization in other regions of modern capitalist agriculture; it was imperative, via this demonstration, for the government to show both the political viability and the economic superiority of collective farming as compared to private property. Furthermore, enough popular strength had to be mobilized to offset the reaction of *hacendados* when their farms were threatened with expropriation. After land redistribution, beneficiary producers had to maintain a solid organization to both resist attacks from ex-*hacendados* and produce at an exemplary level.

The plan was aimed at achieving self-management by *ejidatarios*. In La Laguna, this goal was to be achieved through the organization of beneficiaries into fifteen regional unions, which would eventually substitute for the Ejidal Bank (*Banco Ejidal*, a state credit-granting agency). The fifteen unions would be coordinated by the Central Union of Collective Credit Societies, which was intended to perform the *ejido*'s economic and marketing functions.

This plan was proposed and elaborated through the interaction of the *Ejidatarios*' Central Union and government technicians. The initial impetus for the fifteen regional unions and the Central Union came from beneficiary producers; Cárdenas not only approved the plan but helped to convert the organization into a legal entity. President Cárdenas was so impressed by the La Laguna organization that he thought all future collectives should adopt a similar pattern (Rello 1984).

After months of preparation and labor mobilization, La Laguna agricultural workers finally were awarded *ejido* land grants on 6 October 1936. The total grants consisted of 468,386 hectares, of which 147,710 were irrigated. This meant that 31.2 percent of total cropland, which included 77 percent of total irrigated land in La Laguna region, was granted to *ejidatarios*. The number of beneficiaries totaled 38,101 *ejidatarios*, who were organized into 311 *ejidos* (Whetten 1948, 216–217). (For a more detailed exposition of the La Laguna experience, see Otero 1986, 167–228).

In the first few years, the La Laguna collectives were well supported by government agencies. Thus, their productivity was comparable and, in many cases, superior to that of former capitalist haciendas. This tendency lasted only through 1947 in La Laguna (Restrepo and Eckstein 1975, 93–96).

As in La Laguna, the collectives organized in the Yaqui Valley of southern Sonora also illustrate that production in the initial period was satisfactory. Established later than in La Laguna, agricultural workers at El Yaqui got 17,000 hectares of irrigated land in 1937, on which they cultivated rice, beans, wheat, corn, cantaloupe, and some vegetables. About 2,000 landless workers obtained land in the process. Private holders kept the remaining 27,638 hectares of irrigated land in the valley. This meant that productivity in both sectors could easily be compared.

Productivity tendencies in the Yaqui Valley were similar to those in La Laguna. Availability of credit, technical assistance, and water resources in the first few postreform years was reflected in superior yield per hectare in collective *ejidos* when compared to private farms.

When the state withdrew its support from collectives, a dramatic reversal in production performance occurred. Hewitt de Alcántara (1978) and Silos-Alvarado (1968) present similar figures, which show deteriorating production yields for the post-Cárdenas period. In 1951-1955, the private sector began to show superior yields when compared with those on ejidos financed by the *Banco Ejidal*. For 1956-1960, the advantage of the private sector was accentuated, and this trend continued until at least the mid-1960s (Silos-Alvarado 1968, 27–44). After Cárdenas, state policies toward *ejidos* turned adverse, as succeeding governments came to favor the private sector. In the 1938–1943 period, therefore, *ejidos* showed an advantage of 9 percent in production per hectare when compared to private farms. By 1960, private properties had a 25 percent yield advantage over *ejidos* (Hewitt de Alcántara 1978, 191).

A collective *ejido* was also organized in Atencingo, Puebla. But here the story differs from that in the North. Those pressuring for land were not landless agricultural workers who lived as resident peons on haciendas; they were peasants like those who had rebelled in Morelos under Zapata. In Atencingo, peasants were still demanding redress for the dispossession of communal lands which occurred in the late 1800s.

Sugarcane-producing lands in question in Atencingo included nine villages, which belonged to William Jenkins, former U.S. consul in Puebla. Indeed, he had built an agroindustrial sugar empire of sorts: the harvested cane was destined for a sugar mill which he owned. In order to end the struggle of the Zapatistas, Jenkins decided to circumvent the problem by "donating" his cropland to the *peónes acasillados* on his farm. (A legislative change that was already under way rendered resident peons eligible for *ejido* land grants.) A total of 8,268 hectares, of which 8,076 were irrigated and 192 seasonally cultivable, were allocated to 2,043 of the eligible peons in Atencingo (Paré 1979; Ronfeldt 1973).

Thus, while many of the villagers of this region had fought for the revolution because it promised the return of their lands—and had remained fervently Zapatista—they lost the decisive battle to Jenkins. At his behest, the least revolutionary, least "mobilized" workers in the valley were granted land. The new *ejidatarios* were obliged to produce sugarcane and sell it to Jenkins's mill, thus guaranteeing him a continued supply and, perhaps, a more comfortable living than before.

De facto, then, the Atencingo *ejidatarios* continued to be the mill's peons, as Jenkins played fast and loose with loopholes in the law. They were hired and fired as before and had no real rights over the new collective *ejido*. They lived from their wages only, since no profits were distributed to them between 1938 and 1947. Any grievance they had could be repressed, and corporal punishment was common.

Interestingly, the Atencingo *ejido* produced profits for the first time only in the 1947–1952 period, after the *ejidatarios* freed themselves from Jenkins's control and when their elected representatives ran the cooperative. Because internal divisions were threatening productivity in the early 1950s, however, government authorities imposed a military manager on the cooperative in 1952 as a way to assure a continued supply of sugarcane to Jenkins's mill. A decade of state control of the *ejido* followed, but the collective never showed better economic results than when it was run by the *ejidatarios* themselves (Otero 1986, 112–166).

These three cases of collectivization serve to describe how the sociocultural differences in various parts of Mexico shaped the reform's outcome. In La Laguna, the state eventually controlled most ejidal production, mainly through the Ejidal Bank (now called BANRURAL, *Banco Nacional de Crédito Rural*). In El Yaqui, the agrarian bourgeoisie was consolidated, aided by huge public investments in irrigation infrastructure, while such infrastructure was largely denied to *ejidos*. By the mid-1960s, 80 percent of *ejido* land in the Yaqui Valley was illegally rented out to private entrepreneurs, while *ejidatarios* often worked for a wage on their own land (Hewitt de Alcántara 1978, 193).

Atencingo was the only collective *ejido* in the entire state of Puebla. It represented a sort of capitalist island within a sea of subsistence, peasant-production units, most of which were farmed with only family labor. In 1971, the *ejidatarios* of Atencingo won their decades-long struggle to divide up the immense *ejido* into nine *ejidos*, one under the jurisdiction of each original village, and to parcel the land into individual family plots.

CARDENISMO: THE END OF THE AGRARIAN BOURGEOISIE?

The 150 irrigated hectares (or the equivalent in lower quality land) left to the former owners at the time of reform were the best on the ex-haciendas. They left the proprietors with a precious enclave, complemented by latent contacts with at least some of the agrarian reform beneficiaries. It did not take long, therefore, for many landlords to renew their patron-client domination. Additional leverage was provided to them by the fact that *ejidatarios* often lacked the infrastructure, resources, and credit which, for a price, the *pequeños propietarios* could supply. This sometimes resulted in so much landlord domination that some observers have labeled the phenomenon "neolatifundismo" (Stavenhagen et al. 1968; Warman 1975).

Thus, Cardenismo did not really mean an end to the agrarian bourgeoisie; it did mean a restructuring of the power bloc (Contreras 1977). In a sense, Cardenismo created an opening into which the industrialists stepped with investment; they were abetted by an agreeable state. The state adopted its contemporary form and structure at that time. Personalistic politics of yesteryear were left behind in favor of more impersonal and institutional forms. For example, the man wearing the presidential sash could have extraordinary power, but that power would last for only six years (cf. González Casanova 1964, and Bartra 1986).

After 1938, the consolidated Mexican state geared up in earnest to promote industrialization. Because this meant acquiring large quantities of foreign exchange, agriculture had to be modernized rapidly; crops were to be exported to pay for industrial machinery, raw materials, and technology. The consolidation of this industrial power bloc was one of the new features of the two administrations which followed that of Lázaro Cárdenas, especially that of Miguel Alemán.

ALEMANISMO: RESTRUCTURING THE POWER BLOC UNDER THE HEGEMONY OF THE INDUSTRIALISTS

The end of the peasant-oriented agrarian reform came in 1938. Cárdenas's reformism was limited by negative foreign reactions to the expropriation and nationalization of the petroleum industry and the resultant discontent of the internal bourgeoisie (Hamilton 1982). Thus, a private-sector development philosophy set in before the end of the Cárdenas administration. While World War II called for a policy of "national unity," Mexico awoke after the war to find that its working class and mass organizations had been co-opted by the state. In particular, the National Peasant Confederation (*Confederación Nacional Campesina*, CNC) and the Workers Confederation of Mexico (*Confederación de Trabajadores de México*, CTM) were converted into governmental political arms so that the state could control both peasants and workers. One additional target was the collective *ejido*: it had become a stronghold of opposition and socialist organization and its example was threatening to private firms.

In the late 1940s, the government's productivity drive was combined with a commitment to individualism. Collectivism was equated with the "threat of communism," an epithet of the Cold War era. This was a global change and, reflecting it, "the CNC took an increasingly individualistic position toward land tenure and exploitation during the 1940s, even joining with private property-owners in some states to pressure the regime for stabilization of land tenure" (Sanderson 1981, 138).

All of this was anticipated by two ejidal policy laws in 1942 which sanctioned the individualistic tendencies: the Agrarian Code and the Law of Agricultural Credit. The former placed great emphasis on granting ejidal title (which fell short of full ownership and a fee-simple title) to each beneficiary.

The emphasis on security of possession and on titling accompanied bourgeois pressure for government to extend *certificados de inafectabilidad* (certificates of immunity) to landlords. These certificates were guarantees that holders would never be expropriated. To protect the livestock industry, owners of large acreages got certificates for "enough grazing land for 500 head of cattle" (or the equivalent in smaller livestock) or for "land without irrigation." When they eventually improved their land, the immunity certificates still held, leaving some with substantial farms. Providing these certificates was central to the free-market spirit of the government of Miguel Alemán (1946-1952). Clearly, several paragraphs of the Agrarian Code were amended to promote commercial agriculture. For this reason, Alemán's presidential term has been called the "period of counterreform." His initiatives were further strengthened in later administrations (Gutelman 1974, 115–119). Under Alemán alone, 11,957 certificates of immunity were granted to private landholders and safeguarded over 1,000,000 hectares of cropland for their owners. Also, 336 certificates were granted to protect 3,449,000 hectares of grazing land. During the same period,

56,108 peasants received 3,000,000 hectares, much of which was marginal and infertile.

DISMANTLING THE COLLECTIVE *EJIDOS*

Although the legal strictures meant to dismantle collectives were in place at the end of 1942, government agencies did not begin their campaign against them until 1947, at the beginning of Alemán's term. Representatives of the Ejidal Bank, the Ministry of Agriculture, and other governmental departments tried to convince *ejidatarios* that they could earn more by working their own plots without paying technical and managerial functionaries or contributing to a machinery fund (Hewitt de Alcántara 1978, 174).

Mexico's World War II involvement resulted in its forging close economic and political ties with the United States. This took place during the wartime administration of Manuel Avila Camacho (1940–1946). It was his successor, Alemán, however, who carried out the Cold War's extension in Mexico. The manner in which this hardening of ideological position was effected in Mexico's agrarian structure was dramatic. Not only was financial and technical support withdrawn from the collectives, but the *ejidos'* efforts to become self-managing enterprises were ignored by the government. During this period, there was heavy federal expenditure for irrigation infrastructure (much of it to transform former pastureland into cropland); large-scale capitalist agriculture was given strong impetus under Alemanismo. The government's spending for irrigation in private agriculture is shown in Table 1.

Table 1
Land irrigated through the government's Irrigation for Rural Development Program, 1937–1970[a]

Years	National (hectares)	Sonora (hectares)
1937–1940	5,031	0
1941–1946	37,044	540
1947–1952	146,442	481
1953–1958	147,993	2,415
1959–1964	109,698	2,260
1965–1970	85,108	0

[a] Source: Steven E. Sanderson, *Agrarian Populism and the Mexican State* (Berkeley: University of California Press, 1981), p. 154.

Not by accident, irrigation was chosen as a primary vehicle for modernizing agriculture: it was the infrastructure most needed by the strongest agricultural pressure group in the country, the entrepreneurs of northwestern Mexico.

Alemán's policies consolidated the private-sector orientation which still prevails in Mexico, though there was a brief hiatus (1970–1976) during the administration of Luis Echeverría. In addition to providing heavy investment in large-scale irrigation projects which would benefit large farms, Alemán's presidency shifted much rural credit from the ejidal to the private sector, gave strong impetus to the seed- and yield-improvement centers which would eventually be the linchpin of the green revolution, and emphasized production for export by downplaying the provision of ample foodstuffs for the domestic market (Sanderson 1981, 145). All of these policies were consistent with the consolidation of the industrial bourgeoisie and the formation of a tight alliance with its agrarian counterpart.

The ejidal policy treated thus far has referred predominantly to those *ejidos* organized originally as "collectives" during Cardenismo. However,this type of organization was implemented only in those places where modern haciendas had been expropriated. By 1970, collectives constituted only 12 percent of all *ejidos*. What happened to the vast majority of *ejidos* which was organized on an individual basis from the outset?

A few *ejidatarios* managed to become wealthy from their individual *ejido* plots, often renting in land belonging to their peers. But these were exceptions. Because most individual *ejidos* were in areas of rain-fed agriculture, they did more poorly economically, in general, than the collectives. Individual *ejidos,* in fact, constituted a *minifundio* sector.

Ann Craig (1983) has documented the agrarian history of Los Altos de Jalisco as a case in point. She argues that the *ejidos* in this region are representative of most in the country. As Craig notes, Los Altos de Jalisco is a region "characterized by poor soil and highly variable rainfall, an overwhelmingly *mestizo* population, a pattern of small landholdings, devout Catholicism, conservative politics, and an economy based on dairy farming and small-scale cultivation of maize, beans, and chiles" (Craig 1983:13).

Unemployment in Los Altos is still a major problem, and today there are more landless young men and families than *ejidatarios* in most municipalities of the region (Craig 1983, 245). Agriculture has provided so few rewards and so much hardship that young men now speak more about the need for sources of nonagricultural employment in the countryside than about land. Such perceptions are reinforced by short-term work experiences in Mexican urban centers and in the United States. Thus, in this type of agricultural region, wage labor is highly valued by rural people, but not enough is offered. The region's hacienda class, in contrast, adapted quickly to new conditions after land reform; today, its members are still wealthy.

Several economists have defended the Mexican agrarian reform, arguing that the "social productivity" of small holdings was greater than that of large landholdings (Barchfield 1979; Dovring 1969). They assume that family labor costs can be calculated at zero for the *ejido* sector and for private holdings of 5 hectares or less, where family members provide the bulk of the required labor power. Thus, they calculate an inverse relationship between size of farm and land productivity. "Social productivity" labor costs are acknowledged only for the case of capitalist enterprises where wages are monetary and an actual operating cost to the operator. Their justification for this assumption is that, in societies such as Mexico, where there is an unlimited supply of labor, opportunity costs are virtually nil. Dovring acknowledges that the greater production per hectare in *ejidos* and *minifundios* is due to greater labor intensiveness. This approach disregards the economic consequences for the individual economic unit, focusing only on the macroeconomic or "social" productivity aspects. As recent Mexican experience can attest, such an approach has proved myopic, even at the macroeconomic level. In the long run, what appeared to be macroeconomically productive ended up as agrarian crisis. For the peasant economy, providing free labor to society has had its limit. This was militantly demonstrated by the agrarian movement of the early 1970s, and signs of it are again being manifested in the mid-1980s [for an extended critique of this position, see Bartra (1974) and Bartra and Otero (1987)].

Thus, the agrarian reform has not been able to solve the problems of the rural poor in Mexico. Capitalist development in agriculture expelled a large number of workers, while industrial growth was not sufficient to absorb them. In fact, the optimistic expectations that politicians had in the 1940s about industry and employment never materialized at the required levels. Large numbers in the countryside have been forced to confront counterreform and an industrialization process incapable of absorbing their labor power productively. The net result has been social polarization.

THE RESULT: AGRARIAN CRISIS AND SOCIAL DIFFERENTIATION

The crises of Mexico's rural economy, with capitalist agriculture on the one hand and peasant farming on the other, have resulted in social differentiation among the peasantry within a capitalism that has not expanded the proletarian class proportionately. Instead, an extensive semiproletariat, torn between peasant production on small plots and wage labor for capitalist enterprises, became the largest group in rural society. As the peasant economy continues to deteriorate, depeasantization occurs: increasing numbers of peasants are separated from their means of production and pushed onto a wage-labor market that is incapable of productively absorbing them (cf. Coello 1981).

The first problem is with increased commercialization of agricultural production. From 1940 to 1970, the proportion of output sold by all production units in the country rose from 53.6 to 87.1 percent. If this jump seems impressive, it is all the more so considering that most of the change took place during the first decade of the period. In fact, the percentage of production sold in the market increased from 53.6 percent in 1940 to 82.1 percent in 1950. After the Cardenista agrarian reform, most agricultural production passed through the national market.

Of course, there are differences in the proportion of total output sold by the various land-tenure types (see Table 2). In general, private production units with more than 5 hectares always sold a greater percentage of their output than any other type of producer; performance on these private farms was closely followed by ejidal units. Private operations with 5 hectares or less, the vast majority of them being peasant units, have a more erratic behavior. In 1950 they sold a greater proportion of output than *ejidos* (78.7 versus 72.4 percent), but in 1960 the percentage fell to 67.0, only to increase again in 1970 to 81.0 percent.

The decade of the 1970s began with decreases in production in most crops. Corn production (which stagnated in the mid-1960s) collapsed in 1972, and crop output was not really satisfactory again until the early 1980s—and then, only briefly. A similar pattern occurred with beans (Bartra and Otero 1987).

Table 2
Percentage of production sold, by land tenure type, 1940–1970[a]

Tenure Type	1940	1950	1960	1970
Total	53.6	82.1	82.0	87.0
> 5 hectares	55.7	89.4	87.0	88.2
≤ 5 hectares	40.0	78.7	67.0	81.0
Ejidos	54.2	72.4	77.0	86.2

[a] Source: Elaborated from Dirección General de Estadística, *Censo agrícola-ganadero y ejidal, 1940; 1950; 1960; 1970* (Mexico: DGE, n.d.).

Commercial crops such as cotton, sesame, sugarcane, and tomatoes also were in crisis in the early 1970s. For cotton and sesame, there was no recovery during the early 1980s. The cash crops that did best are those directly linked to agribusiness with export interests, namely, citrus, pineapples, and strawberries: "All these commodities grew rapidly, while the basic foodstuffs sector barely grew at all" (Sanderson 1986, 279). The growth of these cash crops, which might be referred to as "luxury foodstuffs," along with the growth of grain production for feeding livestock, expresses the internationalization of Mexican agriculture (Sanderson 1986).

Mexican cities absorb major quantities of corn, making it possible for peasants to purchase industrial products indispensable for sustenance in the countryside. On farms, corn is usually stored as insurance against bad times. Thus, when corn prices rise, a lower quantity is required to achieve a balance between work and consumption (Chayanov 1974). Given capital scarcity and low land quality, peasants cannot shift their production to other crops easily. And since access to land is usually restricted, peasants can rely only on extending the use of the single resource over which they have control: domestic labor power.[2]

In a few years, Mexico's agriculture went from providing ample foreign exchange necessary for industrialization to not even being able to feed its own population (Sanderson 1986). For this reason, the José López Portillo administration (1976-1982) implemented the Mexican Food System (*Sistema Alimentario Mexicano*, SAM) in 1980, a strategy to gain self-sufficiency in basic grain production (*Nueva Antropología* 1981). Although the official declarations presumed that self-sufficiency would follow from strengthening the peasant economy in rain-fed agricultural zones, most production increases really took place in irrigation districts. This indicates that government prices were so high that members of the agrarian bourgeoisie seized the opportunity to profit from basic grains. In fact, production rose markedly for both beans and corn in 1980 (Redclift 1981).

Mexicans were paying dearly for these production increases, it turned out, for they involved massive subsidies. And, while there was some progress, it was transitory—the results in 1982 were disappointing, due in part to lower than normal rainfall. When Miguel de la Madrid took office, in December 1982, SAM was abandoned.

Despite the fact that the 1960s witnessed a large redistribution of land, the erosion of the peasant economy was considerable. Part of the reason was that poor land was distributed during the Gustavo Díaz Ordaz presidency (1964–1970). While 25 million hectares were distributed, a larger quantity than under Cárdenas, only about 10 percent of it was arable (Gutelman 1974).

In 1970, a large proportion of small agricultural producers were no longer able to sustain themselves by relying only on their farmland. The process of semiproletarianization was already under way: an increasing number of rural producers were caught between a situation of insufficient peasant production and a wage-labor market offering few alternative employment opportunities.

As such, the 1970s saw the beginning of a simultaneous explosion of two crises: an accelerated retrogression in the living standards of small peasants and a fall in export prices which profoundly affected the commercial sector. Politically, this resulted in a renewed tendency of peasant producers to struggle for land (Otero 1981, 1983).

AGRICULTURE-INDUSTRY RELATIONS AND INTERNATIONALIZATION OF PRODUCTION

What changes have been introduced into the production structure by the Mexican agrarian reform process? Specifically, what has happened in terms of agriculture-industry relations, the relative importance of the subsectors in agriculture, the polarization between entrepreneurial and peasant agricultural regions in the countryside, and, finally, the growing internationalization of production?

During the 1970s, the chemical industry increased its participation in manufacturing to become the second most important subsector, closely followed by the metal-mechanics subsector (Montes de Oca and Zamorano Ulloa 1983, 78). The food-and-textiles industry accounted for the largest percentage of gross domestic product (GDP) contributed by the manufacturing industry in Mexico, ranging from 24.5 to 27.9 percent of manufacturing output in the 1970–1978 period. However, its high point appeared in 1970, with slow decreases until it reached its lowest point in 1978. While the food-and-textiles industry once accounted for the largest proportion of manufactured exports (60 percent in 1970/71), and despite the fact that Mexican-American trade relations increased by a factor of eleven in the last decade, this industry's exports decreased to 15 percent of total manufactured exports by 1983. In contrast, the manufacturing subsectors producing metals, equipment, and machinery increased their exports from 11 percent of that total to 33 percent in the 1970–1983 period; this would probably reach 45 percent by the end of 1986 (Dehesa 1986, 33–34). Thus agricultural products and their industrial derivatives lost their traditional role of producing foreign exchange for the Mexican economy.

Furthermore, there has been an increasing "disarticulation" between industry and agriculture over the past two decades. The two sectors were "articulated" in 1945–1955 in that there was a tendency for technological homogeneity, both across and between sectors, and industry had an encouraging effect upon agricultural production by absorbing much of its raw material output. Disarticulation has been the result partly of green revolution technologies and partly of state price policies. The introduction of high-yielding varieties and chemical fertilizers effected a deepening technological heterogeneity between and within the two sectors: the green revolution technologies were biased toward irrigated zones and better off farmers who could afford purchased inputs. The other major factors contributing to the deterioration of agriculture and its links with industry were the state's price policies combined with the lack of dynamism in the tortilla industry itself. "Guaranteed prices," supposedly designed by the state to support farmers, actually functioned to lower agricultural prices for industry. For example, the guaranteed price for corn remained fixed from 1963 to 1972, while that for wheat was constant from 1960 to 1972 (Appendini and Almeida Salles 1980). In 1972, when prices were finally raised, the new prices were inadequate to restore profitability to corn and wheat production. By 1979, as a result of their insufficient output, 69 percent of the national wheat supply had to be imported to meet internal demand, although this figure diminished to 30 percent by 1983. The tortilla and *nixtamal* subsectors, partly due to large subsidies through guaranteed prices, have maintained typically artisan forms of production. Thus, industry has not encouraged expanded corn production.

In contrast, the growth of oleaginous crops, particularly soybeans and safflower, along with sorghum, has been impressive, although their combined weight in agricultural production is still less than 8 percent (Rodríguez Gigena 1983, 10). The expansion of these crops has taken place mostly in the northern regions where irrigation predominates. Soybean farmers use improved seeds on 100 percent of their acreage, while the proportion is 80 percent for safflower producers. Although there is some articulation with industry in these two crops, in the 1977–1979 period, 45 percent of national production had to be imported because agriculture did not produce enough to supply local industry. Sorghum was controlled by transnational corporations (TNCs) located in the livestock-feed industry. These transnationals control sorghum production through contract farming and through the feed, hog, and poultry industries. Such control is partly guaranteed by the TNCs' monopoly over genetic lines of poultry (Montes de Oca and Zamorano Ulloa 1983).

Regional polarization tendencies have gone hand in hand with the expansion of irrigation infrastructure and the increased use of high-yielding varieties introduced with the green revolution. With increased investment in irrigation works, beginning in the 1940s, commercial producers came to be very concentrated in a small area: almost 50 percent of agricultural production comes from 23 percent of the total cropland and is produced by 19 percent of the rural work force. By contrast, the vast peasant and semiproletarian regions account for half of the total cropland, for more than half of the total rural work force, and for only one-third of the total agricultural production (Appendini 1983, 192).

Irrigation districts in the North have been the real locus of the green revolution. Countrywide, 80 percent of the irrigated acreage with alfalfa, sorghum, soybeans, rice, corn, beans, or wheat is planted with improved or hybrid seeds. Moreover, the production of seeds increasingly has been by private firms, mostly by TNCs. Whereas the National Seed Producer (*Productora Nacional de Semillas,* PRONASE), the government's seed-producing firm, sold 41.1 percent of the high-yielding seeds and private firms sold 58.9 percent in 1970, these figures were 26.9 and 73.1 percent, respectively, in 1977. TNCs not only control the market but often have to import seeds from the United States to complement their supply.

Apart from wheat, half of the improved seeds imported by industries with dynamic growth rates in the 1970s were related to livestock and feed (Suárez 1983). The increased importance of livestock production and its associated crops has brought internationalization to Mexican agriculture. Whether it is importing seeds, producing feed, importing genetic material (for both plants and animals), or selling the final product, most of these activities are carried out by TNCs (Barkin and Suárez 1983). Much of this meat is being exported. Domestically, increased demand for meat comes from the middle- and high-income social classes. By the increased internationalization of agriculture, the Mexican nation is losing control of its agriculture at the same time that it is losing the capacity to produce basic grains to feed its population [for an extensive treatment of these issues, see Sanderson (1986)].

SOCIAL DIFFERENTIATION OF AGRICULTURAL PRODUCERS

Data on peasant differentiation in Mexico have been provided by the Economic Commission for Latin America of the United Nations (*Comisión Económica para América Làtina y el Caribe,* CEPAL), which analyzed the 1970 Mexican population and agricultural censuses (CEPAL 1982). CEPAL's study resulted in a typology of agricultural producers in Mexico.[3] Its goal was to distinguish between peasant and entrepreneurial farms. CEPAL's assumption was that small-farm units worked by campesinos have different "rules of the game" from capitalistic agricultural enterprises. While the latter seek to maximize profits, peasant units seek to maximize the returns to family labor, since subsistence is the *minifundio* family's prime objective. Therefore, peasant farming operations are usually much more labor intensive than those of capitalist enterprises.

Table 3 shows the distribution of agricultural production units in Mexico according to CEPAL's typology. The figures for the ejidal and private land-tenure sectors have been merged, because the pattern of social differentiation is similar under both tenure systems (CEPAL 1982, 278–281). Entrepreneurial producers are concentrated in the private sector. Merging the data for the two systems gives the best overall picture of social structure differentiation in rural Mexico, but, when the two are combined, the proportion of "entrepreneurs" declines.

CEPAL used two central criteria to distinguish between peasant and entrepreneurial categories in its typology. (1) Did the farm unit hire wage labor? (2) Did the farm attain or exceed subsistence production levels? "Peasant units" were those worked with family labor that occasionally hired wage labor. "Hiring" was measured by wage payments, which were not to exceed the equivalent of twenty-five hired workdays per year (calculated by yearly expenditures for wages divided by the daily legal minimum wage in each region or state). Most peasant units do hire some workers beyond the family during a few days at harvest. And members of such *minifundio* farms usually worked as wage laborers

Table 3
Mexico: Distribution of agricultural producers in CEPAL's 1970 typology[a]

Type of Production Unit[b]	Percentage
Peasant	
I (infrasubsistence)	55.6
II (subsistence)	16.2
III (stationary)	6.5
IV (surplus-producing)	8.2
Transitional	
V (transitional)	11.6
Entrepreneurial	
VI (small)	1.2
VII (medium)	0.4
VIII (large)	0.3

[a] Source: Comisión Económica para América Latina y el Caribe, *Economía campesina y agricultura empresarial (tipología de productores del agro mexicano)*, by Alejandro Schejtman (Mexico City: Siglo XXI Editores, 1982), pp. 118–119.
[b] Total number of production units = 2,557,070.

laborers on other peasant farms for a few days a year. (This exchange of labor is, in many cases, the monetized form of previous reciprocity relations in peasant communities.)

By CEPAL's criteria, infrasubsistence production units do not meet household food requirements. I would prefer to call this group of families "semiproletarian"—their livelihood is predicated on an increased level of off-farm economic activity by those members of the family who hire out. The expansion of this category expresses the crisis in the peasant economy, which is losing its capacity to provide the rural masses with a livelihood. This is "depeasantization without full proletarianization."[4]

To find out whether peasant producers are becoming more viable or are failing, the proportion of agricultural producers in the various land-tenure categories between 1960 and 1970 can be compared by utilizing the Center of Agrarian Research (*Centro de Investigaciones Agrarias*, CDIA) study of the 1960 census (CDIA 1974). While the CDIA study classifies rural producers into only five categories (infrasubsistence, sub-family, family, medium-sized multifamily, and large-sized multifamily), the CEPAL study defines eight types of production unit. To achieve some comparability, I have merged CEPAL's three entrepreneurial types into one to form six categories: infrasubsistence, subsistence, stationary, surplus-producing, transitional, and entrepreneurial. A graphic comparison is presented in Figure 1.

These data show the decline of the peasant economy between 1960 and 1970. Specifically, the middle units appear to be going bankrupt, thus reinforcing the polarization of agriculture: both the semiproletarian and the bourgeois sectors are increasing while there is a "disappearing middle" group. Moreover, a large proportion of former peasants or semiproletarians simply fall out of the analysis: they are ex-peasants who cannot hold onto at least a semiproletarian position and have become day laborers or have moved to the cities.

Table 4 categorizes the economically active rural population, using census terminology.[4]

The absolute numbers of the agricultural work force decreased from 1960 to 1970, continuing a several-decades-old trend. Similarly, it is not surprising that "workers" have decreased in absolute numbers. This decrease reflects the secular decline of the agricultural sector as the economy develops; rural-to-urban migration brings it about, and agricultural mechanization hastens it along. However, it should be noted that the "peasant" category decreased more drastically than "workers," from 2.5 to 2 million people. The relative number of workers in the labor force increased from 57.4 to 59.3 percent, whereas that of peasants decreased from 42.3 to 38.2 percent.

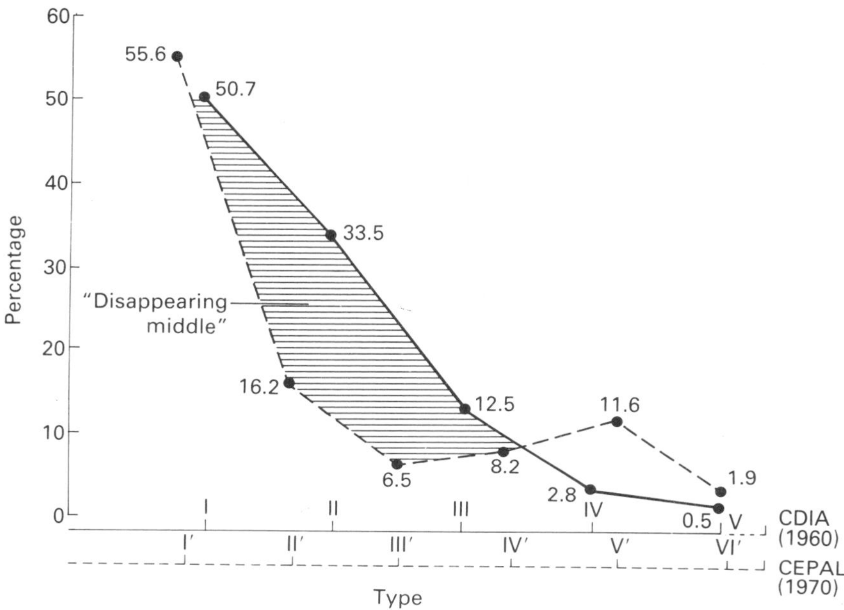

Figure 1
Changes in Mexican agrarian structure, 1960–1970.

CDIA typology (—), 1960: I, Infrasubsistence; II, subfamily; III, family; IV, medium-sized multifamily; V, large-sized multifamily. CEPAL typology (------), 1970: I', Infrasubsistence; II', subsistence; III', stationary; IV', surplus producing; V', transitional; VI', entrepreneurial. Elaborated with data from Centro de Investigaciones Agrarias, *Estructura agraria y desarrollo agrícola en México* (Mexico: Fondo de Cultura Económica, 1974), and Comisión Económica para América Latina y el Caribe, *Económia campesina y agricultura empresarial (tipología de productores del agro mexicano)*, by Alejandro Schejtman (Mexico: Siglo XXI Editores, 1982).

Table 4
Economically active rural population (rural workforce), 1960 and 1970[a]

	1960		1970	
Sector	Millions	Percentage	Millions	Percentage
Workers	3.4	57.4	3.0	59.3
Peasants	2.5	42.2	2.0	38.2
Employers	0.02	0.3	0.13	2.5

[a] Source: Dirección General de Estadística, *Censo general de población, 1960; 1970* (Mexico City: DGE, n.d.).

CONCLUSIONS

Mexico is currently undergoing the most severe economic crisis of its postrevolutionary history. After agriculture had became unable to provide foreign exchange by the mid-1960s, the Mexican economy turned increasingly to foreign indebtedness to sustain industrial growth. During Echeverría's term in office, the foreign debt grew by a factor of five. A short break followed when large oil reserves were discovered in 1977. And, from 1978 to 1981, Mexico experienced growth rates of about 8 percent on the basis of its "oil boom." Unfortunately, this boom was short lived, and it was the basis for further foreign indebtedness. In mid-1981, oil prices began to fall at a time that oil constituted close to 75 percent of Mexico's exports. February 1982 was the beginning of a series of major devaluations in Mexican currency.

The agrarian policy of the Mexican government since López Portillo's administration has again come almost militantly to favor the private sector. De la Madrid has officially ruled out land distribution as a solution to Mexico's agricultural problems. Government rhetoric now talks of a "higher stage" of agrarian reform, referring to the need for increasing productivity on the land currently available to *ejidatarios*. Meanwhile, the right wing is exerting pressure to do away with the legal barriers which *ejidos* impose for investment. Some barely disguise their antipathy to reform. For instance, the Mexican Confederation of Employers (*Confederación Patronal Mexicana,* COPARMEX) recently advocated giving the *ejido* land to those who work on it in private ownership (COPARMEX 1985, 6). COPARMEX proposes that the only way to generate food self-sufficiency and foreign exchange from agriculture is by privatizing all land. The true solution, says COPARMEX, "consists in giving peasants the land in private ownership...to avoid the *latifundio*" (COPARMEX 1985).

In fact, however, the brief experiences of *ejidatarios* with self-management and democratic institutions showed them to be capable of greater production per hectare than private agricultural enterprises when aided by state institutions. The all-out development of state-sponsored capitalistic agriculture is what decimated the *ejido* sector. Only a postcapitalist global outlook and development strategy, predicated on self-management and democratic production and concerned with expanding employment opportunities for direct producers, will solve the problems of the agricultural semiproletariat and provide for the food self-sufficiency of the country (Otero 1986, 1987).

In the Mexican context, distributing titles of private landownership to *ejidatarios* would only further aggravate the polarizing tendencies of social differentiation. Even if *ejidos* are to be organized on an individual basis, depending on the specific preference of direct producers, the *ejido* as an institution cannot be eliminated in Mexico without causing a greater social upset than has already occurred.

It is clear that Mexico's peasant economy is not advancing satisfactorily. *Minifundistas* continually become more semiproletarianized, and the capitalist sector is incapable of providing full employment or self-sufficiency in food production.

The semiproletariat is the most rapidly growing group in numbers in rural Mexico. The character of new agrarian struggles and the organizations that emerge will depend greatly on the political direction taken by this semiproletariat, which, in turn, will depend on the sociocultural specificities of the region where each has developed. In the North, direct producers may be ready for cooperative arrangements of a self-managing and democratic nature, whereas in central and southern Mexico, producers are probably more inclined to individual production. In either case, it is clear that other sources of employment in addition to agriculture will be badly needed in order to absorb the large proportion of workers without adequate and secure sources of income.

NOTES

1. Zapata earned his livelihood from training horses on a hacienda in exchange for a wage. Thus, strictly speaking, he was not a peasant. Yet, he was a respected member of the community.

2. Use of this resource also has a limit, however, when its productivity drops below zero. When hired labor is used, such a limit is reached when labor's marginal product equals the wage. Those who assume the value of labor power to be zero in the peasant unit are actually looking at its lower limit, below which agricultural production makes no sense to peasant farmers. Whereas peasants usually sacrifice their ground rent and often part of their self-imputed "wage," assuming the latter to be zero from the outset actually places the analysis at the point of peasant bankruptcy.

3. For a discussion and critique of the criteria for devising each category, see Otero (1986) and Bartra and Otero (1987).

4. For an extended discussion of CEPAL's typology, see Bartra and Otero (1987).

REFERENCES

Aguilar Camín, Hector. 1977. *La frontera nómada: Sonora y la revolución mexicana*. Mexico City: Siglo XXI Editores.

———.1982. *Saldos de la revolución*. Mexico City: Siglo XXI Editores.

Appendini, Kristen A. de. 1983. La polarización de la agricultura mexicana: Un análisis a nivel de zonas agrícolas. In *Economía Mexicana*, edited by

Gonzalo Rodríguez Gigena, pp. 181–216. Mexico City: Centro de Investigación y Docencia Económica.

Appendini, Kristen A. de, and Vania Almeida Salles. 1980. Precios de garantía y crisis agrícola. *Nueva Antropología* (Mexico) 4(13/14):187–218.

Barchfield, John W. 1979. Land tenure and social productivity in Mexico. LTC paper, no. 121. Mimeograph. Madison: Land Tenure Center, University of Wisconsin, January.

Barkin, David, and Blanca Suárez. 1983. *El fin del principio: Las semillas y la seguridad alimentaria*. Mexico City: Centro de Estudios de Ecodesarrollo y Oceano.

Bartra, Roger. 1974. *Estructura agraria y clases sociales en México*. Mexico City: Ediciones Era.

———.1986. *México: La democracia ausente*. Mexico City: Grijalbo.

Bartra, Roger, and Gerardo Otero. 1987. Agrarian crisis and social differentiation in Mexico. *Journal of Peasant Studies* 14(3):334–362.

Beals, Ralph L. 1932. *The comparative ethnology of northern Mexico before 1750*. Berkeley: Univ. of California Press.

Carr, Barry. 1973. Las peculiaridades del norte mexicano, 1880–1927: Ensayo de interpretación. *Historia Mexicana* 22(3):320–346.

———.1980. Recent regional studies of the Mexican revolution. *Latin American Research Review* 15(1):3–14.

CDIA (Centro de Investigaciones Agrarias). 1974. *Estructura agraria y desarrollo agrícola en México*. Mexico City: Fondo de Cultura Económica.

CEPAL (Comisión Económica para América Latina y el Caribe). 1982. *Economía campesina y agricultura empresarial (tipología de productores del agro mexicano)*. By Alejandro Schejtman. Mexico City: Siglo XXI Editores.

Chayanov, A.V. 1974. *La organización de la unidad económica campesina*. Buenos Aires: Nueva Visión.

Coello, Manuel. 1981. ¿Recampesinización en la descampesinización? *Revista Mexicana de Sociología* 43(1):329–342.

Contreras, Ariel José. 1977. *México 1940: Industrialización y crisis política*. Mexico City: Siglo XXI Editores.

COPARMEX (Confederación Patronal Mexicana). 1985. La COPARMEX frente al *ejido*. *El Día* (Mexico City), 17 August.

Córdova, Arnaldo. 1972. *La formación del poder político en México*. Mexico City: Ediciones Era.

Craig, Ann L. 1983. *The first agraristas: An oral history of a Mexican agrarian reform movement*. Berkeley: Univ. of California Press.

———.1986. Popular mobilization in the Comarca Lagunera: 1918–1936. Monograph. San Diego: Department of Political Science, University of California.

Cumberland, Charles C. 1975. *La revolución mexicana: Los años constitucionalistas*. Mexico City: Fondo de Cultura Económica.

Dehesa, Mario. 1986. El patrón de especialización de las exportaciones mexicanas. Mimeograph. San Diego: Center for U.S.-Mexican Studies, University of California.

Dovring, Folke. 1969. Land reform and productivity: The Mexican case, analysis of census data. LTC paper, no. 63. Mimeograph. Madison: Land Tenure Center, University of Wisconsin, January.

Eckstein, Salomón. 1966. *El ejido colectivo en México.* Mexico City: Fondo de Cultura Económica.

Falcón, Romana. 1977. *El agrarismo en Veracruz: La etapa radical (1928-1935).* Mexico City: Colegio de México.

Fowler Salamini, Heather. 1979. *Movilización campesina en Veracruz (1920-1938).* Mexico City: Siglo XXI Editores.

Gilly, Adolfo. 1974. *La revolución interrumpida,* 4th ed. Mexico City: Editorial el Caballito.

González Casanova, Pablo. 1964. *La democracia en México.* Mexico City: Ediciones Era.

Gutelman, Michel. 1974. *Capitalismo y reforma agraria en México.* Mexico City: Ediciones Era.

Hamilton, Nora. 1982. *The limits of state autonomy: Postrevolutionary Mexico.* Princeton, N.J.: Princeton Univ. Press.

Hansen, Roger D. 1974. *La política del desarrollo mexicano.* Mexico City: Siglo XXI Editores.

Hewitt de Alcántara, Cynthia. 1978. *Modernización de la agricultura mexicana.* Mexico City: Siglo XXI Editores.

Katz, Friederich. 1982. *La guerra secreta en México.* 2 vols. Mexico City: Ediciones Era.

Landsberger, Henry A., and Cynthia Hewitt de Alcántara. 1970. *Peasant organizations in La Laguna, Mexico: History, structure, member participation and effectiveness.* Research Papers on Land Tenure and Agrarian Reform, no. 17. Washington: Inter-American Committee for Agricultural Development, Organization of American States.

López Cámara, Francisco. 1967. *La estructura económica y social de México en la época de la reforma.* Mexico City: Siglo XXI Editores.

Loyola Díaz, Rafael. 1980. *La crisis Obregón-Calles y el estado mexicano.* Mexico City: Siglo XXI Editores.

Matute, Alvaro. 1980. *Historia de la revolución mexicana, 1917–1924,* vol. 8, *La carrerra del caudillo.* Mexico City: Colegio de México.

Medin, Tzvi. 1982. *El minimato presidencial: Historia política del maximato (1928–1935).* Mexico City: Ediciones Era.

Montes de Oca, Rosa Elena, and José Zamorano Ulloa. 1983. La articulación agricultura-industria en los principales granos y oleoginosas. In *Economía Mexicana,* edited by Gonzalo Rodríguez Gigena, pp. 55–82. Mexico City: Centro de Investigación y Docencia Económica.

Nueva Antropología (Mexico). 1981. 5(17), May.

Nugent, Daniel. 1985. Anthropology, handmaiden of history? An answer from the field. *Critique of Anthropology,* 5(2), September.

Otero, Gerardo. 1981. El campesinado como sujeto revolucionario. *El Machete: Revista de Cultura Política* (Mexico), no. 9, January, pp. 25–28.

———.1983. Lucha por la tierra y organización clasista del campesinado. *Crítica* (Puebla), no. 14, February.

———.1986. Political class formation in rural Mexico: Class, state and culture. Ph.D. dissertation, University of Wisconsin-Madison.

———.1987. El nuevo movimiento agrario: Autogestión y producción democrática. Paper presented at the First Meeting Regarding Rural Issues in

Northwestern Mexico and Southwestern United States, Coliacán, Sinaloa, Mexico, 13–16 January.

Paré, Luisa, ed. 1979. *Ensayos sobre el problema cañero.* Mexico City: Universidad Nacional Autónoma de México.

Redclift, M.R. 1981. El estado frente al campo. *Nexos* 4(47), pp. 11–16.

Rello, Fernando. 1984. El leviatán lagunero: Ensayo sobre una agricultura Estatizada. n.p.

Restrepo, Iván, and Salomón Eckstein. 1975. *La agricultura colectiva en México: La experiencia de La Laguna.* Mexico City: Siglo XXI Editores.

Rodríguez Gigena, Gonzalo, ed. 1983. *Economía mexicana.* Mexico City: Centro de Investigación y Docencia Económica.

Ronfeldt, David. 1973. *Atencingo: The politics of agrarian struggle in a Mexican ejido.* Stanford, Calif.: Stanford Univ. Press.

Sanderson, Steven E. 1981. *Agrarian populism and the Mexican state.* Berkeley: Univ. of California Press.

———. 1986. *The transformation of Mexican agriculture: International structure and the politics of rural change.* Princeton, N.J.: Princeton Univ. Press.

Silos-Alvarado, José S. 1968. The Yaqui Valley of Sonora, Mexico: Its agricultural development, resource utilization and economic potential. Ph.D. dissertation, Cornell University, Ithaca, N.Y.

Stavenhagen, Rodolfo et al. 1968 *Neolatifundismo y explotación: Del Emiliano Zapata a Anderson Clayton and Co.* Mexico City: Editorial Nuestro Tiempo.

Suárez, Blanca. 1983. Las semillas mejoradas y los cambios en el sector agropecuario en México, 1970–1977. In *Economía Mexicana,* edited by Gonzalo Rodríguez Gigena, pp. 99–118. Mexico City: Centro de Investigación y Docencia Económica.

Warman, Arturo. 1975. El neolatifundio mexicano: Expansión y crisis de una forma de dominio. *Comercio Exterior* (Mexico) 25(12):1368–1374.

Wasserman, Mark. 1980. The social origins of the 1910 Revolution in Chihuahua. *Latin American Research Review* 15(1):15–38.

Whetten, Nathan L. 1948. *Rural Mexico.* Chicago: Univ. of Chicago Press.

Womack, John, Jr. 1969. *Zapata and the Mexican Revolution.* New York: Vintage Books.

Chapter 11

Agrarian Reform in the Dominican Republic

J. David Stanfield*

Since Rafael Trujillo's death in 1961, agrarian reform in the Dominican Republic has been conditioned by economic and social factors as well as by the changing international scene. The reform's basic features, however, evolved from the earlier development of the Dominican political economy. During Trujillo's dictatorial rule (1930–1961), significant changes occurred in the country's landownership structure. In that period, some land was transferred from state to individual farmer ownership through some forty colonization projects involving approximately 11,000 beneficiaries. More significant was Trujillo's (and his clique's) consolidation of large holdings, particularly large sugar estates and irrigated rice land, and his acquisition of other agricultural and industrial enterprises. To understand the agrarian reform in the Dominican Republic, some discussion of the legacy of this caudillo and the conditions of life in the Dominican Republic at the time of his death is helpful.

THE TRUJILLO LEGACY AND AGRARIAN REFORM

In 1960 the country's population was about 3.7 million with 71 percent living in rural areas; in Latin America, only Haiti and Honduras were more rural. The population density of the Dominican Republic was about 62 people per square kilometer, again the third highest in the region after El Salvador and Haiti.

As revealed by social indicators, the standard of living in 1960 in the Dominican Republic was low: only 12 percent of the homes had

* Latin American Program Coordinator of the Land Tenure Center, University of Wisconsin-Madison.

piped water and just 2 percent had electric lights; over 80 percent of the rural population was illiterate. There were only three graduates of an agricultural university in the entire country, making it the nation with the least trained rural talent pool in Latin America.

The agricultural sector was the focal point of the economy. In 1960, agriculture provided 41 percent of the country's gross national product and nearly 90 percent of its exports. Sugar represented 60 percent of agricultural export value. Agriculture was also the seat of great wealth and deep poverty. By 1960, two owners, Trujillo and the Gulf and Western Company, owned roughly three-fifths of the sugar-producing lands and sugar-processing facilities. In 1960, there were roughly 450,000 farmers; about 1 percent of this number owned over 50 percent of the land. There were at least 200,000 landless rural families dependent on day labor for their sustenance. The mean per capita income was $200 (U.S. dollars) yearly. On this variable, the Dominican Republic ranked tenth among Latin American countries. The index of gross domestic product per capita, on the other hand, was 27 percent below the average for all of Latin America. The country's agriculture operated from a relatively small land base: only 2.5 acres of cultivated land were available per inhabitant, the second lowest area per person in Latin America after El Salvador.

THE POST-TRUJILLO PHASES OF THE AGRARIAN REFORM

Following Trujillo's assassination, there were several months of junta rule; Dr. Joaquin Balaguer was named president in August 1961. During 1961 and for some time thereafter, a major reassignment of rights to land was instituted. Since Trujillo and his associates were among the country's major landowners and industrialists, their holdings became the focus of attention. Using Decree 6988 of 1961, the state confiscated these properties.[1] Of particular importance were the extensive sugar estates and refineries. The State Sugar Council (*Consejo Estatal de Azúcar*, CEA) was created to manage the 1.4 million tareas[2] of sugarcane. Some Trujillo lands in other areas were "repossessed" by those who had previously lost them in Trujillo's various maneuvers. Still others were invaded by squatters and small farmers and by neighboring large landowners, who felt the time opportune to take advantage of the power vacuum created by the dictator's death.

Hemispheric and domestic events coalesced to play a role in Dominican discussions of agrarian policies. The Punta del Este declaration of the Inter-American Economic and Social Council encouraged "programs of comprehensive agrarian reforms, leading to the effective transformation...of unjust structures and systems of land tenure and use with a view to replacing latifundia...by an equitable system of property...." (Inter-American Economic and Social Council 1961, I:par. 6). This declaration placed a discussion of property rights on the public policy agenda in many countries; in the Dominican Republic, where deciding on what to do with the Trujillo holdings was of paramount importance, the timing was opportune. The Charter of Punta del Este fortified the position of those who argued for agrarian reform.

In late 1961 and early 1962, the country was immersed in a ferment of political discussion. In addition to a pending agrarian reform, a new constitution had to be written and a presidential election was upcoming. The constitution, when it emerged, had two implications for agrarian reform. First, the social function of property was recognized to be superior to the right of private ownership, that is, the state could expropriate private property provided there was a clear social benefit to be obtained and the owner was paid just indemnification. Second, the new constitution gave the right to vote to all Dominican citizens over 18 years of age, and the large, young, rural population became a new center of gravity for the political process and for the political parties which aspired to run the new government.

During the presidential campaign, Juan Bosch and his Dominican Revolutionary Party campaigned openly for an agrarian reform, thereby making an appeal for the rural-poor vote. Resulting partly from this pressure, Agrarian Reform Law 5879, which established the Dominican Agrarian Institute (*Instituto Agrario Dominicano*, IAD), was approved in April 1962 and signed into effect by acting President Rafael F. Bonnelly and the Council of State. IAD, as formalized, had the primary function of distributing state lands to individual farmers (*parceleros* or *asentados*) in separate lots of sufficient size to support a farm family. IAD was charged with the initial selection of agrarian reform beneficiaries and the assignment to each of provisional property rights. Another mandate of the agrarian reform agency was to help beneficiaries obtain credit and to provide them with technical assistance and training. At some future date, IAD was to effectuate the definitive transfer of land rights to reform beneficiaries. Conspicuous for its absence was any provision in Law 5879 for the acquisition of land for reform other than the general right of IAD to solicit land from the executive branch of government, to receive land as donations, and to rent or purchase land. Criteria for expropriation were not defined.

A law (no. 5852) controlling the use of water was promulgated at approximately the same time that the Agrarian Reform Law was approved. It specified that landowners who use (or are capable of using) water from a canal of state construction should pay for their use of that water by transferring a prescribed portion of their land to the government for reform purposes. Law 5852 became known as the *Cuota Parte Law*. All land acquired in this manner would become IAD property for use in the agrarian reform. Parcels smaller than 60 tareas were exceptions. Thus, in the absence of an expropriation provision in the Agrarian Reform Law, the state was enabled to acquire land for reform through its water-development laws.

In March 1963, Bosch was elected president with much help from the newly enfranchised peasants. During his 6-month term, he acted to fortify the agrarian reform with two initiatives: (1) he pushed for the new constitution to include a provision whereby the possession of excessive amounts of land would be regarded as contrary to national interest, as would *minifundios* and the ownership of land by foreigners (an early but clear threat to Gulf and Western), and (2) he vigorously applied the *Cuota Parte* and the anti-Trujillo confiscation decrees so that land could be acquired by IAD and assigned to beneficiaries. Productive rice land was of particular interest to Bosch. He created several *asentamientos* (agrarian reform settlements) composed of individual rice-producing parcels on relatively productive land.

In September 1963, a coup deposed Bosch and established a triumvirate headed by Donald Reid Cabral. Continued turmoil, combined with U.S. fears that the Dominican Republic would evolve into another Cuba, resulted in the U.S. invasion of the country in April 1965.

Balaguer returned from exile in 1965; in 1966 he was again elected president. In his first speech to the nation, Balaguer referred to the rigidity of the country's agrarian structure—its system of land tenure—and, in a variant of *Cuota Parte*, offered large landowners shares in state companies in exchange for parts of their lands for redistribution to landless peasants. He received no response. The agrarian reform continued at a snail's pace to settle farmers on state lands, which were still mostly lands acquired upon Trujillo's death.

Balaguer's reform program faced serious institutional constraints. The opposition of the landed class to an invigorated agrarian reform was a major reason behind its slow implementation. The landed aristocracy still held economic and military power and received much international aid and support. An example of how this power was manifested can be found in the composition of the National Development Commission, a governmental policy-making body of seven members. The commission was headed by a well-known representative of the landed elite and was regularly attended by the U.S. ambassador or his representative (Dore y Cabral 1981, 51). While the landed interests approved of a reform that distributed Trujillo lands, they not surprisingly opposed any plans to redistribute other private property (Clausner 1973, 252).

Agrarian reform as a redistributive measure remained on the public agenda, however. One of the more significant institutional changes of the 1960s was a gradual shift in the ideology of the Roman Catholic Church toward the development of programs which would support the peasantry. The social orientation of many younger priests and the development of "liberation theology" led to Church involvement in organizing peasant leagues and incorporating the rural landless as active participants pressuring for agrarian reform. Imperceptible at first, the growth of these organizations increased after the 1966 election of Balaguer (see Dore y Cabral 1984).

Various political and semipolitical organizations began to compete for peasant support in the 1960s. Two such groups proved to be particularly important in organizing peasants and pressuring for a more ambitious agrarian reform. The first, the Dominican Federation of Christian Agrarian Leagues (*Federación de Ligas Agrarias Cristianas*, FEDELAC), a Church-backed association that grouped unionized wage workers, semiproletarian laborers, and small- and medium-scale farmers into cooperatives, had Social Christian Party connections and received substantial support, especially from Venezuela and the Dominican Catholic Church. The second, the Junta for Agrarian Action (*Junta por Acción Agraria*, JUNAGRA), was allied with Balaguer's political party and channeled petitions for land to IAD. When Balaguer became director of IAD in 1970 (while he was also still president), the connections between JUNAGRA and IAD were strengthened.[3]

In large part because of government inaction in agrarian reform in the 1960s, there was substantial political pressure for land from thousands of wage laborers on large farms and large numbers of rural unemployed. Land invasions were commonplace. During and after Balaguer's presidency, he stressed the social turmoil that characterized the times and the need to reduce pressure on the political and economic systems through agrarian reform: "The most serious problem of the country is its high degree of unemployment and the social discontent and political unrest which this situation has engendered.... While this situation is accepted today by everyone, not everyone is disposed to sacrifice part of what they possess to avoid greater evils...." (Balaguer 1979, 213–215).

In the 1962–1965 period, several actions were taken that affected the subsequent development of campesino organizations. In 1962, the Dominican Community Development Office was created, with partial U.S. Agency for International Development (USAID) funding. Between 1961 and 1965, sixty-three cooperatives (consumer, savings, and credit) were founded (Marínez 1984, 122). Although not all of these co-ops operated in rural areas, a large proportion of their members were peasants. During the 1963 triumvirate, the Institute for Cooperative Development and Credit (*Instituto para el Desarrollo Cooperativo y Crédito*, IDECOOP) was created.

Growth of officially recognized peasant organizations, though faster than during Trujillo's days, was slow from 1962 to 1965 but increased rapidly after 1966. The initial post-Trujillo rate of organization was one peasant association, four *asentamientos*, and two cooperatives per year; this annual rate increased between 1966 and 1971 to nearly twenty associations, fifteen *asentamientos*, and six cooperatives (see Table 1).

Table 1
Rural organizations, by type[a],[b]

	Number of IAD settlements		Number of IDECOOP cooperatives		Number of other associations		Total number	
1900–1950	13	(3)	0	(0)	3	(1)	16	(1)
1951–1960	13	(3)	3	(3)	0	(0)	16	(1)
1961–1965	16	(4)	11	(10)	5	(1)	32	(2)
1966–1971	95	(25)	38	(34)	117	(13)	250	(18)
1972–1976	244	(64)	59	(53)	796	(86)	1,099	(78)
Total	381	(100)	111	(100)	921	(100)	1,413	(100)

a Source: Secretaría de Estado de Agricultura, *Inventario de organizaciones rurales: República Dominicana* (Santo Domingo: CNIECA, 1977), p. 14.
b The numbers in parentheses are percentages.

Involvement of the Church in the peasant-organization process also was becoming more significant. As early as 1966, Monsignor Pepén of Santo Domingo issued a public letter which warned the *latifundistas* of the need for reform (Marínez 1984, 138). In 1977, the country's bishops published a "Joint Declaration of the Dominican Bishops on the Peasant Situation" (*Estudios Sociales* 1968). Priests, such as Father Cipriano Cabero de La Vega, were especially active in the organization of peasant associations linked to FEDELAC in the Rincón rice-producing area. Cabero was the manager of a radio station (Radio Santa María); as such, he had a large following and his message was fairly well disseminated (see Clausner 1973, 256–257). Even now, one of the most important federations of reform beneficiaries is called "Padre Cabero."

Revolutionary political groups increased their activities during the late 1960s in the countryside partly because of the anti-United States reaction to the invasion of 1965. The Cuban Revolution provided a hope for some and a threat to others. The organization and mobilization of the peasantry became a central focus of revolutionary and reformist groups.

Nonetheless, while land invasions and pressures for the enforcement of the Agrarian Reform Law and the Irrigation Land Acquisition (*Cuota Parte*) Law mounted after 1966, the elitist politics of the past endured. The government found itself searching for detente with the landed groups; by the late 1960s, little land was being redistributed.

By 1972, however, pressures for a redistributive agrarian reform had increased greatly. Though slow to distribute land, IAD became a focus for peasants who sought land. As of 1972, nearly 90,000 had registered their petitions for land with IAD.

All the while, both the population and the labor force were growing rapidly. In contrast to the increasing number of people who needed land, the concentration of landholdings among the rich continued basically unaltered. Much of the land of Trujillo and his cronies had not been turned over to land-hungry campesinos; most had been transferred to state-run sugar estates. While some settlement of agrarian reform beneficiaries on Trujillo land did occur, this had largely been balanced by the absorption of other such lands by neighboring large landowners. Still other Trujillo land was simply retained by the state. The concentration of landholdings in a few hands remained high. In 1971, 216 families owned the same amount of land as was held by 220,000 smallholder families; there were 200,000 agricultural families with no land at all.

The Dominican agrarian reform through 1972 clearly had been tokenism: only 14,500 parcels, averaging 4.4 hectares each, had been assigned to beneficiaries. The rate of somewhat more than 1,400 parcels assigned per year for the 1966-1971 period neither represented much progress toward satisfying the campesinos' demand nor altered altering the highly skewed landholding pattern.

Even so, by 1972 the number of farm and labor organizations in the countryside had grown significantly. FEDELAC and JUNAGRA both were helping the landless to secure farms. The political environment had become more permissive to the open operation of at least the politically moderate peasant organizations. At the same time, however, governmental and military actions continued to lash out at more radical organizations which were attempting to gain a foothold in Dominican politics (see Dore y Cabral 1980; Balaguer 1979, 214).

A second pressure on the embattled Balaguer government in the early 1970s was from the stagnation of the country's manufacturing industries. Since over 50 percent of the rural population had incomes of less than $50 a month (in U.S. dollars), agriculture was unable to provide a significant demand stimulus for the national market.

A third factor contributing to the national crisis was the continued low productivity of large haciendas. A significant study by Aquino González (1978), a secretary of agriculture under Balaguer, concluded that the Dominican *latifundistas* were not as capable of producing efficiently as were smaller farms, largely because the *latifundistas* used the land extensively and did not invest significantly in their enterprises. In 1971, 56 percent of the land used for agriculture was in mostly unimproved pastureland; 19 percent of the agricultural land was used for the production of sugarcane, coffee, cacao, and tobacco. This left only a quarter of the land for food production for the internal market. What Balaguer had to do was increase the production of food and improve the flagging balance of payments through import substitution, export promotion, or both (Aquino González 1978).

For the Balaguer government, agrarian reform became a policy which could stimulate food production to assure a cheap supply of food to a growing urban population, which was a requisite for industrial growth. The existing private farms would not meet the challenge of increasing food production because (1) the owners were businessmen who preferred to invest in less risky, urban enterprises, and (2) low agricultural prices were necessary for the growing industrial sector, but only peasant farmers, who had no alternative opportunities for investment and did not use hired wage labor, would maintain production at these relatively low prices. Finally, agrarian reform would provide land to some of the landless and thereby stabilize the volatile peasantry (ISA 1979, viii-ix; Aquino González 1978, 154). A moderate reform would also serve to employ the peasants more fully and integrate them into the wider market-based economy.[4]

THE AGRARIAN LAWS OF 1972

The pressure for a thorough and energetic reform from growing peasant organizations, supported by elements of the Church and political parties and combined with the rational *Instituto Superior de Agricultura* (ISA) arguments on reform implications for a profitable economy and greater social stability, made the agrarian reform option sound like an irresistible panacea. Indeed, packaging the arguments this way resulted in a series of laws in 1972 (IAD 1981) which corrected some of the major failings of the 1962 law. The 1972 legislation provided the means for acquiring through expropriation highly productive land for reform. At the same time, an innovative cooperative-farming organizational form for agrarian reform settlements, the collective, was introduced.

Several potentially important pieces of legislation designed to stimulate the agrarian reform were approved in 1972. One of them, Law 289 (March 1972), prohibited rental or sharecropping contracts. In its most controversial clause (Article 3), the law required the transfer of property rights to the sharecropper if the piece of land being worked was smaller than 300 tareas (18.9 hectares). The uproar that followed led to a swift backlash from landowners, who hurried to terminate all rental agreements and to evict peasants from the lands that they had been working. Conflict between the government and the landowners became so intense that, by November 1972, executive resolutions were adopted to postpone indefinitely the effective date of the law. As a result, no peasants have received land through the operation of Law 289; some lost land because of landowner reaction.

The most significant piece of legislation, if only because of the quality of land affected, was Law 290 (March 1972), which required the transfer to IAD of all parcels of rice land larger than 500 tareas (31.4 hectares) which were irrigated by canals paid for by the state. This law extended the *Cuota Parte* Law, compelling the transfer to IAD of all rice farmland larger than 500 tareas in size. The land was to be purchased, and the state was to pay the owners 25 percent of the value of the land in cash and 75 percent in bonds and/or in shares of state-enterprise stock, state-owned urban lots, or urban buildings. Owners were entitled to retain 500 tareas if they owned no other land and could prove that they needed the property to sustain a family.

This law was accompanied by Law 391 (September 1972), which specified that rice land in the reformed sector would be operated by collectives[5] under IAD's administration and technical control. This law also detailed a system of beneficiary participation, an organizational pattern for the farm, how collective credit would be granted, and how enterprise management would function. The law set a payment of 2 pesos ($2.00) per day to be given to members of the collective as a cash advance for subsistence; this sum would be deducted from profits obtained after the sale of rice and the repayment of loans and other production costs.

This law, and others that followed, established a collective operational structure and defined who could benefit from reform. Eventually, IAD developed administrative structures and procedures for dealing with the collectives that were different from those directed at family-farm *asentamientos*. The priority area for the creation of collectives was the state-acquired rice land. Prior to 1972, the production unit used in reform distribution was the individual parcel. A few *asentamientos* had been created on Trujillo land in the rice-producing area, but this happened mostly during the 7 months of the 1963 Bosch government on both rice and nonrice lands.

By establishing the collective as the preferred organizational reform unit, the course of Dominican land reform veered considerably. By 1978, the collective was the only organizational form used for giving beneficiaries access to land. In some cases, this manner of group farming was subverted soon after the settlement's creation, with actual cultivation of land being de facto on parcels and not through the IAD-administered collective. Despite those exceptions, however, after 1972 the direction of the reform was clear: the state would acquire rice lands and create collective *asentamientos* on them.

On the collectives, former agricultural laborers became members and, to a degree, participated in the management of the enterprises, although the management of the collectives was clearly the responsibility of IAD administrators. The appropriateness of this decision to collectives was questioned both by the beneficiaries of the reform, who found themselves incorporated into the collectives, and by some of the reform's theoreticians, who remained dubious about the effectiveness of collective production. Ignoring the theorists, the military was used to convince beneficiaries to accept the collective model; this indicates the radically different path which the collective represented. The initial desire of the beneficiaries was for their own parcel, for their own family farm (Delgado Sánchez 1983, 2). But, when the option of accepting the collective or getting nothing was clearly backed by the military, land-hungry peasants dropped their objections and collectives were quickly established.

The decision to make the focus of reform the heretofore capitalist, rice-producing areas was also bitterly criticized. Some felt that this would threaten the country's lifeline, a marketable surplus of rice. Rice producers themselves felt that their rights—and the rights of all private property holders—had been trampled upon severely. The arguments on agrarian reform swirled around two questions: (1) Why the collective, and (2) why "reform" one of the most productive subsectors of agriculture in the Dominican Republic, the capitalistic rice haciendas?

TWO DEBATES: INDIVIDUAL OR COLLECTIVE PRODUCTION UNITS AND CAPITALIST OR PEASANT-BASED RICE PRODUCTION

The discussion on the relative advantages of the individual peasant producer versus the collective production unit is summarized in the debate between Jorge Munguia and Carlos Aquino González (see Munguia 1976; Aquino González 1978). Munguia argued that the individual, private owner-operator model of farm management had proved productive in a number of countries because there were few inherent economies of scale in agriculture; rather, the relative prices of land, labor, and capital determine the most productive mix of these factors at any given time in any given country, and the owner-operated enterprise was most able to efficiently adjust the use of these factors. Munguia also developed a social argument, stating that the self-management of an individual enterprise and the ultimate incorporation of the peasantry into broader society are related. He felt that, in the state-managed collectives, the beneficiaries of the reform would consider themselves as laborers and, as such, would not develop their individual capacities as they would on individual private farms. He also presented arguments on the diseconomies of scale in the collectives.

Carlos Aquino González, Balaguer's Minister of Agriculture, refuted Munguia, asserting that there are indeed economies of scale in agriculture and that larger enterprises facilitated assembly of inputs and products and permitted lower cost marketing (Aquino González 1978, 157). Also, the cost of using machinery was lower per hectare on larger enterprises, inputs were cheaper in large lots, infrastructure per unit of output was less expensive, and technical knowledge and services (such as education, water, electricity, and health) could be obtained more efficiently and at lower cost for concentrated populations than for scattered farmsteads.

Aquino rejected the argument that small, independent units can achieve these economies of scale through the organization of service cooperatives. He felt that such organizations lacked work discipline. The state administrative structure, on the other hand, could provide the needed discipline in collectives of the type used in the agrarian reform.

Aquino came to the position that the collective model would have its greatest relevance in the most capitalist parts of the agricultural sector—agriculture that already had highly improved technology and had taken maximum advantage of economies of scale. The agrarian reform would permit a takeover of that structure and its utilization more or less "as is." It would divert some of what was formerly profit to improving the standard of living of rural salaried workers without increasing (and maybe even reducing) farm-gate prices. The collective model would also have a salutary impact on production levels: if the enterprise that was taken over had adopted advanced technology, such as mechanized land preparation and harvest, chemical control of pests, and the use of new rice varieties, the state technicians could facilitate the continued use of this technology on the new collective. This would likely not be feasible if large farms were broken up.

While not a direct participant in this debate, Crouch used various indicators of farm efficiency and revenue from a sample of over 1,800 private farm units to show that as gross farm income (a proxy measure of farm size) increases, so does efficiency [defined as the ratio of costs to revenue (Crouch 1981, 80–81)]. His conclusion from these observations was that the advantages of large-scale operations, especially in rice, were significant. He argued that if agrarian reform were chosen as a policy objective, "projects should always be of a type which do not impair, and hopefully improve, the original farm's capacity to produce at high levels of output. Thus, collective projects would seem to be called for, at least in the crops already being produced by large farms" (Crouch 1981, 93–94).

Crouch developed more overtly political explanations for the shift in the center of gravity of the agrarian laws toward the rice lands after 1972. He noted that rice was a major food staple in the Dominican Republic, with a monthly per capita consumption in 1969 of around 11 pounds and an income elasticity of demand of only 0.13. Moreover, the per capita consumption of rice nearly doubled between 1962 and 1972 (see Secretaria de Estado de Agricultura 1977). Clearly, rice was (and is) "the most important food crop in the Dominican Republic" (Crouch 1981, 145), and its low price meant that cheap food could substitute for increased wages in the industrial and commercial urban sectors. Crouch felt that while the political pressures from the rural landless and the semiproletariat were strong and vocal, rice-oriented agrarian reform essentially satisfied urban commercial and industrial interests which stood to benefit from low rice prices.

He also argued that rice-farmer organizations had been embroiled in continual conflicts over pricing and state importation policies since 1964. One clash between farmers and wholesalers concerned rice importation. On one side of the debate were the farmers and the Agricultural Bank; their pressure was for higher internal prices. On the other side were the wholesalers who wanted to import rice at a price lower than that prevailing within the country. The confrontation surfaced again in 1966, when the policies of the second Balaguer government were announced, namely, to freeze wages and to lower prices for essential commodities, particularly rice, at the consumer and producer levels. The price of rice remained frozen for several years, although other policies, such as subsidized credit for rice, high-yielding varieties, and low-priced importation of fertilizer and machinery, compensated in large part for low product prices (see Crouch 1981, 153–154).

In 1969, the Price Stabilization Institute (*Instituto de Estabilización de Precios*, INESPRE) was created with the goal of price stabilization through state regulation of market transactions in rice. By 1971, however, INESPRE was operating only marginally in the rice market. Many rice farmers maintained that they were unable to repay their loans from the Agricultural Bank. A cost-price squeeze led rice farmers to declare that if the situation did not improve, they would stop producing (Crouch 1981, 161).

The political debates over the 1972 agrarian laws, particularly the one which permitted government expropriation of rice land, were intense. Less than a month after the Presidential Message of 1972 announcing the proposed agrarian reform legislation, the Association of Rice Producers issued an extensive critique of the proposal. The rice producers accepted the necessity of an agrarian reform, which was understood as continuing the program of settling people on state lands, unused lands, sugar lands, lands of foreign companies, or lands of *latifundistas*—any land, in other words, but that planted to rice. Their basic question was, "Why rice?—or better, "Why us?" (*Listín Diario* 1972, 8A). Their argument was simply put: even if the government meant what it said in the preamble to Law 290, that its purpose was "to assure an increased supply of rice," this would not happen if rice farms were expropriated. Private investments in rice production would decline, state-managed enterprises would be inefficient, and production would drop (*Caribe* 1972, 8).

As the debate raged, there were delays in the law's application, and some large owners took advantage of these postponements by planting their rice fields to other crops, often even sowing pastures: the owners believed that lands no longer planted to rice would not be expropriated. Others used personal contacts in high government circles to escape the law. A few owners agreed to offer their lands to the state in exchange for urban lots or other state property. One exceptional landowner, Canaan Fernández, offered his farm of 19,000 hectares, "because the moment has arrived for those of us who believe ourselves to be Dominicans to adopt a flexible attitude.... [I]f we want to carry out a profound agrarian reform, we have to begin with the rice lands, which are the most intensively farmed" (Dore y Cabral 1981, 59).

As Dore and others have pointed out, the procedure for the acquisition of rice lands was really a purchase offer by the state. In some cases, the owners exchanged their lands for bills showing other outstanding debts to the government. In other cases, cash compensation was made, accompanied by partial payment in long-term bonds, as the law provided. In both types of transaction, the value of the expropriated property was negotiated with the state. In some cases this value was high, enabling the landowner to escape the rigors of reform in a financially favorable condition.

Through the continuing debates, the Balaguer government proceeded with the reform. Article 1 of Law 391 of 1972 introduced four important innovations into the formation and management of the agrarian reform's productive units: (1) the reformed production unit on all rice lands would be the collective, (2) the units would be under the administrative control of IAD, (3) the net income generated from these production units would be divided equally among the collective members, and (4) rice land that had already been assigned as individual parcels would be reorganized into collectives. In this collective phase of the Dominican reform, a provisional title was issued to each beneficiary, naming him or her as a member of a collective with some rights to all of the land but no rights over any family-farm-sized parcel. The property title remained in the name of the state.

Administrative functions on the collectives were carried out by an administrative council composed of a representative of the *parceleros* chosen by majority vote, a representative of the executive branch of the national government, and an IAD administrator. Often in a rather paternalistic fashion, the IAD administrator presided over the council. All three members of the council were to agree on the disposition of the net income of the collective. However, since all purchases of inputs and sales of products were channeled through IAD, the IAD administrator held considerable sway over such decisions. Menendez (1984) among others has noted the predominant role of the IAD administrator in the collective's management. The representative of the executive branch was a functionary, appointed by the president, who dealt with several farms and acted as a general overseer. In all cases, the government, with two-thirds of the council's vote, could overrule the peasant member.

To organize daily work tasks, special committees of *parceleros* were appointed for credit, inputs, marketing, work discipline, and machinery. Other groups might be created if the *asentamiento* was especially large or if its enterprise pattern was complex. These committees were made up of members of the collective, who, in theory, at least, rotated their committee memberships. On most farms, however, the management functions tended to fall on the shoulders of a limited number of members.

ACHIEVEMENTS OF THE REFORM

Bravo Barros (1983) showed the various types of land acquired for the reform between 1970 and 1981. State-owned property, mostly areas from the Trujillo empire, accounted for 53 percent. "Purchased" land, largely rice land or *cuota parte* land in which the state negotiated the price of the property, was second in importance for the reform (see Table 2).

Between 1962 and 1965, IAD created twenty-three *asentamientos* with 3,765 families and a mean allotment of 50 tareas per beneficiary. From 1966 to 1971, 104 *asentamientos* were organized, benefiting 10,490 families. In the three years between 1972 and 1975, the number of *asentamientos* created by IAD increased by 103 percent, most having

Table 2
Mechanisms for acquiring lands distributed by IAD during the 1970–81 period[a]

Year	Form of Acquisition							Area distributed (tareas)
	Purchased	Recovered state lands	unused	"Cuota parte"	Public use	Donation	*Latifundia*	
1970	29,285	36,433	—	—	1,330	14,744	—	81,783
1971	119,927	187,800	—	—	—	68,343	—	376,070
1972	81,837	484,770	—	—	—	30,295	—	596,902
1973	275,127	300,543	51,914	8,965	—	9,628	—	646,177
1974	39,029	97,258	—	8,487	—	—	—	144,774
1975	42,919	56,103	11,762	12,824	17,000	10,811	—	151,419
1976	32,819	53,564	18,084	9,000	48,000	14,994	—	176,461
1977	868	—	3,000	—	3,205	—	—	7,074
1978	11,233	78,726	—	1,166	—	56,384	18,284	165,793
1979	—	59,777	—	5,000	69,223	—	—	134,000
1980	8,200	32,588	—	4,570	29,098	51,373	—	125,829
1981	31,763	145,654	—	1,400	9,829	49,141	—	237,787
Total	673,007	1,533,216	84,760	51,412	177,686	305,713	18,284	2,844,069

[a] Source: Carlos Bravo Barros, "Informe del consultor," TCP/DOM/2201, mimeograph (Santo Domingo: FAO, 1983), p. 39.

been organized in 1973. The rate of *asentamiento* creation in subsequent years was relatively slower, averaging fifteen *asentamientos* with an average of 136,000 tareas for 2,000 beneficiary families each year.

Individual *Asentamientos*

Under the individual-parcel pattern favored in the first decade of reform, the beneficiary received an immediate provisional title to a parcel of state-owned land. The recipient also received the benefits of certain infrastructural investments by the state on some settlements for irrigation canals, electricity, installations, and so on. Table 3 shows the number of individual parcels assigned from 1962 through 1981.

An individual's right to a parcel was not to be transferred without IAD's approval. Article 39 of Law 5879 states, "The *parcelero* will not be able to sell, rent, mortgage or in any other way dispose or transfer

Table 3
Land distributed in individual parcels through the Dominican Republic's agrarian reform[a]

Year	Parcels	Land area (tareas)
1962	863	61,188
1963	719	63,358
1964	2,214	183,386
1965	0	0
1966	321	39,696
1967	1,901	155,865
1968	1,447	109,757
1969	2,057	155,273
1970	1,345	81,783
1971	3,612	378,536
1972	6,498	596,902
1973	5,592	485,853
1974	1,683	138,611
1975	1,108	78,519
1976	1,336	105,977
1977	139	3,074
1978	1,440	92,134
1979	0	0
1980	0	0
1981	0	0
Totals[b]	32,275	2,729,912

[a] Source: Carlos Bravo Barros, "Informe del consultor," TCP/DOM/2201, mimeograph. (Santo Domingo: FAO, 1983), p. 36.
[b] Through 1981.

rights to the assigned parcel without the written approval of the Institute. These restrictions will cease as soon as the *parcelero* has obtained full property rights to the parcel."

Using data from 1971, preliminary tabulations from the 1981 censuses, and IAD data, we can determine the importance of the "individual farm" phase of reform. Table 4 shows the number and size of peasant farms in the country, distinguishing between IAD *parceleros* and private farm peasants.

In 1971, the IAD peasant farms represented 5.2 percent of all farms in the total peasant sector; by 1981, IAD served nearly 12.7 percent of campesino farms. The average size of the reform farm was twice the average peasant enterprise in 1971 and three times larger in 1981. Through 1978, the reform fortified the individual-farm peasant sector of Dominican agriculture.

Regardless of their illegality, de facto transfers of reform farms took place, as is nearly always the case when there are few alternatives for jobs in an economy and when growth of the work force is so rapid. In 1975, Law 145 was written as an attempt to control the demand side of the market by prohibiting the purchase of agrarian reform properties. It specified penalties for those who "purchased" the land illegally or

Table 4
Number and size of individual peasant farms (private sector and IAD individual *asentamientos*), 1971–81[a]

Number and size of individual farms	1971	1981
Number of farms, 8–160 tareas		
Private sector	208,228	253,263
IAD individual *asentamientos*	10,867	32,275
Total number	219,095	285,538
Area of farms, 8–160 tareas (×1000 tareas)		
Private sector	8,229	5,938
IAD individual *asentamientos*	850	2,734
Total area	9,079	8,672
Average farm size (in tareas)		
Private sector	39.6	24.7
IAD individual *asentamientos*	80.3	75.1
Average size	41.5	30.4

[a] Sources: Oscar Delgado Sánchez, "Diagnóstico socio-económico de los asentamientos individuales y colectivos," Report to FAO, TCP/DOM/2201 (Santo Domingo: IAD-PIDELTA, 1983), p. 66; Carlos Bravo Barros, "Informe del consultor," TCP/DOM/2201, mimeograph. (Santo Domingo: FAO, 1983), p. 36.

those who rented or received land as a gift from, took out a mortgage guarantee against, or acquired the usufructuary rights from an agrarian reform beneficiary.

The problem of unauthorized transfers was not the most serious challenge facing the early phase of the reform, however. Meeting the needs of the landless through an active and wide-ranging reform was achieved only in part; mostly, the goal proved illusive. Quezada et al. (1985) observed that this phase of the agrarian reform did achieve a certain income redistribution since the land offered to the landless represented an income-generating resource. The individual settlement modified the structure of land tenure somewhat, for it granted some limited political participation to a previously excluded group.

Despite high hopes for the family-farm parcel model, important factors constrained its success (Quezada et al. 1985). First, much of the distributed land was only marginally productive. Some had little or no access to water. While much of this land was geographically isolated, roads were rudimentary. Of the 2.7 million tareas (170,000 hectares) of land that were distributed as individual parcels, at least three-quarters was so marginal that it was unable to produce significant additions to the country's marketable surplus (Delgado Sánchez 1983, 76). Often, technological packages appropriate to the needs of the small farmer were not made available (see Rodríguez and Fernández 1976, 47–49). Furthermore, there were insufficient training efforts to transform the previously landless into capable entrepreneurs or effective managers. As a result, reform beneficiaries produced what they could, using traditional production methods. This reinforced a traditional, subsistence agriculture on the agrarian reform lands (Quezada et al. 1985, 11–13). The trend toward marginality and subsistence agriculture was nudged still further along by low food prices. This constellation of problems on the individually parceled *asentamientos* provided at least part of the basis for assigning land to collectives beginning in 1973.

The Collectives

Table 5 shows the number of beneficiaries and the amount of land that have been assigned to collectives since 1973. About one-third of the reform beneficiaries has been assigned to collectives, while about one-fourth of the land in the reform has been collectively organized. In 1973, a major effort at assigning land to collectives occurred; following the election of Antonio Guzmán as president in 1978, the collective was again favored.

Despite the theoretical advantages of the collective model, problems developed, especially around two issues: (1) the relation between the payment received by each collective member and the amount of work

Table 5
Number of beneficiaries and lands distributed to collectives[a]

	Number of beneficiaries	Land area (tareas)
1973	2,270	160,324
1974	117	6,163
1975	822	72,500
1976	1,826	70,484
1977	—	—
1978	1,194	73,659
1979	1,962	134,000
1980	1,982	125,187
1981	3,244	237,787
1982	2,259	103,884
Total	15,676	983,988

[a] Source: Carlos Bravo Barros, "Informe del consultor," TCP/DOM/2201, mimeograph. (Santo Domingo: FAO, 1983), p. 36.

the individual performed during the production cycle, and (2) the control of collective management by the IAD administrator, which implied minimal participation by the beneficiaries themselves in the farm's management and resource use.

Income was to be equally divided among the members of the collective after loans had been repaid and variable costs and other incidentals were met; checks were issued from the IAD office in Santo Domingo to each beneficiary. IAD's practice was to calculate the income for distribution by subtracting the loans provided from the value of production (usually the value of rice sold); the resulting net income was divided by the total number of member labor-days that went into the production process. In this way, the value of a day's labor was established. This coefficient was multiplied by the number of days that each beneficiary had worked, thus determining each member's income. The recording of the workdays for each beneficiary was often done by an IAD employee.

One might imagine that this arrangement would give an individual collective member double incentive to work. More done by a member would mean more labor days to be paid, and greater effort by everyone would lead to greater production, thereby increasing the value of each workday. In practice it was not difficult for management to verify the number of workdays; however, it was another matter to figure out how hard each beneficiary had worked: diligence or effort level is not very quantifiable. Furthermore, the IAD field foreman could not supervise everyone's work, so they had to depend on what the workers themselves reported. This arrangement often did not work out, since fellow workers tended not to report delinquents for fear of being branded as betrayers. That workers were often related to one another made the matter even more complex.

Another factor affecting labor productivity was the size of many collectives. The larger the collective, the more diluted were worker incentives to produce. The effort of any given individual on any particular day made up a small percentage of the total effort needed to produce and harvest the crop. Coordination and discipline problems on larger collectives often produced decisions to divide them into units with fewer members (see Stanfield et al. 1985b). The tendency on most collectives was to record all members as having worked the same number of days with the same level of effort.[6]

Since the members of the collectives had been, in most cases, former day laborers on the rice farms or landless laborers from other parts of the country, their entrepreneurial skills were not well developed—or at least they were untested. Furthermore, most beneficiaries were illiterate, had little or no experience with management or credit, had little technical knowledge about the correct and profitable application of technology for the production of rice, and had never really grappled with the market.

Nor had beneficiaries developed an experience with collectives—that is, organizing work or managing large sums of money on the scale required in the collective enterprise. Collective bargaining was unknown on most rice farms. Most new collective members had never belonged to any organization of their peers—or any organization larger than their own families or, perhaps, their church.

The solution to these challenges was to introduce the managerial presence of IAD administrators into the model of the collective management. The administrators provided the skills and expertise that the group lacked. They dealt with the Agricultural Bank and other agencies to obtain the necessary credit and production inputs. The administrators served as foremen—providing the discipline necessary for the work process, laying out the tasks, and overseeing the work. They had the authority to dismiss beneficiaries from the collective for unsatisfactory work.

IAD administrators also guided the investment of profits to assure the future productivity of the collective. Purchase of machinery was the most common investment, typically financed by advances from the Agricultural Bank. The administrators also made certain that rice was planted and harvested in accordance with governmental policy, neither allowing the land to be used for other purposes nor letting it lie idle.

The government's rhetoric surrounding the collective's operation was couched in phrases usually reserved for describing a democratic institution. The new organization, however, tended to be authoritarian. IAD was the owner of the land, and a beneficiary could be deprived of the subsistence advance or even dismissed if IAD so determined. For Aquino, "[t]he State replaces the function of the capitalist in terms of the enterprise organization, marketing, location of credit and ownership of the means of production" (Aquino González 1978, 165).

The Dominican version of the collective redefined the state's role in the reform process. Under the previous agrarian reform strategy of family-farm settlements, the IAD settlement administrators had a fairly infrequent presence—they provided technical assistance and linkages with other governmental agencies and enforced the few rules that pertained to parcel transfer and use. When the collectives were introduced, their management complexities called for substantially larger numbers of highly trained field personnel and the establishment of special administrative units to handle collective management functions and resolve production bottlenecks as they occurred. Under the collective model, the IAD administrators became responsible to the government for the farm's performance.[7]

Administrative control exercised by IAD produced other problems. The need to obtain the signature of both the administrator and the executive branch representative for the sale of production and the purchase of inputs often produced untoward delay. The rapid turnover of administrators meant that whoever was in charge might not know the farm's soils or the farm's workers. Administrators had little time to acquire the detailed knowledge of a farm and its workers necessary to do a good administrative job (see Stanfield et al. 1985b). Most administrators served a single collective for less than a year.

The very nature of the administrative position was problematic. The involvement of the administrators in the day-to-day operations of the farms produced inevitable political conflicts and bureaucratic complications. The administrators were "outsiders," that is, they were typically young technicians who were employees of the state, not the farm. Their professional careers depended on their carrying out bureaucratic regulations, not on improving the incomes of the reform beneficiaries (*asentados*). Thus, inevitably, a certain amount of an administrator's energy was directed to generating contacts and support in the state bureaucracy to assure his personal promotion rather than to resolving the organizational and production problems of the farm. On the other hand, the bureaucratic activities and worries of the IAD administrators produced some positive results. Their dealings with the bureaucracy were key to their carrying out farm-management responsibilities.

The *asentado*-administrator problems and achievements were related to the high priority that the state placed on rice production. Efforts to assure sufficient quantities of rice from the collective *asentamientos* (which provided about one-third of the country's rice) assured the collectives of credit and machinery. At the same time, these priorities collided with the interests of *asentados* who, in order to maximize their incomes and reduce their risks, often wanted to diversify production and develop off-farm enterprises. An example of the friction between state priorities and *asentado* interests is the debate over second-season planting of rice. Many rice farmers preferred not to plant rice after the year's first harvest, relying instead on the lower cost alternative of natural regeneration for a second crop (see de Groot 1983). This method was low in cost, but yields were also low. If many *asentamientos* followed this practice, the country's overall demand for rice might not be met, and if such shortages occurred, IAD would be subject to substantial criticism for not having carried out one of its most important tasks—assuring an adequate supply of rice from the *asentamientos*.

To avoid these pressures, IAD administrators typically tried to obtain the second planting of rice with the same input level as the first, thereby assuring yields but at higher cost to the beneficiary. If there was less IAD control and beneficiaries used the natural regeneration strategy, *asentados* could invest less in the second crop of rice and get higher incomes, but they would, at the same time, achieve lower production levels (see Mendez and Doorman 1984, 85–87). These conflicts were resolved in each farm and for each season depending on a variety of factors, but the divergence of opinion due to the difference in interests between *asentados* and administrators continued (see Rodríguez and Fernández 1976, 51–52).

A COMPARISON OF INDIVIDUAL AND COLLECTIVE ASENTAMIENTOS

Of reform land, 26 percent was assigned to collectives; the rest was to individuals. Under individual assignment, as of 1982, land was distributed to 32,275 reform beneficiaries in 267 settlements, with an average of 84.6 tareas (5.3 hectares) per beneficiary. There were 15,676 beneficiaries in the 118 collective settlements, with an average area of 62.8 tareas (4.0 hectares) per beneficiary. Delgado Sánchez (1983) estimated that 3,713,900 tareas were distributed to reform beneficiaries through 1982 and that 5,695,000 tareas of state-acquired land were available for distribution through reform. He suggests that about one-third of the IAD land was not assigned because it was unsuitable for agricultural production.

An important part of the debate over the collective versus the individual model of production in the reformed sector was focused on lands devoted to the production of rice. After 1975 there was a yearly decline in the number of individual reform beneficiaries producing rice, largely due to the reorganization of some *asentamientos* into collectives or their shift out of rice. It is also likely that some of the individual parcels had been consolidated, since the individual-settlement area harvested declined only slightly.

Table 6 shows that the total production of individual-farm settlements increased dramatically in the 5-year period between 1976 and 1981. Yields and production per beneficiary increased strikingly. Rice production on collectives did not show the same results. While acreage increased, yields per hectare and production per beneficiary

Table 6
Indicators of rice production on reformed sector settlements, with country totals, 1975/76 and 1980/81[a]

Production unit	Area harvested (×1000 hectares)	Production in quintals[b] (×1000 quintals)	Production per hectare (quintals/hectares)	Production per beneficiary (quintals/hectares)
Reformed sector				
Individual parcel				
1975/76	27.8	834.0	30.0	130.0
1980/81	26.7	1,184.0	44.3	206.0
Change	−4%	+42%	+45%	+58%
Collective settlement				
1975/76	9.6	541.0	56.4	197.0
1980/81	16.5	716.0	43.4	178.0
Change	+72%	+32%	−25%	−10%
Totals				
1975/76	37.4	1,375	36.8	n.a.
1980/81	43.2	1,900	44.0	n.a.
Change	+47%	+38%	+20%	n.a.
Country totals				
1975	114.7	4,654	40.6	n.a.
1980	127.4	5,788	45.4	n.a.
Change	+11%	+24%	+12%	n.a.

[a] Source: Pablo Rodríguez Nuñez, "Evaluación económico-social de los *asentamientos* arroceros de la reforma agraria," mimeograph. (Madison, Wisconsin, 1983); Carlos Bravo Barros, "Informe del consultor," TCP/DOM/2201, mimeograph. (Santo Domingo: FAO, 1983), p. 30.

[b] 1 Quintal = 100 pounds.

both decreased. The resulting income decline was certainly a factor in the growing disaffection of members in the collective as a productive unit. Delgado (1983, 102) observed

> [T]he collective organization is accepted by the members to the degree that it responds to their income expectations.... The leaders and beneficiaries interviewed, with a few exceptions, did not appear to appreciate the complex factors that determine their low personal incomes, but rather appeared to believe that the break-up of the collective and hard work were sufficient conditions to increase productivity and therefore, their family incomes.

Table 7 shows the relative importance of the individual and collective rice settlements in comparison with production in the private sector. The reformed sector provided nearly a third of the country's rice production, and the collectives provided roughly one-third of this reformed sector production. Yields on the individual and collective settlements have been roughly similar in recent years, although the trends are different: yields have been falling on the collectives and rising on individual settlements.

Serious efforts have been made to improve the performance of the reformed sector by focusing state attention on technical assistance, organizational support, and credit for the settlements. In 1976, the 12.3 million pesos of credit approved for the reformed sector represented 15

Table 7
Average production of processed rice, by type of producer, 1980/81[a],[b]

Type of producer	Production (×1000 quintals)[c]		Area harvested (×1000 hectares)	Yield (quintals/hectares)
Private sector	3,888	(67)	84.2	46.2
Reformed sector				
Individual	1,184	(21)	26.7	44.3
Collective	716	(12)	16.5	43.4
Subtotal	1,900	(33)	43.2	44.0
Total	5,788	(100)	127.4	45.4

[a] Sources: Pablo Rodríguez Nuñez, "Evaluación económico-social de los *asentamientos* arroceros de la reforma agraria," mimeograph. (Madison, Wisconsin, 1983), p. 15; Carlos Bravo Barros, "Informe del consultor," TCP/DOM/2201, mimeograph. (Santo Domingo: FAO, 1983), p. 30.

[b] One quintal of unprocessed rice yields 0.5655 quintal of processed rice. The data refer to quintals of processed rice.

[c] The numbers in parentheses are percentages.

percent of the total agricultural credit of the Agricultural Bank. Under the Dominican Revolutionary Party (*Partido Revolucionario Dominicano*, PRD) government, elected in 1978, credit from the Agricultural Bank for the reformed sector had risen 354 percent to 55.78 million pesos, which amounted to 37 percent of the agricultural credit portfolio of the Agricultural Bank for that year.

The shift of state support toward the reformed sector under the PRD government also meant substantially more credit and other inputs to collectives. While the levels of credit use on individual *asentamientos* increased from 14.6 million pesos in 1976 to 25.5 million pesos in 1981, credit to collectives increased from 180 thousand pesos in 1976 to 22 million pesos in 1981.

Another indicator of the attention that production credit received on the collectives is the amount of credit per tarea. In 1976/77, the average loan approved per tarea on the individual *asentamientos* was 5.70 pesos, while in the collectives the average was only 0.56 pesos. For the 1980/81 period, the average loan per tarea for the individual *asentamientos* was 10 pesos; for the collectives, it was double that amount or 20 pesos (Bravo Barros 1983, Tables 19 and 20).

Overall, collectives did consistently better than individual *asentamientos* in loan repayment. Repayment rates on the individual *asentamientos* remained at a disastrous 26 percent in the 1976–1981 period. The policy that shifted production credit to collectives was obviously accompanied by greater supervision and control over the use and repayment of that credit.

THE CONTINUING DEBATE ON THE APPROPRIATE PRODUCTION MODEL

Almost from the moment of creation of the first collective *asentamiento*, there were complaints from the settlers about it. Rodríguez observes that, "from the beginning, the majority of the campesinos criticized this system, claiming that it was dictatorial and that it negated principles of self-determination" (Rodríguez Nuñez 1984:10). At times, military force had to be used to establish the collective farms (see Dore y Cabral 1981).

One response to difficulties with the collective model was the establishment, by IAD, of the Commission for the Evaluation of the Rice Asentamientos, which issued its report in 1975. The commission's central recommendation was that the collective's administration should be improved; no attention was given to changing its form. Instead, the report proposed extension of the collective model to the individual rice *asentamientos* that had been organized before Law

391 was passed. The report determined that, for 1974, the amount of land in individually organized *asentamientos* was substantially greater than that in collectives (326,565 tareas versus 92,565 tareas), but that productivity per tarea of the individual projects was 14 percent lower. Access to credit was substantially lower on the individually organized asentamientos, as was use of improved rice varieties (see IAD 1975).

Beneficiaries on the collectives continued to complain, however. Largely because of these pressures and demands, by 1976 IAD had agreed to study the possibility of dividing the larger *asentamientos*. One persistent complaint was that the collectives with more than one hundred members were practically impossible to administer: there were serious delays in getting the work done and maintaining production levels (see Vargas 1984).

By the end of 1977, some of the larger settlement projects had been divided. The twenty-two collective farms in Angelina, for example, had split into thirty-two collective units. The Castellanos farm, which originally had 106 beneficiaries, was subdivided into four blocks; each functioned as an independent farm. Subdivision into units, which were operated as smaller collectives, was a fairly widespread phenomenon.[8]

After the 1978 elections, pressures for changing the collective model increased, partly as the result of more opportunities for *asentado* participation in public debate under the PRD government (see Eusebio Pol 1982). Antonio Guzmán, the PRD candidate for the presidency, had on at least one occasion promised the reform beneficiaries that he would do away with the collective if elected (Mendez and Doorman 1984). After the 1978 election, some collective members responded by demanding the removal of the collective model. IAD began slowly to adjust to these pressures within the framework of assuring that the domestically produced quantity of rice was sufficient to meet demand.

In 1979 and 1980, IAD sponsored a general reassessment of the production model used in the agrarian reform and decided upon introducing more worker management to the *asentamientos* by converting the collectives to Peasant Agrarian Reform Enterprises (*Empresas Campesinas de la Reforma Agraria*, ECRAs) and making these enterprises autonomous and profit oriented (see IAD 1979; Menendez 1984). This idea met with campesino skepticism and was not widely implemented, although a serious effort at organizing an ECRA was made at Limón de Yuna. Numerous workshops were held around the country by IAD officials to convince the *asentados* of the desirability of some form of collective. As Vargas (1984) reports, however, the maintenance of the collective structure did not satisfy beneficiary demands because, as the asentados frequently observed, "to be in a collective is to be a slave." They interpreted the ECRA model as another, if somewhat paler, version of the collective.

In August 1980, an IAD study showed that there was substantial support for modifying the collective model and assigning a separate parcel of land to each *asentado* for weeding, watering, fertilization, pest management, and harvesting, all within the overall farm plan of the *asentamiento* (IAD 1980). However, apart from a seminar held with campesino leaders in late 1980, no action was taken.

The pressure for change continued, however, and in 1981 IAD created an ad hoc commission to review the situation of the collective asentamientos and to present proposals for policy modification (IAD 1982). The resulting suggestions sought to resolve the problem of labor discipline on the collectives by introducing new ways of relating the work that the *asentados* accomplished with the pay that they received. One proposal called for classifying work according to its difficulty and the level of skill it required, thereby producing a system of labor points. The totaled points would be the basis for dividing the profits of the collective at the end of the harvest. This idea was promptly labeled the "Plan Macabre" by the well-organized rice *asentados* in Rincón and was discarded.

During 1982, the number of *asentado* requests for modifications in the collective model and its underlying legislation and regulations increased further. Beginning in August 1982, the Director-General of IAD again encouraged debate within IAD on collective *asentamiento* problems.

This internal IAD debate was enriched by a letter in 1982 from two rice-producing *asentamientos,* "Padre Cabero" and "Gregorio Luperón," from Rincón and Cotuí, respectively. The rice producers proposed substantial modification of the collective model and concluded, "the collective projects of the agrarian reform do not contribute to the country's economy; they make the economic situation of the *parceleros* and their families very precarious" (Comité Ejecutivo de las Asociaciones 1982, 1).

These *asentados* argued that their economic situation would be greatly improved if the collective model were abandoned. They proposed that certain functions—assurance of credit from the Agricultural Bank, land preparation, irrigation, purchase of fertilizers, aerial application of insecticides—be performed by an associated group of beneficiaries, but that all work on parcels and sale of crops be done on an individual-family basis.

The letter clearly expressed a preference for individual production on a specific parcel of land. The value of production from the parcel, less costs of inputs, would be the income of the *asentado* to whom the parcel was assigned.

Also, a proposed administrative council was to wrest control of the association from the state's representatives and tip the balance of power in agrarian reform to favor the *asentados*. With individualization of work and production and with *asentado* control over the administration of associative functions, the *asentados* argued that there would be a direct relation between work done and income received; there would be more self-discipline of *asentados* and higher productivity. The cost advantages of collective action in the limited activities where there seemed to be scale economies would be retained.

This letter represented the first organized, direct, and public outcry from agrarian reform beneficiaries in which they insisted, unequivocally, on a fundamental alteration of the collective *asentamiento* model. The appeal demonstrated a unified demand from the beneficiaries for a specific change. Rejection of the collective model was so widespread by 1982 that continuing the collective on any basis whatsoever became difficult. In a survey of 125 *asentamientos* in late 1982, Bravo Barros (1983) interviewed 61 randomly selected *asentados* in different collectives and found that, "in absolutely all of our visits to collective *asentamientos*, there was a complete frustration with the collective model, and a desire for the individualization of the land" (Bravo Barros 1983:112).

From the point of view of many IAD functionaries who had worked hard for the collective, the proposal to individualize work responsibility and assign individual parcels to the *asentados* appeared to be a reversion to a form that had not proved itself in the past. Individualization of the collective, it was felt, might risk the loss of clear economies of scale and other advantages that the collective organization had provided.

A national-level seminar, held in Puerto Plata in January 1984, brought together congressmen and senators from the national Congress as well as officials and technicians from various agricultural sector public agencies and campesino leaders. Ideas for proposed legislation for permitting and supporting an associative *asentamiento* model were discussed, as was the importance of reaching a consensus concerning the future of the reform-sector collectives.

The *asentado* organizations and the national Congress reached agreement in March 1985; a law permitting the creation of "associative *asentamientos*," Law 269 (March 1985), was passed. Its central point was that production would henceforth be accomplished on individual parcels.

By 1985, the collective farms had been almost entirely subdivided and were then called *asociativas*. Parcel boundaries were not fenced and, hence, were nearly invisible to an outsider, but each beneficiary, who was formerly a member of a collective, had the exclusive use of an identifiable parcel of land. Rice was planted, cared for, and harvested on an individual basis. The parcel holder got the entire production of the plot and, from the proceeds of the rice sale, repaid the loan he received from the Agricultural Bank. The remaining profit belonged to the *parcelero*.

The Agricultural Bank continued to consider the farm as a single unit, as before the subdivision. An association of beneficiaries, organized from members of the collective who had decided to obtain credit, received the production loan and either purchased needed inputs or reloaned the money to the *parceleros* so that they could purchase inputs individually. Since credit continued to flow to the farm as a single unit, the association or group of *parceleros* was responsible for repaying the loan. If one *parcelero* did not show a profit, other members of the association would loan the individual money and keep the account of the group paid in full.

Certain activities continued to be done together, almost as when the farm functioned as a collective. Land was often tilled for seeding as it was before subdivision, and harvesting was still accomplished using the combine that was purchased when the group functioned as a collective. The area irrigated by a single field canal might be divided into three to eight parcels. The planting of rice, however, was coordinated so that water use could be planned; in that way, harvesting by all parcel holders was possible at about the same time.

While care was taken so that subdivision would not prevent members from taking advantage of economies of scale, the basic change introduced in the associative production model was the individualization of profit: the net value of what the parcel of land produced became the property of each working *parcelero*. The organization of labor, the timing of inputs, and the intensity of effort were also the responsibility of the individual *parcelero* family. Hence, labor performed and income received were more clearly linked under this system than under the collective scheme. The associative model has proved to be a partial success on many farms. Production has apparently increased, as have the incomes of most *parceleros* (see Stanfield et al. 1985b).

Severe strains have appeared on other farms, however. Individual default on the collective responsibility for credit—or the inability of some *parceleros* to show a profit—has introduced an element of dissent. Bookkeeping errors or omissions often become another matter for grievances. The internal accounting system of the association must be open to constant inspection, but many *parceleros* are illiterate and only with great difficulty can keep books or understand how they are kept. Furthermore, although machinery needs constant upkeep and frequent repair, some *parceleros* do not agree with such maintenance expenditures. This has led to a gradual paralysis of collectively owned machinery. *Parceleros* who fall ill or for some other reason perform poorly no longer have the group to carry them along as they did under the collective model, and there is no available insurance scheme (see chap. 6 for a discussion of this point). The challenge of making these organizations work well remains a central preoccupation of IAD.

CONCLUSIONS

While the Dominican agrarian reform initially benefited (between 1962 and 1972) from having Trujillo's lands to distribute and did not have to go through expensive and conflictive expropriations, the rate of settlement was slow and the land distributed was not highly productive. In the late 1960s, pressures from the landless increased. The reform was given a new impetus after the implementation of the potentially radical legislation of 1972. Those agrarian laws, however, were never fully applied, and even the most significant of the efforts (that is, the organization of collectives on expropriated rice lands) was only a partial application of the legal mandates.

Nonetheless, the quality of the land and the number of people affected during this phase were significant. Roughly 70 percent of the reform beneficiaries and 67 percent of the land distributions occurred in the 10-year period following 1972. Presently, about one-third of the country's rice is produced by the reformed sector. From the point of view of those who fashioned the agrarian laws of 1972, these efforts must be judged to be at least qualified successes.

The experimentation with collectives has also had positive results. In most cases, the collective experience evolved into a new way of organizing the production process, the "associative farm." The experience with collectives strengthened the capabilities of reform beneficiaries to manage their own affairs and use their lands in a productive manner. The men and women who received access to land through the agrarian reform in the early 1970s are now different people. They have become, in large measure, managers and farmers—something that was almost impossible to imagine when the collectives were first organized. Indeed, these people seem to make up a new class in rural society.

The growing paralysis of the state's service and credit delivery capacities in the past several years has created challenges to these new entrepreneurs (see Moya Pons 1985, 97–110). Since the Agricultural Bank has fewer funds than in previous years, beneficiaries have trouble getting credit. Farmers must also deal with evolving technologies on their own, since government technical assistance has been drastically reduced. INESPRE cannot pay producers a good price and still provide cheap rice to national consumers. The next steps in the continuing reform of the reform (see Moya Pons 1985; Dore y Cabral 1984) may be more individualization and more privatization of both production and marketing structures.

NOTES

1. The state became the owner of twenty-five industrial, commercial, mining, and transport enterprises worth 40 million pesos; ten sugar refineries worth 150 million pesos; and 1,350,768 tareas of sugarcane land plus 1,132,662 tareas of other lands that were used mostly for cattle and timber (see IAD 1979, 9).
2. One hectare equals 15.9 tareas.
3. See Marínez (1984) for a partial summary of the literature on this point; also see the case history in Stanfield et al. (1985b).
4. See also Dore y Cabral (1984) for a summary of various studies that further explore the peasant strategy of the Balaguer reforms.
5. The term "colectivo" (or collective) in the Dominican Republic refers to a production cooperative where state-paid managers exercise substantial control over the production process but where profits are divided among the members after the production is sold.
6. See Carter and Kanel (1985) for a discussion of these "free-rider" labor-discipline problems on collectives.
7. See Stanfield et al. (1985a) for details of the management information systems of IAD.
8. See Stanfield et al. (1985a, 1985b) for the histories of two farms in this regard.

REFERENCES

Aquino González, Carlos. 1978. *Fundamentos para una estrategia de desarrollo agrícola*. Santiago: Instituto Superior de Agricultura.

Balaguer, Joaquin. 1979. *Mensajes presidenciales*. Barcelona: Imprime M. Pareja.

Bravo Barros, Carlos. 1983. Informe del consultor. TCP/DOM/2201. Mimeograph. Santo Domingo: FAO.

Caribe. 1972. Santo Domingo, 9 March.

Carter, Michael R., and Don Kanel. 1985. *Collective rice production in Finca Bermúdez: Institutional performance and evolution in the Dominican agrarian reform*. LTC Research paper, no. 83. Madison: Land Tenure Center, University of Wisconsin.

Clausner, Marlin D. 1973. *Rural Santo Domingo: Settled, unsettled and resettled*. Philadelphia: Temple Univ. Press.

Comité Ejecutivo de las Asociaciones. 1982. "Gregorio Luperón" y "Padre Cabero" al Presidente de la República, Secretario de Agricultura, y Director General del Instituto Agrario Dominicano, 5 de octubre de 1982. Santiago: IAD correspondence files.

Crouch, Luis Arturo. 1981. The development of capitalism in Dominican agriculture. Ph.D. dissertation, University of California-Berkeley.

De Groot, Jan P. 1983. Cómo evaluar el retoño en el cultivo de arroz. Mimeograph. Santiago: Centro de Investigaciones Económicas y Alimenticias, Instituto Superior de Agricultura.

Delgado Sánchez, Oscar. 1983. Diagnóstico socio-económico de los asentamientos individuales y colectivos. Report to FAO. TCP/DOM/2201. Santo Domingo: IAD-PIDELTA.

Dore y Cabral, Carlos. 1980. El aspecto político de la reforma agraria en la República Dominicana: Necesidad de la contrainsurgencia o del desarrollo del capitalismo. Paper presented at Seminario sobre Problemas de Desarrollo Rural del Caribe, Santo Domingo, May.

———.1981. *Reforma agraria y luchas sociales en la República Dominicana, 1966-1978*. Santo Domingo: Editora Taller.

———.1984. Clases sociales y políticas agrarias en la República Dominicana de hoy. *Ciencia y Sociedad* (Santo Domingo) 9(1):41–62.

Estudios Sociales. 1968. No. 1.

Eusebio Pol, Noris. 1982. Las ocupaciones de tierra en la República Dominicana. *Ciencia y Sociedad* (Santo Domingo) 7(2):160–179.

IAD (Instituto Agrario Dominicano). 1975. Informe de la comisión para la evaluación de los asentamientos arroceros del Instituto Agrario Dominicano. Mimeograph. Santo Domingo: IAD.

———.1979. Programa de consolidación de la reforma agraria, 1979–1982. Mimeograph. Santo Domingo: IAD.

———.1980. Niveles de conocimiento sobre la forma de organización del trabajo: Propuesta por los beneficiarios de la zona arrocera colectiva de Rincón-La Vega. Mimeograph. Santo Domingo: IAD.

———.1981. Compendio de las leyes agrarias. Mimeograph. Santo Domingo: IAD.

———.1982. Informe sobre los *asentamientos* colectivos de la reforma agraria. Mimeograph. Santo Domingo: Comisión Ad-Hoc para la Revisión de los Asentamientos Colectivos, IAD.

Inter-American Economic and Social Council. 1961. Special Meeting at Ministerial Level, Punta del Este, Uruguay. *Alliance for Progress; Official Documents*. OEA/Ser.H/XII.1 (English). Washington: Pan American Union.

ISA (Instituto Superior de Agricultura). 1979. *Anteproyecto para el desarrollo y administración de tres asentamientos* del programa de reforma agraria del gobierno dominicano. Santiago: ISA.

Listín Diario. 1972. Santo Domingo, 10 March.

Marínez, Pablo A. 1984. Resistencia campesina, imperialismo y reforma agraria en República Dominicana (1899–1978). Santo Domingo: Centro de Planificación y Acción Ecumenica.

Mendez, Francisco, and Frans Doorman. 1984. *Diferenciación y adaptación en la producción de arroz*. Santiago: Centro de Desarrollo Agropecuario, Zona Norte (CENDA), La Herradura.

Menendez, Antonio. 1984. El proceso de reforma agraria: 1979–1982. *Ciencia y Sociedad* (Santo Domingo) 9(1):63–100.

Moya Pons, Frank, ed. 1985. *Forum 15: Presente y futuro de la reforma agraria en la República Dominicana*. Santo Domingo: Amigo del Hogar.

Munguia, Jorge. 1976. Asentamientos colectivos, fincas estatales y economía de escala. *Estudios Sociales* (Santo Domingo) 9(7):111–142.

Quezada, Norberto A., Ana Teresa Gutiérrez, Jesús de los Santos, and Gabriel Guzmán. 1985. Administración para el desarrollo de la reforma agraria. Paper presented to 19th meeting of Executives of Agrarian Reform Programs in Central America and the Dominican Republic (PRACA), Santo Domingo, 20–23 May.

Rodríguez, Frank, and Otto Fernández. 1976. Notas sobre las políticas agrarias en la República Dominicana. *Revista Ciencia* 3(1):43–57.

Rodríguez Nuñez, Pablo. 1984. 20 años de arroz y reforma agraria en la República Dominicana. Mimeograph. Santo Domingo.

Secretaria de Estado de Agricultura. 1977. Estudio de costa de producción para algunos cultivos principales. Mimeograph. Santo Domingo.

Stanfield, J. David, Richard Powers, Emil Haney, and Heliodoro Díaz. 1985a. Flujos de información en la gestión de la reforma agraria de la República Dominicana. Madison: Centro de Administración del Desarrollo Rural, Instituto Superior de Agricultura, Instituto Agrario Dominicano, Centro de Tenencia de la Tierra, October.

Stanfield, David, Pablo Rodríguez, Juan Ogando, Leo Colón, Heliodoro Díaz, and Ana Teresa Gutiérrez de San Martín. 1985b. El asentamiento campesino Vásquez Quintero: Un estudio de caso de un asentamiento asociativo. Madison: Centro de Administración del Desarrollo Rural, Instituto Superior de Agricultura, Instituto Agrario Dominicano, Centro de Tenencia de la Tierra, October.

United Nations. 1962. *Boletín económico de América Latina*, 7(1), suplemento estadístico. Secretaria de la Comisión Económica para América Latina.

Vargas, Lino. 1984. La transformación del sistema colectiva en asociativo en los *asentamientos* arroceros del IAD. Mimeograph. Santiago, IAD.

Chapter 12

Reform among the Smallholders: St. Lucia, Jamaica, and Implications for the Caribbean

Randy Stringer, John Bruce, and David Stanfield*

Lack of access to land by the greater part of the rural population has been a constant problem in Caribbean countries during the last century; it is a legacy of the plantation system introduced by the English, Dutch, and French in the early sixteenth century, reinforced by recent patterns of trade in agricultural commodities. Analysis has traditionally focused on the dualism of plantation and peasant holdings, of *grande* and *petite propriété*; more recently, attention has shifted to the tenure situation and problems of the land poor and the landless. Some Caribbean governments have addressed the problem of poor access to land by attempting to implement land settlement and colonization programs. The past decades have seen increased complexity of tenure relationships among fragmented and undocumented holdings, often located on resource-poor hillsides and other marginal lands on the periphery of large estates. Because access to large holdings is restricted and employment alternatives are few, a rapid rate of population growth is dramatically increasing the demand for land. Families who need land must rent, borrow, cash-lease, sharecrop, subdivide, squat, or, if their resources permit, purchase small parcels.

This growing heterogeneity of land-tenure relationships has economic, social, and environmental consequences which are raising new concerns about the inadequate legal protection for the smallholders and the high costs and long delays for those involved in land

* Randy Stringer is a Project Associate, John Bruce is the Director, and David Stanfield is the Latin American Project Coordinator, Land Tenure Center, University of Wisconsin-Madison.

transactions. Problems with insecure tenure stemming from the lack of documented title have instigated new policy initiatives. For example, the Cayman Islands, British Virgin Islands, Montserrat, and Antigua have modernized their land records by changing basic legislation governing the operation of their property registries and by surveying and titling agricultural lands. The main objective of such programs is to define rights in land accurately, inexpensively, and dependably, thereby improving tenure security. A second goal is to promote a more effective land market by making transactions less costly and easier. It is often thought that fully operational land markets will lead to more efficient factor combinations and increased productivity.

The St. Lucian government began a land-titling and registration program in 1984. St. Lucia has invested in a modernized property register and cadastral survey as a means for improving tenure security and, hence, the operation of the land market. In Jamaica, the land-resettlement option has been tried, using leasehold rather than fee-simple ownership, as the basic tenure form. This chapter examines tenure reforms in the smallholder sector in these two countries and draws some preliminary conclusions about the relevance of such programs in the Caribbean.

HISTORIC OVERVIEW

The colonization of the Caribbean islands was distinct from that of most of Central and South America. Unlike the Spanish, whose New World activities focused on the search for precious metals, the French and English Caribbean colonizers seemed to be as interested in agricultural production, mostly sugar. The Caribbean islands provided many advantages for agriculture: (1) they were located closer to European markets than the Central and South American coasts, making shipping cheaper, (2) they were small enough so that each plantation could have its own port, thus reducing overland transportation problems, and (3) their small size and rugged terrain meant that it was difficult for slaves to escape (James 1957, 16).

In all the colonized islands, the plantation system dominated nearly every aspect of economic and social life. Because plantations depended on slave labor, a small-farm sector did not really develop in the anglophone Caribbean until after emancipation in 1838 (Marshall 1985, 1). At that time many former slaves, with varying degrees of success from island to island, attempted to acquire land. In some cases, opportunities for obtaining land did not really exist. For example, in Barbados and the Leeward Islands the long-established sugar industry had already incorporated the best lands. In Jamaica, Trinidad, and the Windward Islands some land was available (Axline 1986, 49). In almost every case, however, the plantation sector controlled the flat fertile areas and the peasant sector cultivated the shallow and relatively infertile soils on the hillsides (Beckford 1968, 234).

Estate owners, who depended on an adequate supply of labor for export crops, usually thwarted attempts by the landless to acquire farms throughout the region. Legislatures blocked land-settlement programs by refusing to survey crown land, by establishing licenses for the sale of sugar, coffee, firewood, and charcoal, and by implementing regressive land taxes. In St. Lucia, a tax of four shillings was placed on all cultivated land in 1849. The purpose of this tax was to deter peasants from becoming owner-operators. A similar tax was used in Tobago (Acosta and Casimir 1985, 37).

Large landowners also made it difficult for ex-slaves by refusing to sell them marginal and underutilized lands. They improvised labor-rent-tenancy contracts to keep wage earners from obtaining parcels (Marshall 1985, 5). While generally successful, these efforts did not completely block peasants from obtaining land both legally through purchase and illegally through squatting. In St. Lucia, the number of smallholders rose from 1,345 units in 1845 to 2,185 units in 1861 (Acosta and Casimir 1985, 36); in Jamaica, the number of smallholdings (those between 5 and 50 acres) increased from 13,189 in 1880 to 24,226 in 1902 (Eisner 1966, 220).

In many cases, limited access to land led to the emergence of new types of tenure relationships. For instance, Acosta and Casimir (1985, 34) suggest that the sharecropping system, known as the *métayage* system, developed as a compromise between the opposing economic and social requirements of plantation owners and landless peasants. Peasants exchanged their labor for land. The large landowner and the *métayer* became interdependent (albeit with the landowner as the dominant partner): the estate owner provided the land while the *métayers* provided the labor as well as deducting sugar-manufacturing operating costs from their half of the sales. The *métayer* was also allowed to raise subsistence crops along with the sugarcane. For the landless, this compromise offered an alternative to wage labor, but, as will be seen, tenancy and wage labor are not mutually exclusive possibilities.

In addition to the continuing problem of lack of access to land, a new set of agricultural and tenure-related issues has emerged with the expansion in the number of smallholdings: subdivision of parcels, fragmentation of holdings, and multiple ownership (family lands). The consequences of these three phenomena for agriculture have often been negative. The continuing subdivision of family parcels, often already too small to provide for subsistence needs, may also lead to underutilization of family labor. And, as these individual plots become smaller, families attempt to rent, lease, purchase, or sharecrop additional small pieces of land in the same area. Thus, the family's farmland becomes fragmented. Although in some regions of the world, fragmentation is a rational result of wanting to farm in different ecological zones, in many parts of the Caribbean the existence of fragmented holdings in the small-farm sector is a result of the monopolization of the best land by the estate owners combined with the need for additional resources of those with access to insufficient and/or poor quality land. In addition to population pressure, tourism and mining interests on many islands have also been competing for the available cultivable land (Beckford 1972a, 30).

A second small-farm tenure issue is family land, which is land held by co-heirs and their descendants in undivided co-ownership. This type of tenure relationship may be problematic because all co-owners are required to consent in writing to any land transaction for any purpose—from sale to use of land as collateral.

Land registration involving a comprehensive cadastral survey has been seen as a potential solution for some of these problems.[1] Systematic survey and proper titling of the land, some argue, will increase security of tenure and will permit a more active land market, which in turn should lead to consolidation of holdings and provide a means of remedying the subdivision brought about by inheritance. The market mechanism can, it is suggested, undo some of the damage wrought by adherence to existing inheritance patterns. An attempt has also been made to deal with family-land issues through a "trust-for-sale" mechanism, which would allow only a few of the co-owners to transact for all.

Some versions of land registration have been attempted, but the amounts of land involved differ greatly from country to country. Many of the countries in the region have had a deeds-registry system from early in the colonial period.[2] Often, the coverage of these registries is very spotty.

In 1970, Britain's Overseas Development Authority (ODA) established a technical assistance project on cadastral survey and registration based in Barbados. In the 1970s, the project assisted with major programs of survey and land registration in the British Virgin Islands, the Cayman Islands, and Montserrat. Advisors from the project and ODA's Directorate of Overseas Surveys have made numerous visits to Jamaica and were involved in the planning of the U.S. Agency for International Development (USAID)-funded project in St. Lucia, which until 1986 had relied on a deeds registry.

JAMAICA

Land-Tenure Patterns

Land-distribution patterns in Jamaica appear to be less skewed than those for St. Lucia. Even so, the bimodal structure of agriculture, with plantation agriculture on one hand and a large number of smallholders on the other, characterizes the sector. Farms of less than 5 acres historically have occupied between 13 and 16 percent of the acreage but represent about 80 percent of the total number of farms, which in 1978 was 184,000 (Pollard and Graham 1985, 736). At the other extreme, fewer than 1,200 large farms (those with 100 acres or more) continue to comprise less than 1 percent of the total number of farms but occupy over 50 percent of the country's farmland. The dualistic pattern appears to be becoming more rather than less pronounced; lately, the numbers of very small and very large farms have increased at the expense of intermediate-sized operations. Smallholdings have become progressively smaller in recent times (Goldsmith 1981, 87). Over the most recent decade (1968–1978) for which data are available, there were decreases in the percentage of farms in the medium range of 5 to 24.9 acres (19.4 to 16.2 percent), and the total area occupied by these farms declined from 23 to 19 percent of total agricultural acreage. The percentage of farms of less than 5 acres increased (78 to 82 percent), while the area they occupied remained relatively stable. The largest farms (over 100 acres) increased in number slightly in that decade (from 991 to 1,116), as did their proportion of agricultural land (53 to 57 percent). Table 1 shows that the average-sized holding in the "under-5-acres category" decreased from 1.79 acres in 1954 to 1.44 acres in 1978.

Fragmentation of holdings seems to be a significant phenomenon in Jamaica. In 1961, 42 percent of farms had two or more parcels, and

Table 1
Jamaican farm numbers and size: 1954, 1968, 1978 for holdings under 5 acres[a]

Year	Number	Acres	Average size	Percentage of total farms	Percentage of total acreage
1954	139,043	249,074	1.79	70	13.0
1968	151,705	229,216	1.51	78	15.4
1978	150,633	216,679	1.44	82	16.0

[a] Sources: Stephen K. Pollard and Douglas H. Graham, "The Performance of the Food Producing Sector in Jamaica, 1962–1979: A Policy Analysis," *Economic Development and Cultural Change* 33:(4) (July 1985): p. 736; Government of Jamaica, Ministry of Agriculture, *Agricultural Census, 1968/69*, vol. IA, p. 19, and *Agricultural Census, 1978/79*.

one-third of the farms had two or three segments, while 5 percent had four to ten or more parts. Approximately one-fifth of the 100-hectare-and-above farms were composed of four or more parcels (Igbozurike 1971, 11). It is probable that the fragmentation of holdings is more serious today (Goldsmith 1981, 105).

There are a number of possible reasons for this fragmentation and generally decreasing farm size in Jamaica. One is population pressure, which is forcing people to search for more land as their families become too large for the existing parcel. Blustain (1982, 56), however, argues that population pressure has played a minimal role in the fragmentation of farm holdings because urban migration and emigration have provided an outlet for rural persons. Nonetheless, small property owners do not tend to sell their parcels since ownership of land confers both security and status. Instead, they tend to rent out land. Farmers who wish to increase farm size are often forced to find a piece of land not contiguous with their existing property for rent or purchase.

Another problem that aggravates the tendency toward fragmentation of parcels in Jamaica is the increasing competition for land caused by the decreasing number of alternative employment opportunities and the slowing of rural-to-urban migration. With rural populations still growing in absolute numbers, land remains the principal employment source. The fundamental problem is that many individual households do not have enough land to support themselves adequately. Land-hungry households must find access to additional land to provide necessary food and income. Mitchell (1984, 18) found that 30 percent of the farmers in her survey depended on rented or leased lands.

There is serious concern over the possible implications of fragmentation for farm operations and agricultural production. First, from the farmers' perspective, the distance from their dwellings to their most distant parcels, as well as the distance between parcels, affects both the crop selection and the amount of time they dedicate to each piece of land. While size of holding, soil quality, water availability, and type of crop help determine the cropping pattern, the decision of how many and which crops to plant is also determined by tenure status and ability to reach the parcel. As the distance covered and the time taken to reach a particular parcel grow, the number of visits to that parcel becomes fewer and the duration of each visit may shorten. Likewise, farmers are likely to spend less time on rented land than on purchased and family lands. Furthermore, when land is fragmented it becomes more difficult for extension agents to provide adequate technical recommendations for all the various parcels.

Family land is also common in Jamaica. In the late 1950s, Edith Clarke's book, *My Mother Who Fathered Me*, showed the relationship between family structure and family land. Clarke's research indicated that there are a number of problems associated with the custom of leaving an undivided share of the land to each heir. In Jamaica, family land is often operated as a single unit, even though there are multiple owners who may or may not participate in production. While this avoids the problems associated with subdividing the land into parcels too small to be viable for the household, Clarke (1957, 44), writes that it creates legal confusion:

> Disagreements between members of the family over family land are in Jamaica one of the most common causes of litigation and invariably the reason is the attempt of one or more members to establish an individual right by exploiting the conflict between the traditional system which is current in one segment of the society and the legal code which is applicable to the whole society.

Most research shows a negative relationship between the presence of family land and the amount of agricultural production. However, recent work implies that family land is a fairly small percentage of total land. Igbozurike (1971, 41) concludes that family lands are (1) most often the house lot, (2) usually the smallest parcel used by the farm household, (3) most often the first piece acquired by a farmer, and (4) infrequently subdivided.

Blustain (1985, 54) found that three of forty parcels of family land he studied currently were involved in interfamily disputes. There were only small and insignificant differences between land use on family lands and on purchased lands. Blustain offers several reasons for the similarity of use on family and other lands. First, in many cases, no other heir exists, so that, even without a will, a single family member operates the farm as a de facto sole owner. Second, many co-owners leave the property for jobs in towns and have no intention of ever reclaiming use rights over it. Third, many farmers have access to several parcels, including purchased land, so they have no real need to exercise their rights over the inherited land. Finally, most family members are able to work out informal agreements and any remaining disputes rarely become confrontational.

Land Reform: Plantations versus Smallholders, Leasehold versus Freehold

Land-tenure patterns underlie many of the current maladjustments in agriculture and make it difficult for the sector to respond flexibly to pressures for economic change. The most productive lands in the lowland plains are often organized into large plantations and extensive enterprises of cattle, sugarcane, banana, and coconut production, all of which have experienced serious economic viability problems. In contrast, small-scale hillside agriculture, which produces crops such as yams, sweet potatoes, coffee, cocoa, and vegetables, yields higher returns per acre of land even though utilizing relatively poor and often marginal lands. Furthermore, these small farms employ intensive growing practices, using largely traditional methods. Recently, the contribution of the export-crop sector to the gross national product (GNP) has been declining while the contribution of domestic crops has been steadily rising. However, this increasing intensity of production on the shallow hillside soils has led to serious erosion of the steep slopes (see Arulpragasam 1984, 54).

Thus, Jamaica is faced with a paradoxical situation. The best land in the country, held in large estates, has been extensively farmed and has had the lowest returns per acre (see Beckford 1972a, 88–97; Beckford 1972b, 33–47). These farmers have the physical and financial resources to produce more intensively, but they have not done so. On the other hand, small farmers are situated on the hillsides, performing both land- and labor-intensive agriculture. They contribute a higher return per unit of land and provide greater returns in terms of foreign exchange saved by producing foodstuffs which otherwise would have to be imported, but they seriously damage the hillsides in the process. The possibilities for improving their relatively precarious socioeconomic condition are severely limited by the quantity and quality of land they farm and by the other factors of production available to them.

Pollard and Graham (1985, 731–754) show that in one recent period there were some changes in this relative balance between domestic food production-export crops and the small-farm-large-farm sectors. They conclude that domestic food production increased while export production declined between 1961 and 1978. During the same period, however, agricultural land became more concentrated in a smaller number of large estates while the number of small farms increased dramatically and their acreages decreased.

The historic problem of land access appears to have grown more serious in recent years. While land in larger estates has shifted to some extent from export-crop production, it is still comparatively underutilized while the lower quality land held in small farms is overexploited. Employment opportunities for small farmers continue to be limited, with the country's unemployment rate at about 27 percent officially and, in reality, probably higher. One of the longer term requirements for the rationalization of agricultural land use in Jamaican rural areas is to bring about a more equitable distribution of productive land to provide more income and employment opportunities. To do so would require complex technical, economic, social, and financial innovations in policy.

From the time of Jamaica's independence in 1962, every government has attempted to address this issue. The result has been a bewildering variety of land reform programs, including, for example, settlement and colonization efforts, land-lease schemes, land-sale programs, sugarcane growers' cooperatives with 49-year land leases, communal farms, pioneer farms for landless youths, and integrated rural development programs. These measures have met with varying degrees of success; all have had to deal with a deeply ingrained, rather intransigent agrarian structure.

In general, land reform in Jamaica has traditionally focused on limited acquisition of land by government for reallocation to landless and land-poor farmers. In the 1929–1971 period, 209 properties were acquired by the government. A total of 39,381 allotments of land were made. Once farmers had paid for the land and the cost of the parcel surveys, they were eligible for freehold titles. By 1985, on these traditional freehold settlements, there were 212 properties on which some settlers had not received certificates of title. Table 2 shows that of the 40,452 allotments, 20,167 had been titled to the settlers, leaving 20,287 untitled lots that occupied 103,100 acres.

In the early 1970s, the Michael Manley administration proposed to change this traditional settlement strategy of government land purchases for sale to settlers. Manley sought to acquire large areas for sublet to peasants. The rationale for leasing rather than selling land was fourfold: (1) leasehold would allow the farmers' capital to be used for on-farm investments and it would not be tied up in land purchases, (2) leasehold would give the government leverage to promote productive policies it deemed appropriate (for example, soil conservation), (3) leasehold would prevent land speculation and keep the land in the hands of the allottees, and (4) fragmentation would be discouraged (Perera 1982, 1).

Project Land Lease had three phases. In Phase I, the government leased over 300 properties that occupied over 60,000 acres. Between 1973 and 1981, 48,115 acres were sublet to 28,829 tenants on 5-year

Table 2
Jamaican traditional land settlements through 1985[a]

Enumeration	Land settlements
Number of properties	212
Gross acres	202,262
Number of plots	40,452
Number of titles issued by 1985	20,165
Number of titles to be issued	20,287
Number of acres to be titled	103,100

[a] Source: File records of Jamaica Lands Department, 1985.

leases; these leases were renewable for an additional 5 years. In Phase II, the government purchased 125 properties, and 9,934 tenants received a total of 22,123 arable acres on 49-year leases (Perera 1982, 4–5). These two phases sought to ameliorate near-landlessness by adding land to very small holdings.

Phase III of Project Land Lease attempted to supply the tenant beneficiaries with land sufficient to provide each family with a target income of J$4,000 per year. Some infrastructure was also provided in Phase III, mostly roads, housing, and water supplies. Due largely to high costs, only seven properties, consisting of 4,552 acres of arable land, were purchased. These lands were distributed to 1,006 tenants on 49-year leases.

The second government program developed during the Manley years was the World Bank-supported First Rural Development Project, which began in 1977 and settled 1,400 families on 15,500 acres of government land in the west of the country under 49-year leases. The project provided for housing, roads, and water supplies. A third program, also begun in 1977, was the creation of production cooperatives, known as "pioneer farms." Eleven such farms were established, with fifty farmers per cooperative. These pioneer farms were organized on a total of 1,417 acres.

The Edward Seaga government of the 1980s had a different set of agricultural policies in mind. The Land Lease Program was discontinued, and over one-third of this land was returned to its owners as unsuitable for leasehold cultivation. Much of the remainder is to be transferred to settlers for eventual purchase under freehold title (Perera 1982, 9–11).

Presently, there are some 36,300 small farmers who have been settled on government lands over a period dating as far back as the 1940s but who have no legal, registered title to their lands. Certificates of title for the period 1976 to 1980 were issued at the incredibly slow rate of only 254 titles per year. Under the Seaga government, the number of settlers in possession of land but without title continues to grow. Between 1983 and 1984, fifteen properties were subdivided and 2,434 provisional allotments of land were made. However, only 221 new titles were issued in those years.

Lack of title is an important obstacle to the provision of credit to these farmers, since without it they are unable to offer their land as security for a loan (Seligson 1985, 2–5). Numerous alternative loan-security mechanisms have been attempted with limited success (see Stanfield et al. 1986, 14–16). A majority of landowners can produce some documentary evidence short of a certificate of title or deed for their ownership claims (Blustain 1982, 61), but this evidence frequently is not satisfactory as collateral. The smaller farmer remains especially handicapped because acquiring a legally recognized title is so difficult. The procedure for registration of title at the title office requires that the farmer employ a lawyer, pay at least J$400, go through much red tape, and wait up to 6 months (Blustain 1982, 60). These high costs are, in part, due to Jamaica's adoption, in 1889, of the relatively advanced Torrens-style system of land registration. Unlike the variants of that system more recently adopted in the Caribbean, the Jamaican office that issues certificates of title requires precise boundary surveys and a costly and lengthy review of evidence of possession and ownership as well as public statements from community residents.

Once land is registered, however, transactions in land are relatively simple and rapid. Title searches appear to be less complicated and less expensive in the Torrens-style system than are searches done through the traditional deeds registry and handled by the Island Records Office (IRO). The lawyer fees for transfer are 50 percent higher when they require searches at the IRO. Both systems, however, rely on the parties involved in the transaction to update the record. For a variety of reasons, new holders of land may fail to do so. Some delays are built into the system. One problem on the government land-registration projects has been the settlers' inability to acquire clear title from the government, largely because individual parcel titles cannot be issued until the legally required roads and water systems are installed in the subdivided government properties and until the settlers' debts to the government are paid. Meanwhile, dealing in land does occur and the official record of ownership increasingly varies from the de facto situation.

There has been some concern for making the land records system easier to update by improving the efficiency of public agencies, which are overloaded and slow to issue certificates of title. Existing survey procedures are unwieldy, and the work load is constantly expanding. Changes in survey procedures are called for, and there is a clear need for renewed political and governmental support for modernizing the survey and registry operations. As of 1986, little more has been done than recognize the problem and establish the need for modernizing the property system. Unlike St. Lucia, however, the Jamaican emphasis is currently on restricted cadastral surveying and registration, specifically as adjuncts to resettlement efforts. No plan exists for systematic cadastral coverage of the entire island.

ST. LUCIA

Until 1814, St. Lucia was a colony and the land law was provided by *"la coutume de Paris"* applied by early French colonizers. In 1786, the French prepared a cadastral map of the island. When the British established final control in 1814, they did so under a treaty obligation to continue to apply French law. The British established a deeds-registry system in 1830 and, in 1879, enacted a civil code based on the Civil Code of Quebec, which, as amended, remains in force today (Meliczek 1975, 7–9).

As in Jamaica, however, the key land-tenure issues are a highly skewed pattern of land distribution and "family land." Available data, brought together and analyzed by Meliczek (1975, 9–10, 24), provide an unusually clear picture of land tenure and distribution. Approximately 63,500 acres of privately owned land and about 6,400 acres of government-owned land are in agriculture in St. Lucia (Meliczek 1975, 16; Lawrence 1979, 1). The 1973/74 agricultural census shows seventy-three holdings occupying 52 percent of all agricultural land (despite the fact that some large holdings were omitted from the census). Tax records from 1971 to 1973 show that all property in holdings of 500 acres or more was owned by seventeen civil or legal persons and included 47 percent of all agricultural holdings (Meliczek 1975, 23). Over 80 percent of holdings was smaller than 5 acres and covered only 14 percent of the agricultural land.

Eight families owned 13,251 acres in St. Lucia, while 15,049 acres were owned by six foreign individuals or companies of British or U.S. origin. On the other hand, 4,700 smallholders had less than 1 acre apiece (Meliczek 1975, 23–24). The plantations are largely worked with wage labor and, unlike many Caribbean islands, only a very small amount of land (just 4 percent of agricultural holdings) is farmed in leasehold (Meliczek 1975, 23). There are approximately 7,000 landless laborers (Meliczek 1975, 14, 21).

The pressure on land in the smallholder sector in St. Lucia has been intense largely because of land maldistribution and population pressure. Given the small holding size and the system of intestate inheritance under the Civil Code, it is remarkable that there is not even more fragmentation. Under the Code, all legitimate children inherit in cases where there is no will. However, Lawrence and Bruce characterize this fragmentation as minimal (Lawrence 1979, 8; Bruce 1983, 16-19). The 1973/74 agricultural census showed the average number of parcels per holder as only 1.12. Of the holdings, 80 percent had a single parcel, 20 percent had two to three parcels, and only one hundred fifty holdings were composed of four or more parcels (Meliczek 1975, 23). A more recent study of smallholders (Knudson and Yates 1982, 38) confirms Meliczek's finding on levels of fragmentation.

Low fragmentation may be due in part to a more effective use of family land, where inherited land can be retained as an undivided holding by the group of heirs. In St. Lucia, the family landholding is associated with (and is, perhaps, a response to) limited land, rapid rural population growth, and labor out-migration into unstable markets where labor mobility is high (Bruce 1983, 12–16, 45). Family land is one way the subdivisive impact of the Civil Code is avoided. Several generations of heirs often fail to leave any legal record that they are co-owners of undivided shares. Meanwhile, they have made arrangements for the temporary or permanent division of the land among themselves, often influenced by parents' preinheritance distributions. Illegitimate children are often included in these distributions and divisions, contrary to the provision of the Code. Others who live abroad or work outside agriculture often temporarily give up their access to family land, though they may intend to claim their share in the future.

Estimates of the amount of family land on St. Lucia differ, though it seems to be more common there than in other nations of the Caribbean (Bland et al. 1978, 37). The agricultural census suggests that the percentage of land in different regions of St. Lucia under family land varies from as low as 2 percent to as high as 34 percent, depending on the locality (Meliczek 1975, 19; Lawrence 1979, 5–8). Meliczek concludes that less than 10 percent of the land in private agricultural holdings is family land. This is disputed by survey data which hold that nearly 40 percent of smallholder parcels is held as family land (Knudson and Yates 1982, 40). This survey suggests (1) that 20–40 percent of all parcels of privately owned land is, in fact, family land, (2) that 15–30 percent of the total land in private agricultural holdings is family land, and (3) that 25–45 percent of agricultural landholders hold some family land (Bruce 1983, 30).

Inconsistent use of the term is a major problem in any attempt to determine the amount of family land in St. Lucia. Some informants use the term for any co-ownership, even first-generation co-ownership by two persons, while others use it only for co-ownership by larger numbers of heirs after more than one generation. As might be expected, family land is clearly associated with small parcel size; 82 percent of the parcels under family ownership is under 10 acres, with only a few holdings under family tenure in the 50–100 acre range and none above 100 acres. On average, there are six co-owners for each parcel of family land; fewer than fifty parcels belong to twenty or more persons (Meliczek 1975, 19–20).

While family land tenure has provided a relief from extreme subdivision and fragmentation of holdings, it has created land-management problems. Co-ownership under the Civil Code is intended to last only until the estate is partitioned among the heirs. It requires the consent of all co-owners in management decisions and becomes clumsy for farm-management purposes, especially if it extends across several generations (Bruce 1983, 3–5). For example, co-owners are always aware of family members who have unexercised claims, and the produce of perennial crops on family land may be subject to claims from these nonfarming co-owners. John Compton, prime minister of St. Lucia, said in 1984, "some who have never planted even a *macamboo* in the land, some whom you have never seen for years, can just turn up and reap what you have planted, saying to you, who have toiled in the sun, I have rights, it is *bien minieurs* [equal rights]" (Syrett 1986).

Recent research suggests that because farmers on family lands located on steep hillsides fear claims by co-owners, they do not plant permanent crops. Instead, they cultivate annual crops, which leads to much more severe soil erosion effects on the hillsides than might permanent tree crops, which are planted on purchased land in the valleys (White 1986, 83). Co-ownership also creates insecurity. It excludes most family land from the land market (because all owners must agree to a sale) and, for the same reason, it constrains credit to smallholders because family land cannot usually be used as collateral to secure a loan (Bruce 1983, 19–23).

The main family land issues in St. Lucia have been summarized by Bruce (1983, 45) as follows:

1. Co-owners believe family land is insecure because of the de facto and extralegal nature of the tenurial arrangement. Co-owners do not fear dispossession so much as they are plagued by doubts about whether they can place home sites on the property and disputes over such matters as the division of tree crops with nonresident claimants.
2. Family landholdings cannot be bought or sold without the consent of all the co-owners. This reduces possibilities for land market consolidation.
3. Because family land is inalienable, it cannot be used to secure loans.

Various land reform possibilities have been suggested for family land: the amendment of the Civil Code's provisions on intestate inheritance, forfeiture of shares by nonfarming co-owners, government acquisition and redistribution, adjudication and partition, buy-out programs which would assist some co-owners in purchasing the shares of others, and trust-for-sale arrangements which would allow a few of the co-owners to make a sale as trustees for the others (Bruce 1983, 31–37).

Land Registration and Agrarian Reforms

In 1984, St. Lucia launched a Land Registration and Titling Project (LRTP), partially funded by USAID. The LRTP was justified by the expected increases in investment and the potentially more efficient factor combinations that might result from more secure, more readily marketable titles. By the end of 1987, the LRTP had demarcated, surveyed, and recorded 33,287 parcels, of which 5,944 were in urban Castries. A new Land Registry was operating based on a register of all parcels and a registry map. The title registration model was one which had been promoted by the Overseas Development Administration (ODA), Britain's bilateral, aid-giving agency. The 1984 Land Adjudication Act provided the legal basis for systematic demarcation, survey, adjudication, and registration of the privately held land on the island. A similar land registration program was implemented in the 1970s in the Turks and Caicos.

Only 910 disputes arose that could not be resolved in the field and required a hearing before an adjudication officer. Of these, only a very few had to go to a special appeals tribunal, and only two LRTP administrative decisions were overturned by the tribunal (Syrett 1986). The registration project has enjoyed broad bipartisan political support; the only consistent opposition to the project has come from within the legal profession, which expressed concern for ambiguities and contradictions between the new registration acts and the Civil Code.

How will the LRTP affect land-tenure patterns in St. Lucia? The expected impacts were (1) to individualize family landholdings and (2) to stimulate the land market. At the end of the LRTP, about one-third of the parcels in the new registry were still undivided family holdings (Lemel and Stanfield 1988). The LRTP, then, did not bring about an appreciable individualization of family landholdings.

The LRTP may have a further effect on the land market, which may eventually have a not readily predictable impact on the agrarian structure. In theory, following the creation of the new Land Registry, land transfers should operate more efficiently, but there may also be less palatable side effects: further land concentration, increasing landlessness, and—even though the project has an agricultural production rationale—the shifting of clear titled land out of agriculture entirely as it is purchased by tourist enterprises or retirement communities.

The project's most likely impact on family land is through the development of a more flexible land market. Little was done through the LRTP to promote subdivisions of family lands during the adjudication process, and it is not clear that additional partition would be advantageous.

Where land continues to be held by co-owners as family land, the parcel is registered as belonging to the heirs of the previous owner of the parcel. In a few such cases, the trust-for-sale provision of the new statute was applied. Where a majority of the co-owners who came forward with their claims agreed to a trust for sale, not more than four were registered as trustees. These four usually included the co-owner who applied for registration of the land, and preference was given in some cases to those living and working on the land and the owners of the largest shares. These trustees are able to convey the land on behalf of the other co-owners, subject to the duties and liabilities of trustees. This arrangement is expected both to allow family landholders to secure a loan with family land and to make family land more marketable.

CONCLUSION

Contemporary land-tenure problems of the Caribbean have their roots in the plantation system. Those who want land have had to establish claims to it in areas of less interest to estate owners, usually in the hills and mountains on the plantation's periphery. The property systems through which the state guarantees private landownership functioned relatively well to defend the plantation owners' interests. But the needs of the smallholders and the landless have not been safeguarded. Family land-tenure systems and informal land transactions have resulted in many holdings without a negotiable title. In some countries, governments have responded to tenure insecurity by conducting systematic and comprehensive land-titling and registration programs.

St. Lucia and Jamaica differ in several critical ways. St. Lucia is a small island, with a very limited amount of good agricultural land, where tenure problems are those of a skewed land distribution pattern and family lands. Jamaica has a potentially viable agricultural sector and even good prospects for export. In Jamaica, agrarian policy debates have sometimes focused on distributive issues; the resettlement of plantation land as smallholdings has been significant if sporadic. In St. Lucia, where distribution is more decidedly skewed, national attention has not focused much on distributive issues and resettlement programs, perhaps due to the perennially depressed state of agriculture, which is highly dependent on banana sales. Both countries, however, have recently come to perceive smallholder tenure security and related issues as high priorities, with a resultant strong interest in the issuance of land titles.

The basic question is whether such titling programs are worthwhile. There is recent, solid evidence to support the common-sense conclusion that clear and marketable titles promote increased productivity through increased access to credit and investment in the farming operation (Feder et al. 1986). On the other hand, there are important questions that cannot yet be answered which have to do with the peculiarities of the agricultural histories of the two countries. In St. Lucia, smallholder agriculture is so subject to international banana prices and credit availability that it is not clear over what time period and with what level of incentives new attitudes toward the sector might be created. In Jamaica, tenure policy in resettlement areas has been a political football—leasehold to freehold to leasehold, and so on. It is still not clear whether a titling program will mean an end to this discussion.

The current generation of titling initiatives in the Caribbean will require careful monitoring. Only time will tell how productivity, investment and capitalization, distribution patterns, labor absorption in agriculture, subdivision rates and levels of fragmentation, credit access, farmer income levels, and the balance between food and export crops will be affected. Because operation of the land market is so central to the anticipated benefits of the St. Lucian titling project, the market's operation is central—and not easily predictable—for any evaluative exercise. St. Lucia constitutes part of a regional real estate market in which land is at a premium for tourism. Whether titling will ease the movement of land out of agriculture entirely is also a matter for conjecture. As both the debits and benefits of titling emerge, they must be quantified and examined in relation to the cost of the exercise. Work in St. Lucia shows that costs can be substantial.

It will also be important for governments to monitor the maintenance of a registry system. Are the public and private sectors devoting adequate resources to this aspect of legal and administrative infrastructure? Are landholders finding sufficient benefits for themselves in the system to motivate the voluntary registrations of transactions which are so crucial for system maintenance?

Finally, there are two major questions concerning the adequacy of the titling approach. Does titling suitably address the problems associated with family land, or is a focus on titling of smallholdings too narrow, neglecting, as it does, the origin of the smallholder problem within the skewed pattern of land distribution?

The titling project in St. Lucia has addressed family land issues only through the trust-for-sale mechanism. In Jamaica, titling is being discussed as an approach to the problems of the resettlement sector and little thought has been given to family land.

Once routinely identified as a major constraint on the development of smallholder agriculture, family land has recently received a more balanced treatment. In St. Lucia, it has been suggested that, while it has some negative consequences, it is a positive counterforce to subdivision (Bruce 1983, 16). Blustain urges a much more positive and flexible approach to family land (Blustain 1982). There is sufficient uncertainty as to the value of family land that, rather than requiring an end to it, "reform" proposals should be framed so as to provide exits for farmers who wish to opt out or to adapt the legal system to the implicit rules of family landholdings. The present titling initiatives attack family land tenure head on and may need modification to address the problems of smallholders.

While these projects focus on the smallholder sector, many analyses of land tenure in the Caribbean see the plantation and smallholder sectors as so interrelated that treatments outlined here consider the symptom and not the disease. After all, wage-labor opportunities in the commercial sector do allow farmers to take advantage of peak labor needs in export agriculture while permitting a retreat into subsistence agriculture in the smallholder sector when export markets collapse or at times of the year when labor demands of export crops are low [see, for example, Lassère (1972, 544)]. This more contextual approach would recognize the evolution of the smallholder sector in both St. Lucia and Jamaica as essentially influenced by the evolution and needs of the plantations and the dynamics of the other sectors of the economy. Recent comparative literature stresses the relative efficiency of smallholdings (Berry and Cline 1979) and the advantages of a unimodal as opposed to a bimodal structure of landholdings (Johnston and Kilby 1975). The theoretical superiority of a more egalitarian tenure system, however, has not been reflected in the current generation of land-registration and titling projects in the two countries.

NOTES

1. Land registration is a parcel-based landownership recording system in which the public record is guaranteed by the state. The land registry may provide information on items such as property ownership, boundaries, and parcel shapes. A cadastral map is usually associated with these systems and shows how an area is divided into units of ownership. A fiscal cadaster is an identification of landowners who can be taxed on the basis of their property ownership; a legal cadaster is an identification of legally recognized interests in land, particularly ownership claims. Land registries and legal cadasters are often used by banks to determine whether or not a piece of property may be used as collateral. If the property has a previous lien, it should be recorded in the land registry.

2. A deeds registry provides information for public use about property transfers. While a system of land registration is an authoritative record of ownership rights, the recording of deeds proves only that a transaction has taken place; proof of ownership by the seller requires a title search. For a comparison of the deeds and title registration systems, see Simpson (1976, 19–23).

REFERENCES

Acosta, Yvonne, and Jean Casimir. 1985. Social origins of the counter-plantation system in St. Lucia. In *Development in the Caribbean*, edited by P.I. Gomes, pp. 34–59. London: C. Hurst and Co.

Arulpragasam, L.C. 1984. Major issues of land policy in Jamaica. *Land Reform, Land Settlement and Cooperatives* (FAO/Rome), no. 1/2, pp. 54–67.

Axline, W. Andrew. 1986. *Agricultural policy and collective self-reliance in the Caribbean*. Boulder, Colo.: Westview Press.

Beckford, George L.F. 1968. Toward an appropriate theoretical framework for agricultural development planning and policy. In *Selected papers from the Third West Indian Agricultural Economics Conference, Mona, Jamaica, 1968*, edited by G.L. Beckford, pp. 233–242. St. Augustine, Trinidad, West Indies: Univ. of the West Indies, Department of Agricultural Economics and Farm Management.

———.1972a. Land reform for the betterment of Caribbean peoples. In *Proceedings of the Seventh West Indian Agricultural Economics Conference, Grand Anse, Grenada, 1972*, pp. 25–39. St. Augustine, Trinidad, West Indies: Univ. of the West Indies, Department of Agricultural Economics and Farm Management.

———.1972b. *Persistent poverty*. New York: Oxford Univ. Press.

Berry, Albert R., and William F. Cline. 1979. *Agrarian structure and productivity in developing countries*. Baltimore: Johns Hopkins Univ. Press.

Bland, A.J. et al. 1978. *Legal and sociological survey of land use and tenure in Antigua, Belize, Dominica, Grenada, Montserrat, Nevis, St. Kitts, St. Lucia and St. Vincent*, vol. 1. Cave Hill, Barbados: Univ. of the West Indies, Faculty of Law, December.

Blustain, Harvey S. 1982. *Resource management and agricultural development in Jamaica: Lessons for a participatory approach*. Ithaca, N.Y.: Cornell Univ., Rural Development Committee.

———.1985. Customary land tenure in rural Jamaica: Implications for development. In *Strategies for organization of small farm agriculture in Jamaica*, edited by Elsie LeFranc and Harvey Blustain, pp. 47–65. Ithaca, N.Y.: Cornell Univ., Rural Development Committee.

Bruce, John W. 1983. *Family land tenure and agricultural development in St. Lucia*. LTC Research Paper, no. 79. Madison: University of Wisconsin, Land Tenure Center, December.

Clarke, Edith. 1957. *My mother who fathered me*. London: George Allen and Unwin.

Eisner, Gisela. 1966. *Jamaica, 1830–1950: A study in economic growth*. Manchester: Manchester Univ. Press.

Feder, Gershon, Onchon Tongro, Chalamwong Youngyuth, and Chira Hongladarom. 1986. *Land ownership security, farm productivity, and land policies in rural Thailand*. Washington: World Bank, August.

Goldsmith, Arthur Austin. 1981. The politics of rural stagnation: Development policy, local organizations and agrarian change in Jamaica. Ph.D. dissertation, Cornell University, Ithaca, N.Y.

Igbozurike, M.U. 1971. Fragmentation in tropical agriculture: Concept, process and result—a Jamaican case study. Ph.D. dissertation, University of Florida, Gainesville.

James, Preston E. 1957. Man-land relations in the Caribbean area. In *Caribbean studies: A symposium*, edited by Vera Rubin, pp. 14–20. Seattle: Univ. of Washington Press.

Johnston, Bruce F., and Peter Kilby. 1975. *Agriculture and structural transformation: Economic strategies in late developing countries*. New York: Oxford Univ. Press.

Knudson, Barbara, and Barbara Yates. 1982. The economic role of women in small-scale agriculture in the eastern Caribbean: St. Lucia. Interim report of research. Madison, Wisc.: MUCIA Women in Development Network, March.

Lassère, Guy. 1972. La petite propriété des Antilles françaises dans la crise de l'économie de plantation. In *Etudes de géographie tropicale offertes à Pierre Goureau*, pp. 539–555. Paris: Mouton.

Lawrence, J.C.D. 1979. Land tenure—St. Lucia. Mimeograph. London: Overseas Survey.

Lemel, Harry, and David Stanfield, eds. 1988. *Land registration, tenure security, and agricultural development in St. Lucia: A research report*, vols. 1–5. Draft. Madison: Land Tenure Center, University of Wisconsin, April.

Marshall, Woodville K. 1985. Peasant development in the West Indies since 1838. In *Rural development in the Caribbean*, edited by P.I. Gomes, pp. 1–14. London: C. Hurst and Co..

Meliczek, Hans. 1975. *Land tenure: St. Lucia; project findings and recommendations*. Rome: United Nations Development Programme/Food and Agriculture Organization.

Mitchell, Rutty. 1984. *Small hillside farmer development programme study*. Kingston, Jamaica: Ministry of Agriculture.

Perera, M.S. 1982. Project Land Lease I-III. Mimeograph. Kingston, Jamaica: FAO.

Pollard, Stephen K., and Douglas H. Graham. 1985. The performance of the food producing sector in Jamaica, 1962–1979: A policy analysis. *Economic Development and Cultural Change* 33(4):731–754.

Seligson, Mitchell. 1985. Land tenure security as a constraint on agricultural development in Jamaica: A preliminary assessment. Report to AID. Mimeograph. Kingston, Jamaica.

Simpson, S. Rowton. 1976. *Land law and registration*. London: William Clowes and Sons.

Stanfield, J. David, Bernard Darnell, and Rutty Mitchell. 1986. Land tenure patterns and the property system in Jamaica. Mimeograph. Madison: University of Wisconsin, Land Tenure Center.

Syrett, Keith J. 1986. Presentation to FY 86 USAID Agriculture and Rural Development Officers (ARDO) Conference, Miami, Florida, 25–30 May.

White, Marcia. 1986. Limited resource countries and agricultural development: A methodology used for the Caribbean. Draft. Ph.D. dissertation, University of Illinois at Urbana-Champaign.

Chapter 13

Honduras: Toward Conflict and Agrarian Reform

Randy Stringer*

In many ways, the Honduran agrarian reform is similar to others in Latin America in the early 1960s. The agrarian reform legislation and land policies began with an impetus from the Alliance for Progress, an international agreement signed by nineteen Western Hemisphere countries. The reform had political and social motives as well as economic objectives. As in Chile, Peru, Colombia, Panama, and the Dominican Republic, the production cooperative—in which large farms are worked "in common" by beneficiaries and profits are divided among members—became the predominant ownership structure on the agrarian reform farms. Like others, the Honduran agrarian reform is generally considered unsuccessful not only in terms of its failure to deliver on the widespread expectation that it would provide wider access to land, capital, and technical assistance, but also in terms of making a significant contribution to agricultural output, rural employment, and improved standards of living for the majority of the small-farm households in the country. Furthermore, thousands of landless families were left out of the reform altogether.

At the same time, the Honduran agrarian reform has some distinguishing features, the principal one being the way in which it has been influenced by national-level campesino organizations. These farmers' associations have played an important role in forming government agrarian policies and programs for some 25 years. They also have had a decisive influence in determining the shape of the postreform agrarian structure. In most of Latin America, campesino organizations

* Randy Stringer is a Project Associate, who works on Latin American and Caribbean area studies, at the Land Tenure Center, University of Wisconsin-Madison.

rarely affect agrarian policies and production organization to the extent seen in Honduras.

DEVELOPMENT STRATEGIES IN HONDURAS: AN OVERVIEW

Standard economic measures characterize Honduras as a small, poor, export-dependent country with a very weak domestic economy. Available human-welfare indicators reveal a deficient social infrastructure: Honduran infant mortality rates, life expectancies, and illiteracy rates are among the worst in the Western Hemisphere. In fact, only Haiti and northeastern Brazil exhibit a bleaker picture. The social structure, income distribution pattern, and agricultural technology use can all be characterized as bipolar. Close to 80 percent of the agricultural labor force grows subsistence food crops in rain-fed conditions: floods and droughts are chronic problems. The resource base of the country is narrow, with few minerals and a low percentage of arable land. Industrialization is rudimentary.

The overall economic outlook for the country is not promising. The population is growing rapidly, and the most optimistic of current unemployment estimates is 25 percent. International reserves are shrinking while external public debt expands. Between 1983 and 1985, net international reserves fell by 34 percent, total external debt rose by 28 percent, and arrears on publicly guaranteed external debt rose by 70 percent.[1]

Throughout this century, the stimulus for economic growth has been provided by a few agricultural exports, primarily bananas and coffee. As recently as the 1982–1984 period, these two crops accounted for 53 percent of total exports and, when combined with lumber and meat, contributed over two-thirds of total export earnings. Relying on traditional agricultural products for subsistence while diversifying into a few different primary commodities for export purposes has been the prevailing economic development strategy of Honduras for decades. This dependence on trade has affected all economic sectors. Price fluctuations in international markets have immediate repercussions on the stability of the entire domestic economy. Cycles in the pattern of economic growth in Honduras mirror the trade cycles of bananas and coffee.

Compounding the export-dependence problem is rising regional unrest. The violence in Guatemala, El Salvador, and Nicaragua has been the primary cause of declining investment and capital flight from Honduras throughout the 1980s. The United States is contributing heavily to this problem: military assistance to Honduras has increased from $4 million in 1981 to an astounding $62.5 million in

1985.[2] In addition, the United States is openly supporting Nicaraguan counterrevolutionaries operating from within Honduras. As political uncertainty and external manipulation have increased, capital investment has declined. Private-sector capital investment in 1985 was only 62 percent of the 1981 figure in real terms.

Since the beginning of the century, the Honduran economy has depended heavily on the banana enclave, which is located on the northern coast with San Pedro Sula as its epicenter. Throughout the 1950s, the banana industry accounted for about 58 percent of the value of exports. The banana companies paid around 20 percent of all wages and salaries earned in the country while employing only around 5 percent of the work force (Slutzky and Alonzo 1982, 18).

Export-oriented growth with dependence on one crop continued until Honduras joined the Central American Common Market and, between 1960 and 1969, pursued what turned out to be a faltering import-substitution development strategy. Honduras experienced strong but uneven growth in the 1960s both by adhering to the Common Market's policies of internally free trade with common external trade barriers and by expanding resources for public goods, particularly roads and ports. Between 1961 and 1969, the average annual growth rate of gross domestic product (GDP) was 5.9 percent; between 1973 and 1983, it was 4.0 percent. During this latter period, beef and coffee production increased substantially, which relieved the country's dependence on bananas.

The relatively strong economic performance during the 1960s came to an abrupt halt about 1969. Adverse weather conditions plus a war with El Salvador, which precipitated Honduras' eventual withdrawal from the Central American Common Market, combined to dampen growth. The rate of GDP growth fell to an average of only 2 percent for the 1970–1974 period, implying a negative per capita rate. The government responded by defining a 5-year development strategy. This plan aimed to provide the benefits of growth to the whole society by exploiting the country's comparative advantage in primary agricultural products and what was, at that time, a low level of foreign indebtedness.

However, a series of unfortunate events blocked achievement of the plan's optimistic production goals and economic projections. First, Hurricane Fifi, which devastated the northern coast in September 1974, caused immeasurable human suffering and had severe economic consequences. It destroyed over 32 percent of the area under banana cultivation, which reduced banana exports by 55 percent in 1974–1975. Agricultural output dropped 10 percent in 1974 and an additional 9 percent in 1975. The high cost of reconstruction forced government planners to reprogram funds intended for the National Development Plan.

Second, beginning in the early 1970s, petroleum prices increased sharply. This situation, and the subsequent instability of the international financial system, caused even more difficulty for Honduras since the value of exports did not keep up with that of imports. This affected the nascent industrial sector and the petroleum-based agricultural input sector. Thus, public and private borrowing from international banks increased just as interest rates were climbing to historically high levels.

Deterioration of the political stability of each of Honduras' neighbors, which also occurred in the mid-1970s, was still another factor that prevented the economy from performing optimally. The Sandinistas came to power in Nicaragua in 1979 after several years of hard fighting. El Salvador began what has turned out to be a long and desultory civil war. The U.S. government became estranged from Guatemala because of its dismal human-rights record. Violence and uncertainty in the region prompted investors to take their capital to countries with more stability.

The 1979–1983 National Development Plan was largely a reprise of the first one and included many of the development projects delayed because of the hurricane. But, because of the critical state of the economy in early 1980, an austerity plan for 1981/82 had to be drawn up. To date, disinvestment, unsatisfactory commodity prices, and regional war have prevented any real chance of recovery and sustained economic progress.

The Role of Agriculture

For Honduras, agriculture is the most important economic sector. The economy depends heavily on it for tax revenues, employment, foreign exchange, and food. It typically accounts for about 30 percent of the GDP, 60 percent of total employment, and 65 percent of the total value of exports (Ponce 1986, 135). The most notable characteristic of this sector is its bipolar technological and social structure. There are high-technology export crops, dominated by bananas, and low-technology subsistence crops, like beans and corn. Table 1 compares the relative contributions of these crops to value added in agriculture for the 1977–1979 period. While basic grains are planted on 65 percent of the crop area, they contributed only about 14 percent to value added in agriculture. The banana industry contributes about 21 percent of the value added while using an average of only 4.7 percent of the crop area.

Recognizing the importance of both export and food crops, the government has emphasized a balanced approach to overall agricultural development; government helps agricultural exports by supporting research and extension services, while minimum prices are established for basic grains. There are government credit programs for both export crops and basic grains. In addition, new public

Table 1
Percentage contribution of selected crops to value added in Honduran agriculture, 1977–1979[a]

	1977	1978	1979	Percentage of area planted to principal crops
Bananas	22.1	20.3	21.7	4.7
Coffee	14.7	16.9	17.2	18.7
Sugarcane	3.1	3.2	3.1	7.4
Timber	13.0	12.5	11.9	—
Livestock	14.8	14.9	14.8	—
Basic grains	14.6	14.4	14.1	65.1
Others	17.7	17.8	17.2	4.1
Totals	100.0	100.0	100.0	100.0

[a] Source: Central Bank of Honduras, Economic Studies Department, compiled statistics, August 1981.

agencies to assist agricultural producers have been created over the past two decades, central and sectoral offices and planning procedures have been reorganized, and interagency coordinating committees have been established. The agricultural sector averaged 14 percent of total public-sector spending in 1979–1981, a substantial increase from the 4 percent average during the 1960s and early 1970s. A major factor in public-sector expansion has been the increased involvement of international agencies since the 1960s.

The evidence suggests that a great deal could be done to improve agricultural performance in Honduras. While recent estimates suggest that underemployment in agriculture is around 75 percent (Ponce 1986, 133), Table 2 indicates that the area in crops is only about 43 percent of that available for use.

In all, about 30 percent of the country's total area is appropriate for agriculture: half for crops and half for pasture. Most of the country is mountainous and forest covered. In many areas where basic grains are raised, farmers can obtain two crops a year. Most production increases come from increasing the area planted; yields of basic grains remained constant and low throughout the 1970s.

AGRARIAN REFORM IN HONDURAS

As in much of Latin America, Honduras is characterized by numerous landless farmers, another large group of *minifundistas*,

Table 2
Land use and potential use in Honduras[a]

	Land use: Actual (×1000 hectares)	Land use: Potential (×1000 hectares)	Percentage of total area	Actual land use as a percentage of potential area
Forestland	7,350	6,800	61	108
Pastureland	2,093	1,700	15	126
Cropland	737	1,700	15	43
Annual	525	800		
Perennial	212	900		
Nonagricultural[b]	2,028.8	1,008.8	9	
Total area	11,208.8	11,208.8	100	

[a] Source: World Bank, *Honduras: A Review of Selected Key Problems of the Agricultural Sector*, Report no. 3606a-HO (Washington: World Bank, 1981), p. 4.
[b]Wetlands, cities, and so on.

and a few very large landowners. Over the years, the increase in the number of very small holdings has been the only basic change in the agrarian structure. The 1974 Honduran agricultural census showed that 4 percent of the farms occupied almost 56 percent of the total farm area, and 58 percent of the farms were located on about 7 percent of the land (see Table 3). The majority of the *minifundistas* is squatters on national lands. The available data suggest that over 50 percent of all Honduran farmers occupies public lands as squatters, that is, without documents to verify their ownership (Greenwood 1982). While the small producers may not have officially recognized documents verifying their landownership, the majority does have private documents, known as *mejoras*, which detail their ownership, including all improvements made on the land.

The agrarian reform represents the government's major effort to improve income distribution, enhance social mobility, and increase political participation in rural areas. Both national development plans identify land reform as a top-priority objective for Honduran development. However, the reformed sector, the fruit of a 25-year effort, is relatively small when compared with the total size of the agricultural sector, encompassing only 8 percent of the nation's farmland and 10 percent of the rural families. The majority of the redistributed land was public property prior to the reform; only 15 percent came through expropriation of good quality, private, agricultural lands (INA 1976, sec. 3:11). By 1985, over 61,000 families had benefited, but around 21 percent of this number had deserted their lands. (While no studies

Table 3
Number and size of farms in Honduras[a]

Hectares	Number of farms	Percentage	Cumulative percentage	Total area (hectares)	Percentage	Cumulative percentage
0–1	33,771	17.3	17.3	21,542	0.8	0.8
1–2	38,650	19.8	37.1	53,648	2.0	2.8
2–3	28,703	14.7	51.8	69,880	2.7	5.5
3–4	11,659	6.0	57.8	40,790	1.6	7.1
4–5	11,998	6.1	63.9	53,133	2.0	9.1
5–10	28,264	14.5	78.4	201,274	7.6	16.7
10–20	19,220	9.8	88.2	268,145	10.2	26.9
20–50	15,170	7.8	96.0	461,216	17.5	44.4
50–100	4,433	2.3	98.3	301,228	11.4	55.8
100–200	1,971	0.7	99.0	266,697	10.1	65.9
200–500	1,057	0.5	99.5	313,207	11.9	77.8
500–1,000	276	0.4	99.9	183,769	7.0	84.8
1,000–2,500	129	0.05	99.95	185,980	7.1	91.9
> 2,500	40	0.05	100.0	209,350	8.1	100.0
Total	95,341	100.0		2,629,859	100.0	

[a] Source: Ministerio de Economía, Dirección General de Estadísticas y Censos, *Tercer censo agropecuario*, vol. 2 (Tegucigalpa: DGEC, 1978), p. 2

document the reasons for the high desertion rate, one can imagine that the poor-quality land and paucity of agricultural services are primary reasons.) Moreover, landlessness in the country increased from 26 percent of the rural population in the mid-1960s to 36 percent by the early 1970s (CEPAL 1973; Honduras 1978). In brief, land reform has not made much of a dent in the numbers of rural landless or the landownership-distribution pattern; in addition, off-farm jobs have not been provided in sufficient numbers to employ the rapidly growing labor force.

Honduran land reform has been in progress since 1962. The progress shows decided ebbs and flows, while the overall pace has been very slow. Today agrarian reform farms are struggling to remain economically viable. Few agrarian reform groups have received management training, and the poor input-market structure, lack of storage facilities, and inadequate transportation systems all contribute to the problem. A great deal of marginally cultivable property has been incorporated into the sector since the reform began.

Historic Background of the Agrarian Reform

The history of the country's land policies can be divided into three periods. The long initial period, from 1829 to 1962, is made up of executive decrees and legislative acts to adjudicate and settle uncultivated public lands (Stanfield et al. 1986, 9). In the second period, from 1962 through 1972, Honduras established a token land-reform program to comply with the requirements of the Alliance for Progress. The third, after December 1972, is a period of rapid land redistribution which ended in 1975 and was followed by a period of lesser activity.

Period 1: 1829–1962

The Agrarian Law of 1829 provided for the settling and development of public lands and became the first in a series of governmental activities to bring productive public lands into cultivation. Over the following 130 years there were numerous government decrees to set aside specific lands in family-farm-sized units, which a 1924 decree defined as 20 hectares (Stokes 1947, 151). However, despite these laws, no significant settlement occurred until the government undertook programs, starting in 1951, to homestead larger numbers of rural families (Parsons 1976, 3). From 1951 through 1961, the government provided 33,300 hectares of land to 2,300 families.

The various decrees and settlement projects had several broad objectives (Villanueva 1968, 21). The primary objective was to develop the unused portion of public lands in order to expand the agricultural base and the potential for exports. Generating tax revenue was another objective. The government recognized that a colonization program which provided land titles was needed before a land tax could be levied. Squatters who occupied public lands illegally would not pay land taxes without documented ownership.

Period 2: 1954 to December 1972

Before a land reform law had been enacted, campesinos organized only when they needed to defend their properties against encroachment by larger landowners (Posas 1981b, 5). This changed after passage of the 1962 Agrarian Reform Law which granted tenant farmers and landless agricultural workers a legal basis for attaining land. Together with the 1954 banana workers' strike, this law was the precursor of three national-level campesino associations which are among the most active and well-organized farmers' unions in Latin America.

The banana strike helped the campesino movement in two ways. First, it produced a number of qualified and experienced union organizers. Success in the strike led campesinos to recognize the advantages of collective action in the face of politically powerful companies and the government. As a result, they increasingly turned to these proven strike organizers for assistance and even leadership. Second, as a result of both the strike and technological advances in banana production, the number of workers employed by the two major banana companies (Standard Fruit Company and United Fruit) dropped from 35,000 workers in 1953 to 16,000 in 1959 (IHDER 1980, 58). Consequently, there were a large number of recently unemployed rural people who needed land and jobs.

The banana strike began in early May of 1954 when workers at the Tela Railroad Company, a subsidiary of United Fruit, refused to work. They demanded a 50 percent wage increase, better working conditions, and legal recognition as a union. By mid-May, more than 25,000 workers at the Tela Railroad Company and Standard Fruit Company were on strike (Posas 1981a, 5). The strike was well organized, and on 17 May a Central Strike Committee was established to coordinate what had turned into a very popular movement throughout the country, one that had garnered strong support from workers in many industries.

The popularity of the strike caused several problems for the country's president, Juan Manuel Gálvez, who faced an upcoming election in October 1954. The situation was further complicated by the presence of the U.S. military, which was in Honduras to carry out operations leading to the overthrow of the progressive government of Jacobo Arbenz Guzmán in Guatemala (Schlessinger and Kinzer 1982; Rosenberg 1986:7). The Honduran government was caught: it could not crush a popular strike against two U.S. companies and expect to remain in power, nor could it lash out against a U.S. company with U.S. military forces present in the country.

So there was need for a compromise solution. The Inter-American Regional Organization of Labor (*Organización Regional Interamericana de Trabajadores*, ORIT) sent advisors to Honduras to mediate the strike and convinced United Brands and Standard Fruit to meet some of the strikers' demands (Spalding 1977, 256ff).[3] As a result, wages increased by around 15 percent, but, more importantly, rural trade unions gained legal recognition in Honduras.

Meza (1981) and Posas (1981b) point out the link between the strike leaders and the campesino movement. The first president of the Honduran Federation of Reformed Sector Cooperatives (*Federación de Cooperativas de la Reforma Agraria Hondureño*, FECORAH), Efraín Díaz Galeas, was a former labor leader and the elected spokesman of 5,000 banana workers on the northern coast. Moreover, Lorenzo Zelaya, the founder of the first farmers' union in Honduras, was a member of the Central Strike Committee in 1954.

The banana companies laid off thousands of workers during this period both because of the strike and because more sophisticated husbandry practices and new packaging technology had lessened the need for wage labor (Volk 1983, 209). Also during this period, the Alliance for Progress, a program which required Latin American countries to undertake land reform in order to be eligible for foreign aid, began its operation. The Cuban revolution, and the extent to which its example might penetrate the psyche of Latin America, was still on the minds of the U.S. "aid givers" and the elites of the region. To comply with Alliance conditions, in March 1962 the Honduran government of President Ramón Villeda Morales established the National Agrarian Institute (*Instituto Nacional Agrario*, INA) to develop land reform legislation and administer the process. In September 1962, the first Honduran Land Reform Law was passed, containing provisions for redistributing public and idle private lands. In October 1963, Villeda Morales was overthrown in a military coup headed by Colonel Oswaldo López Arellano, a conservative who had little interest in the goals of land reform. Subsequently, until the 1970s, INA became virtually inactive.

By 1965, a relatively new campesino organization, the National Association of Honduran Campesinos (*Asociación Nacional de Campesinos Hondureños*, ANACH), which was disgusted with the lethargy of the land reform program, began to pressure the López government. An extensive propaganda campaign and the threat of a massive ANACH-organized "hunger march" on Tegucigalpa eventually caused the government to agree to revitalize INA and to begin land reform.

The López government finally committed itself to act on the petitions of ANACH for more land transfers and sustained institutional support to INA, a commitment that resulted in the appointment of Roberto Sandoval Corea as director of the INA in 1967. The arrival of Sandoval, who left his position with the Inter-American Development Bank to take the appointment, had two profound consequences for the future of agrarian reform in Honduras. First, instead of individual family parcels, Sandoval encouraged production cooperatives—the organizational style that persists today. The second major Sandoval influence is the colonization project, Bajo Aguan. The Aguan project is the largest land-settlement project in Central America. It comprises over 51,000 hectares, or 25 percent of the cultivable area of the entire reform sector.

The concept of collectively managed farm units coincided with the goals of the campesino organizations that had been inspired by the success of the Guanchias Cooperative (White 1978, 177). This cooperative, located near El Progreso in the department (state) of Yoro, began in 1965 when eighty-five campesinos invaded a farm abandoned by United Fruit. In 1968, Guanchias acquired a contract with Standard Fruit Company, which provided for inputs, product sales, and technical assistance. Marketing was transacted through ordinary Standard Fruit channels. A recent evaluation of the Guanchias Cooperative concluded that its success was due to the members' strong cooperative commitment and Standard Fruit's financial support, technical assistance, and guaranteed market for bananas (McCommon et al. 1985). The early success of Guanchias prompted the campesino organizations to encourage their members to adopt the collective style of production and marketing on their lands.

Sandoval's agenda became clear with the increased pace of land redistribution by 1969. Between 1969 and 1972, a total of 158 reform groups had been organized, benefiting 8,043 families and redistributing 26,038 hectares of land. Compared to the 1962–1968 period, when only 721 families had benefited and 3,538 hectares were distributed, this was an enormous acceleration (INA 1985, 5).

Ramón Ernesto Cruz came to power in 1971 after the two major political parties formed a coalition and held elections. Sandoval resigned as INA director, and the pace of agrarian reform dropped so precipitously that it no longer satisfied the campesino organizations. Not surprisingly, land invasions increased and ANACH threatened to stage a hunger march on Tegucigalpa on 6 December 1972. ANACH had strong support from the other major farmer associations, the National Union of Campesinos (*Unión Nacional de Campesinos*, UNC), FECORAH, and the banana workers' unions on the northern coast. The hunger march did not reach Tegucigalpa, because, on 4 December, with the handwriting on the wall, General López Arellano again came to power with a military government that would embark on the most extensive land redistribution program in Honduran history.

Period 3: December 1972 to the Present

The 1972 Oswaldo López Arellano military regime had an agenda very different from the one that took power in October 1963. This time López was reform oriented. He also favored the agrarian sector (Posas 1981b, 31). One of the first acts of this military government was to issue Decree 8, which provided for a temporary program of land reform until a law could be enacted. In January 1975, the Land Reform Law was issued as Decree 170.

Under Decree 8, land reform burgeoned. Some 623 groups were organized on 76,262 hectares of land that benefited 23,627 families. Much of this redistribution came about as a result of pressure brought to bear on the government by systematic land invasions organized by ANACH and UNC. As of 1980, about 32 percent of the total groups organized, 39 percent of the families benefited, and 26 percent of the land redistributed could be traced to activity between 1973 and 1974.

Both of INA's directors under Decree 8 were activists. Mario Ponce Cámbar, an agricultural economist, and Lieutenant Colonel Mario Maldonado, who was influenced by the ongoing Peruvian experience, increased the transfer of public lands and private property. Maldonado became the first director to expropriate banana-company land. This incursion onto previously sacrosanct private foreign property was too much for the more conservative military leaders, and both Maldonado and General López Arellano were forced from office in 1975. (General López was also involved in a bribery scandal, in which United Brands tried to persuade various government officials to repeal an export tax on bananas.) Juan Alberto Melgar Castro replaced López and, with the new, more complicated Decree 170, forced the pace of land reform to slow considerably, much to the dismay of the campesino organizations.

Decree 170 specifies expropriation conditions for privately held lands and sets limits on farm size depending on land quality, geographic location, and production potential. Conservative interpretation of this law and the landlords' ability to adjust their property to the size ceilings (set out in Article 25), however, meant that instead of an acceleration of reform under a clear mandate, activity was all but paralyzed (Thiesenhusen 1980, 2).

In an unprecedented event in October 1975, ANACH, UNC, and FECORAH joined forces to form the Campesino Unity Front (*Frente de Unidad Campesina,* FUNC) to protest the Melgar government's lack of concern for campesino needs. The INA director appointed to follow Lieutenant Colonel Maldonado was unsuccessful in meeting the campesinos' demands.

General Policarpo Paz García replaced Melgar in August 1978 and remained in power through early 1982, when Roberto Suazo Córdoba became the first democratically elected president in Honduras since the 1950s. Under Paz García's administration, land distribution decreased to an even slower rate. The campesino unions again voiced their protests. In November 1979, for the second time, the competing organizations joined together, this time as the Honduran National Campesino Front (*Frente Nacional Campesino Hondureño,* FUNACAMH), to lay their demands before the government. As in 1965 and 1975, they were successful in replacing the head of INA but in little else. In March 1980, FUNACAMH organized a land invasion on some 6,000 hectares of unoccupied lands located in four departments, which resulted in many new groups being organized in that year (Posas 1981b, 39).

The elected government of Suazo Córdoba paid little attention to the agrarian reform sector between 1982 and 1985. Instead, INA began a large land-titling project aimed at providing greater tenure security to thousands of coffee farmers cultivating national lands. The land-titling program's major goal is to help increase small-farmer productivity through an anticipated increase in access to formal bank credit provided by the collateral made possible by land titles. The assumptions are that the newly titled small farmers will adopt more modern technology, invest more labor and money in long-term capital improvements for their properties, and improve their soil-conservation practices both by planting permanent crops on hillsides and by terracing. By May 1986, the titling project had issued 21,829 property titles.

CAMPESINO ORGANIZATIONS

By practicing a variety of tactics, which include organizing land invasions, participating in protest marches, writing open letters, and signing land petitions, the campesino organizations represent the interests of reform groups and landless campesinos before the governing administration, international institutions, and the public. Although not always successful, they have been responsible for acquiring thousands of manzanas of land (1 manzana = 1.75 acres), for the dismissal of three INA directors, for electing one of their officers to Congress, and for obtaining key appointments on the National Agrarian Council. Each campesino union works to strengthen its membership by establishing and affiliating reform groups. The unions assist the groups during the critical initial stages of organization and then offer or broker various services, such as cooperative and management training and assistance in obtaining credit.

In 1985, 75 percent of the reform groups was affiliated with one of the three main campesino organizations—ANACH, FECORAH, and UNC. ANACH is the largest farmers' union, with 37 percent of the groups. UNC and FECORAH follow, with 25 and 13 percent, respectively. About 12 percent of the other groups belong to one of eight local campesino organizations, and 13 percent are unaffiliated and are known as independents.

Campesino organizations have two major objectives: obtaining land for their landless groups and providing agricultural services to members. In 1986, the three national organizations had 628 landless groups organized and petitioning INA and the president of the country for land.

After numerous groups had settled under Decree 8, these unions turned their attention to promoting income-generating services. They helped beneficiaries obtain credit, find markets for their products, and improve the budgeting and farm-planning process. Since the mid-1970s, the three national organizations have established regional cooperatives. These regional cooperatives have organized from ten to fifty reform groups to coordinate credit-related services, help with farm planning, and facilitate market access.

The Organization and Structure of Agrarian Reform Groups

Most reform groups begin their work in an area with a land invasion by the rural landless. Sometimes a presence is first established through petition. Honduran law allows three distinct types of organizational structures for the agrarian reform groups. The first is *asentamientos*, which formally require twelve members, although many have less. A few asentamientos have as many as 200 families as members. In 1975 after Decree 170, reform groups could also be organized as *empresas asociativas*, or agricultural enterprises, which require a minimum of only five members. The third organizational structure is cooperatives, which are established under Honduras cooperative legislation. All three organizational structures require joint ownership of both land and capital. In 1984, 73 percent of 1,939 reform groups was organized as *asentamientos*, 24 percent as cooperatives, and 3 percent as *empresas asociativas*.

Each group is administered by a set of officers, who are elected in a meeting of all beneficiaries, known as the "general assembly." This general assembly discusses and tries to settle all conflictual and planning matters that affect the group as a whole.

INA has divided the reform sector into two subsectors for administration and policy-implementation purposes. The first, the export-oriented subsector, consists of reform groups located in one of the designated areas that specialize in commercial crops, such as African palm, cocoa, citrus, nuts, sugarcane, tobacco, livestock, and cotton. This subsector, with about 30 percent of all reform groups and 55 percent of the cultivable land, receives the majority of INA's budget resources and staff assistance. In 1982, all of INA's thirty-two agronomists worked in the export-oriented subsector. Almost 65 percent of INA's 1981 budget was designated for this subsector, compared to 8 percent for the basic grains subsector, which consists of all of the other reform groups. The export-oriented subsector provides most of the examples of economically successful groups.

The reform groups are organized and structured according to the 1975 land reform law, the aim of which is to create commercial farms. The reform group assumes the responsibility for paying off its land to the Honduran government over 20 years. Thus, the intention of the Honduran agrarian reform remains to transform the entire agrarian reform sector from its present subsistence nature into a capitalist structure. This transition threatens expropriation and legally prohibits precapitalist social relations (de Janvry 1981). To accomplish this, Honduras established size limits on ownership and abolished rental arrangements on agricultural lands.[4]

The organizational structure influences the manner in which the land will be farmed. In cooperatives, most of the land is farmed as a collective unit and crops and livestock are marketed together. In addition, members are assigned small, individual garden plots, usually adjacent to their homes, for production of subsistence for the family.

On the collective property, the general assembly decides what combination of enterprises will be undertaken. Individual members are then assigned tasks in the production process by the elected officers. Records are kept of the number of days worked, and each member is paid a predetermined and uniform daily advance out of the group's working capital.[5] At the end of the crop season, the net income, less the advances, from the enterprises is held as retained earnings (to be used as capital for reserves as well as future operations and investments) or is distributed to members. If the group opts for whole or partial dividends to be paid, members then receive an amount proportional to the number of days worked.

On most *asentamientos*, farmers usually have more sizable individual-family parcels than in the cooperatives, but they also have collectively operated enterprises on common land for commercial crops or livestock. Groups affiliated with farmers' associations follow the collective or mixed mode. Their ideology strongly favors working together as a group in the production process.

Asentamientos unaffiliated with campesino organizations are found in all regions of the country, and, in contrast to those affiliated with unions, most families farm individually rather than as a group. Some of these *asentamientos* rotate the individual plots among members to adjust for land-quality differences.

There appear to be a variety of reasons for why these groups have chosen to remain unaffiliated or have drifted from their association with the farmers' organizations. In some cases, there were problems with organization, lack of interest in the production-cooperative mode, inability to pay union fees, or dissatisfaction with the services provided by the campesino union. Also, the unaffiliated groups seem to be located on the poorest quality land and are the least accessible of all reform groups in the sector. They elect officers who act as their representatives when needed. Few have access to the government credit programs which require cooperative farming, but some of these groups obtain credit for livestock by using their pastureland as a collective project.

Reform groups may obtain credit from the public-sector agricultural bank [National Agricultural Development Bank (*Banco Nacional de Desarrollo Agrícola*, BANADESA)] only for collective projects, not for individual enterprises. Both groups and individual members obtain informal credit for production purposes from merchants, local stores, and individuals who provide production services such as land preparation or harvesting. The BANADESA loans are made to the group, and the members assume joint liability for repayment. Collateral is typically chattel mortgages on the group's livestock and machinery. In the case of short-term credit, a lien on the expected crop is usually sufficient. In some cases, the INA may serve as a guarantor in order to provide additional collateral when the group lacks sufficient mortgageable property.

Table 4 displays estimates of agricultural credit flows to groups for 1980. It is estimated that 768 groups received loans in 1980, that is, 56 percent of all reform groups. Of this number, 57 percent received loans from BANADESA and 43 percent from other sources, including commercial banks, marketing and processing firms, moneylenders, and development foundations. Measured in terms of loan volume, nearly 80 percent of the estimated 40,800 lempiras loaned came from BANADESA and 20 percent from the other sources. By either measure, BANADESA is the most important lender to the reformed sector.

Providing credit and furnishing technical assistance are the main services offered by the Honduran government to assist the reform groups. Unfortunately, these practices have not been too successful.

Table 4
Estimated agricultural credit flows to Honduran reform sector groups, by credit institution, 1980[a]

	Number of reform groups receiving new loans		Amount of loan volume (×1000 lempiras)[b]		Number of farm families benefited	
BANADESA	438	(57.0)[d]	32,425.3	(79.5)[d]	11,388	(57.0)[d]
Other[c]	330	(43.0)	8,365.5	(20.5)	8,580	(43.0)
Total	768	(100.0)	40,781.8	(100.0)	19,968	(100.0)

[a] Source: Jerry Ladman and Randy Stringer, "Agricultural Credit Use by the Honduran Reformed Sector: An Analysis and Recommendations for the Future," in *An Assessment of Rural Financial Movements in Honduras*, vol. 2 (Columbus: Ohio State University, December 1981), p. 31.
[b] 1 lempira = $0.50 (U.S. dollars).
[c] Includes commercial banks, farm-supply firms, marketing and processing companies, moneylenders, middlemen, friends, and relatives.
[d] Percentages are in parentheses.

Delinquency is a major problem, not only for the reform groups but also for the credit institutions. Over time, a large proportion of the groups have obtained credit from BANADESA but have not repaid the loans. In 1982, the ratio of the volume of all delinquent loans to total outstanding loans was 67 percent. Furthermore, 57 percent of the number of loans to the reform sector was delinquent. Nonrepayment makes the borrowers ineligible for succeeding BANADESA loans and often for other loans as well. This catches groups in a vicious circle of poverty.

In a recent study, forty-eight surveyed reform groups had obtained credit from BANADESA at least once, and 73 percent of those groups was delinquent (Stringer 1984). The reason for the delinquency given by the surveyed groups and extension agents was often weather connected: floods, wind, drought, and so on. That more than half the respondents listed flooding strongly suggests the need for land improvements or flood control.

These findings support the recognition that land quality in the reformed sector is important in determining the economic viability of the groups. Most of the redistributed property has come from lands in the public domain that private individuals did not claim for their own. That implies low-quality land or, at least, land in need of improvements given the climatic uncertainties. Without improvements, the economic viability of these lands is in question. This condition, in combination with problems in marketing, lack of good technical assistance, and inadequate infrastructure, as well as with the problems inherent in establishing and organizing any group, makes delinquency difficult to avoid.

Reform Group Members

The agrarian reform's weak institutional structure and the low socioeconomic position of agrarian reform families combine to form a troublesome set of issues for Honduran policymakers. In part, this is caused by the large family size and semisubsistence nature of the beneficiaries' lifestyle which, in turn, directly affects the economic performance of the reform group as a whole.

The average family has six members and must support itself by working on the group's collective project, by growing basic grains on its 1-manzana parcel, and by seeking off-farm employment for about 6 to 8 weeks each year. They live in a dirt-floor house without electricity or potable water. Around 40 percent of the group members cannot read, write, or even sign their names, and fewer than 15 percent has studied past the third grade.

Over the past decade, a number of studies have documented the beneficiaries' very poor living conditions (ATAC 1975; INA 1976; White 1978; IHDER 1980). For instance, a study of 720 beneficiaries located in three geographical regions revealed that 85 percent lived in dirt-floor houses, 88 percent did not have latrines, and only 19 percent was able to pay for emergency medical expenses for their families. But, remarkably, 73 percent responded that their living conditions had improved since affiliating with a reform group (ATAC 1975). Clearly, a major factor contributing to this perceived improvement is the members' newly acquired access to land, which represents the household's primary resource for producing food and income.

Table 5 shows how individual group members often turn to informal credit sources such as moneylenders, relatives, friends, and commercial stores for a variety of purposes. Over a 1-year period, 128 of 271 surveyed agrarian-reform-group members borrowed cash (for medical, personal, and agricultural purposes), agricultural inputs, or food grains; some even borrowed to finance a consumer product during the period of analysis (1980/81).[6] When combined, the cash loans from moneylenders, relatives, and friends accounted for 43.3 percent of the number of loans and 53.4 percent of the amount of credit.

This survey also obtained information on whether or not the families had ever borrowed for medical or subsistence purposes at any time (as opposed to just in the previous 1-year period). Subsistence loans consisted of borrowing basic grains (chiefly corn) in order to cover shortfalls in their own supplies. By the large number of positive responses, it is quite obvious that many borrow because they lack cash savings. This dependence on informal credit for both subsistence

Table 5
Number and volume of loans: A sample of Honduran agrarian reform beneficiaries, August 1980 to September 1981[a], [b]

Loan category	Number of loans	Percentage	Average loan size (lempiras)	Total loan volume (lempiras)	Percentage
Moneylender	11	6.0	179	1,970	16.0
Relatives	15	8.2	85	1,274	10.4
Friends	53	29.1	62	3,305	27.0
Forward sales	18	9.9	94	1,700	13.9
In-kind advances	42	23.1	22	931	7.6
Subsistence loans	36	19.9	41	1,494	12.2
Retail loans	7	3.8	227	1,582	12.9
Total	182	100.0	63	12,256	100.0

[a] Source: Randy Stringer, "An Analysis of Credit Use in the Honduran Agrarian Reform Sector," Ph.D. thesis, University of Wisconsin-Madison, 1984, p. 115.
[b] The data represent the findings from a survey of 271 agrarian reform beneficiaries.

production and nonmarket purposes highlights the very poor economic position of agrarian reform beneficiaries in Honduras.

Families on production cooperatives have three basic income sources: the collective project, the family parcel (including small family enterprises), and off-farm employment. Table 6 demonstrates the relative importance of these three sources for the sample of 271 group members. Some 84.5 percent of these beneficiaries indicated that they farmed a family parcel, while 76 percent had access to the group's collective project; 41.3 percent also worked at part-time jobs. At the same time, 79 percent depended on at least two of these income sources.

Two-thirds of the surveyed members had access to both collective and individual land. Table 6 also shows that of the 229 members with individual parcels, 45 percent ranked such parcels as the family's most important income source and 49 percent listed them as second. On the other hand, 206 beneficiaries took part in the group's collective project, and 71 percent named this as their primary source of earnings; 24 percent listed it as second.

In contrast, of the 112 members reporting that they worked at part-time jobs, only about 19 percent said that this activity provided the household's major income source. The average number of weeks worked at off-farm jobs for these 112 members was 11, and the average wage (in 1981) was $3 per day (in U.S. dollars). Nearly 10 percent of the surveyed members depended on off-farm income as their primary

Table 6
Relative importance of income sources to group members[a], [b]

	Percentage of all members indicating access to income source	Number of members with this income source	Percentage ranking importance of this income source			
			1st	2nd	3rd	Total
Family parcel	84.5	229	45.0	49.0	6.0	100.0
Collective project	76.0	206	71.4	24.2	4.4	100.0
Off-farm labor	41.3	112	18.8	47.3	33.9	100.0

[a] Source: Randy Stringer, "An Analysis of Credit Use in the Honduran Agrarian Reform Sector," Ph.D. thesis, University of Wisconsin-Madison, 1984, p. 56.
[b] N = 271.

income source, certainly part of the sad explanation of why the desertion rate in the reformed sector is so high.

The most important source used by families with individual parcels to finance the production costs was, by far, their own savings, which included cash and in-kind savings in the form of seeds or inputs left over from the previous harvest. Overall, 88 percent of the members utilized their own savings, while 36 percent borrowed equipment or tools. Many members made use of tractors or oxen teams, especially during planting.

The group members' understanding of the decision-making process on reform groups is important for the success of the reform. While a purely commercial farm is primarily interested in maximizing net income from its various enterprises, the semisubsistence, semicommercial reform groups combine many additional objectives in order to meet group and family requirements. Assuring subsistence, lowering risk, and increasing security are usually the most important considerations of these families. While in many cases these circumstances do not appear to interfere with the members' enthusiasm and willingness to adopt new credit-dependent technologies, most members are unskilled in programming large amounts of bank credit, obtaining timely inputs from a variety of sources, and finding markets for their production—all necessary managerial skills if commercial farms are to be established.

THE POLITICAL CONSEQUENCES OF REFORM

One reason often cited for the relative political and social stability found in Honduras compared to El Salvador, Nicaragua, and Guatemala is that Honduras has had broader access to national and ejidal lands

(Morris 1981, 38; Reina 1981, 30; Stokes 1966, 22). For example, in Honduras, around 51 percent of the rural families is considered landless or land poor versus 75 percent of the rural families in El Salvador (Ruhl 1984, 57). Nevertheless, because Honduras is one of the poorest countries in the Western Hemisphere, the relative political stability has been the focus of some important research by social scientists over the past decade.

Ruhl (1984, 33) summarizes the three main explanations offered as to why Honduras has experienced lower levels of social unrest. In addition to the broader-access-to-land hypothesis, one line of reasoning suggests that the Honduran military and political elites have been less repressive than in other Central American countries (Anderson 1982, 142; Rosenberg 1980, 17; Reina 1981, 30). For instance, labor unions and farmer organizations have not been suppressed in Honduras, and, even though it has hardly been thorough, Honduras has had a land reform program. Often, expectations alone can contribute to social and political stability. On the other hand, El Salvador did not begin any program that could be called land reform until 1980, after several years of fighting between rural-based guerrillas and the military. Nicaragua began a legitimate land reform only after the overthrow of the Somoza dictatorship. Thus, this group of writers suggests that a greater willingness to allow moderate reforms contributes to the more stable rural political environment in Honduras in spite of severe economic inequalities.

Finally, a third explanation for the relative calm is that because Honduras is still so poor, the rural population is unaffected by economic cycles. Most families have never been incorporated into the monetary economy; they have never received social or economic services from the government. Instead, they depend on traditional subsistence systems and barter trade. Their expectations have never been raised and, since Honduras is the least literate and least industrialized country in Central America, the rural population does not demand radical change (Leogrande 1981, 19; Rosenberg 1980, 21).

Certainly, broader access to land, less repressive regimes, and the very poor socioeconomic condition of the landless have all played some role in the political evolution of rural groups in Honduras. However, another important reason for the greater social stability found in Honduras is clearly due to the political access provided to the more activist rural groups by the campesino organizations. Even though the economic and social demands of these organizations have met only limited success, they still represent a fundamental political force.

Over the past two decades, the campesino organizations have maintained a strong presence in Honduran politics and survived several military dictatorships, a coalition government, and two elected presidents. The only campesino organization to be eliminated was the first to be

Table 7
Agrarian reform groups and membership by campesino organization, 1984[a]

Campesino organization	Number of reform groups	Members		Area (hectares)	
		Initial	Current	Adjudicated	Arable
ANACH	728	23,477	17,584	97,713	72,208
UNC	478	13,867	10,234	56,328	37,004
FECORAH	255	9,896	8,026	73,870	60,134
ALCONH	80	2,112	1,741	7,228	5,840
UNCAH	7	409	355	2,050	1,358
FRENACAINH	32	951	954	3,763	3,081
UNACOOP	3	61	74	665	549
ACAN	47	1,109	1,258	8,177	5,109
ACADH	4	179	78	569	336
FUNCACH	25	1,039	803	2,544	2,190
UNCACH	13	379	248	1,476	670
Independents	257	7,697	6,774	40,039	26,657
Total	1,939	61,176	48,129	294,422	215,136

[a] Source: Instituto Nacional Agrario, Departamento de Planificación, Sección de Estadística e Información, "Resumen básico de los grupos campesinos beneficiarios de la reforma agraria" (Tegucigalpa, January 1985), p. 7.

established in Honduras, the National Federation of Honduran Campesinos (*Federación Nacional de Campesinos Hondureños,* FENACH). This occurred shortly after Colonel Oswaldo López Arellano took power in the military coup of 3 October 1963. The continuing existence and pervasive influence of these campesino organizations clearly distinguishes the political structure of Honduras from that of its neighbors.

Table 7 presents the number of groups and members affiliated with campesino organizations as of 1984. Around 87 percent of the agrarian reform groups and reform beneficiaries was organized and established with the assistance of campesino organizations. The majority of these groups continues to receive agricultural and social services from their sponsoring organization. In addition, more than 600 landless groups are working through one of the national or local campesino organizations to gain access to land. The organizational skills, together with the large membership, mean that the campesino organizations will remain a growing political force in Honduras.

CONCLUSION

Agrarian reform in Honduras is a relatively recent process with more than 90 percent of the redistribution taking place since 1972. The majority of the agrarian reform farms came from national lands and not from the expropriation of large private holdings; more than 25 percent of the agrarian reform took place in previously uninhabited areas. The initial motivation for reform came from the Alliance for Progress and not from internal political, social, or economic concerns. Only during two brief periods, when Sandoval was director of INA in 1969 and under the Lopéz Arellano regime from 1973 to 1974, did the Honduran government actively promote land reform.

The Honduran government, campesino organizations, and reform group beneficiaries have had serious difficulties establishing economically viable farm units because of the poor land base. Only marginal and ecologically fragile public lands or frontier areas remained unclaimed by 1962 when the agrarian reform legislation was passed. This means higher costs for the Honduran government if it wishes to establish an effective institutional and economic infrastructure to provide production services, including credit, roads, irrigation, and other needed land improvements. The economic unattractiveness of existing reform hinders the ability of campesino unions to organize landless groups to obtain farmland. Also, instead of concentrating their efforts on organizing campesinos to petition INA for land, unions must take on the additional role of providing production and social services. For many of the beneficiary families, reform has meant unfulfilled expectations as beneficiaries find themselves on poor quality land without the resources required to establish a productive farm.

NOTES

1. These data are from AID 1986; the information is from unpublished reports of the Honduran Central Bank.

2. Military assistance data are from "U.S. Overseas Loans and Grants and Assistance from International Organizations," a report prepared by the Office of Planning and Budgeting in the Bureau for Program and Policy Coordination of the U.S. Agency for International Development.

3. ORIT was the precursor to the American Institute for Free Labor Development, a branch of the American Federation of Labor and Congress of Industrial Organizations (AFL-CIO), with its headquarters in Washington, D.C. For a detailed description of the labor movement in Honduras, see Posas (1981b).

4. In September 1981, the Honduran Constituent Assembly passed Decree 78, which permitted titling farms under 5 hectares that had coffee plantings. Parcels under 5 hectares, with the exception of those with coffee, cannot be issued a title under Honduran land laws. Decree 78 also permitted the INA to issue titles in *dominio pleno,* based on a loan agreement between the INA and the farmer purchasing the land. This decree then cleared the way for titling coffee farms that occupied national lands.

5. Only the agrarian reform groups receiving credit from the National Agricultural Development Bank (BANADESA) are able to pay advances to their members in the form of wages. BANADESA establishes a maximum daily-wage rate for its loans.

6. In August-September 1981, a sample of 271 agrarian reform beneficiaries affiliated with 48 agrarian reform groups were interviewed to obtain information about both group and household credit use. The 48 groups were selected from a population of 980 groups (72 percent of the total number of reform groups in 1981). The groups were stratified by affiliation with campesino organizations, by region, and by use of BANADESA credit. For more detailed information, see Stringer (1984).

REFERENCES

Anderson, T.P. 1982. *Politics in Central America: Guatemala, El Salvador, Honduras, and Nicaragua*. New York: Praeger.

ATAC (American Technical Assistance Corporation). 1975. *Honduras: Pequeños agricultores y grupos de la reforma agraria*, vols. 1–5. Tegucigalpa: ATAC.

CEPAL (Comisión Económica para América Latina). 1973. *Tenencia de la tierra y desarrollo rural en Centroamérica*. San José: Editorial Universitaria Centroamericana.

de Janvry, Alain. 1981. *The agrarian question and reformism in Latin America*. Baltimore: Johns Hopkins Univ. Press.

Greenwood, David. 1982. Proposals for a titling system for coffee producers occupying public lands. Tegucigalpa: Agency for International Development.

Honduras. 1978. Dirección General de Estadística y Censos. *Censo nacional de agropecuario, 1974*. Tegucigalpa: La Dirección.

IHDER (Instituto Hondureño de Desarrollo Rural). 1980. *84 meses de reforma agraria del gobierno de las fuerzas armadas*. Tegucigalpa: IHDER.

INA (Instituto Nacional Agrario). 1976. *PROCCARA 46 meses* [Programa de Capacitación Campesino para la Reforma Agraria]. Proyecto FAO-Honduras. Tegucigalpa: INA.

———.1985. Departamento de Planificación. Sección de Estadística e Información. *Resumen básico de los grupos campesinos beneficiarios de la reforma agraria*. Tegucigalpa: INA, January.

Leogrande, W.M. 1981. Prepared statement. Prepared for Subcommittee on Inter-American Affairs, Committee on Foreign Affairs, U.S. House of Representatives, 21 July.

McCommon, Carolyn M., Norlin G. Rueschhoff, Lee A. Tavis, and Jean Wilkowski. 1985. *Guanchias limitada: A case study of an agrarian reform cooperative and its long-term relationship with a multinational firm in Honduras*. AID Special Study, no. 22. Washington: Agency for International Development, March.

Meza, Victor. 1981. *Historia del movimiento obrero hondureño*. Tegucigalpa: Guaymuras 2.

Morris, J.A. 1981. Honduras: An oasis of peace? *Caribbean Review*, 10:38–41.

Parsons, Kenneth H. 1976. *Agrarian reform in southern Honduras*. LTC Research Paper, no. 67. Madison: Land Tenure Center, University of Wisconsin, March.

Ponce, Mario. 1986. Honduras: Agricultural policy and perspectives. In *Honduras confronts its future: Contending perspectives on critical issues*, edited by Mark B. Rosenberg and Philip L. Shepherd, pp. 129–152. Boulder, Colo.: Lynne Rienner Publishers.

Posas, Mario. 1981a. *Lucha ideológica y organización sindical en Honduras (1954–65)*. Tegucigalpa: Editorial Guaymuras.

———.1981b. *El movimiento campesino hondureña*. Tegucigalpa: Editorial Guaymuras.

Reina, J.A. 1981. *Honduras: Cambios o violencia*. Tegucigalpa: Artes Gráficas de Centroamérica.

Rosenberg, Mark B. 1980. Are the dominoes falling in Central America? Context, conjuncture and their impacts in Honduras and Costa Rica. Paper presented at Conference of Latin Americanists, Northern Illinois University, DeKalb.

———.1986. Honduras: An introduction. In *Honduras confronts its future: Contending perspectives on critical issues*, edited by Mark B. Rosenberg and Philip L. Shepherd, pp. 1–19. Boulder, Colo.: Lynne Rienner Publishers.

Ruhl, Mark. 1984. Agrarian structure and political stability in Honduras. *Journal of Inter-American Studies and World Affairs 26*(1):33–68.

Schlessinger, Stephen, and Stephen Kinzer. 1982. *Bitter fruit: The untold story of the American coup in Guatemala*. Garden City, N.Y.: Doubleday.

Slutzky, Daniel, and Esther Alonzo. 1982. *Empresas transnacionales y agricultura: El caso del enclave bananero en Honduras*. Tegucigalpa: Editorial Universitaria.

Spalding, Hobart, Jr. 1977. *Organized labor in Latin America*. New York: Harper Torchbooks.

Stanfield, David, Ricardo Zeledón, Santiago Moquete, Alex Coles, Mario Fandiño, Lily Caballero, and Randy Stringer. 1986. Land titling in Honduras: A midpoint evaluation of the small farmer titling project in Honduras, project no. 522–0173. Madison: Land Tenure Center, University of Wisconsin, April.

Stokes, William S. 1947. The land laws of Honduras. *Agricultural History*, 21:151–152.

———.1966. Honduras: Problems and prospects. *Current History*, January, pp. 22–26.

Stringer, Randy. 1984. An analysis of credit use in the Honduran agrarian reform sector. Ph.D. dissertation, University of Wisconsin-Madison.

Thiesenhusen, William C. 1980. Report on "posibles medidas para apoyar el proceso de reforma agraria en Honduras," 17–21 March 1980. Memorandum to Secretariat, Agrarian Policy Commission, Government of Honduras. Tegucigalpa, March.

United States. 1986. Agency for International Development. Tegucigalpa Mission. *1988 action plan for Honduras*. Tegucigalpa: AID, May.

Villanueva, Benjamín. 1968. Institutional innovations and economic development: Honduras, a case study. Ph.D. dissertation, University of Wisconsin-Madison.

Volk, Steven. 1983. Honduras on the border of war. In *Trouble in our backyard*, edited by Martin Diskin, pp. 203–244. New York: Pantheon Books.

White, Robert. 1978. Prestación de servicios públicos en el sector agropecuario. In *Compilación de los estudios básicos del diagnóstico del sector agrícola*, pp. 175–363. Tegucigalpa: U.S. Agency for International Development.

Chapter 14

The Role of Decentralization in the Recent Nicaraguan Agrarian Reform

David Kaimowitz*

In late 1980 and accelerating into mid-1982, partly for reasons of administrative efficiency, the Nicaraguan government decentralized its agrarian reform. In a very real sense, however, this was as much a military as an agricultural decision. Decentralization was also partly a response to demands for local autonomy coming from the ethnic minorities of the Atlantic coast. This chapter examines the factors that led to this decentralization decision and evaluates its results.

DECENTRALIZATION AND POLICY

After a period of academic neglect in the late 1960s and early 1970s, the role of decentralization as a policy tool has recently received greater attention (Montgomery 1976; Rondinelli et al. 1983; Conyers 1983, 1984). Disillusioned with centralized planning and concerned with fostering participation and eliminating regional inequalities, policymakers, academics, and international aid agencies have looked toward decentralization as a policy alternative.

Decentralization is more easily proclaimed than implemented, however, since obstacles usually prove greater than anticipated. Given a highly centralized government structure, state and local governmental agencies in Latin America traditionally have not had the necessary

* The author is a Research Fellow with the Rockefeller Foundation at the International Service for National Agricultural Research (ISNAR) in The Hague. He acknowledges the help of Michel Merlet, Carlos Manuel Morales, Miguel Barrios, Amanda Lorio, Charles Downs, and other colleagues at the Center for Investigation and Study of Agrarian Reform (*Centro de Investigaciones y Estudios para la Reforma Agraria*, CIERA) in Managua and the regional office of the Ministry of Agriculture in Las Segovias.

power or the finances for decentralization to be successful. In addition, in a number of areas the resources granted to local and regional government bodies have been monopolized by local elites.

In this context, Nicaragua is somewhat of an exception. Beginning in mid-1982, Nicaragua undertook an ambitious process of regionalization that succeeded in adapting agrarian reform strategies to local conditions, increasing popular participation in the reform process and improving the efficiency of public administration.

This outcome is surprising given Nicaragua's historical tendency to centralize government functions. Most observers of the revolution felt that, over time, more rather than less centralization would result. Indeed, in the revolution's first years (1979–1981), centralization reached unprecedented proportions.

THE POST-1979 AGRARIAN REFORM

The post-1979 Nicaraguan agrarian reform can be divided into three periods. From 1979 to 1982, attention focused on state farms, and policy reflected an increased government role in agricultural services. In 1982, emphasis shifted to redistributing land to production cooperatives. Since 1984, property titling and land distribution for small individual producers have been stressed.

Acting under Decree 3 of 20 July 1979 and Decree 38 of 8 August 1979, the Nicaraguan government expropriated all holdings of Somoza and his close associates—a total of 1,500 estates with an area of 800,000 hectares, 20 percent of Nicaragua's cultivable land. Because these were mostly large, modern farms with considerable infrastructure, it was felt that production would decline if they were parceled into small holdings. There were also concerns that, left to their own devices, land reform beneficiaries would shift from growing export crops to producing basic grains for domestic consumption, like corn and beans, and that export earnings would thereby fall. Thus, the decision was made to operate the confiscated holdings as state farms administered by the Nicaraguan Agrarian Reform Institute (*Instituto Nicaragüense de la Reforma Agraria*, INRA), a special agency created in July 1979.

The government's role in regulating and providing services for agriculture grew dramatically in this period. The financial system and the export of agricultural products were both nationalized, and government participation in domestic commerce increased. The provision of government services to rural areas—credit, education, health care, technical assistance, and agricultural machinery—was greatly expanded. Production credit to the peasant sector, for example, increased by over 300 percent in real terms between 1978 and 1980, and the number of recipients rose from 23,000 to 97,000. Some 60,000 families joined credit and service cooperatives (*Cooperativas de Crédito y Servicio,* CCS) in order to receive credit and technical assistance. Through the 1980 national literacy crusade, illiteracy was reduced from 50 to 13 percent.

Social legislation for agricultural workers was passed and enforced for the first time. In addition, a national organization for agricultural workers and small producers, the Rural Workers Association (*Asociación de Trabajadores del Campo,* ATC) was created. By mid-1980, the ATC had over 100,000 members.

Finally, although the confiscated farms were not redistributed, some measures were taken to make more land available to the landless. Laws controlling rents and obligating landowners to lease out underutilized lands were passed. Some 1,300 production cooperatives (*Cooperativas Agrícolas Sandinistas,* CAS) with 13,000 members were created. These cooperatives were usually small, and farmed lands were rented from the state or large private farms. Decision making in these units, unlike the state farms, was completely controlled by the members themselves.

Although the agrarian reform's second period began in mid-1982, its major features can be traced to two events in 1981. In April 1981, the Sandinista leadership had come to the conclusion that both small agricultural producers and agricultural wage workers could not be viably served by a single organization. As a result, the ATC was divided into two bodies. The first, still to be called the ATC, became primarily a union for agricultural workers, while the second, the National Union of Farmers and Ranchers (*Unión Nacional de Agricultores y Ganaderos,* UNAG) became a producers' association for small- and medium-sized producers. The UNAG began to strive for greater land redistribution for its near-landless members.

An agrarian reform law was passed in July 1981. It had been discussed since early 1980, but no action had been taken. With time, demands for land by the landless had grown, however, and the government was obliged to respond. Under the new law, landowners with over 350 hectares in the Pacific regions or over 700 hectares in the central regions could have their lands expropriated for underutilization, sharecropping, or disinvestment, or if areas were declared to be agrarian reform zones. While the law guaranteed the right of private property for efficient producers, emphasis was placed on the need for property owners to perform a social function. As of 1985, 394 landowners and 327,000 hectares of land had been expropriated under the law. Of these expropriations, 61 percent was for underutilization (generally cases where large land areas were being used to maintain only small numbers of cattle), while 20 percent was for complete abandonment (CIERA 1985, 22).

The law stipulated that postreform organization could be as production cooperatives, individual enterprises, or state farms. In practice, however, the cooperatives (CAS) were the principal beneficiaries (see Table 1). Beginning in 1983, agricultural policy had concentrated less on the state farms and more on the cooperatives. The amount of cultivable land in CAS rose from 1 percent in 1981 to 10 percent in 1984. The percentage of rural credit allocated to the CAS rose from 5.9 in 1981 to 28.6 in 1983 (Enríquez and Spalding 1985, 28). By 1986, 35,734 families (some 37 percent of potential beneficiaries) had received access to new land as members of CAS.

The CAS that received title under the 1981 Agrarian Reform Law were quite different from those of the first period. They had, on average, three times as many members (thirty-four versus ten) and greater access to resources. In 1985, the CAS had an average of 14 hectares per member, compared with 1.5 hectares in 1980 (see Table 2). They were also more stable and more diversified and placed a greater emphasis on collective production.

Now, in the third period of the agrarian reform, greater government attention has gone to small individual producers. This change reflects an increased government awareness that previous attempts at agrarian reform had failed to incorporate a large percentage of the potential beneficiaries. Rural poor families, who had hoped to receive land

Table 1
Evolution of the structure of Nicaraguan land tenure by sector[a], [b]

	1978	1981	1982	1983	1984	1985
Type of Property						
Private (noncooperative)						
<7 hectares	2	1	1	1	1	1
7–35 hectares	16	7	7	7	7	7
35–140 hectares	30	30	30	30	30	30
140–350 hectares	16	13	13	13	13	13
>350 hectares	36	18	14	14	13	11
Production cooperatives (CAS)	0	1	2	5	7	9
Credit and service cooperatives (CCS)	0	10	10	10	10	10
State farms	0	20	23	20	19	19
Total	100	100	100	100	100	100

[a] Sources: Central American Historical Institute, "The Nicaraguan peasantry gives new direction to agrarian reform," *Envio* 4(51), September 1985, p. 4c; Dirección General de Reforma Agraria, "Avance y perspectivas de la reforma agraria," mimeograph. (Managua, 1986), p. 3.
[b] All values are percentages.

Table 2
Land titles granted under the agrarian reform in Nicaragua, 1979–1985[a]

	Area titled (in manzanas)					Number of families				
	1981–1982	1983	1984	1985	1981–1985	1979–1982	1983	1984	1985	1979–1985
Type										
Cooperative (CAS)	108,096	269,187	247,297	180,510	805,090	7,024	11,344	11,730	9,266	39,364
Individual	23,761	13,144	15,348	142,686	194,939	408	241	360	6,204	7,213
Legalization	—	198,634	1,089,701	133,616	1,421,951	—	3,805	26,192	3,400	33,397
Indigenous communities	—	21,352	28,284	51,772	101,408	—	1,548	1,600	200	3,348
Total	131,857	502,317	1,380,630	508,584	2,523,388	7,432	10,938	39,882	19,070	83,322

[a] Source: Dirección General de Reforma Agraria, "Avance y perspectivas de la reforma agraria," mimeograph. (Managua, 1986), p. 2.

but were either unwilling to join productive cooperatives or living in locations where large areas of land for cooperatives were unavailable, increasingly pressured the government for land and forced it to become more flexible in its policies.

In 1984, the agrarian reform focused on providing property titles to squatters. Between 1984 and 1985, 29,952 families received titles to land they farmed but did not legally possess. There was also a greater emphasis on redistributing new lands to individual families. Six times more individual titles for new lands were granted in 1985 than in the previous 5 years. In early 1986, the minimal landholding size expropriable under the Agrarian Reform Law was lowered, and the government purchased large tracts of unexpropriable land to make more distribution possible. Government officials became increasingly receptive to a wide variety of forms of cooperative organization. Finally, more attention was paid to providing technical assistance to noncooperativized producers and increasing their access to government investment projects. Like many agrarian reform policies since 1982, these measures especially favored the rural populace in areas of military conflict [see section entitled "The Early Years of Revolution (1979–1981)].

From 1979 to 1984, agricultural performance was quite satisfactory (see Table 3). Beans, rice, coffee, sorghum, and poultry all experienced rapid rates of growth. Only production in livestock and cotton remained below pre-1979 levels. Agricultural investment was maintained via large public sector expenditures on capital goods. Military conflict and increasing foreign exchange difficulties, however, led to a decline in agricultural production in 1984 and subsequent years.

DECENTRALIZATION AND AGRARIAN REFORM

Decentralization itself is "any transfer of the authority to plan, make decisions, and manage public functions from the national level to any organization or agency at the sub-national level" (Conyers 1983, 101). The process can take a variety of forms, the most important of which are deconcentration, devolution, and delegation. Deconcentration is "the handing over of some amount of administrative authority or responsibility to lower levels within central government ministries and agencies" (Rondinelli et al. 1983, 10). Devolution is the creation or strengthening of subnational units of government (Montgomery 1976). Delegation is the transfer of certain managerial responsibilities to organizations, such as parastatal groups, only indirectly controlled by the central government (Rondinelli et al. 1983, 15, 19). All three have played an important role in recent Nicaraguan history.

Table 3
Indices of agricultural output, 1977–1984[a], [b]

Product	1977/78	1979/80	1980/81	1981/82	1982/83	1983/84
Rice	100	132	133	193	204	202
Beans	100	71	70	101	115	155
Corn	100	80	101	107	102	129
Sorghum	100	143	209	225	124	226
Cotton	100	15	53	45	55	62
Coffee	100	98	103	106	125	86
Sugar	100	86	98	114	112	102
Cattle	100	111	83	64	79	81
Chickens	100	51	113	125	174	184
Eggs	100	99	291	384	450	465

[a] Source: Carmen Diana Deere, Peter Marchetti, and Nola Reinhardt, "The Peasantry and the development of sandinista agrarian policy, 1979–1984," *Latin American Research Review*, 20:3 (1985), p. 86.
[b] In crop years.

Among the most common objectives of decentralization are (1) greater flexibility in decision making, (2) better coordination between regional or local-level government agencies, (3) increased participation by those affected in policy making, (4) improved adaptation of policies to different local conditions, (5) reduced income and resource inequalities between regions, and (6) increased incentives for optimal decision making by local management (Conyers 1981; Rondinelli et al. 1983).

These are particularly relevant in rural development and agrarian reform, for agrarian conditions and structure vary markedly by region. Rural development involves a wide range of government agencies whose activities must be coordinated in order to avoid duplication of effort, to prepare appropriate development plans for individual localities, and to maximize local resource use. Because poor communications with the capital frequently characterize these rural areas and information for policymakers often is inadequate, the need for subnational decision making in rural development is accentuated.

THE HISTORIC LEGACY OF CENTRALIZATION

In Nicaragua, the origins of government centralization can be traced to the end of the nineteenth century. Before then, Nicaragua had a series of weak central governments, and the result was constant internecine conflict between the local oligarchies of Grenada and

León. Furthermore, Nicaragua's rainy and forested Atlantic coast, separated from the rest of the country and with over 50 percent of the country's territory, was controlled first by the British and later by the United States.

A change began with the expansion of coffee production, which required infrastructure such as roads, ports, and railroads. Government had to provide technical services and subsidies and enforce land rights. Coercive labor laws were necessary to ensure an adequate labor supply for the harvests. Stability was necessary, and that required a strong central government. Coffee shifted the power balance of the regional oligarchies. Managua had been chosen as the republic's compromise capital as early as 1851. Then, in the 1880s, with the concentration of coffee production in the departments of Managua and nearby Carazo, Managua became the nation's true power center. The liberal regime of José Santos Zelaya (1893–1909) gave political expression to this new coffee elite. Zelaya established a strong centralized government; he reasserted Nicaragua's sovereignty over the Atlantic coast and, in 1894, brought it under Nicaraguan administration.

In 1909, Zelaya resigned the presidency under U.S. pressure. From then until 1979, the United States was the dominant force in Nicaraguan politics, and, for most of the period between 1912 and 1933, Marines were maintained in the country to protect U.S. interests. The United States was not indebted to any of Nicaragua's regional oligarchies; it felt that it could guarantee its interests by fostering a strong, centralized government. Under U.S. tutelage, efforts were made to create a national army, a viable currency, and a central bank. Thus, the United States circumscribed the power of local elites and accentuated the central government.

Strong central government continued under the administrations of the various Somozas (1937–1979). Municipal governments remained weak, with functions limited to collecting some local taxes, gathering vital statistics, providing refuse collection, and maintaining minimal basic infrastructure. Local governments had little autonomy. Politically, they were "docile instruments under the control of the central executive power" (Downs and Kuznetzoff 1981, 52). Despite Nicaragua's political division into sixteen states (known as *departamentos*), there were no state or regional governments.

The local offices of the Ministry of Agriculture (*Ministerio de Agricultura y Ganadería*, MAG), the public banking system (*Banco Nacional de Nicaragua*, BNN), and other programs were limited to the provision of services. All policy decisions were made in Managua; most operative funds were collected and distributed from there. Professionals also were concentrated in the capital city, where they generally enjoyed higher salaries and greater access to life's amenities.

Centralization did not imply the creation of a national market or the reduction of regional disparities. Strong regional differences in income level, population pressure, modernization, and access to government services and infrastructure continued despite relatively small distances between regions.

The Atlantic coast continued to be isolated and distinct. No telephone lines or roads connected the Atlantic and Pacific coasts until after 1979, and the Atlantic region remained economically, ethnically, religiously, and linguistically separate from the Pacific.

There were sharp variations among the other regions as well. For example, in parts of León and Chinandega, agriculture was highly capital intensive and produced cotton, sugar, and bananas. Rural populations were mostly semiurban and landless and had complete access to a variety of markets and social and economic infrastructure. On Nicaragua's agricultural frontier, only 5 or 6 hours away by land vehicle, farmers practiced slash-and-burn agriculture and lived a primitive existence with very limited access to roads, markets, and social services. In still other areas, including much of Nicaragua's northern regions, large coffee and cattle producers interacted with small grain producers through traditional patron-client relationships based on sharecropping, labor rents, and interlinked markets. In these areas, there was little technological development.

THE EARLY YEARS OF THE REVOLUTION (1979–1981)

The first years of the revolution reinforced centralization. In 1979 and 1980, the concentration of resources and decision making in Managua rose to unprecedented levels. Policy decisions and a large proportion of day-to-day administration and management were carried out in the capital.

Only slowly did revolutionary institutions begin to develop some local functions. Few people had both political confidence in the new government and professional skills, and these people were largely in Managua. Those working locally were frequently Somoza holdovers, and the government was understandably reluctant to grant them authority. Because of the political sensitivity of many decisions to be made by the new government, such as those on agrarian reform, the Sandinista government was concerned that policies be equitable and as uniformly administered as possible—something that could be better assured by central coordination and management. The decision to confiscate a certain producer's land and not another's—or to permit a land invasion by landless families in one instance and not in another—would raise questions about the evenhandedness and, hence, the legitimacy of the new government.

It is true that soon after its creation, INRA opened eighteen offices in the departments. From the beginning, however, emphasis was placed on their role in "guaranteeing compliance on the regional level of the official line of the agrarian reform [developed in Managua] in all its aspects" (INRA 1980). They were not expected to play an important role in regional planning, nor were their policies allowed to be inconsistent between regions.

The regional offices handled state-farm finances; production departments in the regional offices drew up each farm's production plan. Financing came directly from the central government.

As Austin et al. (1985, 22) note, the high degree of centralization created a number of problems:

> Since all MIDINRA agency decisions had to be cleared through provincial and regional levels, the sheer volume of decisions clogged the channels. The centralized structure drew the best trained people to the capital, thus leaving the operational and provincial levels relatively understaffed. Furthermore, in spite of its centralized structure, the lack of an adequate administration system limited control over production.

In fact, ministerial offices in Managua and in the departments had very little information on which to base their decisions. Accounting practices were inadequate for true financial oversight. Even in the best of cases, operating-cost data were available only by broad category. Often, even information such as farm size, area in production, capital stock, employment, production, and input needs was not at hand. So there could be little attention, and few incentives, to make production decisions based on efficiency criteria.

The direct management from Managua of certain agricultural operations led to other problems. Although these operations were located throughout the country, INRA's regional offices had no control over them. This often led to administrative conflict. Disputes arose over input use, pay scales, and other issues. Coordination between farm-level production decisions and marketing and processing activities also suffered.

Another problem during this period was the lack of coordination on the local or regional levels between INRA and other government agencies. In fact, because it aspired to "superministry" status, INRA tended to ignore the other ministries. As such, it became involved in providing all manner of services to the rural population, from the distribution of credit and health care to road and infrastructure construction. INRA even had its own literacy campaign in one department (León) (MIDINRA 1982, 12). This tendency created great tensions between INRA and other government agencies that were empowered to carry out these tasks; it made interinstitutional coordination practically impossible.

A year after the revolution, many problems associated with overcentralization had become apparent, and steps were taken toward their resolution. The first major restructuring of the Ministry of Agriculture took place in October 1980 when a merger with INRA occurred:[1] the name was changed to Ministry of Agricultural Development and Agrarian Reform (*Ministerio de Desarrollo Agropecuario y Reforma Agraria*, MIDINRA), the number of local offices was reduced from eighteen to eight, the regional directors were given somewhat greater decision-making authority, and more resources were allocated to each office. In addition, a MIDINRA secretary-general's office was created and charged with coordinating relations between central and regional offices and between the agricultural ministry and other government agencies (MIDINRA 1982, 16). Local production committees were created and included representatives of MIDINRA, the government banking system and market agencies, and the rural popular organizations. These committees were supposed to handle a variety of small-farm problems, but in practice concentrated mostly on rural credit issues.

There were further administrative reforms. The Agrarian Reform Enterprise Law (Decree 580) of 2 December 1980 gave greater financial and managerial autonomy to the state farms, which were grouped into seventy-six corporations (*empresas*).[2] They were to solicit credit from the financial system based on profitability and strict cost accounting. While "clearly the Central Ministry retained a great deal of influence...most operating decisions...[began to be] made at the enterprise level" (MIDINRA 1982, 22).

The increased decentralization of authority had a number of effects. Increased financial autonomy led state farms to eliminate excess workers, limit improvements in working conditions, and increase emphasis on profitable product mixes. This increased productivity and profitability somewhat, although most state farms continued to show losses and had to be subsidized by the central government (MIDINRA 1982, 24). But it brought state-farm workers and the nearby communities to see the state farms as little different from the large private farms.

Decentralized management also led to some increase in worker participation in management, although its extent should not be exaggerated. An earlier attempt at workers' participation, the Economic Reactivation Assemblies (*Asembleas de Reactivación Económica*, ARE) conducted in mid-1980, had largely failed, partially due to overcentralization of state-farm administration. Under the new law, however, the various management councils in which the workers' organizations participated were given authority to carry out agreements made regarding working conditions, work norms, the enterprise plan, and other matters. By December 1982, 66 percent of state farms had consultative councils at the corporation level and broadened councils and production committees at the individual farm level in which worker representatives participated (MIDINRA 1982, 22).

With time, the quality of administration and planning improved. A unified accounting system for the state farms was begun in 1980 and, although this system had not been fully installed at the time of writing, financial information needed for cost accounting was more readily available. The planning process became more structured with the first full state-farm technical plan produced in early 1982.

To eliminate overlaps with the duties of other ministries, MIDINRA eliminated most of its nonagricultural functions. It stopped providing credit and social services and reduced its construction activities. Attempts were made to improve interinstitutional coordination on the regional level through the creation of coordinating committees (*Comités Programáticos de Coordinación Regional*, CPRC) for different sectors. MIDINRA, the financial system, the peasant organizations, and the Ministry of Planning made up the agricultural CPRC, which was coordinated by the Ministry of Planning (*Ministerio de Planificación*, MIPLAN) (Downs and Kuznetzoff 1981, 132–133). But the CPRCs were largely ineffective and were ignored by many government ministries, including MIDINRA. Excessive ministerial centralization left local delegates little flexibility to adjust their plans to decisions made in the meetings. This problem was rendered more acute by the limited authority of MIPLAN (Downs 1985, 51).

To the extent that regional interinstitutional coordination was achieved at all, it was largely under the auspices of the local delegates of the Sandinista Front (*Frente Sandinista de Liberación Nacional*, FSLN).[3] The political clout of the FSLN often allowed these delegates to resolve regional disputes and promote coordination where other mechanisms failed. This led, however, to party officials' spending much of their time on government rather than party affairs and added to the already substantial confusion created by the duplicate, parallel chains of command in the government and party structures.

The creation of a number of regional integrated rural development (IRD) projects was another decentralizing initiative of this period. The most important of these were the Carlos Fonseca project in Waslala, Matagalpa, CHINORTE in eastern Chinandega, and PRONORTE in the western portion of the Segovias (the case of PRONORTE will be examined in greater detail later). These projects faced many of the problems characteristic of IRD projects in other Third World countries: Should administrative agencies separate from the already existing ministries be created? How should interinstitutional coordination be encouraged?

How should bureaucratic rivalries be handled? Nicaragua was no more successful than other countries in resolving these issues.

Despite these efforts, major problems remained. Regional innovation was discouraged, and a number of creative initiatives, such as the trade-union self-sufficiency groups (*Grupos de Autoconsumo Sindical*, GACS) in Estelí and the village-level agrarian reform committees (*Comités de Reforma Agraria Comerciales*, CRACs) in Masaya, were discontinued at Managua's insistence.

Centralization led to the neglect of the more isolated and peripheral areas such as the agrarian frontier. The farther one went from Managua and the more difficult communications and transport became, the less likely a region would be to receive attention or quality resources. Thus, the time-honored bias toward the Pacific region was maintained.

Centralized bureaucracy continued to reign in decision making. One example of this is the 1981 Agrarian Reform Law that empowered the government to redistribute lands to production cooperatives and independent individual producers. Its implementation was slow, partially due to disagreements within the government on how fast the reform should be carried out (see Kaimowitz 1986). But implementation was also retarded by procedures that required approval from Managua of each expropriation and each title.

REGIONALIZATION AND AGRICULTURAL POLICY (1982–1985)

Three additional factors were key in the decision to undertake major decentralization. Most important of these was the war between the United States and Nicaragua (DEPEP 1982, 31). In November 1981, the U.S. Congress approved a program of covert military activities to be carried out by counterrevolutionary forces (Contras) against Nicaragua; during the following years, episodic battles escalated to generalized warfare (Dickey 1985).

Starting in 1982, agricultural policy in Nicaragua became inextricably linked with military policy. The conflict had made increased regional decision-making authority necessary, for certain regions possibly could find their commerce and communications with Managua obstructed by war. Following the U.S. invasion of Grenada in 1983, plans were formulated by the Nicaraguan government that would allow the regional structures of government to operate in the event Managua were occupied by American troops. Decentralization in food and energy supplies and investment projects was carried out to limit the country's vulnerability to attacks on strategic economic infrastructure.

Because the war was a political as well as a military problem, it was necessary to respond flexibly to the economic and social difficulties of the rural people living in isolated regions of military conflict. This, in turn, required increased decentralization to allow for rapid decision making based on local conditions.

A second factor was the process of meeting the demands for regional autonomy voiced by the ethnic minorities of the Atlantic coast. In this area, there was growing discontent among the region's Creole blacks and Miskito, Sumo, and Rama Indians over what they viewed as the Sandinista government's disregard for historic differences between the Atlantic and the Pacific coasts. This discontent spilled over into an armed revolt by indigenous minorities in 1981, and the government realized that a definite policy was needed to incorporate these strong regional differences and to allow for more self-determination.

A third factor was the process of institutionalization that began in 1982. Institutionalization was the name given to the transition from personalized, de facto government to the establishment of legal norms and institutionalized government forms. A general review of the institutional structures inherited from the Somoza period and those developed spontaneously during the first years of the revolution was followed by measures such as a law regulating the operations of political parties, an electoral law, an increased separation between party and state, and several juridical attempts to define clearly the attributes of different institutions. There was an official review of the level of responsibility and autonomy to be given to subnational entities.

A program of regionalization was officially announced on 19 July 1982,[4] which divided the country into six regions and three special zones; the latter were on Nicaragua's Atlantic coast in recognition of its unique situation. Regional governments were created for the first time and were endowed with an administrative structure to oversee governmental operations in their regions, develop regional plans, and coordinate the activities of municipal governments. They were also given significant budgets, which allowed for the recruitment not only of a substantial technical staff but also of discretionary funds for specific regional investments.

A governor, to be the highest decision-making authority on the regional level, was appointed for each region by the national junta (Downs 1985, 57). Regional ministry officials were made responsible not only to their national offices but to the regional governor as well.

New mechanisms were created for regional interinstitutional coordination under the auspices of the regional government. These included a regional cabinet, with strong decision-making powers, in which all ministries, popular organizations, and the FSLN participated, as well as a number of commissions designed to coordinate governmental activities. While these structures had their share of problems, they were more successful than their predecessors. The coordination mechanisms succeeded in creating a unified outlook regarding regional problems. Well-functioning commissions were able to coordinate specific tasks such as agroexport-crop harvests and population resettlement.

Increased decentralization was evident in agricultural policy. The regional offices of MIDINRA (along with six other key ministries) received major budget increases in recognition of their new responsibilities. The demarcation of regional offices was changed to correspond with the new national regionalization, and the regional office on the Atlantic coast was divided into three, with one office for each special zone. The ATC and the UNAG also regionalized their structures.

An attempt was made to transfer skilled personel from Managua to the regions (Austin et al. 1985, 22). Higher salaries and special bonuses were paid for working outside of Managua. Housing was constructed for regional personnel. Beginning in 1984, special professional brigades were organized for regional reinforcement, particularly in areas of military conflict. Through these brigades, professionals from Managua and León would spend from 6 months to 1 year in the regions. While the overconcentration of resources in Managua was not completely overcome and problems of high turnover in the regions persisted, significant accomplishments were achieved through these measures.

In late 1983, MIDINRA was again restructured in order to decentralize still further (MIDINRA 1984, 16, 17). Particular emphasis was then placed on reinforcing regional planning capacity, especially in the area of investment planning. Nicaragua's Minister of Agriculture complained that, at the time, regional offices lacked "trained personnel, adequate information to elaborate investment projects, and an organized structure to monitor them" (MIDINRA 1984, 18).

On the policy level, the territorial rather than sectoral approach of regionalization resulted in greater attention being paid to cooperative and private agriculture rather than just state farms. In addition, the state farms that were isolated and less amenable to central control were dissolved and their lands distributed to production cooperatives or to individual producers (MIDINRA 1984, 16).

Because of military concerns, special priority was given to areas of military conflict (this included all of Nicaragua's regions except those on the Pacific coast). Every attempt was made to keep the regional populations satisfied and disposed to support the government's war efforts. Additional financial assistance and more trained personnel were sent to these regions. Special attention was given to shortages of consumer goods, marketing problems, agrarian reform needs, and problems of coordinating military and resettlement strategies with economic development policies. Ironically, the war succeeded in shifting the government's resources and attention from the Pacific coast to the previously neglected interior and Atlantic coast.

Moreover, to ensure that this new plan was implemented in mid-1982, key national leaders were assigned permanently to oversee the affairs of each prioritized region (DEPEP 1982, 37). Nicaragua's minister of agriculture (Jaime Wheelock) was assigned to Matagalpa-Jinotega, its minister of interior (Thomas Borge) to the Atlantic coast, its vice-minister of interior (Luís Carrión) to Boaco-Chontales, and a fourth member of the FSLN leadership (Victor Tirado López) to the Segovias. Each of these national leaders spent long periods of time in the regions to which they were assigned, and their presence gave added political weight to regional decisions, which allowed them to be made more rapidly and with greater flexibility.

A REGIONAL CASE STUDY: LAS SEGOVIAS (REGION 1)[5]

Las Segovias, the region that covers the Nicaraguan departments of Estelí, Nueva Segovia, and Madriz, stands out as a model for regionalization. It was the first region to experiment with "regionalization" in January 1982 (DEPEP 1982, 36). There was a strong regional identity in the Segovias, dating back to the 1920s when it was the center of operations for Sandino's army. This historic tradition made the region one of the areas of strongest support for the FSLN, and it was there that participation in the popular organizations and government-sponsored campaigns was highest.

Institutional Aspects of Decentralization in the Region

Prior to its 1980 reorganization, INRA maintained a regional office in each of the region's three departments.[6] Before 1982 there was no regional strategy, and problems with centralization were similar to those described for the rest of the country.

There was one early attempt, however, at regional decentralization and interinstitutional coordination—PRONORTE, an integrated rural development project. In early 1980, the national government, concerned about the extreme poverty of portions of the region's western section and its proximity to Honduras, decided to initiate a regional development project covering eight of the region's western municipalities. The project was initially coordinated by the departmental office of the FSLN and involved the participation of a number of ministries. Its activities concentrated on providing social services, roads, nonagricultural employment, and small agricultural investments. Its purpose was to raise the income levels of the farmers and to ensure that each of the region's several hundred dispersed communities obtained access to adequate services. Unfortunately, though, there was little coordination between PRONORTE and MIDINRA's regional development activities.

Subsequently, a special management office was created to coordinate the project and administer two foreign loans negotiated in 1981 for financial support. The coordination function failed, however, because of delays in funding, a lack of political authority on the part of the project's management, and the fact that the different ministries involved responded only to Managua rather than to the regional foci of the project.

Thus, it was not until the regional government was created in 1982 that serious decentralization began. For the first time, it became feasible for a region to resist inappropriate national policies and to coordinate effectively the activities of different regional agencies.

Decentralization was aided by the fact that the delegated governor, Carlos Manuel Morales, brought a great deal of political authority to his job. He was a longtime member of the Sandinista Front and knew the region well, for he had worked there prior to the revolution. He had been head of the FSLN regional office from 1979, and no other figure in the region had similar authority.

Two exercises played an important role in building a coherent regional plan in the Segovias and incorporating popular participation. In mid-1982, Managua asked each regional office of MIDINRA to create a medium-run regional plan of agricultural development and agrarian reform (MIDINRA Region 1, 1983). This was the first attempt to create a plan that would incorporate all of the region's microzones. MIDINRA, the FSLN, the regional government, and the peasant organizations all participated in this planning exercise.

There was also a great deal of local participation. Each of MIDINRA's ten local offices in the region, in collaboration with the local representatives of the FSLN and the peasant organizations, was asked to (1) summarize the agricultural history of the zone, (2) describe the economic and political characteristics of the different types of producers, and (3) make recommendations regarding land redistribution, investment projects, and other policies. These documents were consolidated and discussed at the regional level. A regional plan was the result.

Regionalization received another push in early 1983. As a result of increased military activity, the central government in Managua requested that the war-affected regions create special plans that took the military situation into consideration. For this purpose, a commission was created by MIDINRA that included the regional government, the FSLN, and the peasant organizations. The generation of the 1982 and 1983 plans was instrumental for developing a unified regional development plan and incorporating all needed governmental agencies and ministries.

The human and material resources available to the MIDINRA regional office increased substantially with regionalization. With the emergency plans of 1983, they underwent another major jump. There was especially large growth in the departments concerned with planning and in technical personnel providing services to the small- and medium-sized producers and the cooperatives (see Table 4). Twelve major regional investment projects were initiated in the regional development plan, giving the region control over large sums of capital.

Adaptation to Local Conditions

The Segovias have five basic characteristics which must be taken into account for any effort at adapting agricultural policy to local conditions to be successful. (1) Small- and medium-sized private producers predominate—70 percent of the region's land and the bulk of its livestock and basic-grain production are controlled by private producers who have farms smaller than 350 hectares. (2) As a result of its long and poorly delineated border with Honduras to the north and west, the region is a center of military conflict. (3) The region is subdivided into semiarid western and high-rainfall eastern areas—enterprises in the west concentrate on low-productivity, basic-grain and livestock production; productivity in the east is higher, but the area has little

Table 4
Changes in the number of technical and managerial personnel in the regional office of MIDINRA, Las Segovias, 1982–1984[a], [b]

	January 1982	May 1984
Department		
Director's office	2	7
Planning	14	23
Agricultural production	3	34
Livestock production	0	17
Agrarian reform[c]	103	158
Personnel and training	6	6
Engineering and development	0	11
Total	128	236

[a] Source: MIDINRA Region 1, Las Segovias, primary data, 1983.
[b] Not including state-farm employees. There were 104 technical and 146 managerial employees on the state-farms in 1984, but no comparable data are available for 1982.
[c] This includes all of the agronomists and other technicians assigned to the local (zonal) MIDINRA offices.

Table 5
The contributions of small and medium private producers to total production of selected agricultural products, and land area held, in Segovias, 1983/84[a], [b]

	Percentage
Products	
Corn	94
Beans	97
Coffee	53
Light tobacco	50
Dark tobacco	0
Total land area	71

[a] Source: Ministry of Agricultural Development and Agrarian Reform, Region I, Las Segovias, "Plan de desarrollo agropecuario y reforma agraria a mediano plazo" (1983).
[b] Small and medium private producers are producers with fewer than 350 hectares.

economic and social infrastructure. (4) Within the region there are a handful of key valleys and prime coffee areas with high agricultural potential; the remaining lands are largely marginal pastures, forest, and low-quality basic-grain lands. (5) There are a few pockets of large, capital-intensive, modern farms on which coffee, tobacco, and irrigated rice are produced using wage labor (see Table 5).

Centralization was poorly adapted to this reality. The 1979 decision to maintain expropriated lands as state farms was based on the premise that most of these farms were capital-intensive, agroexport farms with significant economies of scale which needed to be preserved. In the Segovias, however, most confiscated farms were livestock operations, and labor relations were of the patron-client type. By the time they were confiscated, moreover, they had been largely decapitalized.

Thus, while state management may have been appropriate for the modernized farms of the Pacific, it was impractical for most of the expropriated farms in the Segovias. Extensive livestock production neither created much employment nor resolved the issue of how landless families could obtain property. The low productivity on these farms did not justify the high overhead costs associated with state farms. But despite the small overall importance of state farms in the region's agriculture, their management still required practically all of INRA's departmental office resources, thus depriving the small- and medium-sized producers of these skills.

Centralization and emphasis on state farms also led to the neglect of isolated areas. In the Segovias, this meant that the humid eastern portion of the region, where there were few roads and almost no state farms, was largely forgotten. Consequently, this area was susceptible to the overtures of the antigovernment insurgents who began operating there.

Little priority was given to the valleys and high-productivity coffee areas or to the modern agricultural enterprises located in these areas. The lack of territorial planning led INRA to focus on wherever large farms might have been confiscated.

Finally, there was nothing in the agricultural strategy that responded to the military concerns of the government. State farms were dispersed and often isolated, making them difficult to defend militarily. Moreover, the government's neglect of isolated areas and lack of response to popular demands for land redistribution limited its political support in rural areas.

INRA's departmental offices lacked sufficient authority to adjust national policy to local conditions. In one case when an attempt was made to do so, it was overruled by Managua—this was with the idea of the trade-union self-sufficiency groups (GACS), originally developed by the departmental office of INRA in Estelí. The GACS were designed to solve simultaneously the problems of state-farm workers (who increasingly demanded access to land) and of state farms themselves (which required staples to feed their workers but had been unable to produce them profitably using wage labor). The ATC organized the workers into basic-grain cooperatives on state lands. The cooperatives came to cultivate areas not part of the state-farm production plans; in turn they received credit, oxen, and technical assistance from the state. In recompense for this land, co-op members agreed to assist the state farms in harvesting and to sell basic grains to the state farms.

Overall, the GACS were rather successful. Production was high, and most loans were repaid. In a November 1980 regional seminar of INRA and the ATC, the GAC concept was reaffirmed and proposed as a model for the entire northern area of the country. In 1981, however, as a result of shifts in national priorities, Managua decided to eliminate the GACS irrespective of their regional success.[7]

Regionalization in 1982 allowed agricultural policy to adapt to local conditions for the first time. The new governor brought strong views and a specific vision of regional development. This vision was based on (1) limiting the role of the state farms to those few producing tobacco, coffee, and irrigated rice, enterprises that could be profitably managed as state farms, (2) giving greater attention to the eastern, humid portion of the region, and (3) concentrating the dispersed population into a few valleys where they would receive land, be organized into production cooperatives, and be given large amounts of investment capital. These valley settlements, organized after the kibbutz model, would be militarily defensible, and it would be easier to provide them with social services and economic infrastructure. Moreover, when the populations saw concrete economic benefits from these projects, they would be more supportive of the government. Similar policies were eventually adopted in other regions and received Managua's approval; in the Segovias, however, they were adopted earlier and formed part of a more integrated conception.

Through the two regional agricultural development plans previously mentioned, this vision was realized. As a result, the state-farm area was reduced by 55 percent between 1982 and 1984. Almost all of the extensive livestock operations were relinquished (see Table 6).

The regional plans emphasized the predominance of small producers and the need to support cooperatives. By mid-1984, 12 percent of the region's agricultural labor force had received land in production cooperatives. Cooperative development zones were defined together with a series of investment projects, and these investment projects were prioritized. The humid areas and the valleys were given first priority. Plans were also made to create some 76 resettlements to house more than 2,000 families between 1984 and 1985.

Regionalization achieved many of the basic goals of decentralization in the Segovias. Policies became better adapted to local conditions. Resources were transferred to traditionally underprivileged zones. Interinstitutional coordination and popular participation increased.

Political authority granted to the regional government, the personal attributes of the regional governor, the strong regional tradition of popular participation, and the willingness on the national level to both

Table 6
Changes in land tenure in Las Segovias, 1978–1984[a], [b]

	1978	1981[c]	1982[c]	1984[d]
Type of farm				
State farms	0	14	10	6
Production cooperatives	0	2	6	8
Private (< 350 hectares)	29	14	13	8
Private (> 350 hectares)	71	71	71	57
Abandoned due to war	0	0	0	21
Total	100	101[e]	100	100

[a] Source: Tenencia de la tierra, Dirección General de Reforma Agraria, Region 1, Las Segovias, primary data, 1983.
[b] Changes are given as percentages.
[c] December.
[d] May.
[e] Not equal to 100 due to rounding error.

transfer resources and permit greater regional flexibility were essential to the success of this effort.

CURRENT TRENDS AND PERSPECTIVES FOR THE FUTURE

Recent efforts toward regionalization and decentralization have stressed two areas—local-level decentralization and autonomy for Nicaragua's Atlantic coast. In the first, Nicaragua's 136 municipalities have been grouped together into some 80 or so "zones" that are to become the basic level of subregional administration. In each, a delegate has been appointed by the regional governor, and the various ministries have named zonal representatives (Downs 1985, 61).[8] Increasingly, attempts are being made to plan at this level. Correspondingly, MIDINRA's 1985 work plan placed a high priority on the consolidation of zone-level planning and administration (MIDINRA 1985, 93).

Village commissions (*consejos comunales*) have been developed in the rural areas under the auspices of the UNAG. These commissions, which include the local teacher, religious leaders, cooperative presidents, and other community leaders, have taken the initiative in handling local affairs and representing the communities' interests before government bodies. In addition, although the official announcement has not been made at the time of writing, it is likely that the country's first municipal elections will be held in the next few years.

The Nicaraguan government has also moved ahead with plans to provide regional autonomy for the Atlantic coast. A commission has been created to formulate a proposal for regional autonomy, and consultations have been held with the different parties involved on both the local and regional levels. Through negotiation, it has been possible to incorporate into these consultations one of the rebel Miskito groups that had taken up arms against the government. While many details of the Atlantic coast's autonomy are still undetermined, it appears virtually certain that the autonomous regional governments will have a great deal of authority over the strategy of regional economic development and agrarian policy. Currently, the Atlantic coast agrarian reform process is sharply different from that in the Pacific area. It places a premium on the titling of lands to indigenous communities and not on organizing cooperatives or individuals.

There are problems for which no adequate solutions have been found. There are conflicts between projects operating on a national level, such as the Tipitapa-Malaycatoya sugar complex and the national Burley tobacco project (CATRA) and the regional offices in which they are located. These projects infrequently fit into the regional development plans, yet they compete for land, labor, and other scarce resources and frequently make unilateral decisions without consulting the regional offices.

The government has also been only partially successful in its attempts to provide state-farm managers sufficient flexibility and incentives to operate efficiently on a local level. While productivity has improved somewhat and the state has turned over many of its less profitable operations to cooperatives and individual farmers, there is still no adequate incentive system to motivate the administrators to make rational decisions or to promote more worker participation in management.

In addition, certain regions have decentralized more slowly than others. In the Pacific regions of Managua and Carazo-Rivas-Grenada-Masaya, in particular, it has been difficult to develop a regional strategy and consciousness due to the diversity of economies in these regions, the importance of their urban areas, and their proximity to the capital.

Whether Nicaragua's decentralization efforts will be further strengthened and institutionalized remains to be seen. While signs of institutionalizing the process abound, it is true that decentralization has partially been an ad hoc solution to an exceptional situation created by the war. Be that as it may, the experience with decentralization to date has been rather positive.

NOTES

1. The Ministry of Agriculture itself had been practically inoperative since the revolution. The merger acknowledged that fact and incorporated the ministry's resources into INRA.

2. By 1984, the number of *empresas* had risen to ninety-six.

3. These delegates often had been military commanders during the revolution and continued to exercise a great deal of authority.

4. The Regionalization Decree, Decree 1081, became law on 26 July 1982.

5. The material in this section is based on fieldwork in the Segovias region between 1982 and 1984 and, in particular, on a regional evaluation conducted in mid-1984 in which the author participated.

6. The three departmental offices were fused into one regional office located in Estelí in November 1980.

7. The national government was concerned that increasing agricultural workers' access to land would reduce the wage-labor supply for the agroexport harvests—thus the cutback in government support for informal cooperatives and the provision of state lands to cooperatives and individual producers.

8. It is to these zonal offices that I was referring when discussing local participation in the section entitled "Regionalization and Agricultural Policy (1982–1985)."

REFERENCES

Austin, James, Jonathan Fox, and Walter Krueger. 1985. The food system in revolutionary Nicaragua. *World Development 13*(1):15–41.

CIERA (Centro de Investigaciones y Estudios para la Reforma Agraria). 1985. Informe anual del sector agropecuario, 1984. Managua: CIERA.

Conyers, Diana. 1981. Decentralization for regional development: A comparative study of Tanzania, Zambia, and Papua New Guinea. *Public Administration and Development 1*(2):107–120.

———.1983. Decentralization: The latest fashion in development administration? *Public Administration and Development 3*(2):97–109.

———.1984. Decentralization and development: A review of the literature. *Public Administration and Development 4*(2):187–197.

DEPEP (Departamento de Educación Política y Propaganda). 1982. *La regionalización: Un paso firme en la transformación de la sociedad.* Managua: DEPEP.

Dickey, Christopher. 1985. *With the Contras: A reporter in the wilds of Nicaragua.* New York: Simon and Schuster.

Downs, Charles. 1985. Local and regional government. In *Nicaragua: The first five years,* edited by Thomas Walker, pp. 45–64. New York: Praeger Publishers.

Downs, Charles, and Fernando Kuznetzoff. 1981. *Decentralization from above and below: The case of Nicaragua.* Berkeley, Calif.: Institute for International Studies.

Enríquez, Laura, and Rose Spalding. 1985. Rural transformation: Agricultural credit policies in revolutionary Nicaragua. Paper presented at meeting of Latin American Studies Association, April, Albuquerque, N.M.

INRA (Instituto de Reforma Agraria). 1980. Organización de la producción y organización interna de las delegaciones regionales del INRA. Managua: INRA.

Kaimowitz, David. 1986. Recent debates regarding Nicaraguan agrarian structure and the rural poor. *Journal of Peasant Studies,* in press.

MIDINRA (Ministry of Agricultural Development and Agrarian Reform). 1982. *Tres años de reforma agraria.* Managua: CIERA.

———.1983. Region I, Las Segovias. Plan de desarrollo agropecuario y reforma agraria a mediano plazo.

———.1984. *Sector agropecuario: Resultados 1983, plan de trabajo 1984.* Managua: CIERA.

———.1985. *Plan de trabajo: Balance y perspectivas 1985.* Managua: CIERA.

Montgomery, J. 1976. Allocation of authority in land reform programs: A comparative study of administrative processes and outputs. *Administrative Science Quarterly 17*:62–75.

Rondinelli, Dennis, John R. Nellis, and G. Shabbir Cheema. 1983. *Decentralization in developing countries: A review of recent experience.* Staff working papers, no. 581. Washington: World Bank.

Chapter 15

Unfinished Business: Consolidating Land Reform in El Salvador

John Strasma*

Land reform was hardly a new idea in El Salvador in 1980; it had been part of the platforms of Christian Democrats and other parties for years (Alvarenga 1981). However, little had been done because they were never in power. Christian Democrat José Napoleón Duarte won the presidency in 1972, in one of the few elections held during fifty years of military dictatorship, but a new coup forced him to flee to Venezuela before he was inaugurated. The 1979 coup by younger, reform-minded officers changed all that, and reform was suddenly transformed from theoretical possibility to contentious policy.

ORIGINS AND GOALS OF LAND REFORM IN EL SALVADOR

As a member of the civilian-military junta that seized power in 1979, Guillermo Ungo led initial land reform planning for the new government. When Ungo resigned, the Christian Democrats joined the junta, but only after receiving commitments from the military that it would carry out a reform. One major author of the actual reform law was Antonio Morales Ehrlich, a Christian Democrat intellectual and leader, who is still very influential in reform policy decisions.

The U.S. Agency for International Development (USAID) Mission in El Salvador agreed to finance much of the initial cost of carrying out

* The author is Professor of Agricultural Economics, University of Wisconsin-Madison. Most of the information herein was obtained in the field, while working with former students and others at the U.S. Agency for International Development and the Ministry of Agriculture in El Salvador, on numerous trips from 1976 through 1986. The author is solely responsible for the interpretations and views here expressed.

the reform. It paid many of the personnel and administrative expenses of the reform agencies for several years; this aid will probably end after 1987, when the task is to be largely completed.

In El Salvador, one has the novel experience of hearing wealthy conservatives (as well as the left wing) complain about "U.S. intervention in the internal affairs of a Latin American country." Several assured me in 1983 that both Jimmy Carter and José Napoleón Duarte were communists. Most of all, the wealthy longed to recover the full and authoritarian power they had enjoyed, as a class, until 1979. Some extremists hated sharing political power with the middle class almost as much as they hated sharing the benefit of property ownership with half a million campesinos.

As a counterpoint, U.S. leftists also snipe at the reform. They and Salvadorans of their persuasion see reform solely as a U.S. counterinsurgency plan. As evidence, they quote Professor Roy Prosterman, from the University of Washington Law School, who advocated reform mainly for that reason. He claimed that the war in Vietnam would have been won and that South Vietnam would be free and democratic today had South Vietnam redistributed land to peasants early on. Although Prosterman appears to have played a major role in "selling" Phase III of the reform to conservatives in the military, the reform was essentially a Salvadoran initiative and plan.[1] In 1980, its time had come.

RESULTS OF THE REFORM, AFTER SIX YEARS

Phase I of the Salvadoran land reform expropriated the landholdings of all persons believed to own more than 500 hectares as of March 1980. Owners were allowed to retain 100–150 hectares (the higher limit if soil quality was poor), and the rest was to be farmed via a production cooperative run by a committee elected by the workers. The state provided a co-manager (*co-gestor*), with veto power over major decisions and the checkbook, to help ensure continued productivity, honesty, and compliance with the new rules. Government functionaries, supported by armed troops, seized some 300 farms in a few weeks in 1980. They took inventory, called the resident workers together to elect a management committee, and told the former owners to go to the reform agency to negotiate compensation and reserve rights.

Phase II, envisioned originally as extending the same process to persons with more than 100 but less than 500 hectares, has been postponed. The Constitution of 1983 raised the allowable landownership limit from 100–150 to 245 hectares, regardless of quality, for any future expropriations. It also allowed two years before a new implementing law could be enacted, to permit owners in that range to sell the "excess" to other farmers (transfers to their own family members were specifically prohibited). A 1985 national survey of the remaining owners found only twenty-two who did not intend to sell or otherwise transfer the excess land by December 1986 to escape the possibility of expropriation under a new law (PERA 1986). (The twenty-two stated that they did not expect such a law to be enacted.)

Phase III is the land-to-the-tiller law, which was modeled in part on the highly successful Japanese reform of 1946-1949, but also reflected an old Latin American ideological view that farmland ought to belong to those who cultivate it rather than to a rentier class. Under Decree 207, all tenants and sharecroppers could file claims and become owners of whatever small plots they rented in March 1980, up to 10 manzanas (7 hectares) in total.

This process began in late 1980, but was stalled in 1982 when a coalition of two conservative parties won a majority in the constituent assembly. The coalition quickly enacted Decree 6, under which land rented out in the future could not then be claimed under the reform law. Many landowners told their former tenants that the reform was annulled, even though it was not. Under the threat of violence, many ex-tenants decided to renounce their claims or even to flee from the area. The foreign news media, and many critics of the U.S. policy of supporting El Salvador, stated flatly that the reforms had ended and would be reversed.

In fact, however, the U.S. Embassy—vociferously urged on by the U.S. Congress—advised the Assembly members that if El Salvador reversed the social reforms, there would be no reason for U.S. support, so economic and military aid would end. After some shuffling, the Assembly rejected Roberto D'Aubuisson and elected a technocrat, Alvaro Magaña, as interim president. The Assembly then enacted several laws "clarifying" Decree 6. Specifically, all land that had been rented in 1980 could still be claimed. After effective street demonstrations by the Salvadoran Community Union (*Unión Comunal Salvadoreña*, UCS), the deadline for filing claims was extended to June 1984 to allow more time for those campesinos who had held back out of fear of landlord reprisals.

To lead the National Finance Office for Agricultural Lands (*Financiera Nacional de Tierras Agrícolas*, FINATA), the agency in charge of Phase III, President Magaña rejected the candidate of the rightist parties. Instead, he named an energetic, honest army officer (Colonel José Galileo Torres, who had earlier served as vice-minister of agriculture). Colonel Torres used the authority of his rank to persuade most younger officers to support the ex-tenants instead of the former landlords. Thousands of beneficiaries who had fled their parcels under landlord pressure were reinstated with army backing.

Torres also sent field teams to accept applications in villages instead of requiring applicants to come to the cities, and the number of claims soared. A field study by four land-grant university researchers verified that the reforms were continuing (Strasma et al. 1983), and U.S. aid continued to flow.

Table 1 shows the number of beneficiaries under each phase of the agrarian reform at the end of the 1984/85 crop year.

The original goal of the Salvadoran authors of the reform was to reach 100,000 direct beneficiaries (Morales Ehrlich 1985) or, counting family members, about 600,000 persons. Other accounts set the goal at anywhere from 90,000 to 160,000 direct beneficiaries. Based on 1971 census data and some assumptions, which hindsight reveals to have been erroneous, the goal setting was clearly "quick and dirty." However, the planners felt it necessary to move rapidly, lest the powerful landowning class manage to halt the reform. There was no time for refined estimates.

In any event, the two reforms have actually changed land tenure for almost 80,000 direct beneficiaries. When family members are included,

Table 1
Labor force in the Salvadoran land reform, 1984–1985[a]

Sector	Decrees 154/842[b]	Decree 207	Total
Direct beneficiaries[c, d]	27,436	52,000	79,436
Total labor force[e]	65,134	180,682	245,816
Total, including families[f]	164,616	312,000	476,616
Percentage of rural poor[g]	7.4	14.2	21.6

[a] Source: Proyecto de Planificación y Evaluación de la Reforma Agraria, *Quinta evaluación de la reforma agraria* (San Salvador: Ministerio de Agricultura y Ganadería, Oficina Sectorial de Planificación Agropecuaria, December 1985); Michael P. Wise, *Agrarian Reform in El Salvador: Process and Progress* (San Salvador: USAID Rural Development Office, September 1986).

[b] Decree 154 expropriated farmholdings over 500 hectares (Phase I). Decree 842 refers to 109 "traditional" cooperatives created before 1980 on land purchased by the government. In 1984–1985, they had 3,900 members and 14,000 hectares. They, along with Phase I, are administered by the *Instituto Salvadoreño de Transformación Agraria* (ISTA).

[c] Omits some 3,600 beneficiaries (or 20,000 persons) of the 29 co-ops that have been abandoned or are farmed only intermittently because of the guerrilla war.

[d] Some Decree 207 beneficiaries rented more than one parcel. These 52,000 beneficiaries will own about 60,000 parcels (Wise 1986,55).

[e] Includes spouses and others over 14 living or working on reform land. Most tend family *milpas* and migrate elsewhere for the coffee harvest; some work as day laborers or probationary members of reform co-ops.

[f] Same as above, plus children, elderly, and disabled, in beneficiary families. Estimated as an average of six persons to a beneficiary household.

[g] Estimated as 2,200,000 (Wise 1986).

the total involved is almost half a million people (Wise 1986a). By Latin American standards, the reforms are clearly "massive." Yet, in densely populated El Salvador, an even greater number of campesinos owned or were employed on parcels under 100 hectares. They were not involved in the land reform, nor were they intended to be.

However, there were also many thousands of landless campesinos. The land reform planners intended that they benefit, too, but in the haste of designing and carrying out the 1980 reforms, they did not provide an effective mechanism for doing so.

The last agricultural census in El Salvador was taken in 1971; the distribution of farmland by tenure at that time is shown in Table 2. Note that in El Salvador, unlike much of Latin America in 1971, land was usually rented for cash, which was payable in advance. Sharecropping (part of "other" in Table 2) was less common. And, whereas in other countries units under 1.0 hectare would often be simple house plots, in El Salvador the population is so dense that almost all are farmed. In the 1971 census, 28,125 hectares in such units were rented (on an annual basis), and only 17,776 were tilled by their owners. Another 6,909 hectares were farmed by *colonos* (tolerated squatters) who were allowed to use small *milpas* (plots on which campesinos could grow staples on hacienda land), in order to have laborers available in the peak season; 7,143 more hectares were owned and rented in part (that is, the campesino farmed two or more plots adding up to less than 1 hectare, but at least one plot was not his property). It is also notable that there were some large units under rental; along the coast, these were usually cotton lands rented by urban investors, although some were cattle ranches in the hills.

Population density in El Salvador is greater than that of India. There is also massive underemployment, with many campesinos finding regular work only in the peak coffee, cotton, and sugarcane harvest seasons. Part of the problem is that two major events greatly increased the number of landless campesinos between 1969 and 1979. In 1969, a war with Honduras ended with half a million Salvadorans returning to El Salvador as refugees; many had been farmers in Honduras, where land was more plentiful. On their return to El Salvador, they sought land or work in the countryside, but little of either was available. Furthermore, well-meaning legislation in 1975 established a minimum cash wage for farm labor. This led many landowners to evict *colonos*.

At least 18,000 of the landless live on or near the land of Phase I cooperatives but are not members. They were rejected because they were not full-time workers on the farms prior to expropriation. Many are now day laborers for the cooperatives. Some rented land from the hacienda in 1980 and are eligible for Phase III benefits, but the cooperatives refuse to yield those parcels. The government is now

Table 2

Land tenure in El Salvador by size of unit, 1971[a]

Size (Hectares)	Number[b]		Area[b]		Form of Tenure (hectares)				
					Owned	Cash rent	Mixed[c]	*Colonos*	Other
<1.0	132,464	(49)	70,287	(5)	17,776	28,125	7,143	6,909	10,334
1.0–1.99	59,063	(22)	81,039	(6)	25,736	24,809	16,222	2,743	11,529
2.0–4.99	43,414	(16)	131,985	(9)	72,661	16,827	28,426	638	13,433
5.0–9.99	15,598	(6)	110,472	(8)	80,788	3,919	18,640	—	7,125
10.0–19.99	9,164	(3)	126,974	(9)	104,842	2,913	14,450	—	4,769
20.0–49.99	6,986	(2)	215,455	(15)	188,633	5,497	15,480	—	5,945
50.0–99.99	2,238	(1)	154,164	(11)	134,801	3,557	9,416	—	6,390
100.0–999.99	1,878	(1)	437,939	(30)	374,745	19,015	20,541	—	23,637
>1,000	63	—	123,579	(8)	105,512	—	3,269	—	14,798
Totals	270,868	(100)	1,451,894	(101)	1,105,494	104,662	133,587	10,290	97,960

[a] Source: "Censo agropecuario de 1971" (San Salvador, n.d.).
[b] The numbers in parenthesis are the percentages. They may not add up to 100 percent due to errors in rounding.
[c] Mixed: Respondent owns some land and also farms some rented land.

trying to persuade the cooperatives to admit them as full members (see PERA-CLUSA 1985).

Further complicating the numbers game, critics often erroneously assert that the owners of 100 to 500 hectares of land have not been affected. In fact, about sixty of these farms were seized in 1980, in the belief that the owner held over 500 hectares. Many, but not all, of those owners sold "voluntarily" rather than suffer the indignity of returning to the farms that their former workers were now running. Also, the parts of the 100–500 hectare landholdings that had been rented out to small tenants in 1980 were eligible for inclusion in Phase III, and much of this land was so claimed.

THE IMPACT OF THE WAR

El Salvador is the first Latin American nation to carry out a land reform during a war. In other cases, such as Bolivia and Mexico, the reform legalized de facto land seizures that occurred during a successful insurrection and extended them to other parts of the country. In El Salvador, the reforms were launched by a progressive civilian-military junta in 1980, slowed by conservatives elected in 1982, and then reasserted both when Duarte defeated D'Aubuisson for the presidency in 1984 and again when the Christian Democrats won a clear majority in the legislature in early 1985.

The guerrilla war broke out in 1979. It peaked in 1981 when the Faribundo Martí National Liberation Front (FMLN) announced its "final offensive." The guerrillas entered the cities, but the army, weak as it was, defeated the guerrillas and drove them back into the countryside. Since 1983, the army has become more professional, and the guerrilla movement appears to be shrinking. Two rounds of peace talks were held in El Salvador in 1984 and 1985, and another was aborted in August 1986. It is presently unclear whether talks can ever succeed.

The war has exacted a severe toll on the campesinos. Initially seizing about a third of the countryside in 1980, the guerrillas murdered local officials and persons they considered to be possible informers for the government. Paramilitary groups associated with the extreme right responded in kind in the rest of the territory, killing persons they suspected of either being or supporting guerrillas.[2] Thousands of people fled rural areas between 1980 and 1983. By 1986, however, many were able to return safely.

During military operations by either side, campesinos report that cattle were stolen and crops trampled.[3] Many land reform cooperatives report that guerrilla groups visit them to exact a "war tax" of food, horses, cattle, or money. (Some would call this "protection money.")

As a result, at any given time a certain number of reform cooperatives are abandoned. The people flee because their crops or cattle have been stolen or because they fear death since they refuse to pay. As the war dies down, the number and area of reform cooperatives abandoned have declined somewhat.

While there are few reliable damage estimates, it appears that the farms abandoned in 1985 represented a loss of about 6 percent of national output. There is also the cost of "protection money" extorted by guerrillas in some areas. (Until 1984, pro-government paramilitary groups made similar demands in regions they controlled; both seem to want about 5 percent of the gross value of co-op production.) Since farm costs have risen faster than farm product prices, especially in the inflation that accompanied the devaluation of 1985/86, this cost is a significant blow to net profits. It accounts, in part, for the inability of many co-ops to make full payments on their land debt as originally scheduled.

The war has had a severe impact on crop choice, at least for cotton-growing cooperatives along the coast. Guerrillas visited them, demanding that the cooperative plant basic grains (and give them part of the harvest) instead of cotton. When cooperatives ignored this demand and planted "too much" cotton, the guerrillas seized and burned tractors and implements.

All cotton growers in the areas of conflict, reform beneficiaries or not, were hurt when the guerrillas ordered a halt to aerial spraying. Crop dusters must fly "low and slow," and the guerrillas easily shot down the first pilot who defied their orders. Because it never freezes in El Salvador, there is no insect winterkill. Therefore, a successful cotton harvest requires about eighteen pesticide applications a year. It is prohibitively expensive to do this by backpack sprayer. As a result of the guerrilla threat, combined with low world cotton prices, cotton recently has been highly unprofitable and many cooperatives are diversifying.

As part of their campaign to "destabilize" the constitutional government by limiting its foreign exchange earnings from exports, the guerrillas have also destroyed coffee and cotton crops in warehouses. The tactic is much like one used by the Contras in Nicaragua. And, like the Contras, the guerrillas hurt the campesinos more than they hurt the government. The campesinos lose the money they expected to get for their harvests; there is no insurance.

By late 1985, twenty-four cooperatives were still considered abandoned; ten of these had debts for production credit adding up to about $60,000 (U.S. dollars). Most of this had to be written off by the lending bank, which reduced the funds available for financing other campesinos in 1986 (Strasma 1986a).

SITUATION AND NEEDS OF THE PRODUCTION COOPERATIVES (PHASE I)

Production

Overall, and in spite of the war, production on the land reform cooperatives has held up fairly well. Their output is a significant share of the national total, and yields per hectare are similar to those of nonreform farmers in El Salvador.

Table 3 shows the evolution of production on Phase I cooperatives from 1980/81 through 1984/85. Note, however, that these figures refer only to the land which is farmed collectively. Most cooperatives also give or rent small parcels (*milpas*) to their members, whose families till them for cash crops or for subsistence. (*Milpa* production is given in Table 5.)

Several facts are obvious from the data in Table 3. In their first year, most cooperatives plunged deeply into growing basic grains. Many reform agency staffers believed firmly that priority should be given to those subsistence crops rather than to cash crops for export.[4] The result was a huge glut of basic grains in 1980/81, low prices, and financial losses for the co-ops. The co-ops learned from this experience, and much of the land was quickly put back into sugarcane. In many cases, they also responded to the desire of their members for individual parcels by renting or lending small parcels of the lower quality land to the members, who raised basic grains there with family labor. With no

Table 3
Production, in Phase I co-ops, 1980/81 through 1984/85[a]

	Production (cwt)[b]				
Crop	1980/81	1981/82	1982/83	1983/84	1984/85
Corn	977,605	799,700	383,282	461,012	310,721
Rice	224,190	300,113	154,649	194,459	223,765
Beans	86,630	90,784	44,151	48,420	9,656
Sorghum	202,538	91,470	37,623	56,124	31,651
Coffee	404,067	439,970	527,350	369,474	501,334
Cotton	970,794	854,420	898,918	680,406	691,473
Sugarcane[c]	850,887	878,968	933,970	1,152,266	1,234,998

[a] Source: Proyecto de Planificación y Evaluación de la Reforma Agraria, *Quinta evaluación de la reforma agraria* (San Salvador: Ministerio de Agricultura y Ganadería, Oficina Sectorial de Planificación Agropecuaria, December 1985).
[b] cwt = Hundredweight, or 100 pounds (Spanish usage in El Salvador, quintal).
[c] Sugarcane numbers are short tons (2,000 pounds) of cane, not hundredweight.

cash labor costs and negligible opportunity costs for family labor, the beneficiaries could feed themselves and run the risk of low prices for the surplus grain they marketed.

Also, year-to-year crop yields in El Salvador are highly susceptible to rainfall variations; little land in El Salvador is irrigated. Table 4 compares yields for 1980/81 through 1985/86.

Table 4
Yields obtained in collective production by Phase I cooperatives, compared to national average yields for El Salvador, 1980/85[a], [b]

	1980/81		1981/82		1982/83		1983/84		1984/85		1985/86	
Crop	I	All	I	All	I	All	I	All	I	All	I	All
Corn (maize)	64	39	50	39	43	38	68	40	67	47	57	42
Rice	67	79	73	82	52	69	75	75	78	90	57	86
Beans (frijoles)	16	16	21	17	17	15	21	16	19	18	19	13
Sorghum	39	25	31	26	22	23	42	24	33	26	33	25
Coffee	18	21	23	22	27	23	20	20	26	21	23	20
Cotton	50	36	45	39	56	41	50	37	51	47	49	53
Sugarcane[c]	80	75	80	78	73	86	83	91	84	82	79	91

[a] Sources: For national averages, see Ministry of Agriculture and Livestock (MAG), as cited in Michael P. Wise, *Agrarian Reform in El Salvador: Process and Progress* (San Salvador: USAID Rural Development Office, September 1986), p. xx; for reform sector yields, Proyecto de Planificación y Evaluación de la Reforma Agraria, *Quinta evaluación de la reforma agraria* (San Salvador: Ministerio de Agricultura y Ganadería, Oficina Sectorial de Planificación Agropecuaria, December 1985), [but see Wise (1986) for the 1985/86 crop year].

[b] Except for sugarcane, all yields are in quintals per hectare (1 quintal = 100 pounds, 1 hectare = 2.47 acres). Yields are on Phase I cooperatives, including both those expropriated under Decrees 153 and 154 and the pre-1980 cooperatives governed by Decree 842. Note that these yields are strictly for the portion of the cooperatives' land that is farmed collectively. Most cooperatives also assign small parcels to members in rental or as a fringe benefit. National averages are estimated by MAG. While probably consistent from year to year, the civil violence has prevented normal yearly replacement of part of the sampling frame, and access to some fields in the sample is not always possible. Thus, the figures for national averages should probably not be used for international comparisons with countries in which sampling is not hampered by violent attempts to overthrow the constitutional government.

[c] For sugarcane only, yields are in short tons per hectare (1 short ton = 2,000 pounds).

On average, Phase I co-ops obtain better yields than national averages for all crops except rice; however, it must be remembered that these tables show only the collective production of the co-ops and that most co-ops have better land than the national average. Thus, the data in Table 4 prove mainly that the cooperatives have been able to produce about as efficiently on their collective lands as other farmers in El Salvador in spite of various problems. The data refute those critics who assert that land reform leads to declining production and that collective operation is always less productive than private operation. However, the data do not prove whether the same beneficiaries and the same land produce more in collective operation than they would in some other production structure.

Critics of the Salvadoran reform have sometimes stressed that national total food production has not been as high as that of 1979, the year before the reform. However, 1979 was the best year for production ever recorded in El Salvador, and, since 1980, the war has affected both the reform units and all other farmers. Comparisons should therefore be made with the 1975–1979 five-year average, which is more representative.

Individual Production

Within the Phase I cooperatives, most members rent a *milpa*, a small plot on which they raise whatever they like for family use or for sale. Just as landowners formerly decided which lands to rent, the cooperatives tend to use the land that is relatively unproductive, and hence not profitable for farming with wage labor for *milpas*. This is not a problem for *milpa* operators, who farm with their own or family labor and in neither case need to cover the full legal minimum wage. As long as the returns to the *milpa* meet or exceed the opportunity cost of family labor—what could be earned doing something else—it is worthwhile to till the *milpa*. Case studies have found that the cooperatives and their members fully understand the economics involved and manage their land quite rationally.

Table 5 compares the productivity of two sets of land reform beneficiaries: former tenants receiving land under Decree 207 (Phase III) and members of Phase I cooperatives who till individual parcels. However, it must be noted that the Phase III beneficiaries generally received marginal land, often on steep slopes, that the former owner found more profitable to rent out than to farm directly. Also, Phase III beneficiaries generally get just one crop a year and earn most of their annual income from seasonal work harvesting coffee. Phase I beneficiaries usually have better land, some of it irrigated, and farm it all year with intercropping and easier access to credit, inputs, and markets.

The data in Table 5 are strictly for the grains produced by beneficiaries in Phase I on individual parcels loaned or rented to them by the cooperatives. Output and yields of collective production of basic grains by the cooperatives are shown in the preceding tables. As a group, Phase III beneficiaries have much more area and, hence, produce more corn, beans, and sorghum than do Phase I beneficiaries even though their inputs and yields per hectare are lower.

Table 5
Production and yields, of basic grains, obtained by Phase I beneficiaries on individual parcels and by Phase III beneficiaries on the parcels they previously rented, 1983/84[a]

Crop	Production (cwt)[b]		Yields[c]	
	Phase I	Phase III	Phase I	Phase III
Corn (maize)	422,738	1,671,029	52.3	35.9
Rice	21,334	100,704	88.3	33.6
Beans (frijoles)	64,727	254,132	22.5	14.3
Sorghum	60,958	442,593	32.0	20.9

[a] Source: Proyecto de Planificación y Evaluación de la Reforma Agraria, *Quinta evaluación de la reforma agraria* (San Salvador: Ministerio de Agricultura y Ganadería, Oficina Sectorial de Planificación Agropecuaria, December 1985).
[b] cwt = hundredweight, or 100 pounds.
[c] Yields are in cwt/hectare.

Problems in Phase I Cooperatives

Despite the progress made, there are significant problems in many Phase I cooperatives which should be addressed as the reform is consolidated. Many cooperatives do not fully utilize all of their land resource and hire wage labor rather than admit more members. Some members see themselves as workers on state farms rather than as owners of the land they till. Accordingly, they will sit idle if disbursement of a bank loan is late rather than work anyway in order to protect their expected future profits. They prefer receiving costly social benefits now rather than maximizing profits in order to pay off the debt on the land assigned them.

Some of the state-supplied co-managers are incompetent, dishonest, or slothful. Sometimes they are just unavailable to sign critical documents, so the production process is delayed. There is no clear policy on when a cooperative "graduates" to worker self-management (*auto-gestión*), free of a state co-manager, even though this is the stated goal. Some cooperative leaders have stolen funds or sold crops and pocketed the proceeds. Many cooperatives are too large for the members to know everything that goes on or to watch their leaders closely.

The legal system that rules all cooperatives in El Salvador was not designed for agricultural production cooperatives; amendments are needed. Like most farms in El Salvador (and in many other countries, including the United States), reform cooperatives are making little progress in paying off debts from the past or for the land received. In some cases, the land farmed by a cooperative still has not been legally acquired by the government and, therefore, has not been legally assigned to the cooperative. In several instances, the holding was not 500 hectares or more. The owner may refuse to sell, yet the land has already been turned over to the workers because, in 1980, the records made it appear that the land was eligible for expropriation.

In other cases, the land was expropriated but the government did not have the money for the small cash down payment until late 1986. The government was about a year late in payment of interest and redeeming the small set of bonds that matured in 1985 (Strasma 1986a). Had this compensation not been paid, a future conservative government might have had a pretext for returning that land to its former owners.

Some cooperative members are dissatisfied with equal pay for all members, judging that a number are "free loading." This group would much rather have individual parcels. In response, many cooperatives are ceding or renting a large part of their lands to members for individual cultivation. De facto, some co-ops are evolving into groups much like the "associative" rice production cooperatives of the Dominican Republic (see chap. 11 in this volume). In these, each member receives the profits from the production of an assigned plot, although landownership and heavy-machinery services remain in the hands of the service cooperative, which prorates its costs among the members.

Debts have been burdensome to many cooperatives, although most are current on their production credit. The land debt was eased in 1986 by President Duarte in response to demands by the worker and campesino groups who supported his election in 1984. Duarte ordered the board of the Salvadoran Institute for Agrarian Transformation (*Instituto Salvadoreño de Transformación Agraria*, ISTA) to use the discretion the present law gives it to lower the interest rate on the land debt from 9.5 percent to 6.0 percent, to start the grace period when the co-op receives title to the land rather than when the land is expropriated, and to lengthen the grace period and the time to pay off the mortgage.

Nonetheless, farm-product prices paid to producers barely moved in early 1986 while input prices (costs) rose sharply to reflect devaluation. It appears that higher support prices (or higher price ceilings where price controls apply) are badly needed by all producers. Likewise, actual payment to the former owners and assignment of the land in registered title to the co-op and/or its members will be needed before the reform can be considered fairly irreversible. One imaginative proposal would have the government privatize a number of state-owned enterprises in exchange for land-reform bonds (FUSADES 1983; MIPPE 1986; and Strasma 1986b).

All of these problems are being discussed openly in El Salvador (for example, CARA 1985a, 1985b). However, solutions must be designed and implemented before the reforms will be truly consolidated.

THE FUTURE OF LANDHOLDINGS BETWEEN 245 AND 500 HECTARES (PHASE II)

During the drafting of the Constitution of 1983, the Constituent Assembly provided that no action be taken on a land reform affecting landholdings of 245 hectares or less. By raising the maximum holding from 100 hectares, the Assembly effectively reduced the number of possible future cases from about 1,800 to about 400 (Wise 1986a). The constitution also provided that no law could be enacted before December 1986 to provide expropriation of holdings even above 245 hectares. Meanwhile, owners could sell or otherwise rid themselves of the excess land before the law would operate. (However, Art. 105 specifies that the land may not be sold or transferred to family members.)

Many holdings have apparently already been divided or sold to reduce them below the new ceiling. Some 11,000 hectares were sold to ISTA and added to Phase I. Tenants on holdings in the Phase II range claimed 13,000 hectares under Phase III. Still other holders have simply sold off the excess to small farmers. Although there are only a few dozen holders left in the 245 to 500 hectare range, the government is interested in resolving uncertainty, and therefore legislation may be forthcoming.

The Phase I implementing agency, ISTA, still has its hands full trying to consolidate that part of the reform. FINATA is equally busy completing Phase III, though it may be somewhat closer to solutions for its problems. The framers of a law for Phase II will thus have to decide whether to seek some form of land transfer mechanism either using these existing agencies or using an entirely different mechanism. They might, for example, enlist both FINATA and commercial banks to transfer land through the market.

The Ministry of Agriculture recently completed a study of the amount of land that is still available for the landless and for resettling internal war refugees (Moquete 1986). It appears that there may be enough land to settle the bulk of the landless with or without the remaining land in Phase II holdings. It also appears that the persons whose holdings do fall into that size range are, in general, quite willing to sell, but that they hope to get a better price than the value they declared for tax purposes in the 1976/77 fiscal year, ten years ago and before the 2:1 devaluation of the colón. (The 1976 and 1977 tax declarations were the main basis for compensation in Phases I and III.)

Additional land is available in the portfolios of the banks (mixed state and private ownership) as collateral for loans long overdue. In many cases, this land is grossly underutilized. The banks have been reluctant to turn it over to the state, in part because many of these farms are worth less than the debt, with interest, the land supposedly secures. Thus, transfer will force the banks to recognize the losses for these uncollectable loans on their balance sheets.

A significant part of the Phase II land is in coffee production. Salvadoran plantation owners insist that there are great production economies of scale justifying large units, although it is not clear why this is so. Neither Costa Rica nor Colombia is dominated by large production units; both produce excellent coffee very efficiently on units which are, on average, small enough to be tended by one or two families. Phase II may offer an opportunity to test the theory that, in El Salvador, coffee can be produced efficiently on small family units. (A cooperative could run the processing operation, where scale is important.)

THE SITUATION AND NEEDS OF THE FORMER TENANT FARMERS (PHASE III)

The former tenants are an especially interesting case that deserves further field-case studies. The Phase III beneficiaries did not support themselves solely with their parcels when they rented them; now at least they cannot be evicted arbitrarily by a landlord. They received much of their previous yearly income from harvesting coffee, and they still do. Now they have some security, and they can plant fruit trees and build a house or a set of terraces. They can even start to increase productivity and retard erosion. As tenants, they could do none of these profitably.

Research thus far indicates that the beneficiaries have increased their incomes[5] but are still, on average, at what USAID deems a "poverty" level. Even so, many are investing to improve their parcels. A 1984 sample survey found that 21 percent had made soil-conservation investments (terracing or other labor-intensive measures), 13 percent had planted permanent crops (which usually increase income once they come into full production), and 6 percent had installed irrigation or drainage improvements (PERA 1985).

Despite their poverty, many beneficiaries signed up to pay off their parcels much faster than the 30 years allowed them by law; FINATA encourages this with discounts of one-third if the full price is paid in cash and 10 percent if paid within the first 5 years (Strasma 1986a; Wise 1986b). However, actual payments are running far behind schedule.

The number of claims is only about half what was expected by planners, who used 1971 census data and assumed that "landowners" and "tenants" were homogeneous groups: rich and poor, respectively. Landowner intimidation, significant between 1980 and 1982 even though often exaggerated in extent, is apparently not at all the main cause. Rather, much rented land turned out to be owned by other campesinos just as poor as the tenants. Few tenants filed claims against their own parents, say, for whom the rent amounted to a pension. Rather than merely redistributing poverty, FINATA resolved administratively not to process claims against owners who themselves possessed fewer than 7 hectares. FINATA does attempt to buy land elsewhere to resettle the tenants who present such claims.

From the field-based research to date, it appears that the consolidation of Phase III requires at least the following:

1. *Clarification of rules for revision of the terms agreed to by beneficiaries for purchase of their plots.* Some ex-tenants signed up for quick payoff and then found that they had been too optimistic. Although it could foreclose, FINATA does not. However, FINATA needs a simple procedure for refinancing over a longer term.

2. *Some plot consolidation.* Phase III beneficiaries are often scattered across hillsides because of the manner in which the landlord assigned land in 1980. In some cases, landlords rotated parcels every year to preserve fertility, and in others they did so to reduce the temptation for a tenant to identify a parcel as "his" when there were rumors of land reform in the air (Strasma et al. 1983). The scattering of farmsteads makes it more costly for banks or state agencies to provide supervised credit and other services. To remedy this, FINATA has purchased the remainder of some landlords' holdings and then laid out a new and more accessible set of parcels of slightly larger size. This consolidation is expensive and not always feasible (Torres 1985).

3. *Granting titles.* The title-granting process began slowly but is currently moving at a reasonable pace, thanks in part to a recently passed law changing the basic concept of property records. (See Weisleder and López-Calleja 1982; Wise 1986b.)

Consolidation requires completing the titling process, which in some cases is delayed by legal challenges by ex-landowners and is still in the courts. However, a recent law (Decree 467, 1986) clears away the biggest source of delay by specifying that land may be expropriated and transferred to ISTA or FINATA even if it has an outstanding mortgage debt. The compensation is paid to the lender and, if the debt and accumulated interest is greater than the compensation, the lending bank must try to collect it from the borrower—the bank can no longer hold up the legal land transfer.

4. *Relax restrictions on transfers.* Under present law, even after title is issued (and even after the mortgage loan for the purchase price is paid off), the beneficiary is not at liberty to sell, mortgage, or transfer the land to anyone else without FINATA's permission for 30 years. This makes the otherwise valid title all but worthless as security for credit unless FINATA co-signs the loan.

5. *Beneficiaries need to know the rules of the game.* As of late 1986, FINATA has not spelled out the rules under which approval will be granted for transfers. Thus, beneficiaries are unsure of their rights should they be injured, become ill, or, for whatever reason, want to sell their parcels and move elsewhere before the end of the 30 years. Experience in other countries with similar prohibitions on transfer and a similar lack of clear rules of the game for such cases indicates that campesinos wanting to sell will do so privately and illegally. Ownership registries soon will become obsolete again. This happened in nearby countries attempting to impose a heavy bureaucratic hand on transfers of small parcels (for example, Costa Rica and Honduras); FINATA staff admits that it happens in El Salvador as well.

In a 1985 seminar on beneficiary rights and responsibilities, the only reason given for the 30-year entailment of land titles was a paternalistic concern that the beneficiary might lose the land in a card game or sell it for alcohol, or that the despised former landlords might offer a great deal of money and buy back the land. Former landlords interviewed have shown little interest in recovering their lands on a piecemeal basis, and many are now working in urban activities. Consolidation would appear to require doing away with the 30-year ban or cutting it sharply.

LESSONS FOR THE PLANNING OF FUTURE REFORMS

Chilean reformer Jacques Chonchol often insisted that, to be effective, a land reform must be "massive, drastic, and rapid." The Salvadoran reform appears to meet these criteria. It involves almost half a million people, no large landholders escaped, compensation was paid but only at values declared for tax purposes, and the bulk of the land was taken over in the first few weeks before the landowners could get organized to fight back.

The Salvadoran Phase I cooperative is based on the Chilean model (Frei period) of the *asentamiento* (see chaps. 7 and 8 in this volume) However, the Chilean model called for a 3-year period of modest state tutelage followed by a decision by the beneficiaries themselves as to whether they wanted to continue farming collectively, divide the farm into individual parcels, or do a combination of both. There were fewer problems in Frei's reform than there have been in El Salvador, in part because everyone knew when the state was supposed to pull back and let the beneficiaries decide for themselves.

At the same time, two fundamental errors were made in both Chile and El Salvador. First, it was assumed that the former owner had somehow determined the optimal size for the unit. Thus, cooperatives were formed mainly with whatever land the ex-owner happened to have. In real life, however, those holdings reflected speculation, divorce, inheritance, and many other nonmarket forces. The notion that "big is beautiful" guided land reform planners, who genuinely believed that large-scale operation would somehow increase both employment and production in both countries (Majano 1985).

In El Salvador, as in Chile and Peru, reformers organized many units so large that scale brought diseconomies and individual members could not know what was going on. Some cooperative boards and state co-managers thus found themselves operating two, three, or four separate farms (as the former owner had done). The members on each of the farms cannot easily see what happens with cooperative assets on the others, and that tends to corrupt board members. When an operation is large and complex, it is relatively easy to steal cooperative assets while shuffling inputs, products, or money among the parts (see PERA-CLUSA case studies 1985).

Second, even though seeking to reduce landlessness, the actual reforms in Chile, Peru, and El Salvador only admitted those persons who already had at least steady employment or who had rented the land. Persons who had no access to land before the reform still had no access after the reform. Many found themselves working as day laborers for the land reform beneficiaries. Those who got land became a "new class" seeking to live off the sweat of others.

For future reforms, it is clear that if substantially all of the landless are to be included, they must be included from the start. That means starting with a ratio of land per beneficiary that reflects the real land supply and demand rather than the peculiar employment intensity on each given farm that is expropriated. In El Salvador, for instance, a national average would be about 6 hectares per campesino. (Phase I cooperatives have nearly 11 hectares per beneficiary.)

Since rural society is far from a homogeneous class of campesinos, in many cases it will not work well to just "blanket in" the migrants, the landless, and the long-term resident laborers and expect them to function as one happy family. For example, many resident workers consider themselves relatively high on the rural social scale. For generations they have looked down on the migrants as thieves and rapists rather than seeing them as fellow campesinos.

In most cases, expropriated farms should be divided into coherent units just large enough to get reasonable economies of scale in the prevailing or projected enterprise pattern. In El Salvador, that might be an average of thirty families and about 180 hectares, adjusted up or down depending on soil type and the availability of irrigation. Each thirty or so resident laborers on the farm should be assigned to one of the co-ops. The land left over should be assigned to other new cooperatives, organized with landless migrant workers or unemployed campesinos from the area.

An additional lesson, done correctly in El Salvador, is that speed is of the essence when conducting a reform against a strong landlord group or class. Had Phase I been planned at length and implemented one zone at a time, it would probably have been aborted by massive, violent opposition in 1981. At the same time, the errors and organizational problems encountered by ISTA in trying to run just its part of the land reform suggest that it certainly could not have also managed Phase II. It may be just as well that Phase II is taking place largely through defensive actions by owners, selling part of their holdings in order to avoid a future expropriation. Finally, land reform is not conducted in a vacuum, nor is its consolidation. The earthquake of 1986 destroyed the Ministry of Agriculture's main offices in San Salvador but had relatively little impact on the reform beneficiaries in the countryside. In September 1986, President Duarte had ordered steps to consolidate the reform along many of the lines described previously. Now, this may have to take a back seat to earthquake reconstruction. However, consolidation of the reform will strengthen the whole economy. Thus, it should help reconstruction rather than compete with it for resources.

CONCLUSION

The 1980 agrarian reform in El Salvador was massive and drastic; some 476,000 persons (21 percent of the rural poor population) are involved. The reforms were designed and implemented by Salvadorans with U.S. financial and political support. Crop yields and production have held up well, equaling or exceeding those of the nonreform sector. Duarte and the Christian Democrats won the presidency in 1984 and the legislature in 1985; they now have the power to consolidate the reform, make it irreversible, and achieve its full potential.

Duarte recently cut the land debts; now it is time to admit more members and to move from paternalistic state control to genuine self-management. Those cooperatives too large for effective participatory operation should be divided. Phase II (holdings between 245 and 500 hectares) could be implemented for the few cases in which owners have not already sold the excess. Phase III appears particularly successful, and the issuing of definitive titles has been accelerated by recent legal changes. For many beneficiaries, as for thousands of other small farmers in El Salvador, the worst problems are now the usual ones: prices, costs, marketing, and credit.

NOTES

1. Duarte and Page (1986, 165). A favorite claim, by both leftist and rightist critics of the reform, is that Decree 207 was "written in English and had to be translated into Spanish." Professor Prosterman spoke with fatherly pride to U.S. congressional committees; this does not prove paternity. In my view, attributing the reform to him is grossly unfair to Antonio Morales Ehrlich, Guillermo Ungo, Rodolfo Viera, and the other real authors of El Salvador's reform.

2. The right-wing death squads have been much less active since 1984. The reasons are not clear. One theory is that they have gone to join the Contras in Honduras. Another is that they have gone unpaid since the 1985 arrest (in Texas) of an assistant to D'Aubuisson, who had $5.9 million in banknotes that were confiscated under U.S. drug laws (*Washington Post*, Feb. 16, 1985).

3. Accounts of events in El Salvador tend to be exaggerated; "eyewitness" reports are typically inflated, much like the "Texas tall tale" more familiar to U.S. and European readers.

4. I call this "supply-side economics of the Left"; its adherents, concerned for the hungry, often assume implicitly that the demand for basic grains is infinite at present prices. In the real world, the problem is seldom a shortage of corn. Rather, it is a lack of opportunity to earn money with which to buy corn. Families may well produce their own requirements, using their own (unpaid) labor and cutting out middlemen. However, those who have access to more land than they need for their own consumption generally find it more profitable to grow cash crops on the extra land to which they have access.

5. Between the 1982 and 1984 sample surveys, family income from the Phase III parcels rose from $303 to $417 (in U.S. dollars), outrunning inflation by 9 percent. Off-farm income rose even more sharply, perhaps because the former tenants now had a secure base. No longer did they have to spend time and energy to please a landlord or to find a parcel to rent the following year. Total average family income of the Phase III beneficiaries rose from $371 in 1982 to $732 in 1984 (PERA 1983 and 1985).

REFERENCES

Alvarenga, Ivo P. 1981. Carta a Héctor Oguelí. Typescript. San Salvador.

CARA (Consejo Asesor de la Reforma Agraria). 1985a. Análisis de la deuda agraria de las cooperativas de la Fase I del proceso de reforma agraria en El Salvador, y deuda agraria: Principales problemas y medidas. Mimeograph. San Salvador: Ministerio de Agricultura y Ganadería, January.

———.1985b. Políticas de reforma agraria. Paper prepared for National Seminar on Agrarian Reform and Rural Development, San Salvador, January.

Duarte, José Napoleón, and Diana Page. 1986. *Duarte: My story*. New York: Putnam.

FUSADES (Fundación Salvadoreña para el Desarrollo Económico y Social). 1983. Utilización de los bonos de reforma agraria para la reactivación económica. San Salvador: FUSADES, September.

Majano, Colonel Adolfo. 1985. What we sought to accomplish with the agrarian reform. Paper presented to Symposium on El Salvador, American Agricultural Economics Association annual meetings, Ames, Iowa, August.

MIPPE (Ministerio de Planificación). 1986. Propuesta específica para resolver el problema de la deuda agraria con la venta de las acciones de las empresas de CORSAIN. Mimeograph. San Salvador: MIPPE, April.

Moquete, Santiago. 1986. *Estudio de base para la reubicación de familias desplazadas en actividades agropecuarias*. San Salvador: USAID, June.

Morales Ehrlich, Antonio. 1985. Oral presentation at PERA-CLUSA - Seminar (San Salvador, September) on Capacity and Rights and Responsibilities of Beneficiaries.

PERA (Proyecto de Planificación y Evaluación de la Reforma Agraria). 1983. *Tercera evaluación del proceso de la reforma agraria*. San Salvador: Ministerio de Agricultura y Ganadería, Oficina Sectorial de Planificación Agropecuaria, October.

———.1985. *Segundo perfil de beneficiarios del Decreto 107*. San Salvador: Ministerio de Agricultura y Ganadería, Oficina Sectorial de Planificación Agropecuaria, December.

———.1986. *Estudio sobre la oferta potencial de tierras agrícolas en El Salvador*. San Salvador: Ministerio de Agricultura y Ganadería, Oficina Sectorial de Planificación Agropecuaria, June.

PERA-CLUSA (Proyecto de Planificación y Evaluación de la Reforma Agraria and the Cooperative League of the USA). 1985. *La cabida y los derechos y deberes de los socios de las cooperativas de la Etapa I de la reforma agraria salvadoreña*. San Salvador: Ministerio de Agricultura y Ganadería, Oficina Sectorial de Planificación Agropecuaria, October.

Strasma, John D. 1986a. *The agrarian debt: An update*. San Salvador: USAID, May.

———.1986b. Spinning gold from straw: Proposals to exchange Salvadoran government holdings in business enterprises for agrarian reform bonds. Report to USAID/El Salvador. Typescript. Madison, Wisc., May.

Strasma, John D., Peter D. Gore, Jeffrey Nash, and Refugio Rochin. 1983. *Agrarian reform in El Salvador*. San Salvador: Checchi and Co. (Available in Spanish. *Reforma agraria en El Salvador*.)

Torres, José Galileo. 1985. The future of the agrarian reform in El Salvador. Paper presented at the Symposium on El Salvador, American Agricultural Economics Association annual meetings, Ames, Iowa, August.

Weisleder, Jaime, and Alfredo López-Calleja. 1982. *El problema del sistema registral inmobilario de El Salvador frente al otorgamiento de títulos originadas en la aplicación del Decreto 207, y posibles soluciones*. San Salvador: Servicios Técnicos del Caribe, USAID, November.

Wise, Michael P. 1986a. *Agrarian reform in El Salvador: Process and progress*. San Salvador: USAID Rural Development Office, September.

———.1986b. *Report on Phase III of the agrarian reform in El Salvador*. San Salvador: USAID Rural Development Office, August.

Chapter 16

El Salvador: Reform Prevents Change

Martin Diskin*

Although agrarian reform has long been a central concern for Salvadoran social scientists, activists, and peasant organizations, it was not until after the 15 October 1979 military coup that one was instituted. In early 1980, the reforms were decreed by the military-civilian junta. Now, more than 6 years later, with the distributive phases of the reform in the past, there is sufficient experience and information to answer two crucial questions. Is the Salvadoran agrarian reform a success? Who has benefited?

The circumstances leading to an agrarian reform and the manner of its implementation are conditioned by the nature of the government, its political orientation, and often, as in this case, its international links. In El Salvador, the civilian-military junta that took power in 1979 began with a progressive, even radical, vision of reforming the agrarian structure of the country. Although it succeeded in launching the beginning of an agrarian reform, as military hardliners and the traditional agrarian oligarchy recouped their power and replaced the reformers, the reform effected less and less change. Many large land holdings not expropriated during 1980 are still in the hands of their original owners. A much-vaunted smallholders' reform has barely accomplished half of its goals. And the land and resources that have been transferred have burdened their new owners with excessive debt and a lack of auxiliary services, so that many of the reform cooperatives are already bankrupt. Although all of the rural people who have become part of the reform take it seriously, the reform's administrators, have not helped it to accomplish any real improvement in rural welfare.

* Professor of Anthropology, Massachusetts Institute of Technology, Cambridge, Massachusetts.

The Reagan administration publicly approved the agrarian reform, particularly when it was trying to convince Congress to appropriate military and economic support for the government of El Salvador. At that time, Washington called the military funding requests a "shield" behind which reforms could be implemented. Once Congress began to acquiesce and appropriations flowed freely, from about mid-1984 (and the election of Duarte), land reform ceased to be of interest to the Reagan administration, the press, or Congress. The reform helped to protect the economic and military aid from the United States as well as the essentially military policy pursued by the Reagan administration and willingly agreed to by President José Napoleón Duarte.

WHAT IS AGRARIAN REFORM?

Agrarian reform is meant to correct or eliminate some or all of the conditions of agrarian production that give rise to inequality, poverty, and political powerlessness. "Reform" means that access to the means of production must cease to be a privilege of the few. Measures such as land redistribution, tenurial change, extension and credit services, and wage and welfare improvements must be fairly enacted. Hand in hand with this must go the organizational tools to allow new beneficiaries to participate actively in the process of change and become qualified to direct their own futures. In short, agrarian reform is one aspect of a process of social change which involves more openness, representativeness, and democracy in the entire social system.

Land redistribution is a necessary but not sufficient condition for real reform. Whether land reform is redistributivist, collectivist (Lipton 1974), or simply involves regularization of tenure (such as giving titles to squatters), the material and political support for the reform will be a determining factor in its success. Direct changes in the welfare of the peasantry (minimum wage legislation or specification of working conditions for farm laborers) and their greater access to the political process (creation of peasant or farm-worker unions) are other measures to support the peasantry.

The sequence and timing of changes are matters of great importance. Reform should be rapid and firm. Based on a survey of many reforms, Tai states, "a public program of land reform that seeks compulsory, drastic, and rapid tenurial changes is one of substance and meaning. A public program that aims at voluntary, moderate, and gradual tenurial adjustments is bound to be perfunctory and ineffectual" (Tai 1974, 18). For John K. Galbraith, "a land reform is a revolutionary step; it passes power, property and status from one group to another" (Tai 1974, 17).

One determining factor in any agrarian reform is who initiates it. Although there are advocates of "top-down" reform, involving a process of "trickle-down" benefits (Millikan, in Tai 1974, 108), it would be naive to assume that those who monopolize power and land will simply step aside and divest themselves of their wealth and social position. The Salvadoran rural oligarchy regularly advocates a "trickle-down" argument while lobbying for less "statism," that is, less reform.

Related to this is the "radicalness" of the reform—whether a proposed reform goes far enough to correct the situation. On the surface, this debate is between those who say "half a loaf is better than none" and the purists. Even a little reform will be of some help where the state is relatively pluralistic and at least somewhat inclusive of all social sectors. But where power is monopolized and repression is widespread, a little reform (especially if it is initiated by an elite) is subject to the caprice of those in charge, and momentary gains may be quickly undone.

THE SALVADORAN REFORM

Antecedents

In the nineteenth century, the "liberal" reform provided the instrument for the new coffee elite to acquire control of Indian lands previously planted to grain (mostly maize) under communal tenure arrangements (Browning 1971, 174–212). Once the pattern of land use was well established in a coffee-dominated agrarian economy, unrest and misery grew in the countryside. The response to strikes by coffee workers was the infamous government *matanza* of 1932, where as many as thirty thousand peasants were murdered (Anderson 1971).

Since then, the rural population has been deprived of land and political rights and impoverished. In 1950, 60.6 percent of all farms were in holdings of 2 hectares or less, and that percentage increased to 70.1 percent in 1971, making the Salvadoran land distribution one of the most skewed in the world (Deere and Diskin 1984). In 1950, 43 percent of farms of less than 1 hectare was held in ownership and 57 percent in nonownership land-tenure forms such as rental (*arrendamiento simple*) or service tenure (*colonia*). By 1971, only 28.5 percent of farms of less than 1 hectare were owned and 71.5 percent were in other tenure forms, mostly rental. By 1975, 40.9 percent of all rural families was classified as landless, a marked increase from 1971 (29.1 percent) and 1961 (11.8 percent) (Deere and Diskin 1984, 17–19). The U.S. Agency for International Development

(USAID) estimated the number of Salvadoran "rural poor" in the 1970s at 2,040,607, or 83.5 percent of the rural population. Of that number, at least one-third was landless farm-worker families. This population of rural poor lived below an income of about $225 (U.S. dollars) per capita in 1977 (Daines and Steen 1977, 19–24, 35–36), with all the attendant low indices of welfare associated with this situation (Deere and Diskin 1984, 9–15).

In general, smaller holdings were more intensely cultivated and devoted to basic grain production while large properties were kept in a combination of fallow and lucrative agroexport crops like coffee, cotton, and sugar. The pattern of land use by those who controlled the larger holdings was neither rational nor productive.[1] If land was really the "scarce" factor of production in the countryside, most landlords made no effort to maximize production from it.

The predominant condition of the rural poor is frequently described as one of "semiproletarization" (Cabarrús 1983). The relative stasis and traditional equilibrium of the peasant community had been shattered, but new forms of social action, such as labor unions, appropriate to wage earners were severely repressed.

During the 1970s there was increasingly brutal repression, on the one hand, and more focused political organization among campesinos (with the Church as an important actor), on the other. It was also a time of such intense ferment that opposing forces appeared to be headed toward an explosion. The repression of political expression was carried out by the military and the security forces (army, treasury police, national police, national guard). They served as the defenders of the landowning oligarchy, who in turn monopolized political power. This system, which was part of a general philosophy of national development, has been identified by Enrique Baloyra as a "reactionary despotism" (Baloyra 1982). Christian-based communities and organized peasant groups suffered violent retribution from any effort to even discuss the need for change.[2] In 1976, Colonel Arturo Molina, the president, sponsored a modest attempt at reform, called an "agrarian transformation". Although Molina, the candidate of the military and the oligarchy, came to power in a universally acknowledged fraudulent election, his land experiment was seen as too permissive and his replacement (through another fraudulent presidential election in 1977), Colonel Carlos Humberto Romero, instituted even more repressive measures to ensure public "order." In spite of the denunciations of election fraud, massive suppression of human rights, and wholesale violence (Diskin and Sharpe 1986), this Salvadoran regime did not evoke any strong reaction from the Carter administration at the time. The setting was propitious for a reprise of the 1932 *matanza*.

Origins of the 1980 Reform

The military coup of 15 October 1979 was an effort to halt this destructive process and introduce reformist measures that would prevent a bloodbath while preserving the integrity of the armed forces.[3]

In the armed forces, proclamation on the date of the coup, the government was blamed for violations of human rights and for public and judiciary corruption; the army accused the government of having "brought about a veritable economic and social disaster" and of having "disgraced the country and the armed forces" (AWC and ACLU 1982, 260–263). Further, the problems of the country were said to be "the result of the antiquated economic, social and political structures...structures that do not offer the majority of the inhabitants the minimum conditions essential for their human self-fulfillment" (AWC and ACLU 1982, 260). The 1976 Agrarian Transformation was described as "timid structural changes [that] have been halted by the economic and political power of conservative sectors, which have always defended their ancestral ruling-class privileges" (AWC and ACLU 1982, 261). The proclamation advocated an agrarian reform as well as other reforms to the financial and foreign trade systems. The stated goals of agrarian reform were to "bring about an *equitable distribution of national wealth, while at the same time rapidly increasing the gross national product*" [AWC and ACLU 1982, 262 (italics added)].

The goals of income distribution, fuller employment, and welfare were also elaborated in the Agrarian Reform Law (Decree 153) of 6 March 1980. The first paragraph of the preamble to the decree ensured "the right to private property *within a communal framework*" (italics added). The second paragraph stated that "[t]he present law...does not satisfy the demands of the destitute majority of the population of this country, *their situation being the result of a single privileged class, contrary to the objectives of real economic, social and political development*" (italics added). The next paragraph spoke of developing "a new social order...thereby rejecting the prevailing interests of the minority."[4]

Decree 154 was the implementing instrument for the basic law which ordered expropriation of estates over 500 hectares and converted them into producer cooperatives for peasants. This became known as Phase I. Phase II was to have been the confiscation of estates of 100–150 (depending on soil quality) to 500 hectares. Phase III, or Decree 207, gave individual titles to those who worked land under tenancy arrangements. The basic law did not spell out how the cooperatives were to be established and run, how credit was to be supplied, or how the technical and social assistance was to be provided—all of these matters were to be specified in subsequent regulations and implemented by the Salvadoran Institute of Agrarian Transformation

(*Instituto Salvadoreño de Transformación Agraria,* ISTA), the reform agency created in 1976. But since most of the framers of the basic law were going into exile and joining the Democratic Revolutionary Front (*Frente Democrático Revolucionario,* FDR) to express their opposition to the wave of human-rights violations sweeping the countryside, implementing the regulations became the responsibility of an increasingly right-wing military-civilian junta.

At its inception, the basic law enjoyed a good deal of Salvadoran support. But the design of Decree 207 was, by many accounts, a U.S. import (see Prosterman 1972, 1969). One Salvadoran landowner told me that it was the only piece of legislation in the history of the country that had to be translated into Spanish. It was authored by Roy Prosterman, a professor at the Law School of the University of Washington.[5] With experience on other agrarian reforms, including one in Vietnam in 1969, Prosterman worked on the basic law as well as Decree 207 on behalf of an AFL-CIO-sponsored group, the American Institute for Free Labor Development (AIFLD) that, in turn, sponsored a Salvadoran peasant association, the *Unión Comunal Salvadoreña* (UCS). Most of the AIFLD budget came from USAID and, more recently, from the National Endowment for Democracy.

Prosterman elaborated a set of ideas explaining how the kind of tenurial change he proposed ("land to the tiller") would produce economic development and political stability. According to him, the plots previously worked under tenancy and share arrangements would show increased productivity and higher rates of capitalization once they became the property of the "tillers." Because they would have land, the attractiveness of the armed opposition in the eyes of the peasantry would be reduced (Prosterman 1976). In Prosterman's (1982) terminology, land reform would reduce the "index of rural instability." He also offered an estimate of the affected population, stating that if Decree 207 were fully implemented, between 137,000 and 183,000 families would actively claim title to the plots they worked. Furthermore, he calculated that 50,000 families were cooperative members in Phase I. This total number (187,000 to 233,000 families) represented for Prosterman about "two-thirds of the number of such potential-beneficiary groups." That is, the grand total of beneficiaries, excluding those who might benefit from Phase II, would be between 279,000 and 347,000 families, or between 66 and 83 percent of the rural population. The consequence of reform in El Salvador would be to transform the agrarian landscape into one dominated by small- and medium-sized private landowners with a few cooperatives. He immodestly called this the "most sweeping land reform in Latin American history." Table 1 shows the initial goals of the reform.

Table 1
Estimated benefits at the beginning of agrarian reform (1981)[a]

	Area		Beneficiaries	
	Number of hectares	Percentage of Total land in farms[b]	Number of families	Percentage of rural population[c]
Phase I	223,000	15.4	50,000[d]	11.9
Phase II	343,000	23.6	50,000[e]	11.9
Phase III	175,000[f]	12.1	150,000[g]	35.7
Total	741,000	51.1	250,000	59.5

[a] Sources: Donald Paarlberg et al., *Agrarian Reform in El Salvador* (n.p.: Checchi and Co., 1981); Roy Prosterman, "The Demographics of Land Reform in El Salvador since 1980," in *Statistical Abstract of Latin America*, vol. 22, ed. James M. Wilkie and Stephen Haber (Los Angeles: UCLA Latin American Center, University of California, 1982), pp. 589–598.
[b] The basis for total land in farms is 1,452,000 hectares, from the 1971 agrarian census.
[c] Total number of agricultural families equals 420,000. This uses the Prosterman figure and is less than the Paarlberg et al. (1981, 96) number of 480,000. The higher number would produce a smaller relative effect of the reform.
[f] Agrees with Paarlberg et al. (1981,1616) and is within range of Prosterman's "active participation" estimate (1982,table 3705).
[d] Prosterman's number, revised downward from 62,000 (1981); Paarlberg et al. uses the number for cooperative membership (Paarlberg et al. 1981,96).
[e] Paarlberg et al. 1981,96.
[g] Paarlberg et al. (1981). Prosterman (1982) claims 183,000 "active families" with several thousand more to be identified.

The optimism of Table 1 loses much of its sheen when measured against the needs of the entire rural population. First, 40 percent or more of the rural population (800,000 to 1,000,000 landless people) are not statutorily included in the reform, even though, from Prosterman's criteria of economic development and allegiance to the government, they are the most important segment of the rural population. Except for the landless among the resident work force on confiscated landholdings of Phase I, none of the hard-core rural poor received any benefits.[6]

Second, for the most part the acreage definitions for reform ignore land use. Although the 1971 agrarian census lists 30 percent of all land in farms as "natural [that is, unimproved] pasture," it is likely that this represents larger landowners' penchant for raising cattle rather than the most productive use of land. Indeed, the situation seemed to cry out for an idle lands law to stimulate large, well-run farms to produce more and to threaten those holdings that were decapitalizing and/or failing to produce with expropriation. Further planning could have created incentives to achieve a balance among the population's food needs, especially in basic grains (maize, sorghum, and beans) and hard-currency-producing agroexport crops (coffee, cotton, and sugarcane).

Some attention to crop mix could have had an impact on income for the poorest rural families. Simply planting 1.1 hectares of specialty or permanent crops would lift a rural family out of the poorest category. Those families with less land (the average holding in the less-than-2-hectare category is 0.97 hectare) would still benefit enormously from this cropping pattern (Daines and Steen 1977, 41).

Shortly after the implementation of Phase I, it was announced that Phase II would be "indefinitely suspended." Phase II accounted for some 24 percent of all land in farms, including about 31 percent of national coffee production, and was made up of a large percentage of prime land and well-capitalized farms. Salvadorans refer to this as the "spinal column" of the country's agrarian production structure. To minimize its significance, Prosterman emphasized that it amounted to only 17 percent of all cropland. This low index of land-use intensity should have been even more reason to include it in the agrarian reform (Prosterman et al. 1981, 67, n.).

Others knowledgeable in matters of agrarian reform, such as members of the Land Tenure Center (LTC) at the University of Wisconsin, were aware of the complexity and variety of land-tenure arrangements that existed in El Salvador. Somewhat perturbed by the simplistic way Prosterman dealt with the category "tenancy," in one memo they say, "in El Salvador tenancy implies far more than a big landlord renting parcels of his land to others; it makes the Philippine situation look much simpler by comparison, though even that situation is far more complex than originally perceived" (Kanel and Thiesenhusen 1980). Land Tenure Center specialists were in San Salvador during the spring of 1980 when Prosterman was writing Decree 207, but they were effectively frozen out of the process. The former U.S. ambassador to El Salvador, Robert White, explained to me that while he was not involved with the details of land reform policy, he was somewhat suspicious of the "experts" of the LTC and liked the logic of Prosterman's approach.[7]

Norman Chapin, an AID employee with considerable experience in El Salvador, wrote a valuable account of the rural situation on the eve of the reform (Chapin 1980a, 1980b). He found widespread ignorance of the reforms among the potential beneficiaries. He was able to draw several useful distinctions among different types of agricultural operations, each of which would require a slightly different reform approach. For example, among Phase I cooperatives, he felt that small, peasant-run cooperatives, although they were embryonic examples of the democratization of the countryside, needed significant support to handle the burden of paperwork and extension help with crop and farm management. In contrast, on the larger properties, occupational and class stratification still existed after the reform; for the peasant beneficiary this meant merely the exchange of one boss for another.

After Decree 207 had passed, Chapin found vast confusion among those who were to administer it and those who were to benefit from it. Although Prosterman repeatedly called Decree 207 "self-implementing," that is, ownership was to transfer automatically to the beneficiary with the passage of the decree, Chapin found that none of the potential beneficiaries believed that the land was theirs simply because of a junta proclamation.

One glaring weakness of Phase III is illustrated by Chapin's useful discussion (see Chapin 1980b, 11–12) about the varieties of rental arrangements, especially the fact that very small properties are often rented by poor owners to poor neighbors, friends, and kin in villages. The transfer of these small properties would only marginally benefit the new owners while devastating the old ones, who often needed the small income as support because of age or infirmity.

After field study, Chapin concluded that the land reform program was ill-conceived with inadequate appreciation of the rural situation. Especially with regard to Decree 207, the "self-executing" provision was not working. For the prospective beneficiary, after submitting an application for ownership (itself a brave act, given the violence of the countryside), there were still the complexities of proving that one had worked the land, providing a precise description of the parcel, and coping with numerous bureaucratic ambiguities. The more important reason, though, was the understandable reticence on the part of peasants to begin applying for land without any sign that there was political will to support such applications. Chapin states, "Thus far most rental arrangements among small renters and small property owners have been apparently continued as if Decree 207 had never been announced" and "[t]he reaction of owners of large properties has been largely hostile." Further, "There are indications that some of the highest officials in the Ministry of Agriculture and other corners of the government are not committed to Decree 207. Some have been actively opposing it" (Chapin 1980b, 1–2).

Within 6 months of the military coup of 15 October 1979, agrarian reform legislation was on the books. Those who could contribute to the planning of the reform were kept at arm's length, while those who had a special ideological axe to grind were given center stage because of the counterinsurgency element of their argument. Those who opposed change in 1976, those "privileged sectors" referred to in the October Proclamation, became active enemies of reform along with their historic allies in the system of "reactionary despotism." In all of this, the government of the United States actively complied. The "Revolutionary Junta of Government," as the junta was called in U.S. Embassy cable traffic, quickly underwent a move to the right through the successive replacement of reformist elements with the old guard, especially military figures. Concurrent with the agrarian reform decree was the imposition of a state of siege, which granted vast and extraordinary powers to the military and was renewed every 30 days from March 1980 until January 1987. Thus, after a moment of euphoric optimism, the agrarian reform quickly fell under the control of those who had historically opposed it.

Implementation: 1980–1982

Phase I became a de facto reality in short order. The military, in coordination with the ISTA staff, planned the confiscation even before the actual decree was announced on 6 March 1980. By the time the reform was announced by the Armed Forces Press Commission (COPREFA), the ISTA technicians, together with army and security-force units, were already arriving at those properties over 500 hectares. After the military would secure the property and inform the owner of the reform, the ISTA personnel would explain the new organization to those people who were working the property. At that moment, an election was held for officers of the new cooperative that was organized on the spot. On 6 and 7 March alone, 96 properties were expropriated. Most of the 300-odd properties were expropriated by May 1980.

Almost as quickly, reports of killings by the armed forces of the new cooperative leadership began to arrive from Phase I properties (Simon and Stephens 1982,11). Reports of demands for extortion payments arrived as well. These demands were made by the armed forces to ensure "security," food and fuel, and other "services" (Diskin 1982, 37) from the fledging organization. In the 1980–1982 period, human-rights abuses reached gruesome levels (Neier 1985, 115–140). The state of siege ensured a free hand for the military and made monitoring the situation difficult. It is clear, nevertheless, that an overwhelming majority of the victims were rural people; those with most to fear were men in the draft-age category.

In the 6 months following the October coup, swift change occurred. The reformist excitement was challenged by structural backsliding by the junta, the increasingly repressive measures of the armed forces, and the free operation of the death squads (Neier 1985, 130–133). During these 6 months, the political equilibrium moved from somewhat positive toward reform to a position of outright hostility to it. Phase I was set in place, but the political mood would not permit the implementation of the more significant Phase II. Phase III was born with difficulty. This land-to-the-tiller program was not very threatening to the power structure, so it was allowed to commence but not to thrive.

Phase III was far from self-implementing. "Utter paralysis" might be a better description. Between April 1980 and January 1981, funds had to be raised to pay for an administrative staff and a mechanism had to be devised for implementation. The *Financiera Nacional de Tierras Agrícolas* (FINATA), the government agency offering administrative support, was set in motion 8 months after Decree 207 was passed in April 1980. However, the constant violence that plagued the countryside continued to cast a pall over the reform.

In a December 1981 document, the UCS claimed that 25,000 Decree 207 beneficiaries had been evicted from their land[8] and gave specific accounts of military complicity in attacking the reform; a list of "promoters" who were killed or had disappeared was also provided (UCS 1981). AIFLD continually denounced the Salvadoran government and threatened to oppose U.S. aid if the murderers of the director of the Agrarian Reform Agency and two members of AIFLD's international staff were not brought to justice. Although the soldiers who did the killing were eventually convicted, their superiors were never brought to justice. In the December 1987 amnesty proclaimed by President Duarte, the killers were also released.

The 1982–1984 Period

Agrarian reform in El Salvador was presented to the American public twice a year when Congress required the president to "certify" that El Salvador was making continued social and economic progress in a number of specified areas, including agrarian reform. Documentation was provided in the form of applications received, provisional titles issued, and definitive titles granted for Phase III and for compensation and titling in Phase I. These numbers revealed deeper problems.

In Phase III (see Table 2), the movement from application to provisional and then definitive titling went slowly. Peasants who submitted applications were not yet legal owners and were vulnerable to violent eviction. About one-third of all beneficiaries were illegally evicted, but eventually three-quarters of those were reinstated. By mid-1984, applications for Decree 207 land first dwindled and then ceased, as did the process of provisional and definitive titling. Only evictions increased markedly, as resistance to Decree 207 hardened. By May 1985, the Legislative Assembly, still with its rightist majority, formally suspended Decree 207. By the end of 1985, a total of 63,668 families had submitted 79,142 applications under Decree 207, accounting for 6.8 percent of the farmland in El Salvador. Of that number, only one-quarter (16,992) had received definitive titles as of July 1986. The rest are still being processed by FINATA. Because of legal challenges by ex-landowners and other difficulties, FINATA

Table 2
Implementation of Phase III, cumulative data[a]

Date	Number of Families	Percentage of all land	Applications received	Provisional titles	Definitive titles	Evictions	Reinstatements
07/81	14,735	—	19,015	1,440	0	—	n.d.
01/82	25,680	—	32,787	22,061	0	—	n.d.
07/82	29,706	3.37	37,235	32,349	251	—	2,138
01/83	45,743	5.06	58,551	35,281	1,146	4,791	2,532
07/83	51,089	5.56	64,874	43,186	2,691	4,907	3,702
01/84	61,652	6.45	76,861	55,634	6,084	4,907	3,702
07/84	63,611	6.65	79,079	56,152	9,205	18,572[c]	15,453
01/85	63,668	6.8	79,142	64,585	12,186	19,113	15,723
07/85	63,668	6.8	79,142	66,652	14,846	19,113	15,723
12/85	63,668	6.8	79,142	65,782	16,992	19,113	15,723

[a] Source: El Salvador agrarian reform monthly reports (USAID).
[b] — = no data.
[c] The enormous increase in evictions (and reinstatements) coincides with the presidential campaigns of March and May 1984.

Table 3
Implementation of Phase I, cumulative data[a]

Date	Number of properties	Number of beneficiaries (co-op members)	Definitive titles (cumulative)	Number of properties compensated[b]
07/81	282	31,000	0	47 ($27,856,818)
01/82	329	34,728	3	85 ($53,383,510)
07/82	329	29,755	18	117 ($77,127,809)
01/83	329	29,755	22	128 ($82,600,825)
07/83	426	32,317	23	156 ($102,810,526)
01/84	426	31,359	47	212 ($136,056,762)
07/84	439	31,359	54	250 ($163,809,221)
01/85	427	31,359	58	266 ($166,577,118)
07/85	472	31,359	94	285 ($175,024,230)
12/85	469	31,359	127	311 ($187,821,611)

[a] Source: El Salvador agrarian reform monthly reports (USAID).
[b] The cumulative amount paid in U.S. dollars is given in parentheses.

expects eventually to complete titling for only about 47,000 of the 63,668 eligible families.

Some beneficiaries made payments against their 30-year mortgages as a way of establishing ownership rights even without definitive title. Those with provisional titles were eligible to apply for credit, although little credit was actually available for them. In the presidential certification reports, these bottlenecks were never described in political terms, nor were they seen as problems. By limiting the evaluation of the reform to quantitative accounts, serious questions of rural welfare, political expression, and the physical security of beneficiaries were bypassed.

Table 3 shows that the number of member beneficiaries remained remarkably constant. Over the entire period, the awarding of definitive titles to the cooperatives lagged far behind the number of properties compensated. This left many cooperatives in a state of insecurity. Many cooperatives were fearful that the reform could still be rolled back, even though ex-landowners were receiving compensation.

Arena Control of the Reform

After elections for the Constituent Assembly in 1982, the country's extreme right-wing party, *Alianza Republicana Nacionalista* (ARENA), was given administration of the Ministry of Agriculture as a patronage plum—the price it had asked for not destabilizing the interim government. Agriculture included one of the largest ministerial budgets in the country and the entire agrarian reform apparatus, ISTA. Although it held control for 2 years, until the presidential elections of 1984, ARENA's antipathy to the reform was well known. ARENA was not as hostile toward Decree 207 (although there were numerous attacks on its constitutionality) as it was toward Phase I. ARENA and other groups of the far right, including the National Association for Private Enterprise (*Asociación Nacional de la Empresa Privada,* ANEP), regarded Phase I as a frontal assault on private ownership and evidence of U.S. socialist tendencies.

Beneficiaries of Phase I complained that the political direction of ISTA was prejudicial to them. ISTA chose to see the UCS staff members who worked on the properties as sympathetic to the Christian Democrats. ISTA antipathy toward the reform it was charged with implementing was expressed in various ways. First, where possible, the ISTA delayed credit, so that key inputs did not arrive at planting time. Furthermore, the UCS staff was frequently transferred from one property to another to impede their organizing efforts. At times, permission was denied for certain cooperatives to sell cattle or to change their production pattern. *Co-gestión* (co-management), designed as an interim partnership between a cooperative and ISTA, was thus being used to retard self-management, the reform's professed goal.

RESULTS OF THE REFORM

Land and Beneficiaries

Accomplishments (see Table 4) fell far short of the enthusiastic predictions made at the the reform's inception. The most optimistic estimates and predictions were made by U.S. officials and consultants who worked as reform advisors. Salvadoran agrarian reform workers were always less sanguine and more realistic about the capacity of their government to carry out reform. They were also more aware of what reform entailed and considered continued services, technical aid, and physical protection of beneficiaries to be as important as land redistribution to the reform's success.

A recent evaluation of the reform states, "Perhaps the most important finding...is that the area and the number of beneficiaries of the agrarian reform have stagnated" (MAG-OSPA-PERA 1985b, ii). Much of this is attributed to underutilized land on the cooperatives, reform land abandoned by beneficiaries, and the unwillingness of cooperatives to expand their membership. The agrarian debt on cooperatives, poor

Table 4
Agrarian reform outcome versus original estimated goals[a]

	Area hectares	Percentage of Goal[b]	Percentage of farmland	Number of families benefited	Percentage of goal	Percentage of rural families
Phase I	218,566	98	15.1	31,259[c]	68	7.5
Phase II	—	—	—	—	—	—
Phase III	96,566	55	6.7[d]	63,668[e]	42[e]	15.2
Total	315,132	42	21.8	95,027	38	22.7

[a] Source: El Salvador agrarian reform monthly reports (USAID).
[b] Based on stated goals (see Table 1 in this chapter).
[c] This is the number of cooperative members in Phase I. Since there may be more than one member per family, a more reasonable estimate of the total number of families would be around 25,000.
[d] This is based on 1,452,000 hectares as the total land in farms. It disagrees slightly with the monthly report figure.
[e] There may be only 47,000 definitive titles finally issued, which is only 31 percent of the original goal.

prices for agricultural commodities, and the low level of technical assistance have all worsened the situation (MAG-OSPA-PERA 1985b, ii).

Comparing the predictions of reform benefits made in 1980 with the reform's actual performance at the end of 1985, there were about 155,000 fewer beneficiary families (about 930,000 people) than originally hoped for and about 425,000 fewer hectares incorporated into the reform. On these two counts, the reform accomplished less than half of its own goals.

To this shortfall in beneficiaries must be added the 150,000 or so families not eligible for benefits. These roughly 1.8 million people excluded from the reform represent at least three-quarters of the rural population, the poorest and most needy rural people in the country.

Aside from the 12 percent of coffee land distributed through Phase I, no other coffee lands were given out (Phase III applies to rented lands, and coffee land is almost never rented). Thus, redistribution of access to wealth was quite negligible. Of all land in farms in the country, 80 percent still belongs to its original owners.

In late 1986, the Duarte government discussed the reactivation of Phase II. In its original formulation, Phase II would have included 343,000 hectares, less possible the amount taken under a right-of-reserve clause; its present content is significantly less. Because of Articles 105 and 106 of the 1983 Constitution (a product of the rightist-dominated assembly), the upper limit of permissible landownership was changed to 245 hectares from the original 100 hectares. Further, owners of Phase II properties were given 3 years in which to divide or sell their property. As this period drew to an end in 1986, the estimated total amount of eligible land has dwindled to only 17,000 hectares (MAG-OSPA-PERA 1986, 30–31). Even if the government makes the gesture of implementing Phase II, an acreage equivalent to 5 percent of the original goal makes this exercise little more than a cruel joke.

Agrarian Debt

The law stipulated that agrarian reform land was to be paid for by beneficiaries. That is, the amount the government paid for a farm became the amount of the mortgage for which the new cooperative was responsible (Nathan Associates 1984, I:v, 1–7; IIE 1985, 4–8). From the outset, Phase I properties were valued at the amount declared by owners during the 1976/77 crop year for real estate tax purposes. The idea was that these valuations might well be fairly low since no one would estimate high values if it meant paying more tax. Also, the self-assessed values would be "just." If landlords paid real estate taxes on this basis, why should not society expropriate using the same figures? Two complicating factors intervened to provide loopholes, however. Some argued that the self-assessments were high because landlords had decapitalized their properties since 1979. Fearing that their property would be incorporated into the reform, many had driven machinery and cattle across the Guatemalan border. Furthermore, since 1980, many landowners claimed higher than declared values for their expropriated properties, arguing that they had since effected improvements (such as planting fruit trees, for example). Most of these claims—however extravagant—were honored by ISTA (Nathan Associates 1984, IV:12). A member of the board that conducted reevaluation hearings told me that the necessary "before-after" documentary support was missing in most of the claims that were approved. Loopholes became, for ARENA, another way to reward its landowner constituency.

Since the final evaluation of many properties was delayed, the proceeds that accrued to cooperatives were held by the Agriculture and Livestock Development Bank (*Banco de Fomento Agropecuario*, BFA) in "restricted accounts." From these accounts, funds were deducted to be used to pay off the land debt and other credit obligations; the remainder was held in escrow. Funds were released only with the approval of ISTA. Since permission was required to pay members' advances (which came to be regarded as wages), this heightened the sense that beneficiaries had simply changed bosses rather than become owners capable of self-management (Nathan Associates 1984, 16–21).

The imposition of "managers" on certain properties proved to be an added financial burden that yielded negligible additional benefit. Often, these managers were sons of the ex-landowners, and they were frequently regarded by the cooperative members as having a surveillance function; few provided the technical and managerial support that the reform required. Indeed, paying the managers' salary was, for some cooperatives, a final factor leading to bankruptcy.

Debts greater than means to repay—the condition on most Phase I co-ops—should not be interpreted as beneficiary inefficiency or incompetence or as the failure of the cooperative model. Inadequate repayment capacity is a measure of the high operating costs and the handsome compensation to the ex-owners.

The amount of compensation is also politically important. Although expropriated, these ex-*latifundistas* still constitute a potent source of influence. Their ties to the military and the industrial private sector, as well as to those rural elite who still own their lands, make them a potential lobby, one anxious to reverse what has been accomplished. Rewarding them handsomely may effectively neutralize them for a while. Instead of burdening beneficiaries with excessive compensation, the needs of the new cooperatives call for subsidization, for income benefits, and for a manageable agrarian debt.

Credit and Services

The beneficiaries of Phase III were eager to own and utilize their land. About 20 percent of them made farmland improvements without any aid. Many have increased the rate of investment on their small plots, diverting their additional income away from consumption (MAG-OSPA-PERA 1985a, 105–110).

However, here again, beneficiary enthusiasm is not matched by government help. The percentage of Phase III beneficiaries receiving credit in 1984/85 is about half of that in 1981/82. Smaller properties, those less than 1.5 acres, receive almost no credit (MAG-OSPA-PERA 1985a, 83). In Phase I, some credit is now being granted for medium- and long-range capital improvements, a helpful tendency (MAG-OSPA-PERA 1985b, 169–170).

While increasing, social services to the beneficiaries are still deficient. About half of the Phase I cooperatives that were surveyed responded that the loss of their social workers would make no difference to them (MAG-OSPA-PERA 1985b, 116). These services are also poorly distributed, leaving many cooperatives without any contact with social workers. A sound cooperative organizational structure has not developed on many land reform properties, so many are similar to prereform plantations or little more than a series of private plots (PERA and CLUSA 1985,1). Since Phase I properties represent about ten times the value of those in Phase III, with only about 40 percent of the population of Phase III, there should be enough capital to solve these problems (MAG-OSPA-PERA 1985b, 166-177). But more than 30 percent of the Phase I cooperatives has no technical assistance. Furthermore, what technical services are offered tend to focus on animal and plant care and not on much-needed marketing and input acquisition (MAG-OSPA-PERA 1985b, 125–132).

Fewer than one-quarter of the Phase III beneficiaries receive any sort of technical assistance. One technical assistance project was found to be so defective that, in some cases, lower productivity was registered where assistance was offered (MAG-OSPA-PERA 1985a, 105–110; cf. FINATA 1985).

Beneficiaries in both Phase I and Phase III report only slight improvements in basic amenities. Although housing is one of the more desired benefits expected from the agrarian reform, in Phase I only 15.9 percent of the cooperatives have initiated housing programs and, in Phase III, 9.6 percent of the beneficiaries have received housing. Other improvements that are highly desired by beneficiaries, such as electricity, water, or sanitary facilities, occur in even fewer cases (MAG-OSPA-PERA 1985a, 151; MAG-OSPA-PERA 1985b, 98).

Rural Organizations

Organizations that could defend beneficiary interests are few and far between (MAG-OSPA-PERA 1985b, 110). Only the UCS constitutes a presence because of its strong support from AIFLD. During the 1970s, the UCS competed with other groups such as the *Federación de Campesinas Cristianas Salvadoreñas* (FECCAS) and the *Unión de Trabajadores del Campo* (UTC) (Cabarrús 1983; Dunkerley 1982). AIFLD often works against labor organizations which it regards as leftist (Fourché and Wheaton 1980) and supports those it considers democratic. Through the participation of the UCS in the labor coalition, *Unidad Productiva Democrática* (UPD), both rural and urban organized labor worked to ensure Duarte's victory as president. During Duarte's first year in office, however, he ignored labor demands, the UPD began to fall apart, and member groups began publicly to express their lack of support for Duarte. A new group was organized, the *Unión Nacional de Trabajadores Salvadoreños* (UNTS), which has incorporated parts of the UPD as well as new elements.

However, the UNTS sponsored public demonstrations and manifested opposition to the Duarte government. UNTS demanded the abolition of the agrarian debt, the implementation of Phase II (with the necessary constitutional changes to make it meaningful), more credit and services for reform beneficiaries, and a negotiated end to the war (*Proceso* 1986, 12–16). The rebirth and vigor of organized labor protest is one consequence of the more open atmosphere created by Duarte. It also expresses the frustration of many at the government's reluctance to embrace these organizations as part of the reform, which Duarte claimed to support during his electoral campaign. It also shows that the agrarian reform has not deflected or eliminated the basic problems of rural inequity in El Salvador. AIFLD now attacks the UNTS and continues to support Duarte and the Christian Democrats as the only "democratic" movement.

The agrarian reform was born during a civil war. It has not had a dampening effect on the open conflict because it has not addressed enough of the longstanding rural injustice to produce allegiance to the government. The Salvadoran military, under U.S. tutelage, has adopted the increased use of high-technology methods such as aerial bombardment, on the one hand, and a more sophisticated political approach (the so-called "low-intensity conflict"), on the other. In a manner reminiscent of Vietnam, the Salvadoran military once again serves up the rhetoric of reform in conjunction with a massive military presence in the countryside (Miles 1986).

CONCLUSION

U.S. policy in Central America has sought to contain radical change through military means and to reassert regional hegemony (LeoGrande et al. 1986). From this perspective—one that does not consider the campesinos, who constitute the majority group in the area, as especially important—Washington claims success for land reform in El Salvador. Land reform was a useful fallback when Congress was uncooperative and questioned the administration's foreign policy objectives. Present congressional acquiescence is a measure of the Reagan administration's "success" in that strategy.

For the rural poor in El Salvador, most of whom received no benefit, agrarian reform remains a distant goal, one yet to be achieved. Washington's cooperation with the Salvadoran military and oligarchy has put real reform on hold.

NOTES

1. Durham (1978, 21–54) shows how rural misery is more influenced by land-use patterns than by neo-Malthusian factors. See also USAID/El Salvador (1980, 3), which points out that "there exists an estimated 150,000 ha., now mostly in pasture or in fallow on larger farms, which is apt for crop production."

2. Cabarrús (1983) is precise in describing the way this process unfolded in the region of Aguilares, where Jesuits and diocesan priests operated in the formation of Christian base communities and peasant political organizing, especially the Salvadoran Federation of Christian Peasants (FECCAS).

3. For a fuller account of this period, see Montgomery (1982, chaps. 1, 6), Armstrong and Schenk (1982, chaps. 5, 6), and Dunkerley (1982, chaps. 9, 10).

4. These quotes from Decree 153 all come from Diskin (1982, 48).

5. Although Prosterman states that Decree 207 was similar to a reform proposed by Ivo Alvarenga in 1971, the essay he cites says almost nothing that resembles Decree 207. Rather, it suggests a 70-manzana upper limit on landowning, states that the government is not obliged to compensate ex-owners, gives priority to cooperative forms of land use, urges adherence to labor laws, and supports campesino organizations (Alvarenga 1977).

6. USAID's "Statistical Analysis of the Rural Poor" (Daines and Steen 1977) calculates around 800,000 landless, and Burke (1976, 476) lists 166,000 families without land.

7. Interview with Ambassador Robert White, Spring 1985.

8. From the outset, UCS defined "beneficiary" in Prosterman's literal sense, that is, anyone who satisfied the definition of eligibility for receiving land under Decree 207, whether or not they made application. AID defined "beneficiaries" as those people who actually submitted applications (Cobb 1983).

REFERENCES

Alvarenga, Ivo P. 1977. Proyecto de ley de reforma agraria. In *Temas de derecho agrario y reforma agraria*, pp. 116-176. San José, Costa Rica: EDUCA.

Anderson, Thomas P. 1971. *Matanza: El Salvador's communist revolt of 1932*. Lincoln: Univ. of Nebraska Press.

Armstrong, Robert, and Janet Schenk. 1982. *El Salvador: The face of revolution*. Boston: South End Press.

AWC and ACLU (Americas Watch Committee and American Civil Liberties Union). 1982. *Report on human rights in El Salvador*. New York: Vintage Books, 26 January.

Baloyra, Enrique. 1982. *El Salvador in transition*. Chapel Hill: Univ. of North Carolina Press.

Browning, David. 1971. *El Salvador: Landscape and society*. Oxford: Clarendon Press.

Burke, Melvin. 1976. El sistema de plantación y la proletarización del trabajo agrícola en El Salvador. *Estudios Centroamericanos 31*(335/336):473–486.

Cabarrús, Carlos Rafael. 1983. *Génesis de una revolución*. Mexico City: Casa Chata.

Chapin, Norman. 1980a. Difficulties with the implementation of Decree 207 ("land-to-the-tiller") in El Salvador's agrarian reform program. Memorandum. Washington, June.

———.1980b. A few comments on land tenure and the course of agrarian reform in *El Salvador. In El Salvador project paper: Agricultural reform organization, AID/LAC/P-060, Annex II.A.* Mimeograph. Washington: U.S. Agency for International Development.

Cobb, Jack. 1983. Survey of illegal evictions of beneficiaries of the Decree 207 agrarian reform program: 1980–83. Final report. Prepared for American Institute for Free Labor Development. San Salvador, September.

Daines, Samuel, and Dwight Steen. 1977. Statistical analysis of the rural poor: Target group: El Salvador, n.p. Prepared for AID Mission to El Salvador, April.

Deere, Carmen Diana, and Martin Diskin. 1984. *Rural poverty in El Salvador: Dimensions, trends, and causes.* Rural Employment Project Research Paper, no. WEP 10–6/WP64. Geneva: International Labour Office.

Diskin, Martin. 1982. 1982 supplement. In *El Salvador land reform, 1980–81: Impact audit,* edited by Laurence R. Simons and James C. Stephens, pp. 29–61. Boston: Oxfam-America.

Diskin, Martin, and Kenneth Sharpe. 1986. El Salvador. In *Confronting revolution: Peace through diplomacy in Central America,* edited by M.J. Blachman, W.M. LeoGrande, and K.E. Sharpe, pp. 50–87. New York: Pantheon.

Dunkerley, James. 1982. *The long war: Dictatorship and revolution in El Salvador.* London: Junction Books.

Durham, William. 1978. *Scarcity and survival in Central America: Ecological origins of the soccer war.* Stanford, Calif.: Stanford Univ. Press.

FINATA (Financiera Nacional de Tierras Agrícolas). 1985. Departamento de Planificación. *Primer evaluación general del proyecto de asistencia técnica a beneficiarios de Decreto 207 (Proyecto FINATA 02/85).* San Salvador: FINATA, December.

Fourché, Carolyn, and Philip Wheaton. 1980. History and motivations of U.S. involvement in the control of the peasant movement in El Salvador. Mimeograph. Washington: Ecumenical Program for Interamerican Communication and Action.

IIE (Instituto de Investigaciones Económicas). 1985. Universidad de El Salvador. Deuda agraria: ¿Quién debe a quién? *El Salvador: Coyentura Económica 1*(2), November.

Kanel, Don, and William C. Thiesenhusen. 1980. Controversial questions: Lowering the ceiling, "land to the tiller". Memo to USAID/El Salvador, 27 March. Land Tenure Center, University of Wisconsin-Madison.

LeoGrande, William M., Douglas C. Bennett, Morris J. Blachman, and Kenneth E. Sharpe. 1986. Grappling with Central America: From Carter to Reagan. In *Confronting revolution: Security through diplomacy in Central America,* edited by M.J. Blachman, W.M. LeoGrande, and K.E. Sharpe, pp. 295–328. New York: Pantheon Books.

Lipton, Michael. 1974. Towards a theory of land reform. In *Peasants, landlords, and governments,* edited by David Lehmann, pp. 269–315. New York: Holmes and Meier.

MAG-OSPA-PERA (Ministerio de Agricultura y Ganadería, Oficina Sectoral de Planificación Agrícola, Programa de Evaluación de la Reforma Agraria).

1985a. *Segundo perfil de beneficiarios del Decreto 207*. San Salvador: PERA, December.

———.1985b. *V evaluación del proceso de la reforma agraria*. PERA-1–07–85. San Salvador: PERA, December.

———.1986. *Estudio sobre la oferta potencial de tierras agrícolas en El Salvador*. PERA-1–04–86. San Salvador: PERA, June.

Miles, Sara. 1986. The real war: Low-intensity conflict in Central America. *NACLA Report on the Americas*, 22(2):17–48.

Montgomery, T.S. 1982. *Revolution in El Salvador: Origins and evolution*. Boulder, Colo.: Westview Press.

Nathan Associates, Robert R. 1984. *Analysis of the agrarian debt of Phase I agrarian reform cooperatives in El Salvador*, 2 vols. Washington: Nathan Associates.

Neier, Aryeh. 1985. El Salvador. In *With friends like these: The Americas Watch Report on human rights and U.S. policy in Latin America*, edited by Cynthia Brown, pp. 115–140. New York: Pantheon Books.

Paarlberg, Don, Ronald J. Ivey, and Peter M. Cody. 1981. *Agrarian reform in El Salvador*. n.p. Checchi and Co.

PERA and CLUSA (Programa de Evaluación de la Reforma Agraria and Cooperative League of the U.S.A.). 1985. *La cabida y los derechos y deberes de los socios de las cooperativas de la Estapa I de la reforma agraria salvadoreña*. San Salvador: PERA, 31 October.

Proceso. 1986. *Proceso: Informativo semanal*. San Salvador: Centro Universitario de Documentación e Información, Universidad Centroamericano "José Simeón Cañas," 6 August.

Prosterman, Roy. 1969. Land reform in Vietnam. *Current History*, December, pp. 67–68, 327–332.

———.1972. Land reform as foreign aid. *Foreign Policy*, no. 6 (Spring), pp. 128–141.

———.1976. IRI—A simplified predictive index of rural instability. *Comparative Politics*, April, pp. 339–343.

———.1982. The demographics of land reform in El Salvador since 1980. In *Statistical abstract of Latin America*, vol. 22, edited by James M. Wilkie and Stephen Haber, pp. 589–598. Los Angeles: UCLA Latin American Center, University of California.

Prosterman, Roy, Jeffrey M. Riedinger, and Mary N. Temple. 1981. Land reform and the El Salvador crisis. *International Security* 6(1):53–74.

Simons, Laurence R., and James C. Stephens. 1982. *El Salvador land reform, 1980–81: Impact audit*. Boston: Oxfam-America.

Tai, Hung-Chao. 1974. *Land reform and politics: A comparative analysis*. Berkeley: Univ. of California Press.

UCS (Unión Comunal Salvadoreña). 1981. *El Salvador land reform update: The land-to-the-tiller program*. Executive summary. San Salvador: UCS, 10 December.

United States. Agency for International Development. El Salvador. 1980. USAID agrarian reform sector strategy paper. n.p. 21 July.

Chapter 17

Contrast and Congruence in the Agrarian Reforms of El Salvador and Nicaragua

Nola Reinhardt*

This chapter compares the post-1979 agrarian reform programs of El Salvador and Nicaragua. Since that year, the basic political and economic models of these countries have diverged; a close analysis of their agrarian reforms reveals several similarities, however. Because these commonalities are often not expected, they are my central focus. I show that they can be explained by an economic development pattern that emphasizes the importance of agricultural exports.

First, pre-1979 reliance on trade created a reluctance on the part of both governments to expropriate land in the agroexport sector for agrarian reform purposes. As a result, the reforms were based primarily on large, traditional estates not involved in export production. The exception in the Nicaraguan case was the confiscation of the holdings of Somoza and his close associates after the revolution. Many of these "Somocista" properties grew agroexports, and the Sandinistas hoped that organizing them as state farms would preserve their value as export producers. Some large properties expropriated under the Salvadoran reform were also agroexport estates, but both reforms left untouched the medium-sized holdings, the principal agroexport producers of both countries.

A second constraining legacy was the strong antipeasant bias of the previous development pattern. Peasant producers historically had had not only limited access to land, but also little or no access to bank credit, modern inputs, technical assistance and training,

* Associate Professor of Economics, Smith College, Northampton, Mass. This chapter is a revised version of "Agroexports and the Peasantry in the Agrarian Reforms of El Salvador and Nicaragua," *World Development* 15(7), July 1987.

good transportation facilities, and nonexploitative marketing channels. Development of a viable peasant sector under the reforms required a concerted effort to build necessary supportive institutions. While the Nicaraguan government has moved much further than the Salvadoran in this regard, both have been constrained by a resource scarcity.

Third, the conditions of the small-producer sector in both countries reflected a negative attitude toward the peasantry on the part of the urban and rural middle classes and the elites. These groups viewed small-scale production as inherently inefficient. These attitudes have affected the progress of agrarian reform in both countries, although the differences between the two reforms on this point have recently become more marked. In 1985, a gradual movement of the Nicaraguan reform in a pro-peasant direction accelerated sharply. In fact, the Nicaraguan reform has continually shown more flexibility and responsiveness to pressure from rural workers and peasants than that in El Salvador.[1] Prior to 1985, however, both reforms had effectively transferred only limited control over land resources to rural workers and peasants.

This conclusion contrasts with the enthusiastic findings of early assessments of these reforms.[2] The differences stem in part from implementation shortfalls. However, these analyses also tend to accept at face value official figures which inflated the numerical accomplishments of the reforms and sidestepped hard questions about the nature of the reform sectors being created.[3]

I divide my analysis into two periods: 1979–1984, when the previously mentioned similarities were most evident, and 1985–1986, when important differences between the two become apparent. I also present some background on the economic development pattern of the pre-1979 period and summarize the basic features of both agrarian reform laws.

BACKGROUND: AGROEXPORT EXPANSION AND PRESSURES FOR LAND REFORM

The agricultural sectors of Central America in the 1970s have been frequently described as dualistic or bimodal—large landowners and impoverished peasants (*minifundistas*) in the case of El Salvador and capitalist farmers and wage laborers in Nicaragua. In fact, the agrarian structure was far more complex. It had been fundamentally shaped in each country by nineteenth and twentieth century agroexport expansion.

By the late 1800s and through the early twentieth century, coffee production dominated economic activity in both countries. There was some development of trade, commerce, and textile manufacturing, but these sectors derived their dynamism from coffee and were not independent sources of economic growth. This heavy reliance for overall economic growth on the expansion of agricultural exports defines an "agroexport economy."

The best lands for coffee in Nicaragua and El Salvador were on the western mountain slopes. These areas, rich in volcanic soil, were centers of smallholder staple-food production. Planters used a variety of mechanisms to displace many of these peasants in order to convert their land to large-scale coffee cultivation.[4] Some of the displaced peasant families migrated farther inland to claim land in less fertile mountain regions; others remained in the coffee zones to become a work force for the newly formed coffee estates.

The peasant household cultivated parts of the coffee plantation in exchange for usufruct rights to a plot of land on which subsistence crops could be grown (the *colonato* system). Since there were no scale advantages in coffee production, an estate was in essence a collection of small farms. Independent coffee-growing peasants were able to compete successfully with larger coffee farms.

As a result, mini-estates and peasant coffee cultivation developed alongside large estates, a pattern that persists to this day. Coffee yields in the 1960s were comparable on small and large farms (Weeks 1985, 110).[5] In 1961, Nicaraguan peasant holdings, considered to be those under 50 manzanas (1 manzana equals 0.7 hectares), accounted for 22 percent of Nicaraguan coffee production (see Table 1). Holdings between 50 and 500 manzanas, the medium (nonpeasant) producers, accounted for 58 percent of that production, while the large holdings (over 500 manzanas) accounted for only 20 percent. In El Salvador, peasant producers (under 10 hectares) accounted for 10 percent of 1961 coffee production. Medium holdings (10–200 hectares) accounted for 56 percent, while large holdings (over 200 hectares) produced 34 percent of that year's coffee crop. Within this latter category, farms of over 500 hectares accounted for only 14 percent of coffee production in 1975 (Simon and Stephens 1982, 13). The differences between the two countries in the criteria for peasant, medium, and large holdings are due to differences in population density.

The depression and attendant export crises of the 1930s had severe repercussions in El Salvador and Nicaragua. Recovery came only as international trade picked up after World War II. In addition to expansion of traditional exports, new agricultural exports began to grow rapidly: cotton in the 1950s, and beef and sugar in the 1960s. Cotton and sugar production expanded primarily in the Pacific coastal lowlands of both countries, while cattle raising became common in the central highlands of Nicaragua.

Table 1
Production of coffee and cotton by farm size, 1961[a]

Farm Size[b]	Total Output (%)	
	Coffee	Cotton
Nicaragua		
< 10 mz	5.0	1.6
10–50 mz	17.0	7.4
50–500 mz	57.9	60.2
> 500 mz	20.1	30.7
Total	100.0	99.9
El Salvador		
< 10 ha	10.4	6.4
10–50 ha	22.8	13.5
50–200 ha	32.9	27.8
> 200 ha	33.9	52.3
Total	100.0	100.0

[a] Source: CEPAL/FAO/OIT/SIECA/OCT/OEA, *Tenencia de la tierra y desarrollo rural en Centroamérica* (San José, Costa Rica: EDUCA, 1973), calculated from Table A-1, p. 159, and Table A-7, p. 164.
[b] One manzana (mz) equals 1.75 acres; one hectare (ha) equals 2.5 acres.

This second period of agricultural export expansion also affected the agrarian structure of both countries. First, the expansion of cotton and cattle resulted in a new wave of displaced peasant producers, primarily tenants on the traditional coastal estates and settlers without land title in the sierra frontiers (Williams 1986, chaps. 3 and 6; Biderman 1982). According to Robert Williams, the escalating conflict of the late 1960s in the Nicaraguan mountain region of Matagalpa had its roots in the displacement of peasants by cattle. Because cattle-raising generated little employment, some peasant farmers were forced to either migrate farther east in search of land or join the tenants evicted from coastal estates in towns and cities.

Cotton, unlike cattle, required a large seasonal labor force. In El Salvador, this labor force was initially assured through the *colonato* system. However, cotton production became increasingly incompatible with this system because it requires liberal applications of pesticides and fertilizers, operations which could be easily mechanized in the flat coastal lands. By the early 1960s in Nicaragua, and by the late 1960s in El Salvador, the *colonos* in the cotton zones had been largely replaced by machinery (especially for planting and spraying) and a large, seasonal wage-labor force (for harvest). This change in labor relations was permanent: even in the cotton slump of the 1960s, when cotton lands were switched to other crops such as sugar and grains, mechanized techniques and wage labor continued to be used and the *colonato* system was not reestablished (Williams 1986, chap. 3).

As with coffee, cotton was produced on small and medium as well as large farms. In both countries, the majority of cotton cultivators was peasant farmers: in 1963, 68 percent of cotton farms was under 50 manzanas in Nicaragua while 58 percent was under 10 hectares in El Salvador (Williams 1986, 32). However, in 1961, the peasant farms accounted for only 9 percent of cotton production in Nicaragua and 6.4 percent in El Salvador (see Table 1). This was due to the small size of these cotton farms, their location on marginal land, and the peasants' lack of access to credit and modern inputs. In 1961, the medium-sized cotton farms (50–500 manzanas in Nicaragua, 10–200 hectares in El Salvador) produced 60 percent of Nicaragua's and 41 percent of El Salvador's cotton output, while large farms accounted for 31 percent of cotton output in Nicaragua and 52 percent in El Salvador. Farms of over 500 hectares in El Salvador produced 31 percent of cotton output in 1975 (Simon and Stephens 1982, 13).

By the 1970s, peasant producers in both countries had lost access to most of the land in the rich, productive Pacific coast region. By 1978, 20 percent of the rural work force (or economically active population, EAP) in Nicaragua was landless, permanent agricultural workers, employed principally on the agroexport farms (see Table 2). Other peasants combined seasonal work, primarily in the cotton and coffee harvests, with income from their own small plots, from rented land, or from casual labor in the towns and cities. In Nicaragua, some 17 percent of the rural EAP was estimated to be landless seasonal workers in 1978; in fact, many were semiproletarian members of peasant smallholding households. After the Nicaraguan revolution, policymakers assumed that these two groups of workers had a "proletarian" consciousness; that is, the aspirations of these workers were for higher wages and better working conditions rather than for land. In El Salvador, 26 percent of agricultural households was landless in 1970, up from 12 percent in 1961 (Baloyra 1982, 30).[6]

Another 36 percent of the Nicaraguan rural EAP in 1978, those with holdings under 10 manzanas, probably relied on seasonal wage labor for part of household livelihood. In El Salvador, households with holdings under 7 hectares, probably inadequate for family needs, accounted for another 67 percent of rural families in 1970 (Table 2). In addition to seasonal wage labor, land-hungry peasants in both countries rented land from large, medium, and even small farms and used it for both export (mainly cotton) and staple-food production. These peasant renters are included along with small owner-operators in the official statistics on land tenure. Land rental by families with less than 2 hectares increased

Table 2
Status of peasant households in the 1970s[a]

	Rural economically active population (EAP) in Nicaragua, 1978 (%)	Rural households in El Salvador, 1970 (%)
Landless permanent workers	20	26[b]
Landless seasonal workers	17	
Poor peasants (0.1–10 mz/0.1–7 ha)	36	67
Medium to rich peasants (10–50 mz/7–35 ha)	22	5
Total peasant households	95	98

a Sources: For Nicaragua, unpublished 1983 data from the *Dirección General de la Reforma Agraria*. For El Salvador, John Weeks, *The Economies of Central America* (New York: Holmes and Meier, 1985), p. 112.
b Landless permanent and seasonal workers in El Salvador are reported jointly.

sharply between 1961 and 1971 in El Salvador (Weeks 1985, 120). Because households with inadequate landholdings depended on such a diversity of livelihood strategies, their characterization (as primarily "peasant" or primarily "proletarian") and the policies most likely to benefit them were to be the subject of considerable debate among Nicaraguan policymakers after the revolution. They are frequently referred to as "semiproletarians" because of their partial reliance on wage labor.

In Nicaragua, another important group of peasants are those who migrated to the mountain frontier in the north, where, on farms of between 10 and 50 manzanas, they combined coffee or cattle enterprises with the cultivation of basic grains. This group accounted for much of the 22 percent of Nicaragua's rural EAP in 1978 referred to as "family farmers" or "medium and rich peasants." This category is considerably smaller in land-scarce El Salvador, where only 5 percent of the farms were between 7 and 35 hectares in 1970. While the Nicaraguan family farmers of the northern highlands had access to land, however, they frequently lacked title and suffered from inadequate infrastructure and lack of agricultural inputs. Nicaragua's services to its farmers were still concentrated primarily in the Pacific region, an area of severe peasant land hunger.[7]

Despite the high population density of the Pacific Coast and some of the North, the growth of export agriculture in Nicaragua was so rapid that the cotton and coffee harvests brought labor shortages in the 1960s and 1970s. To fill this gap, workers were brought from the interior regions of the country and from El Salvador, where the national average population density in 1971 was ten times what it was in Nicaragua (SIECA 1981, Tables 3 and 5). Even where Salvadoran peasant households combined producing exports with staple crops in the interior mountain communities, they frequently relied on seasonal migration to supplement their inadequate farm income (Durham 1979, chap. 3).

There was another sector of considerable importance in the countryside, that of the traditional estates. In the 1970s, much land in both countries was still held by estates which combined extensive methods of cattle production with traditional forms of service tenure, cash rental, or sharecropping. Peasants relying on these arrangements for their access to land were more numerous in El Salvador than in Nicaragua, but were to be an important target population for both agrarian reforms.

Despite industrial promotion under the impetus of the Central American Common Market, what limited industrial expansion occurred in the 1960s did not blunt the fundamental importance of agricultural exports to both economies (Bulmer-Thomas 1983).[8] Agricultural export value continued to grow in the 1970s, especially due to rising commodity prices for coffee and sugar (Bulmer-Thomas 1983, 275).[9] Overall, agricultural growth, although not as rapid as manufacturing growth, continued strong through most of the 1970s.[10]

Agriculture's continued importance is reflected in indicators of employment, output, and foreign exchange. In El Salvador, agriculture accounted for 30 percent of the gross national product (GNP) and employed 47 percent of the labor force in 1977; for manufacturing, the figures were 15 percent each. In Nicaragua, agriculture accounted for 23 percent of GNP in 1977 and employed 44 percent of the labor force, while manufacturing figures were 20 and 14 percent, respectively (World Bank 1979, 130, 162). These figures understate the significance of the agricultural sector, since coffee processing and processing of other agricultural products is included in manufacturing (Weeks 1985, 52). Even more important than its global output and employment impact is the fact that agriculture continued to be a principal source of foreign exchange. In El Salvador, 64 percent of the total value of commodity exports in the 1975–1979 period were agricultural exports: coffee (47 percent), cotton (10 percent), sugar (6 percent), and beef (1 percent). In Nicaragua, five agricultural products accounted for 66 percent of commodity exports: coffee (25 percent), cotton (24 percent), beef (10 percent), sugar (6 percent), and bananas (1 percent) (Weeks 1985, 76–77).[11] These extraregional exports earned the hard currency necessary to import capital goods, spare parts, technology, industrial raw materials, some manufactured products (primarily for the growing middle class), and food, as well as to service international loans.[12] Finally, some crops which began as exports came to be used as raw-material inputs for emerging domestic industries such as textiles, sugar refining, and cooking oil. Thus, Weeks concludes that "production for export has been the dynamic factor in the economies of Central America" and that "within total trade that part which is extraregional has determined the tempo of growth" (Weeks 1985, 98).

Although the growth of agricultural exports resulted in rapid rates of growth of national output, the structural consequences of this reliance on agroexports led to mounting pressure for agrarian reform. In both countries, agroexport expansion had fostered highly concentrated land ownership and operation. By 1971 in El Salvador, 50 percent of the farms was under 2.5 acres, while the largest 2 percent of the farms controlled 50 percent of the land in farms (Browning 1983, 401). Similar inequities existed in Nicaragua, where, in 1978, the largest 5 percent of the farms accounted for 52 percent of the land in farms, and Somoza and his close associates alone controlled 20 percent of the agricultural land (CAHI 1985, 4c). These inequities stimulated rural tensions and generated rural support for nascent guerrilla groups in the 1960s.

Mounting rural tensions were somewhat relieved by migration to urban areas. Migration, however, generated a new set of problems. In Nicaragua, by the late 1970s, some 25 percent of the country's population lived in Managua. The figure was about 20 percent in San Salvador. Rapid urbanization in both countries strained urban resources, underlined the slow growth of industrial employment, and generated new political tensions in the cities. A key element in the maintenance of social order soon became the ability of the economy to provide the urban poor with affordable foodstuffs. This proved difficult because a contrary consequence of the agricultural export boom was the displacement of small-scale producers of staples to marginal land in the mountains. Without access to credit or modern inputs, these small farmers found it increasingly difficult to respond to a growing urban demand for marketed food.[13] Both countries resorted to increasing imports of basic foods, thereby worsening their debtor condition.

The rural elites were able to block reform implementation until the 1979 overthrow of Somoza and the progressive military coup in El Salvador that same year. Pressures for land reform were *not* due to the "failure" of the agroexport model but to its success in generating foreign exchange (Bulmer-Thomas 1983, 291). Concomitant to agricultural export expansion, production methods came to emphasize modern, capital-intensive techniques on medium and large estates. This was the case not only for cotton and sugar, but also to an increasing extent for coffee and cattle (Williams 1986, 70, 88–89, 93–95). Alain de

Janvry has described the general pattern of development of capitalist agriculture in Latin America as the modernization of estate production, arguing that this development has severely limited the possibility of redistributive reforms (de Janvry 1981). His thesis appears to have considerable relevance in the cases of El Salvador and Nicaragua. Their post-1979 agrarian reforms were constrained by the agroexport development legacy.

THE 1980 SALVADORAN AGRARIAN REFORM LEGISLATION

Three phases define the agrarian reform legislation adopted in El Salvador in 1980. The basic Agrarian Reform Law (Decree 153) was announced in March.[14] All holdings over 100 hectares (150 hectares for poorer quality land) were subject to expropriation with appropriate government compensation. Owners were to be granted a reserve of 100 or 150 hectares, which would allow them to retain the most desirable portions of their estates; this amount could be increased by 20 percent if the owners had improved their property between the effective date of the law and the government's acquisition of their land.[15]

The Agrarian Reform Institute (*Instituto Salvadoreño de Transformación Agraria*, ISTA) was charged with implementing this process: identifying lands for expropriation, determining compensation, and provisionally running the estates. Once the final level of compensation was determined, ISTA was to turn the land over to the estate's former workers and renters. The postreform tenure system was to be the production cooperative. The estate would be run as a "joint venture" of the campesino group and ISTA for an indefinite period. The cooperative would assume, as a debt to ISTA, the full value of the former owner's compensation.

This reform was to be implemented in two stages. Phase I, effective March 1980 (Decree 154), applied to estates larger than 500 hectares. It was estimated that this phase would affect 238 properties controlling 218,000 hectares, or some 15 percent of the country's farmland (Simon and Stephens 1982, 9). This was not prime land: approximately 70 percent was pasture, and a fairly small portion of the country's main export crops was grown on these estates. Phase II was to affect all holdings between 100 and 500 hectares. Original estimates were that Phase II reform would affect 1,700–1,800 estates, some 23 percent of the country's farmland (Simon and Stephens 1982, 15). It would have a greater impact than Phase I not only because of the larger amount of good land included, but also because the principal agroexport estates of the country were involved.[16] However, the implementation of this phase was postponed.

In April 1980, Phase III, or the "land-to-the-tiller" program, was established. As with the earlier decrees, it was prepared in haste and involved little discussion with ministry officials or potential beneficiaries.[17] Under Phase III, renters and sharecroppers were to be entitled to acquire up to 17 acres of the land they were working. As with Phase 1, beneficiaries would owe the government the amount paid to compensate the former owner. Beneficiaries had up to 30 years to repay their debt in annual installments, but would lose the land if payment were not made for a year or more. The beneficiary family was not allowed to lease the land or to transfer it for 30 years except as an inheritance.[18] It was estimated that Phase III would benefit some 117,000 families (approximately 22 percent of peasant households) and include as much as 150,000 hectares, or 10 percent of the country's farmland (Diskin 1985, 7, 35).[19] Altogether, some 50 percent of poor rural households was expected to receive land under the three phases of the reform (Wise 1985, 5).

THE 1981 NICARAGUAN AGRARIAN REFORM

Nicaragua has approximately 5,800,000 hectares (7,750,000 manzanas)[20] in farms and a population of between 2.5 and 3 million, while El Salvador has some 1,400,000 hectares in farms and a population of approximately 5 million. Because of these population-density differences, comparisons will be made using percentages of rural population or of land in farms.

The restructuring of Nicaragua's agrarian sector began with the overthrow of Somoza in July 1979 when the new government declared that lands owned by the Somoza family and its close associates were to be confiscated. The decision was made to run these properties, many of them modern agroexport estates, as state farms. This gave the state direct control over some 20 percent of Nicaragua's farmland, making it an important participant in the country's agroexport sector (Deere et al. 1985, 79–80). During 1980, the Sandinistas attempted to calm growing rural tensions with liberal credit to small farmers, particularly those who organized themselves into credit and service cooperatives (*Cooperativas de Crédito y Servicios*, CCS), and with rent controls to help tenant farmers. By spring 1981, however, pressures for land reform had mounted, and a new agrarian reform law was written and promulgated with the participation of rural workers' and peasants' organizations (Deere et al. 1985, 82–84, 88–91).

Under the 1981 Nicaraguan Agrarian Reform Law, Decree 782, land on holdings of over 500 manzanas that was not being efficiently farmed was subject to expropriation (1,000 manzanas in regions other than the Pacific coast), as was any sharecropped or usufruct land on holdings over 50 manzanas (100 manzanas in regions other than the Pacific coast). "Inefficient" included idle or underutilized land. Abandoned land was subject to confiscation (Nicaragua 1981).

Farms operated through wage labor or cash rental that were under the specified size were exempt from the reform regardless of their economic performance. As with Phase I in El Salvador, many of the agroexport coffee and cotton holdings were smaller than the specified maximum (Table 1). In this matter, the Nicaraguan law was more conservative than that in El Salvador; it exempted from expropriation properties of *any* size that were being "efficiently" worked, provided they were not farmed using *colonato* labor relations. The law's intent was to encourage private sector, medium- and large-scale agroexport production carried out with wage labor or under cash-rental arrangements. As with other Latin American agrarian reforms in the 1960s and 1970s, the incentive effect of the legislation on the "nonreform" sector was an important goal of the reform: farmers could avoid expropriation by operating efficiently and with "modern" labor relations.[21]

As in El Salvador, the owners of expropriated properties were to be compensated. Unlike the Salvadoran reform, however, the expropriated land was to be delivered free-of-charge to reform beneficiaries. The legislation did not prescribe the form in which beneficiaries were to farm the property; although production cooperatives were encouraged, individual peasant ownership was permitted.[22] As in El Salvador, the beneficiaries were not allowed to transfer property except through inheritance.[23]

It was originally estimated that up to 1,380,000 manzanas would be affected by the reform (*Nuevo Diario* 1981). That figure was later increased to 1,985,000 manzanas (*Barricada* 1983), or approximately 25 percent of the country's farmland. Including the state farms, it was envisioned that some 45 percent of the country's farmland would be incorporated into the "reform sector," approximately the same percentage as in El Salvador.

ACHIEVEMENTS OF THE TWO REFORMS: 1979–1984

Table 3 presents a summary of the quantitative achievements of the two reforms as of October 1984 (El Salvador) and December 1984 (Nicaragua).

In El Salvador, Phase I affected the largest percentage of the country's land, while Phase III reached the greatest number of rural families. Between 1980 and 1984, Phase I affected 472 properties with over 15 percent of the total agricultural land. Phase III had

Table 3
Area and families affected by agrarian reform, El Salvador and Nicaragua, 1979–1984[a]

Reform	Number of beneficiary families	Percentage of peasant families	Number of cooperatives	Amount of land[b]	Percentage of total land in farms
El Salvador (Oct. 1984)					
Phase I	31,359[c]	6	317 (52 titled)	219,524[d]	15[d]
Phase II	0	0	0	0	0
Phase III	63,024[e]	12	—	96,011	7
Total	94,383	18	317	315,535[d]	22
Nicaragua (Dec. 1984)					
State farms	—	0	—	1,516,900	19
Cooperatives[f]	30,098	20	1,000[g]	624,580	8
Land titling[h]	34,154	23	—	1,390,224	17
Total	64,252	43	1,000[g]	3,531,704	44

[a] Sources: El Salvador: U.S. Embassy/AID, *El Salvador Monthly Report* (San Salvador), no. 40, 26 October 1984; Martin Diskin, "The Direction of Agrarian Reform in El Salvador," mimeograph (Cambridge, Mass.: Massachusetts Institute of Technology, 1985), pp. 7, 47. Nicaragua: Ministerio de Desarrollo Agropecuario y Reforma Agraria, *Plan de trabajo: balance y perspectivas, 1985* (Managua: MIDINRA, 1985).
[b] For Nicaragua, amount is in *manzanas*. For El Salvador, it is in hectares.
[c] As of November 1983.
[d] Total in affected properties, but up to 150 hectares can be retained by former owners of Phase I lands under the reserve-right provision of the law. By November 1984, 156 claims, covering 14,000 hectares, had been approved, reducing the amount of land held by the cooperatives to 14 percent of Salvadoran farmland. Other claims were still being processed. See Wise (1985, 11).
[e] Who have received provisional or definitive title. A total of 63,661 potential beneficiary families have applied.
[f] Production cooperatives (CAS), formed by members who have collectively received land from the state. There are also credit and service cooperatives (CCS), where members retain individual title to their land. The CAS and CCS together number 2,800 cooperatives, with some 68,000 families and 1,430,900 manzanas.
[g] The number cited by MIDINRA is "over 1,000."
[h] Agrarian reform titles involving transfer of land to individuals and legalization of land titles to individuals ("special titles") and to indigenous communities.

granted provisional titles to 63,024 beneficiary families by October 1984, approximately half the original estimate. By the end of 1984, the Salvadoran reform had reached approximately 570,000 individuals, some 18 percent of the rural population, and had expropriated some 315,535 hectares, or 22 percent of the country's farmland, far less than was originally anticipated. The amount of land transferred will be even less, depending on the outcome of the "reserve" claims filed by former owners.

In Nicaragua, 64,252 rural families had individually or collectively received land titles involving 2,014,804 manzanas, or 25 percent of the country's farmland, by December 1984. Another 1,516,900 manzanas, or 19 percent of the farmland, was in state farms, bringing the total of all farmland in Nicaragua affected by the agrarian reform to 44 percent. This was double the percentage of land affected by the Salvadoran reform during this period. The percentage of peasant households benefited by the Nicaraguan reform was somewhat unclear. Estimates of the total number of peasant families in Nicaragua range from approximately 122,600 to 150,000.[24] The higher figure was used to give the lower bound estimate (Table 3) of 43 percent of peasant households benefited.

IMPLEMENTATION OF THE NICARAGUAN REFORM, 1979–1984

The Nicaraguan agrarian reform was a complex process which changed markedly over the 1979–1984 period. Confiscation of Somocista properties sharply reduced the percentage of Nicaraguan farmland held in large and medium estates (see Table 4). David Kaimowitz has argued that, in the vision of agrarian structure held by the Sandinista Front (*Frente Sandinista de Liberación Nacional*, FSLN), the Somocista estates were a principal part of the technologically advanced, dynamic, agroexport sector of the economy, while peasant producers were a nonprogressive group rapidly being converted to either a semiproletarianized or a fully proletarianized labor force (Kaimowitz 1985). As Jaime Wheelock, the Nicaraguan Minister of Agriculture, explained, "material and political" conditions convinced Sandinista officials that the confiscated land should be organized as state farms (Wheelock 1985, 25). To turn confiscated properties—which included sugar plantations and mills, irrigated rice estates, coffee and cotton estates, and the principal tobacco farms of the country—over to individual peasant producers would result in a considerable decrease in productivity, argued Sandinista planners. Another worry of reform administrators was the possibility that peasant producers would, once in control of decision making, switch from export-crop to basic-grain production to satisfy their own consumption needs, thus threatening the availability of seasonal labor for the agro-export harvests (Kaimowitz 1985, 11–12). This was the primary concern on ex-Somocista cattle ranches, which were mostly extensive up-land grazing operations and accounted for over 50 percent of the confiscated land.

However, scale economies could have been maintained on even the most highly capitalized Somocista operations by organizing them as production cooperatives, as in Phase I of the Salvadoran reform. In fact, many of these properties had been seized by their workers during the war against Somoza and were already run cooperatively. The decision to organize the undivided Nicaraguan estates as state farms rather than as cooperatives was due in large part, according to Kaimowitz, to the FSLN view that turning them over to peasants would be "a historic step backward" (Kaimowitz 1985, 10).[25] The antipeasant legacy of the pre-1979 period thus influenced early agrarian policies of the Sandinistas. The state-farm organizational form responded both to a need for foreign exchange and to a distinct theoretical (or ideological) understanding of Nicaraguan reality. The key to the economy was still to be the agroexport estate: whether state or private, it was to

Table 4
Percentage distribution of landownership in Nicaragua, 1978–1985[a]

Sector	1978	1981	1982	1984	1985
Individual	100	69	65	64	62
>500 mz	36	18	14	13	11
200–500 mz	16	13	13	13	13
50–200 mz	30	30	30	30	30
10–50 mz	16	7	7	7	7
<10 mz	2	1	1	1	1
Cooperative	—	11	12	17	19
Production (CAS)	—	1	2	7	9
Credit and service (CCS)[b]	—	10	10	10	10
State farms (APP)	—	20	23	19	19
Total	100	100	100	100	100

[a] Sources: Central American Historical Institute, "The Nicaraguan Peasantry Gives New Direction to Agrarian Reform," *Envio,* 4:(51) (September 1985), p. 13c; Dirección General de la Reforma Agraria, *Avance y perspectivas de la reforma agraria* (Managua: MIDINRA, January 1986).

[b] Affiliations of individual peasant landowners.

be protected and given priority over peasant production, which was seen as marginal.

Some in the Ministry of Agriculture (*Ministerio de Desarrollo Agropecuario y Instituto de Reforma Agraria,* MIDINRA) disagreed with this dominant notion, citing the importance of the peasantry in basic-grain production. This dissenting perspective did not have an impact on early land-distribution policy, however. Instead, the Sandinistas attempted to assist existing peasant producers through land-rental decrees and generous credit policies. One component of this effort was the strengthening of the rural organization of peasants and workers, the Rural Workers Association (*Asociación de Trabajadores del Campo,* ATC). This also reflected the dominant theoretical view of the Nicaraguan peasantry as a proletariat in formation, one which should be encouraged to organize for proletarian interests rather than as a group pressuring for family farms.

The vision was wrong. The peasant farmers of the north and central regions and the "semiproletarians" of the Pacific region saw themselves as farmers, not as wage workers; the land-poor peasants, meanwhile, continued to pressure for land. The success of independent producer organizations in incorporating the family farmers and their reluctance to join the ATC led the Sandinistas to agree to the separation of peasant landowners from the ATC and the formation of a new organization, the National Union of Farmers and Ranchers (*Unión Nacional de Agricultores y Ganaderos,* UNAG), which began to represent the interests of peasants as producers rather than as wage earners (CAHI 1985, 7c-8c; Deere et al. 1985, 85–88).

The passage of the 1981 Agrarian Reform Law reflected growing FSLN pragmatism in this matter and its recognition of the complexity of Nicaragua's agrarian structure and of the importance, and perspective, of peasant producers.[26] Production cooperatives gained favor as a progressive form appropriate to Nicaraguan conditions. Between October 1981 and December 1984, 624,580 manzanas were distributed to production cooperatives (*Cooperativas Agrícolas Sandinistas,* CAS) made up primarily of landless workers (see Table 5). These lands included "inefficient" estates expropriated under the 1981 reform law and Pacific coast grazing land in the state-farm sector that was redistributed in an effort to rationalize state operations (CAHI 1984, 2). A small amount of land was also turned over to individuals. The number of holdings under 50 manzanas declined in official statistics because many of the owners joined together in credit and service cooperatives, which were then reported in the "cooperative" category (Table 4).[27]

Redistribution in the first 15 months of implementation of the 1981 reform was slow, reflecting the obdurate legacy of the pre-1979 period. Of the land expropriated in this period, 70 percent was added

Table 5
Nicaraguan agrarian reform titles by type of recipient, 1981–85[a], [b]

Type of recipient	Oct. 1981–Dec. 1982		1983		1984		1985		Oct. 1981-Dec. 1985	
	Area	Families	Area	Families	Area	Families	Area	Families	Area	Families
Production cooperatives	108,096 (13)	7,024 (18)	269,187 (33)	11,344 (29)	247,297 (31)	11,730 (30)	180,510 (22)	9,266 (24)	805,090 (100)	39,364 (100)
Individuals	23,761 (12)	408 (6)	13,144 (7)	241 (3)	15,348 (8)	360 (5)	142,686 (73)	6,204 (85)	194,939 (100)	7,213 (100)
Titling of indigenous community land	— (0)	— (0)	21,352 (21)	1,548 (46)	28,284 (28)	1,600 (49)	51,772 (51)	200 (6)	101,408 (100)	3,348 (100)
"Special tities" (legalization of individual holdings)	— (0)	— (0)	198,634 (14)	3,805 (11)	1,089,701 (77)	26,192 (78)	133,616 (9)	3,400 (10)	1,421,951 (100)	33,397 (100)
Total	131,857 (5)	7,432 (9)	502,317 (20)	16,938 (20)	1,380,630 (55)	39,882 (48)	508,584 (20)	19,070 (23)	2,523,388 (100)	83,322 (100)

[a] Source: Dirección General de la Reforma Agraria, *Avance y perspectivas de la reforma agraria* (Managua: MIDINRA, January 1986).
[b] Area is given in *manzanas*. The number in parenthesis is the percentage.

to the state-farm sector (CAHI 1986, 5). One reason for this pattern was the desire to create stable cooperatives, which required considerable attention from scarce ministry personnel. Land redistribution accelerated in 1983 and 1984 (Table 5), but 65 percent of the land expropriated in 1983 and 57 percent in 1984 remained in the state-farm sector (CAHI 1986, 5), while marginal state-farm land continued to be distributed to producer cooperatives, made up primarily of former state-farm workers. By 1984, state-farm holdings had been reduced to 19 percent of Nicaraguan farmland, while production cooperatives had increased to 7 percent (Table 4).

One group bypassed was that of the family farmer. This group was significantly helped by generous credit policies in the first few years after the revolution, but their operations were hampered by continued lack of infrastructure and technical assistance and by an escalating contra war, especially in the north. Indigenous communities in the Atlantic region were also becoming involved in the conflict. The government's response was a titling campaign, initiated in late 1983 and implemented on an ambitious scale in 1984. This effort appears in Table 5 as "titling of indigenous community land" and "special titles." Most households whose land was titled in this period were settlers in the mountain-frontier regions (Kaimowitz 1985, 30).

The inclusion of these households in agrarian reform statistics has often given the misleading impression that the titled land was redistributed property,[28] as suggested by the data reported in Table 3. In fact, only a fraction of the 23 percent of peasant households whose land was titled between 1979 and 1984 had actually received land: 1,009 families (0.7 percent of peasant households) received a total of 52,253 manzanas or 0.6 percent of the land in farms (Table 5). Adding this to the CAS figures, 31,107 families (21 percent of peasant households) received land under the Nicaraguan reform between 1979 and 1984, obtaining a total of 676,833 manzanas or 8.4 percent of the nation's farmland.

Table 6 compares peasant households in 1978 with reform properties in the 1979–1984 period. Assuming that redistribution of land affected primarily seasonal workers and poor peasants (although, in fact, some permanent workers became members of CAS as well), we obtain an upper estimate that 37 percent of those households received land through the reform in this period (31,107 out of 83,500), most by joining a CAS.[29] If we include households of permanent workers as potential land recipients, an estimated 31,500, then the proportion of all landless and land-poor households that received land under the reform falls to 27 percent—a significant figure, but by no means a sweeping transformation of rural property relations. By 1985, many assessments of the Nicaraguan reform were pointing to its limited impact on the

Table 6
Number of Nicaraguan peasant households by status in 1978 and category of reform population in 1979–1984[a]

Peasant households, 1978		Reform population, 1979–1984	
Category	Number of households	Category	Number of households
Landless seasonal workers	26,800	Production cooperatives (CAS)	30,098
Poor peasants (0.1–10 mz)	56,700	Individual recipients	1,009
Medium and rich peasants (10–50 mz)	35,000	Legalization	33,145
Total	118,500[b]	Total	64,252[c]

a Sources: Number of households by category in 1978 is calculated from data in Table 2; this is a rough estimate, since there is not necessarily a one-to-one correspondence between the economically active population category and the household category. The total implied by these calculations—of 115,000 households of landless permanent workers, landless seasonal workers, and poor peasants—is a minimum estimate; other sources have put this total at around 122,000. Number of households by category of reform population is from Table 5.

b Not including landless permanent workers, another 31,500 households.

c Not including households of state-farm workers.

poorest rural groups, the landless and the land-poor households, which depended for their livelihood on a combination of seasonal wage labor and income from other sources (CAHI 1985; Kaimowitz 1985).

IMPLEMENTATION OF THE SALVADORAN REFORM, 1980–1984

In El Salvador as well, the amount of land transferred to the peasantry in Phase I and Phase III was significantly less than data in Table 3 suggest.

Phase III was expected to affect a large proportion of the "semi-proletarian" households in El Salvador, those relying on land rental or *colono* arrangements to provide some portion of family livelihood. In 1982, right-wing groups opposed to the reform gained legislative control in the Constituent Assembly elections and proceeded to pass new legislation which established a June 1984 cutoff date for the filing of claims. A total of 63,661 families, or a little over half the original estimate of 117,000 households, had filed claims to 79,135 plots of land by that date (U.S. Embassy/AID 1984). Many potential beneficiaries had been unable or unwilling to file claims against their landlords.

Filing was only the first step in the complicated process of obtaining land under Phase III of the reform, however. Claims had to be investigated. If approved, the level of compensation had to be determined. Finally, clear title to the property had to be established before it could be legally registered to the new owner. All of these steps proved difficult for the claimants.[30] By late 1984, 63,024 provisional titles had been issued, an indication that the claim was in process. Only 11,454 definitive titles had been issued (U.S. Embassy/AID 1984). If we assume one definitive title per household, this would mean that only 18 percent of the petitioners had actually received title. Many definitive titles had not yet gone through registration, a step which was being held up in some cases by previous mortgages on the properties involved. The figures reported in Table 3 are, therefore, an upper limit on the number of households expected to receive land under Phase III of the reform.

Even for those households which had received definitive title, the impact of the reform on their economic status was debatable. The average size of the transferred properties was only 3.8 acres of questionable–quality land per family. A sample survey of Phase III households found that net income from the Phase III parcels accounted for about one-third of the families' total net annual income.[31] While they had been relieved of the burden of paying rent to a landlord, they had acquired the burden of regular cash amortization payments to ISTA. Since payment to landlords was often in kind or in labor services, the new cash mortgage arrangement may be more burdensome. At the same time, the peasant household's access to credit and technical assistance was still extremely limited. Only about one-tenth of the Phase III land was covered by credit in 1983 (Diskin 1985, 37). In 1982 and 1983 surveys, between 86 and 90 percent of beneficiaries claimed that they had received no technical assistance (Browning 1983, 422–423). Beneficiaries must continue to rely heavily on off-farm wage and handicraft income, and on local moneylenders, to maintain precarious claim to their plots.

It was expected that Phases I and II of the reform would affect another 35 percent of poor peasant households: those working on estates of over 100 hectares as permanent laborers, *colonos*, or renters. Legislation passed by the Constituent Assembly in 1983 officially suspended Phase II implementation until 1987, at the earliest. The impact of Decree 153 was therefore restricted to farms over 500 hectares, and these were quickly expropriated under Phase I. The process of turning properties over to their former workers and tenants as production cooperatives, however, was complicated. Titling had to await the disposition of the 271 reserve claims that had been filed by the previous owners within the specified 12-month period, since the cooperatives were to assume an ISTA debt equal to the amount of compensation paid to the former owners. As with the Phase III properties, determining compensation has proved to be an arduous task (Wise 1985, 11). Until all of the steps are complete, provisional title is held by ISTA. By late 1984, 317 cooperatives had been created (Table 3), but only 52 had received definitive titles (U.S. Embassy/AID 1984).

Phase I cooperatives found themselves under considerable financial pressure. ISTA was generous with its owner compensation, particularly after 1982 (when the agency was under right-wing control). Meanwhile, decapitalization at the beginning of the reform had left many new cooperatives in a financially unstable position. (It was not unusual to see cattle being driven over the Guatemalan border by landlords, for example.) This was exacerbated by delays in credit delivery and in payment for products which co-op members delivered to ISTA marketing agencies (Browning 1983, 417–418). AID studies concluded that "most [Phase I cooperatives] are in serious financial trouble" (Diskin 1985, 24–29; Wise 1985, 14–20). Although there was originally an emphasis in the Phase I reform on "social promoters" to train peasant members for general cooperative participation, financial difficulties led ISTA to downplay participatory management in favor of a more "businesslike" approach to cooperative functioning. Under this approach, ISTA picked those whom they thought were most able for management and technical training, and the trainees were moved into administrative positions on their cooperatives. The status of the majority of the members remained unchanged, except that they had become employees of the state rather than of private producers (Diskin 1985, 30–33).[32]

This raises a fundamental question of how to compare the numerical achievements of the Salvadoran and Nicaraguan reforms. The evidence suggests that the Salvadoran cooperatives were comparable in their functioning to the Nicaraguan state farms. Although the state farms with the ATC were originally envisioned as a vehicle to empower the workers (Deere et al. 1985, 80–81), in fact, worker participation developed along the same lines as that of the Salvadoran cooperative members. The state farms are run by MIDINRA, which selects people to be trained in management and accounting and assigns them to the farms. The ATC functions solely as a union.[33]

The Nicaraguan production cooperatives, on the other hand, were more successful vehicles for the establishment of peasant participation in decision making. Although destruction caused during the war against Somoza, decapitalization by former owners, and effects of the contra aggression created pressures to put short-term financial needs before the goal of participatory cooperative development, the majority of the Nicaraguan cooperatives withstood these pressures and eventually became vehicles for peasant empowerment. In many, the cooperative members received training in cooperative management and came to participate in basic decision making and administration.[34] UNAG played an important role in the development of these programs. Also important to the success of the cooperatives was the fact that they received the land unencumbered by a debt to the government. Based on available evidence, David Stanfield and David Kaimowitz have concluded that the economic status of the Nicaraguan cooperative members up to 1984 had improved (Stanfield and Kaimowitz 1985, 10–11).

These considerations suggest that the Salvadoran cooperatives are far more comparable in their organization and operation to the Nicaraguan state farms than to the Nicaraguan cooperatives. This is particularly true in the case of the Salvadoran cooperatives that have not yet received title from ISTA. Only some 5,645 families, 18 percent of the 31,359 reported in Table 3, had actually received title by late 1984. As with the Nicaraguan reform, by the end of 1984, a sizable proportion of land taken from the large estates remained under the control of the state rather than having been transferred to the rural poor. Adding the estimate of 11,454 families that had received definitive title under Phase III yields 17,099 households that had received property title, or 18 percent of the potential beneficiaries, under the Salvadoran reform between 1980 and 1984. The number of rural poor in that country has been estimated by one USAID study as 2,202,700 persons, with an average of six persons per rural household (Wise 1985, 5, n. 2). Thus only 5 percent of poor peasant households received titled land in this period. Even including all of the potential beneficiaries (Table 3), we still find that only 26 percent of the landless and land-poor households in El Salvador was touched by the reform from 1980 to 1984. Somewhere between 74 and 95 percent of Salvador's landless and land-poor households had not received land from the reform between 1980 and 1984.

PEASANTS AND AGROEXPORT PROPERTIES IN THE TWO REFORMS, 1979–1984

This review suggests several conclusions about the first period of reform implementation. In each country, the majority of the rural poor received no land during this period. In each country, a significant proportion of the land affected by the reform was being operated by the Ministry of Agriculture. Finally, the first period of the agrarian reform affected primarily the large, traditional estates. The private agroexport sector, it was decided, was to remain strong in both countries.

The medium holdings in Nicaragua accounted for almost 60 percent of both coffee and cotton production in 1961; the large holdings accounted for only 20 percent of coffee and 30 percent of cotton (Table 1). The confiscation of Somocista properties resulted in only a slight decline in the land in medium-sized holdings (between 50 and 500 manzanas). The greatest impact was on the large holdings (over 500 manzanas), which were reduced from 36 to 18 percent of the nation's farmland. The confiscations gave the state control over 15 percent of cotton production, 12 percent of coffee production, and 8 percent of cattle production (Weeks 1985, 160). This still left over 80 percent of these exports in the private sector.

The large holdings were also the properties most affected in 1981-1984 by the implementation of the 1981 reform legislation: by 1984, the holdings of this sector had been further reduced to only 13 percent of the total land in farms (Table 4). The untouched properties in this size class were deemed to be "efficient" by government standards. The medium-sized holdings, protected from expropriation unless they were operated under a sharecropping or labor-service arrangement, were virtually unaffected. In some of the more densely populated areas of the Pacific region, the 1981 Agrarian Reform Law had very little impact on agrarian structure. As peasants in Masaya pointed out, "In Masaya the law passes through the clouds—it doesn't touch anybody" (CAHI 1985, 9c). Production figures for 1983 indicate that the private, medium, and large holdings still accounted for 42 percent of the nation's export production (on 43 percent of the farmland). The state farms accounted for another 28 percent, and peasant producers (including those in cooperatives) accounted for the remaining 30 percent (Baumeister and Neira Cuadra 1986, 37).[35]

In El Salvador, the expropriated Phase I estates accounted for less than one-quarter of the value of agricultural exports: 10 percent of coffee production, 38 percent of cotton production, and 43 percent of sugarcane production in 1980–1981 (Wise 1985, 28). The suspension of Phase II in El Salvador preserved the medium-sized agroexport holdings for the private sector. With the creation of 156 additional medium-sized farms through Phase I reservation claims, this sector actually expanded.

The middle-sized agroexport producers in El Salvador had political allies—and some had militias—to protect their lands from expropriation. Military and paramilitary forces, allied with those groups most adamantly opposed to land reform, escalated the level of rural violence in 1980.[36] By 1982, right-wing groups had also gained legislative control in the Constituent Assembly elections; they almost immediately passed new legislation to weaken the agrarian reform. After the 1982 elections, both MAG and ISTA came under the control of the right-wing party, the *Alianza Republicana Nacionalista* (ARENA), which had campaigned on an antireform platform. Soon after, the participation of peasant organizations was curtailed, and landlords were handsomely rewarded for their lands (Diskin 1985, 22–26).

Also of importance was the goal of the agrarian reform itself. Policymakers hoped that a reduction in political tensions and an increase in food production could be accomplished with a minimal transfer of land from the agroexport sector by concentrating instead on the "unproductive" lands of the traditional estates. The continued economic importance and derived political power of agroexport producers protected their lands from reform in a context where the agroexport sector was perceived as dynamic and in no need of restructuring.

In Nicaragua, large and medium landowners also had political and military means to resist the land reform: the "national unity" policy of the Sandinista government reflected the continued political power of these landowners both within the country and internationally, while the *contra* war provided them with the military means to fight land reform.[37] Nevertheless, their power was more limited than that of their counterparts in El Salvador, yet their holdings were just as immune from expropriation. Despite the frequently expressed commitment of the Sandinista leadership to a radical restructuring of rural property relations, the overriding influence on agrarian policy was the perceived imperative of the inherited agroexport economy: Nicaragua needed the foreign exchange which this sector could supply. A second Sandinista priority—improving domestic food production—was dealt with by increasing production on land outside of the agroexport sector by (1) providing liberal credit to existing peasant producers, (2) transferring marginal land from state farms to peasant producers (including the formation of seasonal worker cooperatives), and (3) experimenting on state farms with the planting of food as a second crop following the export-crop harvest.[38]

DIVERGENT PATHS: 1985–1986

Political pressure was of central importance in the formulation of reform legislation in both countries. Because large numbers of rural poor had not received land under the reforms between 1979 and 1984, pressures mounted. In El Salvador, reform was a key issue in the 1984 presidential elections. With the right-wing groups identified as antireform, the victory of José Napoleón Duarte was a clear call for deepening the reform. In the November 1984 Nicaraguan elections, Sandinista support was significantly reduced in a number of departments in the Pacific region that had formerly been important FSLN strongholds, including Masaya. Analysis of voting patterns revealed that support for opposition parties had been strongest in areas where under 10 percent of the peasants had received land (CAHI 1985, 13c). Since taking office in early 1985, the new governments in Nicaragua and El Salvador have responded in quite different manners to these political messages.

In El Salvador, some progress has been made with definitive titling (the figures had risen to 160 Phase I titles and 13,273 Phase III titles by June 1986). Between October 1984 and August 1986, the number of beneficiaries of the Salvadoran reform had increased from 17,099 to 29,266 households, that is, from 5 to 8 percent of the Salvadoran rural poor.[39] However, the total number of potential beneficiaries has been reduced. Between 31 March 1986 and 30 April 1986, the number of Phase III definitive titles reported in USAID documents had decreased from 17,751 to 13,081, the number of provisional titles from 65,978 to 62,160, and the number of potential beneficiary families from 63,668 to 51,800 (USAID/El Salvador 1986a, 1986b). These potential beneficiaries were "disaffected" for various reasons (USAID/El Salvador 1986c). One study has concluded that the number of Phase III titles will be closer to 45,000 (Clapp and Mayne, n.d.). Using the optimistic USAID estimates, the total number of beneficiary families under Phases I and III of the Salvadoran reform will be 83,159, or 23 percent of El Salvador's rural-poor households (8.5 percent in the cooperatives and 14 percent as Phase III owners).

The final number of beneficiaries in the Salvadoran reform will depend on the disposition of existing claims and on the implementation of Phase II. Under 1983 legislation, Phase II property owners were given until December 1986 to sell off any holdings in excess of the minimum allowable size, which was increased from 100 to 245 hectares. The Salvadoran Ministry of Agriculture has estimated that fewer than 14,220 hectares will still be eligible for expropriation in 1987 (USAID 1986, 5–7).

In Nicaragua, the number of beneficiaries increased markedly in 1985: 323,196 manzanas were redistributed to 15,470 families as individuals or as members of production cooperatives (Table 5). This represented almost one-quarter of the cooperative beneficiaries and the land received by them in the entire 1981–1985 period. More significantly, it represented 73 percent of land transferred to individuals and 85 percent of individual recipients in that period. The 1986 reform plan called for the redistribution of another 305,202 manzanas to 16,789 families (DGRA 1986, 4–6). If implemented this would bring up the percentage of rural-poor households receiving land either individually or cooperatively from 27 percent in 1984 to 55 percent by the end of 1986; the percentage of Nicaraguan farmland redistributed would increase from increase from 8 to 16 percent.

The importance of the 1985 redistribution is greater than the statistics reveal. The original plan was to distribute a much smaller amount of land in 1985, primarily to cooperatives. However, pressure from land-poor peasants in the Masaya region was mounting. Those peasants finally convinced the regional UNAG leadership to press their land demands with the Ministry of Agriculture. After a careful study by MIDINRA, the decision was made to respond to this strong peasant pressure. Negotiations were successfully carried out with a number of agroexport landowners. In addition to the private property redistributed to the Masaya peasants, land was also redistributed from state-farm holdings. Bowing to peasant preferences, most of the land was redistributed to individual families rather than to production cooperatives.[40]

The government had been reluctant to move against agroexport estates in the Pacific coast region. The Masaya redistribution was provoked, in part, by a growing alignment of many large and medium producers with the counterrevolutionaries and their refusal to expand agricultural export production.[41] The 1985 transfer of land from some agroexport estates to peasant producers also reflected the fact that the Nicaraguan reform was open to peasant pressure in a way that the Salvadoran reform was not.[42] Nicaraguan policymakers have come to see peasant producers in an increasingly favorable light, due in no small part to the organizational and economic success of UNAG, which has grown in membership among peasant producers. In 1985, UNAG started a cooperative to provide agricultural inputs and consumer goods to members. If this proves successful, the government may turn over to UNAG national responsibility for these marketing functions (Collins 1986, 24). An important factor in UNAG's success has been its inclusion of medium-sized operators. UNAG boasts of its status as the representative of "small, medium, and large producers." This strategic alliance has bolstered the economic and political clout of the organization.[43]

That the perspective of the Ministry of Agriculture has moved in a more pro-peasant direction is indicated by the passage of new agrarian reform legislation in January 1986. This legislation established the means to expand the reform sector by eliminating the previous size exemptions: all holdings are now open to expropriation if operated inefficiently (Nicaragua 1986, 48). This was necessary because of the shortage of expropriable properties in the Pacific Coast region where land pressure was still high. The transfer of state-farm lands to peasant producers is also likely to continue. According to one member of MIDINRA's Department of Land Tenure, the state sector is expected to be reduced to 10 percent in the coming years (CAHI 1986, 4).

Barring new legislation to reestablish Phase II, the Salvadoran reform is, to all intents and purposes, complete; the Nicaraguan reform continues. The Salvadoran reform has transferred land to approximately 8 percent of the rural poor to date, with a maximum future reach of 23 percent under Phases I and III. The Nicaraguan reform, on the other hand, has transferred land to 55 percent of the rural poor to date, and this figure is likely to grow.

NOTES

1. There has been a continuing debate within the Nicaraguan Ministry of Agriculture (MIDINRA) over the relative merits of peasant versus large-scale production. The development of this debate and its influence on the reform process over the 1979–1984 period are analyzed in Deere et al. (1985) and are briefly reviewed here.

2. On El Salvador, see, for example, Prosterman and Temple (1980); on Nicaragua, see Deere (1982).

3. Even later assessments, relying on these figures, were overly enthusiastic about reform accomplishments. See Browning (1983) on El Salvador, and, on Nicaragua, Collins (1982) and Austin, et al. (1985). To some extent, this is also the case in a recent joint paper, with this author, which failed to highlight sufficiently some features of the Nicaraguan reform which are emphasized here; see Deere, et al. (1985).

4. On this process in El Salvador, see Durham (1979) and Browning (1983).

5. In Nicaragua, coffee cultivation over the course of the century was extended from the Pacific mountain zones eastward to the central and northern departments. Peasant producers played an important part in this movement to new coffee zones (Gariazzo 1984, 11–13).

6. Baloyra indicates that the figure had reached 40 percent by 1975.

7. Although the national population density in 1971 was only sixteen persons per square kilometer, all seven Pacific region departments (states) had population densities at least twice the national average (SIECA 1981).

8. Bulmer-Thomas (1983, 271) argues that "during the heyday of the CACM one may observe two models of development co-existing uneasily at the same time. The collapse of the CACM, however, led to further intensification of the traditional export-led model."

9. Overall, as Bulmer-Thomas (1983, 275) shows, export agriculture grew more rapidly in the post-war period than production of foods for domestic consumption. See also Durham (1979, 31).

10. Weeks (1985, 64) shows average annual agricultural rates of growth of 3.8 percent in El Salvador and 5.8 percent in Nicaragua during the 1960s, and 3.2 and 4.7 percent, respectively, during the 1970s.

11. In 1978, 63 percent of El Salvador's merchandise exports was primary products, not including fuels, minerals, and metals, while the figure for Nicaragua was 82 percent (World Bank 1981, 150).

12. In 1970, 44 percent of imports to El Salvador was raw materials and intermediate goods, 17 percent was capital goods, and 32 percent was consumer goods; in Nicaragua, 38 percent of imports was raw materials and intermediate goods, 24 percent was capital goods, and 30 percent was consumer goods. Over the course of the 1970s in both countries, fuel imports accounted for an increasing share of the total (Perez Brignoli and Baires Martínez 1983, 377).

13. In fact, in El Salvador, food production overall lagged behind population increases (Durham 1979, 30).

14. Planning, begun right after the October 1979 coup, initially included peasant groups and Ministry of Agriculture and Livestock (MAG) technicians. After the resignation of the first governing junta in January 1980, the reform was designed with secrecy and, except for one peasant organization, the Salvadoran Communal Union (*Unión Comunal Salvadoreña*, UCS), with no popular or technical participation. Simon and Stephens (1982, 9) quote a MAG official as saying that "it was not known until the fifth of March that there really was going to be an agrarian reform. Everything was kept a big secret.... There was no discussion of it among the technical personnel of the Ministry of Agriculture and Livestock."

15. Decree 153 has been translated into English by Simon and Stephens (1982, 48–51).

16. Simon and Stephens (1982, 15) point out that this phase would affect some 70 percent of the nation's coffee production. They refer to it as the "heart of the reform."

17. Simon and Stephens (1982, 17–18) quote a USAID memorandum, stating, "A sizeable number of people in ISTA and MAG are suspicious of Decree 207 because it was designed virtually in its entirety by Americans and slipped into legislation without their being consulted."

18. Decree 207, translated into English in Simon and Stephens (1982, 52–54).

19. Estimates of potential beneficiaries of Phase III varied widely (from 60,000 to 150,000 households), with the Office of Planning and Evaluation of the Salvadoran Agrarian Reform (Planificación y Evaluación de la Reforma Agraria, PERA) estimate of 117,000 being the most frequently cited. See Wise (1985, 34) and Checchi and Co. (1983, 127–129).

20. While official Salvadoran agrarian statistics are presented in hectares, all official Nicaraguan statistics are presented in manzanas (1 manzana = 0.75 hectares). That convention will be followed here.

21. de Janvry argues that the incentive effect on the nonreform sector has been a primary goal in many Latin American reforms (de Janvry 1981, 203–204).

22. Beneficiaries included tenant farmers, smallholders with insufficient land, landless workers, state farms, and, finally, urban residents interested in producing basic grains.

23. This provision has apparently been relaxed. Researchers at the Center for the Study of the Agrarian Reform (*Centro de Investigaciones y Estudios para la Reforma Agraria*, CIERA) indicated that, due to pressure from peasants in several zones of the country, beneficiaries were being permitted to sell their agrarian reform titles (CIERA interview, 20 June 1985).

24. The lower figure is from official CIERA documents and also would result from the CAHI (1986) data. The higher figure is from CAHI (1985) and MIDINRA (1985). Even this figure may be low, given estimates for the rural population of 1,250,000 in 1980 (SIECA 1981, 37).

25. This decision also reflected a fear that the cooperative recipients of this land would become a new rural elite (Deere et al. 1985, 79–80).

26. See Deere, et al. (1985, 85–88) for a more detailed analysis of underlying pressures.

27. This does not represent a decline in private smallholdings as was reported by the Superior Council of Private Enterprise (*Consejo Superior de la Empresa Privada*, COSEP) (COSEP 1985).

28. The agrarian reform figures are usually presented as an aggregate without making this distinction. The first critical discussion of this issue is to be found in CAHI (1985, 11c-12c). See also the brief discussion in Mayorga (1984, 7).

29. Some households had also benefited from increased employment on the state farms, although Kaimowitz (1985, 23, 39) argues that the overall employment effect for this group was small.

30. See Checchi and Co. (1983, 144–153) for a detailed discussion of these steps.

31. These are results of a study by PERA in July 1985, reported in USAID/El Salvador (1986c).

32. Diskin (1985, 33) concludes: "Although the 317 Phase I 'productive units' (cooperatives) are formally structured as cooperatives, with a board of directors, voting membership, etc., the members have discovered that they remain as dependent as they were when they were merely individual workers on the same farms."

33. Interview with Alba Palacios, International Relations Office, ATC, Managua, 27 June 1985. Although the ATC has two union schools which give general education and training in organizing to selected union members, it gives no training in management or administration.

34. Based on interviews with UNAG regional representatives, El Crucero,20 June 1985, and on visits to cooperatives, "Casa Blanca" and "Ulises Rodríguez," Estelí Province, 22 June 1985. See also case studies of individual cooperatives and the results of a national CIERA survey (CIERA 1984).

35. These figures reflect changes in land use within each sector as well as transfer of land from one sector to another.

36. The undersecretary of agriculture, Jorge Vilacorte, resigned on 26 March 1980—20 days after the announcement of the agrarian reform decrees—charging that "it was useless to continue in a government not only incapable of putting an end to the violence, but a government which itself is generating the political violence through repression. In reality, from the first moment that the implementation of the agrarian reform began, what we saw was

a sharp increase in official violence against the very peasants who were the supposed 'beneficiaries' of the process" (CISPES 1981). In January 1981, Rodolfo Viera, the president of both ISTA and UCS, was murdered along with two U.S. advisors to the land reform program. Viera had previously charged that, between March and October 1980, some 184 murders of agrarian reform workers and beneficiaries had been carried out—most of these by military and paramilitary forces (Camorda 1981). In one cooperative, for example, after the members had elected their leaders, the security forces returned and killed the leadership [see interview with ISTA technician in Armstrong and Shenk (1980, 17)]. It has been charged that the reform was actually being used as a vehicle to identify and eliminate peasant leaders (Armstrong and Shenk 1980; Wheaton 1980).

37. The military option may have been in operation as early as 1980. Deere and Marchetti (1981, 67–68) report that the COSEP vice-president and UPANIC president, Jorge Salazar, who was killed in October 1980 in a shoot-out with the Nicaraguan police, was involved in a counterrevolutionary plot with Somocista exiles. By 1982, the *contra* military operation had been established with covert U.S. funding and CIA direction. The private-sector opposition in Nicaragua has clearly seen the *contra* forces as fighting in their interests, and the connection between the internal and external political and military groups became clear in the 1984 electoral maneuvering and in the formation in 1985 of a unified political/military opposition, the United Nicaraguan Opposition (UNO). In Nicaragua, as in El Salvador, agrarian reform workers and peasant leaders have been particular targets of the right-wing forces opposed to the reform. An important part of the *contra* military campaign has consisted of attacks on beneficiaries of the agrarian reform. During the week of 10 June 1985, for example, there were two major attacks on cooperatives in Nueva Segovia, as well as an attack on a rural community and a particularly destructive assault on a resettlement camp in Jinotega in which all of the homes were burned and twenty children were orphaned (*Nuevo Diario* 1985a; *Barricada* 1985b).

38. The rotation of maize with cotton was implemented under the "contingency plan" (PAN 1983). According to CIERA personnel interviewed in June 1985, this program has had very limited application.

39. This assumes that each definitive Phase III title equals one household and that the 160 definitive Phase I titles, which accounted for 51 percent of the Phase I properties, also accounted for 51 percent of the cooperative households.

40. From *Nuevo Diario* 1985b; *Barricada* 1985a; interviews with Marvin Ortega, member of the CIERA team which carried out the Masaya study for the ministry, 20 and 24 June 1985; interview with regional representatives of UNAG, 20 June 1985. There is another interpretation of the Masaya land reform. Enrique Bolaños, the president of COSEP and one of the landowners affected by this reform, has argued that the peasant demonstrations were engineered by the government as a pretense for taking over his lands because of his political opposition to that government (*Barricada* 1985b; interview with Bolaños, 26 June 1985). The president of the *Partido Liberal Independiente*, Virgilio Godoy, made the same argument in an interview on 18 June 1985. In either case, the

takeover represents the first major move under the agrarian reform against the private agroexport sector in Nicaragua.

41. Interview with COSEP directors, 26 June 1985.

42. This is a principal argument developed in Deere et al. (1985).

43. This alliance has, however, raised important questions about the relative influence within the organization of peasant versus medium producers. It also decreases the possibility of expropriating properties held by the larger UNAG members.

REFERENCES

Armstrong, Robert, and Janet Shenk. 1980. El Salvador: A revolution brews. *NACLA Report on the Americas 14*(4):2–36.

Austin, James, Jonathan Fox, and Walter Kruger. 1985. The role of the revolutionary state in the Nicaraguan food system. *World Development 13*(1):15–40.

Baloyra, Enrique. 1982. *El Salvador in transition*. Chapel Hill: Univ. of North Carolina Press.

Barricada (Managua). 1983. Diez mil manzanas a campesinos del sur. 16 July.

———.1985a. Masaya en manos de los campesinos. 15 June.

———.1985b. Que venga Bolaños para hablarle de justícia. 18 June.

Baumeister, Eduardo, and Oscar Neira Cuadra. 1986. Iniciativas de desarrollo política en la transición Sandinista. Mimeograph. Managua: CIERA.

Biderman, Jaime. 1982. Class structure, the state, and capitalist development in Nicaraguan agriculture. Ph.D. dissertation, University of California at Berkeley.

Browning, David. 1983. Agrarian reform in El Salvador. *Journal of Latin American Studies 15*, part 2 (Nov.):399–426.

Bulmer-Thomas, Victor. 1983. Economic development over the long run: Central America since 1920. *Journal of Latin American Studies 15*, part 2 (Nov.):269–294.

CAHI (Central American Historical Institute). 1984. Nicaragua's agrarian reform. *Update*, 13 January.

———.1985. The Nicaraguan peasantry gives new direction to agrarian reform. *Envio* 4:51, September.

———.1986. Agrarian reform undergoes a change in Nicaragua. *Update*, 7 February.

Camorda, Renato. 1981. Two U.S. union officials gunned down. *In These Times*, 14–20 Jan.

Checchi and Co. 1983. *Agrarian reform in El Salvador*. Washington: USAID.

CIERA (Centro de Investigaciones y Estudios para la Reforma Agraria). 1984. *La mujer en las cooperativas agropecuarias en Nicaragua*. Managua: CIERA.

CISPES (Committee in Solidarity with the People of El Salvador. 1981. El Salvador: Another Vietnam. *Changes*.

Clapp and Mayne, Inc. n.d. Mid-term evaluation of the El Salvador agrarian reform sector support project (0265): Executive summary of the final report. San Salvador: U.S. Embassy.

Collins, Joseph. 1982. *What difference could a revolution make: Food and farming in the new Nicaragua*. San Francisco: Institute for Food and Development Policy.

———.1986. Nicaragua: *What difference could a revolution make?* San Francisco: Institute for Food and Development Policy.

COSEP (Consejo Superior de la Empresa Privada). 1985. Algunos datos sobre reforma agraria y uso de la tierra. *Memorandum de la Presidencia*, no. 5. Managua: COSEP.

Deere, Carmen Diana. 1982. A comparative analysis of agrarian reform in El Salvador and Nicaragua, 1979–81. *Development and Change 13*:1–41.

Deere, Carmen Diana, and Peter Marchetti. 1981. The worker-peasant alliance in the first year of the Nicaraguan agrarian reform. *Latin American Perspectives 8*(2):40–73.

Deere, Carmen Diana, Peter Marchetti, and Nola Reinhardt. 1985. The peasantry and the development of Sandinista agrarian policy, 1979–1984. *Latin American Research Review 20*(3):75–109.

de Janvry, Alain. 1981. *The agrarian question and reformism in Latin America*. Baltimore: Johns Hopkins Univ. Press.

DGRA (Dirección General de la Reforma Agraria). 1986. Plan nacional de transformación agraria. Managua: April.

Diskin, Martin. 1985. The direction of agrarian reform in El Salvador. Mimeograph. Cambridge, Mass.: Massachusetts Institute of Technology, January. (See also *Agrarian reform in El Salvador: An evaluation*. San Francisco: Institute for Food and Development Policy, 1985.)

Durham, William. 1979. *Scarcity and survival in Central America*. Stanford, Calif: Stanford Univ. Press.

Gariazzo, Alice. 1984. *El café en Nicaragua*. Managua: INIES/CRIES.

Kaimowitz, David. 1985. Theory and practice concerning the agrarian question and the rural poor in Nicaragua, 1979–85. Mimeograph. Madison: University of Wisconsin, September.

Mayorga, Salvador. 1984. El carácter democrático y revolucionario de la reforma agraria. *Revolución y Desarrollo* (MIDINRA/Managua), no. 2, July-September, pp. 5–8.

MIDINRA (Ministerio de Desarrollo Agropecuario y Instituto de Reforma Agraria). 1985. *Plan de trajabo: Balance y perspectivas, 1985*. Managua: MIDINRA.

———.1981. Ley de reforma agraria. *La Gaceta*, no. 188, 21 August.

———.1986. Reforma a la ley de reforma agraria. *La Gaceta*, no. 8, 13 January.

Nuevo Diario (Managua). 1981. Wheelock detalla alcances de reforma agraria: Tierra segura a todo productor, 22 July.

———.1985a. Sana increible contra campesinos en *asentamiento*, 14 June.

———.1985b. Tierra a campesinos de Masaya, 15 June.

PAN (Programa Alimentario Nacional). 1983. Plan contingente de granos básicos. Mimeograph. Managua: PAN.

Perez Brignoli, Hector, and Yolanda Baires Martínez. 1983. Growth and crisis in the Central American economies, 1950–1980. *Journal of Latin American Studies 15*, part 2 (Nov.):365–398.

Prosterman, Roy, and Mary Temple. 1980. Land reform in El Salvador. *AFL-CIO Free Trade Union News*, June, 35:6.

SIECA (Secretaría Permanente del Tratado General de Integración Económica Centroamericana). 1981. *Séptimo compendio estadístico centroamericano*. Guatemala: SIECA.

Simon, Laurence, and James Stephens, Jr. 1982. *El Salvador land reform, 1980–81*. Boston: Oxfam-America.

Stanfield, David, and David Kaimowitz. 1985. The organization of production units in the Nicaraguan agrarian reform. Paper presented at Twenty-Sixth Annual Convention of International Studies Association, Washington, 5–9 March. (See also *Inter-American Economic Affairs* 39(1):51–77.)

USAID (U.S. Agency for International Development). 1986. Agrarian reform policy dialogue: Status report, El Salvador. Washington: USAID, July.

USAID/El Salvador. 1986a. Agrarian reform status report, 7 April.

———.1986b. Agrarian reform status report, 7 April.

———.1986c. Report on Phase III of the agrarian reform in El Salvador. Mimeograph. San Salvador, July.

U.S. Embassy/AID. 1984. *El Salvador monthly report*, no. 40, San Salvador: U.S. Embassy, 26 Oct.

Weeks, John. 1985. *The economies of Central America*. New York: Holmes and Meier.

Wheaton, Philip. 1980. *Agrarian reform in El Salvador: A program of rural pacification*. Washington: Epica Task Force.

Wheelock Román, Jaime. 1985. *Entre la crisis y la agresión: La reforma agraria Sandinista*. Managua: Editorial Nueva Nicaragua.

Williams, Robert. 1986. *Export agriculture and the crisis in Central America*. Chapel Hill: Univ. of North Carolina Press.

Wise, Michael L. 1985. Agrarian reform in El Salvador: Process and progress. Mimeograph. San Salvador: USAID/El Salvador, February.

World Bank. 1979. *World development report 1979*. Washington: World Bank.

———.1981. *World development report 1981*. New York: Oxford Univ. Press.

Chapter 18

Conclusions: Searching for Agrarian Reform in Latin America

William C. Thiesenhusen

You can cut the blossoms,
but you can't delay the springtime.

– attributed to Pablo Neruda

The bright promise seen by some analysts in the prospects for Latin American land reform was not realized in the last 25 years. Thus, it is not surprising that the social scientists referred to at the end of chapter 1—Pearse, de Janvry, and Grindle—were pessimistic as they examined the development repercussions that agrarian reforms have had in the region. Another mood is not justified. If agrarian reform was to be a substitute for rural welfare programs and affirmative action in Latin America in the last several decades—and also supply an impetus to production—it fell short of the mark. While the *latifundio-minifundio* structure, *grosso modo,* is still intact, land-tenure patterns in the region are in the process of slow and evolutionary alteration.

NONREFORM STRUCTURAL CHANGE

Some of the changes recorded in these chapters merely continue trends begun earlier than government-backed reforms and would likely have happened in their absence. The time period documented here represents several decades during which the modernization of agriculture in developed countries was advancing rapidly. One spin-off of this trend for Latin America as it imported the resultant technology was that the technological imperative came partially to replace the social rationale as the predominant force shaping and molding the defining features of Latin American agrarian structure. For example, the reason that workers resident on estates as service tenants began to disappear as a tenure class and became *minifundistas* or landless laborers was that a year-round, full-time, labor force was no longer needed, say, on newly mechanized cotton farms. Only peak season workers were required. An additional, more-or-less spontaneous (or market-oriented) development was that while large numbers of campesinos declined in status, often subdividing whatever land they controlled, another group of small-scale farmers became quite viable without much government assistance (chap. 4).

STRUCTURAL CHANGE RESULTING FROM REFORM

Some other changes in the direction of increased intensity of farming were made by landlords to avoid the imposition of agrarian reforms, which tended to target idle but usable land within *latifundios* for expropriation. Hacienda subdivision, sometimes to escape excess-size provisions, also occurred. A group of large- to middle-sized, entrepreneurial, capitalized farms resulted (chaps. 2, 3, and 5). Later, in the late 1970s and early 1980s, decollectivization of agrarian reforms left its legacy of smaller, less capitalized farms (chaps. 6, 9, and 11).

Land reform appears still to be in its infancy in Latin America; even so, some observers question whether it will mature after economic growth resumes in the region. The choice of much of the region seems to be either to reform agriculture, and in so doing provide more jobs in situ, or to ride with the current wave of urbanization. Reliance on the latter will result in the social problems of rural poverty moving en masse to the cities, where they will be focused in the *barrios marginales* and *favelas* (slums), still to be acutely felt. While its locus will have been changed, the problem will be left virtually intact unless more urban jobs and welfare benefits[1] are forthcoming. One can find the future bright if it is assumed that the lessons of the 1960s and 1970s are not lost on state elites and international powers who understand that positive policy must be enacted to help reconstruct the social order on a more equitable basis and forestall the social instability that will otherwise result. Or one can find the future bleak if the never-ending cycle of poverty continues until the result is menacing—and then actual—rural or urban chaos.

An alternative to either a more complete reform of agriculture or to an emphasis on further urban jobs and transfer payments seems to be the "muddling through" picture we have documented in this volume.

Because the contemporary scene involves a growing population, more underemployment, heightened awareness, rising expectations, greater organization, and politicization of the issues, this alternative appears to be less viable for the future than for the past.

REFORM BOTTLENECKS 

A number of formidable agrarian reform bottlenecks have emerged in this volume:

1. The supply of inputs (such as fertilizer, irrigation water, hybrid seed, and so on) that was available to beneficiaries was constrained.
2. Governmental interest in agrarian reform waned as new growth points in the economy emerged, new economic development priorities came to prominence, and a new social agenda emerged (chap. 10).
3. Bureaucratic delay, Byzantine procedures, and even, at times, sabotage occurred.
4. Limited political objectives, once satisfied, often ended the reform (chap. 2).
5. Public opinion, convinced—however incorrectly—that agrarian reform was lowering production and raising prices for wage goods, turned against reform (chaps. 2 and 3).
6. The private sector became determined to fight legally sanctioned reform on an administrative level (chap. 9).
7. The postreform tenure structure was supported neither by adequate services to hold it together nor, at times, even by its beneficiaries.
8. A top-heavy bureaucracy attempted to do everything and did not cede to the private sector even those functions which it is known to accomplish more satisfactorily.

AT THE BENEFICIARIES' LEVEL

By examining beneficiaries, a somewhat more optimistic picture of agrarian reform emerges than can be drawn by analyzing countrywide macroeconomic data. When asked, beneficiaries respond that their level of living is higher than before the reform (chap. 13). This tends to be confirmed when real household budgets are analyzed in a systematic fashion as well as when one looks at postreform productivity per hectare.

While the political right sometimes blamed the agrarian reform for agricultural shortfalls (chaps. 2, 5, and 11), this culpability seems largely to be misplaced; case studies show that production per hectare on reformed land did not usually suffer [though on this point Jarvis (chap. 9) would not agree]. There was, in fact, more of a tendency for production to rise (chaps. 2, 3, 7, and 8).[2] Although macrodata may show that marketable surplus drops as beneficiaries increase their consumption, most authors here feel this trend to be the transitory phenomenon that Clark (1968) pointed out for postreform Bolivia: consumption by beneficiaries becomes higher than before and marketable surplus soon increases and exceeds its prereform level as productivity rises. Pervasive sectoral insecurity as a direct result of reform seemed rather minimal, though Jarvis feels that Chile in the late Allende period was an exception [while Brown (chap. 8) disagrees]. There appears to be a rather large variation in productivity and income between neighboring agrarian reform participants (chaps. 6 and 9).

While, on average, beneficiaries enjoy higher incomes than before the reform, this is at times accomplished at the expense of not making proper amortization payments on debts; thus, gains are ephemeral unless governments forgive indebtedness, an action that challenges the reform's economic integrity (Thiesenhusen 1987). What is not well known is whether any gain for beneficiaries is made at the expense of other public programs for the poor in the agricultural sector, though this is likely. On the subject of helping the poor, it is observed that the sum of beneficiary and nonbeneficiary employment per hectare is usually higher after reform than before, especially if machinery use per hectare is lessened by reform (chaps. 6 and 8). On the other hand, reform beneficiary groups attempt to hire day labor at lower wages than hacendados (chaps. 8 and 9).

BETTING ON THE STRONG

Those who come to the reform with more human and physical resources (for example, a larger family labor force that is better educated) tend to benefit more than those who are initially less favorably endowed, especially if a post-reform family-farm system prevails. For a few beneficiaries, land reform is an almost sure ticket to middle-class agriculture (chap. 9; see also Diskin, Sanderson, and Thiesenhusen 1987).

Indeed, the most common type of reform in the 1960s and 1970s in Latin America was quite partial and granted land to the already more fortunate among the campesinos. Some would interpret this type of reform as a way to turn "transitional peasants" into a group that becomes even more favored [reminiscent of the kulaks in the USSR before collectivization, but a common phenomenon in contemporary reforms as well, such as those in South Asia; see Elder (1980, 171)].

This policy identifies the most able, eager, and motivated producers and grants them land rights and certain benefits of public policy that are not available to nonbeneficiaries, straining the equity principles supposedly inherent in land reform. Some view this approach as the most logical and efficient—an effort to choose those who are most apt to be highly productive and promote them to "farmers." Others, concerned more with distribution than with production, are critical of this view because one of the most universal characteristics of the agrarian reforms documented here is that such large numbers of families below the "superior potential performers" were omitted and the land reforms occurring in the region, as in nearly all rural development programs, continue to "bet on the strong."[3] An exception occurred during the unraveling of the Chilean reform (chap. 9).

In general, the overall number of peasants accommodated in land reform was relatively small, averaging about one-quarter of those who were legally eligible in Latin America and never exceeding 45 percent of the usable land in a country. As such, it is not surprising that time-series data reveal no marked improvement in macroindicators such as the size distribution of income. Much of the distribution of land that took place was to those campesinos already in relatively high-income cohorts.[4]

Besides land, and a counterpoint to the view that some beneficiaries did not obtain enough inputs and services after reform, some recipients were lavished with more subsidized inputs and public services than were optimal given their enterprise combinations—more even than they could possibly repay. At times this occurred because a conservative group, anxious not to push reform further, argued for a "consolidation" of the reform before many potential beneficiaries were accommodated. This inappropriate showering of largesse on a small number of beneficiaries allows antireformers to build Potemkin villages as "showcases" as well as to argue that no more public funds are available for incorporating more beneficiaries in the reform process (chap. 8). What is needed is more research on this allocation problem: What critical minimum of resources is needed by the beneficiaries in order to convert them into productive, tax-paying, or amortizing members of the agricultural society without wastefully overspending on a few? How much of this must be provided by the public sector, and how much can be left to the private sector?

The reforms that have attempted to couple peasants and land without providing a satisfactory number of inputs have resulted in land abandonment, which surely does not serve the government's political or economic aims very well (chap. 13). In this case, a backlash may develop from beneficiaries, who are forgotten by subsequent policy, and their middle-class allies.

Once land is given out, the campesinos face all of the problems with which agricultural advisors commonly deal. These difficulties need not be blamed on the agrarian reform per se; they are the problems of farmers everywhere (for example, paying past-due accounts, whether fertilizer use is appropriate given technical coefficients and the prevailing price-cost ratios, the quality of extension technical assistance, export prices compared to domestic prices, and so on).

WHAT DID REFORM ACCOMPLISH?

The authors in this volume largely agree that reform programs to date in the region have been too small, too late, too underfunded, too dictated from above, too hierarchically organized, and too infrequently responsive to pressure from the grass roots. If land reform efforts had been more inclusive, and if organized pressure from the grass roots had been received more attentively, results might have been quite different than the modest ones reported here.

During the period studied, the Latin American countries examined became steadily more urbanized. Import-substituting industrialization and export promotion became dominant development strategies, and the elites they generated challenged the hegemony of the rural upper classes. As a result, the composition of those in the upper classes shifted somewhat and new pro- and antireform alliances came into being. Also, the middle classes developed and sometimes accepted coalition partners from the upper or lower classes. This tended to change the political complexion and the social agenda quite radically in some countries. As the social structure of most countries was altered, government policies became increasingly biased in favor of the leading urban and export sectors while the income position of most of the poor—the majority in society—remained at a low level. In countries where there was more agrarian reform, one might have expected to find a fairly dramatically altered social structure. In some countries this occurred, but it tended to be a transitory phenomenon. A rollback of the reforms, industrialization and other forms of economic diversification, inflation, and public expenditure patterns which favored the commercial (and export) sectors of agriculture tended to neutralize many of the income gains traceable to reform (chaps. 5, 9, and 10).

The population bulge of midcentury hit the rural labor market at almost the same time as the agrarian reforms did—in the 1960s and 1970s. In a milieu of rapid population growth and fairly weak commitment to reform on the part of most governments, reforms could not keep ahead of population growth in most countries, especially since the rural poor had larger families than either the urban poor or the middle and upper classes. Therefore, even rapid rural-to-urban migration did not substantially alleviate underemployment in rural areas. Meanwhile, urban unemployment grew as the rate of industrialization did not proceed rapidly enough or track a course that was sufficiently labor absorbing for the immense task at hand.

In sum, income and resources did not display much between-class redistribution, new jobs which were created by reform fell short of demand, and domestic markets did not widen much (chaps. 5 and 11).

Even so, more jobs were created than would have been in the absence of reform, and some income additions to the peasantry resulted. Agrarian reform tended to make the peasantry more heterogeneous than would have been the case otherwise.

Given a postreform, individual-farm, labor-abundant, and capital-scarce agrarian structure, campesinos can produce food efficiently because labor is homegrown; these family resources tend to be employed (chap. 6), and labor is utilized until its marginal product approaches zero. Some, however, believe that this is a misguided notion of efficiency and that it really amounts to rural labor-force exploitation (chap. 10).

Much of the literature on the Latin American peasantry associates the campesino with the production of subsistence goods while associating the larger, more commercial farmers with the production of either agroexports or commodities that have rather high income elasticities of demand (like dairy products, livestock, and fruit), products for domestic middle and upper class consumption. The idea is sometimes advanced that there are more economies of size in upscale domestic commodity and export production than in production for lower class domestic consumption. Production of agroexports has been interpreted pejoratively as being the domain of the elite and even of foreigners, a subsector of farming which misallocates resources that ought to be devoted to feeding the country's masses (Sanderson 1986) and, hence, exploits the poor; de Janvry (1981) decries the sectoral disarticulation that results in which the modern sector obtains what capital it needs from the export sector and can, therefore, be indifferent to local market expansion. This stigmatization of trade may be too dogmatic, however. In fact, small countries without a sufficiently wide range of resources and ready technology must rely on importing them; and, in order to import, foreign exchange is essential, even given "dependista" arguments advanced over the last several decades. The "exploitation" argument should not be directed against classes of commodity exports per se, but against those people who may unfairly monopolize these products and benefit excessively from their trade. The issue is how to make certain that the income generated from agroexports contributes to a broader public good than it presently does.

Over the long run in the region, export crops have tended to be more remunerative than cereals, whose price is internally controlled and which are grown for domestic consumption. It is possible for beneficiaries to make higher incomes by producing exports. Stringer (chap. 13) points out that some reform *asentamientos* in Honduras are being encouraged to produce export goods; this is also happening in Nicaragua and El Salvador (chaps. 14, 15, and 17). Both Nicaragua and El Salvador, recognizing the unique role of agroexports, took precautions to protect them from disruption during the redistributive phases of the reforms (chaps. 14–17).

The future of agrarian reform will be clouded if it does not facilitate the production of export crops for which the country in question has a comparative advantage. If economies of scale are a deterrent, Strasma (chap. 15) suggests that there is really no reason why groups of peasants cannot run coffee mills or cotton gins or sugar refineries. (Other scale economies could be realized if individual parcel holders banded together for machinery use, as they did for decades in threshing rings in the U.S. Midwest, for example.)

POLITICAL GOALS OF REFORM

Especially in the 1980s, political and military goals of reform seem to take precedence over economic and social goals in Latin America: reforms seem to have been set in place expressly to blunt political protest. It appears that some economic goals have been shortchanged, though on this point there is some argument (cf. chaps. 15 and 16).

Governments tend not to make land assignments in an agrarian reform arbitrarily. There is good evidence that those campesino groups that have complained vociferously and have been the most socially disruptive, often through strikes and land invasions, have been more likely to obtain property than those that have been relatively more quiescent (chaps. 5 and 7), though governments may make a strong attempt to resist these pressures. There is evidence that most governments have bought at least a modicum of stability with their agrarian reform budgets. This stability has not, in general, resulted in increased plaudits from the political right, even though the right is interested in avoiding social disruption. In Nicaragua, in response to campesino demands, policies aimed primarily at setting up state farms changed to plans favoring production cooperatives and individual titling. The Sandinistas reacted positively because they needed the support of the countryside where the war against the Contras was being waged (chaps. 14 and 17). By decentralizing agrarian reform and granting land to the peasants (chap. 14), they were able to secure more political backing from rural areas.

What has sometimes appeared to be blatant co-optation of peasant groups through agrarian reform may clear a path for more progress in a later period by another route. If the current group of beneficiaries is able to provide schooling, better health care, and more satisfactory nutritional standards for its children, it is probable that the next generation will not be content to remain on its inherited and now subdivided land assignment. Future generations may intensely pressure for agrarian reform, especially if city jobs remain scarce. On the other hand, if city opportunities become more viable, demands for a better life for the next generation may be answered in the cities, and the need for agrarian reform will lessen.

Also, some current nonbeneficiary farmers will chafe because of their disadvantaged position; those who do not receive land will begin to compare themselves to those who did, especially if those who did not benefit believe themselves to be in the same social class as the beneficiaries. Those who receive land thus serve as examples for those left behind. Land seekers will doubtless organize more quickly and coherently even than current beneficiaries did when they publicly petitioned for land reform.

During the several decades under analysis here, new pressure groups have emerged to support land reform: some elements of the Roman Catholic Church and parts of the military. The Church has been important in focusing cries for reform in contemporary Brazil, as it was in the mid-1960s in Chile and later in the Dominican Republic (chap. 11). In the 1970s, the military was a vital element in the reforms in Peru and Honduras (chaps. 5 and 13).

Peasant organization has not been a particularly strong social force for change in Latin America, though Strasma (chap. 15) sees the potency of campesino organization in the El Salvador reform of the early 1980s quite differently than Diskin (chap. 16). In Honduras (chap. 13), however, peasant unions have indisputably made a significant difference in rural life, as they pressured for whatever meager reforms the country eventually adopted. While peasant unionization was not strong enough to prevent the demise of agrarian reform after López Arellano, it was responsible, according to Stringer, for "acquiring thousands of manzanas of land, for the dismissal of three INA directors, for electing one of their officers to Congress, and for obtaining key appointments on the National Agrarian Council....[Peasant unions also] assist the groups during the critical initial stages of organization and then offer or broker services, such as cooperative and management training and assistance in obtaining credit." In those production cooperatives that changed from group to individual farming during the period under examination, beneficiary pressure was crucial to the effort (chaps. 6 and 11), except, of course, in Chile (chap. 9).

When coupled with a permissive government, peasant organization did make itself felt in the last several decades. An example was the Dominican Republic where, after disappointing results throughout the 1960s, several peasant groups organized by the Church pushed tokenism into a much more active reformist stage in the early 1970s (chap. 11).

PRESSURES FOR FURTHER CHANGE

We have learned in this volume that Jeane Kirkpatrick (1979:44) was shortsighted when she claimed, "Because the miseries of traditional life are familiar, they are bearable to ordinary people who, growing up in the society, learn to cope." While they do "learn to cope," miseries among the campesinos are apparently becoming less and less bearable to the disadvantaged majority in Latin America. The question is this: Are the rich minorities able to adapt to the legitimate demands of this more vocal majority group (which is now also somewhat better nourished, more literate, and more aware than previously) as this poverty-stricken group becomes more dependent upon the monetary economy and, at the same time, more economically desperate? The answer from cases examined in this volume has been primarily negative. Governments to date have tended to adapt to any grass-roots clamor for better conditions with a patchwork of short-term expedients, palliatives (which are sometimes reformist actions), and repression. History teaches that a majority group like this is not likely to remain an underclass in the long run.

Even though politics and not economics seem to be decisive in shaping agrarian reform in the 1980s, discussion of government "motivation" rests on quicksand. Since the state speaks through different agencies, branches of government, and individuals in its need to assuage foreign powers and domestic dissidents, it seldom has one voice.[5] We do know, however, that "political" reform must in some sense become "economic" if reform is to survive and become self-sustaining.

What will likely happen if there is a complete lack of flexibility and adjustment by the elite is that society will eventually be led nearer to chaos, perhaps as was the case in 1979 in El Salvador and Nicaragua (chaps. 14–17). During the coming decades, Latin America will have to cope with its homegrown version of the "South Africa problem." The emergent coalitions are not as racially distinct, but the standoff situation created by intransigent elites, on the one hand, and demands for the fulfillment of basic human rights, on the other, is as volatile. Revolution should not be considered a panacea in these cases for, despite its utopian rhetoric, revolution does not end with decisive victories. Revolutions usually beget revisionism, reaction, and further factionalism. Along with undeniable gains, there are often losses, rethinkings, international pressures, unfinished business, and even more war (chap. 14). Revolution, if it is to be successful, must lead as soon as possible to economic recovery, for revolution's supporters can become its bitter enemies if not accommodated by the new government and if living conditions decline.

While prerevolutionary governments may be able to respond to grass-roots pressures with a certain amount of repression, coercion will probably prove to be self-defeating in the long term. States and the international community can, for a time, blame a "communist menace" for any social disruption, but even U.S. administrations may be forced (because of their increasingly bitter experience in Central America) to an official understanding of the need for social change. When the lesson is misread and social change is overturned, Eastern bloc influence is invited—which, some argue, comes from the USSR's desire to capitalize on the United States's lack of empathy with the poor majorities in Latin America.

Radical analysts, like Chomsky (1987), present another argument. Chomsky believes if the United States determines that it "cannot destroy popular resistance movements by force...the next best thing is to drive them into the arms of the Russians so we have justification for the violence and terror that we launch against them." He continues, "The United States is not concerned by the useless Soviet tanks in the streets of Managua, nor is it concerned by the censorship of a newspaper that is funded by the U.S. and supports contra terrorism in Nicaragua. What the U.S. is concerned about is the early substantial success of social reforms—which have been aborted, thanks to the contra war" (Chomsky 1987, 73).

The point is that social revolution and successful accompanying reforms would make a Central American country less amenable to U.S. control, and it is this control which Chomsky believes is the rather single-minded, foreign-policy purpose of the United States in this part of the world.[6] By "covert" actions, withdrawing aid, embargoing trade, sponsoring the counterrevolution, and flaunting the Contadora and the Arias peace processes, the United States does not appear innocent of this charge; Chomsky's ideas cannot be dismissed out of hand.

Chomsky is not alone in his view. According to Robert White, former U.S. ambassador to El Salvador, "The real fear of the Reagan administration is not that the Sandinistas will identify with the Soviet Union and Cuba; its real fear is that the Sandinistas will not identify with the Soviet Union and Cuba. If, out of the revolution, the Nicaraguan people can forge a democratic, non-aligned state, then what pretext will the United States have to prop up a brutal and corrupt military status quo in Central America instead of accommodating U.S. policy to the indigenous forces of political, economic and social change?" (White 1985). White appears to be asserting that the United States does not want the Nicaraguan revolution to be successful under any conditions, for that will make Central America less dependent on the United States and, hence, less controllable. White not only criticizes the Reagan regime but extends his remarks to critique all post-World War II U.S. administrations.

The issue of how the United States reacts to reforms, reformers, and revolutions is a matter which needs to be debated and redebated. U.S. policy is on a perilous track as it continues to contradict the natural aspirations of majority groups in the Third World (La Feber 1983). The question remains this (chaps. 15 and 16): Can future U.S. policy come to be as favorably inclined to homegrown reforms as to ones that are sanctioned and controlled by the U.S. government from the outset?

TITLING AND REGISTRATION

Several other aspects of land policy are worth noting. Titling the land of reform beneficiaries seems to offer regional governments a very desirable opportunity for setting in place programs of land taxation in future years (chap. 12). For their part, beneficiary owners can make a necessary contribution to public savings and investment which, over time, will more than offset their settlement costs. At times, programs which involve titling existing *minifundios* have taken precedence over distribution because they are more acceptable to most conservative governments than agrarian reform (chap. 13). In fact, "titling" and "registration" became two of the rural development buzzwords of the mid-1980s. While these processes help to bring more order to the land market—and to agricultural development in general because a land title serves as collateral for production loans—titles also are the foundation for land acquisition and sale.

Individual titling may lead to parcels of reformed land being sold to more capitalized farmers in lean or difficult years (chap. 9). Avoiding this will take not only interest-group surveillance but also some beneficiary cushion of savings. If there are savings, selling is no longer the only option facing beneficiaries when harvests are bad. More realistically in the short run, some crop insurance scheme or emergency loan procedure might be developed to tide peasant farmers over the bad times.

TYPES OF POSTREFORM INSTITUTIONS

The desired type of postreform tenure structure in many of these countries was a bone of contention during the period. Some still feel that the only workable possibility is group farming (chap. 10); others may have appreciated the theoretical arguments for the production cooperative but documented a rollback of this collective organizational form (chaps. 3, 6, 9, and 11) in response to the collapse of government or beneficiary support, or both. In these latter cases, it is not clear whether the production cooperative should be pronounced a failure, or whether it was a convenient and interim institution, appropriate at the beginning of a reform to keep the new landholders together with some spirit of community, but not appropriate for sustaining it. Group farming did serve initially as a springboard from which to heighten solidarity and a community-wide sharing of infrastructure among a group of divergent peasant families who might otherwise have been or soon become totally isolated from one another. Collectivization after individualization (as in the USSR) is not, of course, an option for Latin America; time and further research will tell how decollectivization, now ongoing in a number of countries, will serve the sector.

It is clear that if the production cooperative is not supported by outside organizations (usually state agencies and their services), it cannot persevere. In Peru, Chile, most of Mexico, the Dominican Republic, and, to the more limited extent it was attempted, Ecuador, it either disintegrated or is now in the process of doing so. However, the production cooperative in the mid-1980s still remains a dominant reform feature in Honduras, Nicaragua, and El Salvador. In Panama, the small remaining agrarian-reform production-cooperative sector was still supported strongly by the state in 1984 (Thiesenhusen 1987). In Honduras, production cooperatives are supported not so much by the government as by campesino organizations.

The production cooperative has other positive and negative aspects. On the one hand, it spares the reform the costs of subdivision and fencing and the attendant costs of building new roads, accommodating the new smaller fields with water and the new farms with other infrastructure such as electricity. It is also fairly easy for the state to provide technical assistance to the production cooperative by giving an employee from the agrarian reform agency co-manager status with the beneficiary officers (though some would proclaim this a continuation of paternalism, such that worker *auto-gestión* is delayed, if not crippled) (chaps. 15 and 16).

In contrast, there is the danger that new beneficiaries continue, under the production co-op, to see their day-to-day responsibilities as so similar to work on the hacienda that they regard their cash advances against future profits as a wage. If governments fail to require repayment of these credits with the harvest, they reinforce this erroneous beneficiary notion, negating genuine feelings of proprietorship among beneficiaries. The idea that no one has an ownership stake in the production cooperative leads land recipients ultimately into wanting to take current profits for consumption purposes rather than allowing capital investment to occur. Moreover, where the production cooperative is the predominant form of postreform tenure, the beneficiaries, anxious to protect heritable land rights for their children, tend not to be willing to take on new peer members, preferring lower cost wage workers who receive less from reform beneficiaries than they got under the ancien régime. Current members usually assume quite correctly that new adherents will be difficult to evict and, moreover, that they subtract more from the year-end profit division than their marginal contribution.

Carter and Alvarez (chap. 6) argue that the production cooperative in Peru had evolved into a low-effort, low-income equilibrium before decollectivization began. They believe that the major advantage of group farming is that it spreads agricultural production risks broadly; meanwhile, owner-operatorship sharpens production incentives. The major disadvantage of the production cooperative is the diffuse production incentives it provides and, perhaps, the inevitable problems of the "free rider." The production cooperative performs better at countervailing against the government for inputs; the individual farm does a more satisfactory job of providing labor because it has better access to and control over family resources.

It is too early to discover whether beneficiaries are responding to decollectivization by switching to a less risky (and also less remunerative or, in Carter and Alvarez's term, "suboptimal") enterprise combination. In the mid-1980s, most campesino beneficiaries in the region have tended to vote with their feet on the matter of their preference: they wish to farm individually [Alvarez and Carter (chap. 6) and Stanfield (chap. 11) document this in Peru and the Dominican Republic, respectively; while Kaimowitz does the same for Nicaragua (chap. 14), he refers to a shift in the reform's center of gravity toward family farming]. Some functions, like marketing and input purchase, are almost indisputably accomplished more efficiently in bulk; this argues for some joint action in all agrarian reforms—even if only in terms of input and output assembling for purchase and marketing purposes. The Dominican Republic (chap. 11) is attempting to preserve these cooperative functions, while the counterreform in Chile destroyed most of them. Alvarez and Carter (chap. 6) argue that beneficiaries developed a "legacy of distrust" in cooperatives after the demise of the CAPs. Strasma (chap. 15) is fairly optimistic about the future of the production cooperative in El Salvador (though he notes that their large scale has brought diseconomies to some); time and continued government support will prove his case. Postreform production structure all over the region is clearly in the process of evolution. Carter and Alvarez (chap. 6) note that there is a need for an intermediate tenure type which could ameliorate the weaknesses while capitalizing on the strengths of the production cooperative.

The paternalism of the land reform agency's hired manager (*gerente*) on agrarian reform settlements, sometimes with veto or vote on the cooperative's plans, but always with a certain coercive power, was nearly universal and probably unavoidable on postreform production cooperatives. Again, the issue becomes that of when a reform group can logically expect to be weaned of this influence, a question to which there is no clear answer. The *gerentes* are easily confused in the beneficiary's mind with the old hacienda administrator, or *mayordomo* (foreman), and sometimes beneficiary-*gerente* social relations tend to settle into that familiar patron-client routine, the new patrons doing little to disabuse the beneficiaries of this convenient, if inappropriate, social relations artifact. A difference is that the land reform technician is usually young and fresh out of agricultural school, while the *mayordomo* was frequently a wily and astute resident farm laborer who enjoyed the landlord's good will and was therefore promoted.

In fact, there is often little the unseasoned manager can teach these seasoned and often crusty beneficiary farmers except the abstract in a situation where the applied is more important; furthermore, the *gerente* is often as much an agent for the government as the *mayordomo* was an agent for the landlord and is considered as such by beneficiaries. Nonetheless, some teaching is the *gerente's* job—and it is more frequently done by decree than by anything approaching a Socratic method. An example is the emphasis that technicians put upon rice output in the Dominican Republic reform (chap. 11). Cost, which would be borne by the beneficiary, was immaterial. The government needed rice and that is what technicians were hired to promote at any cost. On the other hand, the beneficiaries knew that, given a need for optimization, costs had to be kept as low as possible. It appears that economic principles frequently are found wanting in the agricultural technician's training, and there are often other problems. While there is always a need for new agricultural knowledge, there is doubt as to whether the assignment of a *gerente* is the best way for land reform beneficiaries to obtain it. Since they have often lived a lifetime in the area, the beneficiaries know the soils, the irrigation potential, the cropping patterns, and the plant diseases, inter alia, rather well. The technicians, however, are transitory, often remaining less than a year, in what they consider to be outposts, a

Siberia of sorts, that may be marginally acceptable for an internship but never for a permanent position.

SECTORAL DIVERSITY

The chapters presented in this volume seem to show the campesino sector to be more diverse than de Janvry (1981) indicates, though the semiproletarianization of labor which leads to the functional dualism that he documents is important. In Chimborazo (chap. 3), for example, a quarter of gross family income comes from wages. As this happens, female roles change; women tend to assume greater responsibility for on-farm work while males hire out.

Farming is characterized by a great deal of social variegation, making reality complex in Latin America. There is some dualism which is probably not functional, for example. Even within the rural poor, campesinos perceive sharp differences among themselves as far as social status and future livelihood goals are concerned, and these tend to be rooted in their land-tenure status. As Strasma and Brown show (chaps. 15 and 8, respectively), resident workers believe themselves to be relatively high on the rural social scale. Wage labor, especially migratory wage labor, is looked upon with circumspection, pity and even fear by more settled campesinos with some access to land. Those who are landless sometimes see their goal as obtaining a higher wage; in contrast, former or present resident farm workers may have a landownership goal. Indeed, the rural social structure is highly variegated: while this is not easily discernable to outsiders, it is perfectly clear to the resident campesinos. If these differences aren't considered by policymakers, they will make costly and avoidable errors. In Nicaragua, those who considered themselves peasant-operators resented the government's treating their problems as though they were landless laborers; consequently the government had to change its modus operandi (chap. 17). While many campesinos in the area are downwardly mobile, there are [as Forster (chap. 4), Haney and Haney (chap. 3), Lehmann (1985, 1982), and Zevallos (chap. 2) have argued] some upwardly mobile campesinos who have not participated in any agrarian reform program. If there were ways to identify peasants so inclined to better their situation, governments might be able to assist them rather inexpensively.

Surely we have not heard the last of agrarian reform in the region. But whether it is to be merely a method of social control or a valuable tool for promoting agricultural progress and campesino "liberation" cannot be asserted glibly. The "democratic" process of land reform has the disadvantage of having at least four possible points in the establishment of the peasant onto land where dilution of economic policy can occur because the process is subject to publicity, to scrutiny, and, hence, to more than ordinary political pressure: (1) when the country makes a decision to conduct an agrarian reform, (2) when the decision is made to take a specific piece of land away from one group and give it to the beneficiaries, (3) when the expropriation decision is appealed to the courts, and (4) when the decision is made as to whether or not to provide inputs and, if provided, how many inputs will be supplied. Even the last decision requires sustained campesino pressure on government agencies over a fairly long period of time; in some countries, where urgency in this matter never materialized, reforms were more incomplete and unproductive than they might have been.

While most reforms described here were the product of a mixture of motivations, some more than others seem to rest on a single government objective. (1) In the case of Ecuador in 1964 (chaps. 2 and 3), the object of reform was apparently to go just as far as necessary to obtain U.S. support, that is, to meet the conditionality clauses of the Alliance for Progress by showing that reforms were occurring. The goal was to demonstrate tokenism but not to challenge the social structure. (2) There were also those reforms which had an increase in production as a major rationale: the 1971 actions which extended the Ecuadorian reform into the Guayas Valley fall roughly into this category. Perhaps nowhere else in Latin America did the prereform structure of agriculture and the cropping pattern so resemble the analogous structure in countries like Taiwan and South Korea. As in these Asian countries, reforms in this part of Ecuador were indeed accompanied by dramatic increases in rice production. (3) Some reforms were meant to quiet internal protest so that development funds could be redirected to more promising growth points within the country. In Mexico, Cárdenas's reforms in the 1930s accomplished this as they paved the way for the pre-eminence of the industrial and northern elites (chap. 10). (4) There were distributionist-minded reforms which put production in a secondary position, such as the Allende reforms in Chile (chaps. 7 and 8).

In most cases, however, it is difficult to attribute such complex change to a single motive; in fact, there are many. Peru (chaps. 5 and 6) cannot be categorized because it involved a split in the dominant elite, productionist and distributionist arguments, campesino agitation, military direction, and even some Church pressure. The unsettled debate about what political forces were really behind the reforms in El Salvador and Nicaragua is apparent from the material presented here (chaps. 14–17). One might be tempted to categorize the Dominican Republic and Honduras in the first category with 1964 Ecuador, but

Stanfield (chap. 11) and Stringer (chap. 13) reveal that even those situations were more complex.

We could formulate, as some have, an argument which states that future confrontations between the poor and the "establishment" will occur in cities as agriculture steadily becomes a smaller sector. On the other hand, since the agricultural population is still growing in absolute terms in many countries of the region, there are grounds for supposing that, in these countries, demands for rural reform will arise sometime in the future. Meanwhile, those who believe that agrarian reform is the cheapest and easiest way of insuring that the fruits of agricultural progress are more equitably distributed are caught in a moral bind for which there are no good answers: Does the progress of the few who are selected to engage in reform hinder the subsequent progress of the poor rural majority? Does agrarian reform take resources from the majority of poor to build up a small amd more privileged class of formerly poor? Or, by raising the expectations of a few, have the expectations of the many become unquenchable, making subsequent progress by the masses of peasantry in Latin America more probable? All of this neglects a most pressing problem that is not covered in this volume: How can the poorest of the rural population in Latin America, the growing group of landless, be helped (FAO 1985)? We can deduce few clues from extant agrarian reform programs of the region. Specifically, targeting the poorer groups for land grants in a reform would be one possibility, but, given that the landless sometimes specify that their desires are to make higher wages and to become more steadily employed, top-down programs which proceed without grass-roots participation are unlikely to be successful.

While many of the agrarian reforms and social movements of the world have charismatic leadership—larger-than-life figures like Martin Luther King, Jr.—in certain crucial or formative stages, the last 25 years in Latin America have not brought them to center stage. The reform which occurred tended to be directed by technocrats, generally rather quiet, professional types: the Ortegas, the Duartes, the Freis, the Allendes. Thus, there were no Emiliano Zapatas, no Fidel Castros—not even a Lázaro Cárdenas. In fact, those who might have qualified as charismatic died before they left the wings. So there were martyred heroes. Both Farabundo Martí and Augusto Sandino lent their names to their country's respective "liberation movements," and much was done in the names of El Salvador's Archbishop Oscar Arnulfo Romero, assassinated in 1980, and Carlos Fonseca, who was killed in the Nicaraguan revolution. Most Latin Americans might even add to this list John F. Kennedy, who died in 1963. There were only a few towering figures on the right, like Rafael Trujillo and the Somozas, but even the number of dictators was declining rapidly. Social movements of the

1980s are more bureaucratized, grayer, more institutionalized, and less visible, somehow matching the economic depression that has gripped the region. Democratization has become a key phrase of the 1980s, and in countries with democratic forms, social movements which declare the illegitimacy of the extant social structure are becoming more difficult to bring to fruition despite increasing incidences of campesino dissatisfaction.

Is it enough in describing the current Latin American development path to attribute it to a drive to capitalism? In fact, such a capitalist mode has been functioning in Latin American agriculture for a long time, mixed, of course, with some stranger ingredients, such as elements of heavy paternalism. From most of these chapters, it appears that what campesinos in Latin America want is to shake off the institutions that bear the vestiges of paternalism, which directs most of the income benefits of capitalism to a few while the many are exposed to arbitrary personalism. The clients in these paternalistic relationships are becoming more and more unwilling to be subservient. They are now more able than in the past to challenge the system, to make demands of it, to countervail against it. Today the situation may be a standoff in many parts of Latin America, but it will not remain so.

NOTES

1. The use of transfer payments would need to be limited to the hard-core unemployable lest inflation result.

2. In addition to the cases here, see Barraclough and Domike (1966), Clark (1968), Dorner and Kanel (1971), Raup (1967), and Thiesenhusen (1966, 1971, 1972, 1975).

3. This term was used in Erasmus (1967). In a recent manuscript, we called it "betting on winners" (Diskin, Sanderson, and Thiesenhusen 1987).

4. In addition, see Thiesenhusen (1984).

5. In some sense, this contradicts Grindle (1986).

6. Hannah Arendt, in her seminal work, *On Revolution*, argues that fear of revolution has been the guiding force of U.S. foreign policy since World War II. She points out, "[I]n a contest which divides the world today and in which so much is at stake, those will probably win who understand revolution ... and such understanding can neither be countered nor replaced with an expertness in counterrevolution" (Arendt 1963, 18).

REFERENCES

Arendt, Hannah. 1963. *On revolution*. New York: Viking Press.

Barraclough, Solon, and Arthur Domike. 1966. Agrarian structure in seven Latin American countries. *Land Economics* 43:391–424.

Chomsky, Noam. 1987. Banana empire: How America controls the Caribbean. *Utne Reader*, January-February.

Clark, Ronald J. 1968. Land reform and peasant market participation on the northern highlands of Bolivia. *Land Economics* 44:153–172.

de Janvry, Alain. 1981. *The agrarian question and reformism in Latin America*. Baltimore: Johns Hopkins Univ. Press.

Diskin, Martin, Steven E. Sanderson, and William C. Thiesenhusen. 1987. *Business in development: A workable partnership*. Issues in Grassroots Development, Monographs and Working Papers of the Inter-American Foundation. Rosslyn, Va.: IAF.

Dorner, Peter, and Don Kanel. 1971. The economic case for land reform: Employment, income distribution, and productivity. In *Land reform in Latin America: Issues and cases*, edited by Peter Dorner, pp. 41–56. *Land Economics* Monograph Series, no. 3. Madison: Published by *Land Economics* for the Land Tenure Center at the University of Wisconsin.

Elder, Joseph W. 1980. Social justice and political equality: Land tenure policies and rural development in south Asia. In *The politics of human rights*, edited by Paula R. Newberg, pp. 161–186. New York: New York Univ. Press.

Erasmus, Charles. 1967. Upper limits of peasantry and agrarian reform: Bolivia, Venezuela and Mexico compared. *Ethnology* 6(4):349–380.

FAO (Food and Agriculture Organization of the United Nations). 1985. *The rural landless: A synthesis of country case studies*. ESH 805. Rome: FAO, September.

Grindle, Merilee S. 1986. *State and countryside: Development policy and agrarian politics in Latin America*. Baltimore: Johns Hopkins Univ. Press.

Kirkpatrick, Jeane. 1979. Dictatorships and double standards. Commentary, November, pp. 34–45.

La Feber, Walter. 1983. *Inevitable revolutions: The United States and Central America*. New York: W.W. Norton and Company.

Lehmann, David. 1982. Beyond Lenin and Chayanov: New paths of agrarian capitalism. *Journal of Development Economics* 11:133–161.

———.1985. Dos vías de desarrollo capitalista en la agricultura. *Revista Andina* 3(2):343–378.

Raup, Philip M. 1967. Land reform and agricultural development. In *Agricultural development and economic growth*, edited by Herman Southworth and Bruce Johnston, pp. 267–314. Ithaca, N.Y.: Cornell Univ. Press.

Sanderson, Steven E. 1986. *The transformation of Mexican agriculture: International structure and the politics of rural change*. Princeton, N.J.: Princeton Univ. Press.

Thiesenhusen, William C. 1966. Chile's experiments in agrarian reform. *Land Economics* Monograph Series, no. 1. Madison: Published for *Land Economics*, University of Wisconsin Press.

———.1971. Latin America's employment problem. *Science*, 5 March, pp. 868–874.

———.1972. A suggested policy for industrial reinvigoration in Latin America. *Journal of Latin American Studies* 4(1):85–104.

———.1975. Chile's experiments in agrarian reform: Four colonization projects revisited. *American Journal of Agricultural Economics* 56(2):323–330.

———.1984. The illusory goal of equity in Latin American agrarian reform. In *International dimensions of land reform,* edited by John D. Montgomery, pp. 31–62. Boulder, Colo.: Westview Press.

———.1987. Incomes on some agrarian reform *asentamientos* in Panama. *Economic Development and Cultural Change* 35(4):809–831.

White, Robert. 1985. Aiding Contras harms democracy. *Christian Science Monitor*, 23 April.

INDEX

1 3 3 7 7 3